THE ART OF THEATRE

D0026560

THE ART OF THEATRE

FOURTH EDITION

WILLIAM MISSOURI DOWNS

LOU ANNE WRIGHT

ERIK RAMSEY

CENGAGE
Learning·

Australia • Brazil • Mexico • Singapore • United Kingdom • United States

The Art of Theatre, **Fourth Edition**
William Missouri Downs, Lou Anne Wright, Erik Ramsey

Product Director: Monica Eckman

Product Manager: Kelli Strieby

Marketing Manager: Sarah Seymour

Content Project Manager: Dan Saabye

Art Director: Marissa Falco

Manufacturing Planner: Doug Bertke

IP Analyst: Ann Hoffman

IP Project Manager: Betsy Hathaway

Production Service: Lumina Datamatics Ltd.

Compositor: Lumina Datamatics Ltd.

Text Designer: Ke Design

Cover Designer: Diana Graham

Cover Image: Joan Marcus
 /Shane Marshall Brown

© 2018, 2013, 2010 Cengage Learning

ALL RIGHTS RESERVED. No part of this work covered by the copyright herein may be reproduced or distributed in any form or by any means, except as permitted by U.S. copyright law, without the prior written permission of the copyright owner.

For product information and technology assistance, contact us at
Cengage Learning Customer & Sales Support, 1-800-354-9706.

For permission to use material from this text or product,
submit all requests online at **www.cengage.com/permissions**.
Further permissions questions can be emailed to
permissionrequest@cengage.com.

Library of Congress Control Number: 2016944072

Student Edition:
ISBN: 978-1-305-95470-0

Loose-leaf Edition:
ISBN: 978-1-337-11800-2

Cengage Learning
20 Channel Center Street
Boston, MA 02210
USA

Cengage Learning is a leading provider of customized learning solutions with employees residing in nearly 40 different countries and sales in more than 125 countries around the world. Find your local representative at **www.cengage.com**.

Cengage Learning products are represented in Canada by Nelson Education, Ltd.

To learn more about Cengage Learning Solutions, visit **www.cengage.com**.

Purchase any of our products at your local college store or at our preferred online store **www.cengagebrain.com**.

Printed in the United States of America
Print Number: 01 Print Year: 2016

This book is dedicated to

Kelli Strieby,

David Hall,

Holly Allen,

Greer Lleuad,

Stephanie Pelkowski Carpenter,

Megan Garvey,

and

Michael and

Barbara Rosenberg,

each a vital link

in the long chain that

brought this book

to publication.

BRIEF TABLE OF CONTENTS

CONTENTS

PART 2
THE ARTS WITHIN THE ART

5
A DAY IN THE LIFE OF A THEATRE   88

6
THE ART OF PLAYWRITING   109

7
THE ART OF ACTING 127

8
THE ART OF DIRECTING 148

9
THE ART OF DESIGN 169

PART 3
A CONCISE HISTORY

12

THEATRE AROUND THE WORLD 229

We live in a distracted age where technology has left a lot of digital distance between us. Yet, in this contemporary world theatre still thrives—an ancient art form that, at its very core, is driven by compassion and human-to-human contact.

As theatre professors we looked for a text that would speak to this new digital generation. Not finding one, we wrote our own. *The Art of Theatre* employs popular screen entertainments as a touchstone to exploring the unique art of theatre as it challenges students to analyze and appreciate the roles dramatic production plays in society. From theatre's ritual origins to modern musicals, from controversies surrounding the NEA to the applicability of acting lessons to everyday life, this book provides a first step toward a deeper awareness of theatre's enduring significance.

The Art of Theatre is divided into 17 standalone chapters that can be taught in any order, giving each professor unique flexibility. Using the custom option, you can design a textbook that explores the precise subjects you wish to cover. In addition, we have arranged the chapters into three sections, each embracing a distinct aspect of theatre:

Part 1: Theatre Literacy

Because most theatre departments stage their first play four to five weeks into the term, Part 1, "Theatre Literacy," prepares students to be knowledgeable theatregoers. This section explores the differences between art and entertainment while illustrating the many diverse forms of world theatre: commercial, historical, political, experimental, and cultural. We explain how screen entertainment differs from theatre in purpose, medium, and financing, and describe theatre's relationships to our many world cultures. We also discuss theatre etiquette, play analysis, and free speech. By introducing students to these fundamental topics early on, we provide a bridge between what students already know about screen entertainments and what they need to know about culture and theatre.

Part 2: The Arts within the Art

Part 2 opens the door to the timelines and techniques employed in creating theatre, exploring the nuts and bolts of the art form. We concentrate first on a day in the life of a typical theatre, and then move to playwriting, acting, directing, and design. We also include a chapter on how students, like theatre artists, can employ creativity, and how they can use acting and design techniques as well as character analysis and story structure in their own lives. In addition, this section includes a chapter on the evolution of the musical, a fun and popular theatrical form with which students are often familiar. By the time they are finished with this part, students should be ready to see their second production with a richer understanding of the full spectrum of skills, talents, arts, and creativity needed to stage a play.

Part 3: A Concise History

Part 3 provides students with a broader understanding of theatre's role in society. Our approach ties the major episodes of world theatre history to the social, cultural, and philosophical movements that the art has both sparked and reflected. We make theatre history interesting by drawing connections, making analogies, and joining together what might seem random events into a logical, unified whole.

Features of This Book

- Thorough coverage of the many forms of theatre and the people who create it
- Broad coverage of cultural and social events that illustrate theatre's place in world history
- A chapter devoted to what makes theatre different from film and television
- A chapter dedicated to creativity and how students can be more imaginative
- Spotlights that highlight the people, trends, and events that have shaped theatre
- Interesting and relevant timelines
- A detailed glossary (including pronunciation) of theatre terms
- Discussions on freedom of speech, censorship, and copyrights
- A chapter on how to attend the theatre, from etiquette to criticism
- A complete examination of everything that happens during the day and night at a typical theatre
- A wide-ranging look at the life and art of playwrights, actors, designers, and directors
- A chapter devoted to the history and art of musicals
- Chapters that make theatre history interesting and relevant

New to This Edition

There are many new features in the fourth edition, including new photographs, new and revised spotlights, and enhanced material:

Part 1: Theatre Literacy

Chapters 1 and 2 contain updated coverage about the art of theatre and its place in the modern world. Included is an expanded section on the difference between art and entertainment, updated information about the funding of theatre versus funding of film and television, more about the media moguls that control our screen entertainments and expanded coverage on copyrights. Chapter 3 has been extensively updated with more information about the diverse forms of theatre and how the theatre gives a voice to everyone, not just privileged groups. Chapter 4 has expanded information about how to find and attend the theatre, new information on curtain speeches, and expanded coverage of censorship.

Part 2: The Arts within the Art

All of the chapters in this section have new photos and examples to help students understand the many arts and techniques involved in producing a play. Chapter 6 has new information about the writer's life and expanded coverage of the art and craft of writing a play and structuring a story. Chapters 7, 8, and 9 have been updated with the latest examples and information about acting, directing, and design; Chapter 10 has new information on the need for solitude in order to be creative and how multitasking interferes with creativity. This section of the book now contains the revised musical theatre chapter, which includes a new spotlight on women and the American musical.

Part 3: A Concise History

This section of the book has been revised to be more concise. Changes include new photos, updated timelines, and new spotlights, including one on Nell Gwyn. In addition we look at how theatre might fare in the digital age.

Teaching and Learning Resources

Cengage Learning's **MindTap for *The Art of Theatre*** brings course concepts to life with interactive learning, study, and exam preparation tools that support the printed textbook. Student comprehension is enhanced with the integrated eBook and interactive learning tools, including learning objectives, activities, quizzes, and videos.

The **Instructor Companion Website** is an all-in-one resource for class preparation, presentation, and testing for instructors. It is accessible by logging on to login.cengage.com with your faculty account. You will find an **Instructor's Resource Manual**, **Cognero®** test bank files, and **PowerPoint®** presentations specifically designed to accompany this edition.

The **Instructor's Resource Manual** provides you with assistance in teaching with the book, including sample syllabi, suggested assignments, chapter outlines, activities, and more.

Cengage Learning Testing Powered by Cognero® is a flexible online system that allows you to import, edit, and manipulate content from the text's test bank and deliver tests from your LMS, your classroom, or wherever you may be, with no special installation required.

PowerPoint® Lecture Tools are ready-to-use outlines of each chapter. They are easily customizable to your lectures.

Acknowledgments

A very special thank you goes to Mike Earl for his help with the chapters on design, and to Sean Warren Stone for his help with the chapter on musical theatre. We also send our gratitude to other colleagues who gave us valuable assistance, including the University of Wyoming's Oliver Walter, Tom Buchanan, Jack Chapman, Don Turner, Ron Steger, Adam Mendelson, and Ohio University's Charles Smith. Special thanks to Dr. James Livingston, Linda deVries, Peter Grego, Shozo Sato, and our amazing students, past and present, at the University of Illinois, Colorado State, University of Colorado, University of Nevada Las Vegas, University of California Los Angeles, University of Wyoming, and Ohio University.

Thanks also to the many reviewers of this book, including, for the fourth edition: Robert Alford, Louisiana State University in Shreveport; Karina Balfour, West Chester University of Pennsylvania; Wendy Coleman, Alabama State University;

John Countryman, Berry College; Raquel Davis, Boise State University; Rachel Dickson, University of Houston–Downtown; Gail Medford, Bowie State University; Iva Kristi Papailler, Georgia College & State University; Sally Robertson, Georgia Perimeter College–Clarkston; Judith Ryerson, University of Nevada, Las Vegas; and Stephen Thomas, Tarrant County College–Northeast.

We also want to thank all those reviewers who worked on earlier editions with us, including: Christopher R. Boltz, Fresno City College; Mary Guzzy, Corning Community College; Nadine Charlsen, Kean University; William Godsey, Calhoun Community College; and Joe Jacoby, North Idaho College. For the second edition: John Bagby, State University of New York College at Oneonta; Paula Barrett, Gannon University; Robbin Black, Utah State University; Ro Willenbrink Blair, Edinboro University of Pennsylvania; Christopher Boltz, Fresno City College; John R. Burgess, University of Tennessee at Chattanooga; Suzanne Chambliss, Louisiana State University; Donald Correll, Lower Columbia College; Florence Dyer, Lambuth University; Oliver Gerland, University of Colorado; Rebecca Gorman, Metropolitan State College of Denver; Cleo House, The Pennsylvania State University; Dennis Maher, The University of Texas Arlington; Leslie Martin, California State University Fresno; Elena Martinez Vidal, Midlands Technical College; Jason Pasqua, Laramie County Community College; Tony Penna, Clemson University; Sheilah Philip, Johnson County Community College; Pam Reid, Copiah Lincoln Community College; Rick Rose, Piedmont College; Korey Rothman, University of Maryland; William G. Wallace, Hamlin University; Darby Winterhalter Lofstrand, Northern Arizona University; and Rhea Wynn, Alabama Christian Academy. We also want to thank reviewers of the first edition, whose influence can still be seen on these pages: Stacy Alley, Arkansas State University; Blair Anderson, Wayne State University; Robin Armstrong, Collin County Community College; Dennis Beck, Bradley University; Robert H. Bradley, Southwestern Missouri State University; B. J. Bray, University of Arkansas Little Rock; Mark Buckholz, New Mexico State University Carlsbad; Lon Bumgarner, University of North Carolina Charlotte; Carol Burbank, University of Maryland; Katherine Burke, Purdue University; Gregory J. Carlisle, Morehead State University; Dorothy Chansky, College of William and Mary; Leigh Clemons, Louisiana State University Baton Rouge; Patricia S. Cohill, Burlington County College; Anita DuPratt, California State University Bakersfield; Thomas H. Empey, Casper College; Jeff Entwistle, University of Wisconsin Green Bay; Rebecca Fishel Bright, Southern Illinois University; Anne Fliotsos, Purdue University; Christine Frezza, Southern Utah State University; Keith Hale, State University of New York Albany; Ann Haugo, Illinois State University; Charles Hayes, Radford University; Robert A. Hetherington, University of Memphis; Allison Hetzel, University of Louisiana Lafayette; Helen M. Housley, University of Mary Washington; Jackson Kesler, Western Kentucky University; Yuko Kurahashi, Kent State University; Howard Lang Reynolds, Marshall University; Don LaPlant, California State University Bakersfield; Jeanne Leep, Edgewood College; Nina LeNoir, Minnesota State University Mankato; Sherry McFadden, Indiana State University; Ray Miller, Appalachian State University; Joel Murray, University of Texas El Paso; Kevin Alexander Patrick, Columbus State University; Paula Pierson, San Diego State University; Ellis Pryce Jones, University of Nevada Las Vegas; David Z. Saltz, University of Georgia; Kindra Steenerson, University of North Carolina Wilmington; Jennifer Stiles, Boston College; Shannon Sumpter, University of Nevada Las Vegas; Stephen Taft, University of Northern Iowa; Vanita Vactor, Clemson University; Thomas Woldt, Simpson College; Boyd H. Wolz, University of Louisiana Monroe; and Samuel J. Zachary, Northern Kentucky University.

ABOUT THE AUTHORS

WILLIAM MISSOURI DOWNS is a playwright and director. His plays have been produced by The Kennedy Center for the Performing Arts, The Orlando Shakespeare Theatre, The InterAct Theatre in Philadelphia, The San Diego Rep, The Berkeley Repertory Theatre, the Salt Lake City Acting Company, the Actors Theatre of Charlotte, the International Theatre Festival in Israel, the Stadt Theater Walfischgasse in Austria, the Jewish Theatre of Toronto, The Bloomington Playwright's Project, the Detroit Rep, the New York City Fringe Festival, the Durban Performing Arts Center in South Africa, and 150 theatres worldwide. He has won numerous playwriting awards including two rolling premieres from the National New Play Network (*Women Playing Hamlet* & *The Exit Interview*), and twice been a finalist at the Eugene O'Neill (*Mad Gravity* & *How to Steal a Picasso*). Samuel French, Playscripts, Next Stage Press, and Heuer have published his plays. In addition, he has authored several articles and three other books, including *Screenplay: Writing the Picture* and *Naked Playwriting*, both published by Silman/James. In Hollywood he was a staff writer on the NBC sitcom *My Two Dads* (which starred Paul Reiser). He also wrote episodes of *Amen* (Sherman Helmsley), *Fresh Prince of Bel Air* (Will Smith), and sold/optioned screenplays to Imagine Pictures and Filmways. He was trained in directing under the Oscar Nominated Polish Director Jerzy Antczak and has directed over 40 college and professional productions. Bill holds an MFA in acting from the University of Illinois, an MFA in screenwriting from UCLA; Lanford Wilson and Milan Stitt at the Circle Rep in New York City trained him in playwriting.

LOU ANNE WRIGHT is an actor, dialect coach, professor, and writer; she holds an MFA in Voice, Speech, and Dialects from the National Theatre Conservatory and is a certified Fitzmaurice Voicework teacher. Lou Anne has served as voice/ dialect coach for such companies as the Colorado Shakespeare Festival and the Denver Center for the Performing Arts. Film roles include Judy Shepard in HBO's *The Laramie Project* and Nell in *Hearsay*. As a playwright, she authored the play *Kabuki Medea*, which won the Bay Area Critics Award for Best Production in San Francisco. It was also produced at the Kennedy Center. She is the coauthor of the book *Playwriting: From Formula to Form*, and her screenwriting credits include the film adaptation of Eudora Welty's *The Hitch Hikers*, which featured Patty Duke and Richard Hatch (for which she was nominated for the Directors Guild of America's Lillian Gish Award). Lou Anne teaches acting, voice, speech, and dialects at the University of Wyoming, where she has won several teaching awards.

ERIK RAMSEY is an Associate Professor of Playwriting in the MFA Playwriting Program at Ohio University. His plays have been developed at various theaters including Cleveland Public Theatre, American Stage, Victory Gardens, and Pittsburgh Irish and Classical Theatre, and been published by Samuel French and Dramatic Publishing. As a new play dramaturg, he has worked in diverse settings from Steppenwolf Theater to WordBridge Lab. Over the past decade he has been a guest artist and taught playwriting, new play development, and narrative theory in a variety of national and international venues, including the St. Petersburg Academy of Dramatic Arts "New American Plays" Conference and Lubimovka Playwrights Laboratory at Teatr.doc in Moscow. Erik's newest play, a two-hander for actresses in their 40s, explores the intersection of rodeo clowning and time-travel.

The theatre often expresses points of view not easily found in mainstream movies and television. Plays will typically explore themes and issues that film and T.V. gloss over or ignore such as religion, sexuality and politics. Pictured here are some of the cast of the mega hit musical *The Book of Mormon* at the Eugene O'Neill Theatre in New York.

Chapter 1

THEATRE, ART, AND ENTERTAINMENT

Sara Krulwich/The New York Times/Redux

Outline

On a recent January morning in Washington, D.C., at the L'Enfant Plaza Metro Station, a street musician began to play beside a trash can. A thousand commuters rushed by over the next hour. Many failed to hear the recital—barely six people stopped to listen, and only one person realized that the musician was no ordinary violinist, but the internationally acclaimed virtuoso and heartthrob Joshua Bell. The violin he played was a one-of-a-kind Stradivarius made in 1713, worth over $3.5 million. Only three days before, Mr. Bell had played to a standing-room-only crowd at Boston's Symphony Hall. Cheap tickets for that performance cost $100, meaning Bell's concert raked in approximately $1,000 per minute. But three days later, in the cold D.C. Metro station,

MindTap®

Start with a quick warm-up activity and review the chapter's learning objectives.

William Missouri Downs

Art is a puzzle that must be assembled by the individual. The fact that millions of people think that the Mona Lisa is the greatest painting ever made should not be your only justification for calling it "art." You must create your own definition.

Mr. Bell's open violin case pocketed $32.17 in donations. It would have been $12.17, except that the one person who did recognize him tossed in a twenty.

Two hundred years ago, a performance by a great artist like Joshua Bell would have been, for the majority of us, a once-in-a-lifetime experience. Today, if you want to hear Joshua Bell you can download his music to your smartphone. Two hundred years ago, if you wanted to see the great painting *Mona Lisa,* you would have had to travel hundreds, perhaps thousands, of miles. Today, in seconds you can make the *Mona Lisa* the screen saver you never look at.

If you wanted to attend a play 200 years ago, it meant making detailed plans, buying tickets, waiting weeks, and dressing up. Today you can push a button and see great actors in an instant on your tablet without having to get out of bed. Technology makes enjoying art an almost effortless activity, but has that same technology also devalued the arts? Have we cheapened the *Mona Lisa,* made dramatic performances commonplace, and made Joshua Bell playing his Stradivarius on the street little better than an annoyance on our rush to work?

The *Washington Post* staged Bell's Metro station violin concert as an experiment to test people's perceptions and priorities. It led to many questions. Perhaps the most important question was, "If we do not have a moment to stop and listen to one of the best musicians in the world, playing some of the finest music ever written, on one of the most beautiful and expensive instruments ever made . . . how many other things are we missing?" The true value of art is not its price tag, but its ability to make us feel and think. Because of this, art can be a powerful force within our lives, but there is one obstacle art cannot overcome: an individual's *inability* to perceive and enjoy it. Before you read this first chapter, take a moment to watch Bell's Metro station concert on YouTube. Would you have been one of the walking masses who never heard him, or one of the rare few who knew how to appreciate fine art?

The reason most people don't appreciate the arts is because art takes time and education. The philosopher, mathematician, and social critic Bertrand Russell wrote, "When the public cannot understand a picture or a poem, they conclude that it is a bad picture or a bad poem. When they cannot understand the theory of relativity they conclude (rightly) that their education has been insufficient." There is no difference between art and the theory of relativity in that they both take time and education to fully experience.

In this book, you will learn about one of the most unique art forms humankind has ever invented, including its history, techniques, and methods. If you take the time you will discover an art brimming with creativity, philosophy, emotion, intellect, and inspiration that will lead to a greater understanding of yourself and the world around you.

Art, or Not Art, That Is the Question

Think about how often the word *art* appears in everyday conversation. It is used in a wide array of contexts but generally conveys three main ideas: art as "skill," art as "beauty," and art as "meaning." Recently, a sports reporter on

ESPN described the American Women's World Cup champions as "artists." In this sense, the word *art* means "skill," and it is derived from the Latin word *ars,* synonymous with the ancient Greek word *techne,* which means "skill" or "technique." An *artist* is a person who has a great deal of skill or talent or whose work shows considerable technical proficiency or creativity. This is why we have phrases such as "the art of war" or the "mechanical arts."

We use *art* in the second sense when we make such comments as "The sunset at the beach was a work of art." When we use the word *art* to describe something of great beauty, whether it's a real and magnificent sunset or an exact watercolor replica of that same sunset, we are talking about aesthetics. **Aesthetics** is the branch of philosophy that deals with the nature and expression of beauty. Aestheticians ask questions such as: Does beauty have objective existence outside the human experience? What environmental factors or moral judgments affect our perception of beauty? What purpose does art serve other than to delight the eye, please the ear, and soothe the senses? The highest level of aesthetic beauty is often called the **sublime**. This happens when beauty is so intense that it gives us the sense of awe and grandeur, as if we are in the presence of the divine.

In the third sense, *art* can be defined as conveying "meaning." Artists commonly view their art as their own interpretation or judgment of existence, rather than simply as an act of skill or a work of beauty. When the word *art* is used in this way, the implicit meaning is "this is life as I, the artist, see it. This is my personal take on things." Certainly, when artists set out to create meanings, they may choose to do so in a socially acceptable manner. They may even choose to support their meanings with great skill and beauty. However, an artist may also choose to ignore, challenge, or utterly defy traditional social values and disregard common standards of technique and beauty. The idea that art can reflect no skill, contain little beauty, and be unpleasant is hard for some to comprehend.

Theatre, or any kind of art that confronts or violates the popular understanding of skill, aesthetics, and meaning, can be dangerous to create. What if

MindTap®

Read, highlight, and take notes online.

Art is not supposed to repeat what you already know. It is supposed to ask questions.

Kutluğ Ataman,
Filmmaker, artist

"Beauty is no quality in things themselves: It exists merely in the mind which contemplates them; and each mind perceives a different beauty."

David Hume,
Philosopher

William Missouri Downs

According to most dictionary definitions, only humans can make art. This untitled painting was created by "Add," a nine-year-old elephant in Thailand. Would you call it art?

SPOTLIGHT ON Plato, Aristotle, and the Theatre Arts

The debate over the purpose of theatre has been going on for centuries. Over two thousand years ago great philosophers like Plato and Aristotle pondered the subject—their arguments sound a lot like those we hear today in the modern media.

Plato (427–347 BCE) was a teacher, a philosopher, and an amateur playwright. However, early in his career he was persuaded by the philosopher Socrates (ca. 469–399 BCE) that playwriting was a waste of time, so he burned all of his plays. Later he wrote a series of dialogues between Socrates and others. These dialogues, conversation-like plays meant to be read rather than performed, deal with art, metaphysics, immortality, religion, morals, and drama. Plato also founded "The Academy," which is often called the first university. His most famous student was Aristotle.

Ted Spiegel/Fine Art Premium/Corbis

Plato and Aristotle (l to r), detail from Raphael's *The School of Athens* (1510–1511)

The philosopher Aristotle (384–322 BCE) wrote on such diverse topics as logic, natural philosophy (what we would call physics today), astronomy, zoology, geography, chemistry, politics, history, psychology, and playwriting. His treatise *Poetics* is the first known text on how to write a play. Aristotle founded a rival school to Plato's Academy called the "Lyceum." His most famous student was Alexander the Great (356–323 BCE).

Plato accused those involved with the theatre of promoting "vice and wickedness." In his book *The Republic* he says that people forget themselves and are highly manipulated—even irrational—when under the influence of the arts.

> When people are confronted with a real work of art, they discover that they don't believe what they thought they believed all along. In a way, the great art, the great subversive art, is art that makes you realize that you don't think what you thought you did.
>
> **David Hare,**
> Playwright

the audience disagrees with the artist's interpretation, finds it offensive, or simply refuses to pay attention? For example, when playwright and filmmaker Neil LaBute was a student at Brigham Young University, he directed David Mamet's controversial play *Sexual Perversity in Chicago*. The strong reaction made him think that the purpose of drama is to confront the audience. He now often writes plays and movies about homophobes and misogynists. His play *Filthy Talk for Troubled Times* was so controversial that some audience members shouted, "Kill the playwright!" Later LaBute said that performance was one of the best theatre experiences he has ever had. Many audience members disagreed.

This is nothing new. For millennia people have been debating whether art is simply a means to create objects of beauty, a tool to educate, or designed to incite. Two thousand and four hundred years ago the Greek playwright Aristophanes (ca. 450–ca. 388 BCE) argued that, "The dramatist should not only offer pleasure but should also be a teacher of morality and a political adviser." Yet his near contemporary, Greek astronomer and mathematician Eratosthenes

He felt that the danger of the theatre is its power to instill values hostile to the community, so he banished the poets (by which he meant "playwrights," but the word did not yet exist) from the ideal state in order to protect citizens from being mindlessly spellbound. He worried that when people join together in an audience, particularly young people, their thoughts can be swept away by the power of the crowd and as a result they lose the ability to reason for themselves. He said, "The poet is a sophist, a maker of counterfeits that look like the truth."

If there had to be theatre, Plato felt that it must be subservient to the state and to society: playwrights should be of high moral character, appointed by official decree, and their writing should be closely supervised and their plays checked by a government-appointed panel of judges. He said, "The poet shall compose nothing contrary to the ideas of the lawful, or just, or beautiful, or good . . . nor shall he be permitted to show his composition to any private individual, until he shall have shown them to the appointed censors and the guardians of the law, and they are satisfied with them." Plato justified this call for censorship by asserting that man is an imitative animal and tends to become what he imitates. He cautioned, therefore, that if we allow theatre we should ensure that it only contains characters that are suitable as role models.

Over the centuries, other philosophers have occasionally agreed with Plato. Blaise Pascal (1623–1662) disliked the theatre because he felt that the consciences of audience members stop functioning during performances. Jean-Jacques Rousseau (1712–1778) said that the arts "spread flowers over the chains that bind people, smothering their desire for liberty."

Aristotle disagreed with his mentor, Plato. He felt that art and theatre do not stir undesirable passions, but rather they awaken the soul. He argued that seeing a play in which a son marries his mother, as in the ancient Greek tragedy *Oedipus Rex*, doesn't cause the young men in the audience to run out and propose marriage to their mothers. (As modern independent film director John Waters once said, "No story is that good.") Instead, he believed that good theatre fortifies us because it allows us to release repressed emotions in a controlled, therapeutic way.

Nature, according to Aristotle, tends toward perfection but doesn't always attain it. We tend to be healthy but we become sick. We tend to be nonviolent but there is war. We tend toward love but there is hate. Therefore, we need art and theatre to correct the deficiencies of nature by clarifying, interpreting, and idealizing life.

(276–194 BCE), said the function of the theatre arts was to "charm the spirits of the listeners, but never to instruct them." Similarly, Greek philosophers Plato (427–347 BCE) and his student Aristotle (384–322 BCE) disagreed about the nature of theatre. Aristotle believed theatre is a creation meant to interpret the world and awake the soul, but Plato maintained that art should be a tool of the state and promote the well-being of the body politic. The debate over what art is has been going on for centuries and will continue for centuries to come. (See Spotlight, "Plato, Aristotle, and the Theatre Arts.")

The Qualities of Art

A few years ago, a janitor in a modern art gallery accidentally left his grimy mop and bucket on the gallery floor overnight. The next morning the gallery manager was shocked to find patrons gathered around the mess, admiring it as

> Art was basically functional in far earlier times, a tool by which people could express their inner feelings. Just as they might demonstrate certain desires through dance, or voice joy or sorrow though song, so the mystical, unknown world of these early artists came alive in their drawing and paintings. This search into the visible and unknown worlds was mirrored in their artist creations; not art for art's sake, perhaps, but a tool to find a way, a connection, to the unknown.
>
> **Rabbi Moshe**
> Carmilly-Weinberger

a work of art. This story illustrates how difficult it is to provide an exact definition of a word like *art*. In fact, defining any abstract word can be a challenge, as you've probably noticed when you've looked up certain words in the dictionary and found that they mean a number of different things. In his book *Philosophical Investigations*, British philosopher Ludwig Wittgenstein (1889–1951) points out that trying to find all-encompassing definitions is not only difficult but also introduces boundaries that limit our imagination. Instead, he suggests we define words by pointing out their "family resemblances," or the ways in which the many different meanings of a word resemble one another. So rather than nailing down the exact definition of the word *art*, let's list the five basic qualities that all works of art share to a certain extent: human creation, subject and medium, structure, and reaction.

Human Expression

Human beings and only human beings can make art. The *American Heritage Dictionary* says art is "a *human effort* to imitate, supplement, alter, or counteract the work of nature." *Webster's Deluxe Unabridged Dictionary* says that art is "the disposition or modification of things by *human skill* . . ." (emphasis added). From these definitions it is easy to see how the word *art* springs from the same root as the word *artificial*. It is not the real thing but rather a human creative endeavor that involves the perceptions and imagination of an artist who is trying to say something in his or her own particular way. And so every work of art has an individual style that reflects a person's talent, technique, historical period, and unique way of looking at the world. Therefore, the snow-capped Rocky Mountains, no matter how beautiful, meaningful, or inspiring, are *not* art because humans did not create them, and those same mountains cannot become art until a person interprets them through a medium such as oil paint on canvas.

Subject and Medium

Every work of art has a subject and a medium. The **subject** of the work is what that work is about, what it reflects or attempts to comprehend. The **medium** is the method, substance, style, and technique used to create the work. In other words, the medium is the vehicle for communication. For example, the subject of a painting may be a flower, but the medium is paint on canvas. The subject of a dance might be the beginning of spring, and its medium is choreographed physical movement. The subject of a song might be an "Achy Breaky Heart," but the medium is a combination of words, tone, pitch, and volume. Every genre of art has a different medium that defines it and makes it unique. The **spatial arts,** such as sculpture and architecture, are created by manipulating material in space. The **pictorial arts,** such as drawing and painting, are created by applying line and color to two-dimensional surfaces. The **literary arts** are created with written language. Theatre is classified as a performing art, as are music, opera, and dance. The medium of the **performing arts** is an act performed by a person. In this way the performing arts are unique because they exist only in the time it takes an actor, singer, musician, or dancer to complete a performance. Therefore they also have a beginning, middle, and end. Once a performance ends, the work of art no longer exists, leaving behind no tangible object such as a painting or a statue.

Theatre is unique because it is the only art for which the medium and subject are exactly the same: the subjects of a play are human beings and human acts, and the mediums of a play are also human beings and human acts. The actors' bodies are like canvas and paint to the painter—they are the mediums of the art. But you might ask yourself: what about the musical *Cats?* That's not about humans and human acts; it's about felines, right? Actually, the emotions, thoughts, and actions staged for the musical are purely human—invented by humans to represent an idea of what cats might think and feel. Ultimately, people can only experience the world through their own senses and thoughts, and therefore any "animal," "monster," or even a child dressed up like a "tornado" in a school play is really a human idea of how an animal, monster, or tornado might think, feel, and behave.

Response

The power of art comes from its capacity to evoke a response. Art does not come to life until a spectator, a listener, or an audience breathes life into it by experiencing it. Art provokes in us a reaction that causes us to consider, judge, emote, or perceive meaning in some way. This reaction may be spiritual, emotional, intellectual, rational, or irrational. And that reaction, whatever it may be, often lingers long after the initial encounter. Yet each person views a work of art through the lenses of his or her own experiences, education, preconceptions, assumptions, and interests. And because each of us is unique, what constitutes *art* for one person may not be *art* for another. This is at the root of the difficulty in finding a definition of art on which most can agree. But it also means that arts education is critical. According to the educator and art philosopher Harold Taylor (1914–1993), the spectator must know how to "respond to other people

> In one sense the aim of the scientist and the aim of the artist are the same since both are in pursuit of what they call truth; but the difference between them may be said to consist in this, that while for science there is only one truth, for the artist there are many.
>
> **Joseph Wood Krutch,**
> Author and philosopher

AP Images/Keystone/Georgios Kefalas

Like many artists, playwright and Nobel Prize winner Wole Soyinka has played an active role in politics. His efforts to broker a peace agreement during the 1967 Nigerian Civil War resulted in his arrest and 22 months in solitary confinement. Today, Soyinka continues to be an outspoken critic of political tyranny.

Life is very nice, but it lacks form. It's the aim of art to give it some.

Jean Anouilh,
Playwright

The world of the theatre is a world of sharper, clearer, swifter impressions than the world we live in.

Robert Edmond Jones,
Set designer

and other ideas, different from his own," rather than react against them. Spectators must "learn to accept difference as natural rather than as a threat to their whole style of life." In essence, Taylor is saying that art depends on the open minds of those who experience it. We need not approve of any given piece of art, yet we must attempt to understand the perspective of the artist who created it before we can dismiss it or judge it.

Perception of Order

It is often said that artists "select and arrange" their perceptions of the world and in doing so find or create a structure—a meaningful order or form. "It is the function of all art to give us some perception of an order in life, by imposing order upon it," said poet T. S. Eliot.

American philosopher and novelist Ayn Rand (1905–1982) interpreted the notion of structure in art quite elegantly with the following example. Imagine that a beautiful woman in a lovely evening gown enters a ballroom. She is perfect in every way except for the fact that she has a rather large, ugly cold sore on her lip. What do we make of it? What does it mean? Not much—many people are afflicted with cold sores, and they are perhaps unfortunate but have little meaning. However, if a painter paints a picture of a beautiful woman in a lovely evening gown and portrays her with the same ugly cold sore, the blemish suddenly takes on great importance.

This minor imperfection, says Rand, "acquires a monstrous significance by virtue of being included in the painting. It declares that a woman's beauty and her efforts to achieve glamour are futile and that all our values and efforts are impotent against the power, not even of some great cataclysm, but of a miserable little physical infection."

By including the cold sore—by emphasizing certain parts of life and de-emphasizing others—the artist finds order and imposes meaning. This editorial process troubles some who believe the artist's duty is, as Shakespeare's Hamlet says, to hold a "mirror up to nature." Some people believe art should merely imitate life, nothing more. Yet, if art simply imitates, then it would serve only to reflect what we already see and experience, not help us understand it. Additionally, the process of "holding up a mirror" is inherently editorial anyway—even if one does set out to simply hold up a mirror to nature, what one chooses to reflect in the mirror is, in itself, an editorial process or value judgment that focuses our eyes on one particular setting or idea instead of another.

Art is never a slavish copy. It always is a selective re-creation that is given form by the artist's individual view of existence. Perhaps the Polish sociologist Zygmunt Bauman said it best: "To be an artist means to give form and shape to what otherwise would be shapeless and formless. To manipulate probabilities. To impose an 'order' on what otherwise would be 'chaos'; to 'organize' an otherwise chaotic—random, haphazard and so unpredictable—collection of things and events by making certain events more likely to happen than all others." When artists find order they also cultivate insight and understanding about our world and ourselves. (See Spotlight, "To Be an Artist Means Finding Form and Structure.") This means that inherent in any work of art are the artist's opinions, interpretations, philosophy, and beliefs. In short, art is inherently political and often has political consequences.

SPOTLIGHT<u>ON</u> To Be an Artist Means Finding Form and Structure

French novelist Gustave Flaubert said that emotions are important in art, but that feelings are not everything: "Art is nothing without form." Our need for form and structure is really the need to simplify. At nearly fifteen hundred pages, *War and Peace* is a condensed version of the French invasion of Russia, the play *Long Day's Journey into Night* is an edited version of Eugene O'Neill's family traumas, and $E = mc^2$ is an abbreviated version of Einstein's insights. Why do we need a simplified structure? The great Russian writer Dostoyevsky said humans "crave miracles, mystery, and authority." In other words, we crave a well-structured map through the confounding experiences of life.

Our need for structure shows itself in common phrases like "Everything happens for a reason," "What goes around comes around," or "God helps those who help themselves." Each statement takes the raw data of nature, edits it, and adds structure. The result is theme. Theme comes when one begins to see patterns in nature and life—whether those patterns are imagined or real. Anthropologist Pascal Boyer called this the "hypertrophy of social cognition," which is our tendency to see purpose, intention, and design where only randomness exists.

For example, the first day you walk to your new job, it is novel. Perhaps you pass a house with a red door, a tree shaped like a Y, and a park bench near a bus stop. At first the door, the tree, and the bench have no meaning. But as you walk to work the next day and the next, the walk develops a structure. The red door means you are at the beginning of your walk; the tree denotes the midway point, while the bench signifies the end. If you begin to dislike your employment, the door, tree, and bench can take on new significance. The red door symbolizes how you hate to leave your house, the tree the missed opportunity to take the "Y" in the road, and the park bench your desire to retire. Your walk now has structure, and, as a result, theme and meaning. Years later, long after you have left the job, when you see a similar door, tree, or bench you will read meaning into it even though no inherent meaning, theme, or structure exists.

Humans need structure and theme because the world in which we find ourselves appears to be disorganized or at least lacking in purposeful design. Nature, says Adam Phillips in his book *Darwin's Worms,* does not "have what we could call a mind of its own, something akin to human intelligence. Nor does nature have a project for us; it cannot tell us what to do; only we can. It doesn't bear us in mind because it doesn't have a mind. . . ." Some argue that there is a chaos to nature, others that nature has too much structure. Either way, we must simplify in order to find meaning or to create it.

Art, along with science and religion, helps us find structure; with structure comes meaning.

On the right is a photo of Sawtooth Mountain in Colorado, on the left Sumi-E artist Shozo Sato's painting of the same mountain. An artist takes the raw data of life and edits it into order to find or impose order and meaning.

Shozo Sato

William Missouri Downs

The Politics of Art

Every time artists make a choice about what aspect of existence to select and arrange, they express a value judgment and reveal their beliefs. In this way art is like politics in the broad sense: it reflects people's conflicting ideas about how we should live, how society should be organized, and how the world is. Artists select those aspects of existence they believe are significant, isolate them, and stress them to create meaning. The result is that artists' fundamental views of life are embodied within their art. Therefore, at the core of every artist is a political individual who states an opinion that may challenge an audience's values and shatter their preconceptions.

This is probably why many artists eventually become political leaders, join political causes, or simply stand up and publicly state their opinions. In the United States, most artists have particular political causes that they support—we see them standing on the platforms during national political conventions, testifying before Senate committees, doing public service announcements, and lending their names to political causes, organizations, and campaigns. Bands from Rage Against the Machine to the Dixie Chicks are well known for their political opinions. South African playwright Athol Fugard has spent his life writing plays that attack apartheid, or state-sponsored racial segregation.

Taking the connection a step further, Vigdís Finnbogadóttir, director of the Reykjavík Theatre Company, was elected president of Iceland, and movie stars N. T. Rama Rao of India and Joseph Estrada of the Philippines both became successful politicians in their respective countries. Artists turned politicians represent all political parties. Singer Sonny Bono (*Sonny and Cher*), actor Fred Grandy (*Love Boat*), actor Ben Jones (*The Dukes of Hazzard*), and movie star Arnold Schwarzenegger (*The Terminator*) all served in the national and local governments as Republicans. And, of course, we cannot overlook the former actor, movie star, and president of the Screen Actors Guild who became president of the United States, Ronald Reagan.

Art and politics are often closely related and it is not uncommon for actors, directors and writers to enter politics. In the U.S., actors such as Ronald Reagan and Arnold Schwarzenegger have been elected to office. Pictured here is activist-playwright Vaclav Havel who became the first elected president of post-communist Czechoslovakia.

Pascal George/Getty Images

SPOTLIGHT ON The Life and Death of Ken Saro-Wiwa

During his lifetime, Nigerian author Ken Saro-Wiwa (1941–1995) wrote twelve children's books, eight plays, five novels, two memoirs, and many poems. But it was his outspoken criticism of the Nigerian government, environmental pollution, and the unfair business practices of Shell oil company that got him into trouble. Nigeria is the sixth-largest producer of crude oil in the world, but the people of Nigeria have little to show for their country's wealth. Most people still live in poverty; the infant mortality rate is one of the highest on the planet; and the average life expectancy is only fifty-four years.

Most of Nigeria's oil revenues lined the pockets of the military regime while Shell Oil was allowed to pump crude oil from the Niger Delta with few, if any, environmental regulations. Saro-Wiwa began campaigning to share the government's wealth with its people. He also called for clean air, land, and water. Then he organized peaceful protests, wrote pamphlets on minority and environmental rights, and launched the grassroots, community-based political

Reuters/Corbis

Ken Saro-Wiwa (1941–1995)

movement called the Survival of the Ogoni People (MOSOP), which called for social and ecological justice for the people of the Niger Delta. When asked why a writer of children's books and comic plays was doing this he said, "The writer cannot be a mere storyteller; he cannot be a mere teacher; he cannot merely X-ray society's weaknesses, its ills, its perils. He or she must be actively involved shaping its present and its future."

In order to silence his voice, the military government of Nigeria arrested Saro-Wiwa on trumped-up murder charges and, despite international protests, he was executed by hanging eight days later along with eight of his compatriots. Saro-Wiwa wrote before his execution, "The men who ordain and supervise this show of shame, this tragic charade, are frightened by the word, the power of ideas, the power of the pen; by the demands of social justice and the rights of man. Nor do they have a sense of history. They are so scared of the power of the word that they do not read. And that is their funeral."

Yet the road for artists into politics has often been perilous. For example, before Czechoslovakian playwright Václav Havel (1936–2011) became president of the new Czech Republic in 1993, he was arrested so often by the former communist regime that he carried his toothbrush with him—ready to go to jail at a moment's notice. Nigerian writer and playwright Wole Soyinka, the first African writer to win the Nobel Prize for Literature (1986), spent two years in solitary confinement—secretly writing on toilet paper and discarded cigarette wrappers—after he was arrested for his political views during Nigeria's civil war. In 2007, art students at Maharaja Sayajirao University in India were jailed for making art that "attacked Indian culture." In 2004, filmmaker Theo van Gogh was murdered in the streets of Amsterdam for making *Submission: Part 1*, an

11-minute movie critical of the treatment of women by Islam. And in 1995, playwright and author Ken Saro-Wiwa was executed for his outspoken views about the military government of Nigeria and the environmental and economic practices of the Shell oil company. (See the Spotlight, "The Life and Death of Ken Saro-Wiwa.") As Polish actor Zygmunt Hubner, former director of the Pow-szechny Theatre in Warsaw, said, "Beware of underestimating the theatre! The theatre is . . . a lens that focuses the rays of many suns. And a lens can start a fire." That lens is the artist's interpretation of how the world is or should be. Often it is the artists who get burned, but on occasion art can also stoke an inferno that reduces tyranny to ashes.

Art versus Entertainment

> The presentation of something besides mere entertainment and spectacle is the great function of the legitimate theatre of the world today.
>
> **Lillian Hellman,**
> Playwright

The fundamental difference between art and entertainment is that artists create primarily to express themselves, making little compromise to appeal to public taste, whereas entertainers create primarily to please an audience. Entertainment is designed to amuse us and make us feel good about who we believe we are and the values we hold. Entertainment, according to Dana Gioia, former head of the National Endowment for the Arts, "exploits and manipulates who we are rather than challenging us with a vision of who we might become." Entertainment satisfies a consumer demand by providing commercialized stories that make us forget our troubles for a few popcorned minutes. Entertainment is designed from the beginning to reinforce the consumer's values and beliefs.

Art may also confirm our values and beliefs, but artists do not necessarily *seek* to confirm them. True, artists often desperately want their audience to understand and appreciate their creation, which is why they may pay attention to criticism and audience reaction. But artists do not always take an audience's opinion into consideration when creating work. They do not compromise to make their work line up with public taste. Writer Mark Slouka put it best, "Art is a supremely individual expression. It doesn't ask permission; it doesn't take an exit poll and adjust accordingly . . . Once artists start asking how many "likes" they've garnered, or listening to customer-satisfaction surveys to increase their sales, they're no longer making art; they're moving product." Entertainers are always willing to adjust, change or rewrite their product to please the audience. Many, if not most, major movie and television producers show works in progress to test with audiences before formally releasing the "product." These test audiences, usually recruited from a targeted age or social group, fill out questionnaires after the showing about what they liked and didn't like, what they thought about the story and the characters, after which the producers, writers, and directors rewrite and edit to make it more audience friendly. In essence, a test audience is a tool for producers to match the values of the product to the consumer, thereby making the product more entertaining and marketable.

What are values? **Values** are the principles, standards, or qualities considered worthwhile or desirable within a given society. Entertainers want to confirm our values because they want to make us feel good about who we are and what we believe so that we buy their product. Otherwise, we may change the channel or spend our money on a different movie. When entertainment fails to reinforce the audience's values, it is often suppressed. For example, the

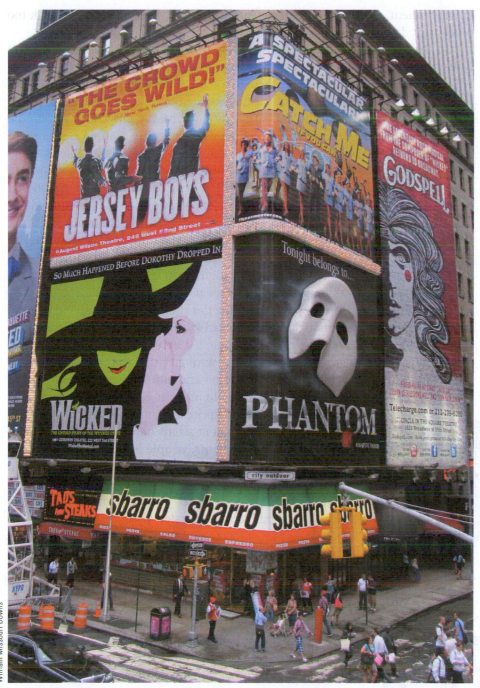

A billboard on Times Square advertises the many musicals available on Broadway. These musicals can be both art and entertainment.

producers of the raucous animated sitcom *Family Guy* made an episode in which the mother (Lois Griffin) has an unwanted pregnancy and contemplates abortion. The episode was so full of frank discussions and outrageous comedy that Fox Network executives felt was a "fragile subject matter at a sensitive time," so they pulled it off the air. Other episodes of *Family Guy* have been rejected even before they made it into production, including one in which the father (Peter Griffin) pushes for his son to convert to Judaism so that he would be "smarter." At other times Fox has insisted that the writers edit individual jokes, including one that contained the phrase "World Trade Center." Fox censored these jokes and episodes because they consider *Family Guy* not a work of art, but pure entertainment, and good entertainment does not make the audience think too much, nor does it challenge the audience's values.

In his book *Life: The Movie—How Entertainment Conquered Reality,* Neal Gabler describes entertainment as a "rearrangement of our problems into shapes which tame them, which disperse them to the margins of our attention." In other words, entertainment is the art of escape. Stephen Sondheim, one of America's leading writers of musical theatre, tells a story about a man walking out on the musical *West Side Story* when it was first produced: "He wanted a musical—meaning a place to relax before he has to go home and face his terrible dysfunctional family. Instead of which he got a lot of ballet dancers in color-coordinated sneakers snapping their fingers and pretending to be tough. His expectation had been defeated." Entertainment fulfills your expectations, it makes you believe that change is not needed, that your way of life is justified; it makes you *think* that you are thinking. Writer Don Marquis said, "If you make people think they're thinking, they'll love you; but if you really make them think, they'll hate you." In short, entertainment fulfills our expectations. Art, on the other hand, makes no compromise for public taste as it inspires us to consider life's complexities and ambiguities. Art is the opposition testing the strength of societal and cultural values—values that are thoughtlessly adopted by the mass of individuals living unexamined lives and all who cannot imagine a different way of seeing life.

All this is not to say there is anything wrong with entertainment—we all need and enjoy entertainment. From sitcoms and amusement parks to the Ice Capades, entertainment is a wonderful way to relax. It adds to the enjoyment of life and is often worth the price of admission. To most people, a life devoid of entertainment seems hardly worth living. Even in the harshest environments, people long to be entertained. For example, the USO (United Service Organizations) has been bringing entertainment to American soldiers on the front lines for more than 60 years, evidence of entertainment's ability to be therapeutic and increase morale.

Never in history have there been so many ways to entertain yourself as there are today, including movies and TV on demand, social media, video games, YouTube, and innumerable websites and other services on the ever-evolving Internet. There are hundreds of thousands of titles that you can rent or download from Netflix, and YouTube has billions of video views per day. According to the Bureau of Labor Statistics, the average American family spends more money on entertainment than on gasoline, clothing, and household furnishings. In addition, Americans watch billions of hours of television every year, even though TV is often not viewed on a television set any more. To get an idea of how much time that is, let's compare it to the amount of time it took to create the popular web encyclopedia Wikipedia. Clay Shirky, in his book *Cognitive Surplus,* estimates that it took about one hundred million hours for human beings to build Wikipedia into what is today—the largest encyclopedia in the world. That means that if Americans turned off the TV for one year they would have enough time to create 2,000 Wikipedia-sized projects.

> Art is an individual experience. It forces us to examine ourselves. It broadens perspective. Entertainment masquerading as art, by contrast, herds viewers and audiences into the collective. It limits perspective to that experienced by the masses.
>
> **Chris Hedges,**
> Journalist and author

Experimental plays test the bounds of theatre. One of the most famous experimental plays is *Paradise Now* (1968), which was staged by The Living Theatre during the Vietnam War. This play directly confronted the audience by staging an "aesthetic assault" on their culture and values.

Courtesy, Living Theatre

With a flick of a remote or a mouse, we can usually find a TV program, movie, or song that makes us feel good about who we are and what we believe. But what happens when we indulge in a diet dominated by entertainment? What happens when we watch and listen only to what confirms our values? We may become apathetic and convinced of our own point of view, but more importantly, we can become intolerant of new ideas and alternative opinions of how the world is or should be. Seth MacFarlane, creator of *Family Guy*, said, "People in America, they're getting dumber, they're getting less and less able to analyze something and think critically, and pick apart the underlying elements. And more and more ready to make a snap judgment regarding something at face value, which is too bad." This same sentiment was paralleled by the great philosopher Ludwig Wittgenstein, who said that philosophical illnesses usually stem from dietary insufficiency. A diet of only one philosophy, religion, or way of looking at the world leads to philosophical illness and a limited view of the world. Art and theatre help balance our diet. They challenge us, teach us, and sometimes even insult us by calling our values into question. In short, here are the differences between art and entertainment:

Art

- Lets us see another's point of view
- Is directed toward the individual
- Makes us think
- Demands an intellectual effort to appreciate it
- Requires active viewing
- Requires self-examination
- Has great potential as an agent of social change
- Challenges the audience
- Offers edification, transcendence, and contemplation
- Does not compromise for public taste

Entertainment

- Pulls us into ourselves, reaffirms our point of view
- Targets the largest possible number of people
- May make us think we're thinking
- Is about sameness
- Makes few intellectual or other demands on the viewer
- Can be done with passive viewing
- May examine life but does not lead to criticism
- Is easily digested
- Has little potential as an agent of social change
- Flatters the audience
- Is about gratification, indulgence, and escape

What Is Theatre? What Is Drama?

Now that you have a basic understanding of art and the differences between art and entertainment, let's look at the theatre and drama. The word *theatre* comes from the ancient Greek word *theatron,* which means "seeing place." The word *drama* comes from the ancient Greek verb *dran,* which means "to take action, to do, to make, or to accomplish." These meanings still apply today—theatre is about an audience witnessing a production or a theatrical event, whereas drama is a form of theatre that tells a story in which characters set out to do, to accomplish, or to take some sort of action.

In his book *The Empty Space,* English director Peter Brook states that all that is needed for theatre to occur is an empty space and someone to walk across that space while someone else watches. In later chapters, we'll discuss the various types of spaces, or stages, used throughout history and today. At this point, simply note that, at its most basic, theatre requires only a space, a performer, and an audience. Story, characters, spectacle, costumes, lights, script, and sets are all unnecessary. They may improve the theatrical experience, but they are optional. As such, many events can qualify as a kind of theatre: weddings, award banquets, football games, political rallies, church services, or even a supermodel walking down a runway. Any time people get together with the common purpose of throwing the focus on a particular person, we have a theatrical event.

Drama is a form of theatre that tells a story about people, their actions, and the conflicts that result. **Conflict** is the key to the movement of a story and is what qualifies a theatrical work as a play. Whether explicit or implicit, conflict is at the core of drama. As Professor David Ball, author of *Backwards & Forwards: A Technical Manual for Reading Plays,* puts it, "People who talk about, write about, or do theatre agree on little. But there is one thing: 'Drama is *conflict*!' we all cry in rare unanimity." If there is no conflict, there is no power struggle, and if there is no power struggle, there is no story. Without a story, there may be theatre but not drama.

Both theatre and drama have three qualities that make them unique art forms. First, theatre is always live. This means that theatre cannot be replayed, like a film. You can watch a movie again and again and it is always the same. This is not so in the theatre, because no two performances are ever exactly the same. No two Hamlets ever ask the question "To be, or not to be . . ." in precisely the same way. So, if you go to the theatre on Monday night and tell a friend that you loved the performance, and your friend goes to the same show on Tuesday night and says that he hated it, you both may be right because the two of you did not see the same exact performance or see it with the same audience.

The second quality that makes drama and theatre unique was introduced earlier in this chapter: they are always about human beings. A painting might be about a flower, a poem might be about the stars, but theatre and drama can only be about human beings and human emotions. At their most basic, theatre and drama always express something fundamental about the human condition with the intention to touch, arouse, inform, entertain, or even enrage the audience by portraying aspects of themselves.

When you come into the theater, you have to be willing to say, "We're all here to undergo a communion, to find out what the hell is going on in this world." If you're not willing to say that, what you get is entertainment instead of art, and poor entertainment at that.

Playwright David Mamet,
Three Uses of the Knife

Patricia Switzer

The third quality that makes theatre and drama unique is that they are often collaborative forms of art, requiring more than one type of art and artist to produce. This is not true of most other forms of art, which are the product of a single individual. For example, art museums are often very quiet. They do not feature music, because it would interfere with the visual art. Similarly, we do not need music, dance, or a director to help us read a book. In contrast, plays often use lights, sound, movement, words, and actions. When you attend the theatre, more often than not you experience art made by an ensemble of artists. Often the final product is a result of how well all these artists coordinated their artistic visions. (In Chapters 5, 6, 7, 8, and 9, we will explore in greater detail the various artists involved in crafting theatre.)

Now let's explore the five most common categories of theatre: commercial, historical, political, experimental, and cultural.

Art and entertainment are not mutually exclusive. Entertaining works can be considered art and art can be entertaining. The musical *Miss Saigon* contains powerful political themes about American involvement in the Vietnam War and yet it can be called entertainment. The production pictured here was staged by the Arvada Center for the Arts and Humanities.

The Common Categories of Theatre

There are many types of theatre, most of which are covered in greater detail in later chapters of this text. However, let's take some time here to survey the most common categories in order to understand the various roles theatre plays in society.

Perhaps the most familiar category of theatre is **commercial theatre,** which includes big musicals as well as comedies and dramas that are intended to be entertaining and profitable.

Commercial plays offer safe themes, plenty of laughs, and spectacle designed to appeal to a majority of people, thereby filling lots of seats and ideally making lots of money. Big Broadway musicals like *Beauty and the Beast* or *Spider-Man: Turn Off the Dark* are perfect examples of commercial theatre, but it can also include familiar plays appealing to the widest possible demographic staged by small local theatres. The commercial theatre has been around for thousands of years. As we will see next, most other types of theatre are not designed to be purely entertaining or to turn a profit.

Historical theatre presents dramas that use the styles, themes, and staging of plays of a particular historical period. And there is plenty of history to be staged, for theatre has been around for thousands of years and has reflected hundreds of styles and themes. From the classical forms of theatre, such as Sophocles' *Oedipus Rex* and Shakespeare's *Hamlet,* to the dawn of modern drama with Henrik Ibsen's *A Doll's House,* historical theatre attempts to show how far humanity has come by presenting costumes, acting styles, language, and subject matter that express universal human concerns rather than ideas that are specific to the current generation. When you attend this type of theatre, you'll probably enjoy it more if you have some knowledge of history and do some research beforehand into the background of the particular playwright and

Political Theatre can be a powerful tool for exposing social ills. For example, Steven Dietz's play *God's Country* is about the 1984 assassination of liberal radio talk show host Alan Berg after he spoke out against the white supremacist movement. This production was staged by the National Theatre Conservatory at the Denver Center for the Performing Arts.

Patricia Switzer

theatrical style. When you attend historical theatre, you are not just being entertained; you are also getting a lesson in history. And one of those lessons may be that though a play is hundreds of years old, the themes are still very relevant.

Political theatre allows playwrights, directors, and actors to express their personal opinions about current issues, trends, and politics. This type of theatre is a bully pulpit, an open mic, and a bullhorn that allows the artist to express ideas that are seldom heard in the mainstream media or in commercial theatre. Political theatre allows artists to ask an audience to join them in a protest or in calling for social change. For example, the play *The Exonerated*, written by Erik Jensen and Jessica Blank, revolves around the stories of six former death row prisoners who were falsely accused, wrongly convicted, and eventually exonerated—several after being imprisoned for decades. Once the play is over, the cast and crew invite the audience to stay afterward to discuss the wisdom of imposing the death sentence and provide information about how they can personally take steps to end the practice of it. In addition to being a voice for the disenfranchised of society, political theatre can be designed by "the powers that be" in order to control the hearts and minds of the people. For example, during World War II, Nazi Germany's rulers produced propaganda plays and highly theatrical political rallies designed to win the people over to their way of thinking.

Plays can also be experimental in nature. Just as automakers display concept cars that try out new designs, theatre artists also experiment with styles and ideas in **experimental plays** that push the limits of theatre. These plays might break down barriers by eliminating the distance between actor and audience, trying out new staging techniques, or even questioning the nature of theatre itself. For example, The Living Theatre of the 1960s dedicated itself to staging such works as *Paradise Now* (1968), in which actors asked the audience to join them in a protest calling for a social revolution. Experimental plays are an attempt to reinvent theatre, for all art forms must avoid stagnation by constantly searching for what the future of the art form might be.

Finally, there is **cultural theatre,** which is designed to support the heritage, customs, and point of view of a particular people, religion, class, country, or community. This theatre celebrates human diversity by providing the audience a window into a world that is different from their own or by preserving the unique traditions of a particular society. As later chapters of this book will discuss, when you attend Japanese Kabuki plays, African ritual plays, or the Peking Opera, you reinforce your own culture or learn about other peoples' cultures by witnessing aspects of their religion, history, customs, folklore, or worldviews.

When attending the theatre, remember that any given performance doesn't necessarily fit neatly into just one of these categories. For example, a play can be both cultural and commercial, and another might be political and experimental. But knowing about these basic categories can increase your enjoyment of the theatre. For example, if you go to the theatre expecting a purely commercial production and find yourself watching an experimental play, you might not enjoy it. Or, you might be offended. But try to keep an open mind, determine what type of theatre you're witnessing, and enjoy or study it for what it is rather than what you thought it would be. And remember that theatre is not always designed simply to entertain us. Sometimes it teaches us, sometimes it insults us, and sometimes it makes us think.

Curtain Call

Why does the ancient art of theatre still exist in a world dominated by movies and television? We need art and theatre because they help us *see life differently*. Entertainment allows us to see life as *we* see it, with our values and perceptions intact. Art, on the other hand, allows us to expand our experience, intensify our perceptions, challenge conventional wisdom, and introduce another frame of reference—that of the artist. Thus, art, as Harold Taylor said, allows us to "move freely into areas of experience which were formerly unknown." The American set designer Robert Edmond Jones once said:

> Here is the secret of the flame that burns in the work of the great artists of the theatre. They seem so much more aware than we are, and so much more awake, and so much more alive that they make us feel that what we call living is not living at all, but a kind of sleep. Their knowledge, their wealth of emotions, their wonder, their elation, their swift, clear seeing surrounds every occasion with a crowd of values that enriches it beyond anything which we, in our happy satisfaction, had ever imagined. In their hands it becomes not only a thing of beauty but a thing of power. And we see it all—beauty and power alike—as a part of the life of the theatre.

SUMMARY

MindTap®

Test your knowledge with online printable flashcards and online quizzing.

Philosophers, artists, and critics have been debating the meaning of the word *art* for thousands of years. Few have been in agreement, and even today the debate continues. Often when we use the word *art,* we are referring to a skill or a talent, the aesthetics of a piece of art, or the meaning inherent in a piece of art. Generally, artists see art as a means of finding or conveying meaning. They create art to educate, inform, influence, and sometimes even offend and enrage an audience.

Rather than attempt an all-encompassing definition of art, we may find it more useful to describe art in terms of the qualities that all works of art have in common. These qualities include human creation, subject and medium, structure, and reaction. By describing art in this way, we can embrace all of the different forms art takes.

Art is important in our lives because it can bring order to what seems to be a chaotic universe. Religion and philosophy help us explain *why* events occur, science can explain *how* events occur, and art can fine-tune our understanding by expressing events in human terms. Artists isolate the aspects of nature they regard as essential and integrate them into a concrete, focused, and organized view of life. With this organization comes meaning and significance. In addition, every artist is a political individual who states an opinion that may challenge an audience's values, shatter their preconceptions, or help them see the world in a new way.

Theatre is a dynamic form of performing art that focuses on the human experience. All that is needed for theatre to occur is an empty space, someone to walk across that space, and someone to watch. We often refer to theatre as drama, but in fact there is a difference. Drama is a form of theatre that tells us stories about people, their actions, and the conflicts that result. Conflict is the key to the movement of a story and is what qualifies a theatrical work as a play. Conflict is at the core of drama.

Theatre is also a unique form of art because it is always live, it is always about the human experience, and it is a particularly collaborative form of art, requiring more than one type of art and artist to produce. There are many different categories of theatre, the most common being commercial theatre, historical theatre, political theatre, experimental theatre, and cultural theatre.

Theatre can be considered artistic, entertaining, or both. The fundamental difference between art and entertainment is that artists create primarily to express themselves and communicate their particular perspective, whereas entertainers create to please an audience. Entertainment is meant to amuse us and make us feel good, not necessarily to challenge our values and beliefs. Art may also confirm our values and beliefs, but artists do not necessarily seek to confirm them. This means that art is far more likely to have controversial themes that make us think.

KEY TERMS

Aesthetics / 3

Commercial theatre /18

Conflict / 16

Cultural theatre / 19

Drama / 16

Experimental plays / 19

Historical theatre / 18

Literary arts / 6

Medium / 6

Performing arts / 6

Pictorial arts / 6

Political theatre / 19

Spatial arts / 6

Subject / 6

Values / 12

Chapter 2
STAGE VERSUS SCREEN

Unlike the movie version of *West Side Story*, which is fixed in time and unchanging, every stage production of the musical is different. It is the live nature of theatre that makes it special. This picture is from the latest Broadway revival of the play at the Palace Theater in New York.

Sara Krulwich/The New York Times/Redux

Outline

For thousands of years the theatre has had little competition, but in the modern world it must vie with movies, television, and other screen entertainments. Although theatre, film, and television have some obvious elements in common, there are key differences when it comes to acting, directing, funding, creative control, ownership, and audience participation that make the theatre unique. In this chapter, we'll look at each of these elements to understand why the ancient art of theatre remains vital and valuable in our modern world of diverse screen entertainments.

The invention of film and television had a major effect on the theatre. For a time, some critics were saying that screen entertainments would lead to the theatre's demise. "The theatre is dying" was a common catchphrase. But today, well over a hundred years after the invention of the movies, and decades after television became a dominant force, the stage is thriving. It has stood the test of time because film and television, as well as the Internet, Xboxes, apps, and avatars, have not improved upon or replaced the art of theatre.

MindTap®

Start with a quick warm-up activity and review the chapter's learning objectives.

The Audience

Movies and television require only passive participation. You can leave the movie theatre if you don't like a movie, or hit Pause or Rewind on the DVD player, and it will not affect the actors. However, in the theatre the performers can hear and often see you. If the audience doesn't laugh at a line that the cast believes is funny, that affects them. If an audience finds a performance amusing, the actors will "hold for laughs" to make sure the next funny line will be heard. And if a cell phone goes off or there is a disturbance in the audience, an actor might be distracted enough to forget lines. Even when the audience is perfectly silent, cast members often say they can feel an "energy" coming from them. One thing is certain: give stage actors your full attention and they will do a better job. *New York Times* theatre critic Margo Jefferson says there is something almost "primal" about the relationship between a theatre audience and the actors because of their physical proximity and the power the audience has to affect the actors' performances. The immediate nature of theatre is why it is sometimes called "the living stage" or a "living art."

Communication flows in only one direction during screen entertainments: from the TV screen to your easy chair, or from the big screen to your sticky megaplex seat. You can throw tomatoes at screens big and small and it won't change a thing about the show. The audience has two choices: to watch or not

MindTap®

Read, highlight, and take notes online.

> Television's hypnotic power lies in the fact that it roasts us with its light like butterflies around a lamp: it produces continuous jets of flowing colors and impressions that we suck down with a never-ending thirst. Television is an animated piece of furniture and it speaks, it serves the function of making dullness bearable.
>
> **Pascal Bruckner,**
> Writer

Theatre is live and immediate. The actors can hear and see you, and your reaction to them changes the production from performance to performance. With screen entertainments, communication flows in only one direction, but in the theatre communication is a two-way street. This is why theatre is often called a "living art."

We're so accustomed to the unchanging nature of film (and recording and computer effects) that we're less tolerant of theatre's human fallibility. Nothing in our responses can change a movie; it's invulnerable, as no actor or play, however great, can be.

Margo Jefferson,
New York Times theatre critic

Think of this moment. All that has ever been is in this moment; all that will be is in this moment. Both are meeting in one living flame, in this unique instant of time. This is drama; this is theatre—to be aware of the Now.

Robert Edmond Jones,
Theatre designer

We're tightrope walkers. When you walk the wire in a movie, the wire is painted on the floor, but when you walk it on the stage, it's a hundred feet high without a net.

Al Pacino,
Actor

to watch. This makes for a very different level of audience participation than at the theatre. For example, when was the last time you were at a movie where the audience applauded at the end? It happens, but only very rarely. When you're watching TV, do you stand and applaud in your own living room? No matter how brilliant the acting, no matter how much the film or television show affected you, you don't usually applaud. Why? Because the performers can't hear you. There is no communication from you to them. In Yoruba, the western part of Nigeria, television is called *ero asoro maghese,* which means "the machine that speaks but accepts no reply." Theatre, on the other hand, accepts replies. Actor John Lithgow, who acts in films, television, and on the stage, says that performing in the theatre is "the purest form of acting," because it belongs to both the audience and the actors.

Theatre is a risky business. The unrepeatable nature of live theatre makes watching it like watching a high-wire act—something can always go wrong and you never know what you're going to get. Not only are no two performances exactly the same, but unless you read a review of a play before you see it, you probably know only the basics of the plot, not the specifics of the play's content. In contrast, movie studios and television networks advertise their products heavily before they're seen. Before you go see a movie or watch a television show, you usually have a pretty good idea of what to expect. Movies and television in the United States also have a rating system that warns you when a show or movie includes sexual content, violence, or adult language, and movie theatres even limit who can attend particular movies. Most of the time you can avoid seeing material you think will insult you or challenge your values. All this information makes for a safety net not generally available in the theatre. In short, when you go to the theatre, you're taking a chance. But this element of chance is also what makes live theatre exciting and rewarding to watch.

Acting: Key Differences

Most people think that acting on a stage and acting in a movie are the same. In many ways they are, but there are also some key differences. Unlike stage actors, screen actors always have a backup. If they can't perform what the script or director calls for, doubles can fill in and perform the dance, jump off the skyscraper, or sing the song. For example, in the movie *West Side Story,* Natalie Wood did not sing her own songs while playing the character of Maria. Rather than spending time and money training her to be a better singer, the film studio simply dubbed in another voice. A stage actress named Marni Nixon was the real singer in that movie—she also dubbed songs for Audrey Hepburn in the movie version of *My Fair Lady,* for Deborah Kerr in *The King and I,* and even sang the phrase "These rocks don't lose their shape" for Marilyn Monroe in *Gentlemen Prefer Blondes.* "Hollywood wanted recognizable stars," Nixon said. "And the fact that a lot of the stars couldn't sing was only a minor inconvenience to the big [Hollywood] producers." But if you see *West Side Story, My Fair Lady,* or *The King and I* on stage, there can be no substitution. The actress playing the part must be able to act, dance, and sing.

Actors in films and TV are sometimes called "talking heads" because there are so many close-up shots in which an actor expresses an emotion with the face or even part of the face. Stage actress Dame Judith Anderson learned about

United Artists/Photofest

Photofest

When you see movie stars singing in films, you're often hearing someone else's voice. This process, dubbing, is common in movies. In the movie *West Side Story*, the singing voice of Natalie Wood (at left) was dubbed by professional singer Marni Nixon (at right), who also dubbed Audrey Hepburn's voice in *My Fair Lady*. But you can't dub in theatre, so actors in musical theatre must sing their own songs.

close-ups in her first movie acting experience. The director called her aside and said, "Watch your eyebrows." He explained that when she moved her eyebrows on stage, it was a matter of only a fraction of an inch, but when she raised them in a close-up shot, it was the same as moving them three feet on screen. In the theatre, there is no such thing as a close-up. Everything is a wide shot, so actors must learn to express themselves with their entire body. Also, the-atre actors spend years training their voices to fill large theatres, often without microphones and amplification. Film actors don't have to project their voices because the boom mic is always right over their heads, just out of the frame. (In fact, if you watch closely enough, you can occasionally see the boom mic accidentally drop into the shot.)

Additionally, screen actors don't have to remember as many lines as stage actors. Many movies and most television shows generally have fewer lines of dialogue than plays, and screen actors seldom have to remember more than just a few minutes' worth of dialogue at a time. Screen actors often learn their lines on the day of shooting; sometimes they don't have to remember lines at all because cue cards and teleprompters can be placed just off camera, allowing them to simply read their lines. This is especially true for television actors in many soap operas and live shows such as *Saturday Night Live*. Stage actors don't have it so easy. They must memorize thousands of lines of dialogue and long speeches before they dare to perform in front of a live audience—and if they forget their lines there is no one there to help. (See Spotlight in Chapter 7, "The Actor's Nightmare—Forgetting Lines.")

Don Arnold/WireImage/Getty Images

One of the most popular musicals for stage and film is *Les Miserables* (pictured here). Unlike film actors, stage actors often perform a play or musical six to eight times a week and must get it right every time.

But the most important difference is that in movies and TV, screen actors are allowed to fail. If they don't get it right on the first take, they can always try again. If they fail a hundred times in a row, they can still win an Oscar if they get it right on the hundred-and-first take. In contrast, stage actors must get it right the first time, night after night after night. For example, in the movie version of the stage musical *Chicago*, Richard Gere tap-dances, Catherine Zeta-Jones struts her stuff, and Renée Zellweger sings. They all look pretty good, yet the director had the luxury of cutting to a new shot or a different take every few seconds, thereby covering up all their missteps and wrong notes.

Not that acting for the camera is easy. Movies are often shot out of sequence, so in the morning a film actor might start shooting a tender love scene, die that afternoon on the battlefield, and in the evening go back to finishing the love scene. In general, though, actors who train for the stage need much more training, more hours of rehearsal, and perhaps even more talent, for there is no safety net in the theatre, no editor to make errors disappear, no cue cards or teleprompters, and no retakes or second chances. This is the very nature of the live theatre: anything can happen!

Directing: Key Differences

Film is often called a director's medium, because the director has a great deal of creative control. The director is all-powerful and tells everyone what to do, except for the producers, who bankroll the production. Directors can change the script, rewrite a scene, and control exactly what the audience will see moment by moment and shot by shot. If they don't like one take, they can shoot a scene repeatedly until they get what they want. Interestingly, the opposite is true in most television sitcoms and dramas. In television, the directors often go unnoticed and are sometimes even subservient to the writers. Television is so fast-paced, delivering new ideas, scripts, and episodes each week, that it makes sense for the person in charge to be the one who produces those scripts: the writer or the producer.

As we will discuss in later chapters, theatre directors can also be very powerful, but they never have absolute control over every moment of the production. Each performance is different, and no matter how skilled they are, no actor can exactly duplicate what he or she did the night before. In most instances, the director chooses, or "casts," the actors, and during rehearsal the director will suggest, urge, and even demand certain things from them. Yet, once the curtain goes up, no director can bring it down to make adjustments. Nor does the theatre director have control over the script—the playwright owns the copyright, except when the script is in public domain, which is the case for plays written long ago, such as Shakespeare's plays. (The ideas of copyright and public domain are covered in greater detail later in this chapter.) The special collaborative aspect of play production usually makes theatre a little more democratic than film or television. You hear the words *ensemble* and *team* used often in the theatre but not always in film and television, even though these mediums also require a collaborative effort. As a result, in a good theatre production—one where egos are not battling for control, and collaboration is based on mutual respect—more voices are heard and more creative individuals are working together, rather than a solitary authority telling everyone what to do. In the theatre, there is no "director's cut."

Funding and Profit

Another major difference between most theatre and screen entertainments is funding and profit. With only a few notable exceptions, such as the big Broadway production companies, theatres are generally nonprofit companies. "Nonprofit" companies do not have stockholders and pay no dividends or federal

William Missouri Downs

. . . acting for film is like a musician playing in a recording studio and acting in the theatre is like playing live in concert . . . .

Willem Dafoe,
Actor

It's much harder to write for the stage because it's got to be really tight; it's got to work—actors are dependent on their cues, they're live . . . In film, they can garble it and mangle it and get it backwards, but if you shoot it and it comes out funny that way, you have it and it's great for all time.

Woody Allen,
Director, screenwriter, and playwright

Theatre is expensive because it is labor-intensive and it plays to very limited audiences. Costs include not only designing, building, and maintaining the costumes, sets, and lights, but also advertising, utilities, insurance, rental fees, maintenance fees, payroll taxes, union benefits, royalties, and salaries for actors, directors, stage crews, technicians, musicians, ushers, box office personnel, accountants, and security.

Unlike Hollywood movies, which can employ dozens if not hundreds of actors, professional theatres often operate on such tight budgets that they can only afford to produce plays with small casts. While this is not the case with college and amateur productions where the actors are not paid, many professional theatres have an unwritten rule that if a play has more than seven roles the chances of it getting produced are small. One popular two character full-length play is Arlene Hutton's *Last Train to Nibroc*. This production featured Katrina DeSpain and Nicholas Linn and was produced at the Snowy Range Summer Theatre.

taxes. The Internal Revenue Service created nonprofit status for companies and organizations that are not designed for private financial gain and that provide the general public with charitable, educational, and recreational services. Most theatres apply for and receive nonprofit status because the sad fact is that most plays—and the theatre companies that produce them—lose money. If it weren't for tax exemptions, donors, and patrons of the arts, most theatres would cease to exist. And even the best for-profit theatres often don't fare much better, because fewer people attend the theatre than watch television or movies. For example, an average of 10 to 11 million people per year attend plays or musicals at one of the 39 Broadway theatres in New York City. By comparison the average Super Bowl football game attracts more than 100 million viewers on a single afternoon. As a matter of fact, on Super Bowl Sunday more people watch Animal Planet's "Puppy Bowl" than attend Broadway plays in a whole year. Broadway's combined gross sales (not profits) average around one billion per year. That sounds good until you realize that one billion is about the same amount of money the average Batman movie earns at the box office worldwide.

Funding the Screen

Each year people all over the world pay tens of billions of dollars to go to the movies, rent DVDs, and watch television. But that is only part of the big media companies' income. They also make money through advertising. When you go

University of Wyoming Photo Archives

Warner Bros/Everett Collection

Product placement is common in Hollywood movies and television. Not only do companies pay billions to have their products placed within a scene, but they also send a representative to the set to make sure the actors prominently display products within the production. There are even public relations and marketing agencies that specialize in forging ties between products and celebrities. In this scene from the movie *Syriana*, Matt Damon and Amanda Peet star with a box of Cheerios.

to the movies or watch television and see a star drinking a particular type of soda, driving a specific type of car, or wearing distinct apparel, it is more than likely that a soft drink, car, or clothing company paid millions to have their product featured. **Product placement** is becoming so big that in 2015 corporations paid more than $15 billion to have their products strategically located within a shot, or weaved into a storyline, and that number will continue to grow in the future. This is why James Bond switches among Smirnoff, Absolut, and Stolichnaya vodka from movie to movie: the company that pays the most gets their product featured. And the same is true of TV. As a matter of fact, 75 percent of all product placement money goes to television. So when you see Adam Sandler enjoying Popeye's chicken in a movie or a Staples paper shredder featured in a television show, it's almost certainly in the shot because a manufacturer paid millions to place it there.

Traditional television makes money not only through product placement but also by selling commercial time. The more commercials a network can pack into an hour, the more money it can make. For example, on average MTV spends 18 minutes and 11 seconds per hour airing commercials and FOX, 16 minutes and 36 seconds. And the amount of commercial time continues to increase—Disney's ABC has augmented the amount of time given to commercials by 34 percent since 1989. Selling commercials can make the television companies a lot of money. In 2015, a 30-second advertisement on a popular sitcom generally cost between $300,000 and $350,000. A 30-second ad on *Monday Night Football* goes for about $400,000, and *Sunday Night Football* can be a whopping $600,000.

Funding Theatre and the Arts

When you divide the cost of a Hollywood blockbuster movie, which can cost hundreds of millions to produce, by the tens, even hundreds, of millions of

National Archives

National Archives

Before the NEA there was the Federal Theatre Project (FTP), established in the 1930s as part of Franklin Delano Roosevelt's New Deal social reforms. During its four-year existence, the Federal Theatre Project employed more than 10,000 theatre professionals and mounted more than 1,000 productions. Many plays staged during this time highlighted the social ills of the nation, such as *Triple-A Plowed Under*, which dramatized the plight of farmers, and *One-Third of a Nation*, which studied the problems of the homeless in America. These sorts of plays got the Federal Theatre Project into deep trouble. By 1939, charges began flying that the FTP was dominated by communists, and politicians accused it of portraying "un-American propaganda." Soon thereafter, funding was cut.

people who will see it on the screen or on video, the production cost per audience member is tiny. The same is true of television. On the other hand, a play costs far less to produce—anywhere from a few thousand dollars for a community theatre production to several million for a big Broadway production. However, when the expenses of producing live theatre are divided by the limited number of seats available, the cost per audience member is high in comparison to screen entertainments.

The problem in funding theatre stems from the nature of theatre: It is a live medium. Theatre is labor-intensive and comparatively low-tech, with few technological innovations to make it cheaper. Screen entertainments benefit from numerous technological advances that replace the expensive labor force once required to produce a movie or TV show. But in theatre, the cost of producing a play is continually on the rise precisely because it depends on human labor, much of which cannot be replaced by machinery. For example, the lighting changes for a play can be programmed into a computer, but no computer can predict what will happen during each live performance. Put simply, inspired human minds are always required backstage to support the inspired human minds and bodies onstage, as they attempt to inspire a live audience.

Another obstacle in funding theatre is that ticket sales at most nonprofit theatres cover only 60 percent of the cost of producing a performance. If most theatres had to depend solely on ticket sales, they would have to raise their prices to the point where only the very rich could afford a seat. As a matter of fact, that is exactly what is happening with Broadway for-profit plays and musicals where ticket prices are commonly well over $100 per seat. Studies show that the average person who attends plays on Broadway has a median household income in excess of $200,000. In order to satisfy demand and make theatre available to more people, nonprofit theatres cut ticket prices and try to make up the difference through alternative forms of funding. A recent poll by the Theatre Communications Group questioned 262 theatres on the sources of their funding. It was found that 59 percent of their income came from tickets and concession sales, and 41 percent had to come from outside sources, including grants and contributions. Individual contributors, corporations, foundations, and federal, state, and local entities keep theatre alive.

Individual contributors to the arts, or **patrons**, come in all sizes. They range from billionaire philanthropists who give away millions, to average Americans who donate a few extra, hard-earned bucks. Most nonprofit theatres print a list of their donors in the program you're handed by the ushers. The people who contribute the least are listed as "donor" or "patron," whereas those who give greater amounts might be labeled "benefactor" or "producer" or given a creative name like "angel" or "protector." Most theatres are nonprofit, so donors' gifts are tax-deductible, or free from federal income taxes. Theatres also offer donors other benefits, such as special opening or closing-night parties, first choice of seats, thank-you gifts, membership in patron clubs, and the opportunity to serve on the theatre's board of directors.

Corporate funding for the arts, whether from the smallest mom-and-pop companies or mammoth corporations, is good for business. Small businesses, such as restaurants, will donate to a local theatre because a successful theatre in the neighborhood can increase dinner receipts. Studies show that for every dollar a theatre spends, it brings in $5 in goods and services for related or neighboring enterprises. Private parking lots, restaurants, taverns, coffeehouses, and retail stores reap the benefits of increased traffic, which boosts the local economy. Large corporations often make donations to gain political clout, tax write-offs, or publicity.

Sometimes corporations make donations to theatres in an effort to suggest that they are "giving something back" to the community. For example, the Metropolitan Life Insurance Company underwrites the PBS television series *Live from Lincoln Center*, which often presents opera and theatre performances. Recently, however, corporate funding for the arts and theatre has been in decline. According to the Giving USA Foundation, an educational and research program of the American Association of Fundraising Counsel, corporate funding of the arts has dropped by nearly one-half in the last decade. And when

Arts groups are notoriously undercapitalized, living year to year (or even week to week). As a result, even mild economic downturns can be devastating. In this era of free market fetishization, it may be difficult for many people to grasp, but the arts don't come close to paying their own way. They need welfare—public or private.

Christopher Shea,
Writer, in The American
Prospect magazine

corporations today do fund the theatre, the money often comes with strings attached. Some corporations will give money only if free tickets are given to their employees; others require that company promotional material be included in the play's programs, posters and other advertisements, and even printed on the tickets. Some corporations fund theatre because they have a vested interest in the subject matter. For example, Serono, a biotechnology company that makes fertility drugs, sponsored the musical *Infertility*. It appears as if today's corporations are less interested in philanthropy and more interested in targeting specific demographics with commercials and product placement, as well as controlling the message of the entertainment produced. In some cases, corporate sponsors attach restrictions on subject matter, forcing theatres to avoid plays about labor unions, pollution, socialism, communism, workers' rights, workers' safety, closing corporate tax loopholes, the need for greater government regulations, or any theme that corporations find objectionable. With more than 150 different corporate sponsors, PBS programming faces similar "side effects" of corporate funding. A common joke in the industry today is that PBS no longer stands for "Public Broadcasting Service" but "Petroleum Broadcasting Service" because so much of their funding comes from large oil corporations that place limits on what they can produce and broadcast using the funds they donate. For example, there is evidence to suggest that PBS pulled a documentary called "Citizen Koch" because they feared it would offend the billionaire industrialist David Koch who has given millions to PBS.

Government funding, the money spent each year on the arts by federal, state, and local entities, is by far the most controversial method of maintaining a healthy arts community in the United States—even though we spend far fewer tax dollars on the arts than any other major industrialized nation. The U.S. government, for example, spends 1/40th of what Germany spends per capita to support the arts.

Hollywood movies often use star power to sell tickets. On the other hand, most theatres do not have the resources to hire big name actors. When a star does accept a contract with a theatre, it is often at a drastically reduced salary and he or she performs mostly for the love of being on stage. Here the Wenham's theatre in London headlines Academy Award Winner Holly Hunter.

William Missouri Downs

The federal agency that disburses our arts tax dollars is the **National Endowment for the Arts (NEA)**, and it is one of the smallest of all the government programs. Funding for the arts takes up a very tiny part of the federal budget. Approximately 29 percent of the federal budget goes to support the military, 19 percent to pay the national debt, 4 percent for education, but only 0.01 percent to support the arts. In fact the amount of money Americans pay in federal tax dollars to support the NEA is less than they pay to support the U.S. Army marching bands. (In 2015 the budget for the NEA was $158 million; that same year the budget for the U.S. Army marching bands was $198 million.) To be fair, it is important to point out that tax money goes to support more than just the NEA. (For up-to-date information on arts funding, check out the *National Arts Index* online.) But if you include the federal tax dollars that go to the Smithsonian Institution, the Corporation for Public Broadcasting (PBS), the National Endowment for the Humanities, the National Gallery of Art, the Kennedy Center for the Performing Arts, the Advisory Council for Historic Preservation, the Institute of Museum and Library Services, and the money the departments of State and Education spend to support the arts, the total is still less than $8 per American per year. Less than the cost of one movie ticket. To put that into perspective: in order to pay just the interest on the national debt, each American must pay nearly $750 in taxes each year.

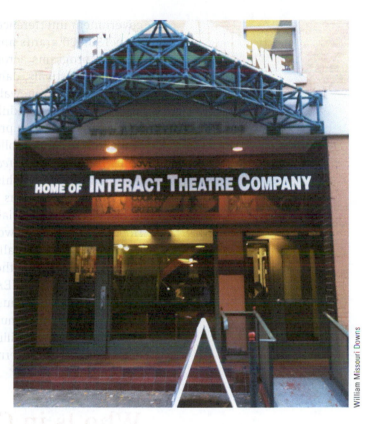

William Missouri Downs

There are thousands of independently owned, smaller theatres all over the United States that are locally controlled and funded. Being independent means they can often present a wider diversity of views than do Hollywood movies. Pictured here is the InterAct Theatre in Philadelphia, known for producing new and sometimes controversial plays.

President John F. Kennedy earned the bipartisan support needed to create the National Endowment for the Arts (NEA), but he was assassinated in 1963 before his dream could be realized. In September 1965, President Lyndon B. Johnson signed into law the bill that created the National Endowment for the Arts as well as the National Endowment for the Humanities. The bill states in part, "While no government can call a great artist or scholar into existence, it is necessary and appropriate for the Federal Government to help create and sustain not only a climate encouraging freedom of thought, imagination, and inquiry, but also the material condition facilitating the release of this creative talent." The first NEA grant went to the American Ballet Theatre and saved the nearly bankrupt ballet company from extinction. Since then, the NEA would become the largest single supporter of nonprofit art in America as it attempted to fulfill its mission "to foster the excellence, diversity, and vitality of the arts in the United States, and to broaden public access to the arts."

The NEA acts as an independent commission, and NEA panels do not have to get their decisions rubber-stamped by the Senate or the president. The law that created the NEA states: "No department, agency, officer, or employee of the United States shall exercise any supervision or control over the administration or operations of the NEA." It is to be an independent government institution, thereby facilitating artistic speech while limiting

We have agencies of the Government which are concerned with the welfare and advancement of science and technology, of education, recreation and health. We should now begin to give similar attention to the arts.

John F. Kennedy,
President of the United States,
1961–1963

government interference and censorship. To date, the NEA has given out more than 150,000 grants and provided funding for a wide variety of artistic and cultural programs across the United States. It has supported concerts, theatres, film festivals, dance performances, orchestras, operas, poetry readings, and downtown renewal projects. It has helped museums with travel costs so that they can take exhibitions to inner cities and rural areas. It has invested millions in K–12 arts programs nationwide. It gives money to preserve historical paintings and public monuments. It helps showcase Native American art, helps fund the PBS *Great Performances* series, and even helped with the PBS documentary on the history of the American music creation known as rock and roll. The NEA has funded projects ranging from the design of the Vietnam Veterans Memorial in Washington, D.C., to the acclaimed documentary *Hoop Dreams* about two inner-city Chicago youths and their quest to become professional basketball players. When a symphony orchestra played at the memorial service for the victims of the Oklahoma City bombing, it was aided by a grant from the NEA.

The relatively minuscule funding our government invests in the NEA helps the national arts community pump nearly $37 billion into the economy and generates more than $5 billion in revenue for federal, state, and local governments. Few, if any, other governmental programs can boast such a high return on such a small investment.

Who Is in Control?

The picture we have painted so far portrays those who control screen entertainments as being far more interested in the audience's values than in the artist's voice. Theatre, on the other hand, has been shown as more interested in the artist's voice than in the audience's values. However, there is no exact dividing line between them. Some commercial theatre productions, such as Disney's stage versions of its films *The Lion King* and *Beauty and the Beast,* are sometimes called **bourgeois theatre** because they pursue maximum profits by reaffirming the audience's values just as rigorously as any big-budget Hollywood film, and many art and independent films stress the artist's vision as much as any noncommercial theatre. But generally speaking, Hollywood more often produces entertainment, and theatre more often creates art. This becomes even clearer when you look at the organizations that produce and fund—and therefore control—entertainment and art.

Who Controls Content?

Who controls screen entertainments and the theatre could not be more different. With combined revenues in the hundreds of billions, most Hollywood screen entertainment companies are owned by some of the largest multinational corporations in the world. In contrast, smaller companies, independent producers, and even mom-and-pop theatre companies produce the lion's share of theatre in the United States.

In 1975, about 50 corporations owned 90 percent of American entertainment companies (which include book publishers, magazines, movie companies, television networks, and newspapers). Today, because of deregulation, the number is down to six. And these multinational corporations, sometimes called **media moguls**, want exactly what all corporations want: low taxes, limited liability, high profits, and no unions. And they tend to produce movies, television shows, and news stories that put forth their corporate views. Patric M. Verrone, former president of the Writers Guild of America (the union that represents screen writers), said, "Because control of the media is concentrated among a few similar corporations, the common interests of the corporations further reduce the range of perspectives and life experiences reflected in the media. The palpable result of consolidation on TV writers has been to reduce them to only those ideas acceptable to the corporate voice."

This new world of media control brings up concerns that were voiced by George Orwell in *1984* and Aldous Huxley in *Brave New World*. Cultural critic Neil Postman spelled out the difference in his book *Amusing Ourselves to Death*: "What Orwell feared were those who would ban books. What Huxley feared was that there would be no reason to ban a book, for there would be no one who wanted to read one. Orwell feared those who would deprive us of information. Huxley feared those who would give us so much that we would be reduced to passivity and egoism. Orwell feared that the truth would be concealed from us. Huxley feared the truth would be drowned in a sea of irrelevance. Orwell feared we would become a captive culture. Huxley feared we would become a trivial culture."

Not only do these multinational corporations control our news and entertainment but they also export American entertainments around the world and affect how the people of the world view Americans. (See Spotlight, "We Hate You But Please Keep Sending Us *Baywatch*.")

Although screen entertainments tend to be commercialized and globalized and have concentrated ownership, most theatre is less commercialized, more provincial, and locally controlled. But this does not necessarily mean that artists at a given theatre have the financial or civic freedom to produce any play they wish. For thousands of years the powerful and elite have subsidized theatre, from monarchs and czars to wealthy citizens and the church. Those who control the funding have a tendency to control content. In short, the theatre has always been a pawn for whoever controls the purse strings, and those who do not control the money often charge those who do with censorship. Joan E. Bertin, executive director of the National Coalition against Censorship, points out that the impulse to suppress ideas comes from both sides of the political spectrum: "The left complains about art that is critical of feminists, civil rights advocates, and gay activists. The right usually objects to artworks that include nudity, have sexual or antireligious themes, or denigrate patriotism or the American flag." The battle to control the funding of the theatre goes much deeper than government leaders and citizens worried about how tax dollars are spent. The core of the issue is who will control content and who will be able to promote his or her point of view and censor those who disagree. Unlike screen entertainments that are run by a small handful of multinational corporations with similar political agendas, theatre is liberated by a multitude of diverse, smaller, independent production companies. Hundreds of differing political points of view are

Television technology is inherently antidemocratic. Because of its cost, the limited kind of information it can disseminate, the way it transforms the people who use it, and the fact that few speak while millions absorb, television is suitable for use only by the most powerful corporate interests in the country. They inevitably use it to redesign human minds into a channeled, artificial, commercial form that nicely fits the artificial environment.

Jerry Mander,
Four Arguments for the Elimination of Television

The danger of media concentration lies not in the risk of prices getting higher. The real danger is much subtler. You're talking about an exponential increase in conflicts of interest. You're talking about few interests having greater market power. You're talking about the rise of trivial programming.

Mark Crispin Miller,
Director of the Project on Media Ownership

SPOTLIGHT ON We Hate You but Please Keep Sending Us *Baywatch*

The Writers Guild of America (WGA) recently held a panel discussion entitled "We Hate You (But Please Keep Sending Us *Baywatch*)," which looked at the influence of American screen entertainments on world culture. Like its fast food, America exports its entertainment worldwide. For example, Hollywood movies can easily reach as many as 2.6 billion people and even the soap opera *The Bold and the Beautiful* is watched by 450 million people in 98 countries. In Britain, U.S. movies account for 95 percent of the box-office revenues, with an average of nine of the top ten films at any Cineplex coming from America. The numbers are similar in Germany, Spain, and Italy. Even in Afghanistan, where only 19 percent of the people now have televisions and censorship laws require that a woman's bare midriff must be electronically covered, American television is prevalent, with Kiefer Sutherland's show *24* being one of the most popular. The bikini-filled *Baywatch* was cancelled after one season on NBC because of low ratings, but continues to play in syndication in 140 countries and in 195 major cities around the world.

On average Hollywood movies make about 50 percent of their ticket sales from overseas markets. But not all American films translate well to other cultures. For example, comedies like *Anchorman: The Legend of Ron Burgundy* and *Talladega Nights: The Ballad of Ricky Bobby* fared poorly in international markets, but action movies such as *Spider-Man* and *Pirates of the Caribbean* do well. Trying to make a film that plays in a multitude of global markets can be problematic. Hollywood directors and editors often adhere to the unofficial maxim that if a movie is to be shown to Europeans, cut the violence; if it is to be shown to Asians, cut the sex scenes; and if it is to be shown to Americans, cut both.

Hollywood moviemakers have also learned that satirizing—even in a good natured, well-intentioned manner—various peoples around the world is a quick way to reduce international profits. For example, the Mike Myers movie *The Love Guru* satirized Hinduism, which led to an uproar in India and an international boycott of the film. The same is true of the sitcom/cartoon *The Simpsons*, which has been accused of including derogatory stereotypical characters like Apu, the convenience store owner from India who is the father of octuplets. In fact, in India the word "Apu" is used to mean any stereotypical perceptions of Indians.

Hollywood movies can also lead to stereotypes of Americans. Most of the world's population knows Americans only through Hollywood movies and television shows. A Council on Foreign Relations report, "Public Diplomacy: A Strategy for Reform," examined polls by Gallup, Zogby, and the U.S. State Department and found that "foreign perceptions of the United States are far from monolithic, but there is little doubt that the stereotypes of United States citizens as arrogant, self-indulgent, hypocritical, inattentive, and unwilling or unable to engage in cross-cultural dialogue are pervasive and deeply rooted." Margaret Tutwiler, former undersecretary for public diplomacy and public affairs at the U.S. State Department, said, "By allowing our society to be represented overseas by popular art that portrays us as secular, violent, undisciplined and obsessed by sex, we are only making it easier for extremists to recruit. . . ." The effect Hollywood has on the world, and the world's perception of the United States, must be considered if any major attempt is ever made to change that perception.

A movie poster for *Iron Man* in China.

Yi chang/Imaginechina /AP Images

promoted by thousands of theatres across the United States. As we stated in Chapter 1, art is political. Art conveys messages about how an artist thinks the world is or should be. A play contains an artist's opinions, values, and political views. Add this to the thousands of actors, playwrights, and directors in America, each working in theatres owned by different producing organizations with different funding sources, and you have a greater possibility that a wealth of diverse points of view will be expressed. Therefore, when you go to the theatre, you can see patriotic musicals and radical anti-government plays; stories that promote traditional family values and stories that champion diverse values; themes that endorse communism and themes that uphold capitalism; plays that glorify Christianity and plays that sing the joys of atheism. Some theatre companies promote African American, Latino, and Asian points of view, and others stage plays with gay, lesbian, and feminist themes. As long as theatre remains locally funded and controlled, a wealth of opinions can be expressed. (For more discussion on these topics, see Chapter 3.)

In short, a particular theatre may be controlled by corporate or local funding that restricts content, and groups may succeed in censoring, delaying, or

> Theatre could have been rendered obsolete years ago, but it hasn't yet. There's still an elemental need to sit around the campfire and tell stories.
>
> ***Allison Narver,***
> Artistic director of the
> Empty Space Theatre

Photofest

When a high school in Utah wanted to do the musical *A Chorus Line,* they decided to cut the gay character and rewrite some of the lyrics to please a more conservative audience. What they didn't take into account is that writers copyright their work, which means that no one is allowed to rewrite scripts without the copyright holder's permission. If the writer has been dead for fewer than 70 years, permission must be obtained to make any alterations. Pictured here is the cast of the original 1975 production of *A Chorus Line.*

even canceling a given production. Yet with so many different theatres located in diverse areas and with diverse funding, more information, more points of view, and more diverse content can be disseminated. Theatre, therefore, has a much greater chance of being a forum for debate and controversy and providing a voice to those parts of our society about which the massive screen entertainments are silent.

Who Controls the Copyright?

There are striking dissimilarities between a typical Hollywood screen entertainment and the theatre when it comes to who owns the copyright. A **copyright** is a legal guarantee granted by the government to authors, playwrights, composers, choreographers, inventors, publishers, and/or corporations that allows them to maintain control and profit from their creative works. A copyright is similar to a patent. When you patent an invention, the U.S. government grants you the right to exclude others from "making, using, offering for sale, or selling" your particular invention without your permission. A copyright, unlike a patent, protects the form of expression rather than the subject matter. When you copyright something, you affirm your exclusive right and ownership of your words, music, photographs, paintings, drawings, computer software, CDs, DVDs, MP3s, or other form of expression.

Playwrights copyright their plays, published or not. This means that in order to stage a play by a playwright who is living or has died within the last 70 years, you first must get written permission from the playwright or the playwright's agent, publisher, or estate. When a play is produced, a **royalty payment** must be made to the playwright or the playwright's estate. This payment is like rent, except that instead of renting property such as a house or a car, you are renting the playwright's intellectual property. Also, because a play is copyrighted, directors, producers, actors, or anyone involved with the production cannot change, rewrite, or rearrange a script without permission from the playwright or the playwright's agent, publisher, or estate. Therefore, playwrights have the right to say who will perform their plays, the right to make money from the production or publication of their plays, and the right to decide what changes, if any, will be made. This gives playwrights one power: Their words, and therefore their thoughts, themes, and messages, cannot be altered without permission. So when a high school or community theatre cuts all the dirty words from a play in order not to offend their audiences, they are guilty of breaking the copyright laws of the United States. (See Spotlight, "Copyright Law: Infringement, Public Domain, and Parody.")

Things could not be more different for Hollywood screen and television writers. They, unlike playwrights, do not retain the copyright but instead sell their words outright. They are known as **writers for hire**. This means that instead of an individual writer owning her intellectual property, usually the Hollywood production company owns it and can hire other writers to change, rewrite, or rearrange the script however they see fit without the original writer's permission. Unlike the art of playwriting, which is dominated by solo writers who develop and own their words, Hollywood movies and television shows are often written by groups of writers who are hired to do the corporation's bidding and

Rewriting is the intrusion of another mind, another personality, another ego, another ethos. Sometimes it is done with good intentions, good will, and sometimes it will seem to improve the script. But it is a violation of what lies at the heart of authorship and that's why . . . I was never happy writing for screen or for TV. I met some nice people, had some fun, and made some money, but was never satisfied.

David Karp,
Hollywood screenwriter

SPOTLIGHT ON Copyright Law: Infringement, Public Domain, and Parody

The copyright laws of the United States can be complicated and in some cases contradictory. But one thing is certain: copyright infringement is a real problem. Dan Glickman, the president of the Motion Picture Association of America, estimates that American companies lose around $18 billion worldwide every year because of copyright infringement. These losses include movies that are copied without permission, illegal downloading of songs, and TV shows that are aired without paying royalties.

Copyright infringement also includes altering copyrighted material without permission. For example, the company CleanFlicks took Hollywood movies and edited out all of the sex, violence, and nudity. They removed Kate Winslet's nude scene from the movie *Titanic*, for example, and eliminated all the violent moments from Jackie Chan's Kung Fu movies. Several Hollywood directors challenged CleanFlicks in court, saying that not only do these edits violate the integrity of their work but that they are also a violation of the copyright laws of the United States.

In the end, the court ruled in favor of the Hollywood directors, reaffirming that if you want to edit a movie for your own personal use, that is allowable under the fair use clause of the Copyright Act, which allows alterations to copyrighted material for teaching, news reporting, comment, scholarship, research, or criticism. However, if you turn around and sell or rent a movie that you've altered without the creator's permission, you are profiting from someone else's intellectual property and therefore breaking the law

Another example of copyright infringement is a high school theatre group that decided to produce the musical *A Chorus Line*, but felt that some of the language (including the song "Dance Ten, Looks Three," a comic number about a dancer getting breast augmentation) was inappropriate, so the group rewrote it. In doing so, the high school had broken the copyright laws and was ordered to do the musical as written or close the show. The high school theatre group could write its own musical, but it couldn't alter a copyrighted musical and publicly perform it without permission.

One loophole in the copyright law that does allow alteration of copyrighted material is **parody**. Parodies are exaggerated imitations that are done for comic effect or political criticism. For example, the rap group 2 Live Crew rewrote the Roy Orbison song "Oh, Pretty Woman" without permission. In their parody, the pretty woman became a "bald-headed woman." The publishing company that held the copyright sued 2 Live Crew for copyright violation. The case went all the way to the Supreme Court, which ruled that parody is allowed under the fair use clause. This means that the high school in the previous example could have rewritten "Dance Ten, Looks Three" if it had been performing a parody of *A Chorus Line*. However, because the school chose to rewrite *A Chorus Line* with the intent of improving or altering the content rather than parodying the content, they broke the copyright owned by James Kirkwood, Jr., Nicholas Dante (book), Edward Kleban (lyrics), and Marvin Hamlisch (music).

A copyright only lasts the lifetime of the creator plus 70 years. This means that 70 years after the creator dies, the copyrighted material passes into the public domain and the copyright no longer applies. Songs, plays, pictures, etc., in the **public domain** are owned by the general public, and everyone has the right to produce or change them, without permission or payment to the creator. The plays of William Shakespeare (1564–1616) are in the public domain and can be produced free of charge and extensively rewritten or altered without permission.

fired if they fail to measure up. Writers for hire are able to make considerably more money than playwrights. However, they usually make money by catering to the needs of the media conglomerates, not by sharing their own artistic visions of the world.

The playwright stands alone, has sole creative control of the script, and decides what can be changed. From the original idea to first draft to finished product, playwrights own their intellectual property. When you see a play, you are hearing the voice of the playwright, not of a committee. Emanuel Azenberg, the Broadway producer, said, "The wonderful thing about the theatre is the writer. Who writes a movie? The theatre is the writer's place." Unlike screenwriters, playwrights see their work produced as written. Unlike screenwriters, playwrights can be part of the total creative process, and unlike screenwriters, playwrights can know the joy that lies at the heart of authorship. When you see a play on stage, you are likely to be experiencing a story that is true to the author's voice rather than one that has been rewritten to please the audience, the producers, or a multinational corporation.

Curtain Call

Far more separates theatre from screen entertainments than most people take into account. True, one is live and the other only "shadows on a screen," but those shadows have far more financial power and it's concentrated in only a few hands. The media moguls of massive corporations have a huge effect on our lives. Not only do they reflect our values more often than question them, which is problematic in itself, but they color their evening news programs, their newspapers, their movies, and their television shows with their corporate values. In contrast, theatre is little, largely independent, and much smaller than it once was. But is it dying? No. It is still very much alive, but its voice is a whisper compared to the roar of endless TV channels, web-connected content, and megaplex cinemas. Yet, as long as it is funded and uncensored, sometimes a whisper can change the world.

SUMMARY

MindTap*

Test your knowledge with online printable flashcards and online quizzing.

There are many differences between screen entertainments and the theatre. In terms of societal impact, one of the most important is that theatre attracts a relatively small audience. A play can run on Broadway for thousands of performances and still not be seen by as many people as watch a popular television show on a single night. Another key difference between theatre and screen entertainments is that theatre is a live, relatively interactive medium. When you watch a movie or a TV show, communication flows only one way: from the screen to you. In contrast, when you watch a play, you and the actors share communication—you each have a direct influence on the other. This is why theatre is called a living art.

Because it is live, theatre is a risky business. Many unfortunate surprises can occur in a live setting, but the show still must go on. As such, stage actors usually need plenty of rehearsal time in order to avoid making mistakes during a performance. Often, they also must be skilled in singing and dancing as well as acting. In contrast, screen actors are provided a safety net in the form of multiple takes, dubbing if they can't sing, and editing if they're not talented dancers.

In film, directors often have a lot of power and can directly influence what the audience will see. They control many aspects of the movie-making process because they can rewrite a script, influence the actors' performances, and dictate the editing of a movie. Stage directors usually do not have as much power or control. Because playwrights copyright their work, directors must obtain the playwright's permission to change a script, unless it is in the public domain. In addition, directors can do nothing to control the actors' performances once the curtain goes up on a performance. Similarly, directors of television programs have limited power over a production and are sometimes even subservient to the writers.

Theatre and screen entertainments also differ in how they are funded and in how profitable they are. Screen entertainments are often controlled by mega-corporations that expect their products—movies and TV programs—to make a profit. To help ensure that these products are profitable, corporations use test audiences to make sure movies and TV shows are appealing and entertaining. These mega-corporations export American entertainment all around the world, open movies in dozens of theatres at once to maximize ticket sales, sell movies to home audiences in the form of DVDs, and sell movie rights to lucrative overseas markets. Although some blockbuster plays and musicals turn a profit, many theatres cannot rely on ticket sales to cover the many costs of putting on a production. Consequently, most theatres seek additional funding from individual patrons, corporations, and government agencies (such as the National Endowment for the Arts) in order to make ends meet. Yet, because theatre is often locally controlled and funded, it can present a wider diversity of subject matter and ideas than screen entertainments do.

KEY TERMS

Bourgeois theatre *34*

Copyright *38*

Corporate funding *31*

Government funding *32*

Media moguls *35*

National Endowment for the Arts (NEA) *33*

Parody *39*

Patrons *31*

Product placement *29*

Public domain *39*

Royalty payment *38*

Writers for hire *38*

Chapter **3**

THEATRE OF THE PEOPLE

The theatre is often controlled by individual artists and can look at complexities of character and story in ways electronic or digital mediums can't or won't deal with. In *Father Comes Home* from the Wars, an African-American man is offered his freedom in exchange for fighting with the Confederate army. This production featured Jenny Jules, Sterling K. Brown, and Peter Jay Fernandez at The Public Theatre.

Joan Marcus

Outline

Never before has there been so much art and entertainment, but today, more than ever, a small group of powerful multinational corporations have the power to decide which art and entertainment will easily find an audience and which will not. These corporations decide which movies will play at your local Cineplex and which television shows will be available for download. They have the power to say which musicians, artists, actors, and writers will be spotlighted and which will not. Because all corporations are interested in making a profit, it is to their benefit to know what the public wants and to make it readily available. But this does not mean these corporations fill the needs of *all* the people. Many points of view are overlooked or ignored. In his book *Four Arguments for the Elimination of Television*, Jerry Mander writes that television is not democratic: "There are still no poor people running television, no Indians, no ecologists, no political radicals, no Zen Buddhists, no factory workers, no revolutionaries, no artists, no communists, no Luddites, no hippies, no botanists, to name only a few excluded groups." In our society, there is no denying that there are people, organizations, and corporations who have more money, status, and/or privilege, and thus they have more say when it comes to deciding what the general public will see, hear, and read.

So let's ask an age-old philosophical question, "If a tree falls in the forest and no one is around to hear it, does it make a sound?" The answer is "no." It does not make *sound*, it makes *sound waves*. In order for sound waves to become sound there must be a living being with ears and a brain that can convert those waves into sound. In other words, there must be an audience. Let's take this philosophical answer and apply it to artists and entertainers. They can create a great work of art, or a splendid evening of entertainment, but if there is no audience they are making only sound waves, not sound. Neither art nor entertainment are possible if they cannot reach an audience. So, even if you have freedom of speech and a work of art worthy of an audience, that does not mean that you have a voice in the political, social, or cultural arena. The fact is that we live in a society—in a world—where some people, because of their money, status, and/or privilege, are empowered to shout their ideas, while many can make little more than a whisper.

MindTap

Start with a quick warm-up activity and review the chapter's learning objectives.

Fox Searchlight/Photofest

As they get older, most women in Hollywood struggle to find substantial and interesting movie roles, whereas men are offered leading roles even into their sixties and seventies. Women also struggle to find directing jobs—in 2004, women directed only four of the top 100 Hollywood films. Many older women turn to the stage or independent movies, such as *Titus,* directed by Julie Taymor and starring Jessica Lange in the lead role of Tamora. Older women are having greater success as movie executives. In 2005, women held top creative decision-making roles in four of the six top studios, including Universal, Paramount, Sony, and Buena Vista.

AP Images/Reed Saxon

In Hollywood, only 25 percent of screenwriters and 20 percent of executive producers are women. A few of these female executive producers are Lynda Obit, Wendy Finerman, Amy Pascal, Jana Sue Memel, Denise Di Novi, Paula Wagner, and Kathleen Kennedy. Pictured here with Christine Lahti is Jana Sue Memel (right), who produced the Oscar-winning short movie *Lieberman in Love*. She has also produced dozens of movies and television shows.

MindTap®

Read, highlight, and take notes online.

In this culture of shouters and whisperers the theatre has found a unique voice. Because most theatres are owned and operated at the local level they have freedom (if they choose to use it) to give a voice to those people who are often overlooked or intentionally ignored by those with money, status, and/or privilege. Now this is not to say that *all* theatres do this. As described in Chapter 1, many theatres are commercial theatres that, much like massive multinational corporations, overlook the underserved voices in their communities. But a growing number of theatres choose to create art and entertainment that gives a voice to those who are too often forced to whisper. In this chapter, we'll focus on this type of theatre, and call it, "the **theatre of the people**."

Art, Entertainment, and Privilege

A **privileged group** is one that has assets such as access to housing, education, jobs, and opportunities for advancement that other members of a society find more difficult to obtain or are denied. The only way a member of a privileged group becomes aware of their privilege is when their lives are contrasted with another group. For example, let's look at the numbers when it comes to Hollywood movies. According to a report published by the Media, Diversity & Social Change Initiative at the University of Southern California's Annenberg School for Communication and Journalism, only 30.2 percent of all speaking roles in the top 100 grossing films released in the United States were written for women. In other words, for every woman who speaks in a major Hollywood movie, there are 2.3 roles written for men. In action adventure movies, the number of women with speaking roles falls to only 21.8 percent. The Annenberg study also found that only 19.9 percent of women's roles were written for women over the age of forty, and not a single top grossing Hollywood film starred a leading role with a woman over 45 years old. In addition, women directed only 4.1 percent of the top-grossing films in the last decade. So, if you are a man and want to be a Hollywood actor or director, you have more opportunities—*you have privilege*. The study also found that 73.1 percent of all speaking roles were white, only 4.9 percent of all speaking roles were written for Hispanic/Latino actors, and of the thousands of speaking roles only 19 total roles were gay, lesbian, or bisexual.

Although theatre has a long history of giving a voice to those outside of privileged groups, its overall record is not much better than Hollywood. For thousands of years those with privilege have controlled the theatre. During most of Western and Eastern theatre history, not only was it considered improper for religious, social, or cultural reasons for women to write plays, but women were also not allowed to set foot on stage. For example, in Shakespeare's day, men and boys played women's roles in drag (see Chapters 14 and 15). Today in the west, there are still more parts written for male characters than there are for females, and more male playwrights than female playwrights. The most recent numbers show that women write only about one out of every four plays produced today. Women of color write only about one out of every 50 plays, and the majority of roles in those plays are still written for men even though women make up more than 60 percent of the theatre going audience (if you are interested in studying this, a good place to start is Emily Glassberg Sands' *Opening the Curtain on Playwright Gender: An Integrated Economic Analysis of Discrimination in American Theater,* which can be found on the web.) What makes the theatre different from Hollywood movies is that many theatres study the problem and take steps to correct it.

Theatre and Culture

The word *culture* often pops up in our society. Our newspapers and television are filled with references to culture wars, **multiculturalism**, counterculture, pop culture, cultural relativism, and corporate culture. **Culture** is composed of the values, standards, and patterns of behavior of a particular group of people. It can include habits, traditions, languages, prejudices, superstitions, religions, rituals, customs, preferences, manners, assumptions, and lifestyle—anything that affects a group of people's particular way of thinking about the world. Culture can connect us to history, be a gateway to our heritage, give us a sense of shared community, and influence how we perceive ourselves.

One of the fundamental conflicts of human existence is the difference between how we perceive ourselves and how others perceive us. Whether at the individual, group, or national level, we have a basic view of who we are and spend a great deal of time trying to convince others that our self-perceptions are correct. We demand that others understand us, but we seldom take time to understand others. Instead, we often view others as stereotypes. **Stereotypes** are shortcuts in thinking that attribute a generalized identity to people who are not like us. In the United States, stereotyped characters include Mexican bandits, bigoted Southern sheriffs, Korean grocers, drunken Indians, and dumb blondes. Stereotypes tend to diminish when communication among groups, races, and cultures increases.

The philosopher and essayist Isaiah Berlin wrote that if you want to understand a person unlike yourself then you must have a direct acquaintance with their actual "sources of life." Anything less than that means that you are putting that person "into a box with a lot of other people," which only classifies that person "as one of the species, one of a type" and thus you miss true knowledge as you apply only "categories" when we should be studying the "palpitating unique, asymmetrical, unclassifiable flesh of living experience."

If there's specific resistance to women making movies, I just choose to ignore that as an obstacle for two reasons: I can't change my gender, and I refuse to stop making movies.

Kathryn Bigelow,
Oscar-winning director

The majority of roles are written by and for men. In addition, during many periods of theatre history, women were not allowed to act on stage so men played the female roles. Today, there is a movement to encourage more female playwrights and more roles for women. *Women Playing Hamlet* is a comedy that features women playing all the male roles. This production at the Unicorn Theatre in Kansas City featured Katie Karel and Kathleen Warfel.

William Missouri Downs

I wrote my first play, *Uncommon Women and Others*, in the hopes of seeing an all-female curtain call in the basement of the Yale School of Drama. A man in the audience stood up during a post-show discussion and announced, "I can't get into this. It's about girls."
I thought to myself, "Well, I've been getting into Hamlet and Lawrence of Arabia my whole life, so you better start trying."

Wendy Wasserstein,
Playwright

Theatre of the people has a unique ability to study and celebrate the "palpitating unique, asymmetrical, unclassifiable flesh of living experience" by privileging all voices.

There are three basic types of theatre of the people:

- *Theatre of identity* promotes a particular people's cultural identity and invites members of that culture and other cultures to experience that culture's joys, problems, history, traditions, and point of view.

- *Theatre of protest* objects to the dominant culture's control and demands that a minority culture's voice and political agenda be heard.

- *Cross-cultural theatre* mixes different cultures in an attempt to find understanding or commonality among them.

Of course, these types of theatre are not always separate. One play can include the characteristics of more than one type of theatre of the people.

Theatre of Identity

Theatre of identity promotes a particular people's awareness of themselves and their experiences, traditions, and culture. The plays of theatre of identity are written by members of a particular culture and staged by actors from that culture. This type of theatre gives a voice to a people and encourages audience members to reflect on, analyze, or reinvent their own self-perceptions. It gives a voice to groups that the privileged cultures ignore or silence. This type of theatre is not closed to outsiders. On the contrary, theatre of identity often welcomes people of other cultures even though they might not completely understand the sensibility in these productions. Theatre of identity can present sugar-coated images of a culture, but it can also feature that culture's defeats and regrets. Images of imperfections are meant to strengthen the bonds of the community as it gives audience members of that culture a self-definition not available from the dominant culture.

In the United States, the theatre of identity grew out of the wide variety of traditions that make up our diverse population. People fleeing the French Revolution in 1789 started the French American theatre. One of the first African American theatres was founded in New York City in 1821, and some Spanish-language theatres were acquired with the conquest of the Southwest. In the 1800s, German, Polish, Chinese, Norwegian, and Swedish theatres were founded across the country. These theatres reached their peak in the opening decades of the twentieth century, providing art and entertainment for millions of new immigrants whose cultural and language differences, as well as outright discrimination, kept them out of mainstream American life. By the 1900s, Finns in Oregon had the Astoria Socialist Theatre; Italians in San Francisco had their own theatre; and in New York City, Second Avenue was known as the "**Yiddish Broadway**" because so many Jewish theatres were located there. The first half of the twentieth century was also a time when the absence of plays written by women playwrights began to be corrected. Zona Gale (1874–1938), Georgia Douglas Johnson (1880–1966), Susan Glaspell (1876–1948), Edna Ferber (1885–1968), Ruth Gordon (1896–1985), Lillian Hellman (1905–1984), and many others were writing plays that presented women as successful scientists, businesspeople, legislators, and screenwriters who dealt with or fought against the male-dominated culture.

Hulton Archive/Getty Images

The Second Avenue Theatre was one of the theatres in New York City that featured Yiddish plays in the early part of the twentieth century. There were so many of these theatres on Second Avenue that the area became known as the "Yiddish Broadway." Initially many of these theatres premiered European Yiddish works that appealed to New York's many Jewish immigrants. Later they featured new works based on the Jewish experience in America.

Theatre performed by African Americans has been around for hundreds of years, but plays written by black people for black people were rare until the twentieth century. Before that, black characters were mainly stereotypes written by whites and even performed by whites. (See the Spotlight "Color Consciousness.") Willis Richardson (1889–1977) was the first black playwright to have a play on Broadway that was not a musical; his play *The Chip Woman's Fortune* appeared in 1923. Richardson went on to write about black historical heroes including Crispus Attucks, who was killed in the Boston Massacre; Alexandre Dumas *père*, the biracial French playwright; and biblical characters such as Simon the Cyrenian, who carried the cross for Jesus. Richardson felt that too many plays by black writers were only about how black people were treated by whites. He said, "Still there is another kind of play: the kind that shows the soul of a people; and the soul of this people is truly worth showing." A few years later, in 1926, poet Langston Hughes said, "We younger Negro artists now intend to express our dark-skinned selves without fear or shame. If white people are pleased, we are glad. If they are not, it doesn't matter. We know we are beautiful. And ugly too." This comment summarized the black struggle for artistic independence that took place during the 1920s and 1930s, in the period known as the **Harlem Renaissance**. This was a time when black artists, actors, poets, musicians, and writers converged in Harlem to tell the stories of their lives, their history, and their people, contrary to white stereotypes of blacks.

SPOTLIGHT ON Color Consciousness

For most of U.S. theatre and film history, blacks, Native Americans, and Asians were discriminated against and even banned from appearing on stage or in films. As a result, whites played "ethnic" characters by wearing heavy makeup, which led to one of the most bizarre forms of theatre: the **minstrel show**. Minstrel shows originated in the nineteenth century and lasted well into the twentieth. These performances contained comic scenes, dance interludes, and sentimental ballads, all based on white people's perceptions of black life in the South. Black music was popular, but it was considered improper for whites to go to a theatre to hear black musicians, so whites would put on black makeup, called **blackface**, and perform as black people. Minstrel shows often contained skits with illiterate and foolish exchanges that made fun of blacks. Blacks did not attend minstrel shows; they were entertainment for white people only.

For many years in Hollywood films, it was considered acceptable for whites to play blacks as well as Native Americans and Asians. The first talking picture, *The Jazz Singer*, was about a Jewish boy (Al Jolson) who becomes a jazz singer. In the movie's final scene he performs in blackface in a minstrel show. In the 1950s, whites playing blacks finally fell out of favor, but the tradition of whites playing Asians and Native Americans continued into the 1970s; for example, David Carradine played the lead in the TV show *Kung Fu*. Katharine Hepburn, Fred Astaire, John Wayne, and Marlon Brando are some of the stars who played Asian roles in Hollywood films.

White domination of ethnic roles was challenged when the British producer Cameron Mackintosh (*Cats, Phantom of the Opera*) announced that the white British actor Jonathan Pryce was going to play the Asian male lead on Broadway in the hit musical *Miss Saigon*. Asian actors protested that they weren't even given a chance to audition. Actor B. D. Wong said, "If Asian American actors aren't good enough to play Asian roles, what are we good for?" Asian actors announced that they would not allow "taped eyelids and yellowface" on a white actor. But when Mackintosh threatened to cancel the production, throwing many actors out of work, the union backed down. In the end, Pryce played the role, but he did not wear the eye prosthetics he had worn when he played the role in London. After he left the show, an Asian actor took over the part.

Is it right for whites to play blacks, or for Filipinos to play Chinese, or for Jews to play Italians? (The practice of casting actors regardless of their race is called *color-blind casting*. For more on this topic, see Chapter 8.) The actors' union said, "Jews have always been able to play Italians, Italians have always been able to play Jews, and both have been able to play Asians. Asian actors, however, almost never have the opportunity to play either Jews or Italians and continue to struggle even to play themselves." As recently as 1995, a book on stage makeup listed "ethnic appearances" including "Caucasian to Oriental" and "Caucasian to Indian," complete with before-and-after photos of a young white model made up to look like Fu Manchu. White to black makeup was not included. Today, the question remains: should the theatre be color-blind or color-conscious?

British actor Jonathan Pryce originated the Asian lead role in the London run of the musical *Miss Saigon*. His casting caused controversy when the play transferred to the United States, where the Actor's Equity union initially refused to allow Pryce to continue in the part because "it would be an affront to the Asian community." After pressure from the play's producer, Pryce joined the Broadway production. However, he agreed to perform without the eye makeup he had used in London to appear Asian.

Joan Marcus/Photofest

August Wilson's *Two Trains Running* uses sharp-edged humor and cutting social analysis to reveal the conflicts that African Americans face. Set in Pittsburgh in 1969 after the assassinations of Martin Luther King, Jr., and Malcolm X, the characters find themselves at a crossroads as they try to come to terms with their pasts and find self-respect in an inequitable world. This 2005 production featuring (l to r) Adolphus Ward, E. Milton Wheeler, James A. Williams, and Erika LaVonn was directed by Lou Bellamy at the Kansas City Repertory Theatre.

During the civil rights movement of the late 1950s and 1960s, theatre of identity continued to grow. In 1959, Lorraine Hansberry (1930–1965) became the first black woman playwright to be produced on Broadway. It would take another 25 years for another African American playwright to succeed on Broadway. However, black playwrights, although they were still locked out of the mainstream commercial theatre, were finding a voice. Some of these playwrights were Amiri Baraka (b. 1934–2014), whose *The Slave* (1965) deals with an interracial couple; Adrienne Kennedy (b. 1931), whose *Funnyhouse of a Negro* (1964) focuses on the human unconscious and the search for meaning and truth; and Douglas Turner Ward, whose *Day of Absence* mocks minstrel shows by having a black cast dress up in whiteface and play white characters.

By 1968 there were 40 black theatre companies in the United States, and 20 years later there were more than 200. However, many of these theatres struggle for funding because their major purpose, unlike the mainstream commercial theatre, is not to make money but rather to tell stories that the privileged culture ignores. Some of the plays created by these influential theatres have become mainstream Hollywood movies: *The River Niger* (1976), which starred James Earl Jones; *Ceremonies in Dark Old Men* (1975) with Glynn Turman; and Charles Fuller's Pulitzer Prize–winning *A Soldier's Play* (1981), which became the movie *A Soldier's Story* (1984) with Adolph Caesar and Denzel Washington.

Today, perhaps no two playwrights represent the growing diversity of the American theatre scene more than August Wilson (1945–2005) and Suzan-Lori Parks (b. 1964). Wilson grew up in the Hill District of Pittsburgh, Pennsylvania. He left school after daily barrages of racial epithets. Rather than tell his mother that he had dropped out, Wilson spent his youth at the public library, where he gave himself an education. In 1984, he had his first big writing success with *Ma Rainey's Black Bottom*, a play about black musicians struggling with their white bosses in the 1920s. The play was first produced by the Yale Repertory Theatre and later on Broadway. His second play, *Fences*, opened on Broadway in 1987. It was set in the 1950s and tells the story of Troy Maxon, a garbage collector who

We have never said that white reviewers cannot understand black theatre—if you can understand Duke Ellington and Ray Charles, you can understand black theatre.

August Wilson,
Playwright

We're not beyond race in this country. We have a lot to learn about existing in a very colorful society.

Tisa Chang,
Founder of the Pan
Asian Repertory Theater

Michal Daniel

Topdog/Underdog by Suzan-Lori Parks is the dark comic tale of two brothers who vie with each other to come out on top. The brothers, named Lincoln and Booth by their father as a joke, experience an intense sibling rivalry and come to understand their shared history only through their obsession with the con game three-card Monte. This 2001 Off-Broadway production featured Don Cheadle as Booth and Jeffrey Wright as Lincoln and was directed by George C. Wolfe at the Public Theatre in New York.

has become embittered by the white-controlled system that has denied him the baseball stardom he feels he deserves. For this play, Wilson won the Pulitzer Prize. The following year he returned to Broadway with *Joe Turner's Come and Gone*, the story of a black man who was unjustly imprisoned in 1910. Then came *The Piano Lesson*. Set in the 1930s, it is the story of a man who wants to buy the land in Mississippi where his ancestors once worked as slaves. But in order to raise the money, he must sell the family heirloom, a piano. This play earned Wilson his second Pulitzer Prize for Drama. In Wilson's plays, the white world is a major character but remains almost entirely offstage. Wilson said, "Blacks know the spiritual truth of white America. We are living examples of America's hypocrisy. We know white America better than white America knows us."

Suzan-Lori Parks represents a generation of playwrights who are not waiting for the mainstream commercial theatre or the dominant culture to recognize their plays. Born in Fort Knox, Kentucky, she lived the transient childhood of an "Army brat." This allowed her to experience many different worlds, but friendships were hard to maintain, so she entertained herself by staging puppet shows. Her life changed when she took a creative writing class from James Baldwin, who suggested that she was a natural playwright. After graduating from college with degrees in English and German literature, she moved to New York and started staging her own plays wherever she could find an empty space. Once, when she couldn't find a stage, she even used a garage at a gas station. To those who run into barriers she says, "To get a play done, you go to a place and do it, or you work your day job and then you do a play; you produce it yourself." Within a few years, she had graduated from garages to such notable theatres as the Public Theatre in New York City and the Arena Stage in Washington, D.C., and in 2001 her play *Topdog/Underdog* was produced on Broadway. A dark comedy about sibling rivalry between two brothers, Lincoln and Booth, *Topdog/Underdog* deals with oppressive systems within society. With this play, Parks became the first African American woman to win the Pulitzer. Parks succinctly summed up the ideas behind theatre of identity when she said, "I know where I am and who I am and what I do."

Theatre often offers opinions and ideas that an audience will not hear from mainstream, corporate-controlled media. Since its inception in 1959, the San Francisco Mime Troupe has performed Commedia dell'Arte influenced and politically themed plays in the city.

Theatre of Protest

The second type of theatre of the people could be called theatre of social agenda or theatre of militancy, because its purpose is protest and change. **Theatre of protest** uses its voice to explore and affect the inequity of governments, religions, and privileged cultures. Protest plays date back to the ancient Greeks. For example, Aristophanes' comedy *Lysistrata* (411 BCE) is often called the first anti-war play. Twenty-four hundred years later, similar anti-war plays were produced during the 1960s and early 1970s as American students demonstrated against inequality and the Vietnam War. The French director Antonin Artaud (1896–1948) summed up the purpose of protest plays when he said, "The action of theatre, like that of plague, is beneficial, for, impelling men to see themselves as they are, it causes the mask to fall, reveals the lie, the slackness, baseness, and hypocrisy of our world." In other words, this type of theatre isn't presented to entertain but rather to demand justice.

One such theatre is El Teatro Campesino ("farmworkers' theatre"), founded in 1965 by Luis Valdez (b. 1940). Spanish-speaking theatre has existed in America since the late sixteenth century, but El Teatro Campesino became a new type of theatre that did more than celebrate Latino culture—it protested social injustice. Valdez and his theatre improvised plays to support Filipino and Chicano migrant farmworkers who, led by Cesar Chavez (1927–1993), were on strike against California grape growers. Performed on the backs of flatbed trucks, these plays were often cast with striking workers, which narrowed the line between performer and audience and made audience participation critical. The dialogue in *The Conscience of a Scab* and other plays was drawn from real conflicts the strikers experienced. The stories focused on the strikers' meager pay and poor working conditions, highlighting the oppressions perpetrated by the white growers. Valdez went on to write plays that addressed not only immediate local issues but also cultural identity and national issues. He has written about members of the Chicano community who deny their heritage as they attempt to blend into the American melting pot and has attacked

Bob Kreisel/Alamy Stock Photo

Universal/The Kobal Collection/The Picture Desk Inc.

Luis Valdez's play *Zoot Suit* dramatizes the powerful racial tensions of 1940s Los Angeles. Shown here is Edward James Olmos playing the part of El Pachuco in a 1979 production of the play, directed by Valdez at the Winter Garden Theatre in New York. The first Mexican American playwright to be produced on Broadway, Valdez observed that "until we [Mexican Americans] had the artists who could express what the people were feeling and saying, we wouldn't really register politically. Art gives us the tools of that expression."

Mexican stereotypes found in mainstream theatre, television, and film. He has written that El Teatro Campesino's purposes are to "replace the lingering negative stereotype of the Mexican in the United States with a new positive image created through Chicano art, and to continue to dramatize the social despair of Chicanos living in an Anglo-dominated society."

Valdez's most famous play is *Zoot Suit* (1978), which is based on the Sleepy Lagoon murder trial and the famous Zoot Suit Riots, now often called the Sailor Riots. These riots occurred when American military personnel claimed that Mexicans wearing zoot suits had attacked them while they were on leave in Los Angeles during World War II. (A "zoot" is a flamboyant suit with wide lapels and oversized pleated pants popular among Mexican American youth in the 1940s.) In response to the allegation, more than 200 uniformed white sailors stormed into the heart of the Mexican American community in East Los Angeles and attacked anyone wearing a zoot suit. The police did nothing to stop the sailors' riot. After several days of rioting, when the Navy feared it had a mutiny on its hands, military authorities finally took steps to end the melee. None of the sailors were ever prosecuted, but many of the Zoot Suiters were.

Zoot Suit takes place in front of a giant newspaper that serves as a drop curtain. The headline reads "Zoot Suiter Hordes Invade Los Angeles. U.S. Navy and Marines Are Called In." The newspaper's fallacious headline becomes a symbol of Anglo racism. The play tells the story of Chicano consciousness and cultural survival in a country in which racism and violence are advocated by the press and the state. *Zoot Suit* ran for more than 11 months in Los Angeles. It was also the first Chicano play to be produced on Broadway, and Valdez was the first Mexican American to direct on Broadway. Since *Zoot Suit*, Valdez has gone on to write many more plays and direct popular movies, including *La Bamba* (1987).

Another example of theatre of protest is the performance art of Karen Finley (b. 1956), who has toured the country performing one-woman plays about sexual abuse, violence against women, prejudice, censorship, AIDS, suicide, and the male domination of politics. Her most notorious piece, *We Keep Our Victims Ready* (1989), satirizes national events, questions the definition of obscenity, and confronts the dehumanization of women that reduces them to sexual objects. She also attacks the idea of a sole deity whose image is masculine, monolithic, and absolute, which she says results in a masculine-dominated society. Her performance includes a scene where she covers her naked body in chocolate and yams, almost like a tar-and-feathering, in order to symbolize the bruising abuse women suffer in our society. Taken out of context, these symbolic acts earned her the epithet "the chocolate-smeared woman." But Finley says, "My critics are people like Jesse Helms. The attacks don't come from people who have actually seen my work." Those who have seen her work, such as critics from the *New York Times*, praise her "highly visceral, startling monologues" in which she confronts pressing social issues. Theatre of protest is often censored or marginalized by the dominant culture, which doesn't want its views or traditions questioned. Such was the case when Finley was denied a grant from the National Endowment for the Arts because of what the head of the NEA called "certain political realities." Finley took her fight all the way to the Supreme Court. (See the Spotlight "Karen Finley and the NEA.")

Cross-Cultural Theatre

Cross-cultural theatre borrows contrasting ideas from diverse cultures and joins them into a single work. At its most basic, cross-cultural plays borrow staging techniques from another culture to create a unique piece of theatre. At its highest level, cross-cultural theatre is an attempt to fuse various cultural rituals, myths, and styles in order to find parallels between cultures, including those of the writers and performers and those of each audience, and merge them in a performance that celebrates our diversities and similarities and promotes cultural pluralism. As Nigerian writer Ben Okri (b. 1959) said, "Literature doesn't have a country. Shakespeare is an African writer . . . The characters of Turgenev are ghetto dwellers. Dickens's characters are Nigerians . . . Literature may come from a specific place, but it always lives in its own unique kingdom."

Cross-cultural plays have been a part of the Western theatre experience for hundreds of years. Irish poet and dramatist William Butler Yeats (1865–1939) was influenced by the masks, mime, and dance techniques of Japanese Noh drama (see Chapter 11) for his poetic dramas *Four Plays for Dancers at the Hawk's Well* (1916). American playwright Thornton Wilder (1897–1975), who spent part of his childhood in China, adopted Chinese staging methods in his masterpiece *Our Town* (1938), a drama about life and death in a small New England town. In the play, Wilder used the character of a stage-manager/narrator to invoke the imagination of the audience, just as the Beijing Opera (see Chapter 11) uses the character of the property man. Yet historically, many other Western cross-cultural plays have done little to promote understanding between cultures. For example, Gilbert and Sullivan's musical *The Mikado* (1885) and Puccini's *Madama Butterfly* (1904) were both influenced by Asian theatre but did little to portray nonstereotypical Asian characters or to promote cultural understanding.

Cross-cultural plays remain a part of the contemporary theatre. Japanese director and theorist Tadashi Suzuki (b. 1939) set the Greek tragedy *Trojan Women*, about the destruction of the ancient city of Troy, in post–World War II Japan, and used both classical Japanese theatrical styles and modern Western staging. The play includes traditional Japanese music and Western punk rock, kimonos and sweatshirts, and a script spoken in both English and Japanese. One critic described the performance as "a controlled crash that celebrates both East and West and finds a common language." Similarly, the Contemporary Legend Theatre of Taiwan creates performances that fuse 400-year-old Shakespeare plays, 200-year-old staging techniques from the Beijing opera, and verse

We are a lot more varied, as a country, than we like to pretend to be. I mean, we give sort of a nodding recognition that the country is multiracial, for instance, but do not do a lot to really integrate, in a cultural-artistic sense, the real currents that flow in this country. That sort of thing has to happen of itself through the daily life of the people, through the daily cultural life.

Luis Valdez,
Playwright

The National Endowment for the Arts was funding work by those who were once rendered invisible by economic, ethnic, or gender differences. What previously had been a private, almost sequestered world, existing only within academia or in galleries, became public. People who had never had the same access that white, middle or upper-class men have traditionally had were suddenly given means to create.

Karen Finley,
Performance artist

SPOTLIGHT ON Karen Finley and the NEA

Over the years several complaints have been lodged against the National Endowment for the Arts (NEA) concerning the social and moral concepts behind the works of art it funds. (For more on the NEA, see Chapter 2.) With all the controversy, one might think that thousands of so-called questionable or obscene works of art must have been funded with federal tax dollars. But the truth is that fewer than fifty out of 160,000 works of art funded over thirty years have received complaints. Compare this to American television, which through the FCC (Federal Communications Commission) has received as many as one million complaints in a single year. Why would so few works of art—including Karen Finley's *We Keep Our Victims Ready*—cause such a stir? In his book *Culture Wars*, artist and writer Richard Bolton points out that many believe that artists are trying to introduce a progressive agenda into society, "an agenda based upon multiculturalism, gay and lesbian rights, feminism, and sexual liberation" that is intended to destroy traditional American values. Somehow this "objectionable" handful of artistic projects funded by the NEA—less than 0.1 percent of all the projects it has ever funded—is seen as a serious threat to the power structure of the United States.

In the 1990s Senator Jesse Helms tried to stop this "progressive agenda" with legislation to ensure that every art grant given by the NEA must take into consideration the general standards of "decency and respect for the diverse beliefs and values of the American public." Some said that the new law, when properly interpreted, had no practical effect. Others felt it was a far-reaching attack on the First Amendment's guarantee of freedom of speech. Finley, who was denied an NEA grant under the new law, immediately challenged the law in court. She felt that it discriminated against nontraditional artworks and that the "diverse beliefs and values" clause unconstitutionally suppressed ideas that challenged the general public's sensibilities.

David Cole, a professor at Georgetown University Law Center and a lawyer for the Center for Constitutional Rights, represented Finley before the Supreme Court. He argued that "one would be hard-pressed to find two people in the United States who could agree on what the 'diverse beliefs and values of the American public' are, much less on whether a particular work of art 'respects' them. . . . Decency is likely to mean something very different to a septuagenarian in Tuscaloosa and a teenager in Las Vegas." In the end the Supreme Court ruled eight to one to uphold the new law. Everyone from Speaker of the House Newt Gingrich to President Bill Clinton claimed it to be a victory, whereas many people in the arts felt it was censorship and an attack on cultural freedom. Actor and former head of the NEA Jane Alexander said, "It is in decisions such as the Supreme Court's that liberties in our society are whittled away slowly and incrementally. Doors to diversity and variety silently close." Theatre producer and critic Robert Brustein said, "The channels that support serious advanced expression are quickly drying up. The big cultural dinosaurs will probably survive and some theaters and dance companies may hang on if they fill their schedules with the equivalent crowd-pleasing holiday shows like *A Christmas Carol* and *Nutcracker*, but high art in America is dying and dying along with it are our hopes for a still significant civilization."

The arguments before the Supreme Court raised many provocative issues: Does the government have the right to favor certain points of view? Does the NEA have the right to exclude grant applicants because they are not in tune with the dominant culture? Is it even possible to make a work of art that respects all of the "diverse beliefs and values of the American public"?

Terry Ashe/The Life Images Collection/Getty Images

Actor Jane Alexander, former head of the NEA, answers charges in front of a congressional committee. Of the 160,000 works of art funded by the NEA in its nearly forty-year existence, there have been only fifty complaints. But this was enough for some members of Congress to slash the NEA's budget and call for its demise. Although they succeeded in reducing its budget, the majority of their colleagues voted for its continued existence.

William Missouri Downs

Director, painter, and master teacher Shozo Sato demonstrates Kabuki movement to dance students.

written in Mandarin (performed with English subtitles) into a single production. Another example is Japanese director Shozo Sato, who stages Western classics such as *Medea, Faust*, and *Macbeth* in Japanese Kabuki style (see Chapter 11). Sato uses a multiracial cast of men and women, although Kabuki traditionally uses only men, and he adds a dash of "Kabuki soy sauce" in order to create what one critic called a "dramatic tension between the stylized beauty of the Kabuki tradition and the visceral action of Western stories."

The purpose of cross-cultural theatre is often to join people of diverse cultural backgrounds. This can mean that the performers come from one culture and the audience largely from another. For example, the play *Black Elk Speaks* (1994), which was adapted from an oral biography of a Sioux holy man, tells the story of white America's westward expansion from the Native American

Peter Kelly Gaudreault (Crazy Horse) and Jane Lind (Eagle Spirit) in the Denver Center Theatre Company's 1994 production of Black Elk Speaks based on the book by John Neihardt, dramatized by Christopher Sergel. Photo Credit: Terry Shapiro.

Black Elk Speaks is an example of theatre as a vehicle for cultural interaction. Dramatizing the life of Black Elk, a Sioux holy man, and the struggles of Native Americans against the policy of Manifest Destiny, the play brings together the Native Americans who perform the play and the largely non-Native American audiences. This 1994 production featured Ned Romero as Black Elk and was directed by Donovan Marley at the Denver Center for the Performing Arts.

David Henry Hwang's plays often blend Eastern and Western styles of theatre. This production of his play *M. Butterfly* was directed by Peter Rothstein and staged at the Guthrie Theater in Minneapolis.

Michal Daniel

perspective. It is a story of broken promises, war, and the white man's quest for land and gold. When the play was originally produced at the Denver Center for the Performing Arts, it employed a cast of Native American actors, dancers, and singers from twenty North American tribes, but it drew an audience that was largely non-American Indian. The play's purpose was to bring people together. As the director, who is white, said, "If *Black Elk* is saying anything, it is that the categorization is not red, white, yellow, and black . . . and all four have to live in this world together."

Other cross-cultural plays expose the complexities among cultures by putting them on stage side by side. Such is the case with *M. Butterfly* (1988) by David Henry Hwang (b. 1957). This play explores the Western psyche and its stereotypical views of Asian culture, race, and gender. Hwang's play combines plot elements of *Madama Butterfly*, an Italian opera, with a story about a French diplomat who, after ten years, discovers that his Chinese mistress is not only a spy but also a man. This play uses a modified Japanese Kabuki stage and choreography from the Beijing Opera as it attacks the cultural blindness that pervades so much of the world—a blindness that reveals itself in many ways.

Cross-cultural theatre does have its critics. Some feel that cross-cultural plays mix cultures without grasping their ideological dimensions. These critics charge that intercultural borrowing merely reduces culture to an interesting stage technique, or amounts to inappropriate cultural appropriation. For example, the great-grandson of Black Elk was bluntly critical of the inclusion in *Black Elk Speaks* of non-Lakota songs, incorrect choreography, and sacred images that should not be put on stage. And some might be justifiably concerned that *Black Elk Speaks* is not an appropriate instrument for conveying native culture to white audiences since white people, rather than Native Americans, controlled how indigenous peoples, stories and behavior are staged or viewed in both the book and the play. Other critics have charged that Shozo Sato's Kabuki versions of Western classics trivialize Japanese theatre because the Western actors lack traditional training and so cannot comprehend Japanese content or culture. But

Anacleto Rapping/Los Angeles Times/Getty Images

Plays often deal with characters who are marginalized by society. One example is *Take Me Out*, a drama about a gay professional baseball player and the difficulties he faces when he comes out of the closet. This Los Angeles production featured Terrell Tilford and Jeffrey Nordling.

from another viewpoint, Ping Chong, a Chinese American creator of avant-garde dance-theatre who often employs Chinese and Japanese aesthetics, says, "I'm not going to allow myself to be ghettoized as an Asian American artist. I'm an *American* artist. The irony is that we are now ghettoizing ourselves by choice. I understand that this act is an affirmation of one's identity. That's important. But we cannot lose sight of the fact that we all live in a society where we have to coexist. It doesn't mean that I have to like your culture. But we have to be *sensitive* to each other's cultures."

Seeing through Another's Eyes

We all see the world from our own point of view, and most people tend to think that their take on it, as seen through their culture, is the correct view. This phenomenon is called **ethnocentrism**. English philosopher Francis Bacon (1561–1626) called ethnocentrism the "idols of the cave" because we often assume that our own social or cultural group is superior to others, that our sheltered and secluded "cave" is better than someone else's. Writer Dinesh D'Souza, who is a Fellow at the Hoover Institution at Stanford University, said, "To some degree ethnocentrism is unavoidable, because human beings have no alternative to viewing the world through some background set of assumptions and beliefs. If ethnocentrism cannot be completely overcome, however, the scope of its errors can be reduced and minimized. The way to do this is to turn assumptions into questions." Most would agree that all cultures should be allowed to express themselves, but what happens when cultures are so different that they come into conflict in their attempt to define a nation's cultural identity? How do we turn assumptions into questions?

Several years ago the mayor of New York City, Rudolph Giuliani, threatened to terminate the funding and possibly take over the Brooklyn Museum of Art because it displayed a painting by English artist Chris Ofili called *Holy Virgin*

I think one of the big problems, ultimately, in the efforts towards cultural diversity in the theater is whether the white establishment is willing to give up control. There have been a lot of well-meaning people, a lot of people trying to do things, but if you look at the administrative staffs of theaters, the decision makers there, nothing much has changed with them. As a result, tokenism remains far too prevalent.

David Henry Hwang,
Playwright

Mary. The painting depicted a woman representing the Virgin Mary. Attached to the painting were clumps of elephant dung, which prompted some critics to call it sacrilegious and obscene. In fact, a retired schoolteacher found it so offensive that he smuggled a container of latex paint into the museum and threw it on the painting. The painting insulted his culture and he reacted, but he failed to take the time to understand the artist's cultural perspective and intention. Few people did. The public debate over freedom of speech, obscenity, and the painting raged in the national news media for weeks. Yet a closer look at Ofili's background reveals that he is a Roman Catholic of Nigerian descent. Although the elephant dung may shock us in the West, he meant it as an affirmative interpretation of Christianity: Because elephant dung fertilizes the soil of Africa, to Africans it is a symbol of all that is good and nurturing. If you think about it, many Americans also have symbols that are not understood by other cultures. For example, a rabbit's foot represents good luck. If you were from another culture, the meaning of a rabbit's foot might confuse you as much as elephant dung confused mayor Giuliani. When cultures come into conflict, it is often a test of how well society as a whole tolerates alternative points of view.

Many plays attempt to combat or minimize ethnocentrism, including Milcha Sanchez-Scott's (b. 1955) *Roosters* (1987), a play about a generational feud between a proud, headstrong Hispanic father and his equally determined son; Anna Deavere Smith's (b. 1950) series of one-woman plays, *On the Road: A Search for American Character* (1983 to the present), which confronts racial and gender identity issues; and Regina Taylor's (b. 1964) *Watermelon Rinds* (1992), a seriocomic exposé of African American family politics. Currently, perhaps the most famous cultural-awareness play is Tony Kushner's (b. 1956) Pulitzer Prize–winning *Angels in America* (1992), a play in two parts that was adapted for television by HBO in 2003.

Kushner grew up Jewish and homosexual in the turbulent South of the 1960s. He said that he had had "fairly clear memories of being gay" since he was six but he did not come out until after he tried psychotherapy to change his sexual orientation. *Angels in America* tells the interwoven stories of several gay men. One is Prior Walter, a young man dying of AIDS who is visited by a frightening and mysterious angel; another is a Mormon, Joe Pitt, who comes to terms with his homosexuality despite its being forbidden by his religion; and another is Roy Cohn, a powerful attorney who denied his gay lifestyle in public and collaborated with Senator Joseph McCarthy in the 1950s persecution of "un-Americans." *Angels* is a perfect example of a play that challenges an audience to think and calls their values into question. By doing so it transmits knowledge, and with knowledge comes understanding.

Just as Ofili experienced with his painting, artists who attempt to produce plays that promote cultural awareness also sometimes come into conflict with the dominant culture. In 1993, when Terrence McNally's play *Lips Together, Teeth Apart*, which includes positive portrayals of gay men, was produced by a theatre in Cobb County, Georgia, the County Commission attempted to silence any further such productions by establishing a "family values" criterion for funding local art. When that proved to be difficult to defend in court, the commission simply eliminated all art funding for the entire county. A similar incident occurred in 1999 when the theatre department at Kilgore College in Longview, Texas, staged *Angels in America*. On the sold-out opening night the building

> People have waged a war against art in the name of decency, in the name of civic stability, in the name of God. But censoring art, even indecent art, isn't decent; it's thuggish, it's unconstitutional, undemocratic, and deeply unwise.
>
> **Tony Kushner,**
> Playwright

Darren Staples DS/RUS/Reuters

had to be surrounded by police because there were so many protesters. The play received a standing ovation, but a county commissioner revoked $50,000 worth of support to the Texas Shakespeare Festival, which was hosted by Kilgore College (but not by the theatre department). The commissioner said that county funds should not be used to support the arts because the "arts are always controversial." The arts are not always controversial, but they can be when they attempt to foster understanding of differing cultures within society. As Tony Kushner put it in a letter to the cast and crew at Kilgore College, "A healthy state needs vigorous, lively, pluralistic debate, not enforced acquiescence to a bullying majority."

Culture Wars

Public opinion polls show broad public support for the arts and artists. The majority of Americans feel that the arts and humanities contribute to the economic health and well-being of society and that they are important to education. Yet today public funding for art that expresses a minority's point of view

Stating your opinion can be dangerous. The theatre often deals with ideas and opinions that are controversial; this has resulted in many protests and, too often, violence. One such example is the 2004 production of *Behzti* by the Birmingham Rep, which dealt with a rape and murder in a Sikh temple. During a protest, some members of the Sikh community tried to force their way into the theatre, causing serious damage to the theatre. The play was canceled on safety grounds, and playwright Gurpreet Kaur Bhatti fled into hiding after receiving death threats.

Patricia Switzer

Theatre of Identity allows us to learn about various people's traditions, culture, and experiences. This rendition of *The Wizard of Oz* was produced by PHAMALY, The Physically Handicapped Actors & Musical Artists League.

is sometimes questioned. At the center of this debate has been the National Endowment for the Arts, whose primary purpose has always been to give a voice to all cultures as it "increases the public awareness of our cultural heritage." This policy has put the NEA into conflict with some people who feel that all cultures are not equal. These people seem to believe that Americans must decide which culture is *the* American culture and government policies and funding must reflect that decision. Others feel that the government should stay out of arts funding altogether. Still others feel that without government assistance only those with the loudest voice—the privileged culture—will be heard.

The U.S. government does have a long history of guaranteeing freedom of speech by financially supporting viewpoints that might otherwise be drowned out. For example, it restricts monopolies by allowing smaller companies access to the marketplace, thereby guaranteeing them a voice. It provides funding for numerous political candidates. It gives tax-exempt status to tens of thousands of organizations, including hundreds of different religions. But should the government simply *allow* for freedom of speech or should it *guarantee* it? And how far should the government go to ensure that all voices are heard? Richard Bolton says in his book *Culture Wars*, "In the end, censorship of the arts reveals the failure of democratic institutions to articulate and defend the complexity and diversity of the American public. The NEA debate contained many lessons about art's relationship to society, but it also raised many questions about the future of American democracy."

Curtain Call

Today, the East/West Players, El Teatro Campesino, Ujima Theatre Company, Repertorio Español, Puerto Rican Traveling Theatre Company, the Hispanic American Arts Center, Pan Asian Repertory, Teatro de la Esperanza, San Diego Black Ensemble Theatre, and many more culturally specific theatres are opening up opportunities for culturally diverse actors, designers, directors, playwrights, and theatre practitioners. In addition, many theatres have been formed to highlight gay and lesbian themes, as well as to advocate feminist ideas and stories written by women, about women, and for women.

The battle over cultural diversity around the world and in the United States continues. Some would agree with this statement in UNESCO's *Universal Declaration on Cultural Diversity*: "Cultural diversity is as necessary for humankind as biodiversity is for nature." Others would agree with William Bennett, the chairman of the National Endowment for the Humanities under President Ronald Reagan, who said that to keep a country together, it must share a common culture, which is our "civic glue" and serves as a kind of "immunological system." Without a doubt our cultural differences will continue to be a source of celebration and conflict and the theatre will be part of both. Recently, playwright David Henry Hwang wrote, "American theatre is beginning to discover Americans: black theatre, women's theatre, gay theatre, Asian American theatre, Hispanic theatre." American theatre, like its audience, is diverse. The only way to fully appreciate it is to see and study its many forms, not just those that reflect our own culture and beliefs.

SUMMARY

We often think of theatre in terms of stars and spotlights, but theatre of the people, where artists outside the dominant culture express themselves, also thrives. This type of theatre is what Brazilian director Augusto Boal calls the "theatre of the oppressed." In its long history the theatre has seldom given a voice to all the people or reflected the many cultures in any society. Instead it has been controlled by the dominant culture through racism, sexism, discrimination, economic power, and social and religious customs. Theatre of the people attempts to give a voice to all members of society as it increases multiculturalism and reduces stereotyping.

There are three types of theatre of the people. Theatre of identity promotes a particular people's cultural identity as it strengthens the bonds of the community. It can also invite members of other cultures to experience that people's joys, problems, history, traditions, and point of view. Theatre of protest objects to the dominant culture's control as it demands that a minority culture's voice and political agenda be heard. Cross-cultural theatre mixes different cultures in an attempt to find understanding or commonality among cultures.

Most people see the world from their own point of view, and they tend to think that their take on things, as seen through the lens of their culture, is the correct view. This ethnocentrism leads to a great deal of conflict between cultures. The theatre of the people attempts to lessen this conflict by raising the cultural consciousness of audiences. Government organizations, such as the National Endowment for the Arts, try to promote cultural understanding by funding art created by non-mainstream cultures and allowing all voices to be heard. These attempts sometimes fail, especially when members of the dominant culture see them as threats to the nation's cultural identity. Yet in order for societies to evolve and progress, artists must be free to voice ideas that challenge the privileged culture's views and values.

MindTap

Test your knowledge with online printable flashcards and online quizzing.

KEY TERMS

Blackface *48*

Cross-cultural theatre *53*

Culture *45*

Ethnocentrism *57*

Harlem Renaissance *47*

Minstrel show *48*

Multiculturalism *45*

Privileged group *44*

Stereotypes *45*

Theatre of identity *46*

Theatre of protest *51*

Theatre of the people *44*

Yiddish Broadway *46*

The theatre is more than just a social gathering. It's a place to hear the opinions of the artists. This cartoon by Adolph Schus makes fun of those who go to the theatre to be seen rather than to think.

Chapter

EXPERIENCING AND ANALYZING PLAYS

Outline

MindTap*

Start with a quick warm-up activity and review the chapter's learning objectives.

We go to the theatre for a variety of reasons: Some want to be amused, others desire to be challenged; some want philosophy, others want magic. Theatre can be a vehicle to make us feel, think, and learn, and perhaps motivate us to discuss, analyze, or even take action on what we've experienced. When we support playwrights, directors, designers, and actors in expressing themselves, not only do we increase our own awareness, but we also fuel public dialogue, which sometimes can help us change our world.

This chapter will explore the dynamics of the audience, what to expect when you go to the theatre, and what is expected of you as an audience member. It will also look at a special kind of audience member, the critic, and explain how to go beyond your own opinion to analyze a play and understand what the theatre artist is trying to convey. Finally, it will explore how the right to freedom of speech applies to the arts and how it affects what audiences see.

A Group Activity

MindTap*

Read, highlight, and take notes online.

> In a theatre, actors and audience meet each other at the moment of performance; they share the experience and each contributes something towards it. Real actors, acting in the presence of a real audience: This is the essence of theatre.
>
> **Stephen Joseph,**
> Theatre director, producer, and designer, in New Theatre Forms

People have a tendency to act differently in a group than they do when they're alone. Group dynamics are the actions and changes that take place when individuals begin to subconsciously follow the consensus of a crowd. For example, when the Beatles first came to North America, concert organizers arranged to have many screaming fans greet them and this helped to generate the nationwide phenomenon of "Beatle-mania".

Theatre is a group activity. Unlike television, which usually is watched alone or with a few family members or friends, theatre is designed to be experienced with a sea of strangers. In fact, unlike television or the movies, without an audience there can be no theatre. Remember the quote from the British director Peter Brook in Chapter 1: At its most basic, theatre requires someone to walk across an empty space while someone else watches. Theatre artists have studied their audiences for thousands of years and have learned to manipulate their feelings, reactions, and even their thoughts. This manipulation is possible primarily because of three factors: group dynamics, the suspension of disbelief, and aesthetic distance.

Group Dynamics

Human beings have a tendency to act and react differently depending on whether they are alone or in a group. Whether that group is a gang, a family,

Fox Photos/Getty Images

a congregation, a rock concert, or a theatre audience, studies have shown that people become less intellectual and more emotional, less reasonable, and more irrational, less likely to react as individuals and more likely to react with the crowd when they are joined together with other people. The psychological processes that occur when humans are in groups are called **group dynamics**. One of the most famous cases of using group dynamics to manipulate an audience may have happened in 1964 when the British rock band The Beatles visited the United States for the first time. To sell John, Paul, George, and Ringo to audiences, it is rumored the show's producers hired a few young girls to scream and faint during the performance. Soon, all the young girls in the audience were screaming and fainting.

Theatres take advantage of group dynamics by seating audience members close to one another. Even if the theatre is half empty, the audience will

SPOTLIGHT ON Ovation Inflation

The play ends, the curtain call begins, and the audience claps. Then an enthusiastic patron, perhaps an actor's mother, stands and a few seconds later someone else stands—before you know it, everyone feels compelled to stand. You have been sitting for a while so it feels good to stretch, but did the performance really deserve a standing ovation? Today, standing ovations, which were once reserved for the most outstanding actors and productions, are becoming commonplace. Blogs, theatre critics, and audience members have all voiced concerns about the frequency of ovation inflation.

Some feel that this surplus of standing is because the theatre is too expensive, so people want to supersize the experience. And it is expensive. The *Wall Street Journal* recently pointed out that four full-price tickets to a Broadway show could cost more than an iPad. In addition, some directors stage plays so that the audience has no choice but to stand. For example, during the last number in the Broadway musical *Mamma Mia*, the audience tends to get up and dance, which means that they just happen to be on their feet as the curtain call begins.

There is also the emotional pressure of the group dynamic. (See "Group Dynamics" in this chapter.) If everyone around you is standing it is hard to not follow the crowd's lead, if for no other reason than to get a better view of the curtain call. Jesse McKinley wrote in "The Tyranny of the Standing Ovation" (*New York Times*), "Whatever the motivation, the effect of the rampant increase in standing ovations has been accompanied by—as with any other form of inflation—a decrease in value. If almost every performance receives one, then it ceases to be a meaningful compliment."

You don't have to stand. If you do not feel it was an exceptional performance, then it is perfectly acceptable to sit while you applaud—even if the friend/date/spouse/family member next to you is standing. If anyone questions you about not standing, let them know that you are a soldier in the fight against ovation inflation.

Richard Ferry/The New York Times/Redux Pictures

Audience members give a standing ovation to the hit Broadway musical *The Book of Mormon*.

be seated as a group, increasing the chances that they will be influenced by group dynamics. Theatres reason that if the people around you are enjoying the play, there is a good chance you will too. Some theatres even go so far as to **paper the house**. In theatre lingo, **house** is the auditorium, and in this case *paper* means tickets. So to "paper the house" means to give away a lot of free tickets to the families and friends of cast members in order to make it appear as though the performance is well attended. Theatres are most likely to paper the house on opening night when they know a critic is attending. They hope that an audience's positive response to the play will rub off on the critic, who may then write a favorable review. (See Spotlight, "Ovation Inflation.)

The Willing Suspension of Disbelief

When we go to the theatre, or watch a television show or movie for that matter, we must enter into a **willing suspension of disbelief**. In other words, we admit that what is happening is not real and so we don't need to rush up and save the actor who is being attacked or call the police to stop the actor playing the criminal. When suspending our disbelief, we put aside our concerns about everyday reality and agree to accept the *play's* particular quasi reality, which communicates some perception about everyday reality.

If an artist crosses the line and we don't know if the moment is real or make-believe, it can make for a very powerful performance, but the audience may feel violated. For example, in 1994, performance artist Ron Athey famously broke the audience's willing suspension of disbelief during a performance at the Walker Art Center in Minneapolis. In his piece, which was based on African tribal traditions and was about the spread of AIDS, Athey purposely nicked the

When you go to the theatre, there is an unwritten contract between you and the performers: although the emotions feel real, you agree to suspend your disbelief. For example, in the play *The Exit Interview,* two people are terrorized by a gunman and yet the audience sits passively and doesn't help. This production of *The Exit Interview* was produced at the Flying H Theatre in California and featured Angela DeCicco and Chad Parker.

William Missouri Downs

skin of another actor—with the actor's permission of course—and blotted the blood onto a paper towel that he then showed to the audience.

People get nicks all the time; they cut their skin shaving, cleaning the yard, or playing sports. But because this nick happened in front of a live audience, it sent shock waves through the auditorium and across the country. When Senator Jesse Helms of North Carolina heard about the performance, he sent a letter to the then head of the National Endowment for the Arts, Jane Alexander, accusing her agency of funding a work in which HIV-positive, "blood-soaked towels" were sent "winging" over the audience. None of this was true; the blood was not HIV positive, nor did it come into contact with the audience. The Minnesota Department of Health affirmed that the Walker Center had taken appropriate safety precautions, but that wasn't enough to squelch the commotion. It's interesting to compare the impact of a few droplets of real blood on stage in front of a live audience to the dozens of bloody and severed limbs in summer blockbuster movies like Quentin Tarantino's *Kill Bill* (Volumes 1 and 2). One type of performance set off a political firestorm; the other simply seems to sell more tickets.

Athey's performance made a powerful statement about AIDS, but he also blurred the lines between art and life. Theatre artists are always attempting to manipulate the audience's willing suspension of disbelief, sometimes engulfing them in total fantasy and at other times taking them to the edge of reality. Suspension of disbelief allows the audience to laugh at a painful beating during a comedy, or come so close to real life that they are moved to tears. For example, the smash Broadway success *Spamalot* (2005), the musical based on the movie *Monty Python and the Holy Grail* (1975), creates a hilarious fantasy world that demands an audience suspend their disbelief in order to find the slapstick violence funny. In contrast, Marsha Norman's play, *night, Mother* (1982) details the last 90 minutes of a woman who has decided to commit suicide. The set of this play features functioning clocks and the actors perform in real time, highlighting the sense of reality for the audience. Yet, because the audience members suspend their disbelief while watching the play, they know the actress is not really going to kill herself, and so don't try to stop her.

Aesthetic Distance

Closely tied to the suspension of disbelief is **aesthetic distance**, the audience's ability to remove themselves from a work of art just far enough so that they can contemplate it—or even judge it. If we allow ourselves to be immersed in a play, movie, or television show to the point that we forget ourselves, forget that time is passing, then we have no aesthetic distance. We are simply using the show as a vicarious experience. For example, we want to live a more exciting life, so we go to an action movie or play a video game and feel that we have been on a mini-escapade. But most artists don't want the audience to totally forget themselves; they want the audience to distance themselves from the work just enough to be semi-objective but not indifferent. This way, the audience can have a vicarious experience, feel empathy for the characters, and be entertained, yet they can also think about the play's themes and meaning and even its artistic merit.

Some writers and directors go further and challenge or even alienate an audience. The German playwright Bertolt Brecht (1898–1956) believed that an

The very nature of theatre encourages audiences to maintain a certain aesthetic distance, keeping us from completely losing ourselves in a story. Some plays ask audiences to maintain more distance than others. For example, in the musical *Urinetown* Officer Lockstock addresses the spectators and acts as a narrator reminding the audience that they are watching a play. This production was directed by John Rando at San Francisco's American Conservatory Theater.

> In its essence, a theatre is only an arrangement of seats so grouped and spaced that the actor—the leader—can reach out and touch and hold each member of his audience. Architects of later days have learned how to add conveniences and comforts to this idea. But that is all. The idea itself never changes.
>
> **Robert Edmond Jones,**
> Theatre set designer

audience's emotional involvement in the characters and story could cloud their grasp of the play's message. He sneered at what he called "culinary theatre," theatre that does not provoke socially meaningful thought but rather feeds us illusion and leaves us feeling content and emotionally satisfied, as we do after a good meal. In his "epic theater" style, he tried to shatter traditional stage illusions and continually remind the audience that they were sitting in a theatre watching a performance. In this way, Brecht did not allow the audience to lose themselves in the play. Instead he consciously urged them to distance themselves from the play so they could think about its message. (For more on Bertolt Brecht and his plays, see Part 3.)

Levels of Participation

Group dynamics, suspension of disbelief, and aesthetic distance also affect the level of audience participation. Audience participation can be divided into two basic levels: active participation and sitting quietly in the dark. The two types of theatre that correspond to these levels of participation are sometimes called *presentational* and *representational*.

Presentational theatre makes no attempt to offer a realistic illusion onstage, and the actors openly acknowledge the audience and sometimes even invite members to participate. When Peter Pan begs the audience to clap their hands to help Tinker Bell, that's presentational theatre. In **representational theatre,** actors never acknowledge the audience and go about their business as if there were no audience present. Almost all movies and TV shows are representational but in the theatre plays are either presentational or representational, and audiences either sit quietly in the dark or are asked to participate. To maximize your and your fellow audience members' theatregoing experience, you need to know what is expected of you for both types of plays and what etiquette you should follow.

Sitting Quietly in the Dark

Sitting quietly in the dark to watch a play is a relatively new behavior for theatre audiences. It started in the late 1850s but did not become popular until Edison invented the lightbulb. Electric lights allowed designers to control the illumination of the stage and to completely dim the house during performances; before this, the audience was as well-lit as the stage. But the major reason for a passive audience was **realism**, a style of theatre that attempts to portray life as accurately as possible. (For more on realism, see Part 3.) By the late 1800s, realism had become the dominant form of theatre in the West, and the idea of an actor talking with an audience was considered passé. Asides, prologues, and epilogues were dropped, and the performers began acting as though the audience didn't exist. The actors' "reality" incorporated a **fourth wall**, an imaginary wall between the actors and audience. In this form of theatre, the audience had to sit quietly.

Not Sitting Quietly in the Dark

Not all plays require the audience to sit complacently in the dark. For some types of theatre, the audience is supposed to express themselves and even participate in the play. These productions do not allow the audience the safety of the fourth wall, and in some cases the actors embrace or confront the audience during the play. Interactive theatre comes in many forms, from Japanese Kabuki theatre to children's shows to comedies such as *Tony n' Tina's Wedding*, a popular satire of an Italian American wedding in which audience members participate in the ceremony, the champagne toast, and the cutting of the wedding cake. The most extreme example of audience participation is the musical *Rocky Horror Show* (1973) or the movie based on the play, *The Rocky Horror Picture Show* (1975), where audience members dance the Time Warp, throw buttered toast, water, rice, and toilet paper at the actors or the screen, and even speak lines of dialogue. You don't go to "see" *Rocky Horror Show*; rather, you "experience" it. In short, when attending the theatre, knowing and obeying the basic etiquette improves the experience for everyone, but you can seldom predict what will be expected of you. Keep an open mind and play along.

Attending the Theatre

Let's explore what you need to know to find a play you want to see, buy a ticket, choose what to wear, and use the program.

Finding a Play

Fifty years ago, there were only a handful of professional theatre companies outside of New York City. Today, thanks to the National Endowment of the Arts and patrons, there are hundreds. Some are **road houses** where touring companies perform Broadway plays and musicals; others are professional theatre companies known as LORT theatres (**League of Resident Theatres**). These large regional theatres hire professional actors and fill their seasons with traditional comedies, dramas, and musicals, as well as challenging new plays. In addition, there are now nearly 1,800 smaller professional and semi-professional theatre companies throughout the United States, not counting hundreds of community and college theatres. You don't have to travel far to see a good play.

Getting Tickets

Theatre tickets must almost always be reserved in advance by calling or visiting the box office or buying tickets online. When you buy your tickets by

Going to the theatre is a special event. People often dress up, go out to dinner before, and stay after for talkbacks or panel discussions. It you treat theatre attendance as you would a movie, you are missing some of the magic.

William Missouri Downs

phone or online, the tickets will be mailed if there is enough time or you can pick them up at the box office before the performance. Many theatres have a "**Will Call**" window for those who are picking up tickets they have already paid for. The words "will call" come from the phrase "the purchaser will call." In other words, the purchaser will show up and pick up the tickets. When you do pick up the tickets, be sure to do it at least 15 minutes before **curtain** (the start of the show), or the theatre may assume you are not coming and sell them to someone else.

Once you have purchased your tickets, you usually cannot return or exchange them. Some theatres may offer an exchange of tickets for another performance or play, but most will not. Because you have purchased your seat in advance, the theatre cannot sell it to anyone else and cannot afford to give you a last-minute refund. The same no-refund policy is true if you misplace your ticket or are dissatisfied with the play. Just as with a fishing license, you can't get your money back if you fail to catch any fish.

Saving Money

If you want to save a little money, be sure to ask at the box office if student tickets are available. Often theatres sell high school and college students discount tickets if they have a valid student ID. The availability of these tickets can be limited and sometimes they don't go on sale until the afternoon of the performance. If you are seeing theatre in New York City, then you can get bargain tickets the day of the performance at the TKTS booth in Times Square. Sometimes you have to stand in line for several hours, but in the end you can save as much as 25 to 50 percent. Another way to get discount Broadway tickets is through the School Theater Ticket Program (http://schooltix.com), which offers discount tickets for students.

Preview performances can also offer a way to save money. Previews are performances open to the public and are staged before the play officially opens. Previews allow the director and actors to identify problems and make improvements before critics are invited to attend. Ticket prices for previews are generally half as much as regular performances. If you do attend a preview, you must remember you are not seeing a final product but a play that is still in rehearsal. On rare occasions, the director or crew may even have to stop a preview to make adjustments. Previews are common in the professional theatre but rare in college, community, and amateur theatres.

Dress Codes

In the United States, you're expected to dress up a little or a lot when you go to the theatre. Unlike movie audiences, theatre audiences are made up of people intending to attend a special event. If you go to the professional theatre, you'll be out of place if you dress the way you do for college classes. Unless you are attending the opera, formal or semi-formal attire is not required, but you will need to reach farther into your closet for something clean and pressed. In other words, a Hooter's T-shirt and old tennis shoes are inappropriate. But there are exceptions: If you are attending an outdoor performance of Shakespeare, then

SPOTLIGHT ON Audiences Behaving Badly

When you enter a theatre your cell phone is turned off and left off for the entirety of the performance. Texting, tweeting, taking pictures, making or receiving calls, checking your Facebook page or anything else you can do on a smartphone or device of any kind are breaches of theater etiquette. Not only do these behaviors annoy the people around you but they also break the actors' concentration and can ruin the play. Actress Mary-Louise Parker, the Emmy-nominated lead actress from Showtime's *Weeds*, famously said, "People think they're watching television. What they don't know is that when you're onstage, one Tic-Tac coming out of the box sounds like an avalanche."

At a recent performance at the Booth Theatre in New York a 19-year-old Long Island college student jumped up on stage before the play began and plugged his smartphone into an electrical outlet that was part of the set; of course, the outlet was simply set dressing and not functional. When asked later his reason for doing so he said, "Girls were calling all day—what would you do?" This too is unacceptable behavior.

Cell phone interruptions have become such a problem that some actors have started taking things into their own hands. Actors such as Kevin Spacey, Hugh Jackman, and Laurence Fishburne have stopped performances to lecture rude audience members. In one case actress Patti LuPone snatched a cell phone away from an audience member who was texting. Benedict Cumberbatch pleaded with audiences not to record him performing the role of Hamlet: "I can't give you what I want to give you, which is a live performance that you'll remember, hopefully, in your minds and brains whether it's good, bad or indifferent, rather than on your phones."

Here is a list of basic rules of etiquette for theatregoers:

1. **Turn off phones and beepers.** A mobile phone ringing (or merely vibrating) not only bothers the actors but other audience members. Doctors or parents who must be available during the performance can leave their phones or beepers at the box office or coatroom. If the phone should

William Missouri Downs

Taking on the phone, texting, or doing anything that involves your handheld devices, is not allowed during a play and ruins a production for both actors and audiences.

dress for the weather. And if you are attending a performance of *Rocky Horror Show*, you might want to dress in costume.

Before the Play

Once you enter the theatre, an usher will give you a program and show you to your seat—unless it's "general seating," in which case you can sit anywhere you like. In the United States programs are free, but in some countries, such as England, programs must be purchased. Try to arrive early enough to spend a few minutes reading the program before the play begins. Programs feature information that will help you better understand the performance, such as the location and time of the scenes and the cast of characters. Some programs also ring or the beeper beep, an usher will come get its owner.

2. **Do not text or tweet during the play.** The actors may not see you using Twitter but it can be very distracting to other audience members. The bright light of your handheld device is extremely visible to those around you.

3. **Do not talk.** Even whispering can bother other audience members and the actors. At a musical, all talking should end when the lights dim or the conductor enters; the overture is part of the performance. However, vocal responses to the play itself, such as gasping or laughing, are okay.

4. **Try not to cough.** If you have a cough, then you should bring cough drops (unwrapped before the show starts, see rule 6) and do everything in your power to suppress the cough until scene changes or the intermission. One cough can obscure a crucial word of dialogue and ruin a scene.

5. **Do not be late.** Latecomers edging down a row to their seats are very distracting. If you arrive late, you will probably have to wait to be seated until a break in the performance. You may be required to stand in the back or sit in a different seat until intermission.

6. **Do not eat.** In most U.S. theatres, food is not allowed (although each theatre is different).

Cough drops should be unwrapped before the performance begins. The crinkling of cellophane wrappers distracts audience members and actors.

7. **Be courteous.** Do not kick or put your feet on the seat in front of you, fidget, squirm, or constantly wiggle in your seat. Do not sing or hum along with the music or make any other disruptive noises.

8. **Go light on the perfume or cologne.** In the theatre you sit close to other audience members; heavy perfume or cologne may bother them or even trigger an allergic response.

9. **Do not leave until the intermission or until the end.** The only reason to leave during a performance is an emergency. Leaving a performance because it bores you or insults you is discourteous and will ruin the play for those who do not find it boring or insulting.

10. **No photos or recording devices allowed.** Not only is the noise distracting, but the flash can disorient the actors. In the past, actors blinded by a flashbulb have actually fallen off the stage. Moreover, taking pictures or recording a performance is a violation of copyright laws. Your ticket allows you to attend the performance once, not to own a copy of it. (For more on copyright, see Chapters 2 and 6.)

include a **director's note** or a **playwright's note** that explains what he or she intended to accomplish with the play. You might also find historical information about the play, playwright, or style of production. Some larger professional theatres sell **souvenir programs** that have more pictures and information about the cast and production. You don't have to buy one unless you really want a souvenir.

Just before the play begins there is often a **curtain speech** during which a member of the theatre staff will make general announcements. They will inform you about upcoming productions, often ask for you to donate money to the theatre, and give the all-important "turn off your cell phone" warning. This is the time to check and make sure your phone is totally off—not on vibrate—totally and completely off. (See Spotlight, "Audiences Behaving Badly.)

After a play, audience members sometimes like to meet the actors. You can do this by staying for the talk-back or by waiting by the stage door, which is the exit where actors leave the theatre after the performance. Here, audience members wait at the stage door after a production of *A Chorus Line* at the Shubert Theatre on Broadway.

William Missouri Downs

After the Play

Occasionally, a theatre will sponsor an audience **talk-back**, a post-performance discussion where you get a chance to meet, and perhaps ask questions of, the director, actors, and sometimes the playwright. If the play is issue-oriented, the theatre might even have experts there to discuss the play's theme. For example, the Broadway producers of David Mamet's play *Oleanna* held such audience talk-backs after every performance. *Oleanna* deals with charges of sexual harassment between a female student and a college professor, so the producers had criminal defense lawyers and professional mediators present to discuss the problem. Such talk-backs were once limited to smaller theatres, but today they are held at theatres of any size; with certain particularly evocative plays, talk-backs have become a regular and expected part of the theatregoing experience as an outlet for the audience to express themselves. "I think talk-backs are being embraced more and more by commercial theatre because we producers sense that when people connect to a show, they want to prolong that experience as much as they can," said Jed Bernstein, one of the producers of the Broadway production of *Oleanna*.

Not all theatres sponsor talk-backs, and when they do, they don't always hold one for every performance. In addition, just because the theatre is holding a talk-back, that doesn't mean you have to attend. However, when you leave the theatre you should have your own talk-back where you and your friends discuss the play's merits, shortcomings, and meaning.

Play Analysis

As a student, you'll probably not only attend plays but also read plays and write about what you've seen and read. To fully appreciate a play and analyze it thoughtfully, it's important to understand the differences between a review, which is an opinion, and criticism, which is a detailed analysis. An opinion tells you what someone thinks about the play, but educated, thoughtful, and justified criticism will lead you to a greater understanding of a play. Let's take a look at what constitutes a review, what constitutes criticism, and how to analyze a play.

Reviews

Reviews, sometimes called *notices* in theatre lingo, are evaluations of a production, often published in newspapers or magazines. They can also be broadcast on television, on the radio, and over the Internet. In a sense, everyone who has ever expressed an opinion about a dramatic performance is a reviewer, whether or not they have published or broadcast that review to a large audience. The reviewer's main goal is to inform the potential audience members whether a play is, in the reviewer's opinion, worth attending. A reviewer assesses the production and gives it a "thumbs up" or "thumbs down," or may rate a production, for example, by giving it three stars out of four. Reviews are a sort of consumer report or comparative shopping guide that rates a performance.

One of the oldest examples dates back to about 1800 BCE, when the Egyptian actor Ikhernofret wrote in hieroglyphics his opinions about a ritual play in which he had performed—he gave himself a positive review, four stars out of four. Today, however, many reviewers' number-one desire is to sell newspapers, so their reviews must above all grab readers' attention. A few years ago, an actor in Denver was mugged and beaten by a gang as he walked home after his performance. The next day, a newspaper reviewer wrote that perhaps the gang had seen the actor's performance and were on a mission of revenge. The reporter was later forced to apologize.

Although some reviews can be insensitive or mean-spirited, regularly reading reviews can help you discover which reviewers' tastes you share. And you'll know that when certain reviewers pan a play, you'll probably love it. In any case, reviews generally do not provide a deep, scholarly analysis of a play, the artists, or the production—that level of analysis is left to dramatic criticism.

Dramatic Criticism

Dramatic criticism, sometimes called *literary criticism* or simply criticism, is not meant to draw people to a particular production or warn them away from it, nor is it based solely on opinion. Instead, criticism offers the reader a discriminating, often scholarly interpretation and analysis of a play, an artist's body of work, or a period of theatre history. Criticism appears in literary quarterlies, in academic books, and in more sophisticated magazines and newspapers. Academics and theatre professionals often study criticism when they research a particular play, playwright, historical movement, or genre. Students of theatre find reading criticism often allows them a greater understanding of the plays they read and see.

Criticism comes in many forms. It can examine the structure of a play; it can compare a play with others of its genre; or it can analyze a play's effectiveness. Criticism can judge a play in relation to a particular period or style of theatre. It can challenge or support a play's philosophical or sociological perspective. Or it can chronicle how the play was created and how history and the artist's background and conscious or unconscious motives affected it. Criticism can also attack or endorse other works of scholarly criticism. In short, criticism has less to do with rating a particular production than with delving into a play's aesthetic effect, history, and dramatic structure.

> [The critic's job is to] improve theatrical standards by educating an audience to a level of taste more receptive to ambitious theatre and less tolerant of mediocrity.
>
> **Richard Palmer,**
> Theatre professor, director, and author, in The Critics' Canon

Donald Cooper/Photostage Ltd.

Understanding a character's motivations is critical for actors such as Ray Fearon and Zoe Walker, playing Othello and his wife, Desdemona, in this scene from Shakespeare's *Othello*. Why does Othello believe his wife has been unfaithful? Why is he so enraged that he is willing to kill her for her supposed crime? Why is Desdemona unable to convince Othello of her innocence? To analyze a play effectively, you must ask similar questions. This 2001 Royal Shakespeare Company production was directed by Michael Attenborough at the Barbican Theatre, London.

Assessment

For students, writing an opinion paper about a production is a lot like writing a review. Often such papers say more about you than they do about the play: if you prefer musical theatre, you may not enjoy a tragedy; if you like serious plays, you may not care for farce. All plays fall into categories known as **genres**. Each genre is characterized by similarities in form, style, and subject matter. A well-rounded theatregoer enjoys many different genres. (See Spotlight, "Genre.")

Opinion papers are a nice exercise, but only when you know the basics of analyzing a play can you take the first steps toward dramatic criticism and analysis. Of course, the greater your knowledge of theatre, the deeper you can delve into the subject. And the more you know about playwriting (Chapter 6) the better you'll be at analyzing a play's structure, theme, and story. The more you know about acting (Chapter 7) the better you'll be at analyzing the actors' performances and the play's characters, emotions, and motivations. This also applies to directing (Chapter 8), design (Chapter 9), and theatre history (Part 3). But you don't have to be a theatre expert to write meaningful criticism after seeing a performance or after reading a play. The key is to ask the right questions and always include examples from the play itself that lead you to your answers or conclusion.

SPOTLIGHT_{ON} Genre

Plays are written in a particular *genre*, or type of story. The most common genres are comedy and tragedy. Other genres include melodrama, realism, romanticism, expressionism, and absurdism. Each genre may also have subgenres. For example, a subgenre of comedy is sentimental comedy, which takes an entertaining look at the troubles of everyday people. *The Dining Room* (1982) by A. R. Gurney and *The Man Who Came to Dinner* (1939) by Moss Hart and George Kaufman are examples of sentimental comedies. Another subgenre of comedy is farce, such as *Noises Off* (1982) by Michael Frayn, in which the characters are caught in a fast-paced story and broadly satirical circumstances. Situation comedy, called "sitcom" on television, is a subgenre that takes a light look at comic situations, such as the TV show *Seinfeld*. Dark comedies, such as *Little Murders* (1966) by Jules Feiffer and the movie *Eternal Sunshine of the Spotless Mind* (2004), allow the audience to laugh at the bleaker or absurd side of life.

Working within a genre means obeying its rules. A playwright who sets out to write a realistic play cannot include supernatural events or dream sequences, because such moments would not be realistic. Romantic plays have protagonists who set out against impossible odds simply because they know in their hearts they're right. Expressionist plays use highly stylized methods to show the characters' inner feelings rather than external realities. Absurdist plays have stories that show the world as cruel, unjust, and meaningless. In Part 3 of this book, you will learn more about the many genres and how they came into being.

Sometimes playwrights deliberately mix genres in an attempt to shock the audience, to increase irony or comic effect, or to express ideas that can't be limited to a single genre. For example, in *Macbeth* (1606) Shakespeare follows the tragic scene where Macbeth returns from killing King Duncan with a broadly comical scene with a drunken porter. By juxtaposing a serious scene with a comic scene, he creates ironic moments and powerful dramatic effects. Playwrights may also mix genres to show different points of view. For example, Arthur Miller's *Death of a Salesman* (1949) is a realistic play but switches to expressionism when it enters into the mind of the main character, Willy Loman, thus allowing the audience to gain greater understanding of the troubled salesman.

William Missouri Downs

Farce is one of the most outrageous forms of comedy. The action is fast-paced and the humor often borders on slapstick. This production of the farce *Mad Gravity* by William Missouri Downs featured Kevin Inouye, Landee Lockhart, Lana Percival, and Peter Parolin.

Three of the most productive questions for analysis were proposed by the great German romantic playwright, philosopher, and critic Johann Wolfgang von Goethe (1749–1832):

1. *What is the artist trying to do?* This question will help determine the direction of your essay. If you understand the intention of the artist, you will understand the reasons for his or her choices. Put aside your opinion of the play and identify the artist's purpose. What is the artist trying to express?

What is the artist's goal? What was the artist trying to accomplish? Can you explain why the artist chose to bring this particular work into being?

2. *How well has the artist done it?* By answering this question, you judge the degree of success the artist achieves toward the goal you identified in the answer to the first question. How do the artist's techniques, methods, and talents help to achieve the goal? How effective is the production in fulfilling the artist's intention?

3. *Is it worth doing?* The final question is whether the finished work of art was worth the artist's and the audience's time and effort. Does the play have new, interesting ideas? Will it help us understand the world, or understand it in a new way? If it didn't communicate to you, did it communicate to anyone else?

Goethe's simple formula has been used for hundreds of years and can lead to a well-structured, intelligent assessment of a play that is useful to audience members as well as to the artist. Another way to evaluate a play, which can be done separately or combined with Goethe's method, is to break the play into its basic components and analyze the effectiveness of each one. An excellent, time-tested definition of a play's elements is derived from Aristotle's *Poetics*. More than 23 centuries ago, Greek philosopher Aristotle deconstructed plays into six elements: plot, thought, character, diction, spectacle, and song. (For more on Aristotle and *Poetics*, see Chapter 1 and Part 3.) A clear and cohesive analysis of a play can be written by investigating how each element works by itself and in relation to the others. Here is a brief description of each element, followed by questions to which you might respond when analyzing it.

- **Plot**

  Aristotle defined *plot* as a unified "arrangement of the incidents" in which characters, meaning, language, and visual elements come together to comment on a single subject. In other words, plot is what happens. Plot is the main story of a play. Because Aristotle believed that a story does not copy but, rather, imitates nature, it is not "real life" logic that determines the order of events but rather the requirements of the story. The action must be both probable and essential to the story.

  - Are all the parts of the plot essential?

  - Are any parts of the plot unclear and why?

  - Is the story told in a linear or nonlinear way and why? That is, does it follow chronological order or jump around?

  - What are the main conflicts of the play, and how are they resolved or left unresolved and why?

  - Why does the playwright make the story a comedy instead of a serious play or a serious play instead of a comedy?

- **Character**

  Character is about the personalities of the story. Characters are made up of motivation and action. We are what we do.

- Which character is the protagonist (the main character around whom the story revolves, and without whom the play could not take place), and why do we care about him or her?

- Which character is the antagonist (not necessarily the villain but rather the person who blocks the protagonist from getting what he or she wants)?

- Are the characters' action and behaviors motivated?

- What are the characters' objectives?

- How does each character advance the play's plot?

- How does each character advance the play's theme?

- What is the psychological makeup of each character?

- What are the characters' relationships?

- Are the characters well developed, or are they caricatures that lack depth or are exaggerated?

- *Thought*

  Thought is what the play means, the ideas it's trying to communicate, and its themes or message. If plot is the series of actions in the play, thought asks what the sum of those actions means. For some plays, thought is a complicated philosophy; for others, it is simply a question or idea about the universal human condition. Usually the meaning of a play is implied, not stated directly.

  - What is the play's thought, theme, or message?

  - How does the play's thought, theme, or message apply to today's social, cultural, or religious climate?

  - What events in the playwright's life motivated him or her to include this thought, theme, or message?

  - To what degree do you agree or disagree with the play's thought, theme, or message, and why?

  - Is the play's thought, theme, or message universal? Does it apply to human beings of any social class in any period? Why?

  - What does the play's theme say about human nature?

  - What do other criticisms say about the meaning of the play?

- *Diction*

  Aristotle describes *diction* as "modes of utterance." It is the dialogue used to create the thought, character, and plot. It is the playwright's mode of expression. From beautiful rhyming couplets to guttural grunts, diction comprises the human sounds that communicate the play.

  - How does the playwright use language to advance the plot?

  - How does the playwright use language to reveal the characters?

  - How does the characters' language reveal their background, education, or social class?

  - How do imagery and symbolism help or hurt the dialogue of the play?

Patricia Switzer

Plays such as Arthur Miller's *The Crucible* have themes that can be applied to generation after generation, regardless of the setting. *The Crucible* concerns the 1693 Salem Witch Trials but is also an allegory to the McCarthyism of the 1950s as well as contemporary attempts to intimidate and censor alternative ideas. This production was produced by the Arvada Center for Arts and Humanities in Colorado.

- What are the most memorable lines of the play and why?
- How does the dialogue reveal the characters' identities?

- **Spectacle**

  Spectacle is the performance's set, costumes, and effects—the sensory aspects of the production. Aristotle said that spectacle is the least important element of any play, but he lived long before electric lights, recorded sound effects, and indoor theatres in which the environment could be controlled.

  - How do the set, lights, sound, and costumes help tell the story? How do they help set the mood?
  - How does the setting tell you about the characters?
  - Why does the playwright set the play where he or she did?
  - How does the director's staging advance the story, characters, and/or theme?
  - What is the style of the production? (For more on style, see Chapter 9.)

- **Song**

  Portions of ancient tragedies were sung, so Aristotle included *song* as a standard part of any play, but today song is optional. However, if you are analyzing a musical or a drama that incorporates music, you will certainly want to consider song.

- How do the songs and music advance the plot, characters, or thoughts of the play?
- How do the songs and music help set the mood?
- Are all the songs and music necessary? If not, which ones and why not?

Using Goethe's and Aristotle's methods, you can break a play into its elements and specify how and why it does or doesn't work. Analyzing a play can also increase your understanding and open your mind to new points of view and forms of expression in the theatre.

Because plays often appeal to smaller audiences than movies and television do, they are more likely to express ideas outside the mainstream. Consequently, Goethe's last question, "Is it worth doing?" is more often asked in regard to plays. When a group takes a negative response further and insists the play *shouldn't* be done, criticism turns into censorship. The right to freedom of speech affects all of us, but theatre artists and critics are particularly concerned about it. Theatre practitioners rarely make a consistent living writing, producing, directing, or acting in plays, so it isn't money that drives them. What motivates many of them is having a forum for expressing ideas they are personally invested in. In the United States, the right to freedom of speech protects that expression.

Freedom of Speech

We live in a society bristling with consumer warnings. Everything from power tools to children's toys has an inventory of warnings and dangers printed on labels. Even the entertainment industries have been pressured to come up with ratings systems and warning labels that let consumers know what age group the producers think a particular program or product is suited for and what questionable content is to be expected. On top of this the FCC (Federal Communications Commission), which regulates radio and television, can impose fines of up to $325,000 on stations that broadcast over the public airwaves anything that does not meet its decency standards—standards that are not particularly well-defined and therefore often force filmmakers, PBS, and other broadcast companies to self-censor to avoid a possible penalty. No such warning labels or consumer protections exist in the theatre. A play may be advertised as a children's play or a theatre may choose to warn theatregoers that a particular production is inappropriate for children, but no government institution such as the FCC regulates the theatre. Instead, audience members must take responsibility for researching a play if they want to know its content before viewing it. The fact that there is no rating system for theatre can lead to problems regarding the right to express ideas freely. Some members of the public want not only to be warned about the content of a particular play, but also to restrict the content of plays so that certain ideas will never be heard, even by those who desire to hear them.

Free speech is most often contested when unpopular or controversial ideas are being expressed. Yet if only popular ideas were protected, there would be no need for the First Amendment, which states, "Congress shall make no law respecting an establishment of religion, or prohibiting the free exercise thereof; or abridging the freedom of speech, or of the press; or the right of the people peaceably to assemble, and to petition the Government for a redress of grievances." **Censorship** is the altering, restricting, or suppressing of information, images, or words circulated within a society. It can take the form of banning or

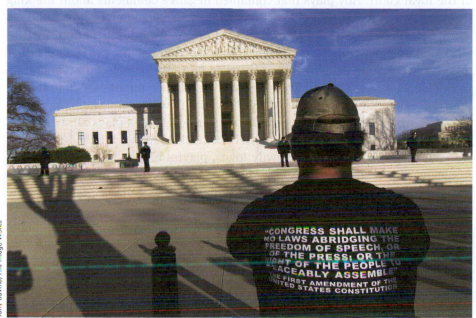

Artists often highlight a society's problems, cultural shortcomings, religious hypocrisy, and corporate greed, and so there are many groups that wish to censor them. Here a protester with the First Amendment printed onto his t-shirt, protests in front of the United States Supreme Court.

altering books, periodicals, films, television and radio programs, video games, content on the Internet, news reports, theatrical productions, or any other expression of thought that someone finds objectionable or offensive.

Today, people who want to censor seldom use the word *censorship*. More often, they hide behind such terms as *speech code, political correctness, decency*, and *morals*. And people who want to restrict speech seldom see themselves as censors; more often they believe that they are protecting basic social institutions and values, such as religion, patriotism, the war effort, or children. The critical questions remain: Who decides what will be censored and what will not? Is it possible to create a society in which the audience is never offended? And what happens if we succeed? One possibility is that we become less tolerant of other people's opinions and right to express themselves. Even though freedom of speech has been a part of America's tradition since its beginning, some people still call for censorship, particularly in the arts.

> What is freedom of expression? Without the freedom to offend, it ceases to exist.
>
> **Salman Rushdie,**
> Novelist

Censorship

Theatre has been censored for thousands of years. Records of censorship go back to antiquity. In 493 BCE, the playwright Phrynichus presented his tragedy *The Capture of Miletus* at the Theatre of Dionysus in Athens. The play was about the fall of the Greek city Miletus, which had been sacked by the Persians the year before. The government felt that the play reminded the citizens of their misfortunes, so it banned the play and fined the playwright. The Roman emperor Caligula ordered actors and playwrights who offended him to be burned alive. In the late Middle Ages and the Renaissance, the church banned or condemned opposing ideas with papal edicts, the Inquisition, and the *Index of Forbidden Books*.

> If the printed word facilitates the working of the imagination, then the staging of dramatic scenes in a public auditorium by presenting these images to our senses in much stronger colors makes a much deeper impression on the spectator and stirs their passion more violently.
>
> **Czar Nicholas I,**
> Russian ruler, justifying censorship of the stage

In 1737, the **Licensing Act** was passed in England. This law placed the censoring of plays under the authority of the Lord Chamberlain, one of the officials of the royal court. Any plays that contained negative comments about the king or queen, unorthodox opinions, or statements considered heretical or seditious could be censored; the term *legitimate theatre* comes from this period. In 1817 Shakespeare's play *King Lear*, about a king who slowly loses his mind rather than believe that his daughters have betrayed him, was banned for several years in England because officials were afraid the audience might associate it with the madness of King George III. In 1818 Thomas Bowdler published *The Family Shakespeare*, in which he had edited out of Shakespeare's plays all words and expressions "which cannot with propriety be read aloud in a family." The result was Shakespeare without the bawdy jokes, playful banter, or any mention of sexuality. This is where the term *bowdlerize* originated. To **bowdlerize** means to remove any possibly vulgar, obscene, or otherwise objectionable material before publication.

For almost 85 years the Comstock Act (1823) was used to censor mail in the United States. If Post Office inspectors decided a book, picture, play, or other item was indecent, they would seize all copies and arrest both the sender and the receiver. The list of items banned from the mail included information on birth control, anatomical drawings, anything written by atheists, agnostics, or freethinkers, and information about cures for venereal disease. They even seized copies of pictures of Egyptian belly dancers that were mailed from the Chicago World's Fair. J. D. Salinger's *The Catcher in the Rye* has the distinction of being the most frequently censored book in the United States since its publication in 1951, primarily because the main character, teenager Holden Caulfield, takes the Lord's name in vain 295 times.

Hollywood has also long been a target of censorship. In the 1930s, complaints by religious leaders were so numerous that Hollywood producers "voluntarily" submitted to the Hays Code, which stated, "No picture shall be produced that will lower the moral standards of those who see it." The Hays Code banned any scene that contained homosexuality, adultery, or sex. It even limited the length of a screen kiss to three seconds. The code also banned a long list of words and phrases, including *fairy, goose, madam, pansy, tart, in your hat*, and *nuts*. The Hays Code was in force until 1968, when the modern rating system took over.

The theatre has almost always been the first of the arts to be censored because it can rouse emotions, create empathy, hide subliminal messages, and stir groups of people to action. A novel may stir emotions but it does so for only one reader at a time—the theatre does it en masse. Another reason the theatre has been heavily censored is the problem of interpretation. The dialogue of a play might appear harmless on the page, but it can be interpreted by an actor to have new meanings. Unlike a film or a novel, a play can be changed from one performance to the next. A wink, a change in vocal inflection, or the slightest gesture can change the meaning. In Poland during the Soviet occupation, every theatre performance had to hold seats for censors so that every performance could be monitored. This is still true in many countries. For example, in Egypt a censorship committee must first see all plays before any can open to the general public.

CBS/Photofest

Although Lucille Ball and Desi Arnaz were married in real life, societal standards dictated that they could not be shown sharing a bed during the run of their 1950s sitcom *I Love Lucy*. Even when Lucy was expecting their first child, network officials prohibited the scriptwriters—who had written the birth of the baby into the show—from using the word "pregnant."

The First Amendment

The First Amendment protects our right to express ourselves not only with words but also with nonverbal, visual, and symbolic forms of expression. A silent candlelight vigil is protected by the First Amendment as freedom of speech. Symbolic gestures are also protected, such as burning the American flag—as long as the flag is your property and you obey local fire codes. Satire of public figures is protected as well. In 1988 the Supreme Court ruled in *Hustler Magazine v. Falwell* that satirical portraits of public figures, such as presidents, religious leaders, and movie stars, are protected under the First Amendment even if the satire is insulting, vulgar, or false. However, freedom of speech is not guaranteed in all situations. Exceptions include defamation; expression that causes a breach of the peace, sedition, or incitement to crime; expression that violates the separation of church and state; and obscenity.

Defamation

Freedom of speech does not cover the publication or statement of alleged facts that are false and harm the reputation of another. This exception to freedom of speech is difficult to apply because the expression of an opinion that is false is allowed. In other words, you have the right to express a factually wrong or politically incorrect opinion. Let's say a theatre critic writes a highly negative review about a play and says that the acting is horrible and the playwright is an execrable writer. Even though none of his opinions are accurate, audiences stay away and the producer has to declare bankruptcy. The critic cannot be sued because the review is his opinion and is covered under the First Amendment. But if the critic publishes a false negative statement, such as a made-up quotation from the city inspector saying that the theatre is unsafe, then the producer can sue because a false statement was published as fact.

Breach of the Peace

In 1919, Supreme Court Justice Oliver Wendell Holmes wrote, "The most stringent protection of free speech would not protect a man in falsely shouting fire in a theatre and causing a panic." This famous maxim has often been cited to underscore the fact that free speech is not a viable defense when such speech is used to perpetrate a fraud. An example is Orson Welles's *War of the Worlds* radio broadcast. On the night of October 30, 1938, Welles, famous for his movie *Citizen Kane*, broadcast to more than 100 radio stations in the eastern United States a play version of H. G. Wells's novel *The War of the Worlds*. In order to make this story of an alien invasion of the earth more realistic, Welles interrupted another show with seemingly real "breaking news" reports about meteors landing on earth and huge mechanical monsters emerging from the debris. Some people who heard the fake bulletins panicked. The newly created FCC (Federal Communications Commission) reprimanded the station and passed rules to prevent such a pseudo-event from happening again.

Sedition and Incitement to Crime

The Supreme Court has affirmed that freedom of speech does not cover unlawful conduct against the government or speech that advocates the violent overthrow of the government. This point can be difficult to argue because we all have the right to criticize the government and demand change. You can write a play in which you advocate "throwing the bums out," but you cannot write a play in which you unequivocally urge the audience to assassinate the president.

This exception to freedom of speech also applies to the laws of the land. If your words incite someone to commit a crime, the First Amendment does not protect your words. This exception to freedom of speech has been used for several years in an attempt to silence rap artists, most notoriously Ice-T and his band Body Count. Their 1992 track "Cop Killer" was condemned by law enforcement officials, who claimed that the song incited crime against police officers. The same charge has been applied to some movies, such as Oliver Stone's *Natural Born Killers*, a story about a young couple who commit a series

In 1938, Hollywood writer and director Orson Welles broadcast a dramatization of H. G. Wells's alien invasion story, *War of the Worlds*. The program was so realistic that Welles eliminated the audience's aesthetic distance and broke their willing suspension of disbelief. As a result some radio listeners panicked, believing that an actual Martian invasion was taking place. The broadcast caused such a commotion that the FCC passed rules to prevent future such breaches of peace.

Bettmann/Corbis

of ruthless murders. In the mid-1990s, a family in Ponchatoula, Louisiana, sued Stone and Time Warner Entertainment for damages after a family member was shot by two teenagers. The family claimed that the teenagers' shooting spree was inspired by repeated viewings of Stone's movie. The case was dismissed in 2001 because the family's lawyers couldn't prove that Stone intended to incite violence.

Separation of Church and State

The part of the First Amendment that states "Congress shall make no law respecting an establishment of religion" is known as the "establishment clause." It means that the government cannot endorse, or appear to endorse, any religion. This is a sensitive point to many people who view the clause as a violation of their personal freedom of speech. This controversy was highlighted when the National Endowment for the Arts (NEA; see Chapter 2) funded an exhibition of work in 1990 by artist David Wojnarowicz. The exhibition, titled "Tongues of Flame," included a painting that attacked prominent religious and political figures and accused them of being indifferent to the suffering caused by AIDS. A lawyer filed a lawsuit against the NEA, alleging that the exhibition displayed "hostility toward religion" and that the art caused him to suffer "spiritual injury" because it was offensive to his "religious sensibilities." He also charged that, because the art was partly funded by the government through an NEA grant, it violated the establishment clause. The idea was that if the government cannot endorse religion, then it should not be allowed to support art that attacks religion.

The court ruled that there is a difference between spiritual injury and physical or economic injury. Freedom of speech can be suppressed if it causes physical or economic injury, but cannot be suppressed if it causes spiritual injury.

AP Images/Mary Altaffer

The rock musical *Hair* is considered by some to be a great example of counterculture art, whereas others consider it obscene for its nudity and antiestablishment messages. This production was performed at the Union Square Theatre in New York City.

In other words, you cannot deny someone an opinion just because it makes you feel bad, such as a critic's negative review. But what about the second part of the lawsuit, that the government should not fund art that insults religion? The court ruled that Congress does not directly decide how the NEA funds are to be spent, because the NEA is an independent government agency; nor is the NEA simply administering Congress's wishes. Thus, the government was not directly attacking religion and the grant did not violate the establishment clause. This decision highlighted a fascinating loophole in the establishment clause: not only is it legal for the NEA to fund art that criticizes or insults religion, but it can also fund art that promotes an appreciation for religion, which it has done on many occasions.

Obscenity

Freedom of speech does not apply to obscenity, but the courts have long struggled to define the word *obscene*. The word means many different things to different people. In 1973, the Supreme Court (*Miller v. California*) established a three-pronged test for obscenity:

1. Whether the average person, applying contemporary community standards, would find that the work, taken as a whole, appeals to the prurient interest.

2. Whether the work depicts or describes, in a patently offensive way, sexual conduct specifically defined by the applicable state law.

3. Whether the work, taken as a whole, lacks serious literary, artistic, political, or scientific value.

These standards remain in effect today but are still controversial. The Court basically said that each community could adopt its own idea of what is obscene, but how do we define *community* in the age of the Internet? A web page that may be acceptable to someone in Los Angeles, California, might be grounds for arrest if it were downloaded in Opp, Alabama. And who decides what is of "serious literary, artistic, political, or scientific value"? Many feel that the Court has not solved the problem of defining obscenity but has only made it more complicated, so obscenity prosecutions are rare.

Curtain Call

Powerful forces are at work when people join together into a group, and many, including the artists, would like to control those forces. The power of the audience may come from being in a group, but every audience is made up of individuals who must decide if a given work has meaning. Too often today, audience members dismiss a play because it isn't to their liking, but if they knew how to analyze plays beyond simple opinion, they could come to a deeper understanding of the work. Only when audiences learn to analyze and artists are free to create does the theatre become a powerful work of art. As Czech playwright Václav Havel said, "[I]f theatre is free conversation, free dialogue, among free people about the mysteries of the world, then it is precisely what will show humankind the way toward tolerance, mutual respect, and respect for the miracle of Being."

SUMMARY

MindTap

Test your knowledge with online printable flashcards and online quizzing.

There are as many reasons to attend the theatre as there are audience members. But even though each member of the audience is unique, when they join together in a group, there are forces at work that can change how they feel and react. These forces include group dynamics, the suspension of disbelief, and aesthetic distance.

When you go to the theatre, you never know exactly how much you will be asked to participate. Some plays require you to be active, and others require you to sit quietly in the dark. Depending on what type of play you are seeing, the rules of etiquette change. These rules cover everything from how to behave to what to wear. Attending the theatre is also different than attending a movie; not only are you expected to behave differently, but tickets are harder to get and there are fewer performances to see. Going to the theatre requires more of an effort than going to movies or watching television, so going to the theatre takes a little more planning.

Once you see or read a play, it is important that you think about it and learn to evaluate it with more than a simple "I liked it" or "I didn't like it." In order to become a connoisseur of the theatre, you must learn to justify your critical thoughts by asking these three questions: What is the artist trying to do? How well has the artist done it? Is it worth doing? Plays can also be analyzed in terms of plot, character, thought, diction, spectacle, and sometimes even song.

Who controls what the audience sees and hears? In a few ideal cases the artist controls content, but usually other entities are involved. The government, corporations, religious institutions, or even the audience themselves can demand, legislate, or enforce censorship. Freedom of speech is important because self-expression is at the core of all works of art. However, limitations are placed on artists by the Constitution and the courts, including defamation, breach of the peace, sedition and incitement to crime, separation of church and state, and obscenity.

KEY TERMS

Aesthetic distance *67*

Bowdlerize *82*

Censorship *81*

Curtain *71*

Curtain speech *73*

Director's note *73*

Dramatic criticism *75*

Fourth wall *69*

Genre *76*

Group dynamics *65*

House *66*

League of Resident Theatres *70*

Licensing Act *82*

Paper the house *66*

Playwright's note *73*

Presentational theatre *69*

Preview performances *71*

Realism *69*

Representational theatre *69*

Talk-back *74*

Reviews *75*

Road houses *70*

Souvenir programs *73*

Will Call *71*

Willing suspension of disbelief *66*

Chapter **5**

A DAY IN THE LIFE OF A THEATRE

Prior to making her entrance as Feste in Idaho Rep's production of Shakespeare's *Twelfth Night*, actor Claudine Mboligikpelani Nako checks her makeup.

Claudine Mboligikpelani Nako

Outline

MindTap®

Start with a quick warm-up activity and review the chapter's learning objectives.

Theatre is a hybrid art. More often than not it is brought to you by an **ensemble**, or dozens of artists and technicians, including playwrights, actors, directors, and designers, as well as painters, carpenters, drapers, stagehands, and electricians, who join together to make it appear as if a performance were the product of a single creative mind. In order for a production to be successful, a theatre must have a well-organized power structure (see Figure 5.1) that allows for unfettered communication as well as a delineation of duties, which gives each member of the ensemble the freedom to create as they share the same artistic vision.

The *ensemble* is so important that many theatre companies—such as the West Coast Ensemble and the Boulder Ensemble Theatre Company—include the word in their name.

To understand how theatre works, let's imagine an average day in the life of a typical large repertory theatre. The word **repertory** means a group of plays performed by a theatre company during the course of a season. For example, the Colorado Shakespeare Festival's repertory might include *A Midsummer Night's Dream*, *Hamlet*, and *Romeo and Juliet*. Many theatres include the word repertory in their name, such as the Milwaukee Repertory Theater, the Seattle

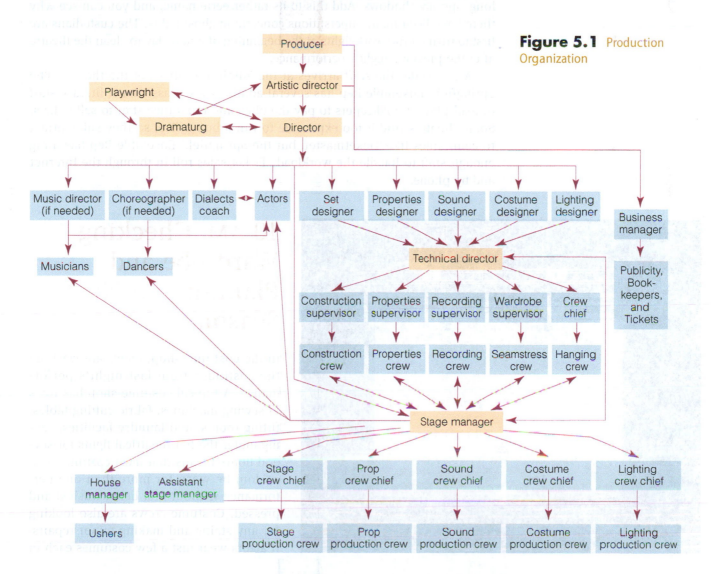

Figure 5.1 Production Organization

Repertory Theatre, and the San Jose Repertory Theatre. Often these theatres shorten the word repertory to "Rep," as in "The Seattle Rep." For the purposes of this chapter, we will call our imaginary theatre the Springfield Ensemble Rep and explore, hour by hour, the ensemble of people who contribute to the work done on stage and behind the scenes during a day in the life of a theatre. Not every theatre follows this exact timeline, of course, but all the people and jobs at the Springfield Ensemble Rep are common throughout the industry.

9 AM: Entering Springfield Ensemble Rep by Ghost Light

MindTap*

Read, highlight, and take notes online.

The dark stage is lit by a single bare light bulb mounted on a portable pole. This solitary illumination is known as the **ghost light**, which was rolled out on stage the night before as a safety precaution. Walking into a jet-black theatre and trying to find the light switch can be dangerous, so the ghost light is left burning all night in the middle of the stage. The flickering of the naked bulb throws long, spooky shadows. Add this to its rather eerie name, and you can see why there have been many superstitions concerning ghost lights. The custodians are first to turn on the work lights at the beginning of a new day to clean the theatre after the previous night's performance.

Meanwhile, the staff arrives at the adjoining offices of the theatre. The Springfield Ensemble Rep has several administrative assistants, literary staff to read plays, bookkeepers to pay the bills, and box-office staff to sell tickets. Some theatres find it too expensive to run a box office, so they subcontract to companies like Ticketmaster, but the Springfield Ensemble Rep has a big enough staff to handle the workload. Ticket sales roll in through the Internet and by phone.

Finding a light switch in a dark, empty theatre can be difficult and dangerous, so a single "ghost light" is often left burning near center stage.

Bob O'Connor/Getty Images

10 AM: Checking Wardrobe and Planning for Next Season

In the **costume shop**, crews are washing the costumes from last night's performance. A typical costume shop has rows of sewing machines, fabric-cutting tables, fitting rooms, and laundry facilities. Acting under the hot theatrical lights for several hours means that most costumes can seldom be worn for more than one performance without first being washed and pressed. Costume crews are also looking for any stains and making minor repairs. If actors wear just a few costumes each in a simple contemporary play, such as the one currently showing at the Spring-field Ensemble Rep, then there may be less work for the costume shop. However, if it is a large, complicated show requiring sequined costumes and wig maintenance, the process can be time-consuming. For example, the Broadway musical *Titanic* needed five wig dressers to care for the show's 71 wigs, and 14 wardrobe people to repair, wash, starch, and press the 180 costumes between performances. In all, *Titanic*'s costume maintenance required more than 275 hours a week.

In the literary department, the **literary manager** has begun another day of reading and evaluating new scripts for next season. The literary manager is a liaison between playwrights, agents, and the theatre. Also, this person often writes grant applications to help support new play development and stage readings of new plays. The literary department at even a moderately well-known theatre can receive up to 1,000 scripts a year from struggling playwrights. Notoriously understaffed, the literary manager and assistant (if there is one) cannot possibly read all the scripts. This is why they commonly ask playwrights without agents to send only sample pages, a synopsis, and cover letter; if the literary manager likes the sample, she requests a copy of the full script. The office is stacked with hundreds of scripts yet to be read—plays by famous playwrights submitted through agents, and by lesser-known playwrights who have been queried to submit plays in their entirety. Because such a backlog is common, some playwrights wait as long as a year to get a rejection letter. The literary department rejects a vast majority of scripts, but chooses perhaps 100 a year for closer scrutiny. In the end, the literary

Patrick Rivière/Getty Images

Oscar-winning actor Cate Blanchett is known for her powerful performances in movies like *Elizabeth* (1998), *Oscar & Lucinda* (1997), and *Notes on a Scandal* (2006). She also serves as the co-artistic director of the Sydney Theatre Company in Australia.

SPOTLIGHT ON The Producers

The word *producer* has different meanings depending on how it is used. For a Hollywood movie as for a play on Broadway, the producer is the person in charge of the business and managerial side of a production. For a television sitcom or hour-length drama, the producer is usually a staff writer who may have a title such as associate producer, producer, or executive producer. However, for other kinds of television shows, the producer has the same business-managerial role as the producer for motion pictures or the theatre. Just to make the definition even more confusing, in England the word producer is often used to denote the person who directs a play.

In the American theatre, producers may be individuals who put up their own money or control an investor's money to finance a production—or they may be institutions such as universities, churches, or community organizations that handle the business side of the production. Depending on the size of the production, the financial responsibilities can range from small to large, sometimes involving millions of dollars. If the theatre is nonprofit, the producer—often called a producing director—must manage all the aspects of the theatre's budget to meet government regulations for nonprofit organizations. If a play is performed for profit, the producer assumes financial responsibility for any losses but also pockets any profit. Because money is involved, the producer or producing organization is one of the most powerful positions in the theatre. It is the producer's responsibility to raise money, negotiate contracts, keep financial records, pay taxes, and hire the creative, production, and construction teams.

AP Images/Paul Sancya

A well-known and prolific director in the theatre, Woodie King, Jr. (pictured at right, with Morgan Freeman and Ruby Dee) has also produced many plays, including *For Colored Girls Who Have Considered Suicide When the Rainbow Is Enuf* and *Reggae*.

> What prepared me for the artistic director job? Everything and nothing . . . One of the biggest problems I face is when to be pragmatic in solving a problem and when to just insist on the art.
>
> **Irene Lewis,** theatre director

manager only forwards a few dozen scripts to the artistic director for possible inclusion in a future season.

A few doors away, the artistic director of the theatre is in a budget meeting with the producing director. In the theatre, a **producer** or a **producing director** is someone who financially backs the theatre or orchestrates funding through grant money and ticket sales (see Spotlight, "The Producers"), and the **artistic director** is in charge of the overall creative vision or goal of the ensemble. The artistic director will often choose which plays to produce, who will direct them, and who will design them. A director is in charge of a single play, whereas the artistic director is in charge of an entire season of plays. The artistic director also manages the ensemble by making sure that all its members work together and have the same artistic goal. On top of this, the artistic director is an ambassador to the community, a fund-raiser, and the theatre's chief promoter. The position of artistic director is so important that it sometimes attracts world-famous stars to the job: the Oscar-winning actors Cate Blanchett and Kevin Spacey have both been artistic directors, of the Sydney Theatre Company in Australia and the Old Vic Theatre in London, respectively.

11 AM: Rehearsing and Building a Show

In one of the rehearsal halls, the director and actors are rehearsing the next play in the repertory. Though not as visible, one of the most important people in the room during rehearsal is not the director or actors but the **stage manager**, also known as the SM (and sometimes known as the PSM, for "production stage manager"). The stage manager not only runs the show during the performance but also helps the director throughout the rehearsal process by taking notes, recording blocking (the movement of the actors on stage—see Chapter 8), scheduling rehearsals, and assisting during auditions. The stage manager has many responsibilities, from getting coffee (although this is often done by the assistant stage manager or ASM) to enforcing safety rules, and therefore she often requires the help of several assistants (see Spotlight, "The Stage Manager").

Down in the scene shop, the set construction crew is building the set for a play that opens in two weeks. Most theatres have well-equipped scene shops with a variety of metalworking and woodworking tools; an electric shop with equipment to maintain, repair, and hang lights; and a paint shop, where paint is stored and mixed. Theatres also have a great deal of storage space for all the costumes, props, wood, platforms, and flats that are used during a production. A **flat** is the standard scenery unit made of wooden frames covered with canvas, muslin, or thin plywood. Most flats are from 12 to 16 feet tall and one to six feet

In theatre it's about emotion. It differs every night and it's the stage manager's job to respond to what's happening on stage and in the audience. The actor says something, the audience responds, and the stage manager responds. At the end of the show, when the audience applauds—yes, of course they're applauding the actors, but they're also applauding everyone backstage who made the production possible.

Alan Hall,
Stage manager of the Tony Awards

Building the set and hanging lights are labor-intensive processes that can take weeks. Here, crews hang lights at the Vienna Opera house in Austria.

William Missouri Downs

SPOTLIGHT ON The Stage Manager

One of the most important positions in the theatre is that of the stage manager. From auditions to closing night, the stage manager is involved in every aspect of the play. The stage manager's job starts in pre-rehearsal meetings with the director and designers. For the audition process, she will post audition announcements, reserve audition and rehearsal spaces, prepare the room for auditions, and assist the director during auditions. Once rehearsals start, the SM maintains contact sheets, obtains rehearsal props, schedules rehearsals, and generates and keeps a **prompt book** in which every aspect of the production is recorded. This book includes light cues, blocking, technical notes, and director's notes. Sometimes the prompt book is called the production's "bible" because everything that is important is recorded in it.

At the end of each rehearsal, the stage manager stays after to write up a **rehearsal report**, which is then e-mailed to everyone involved with the production. This report lets the entire ensemble know how rehearsal went and informs designers about any concerns or ideas that came up that affect the set, lights, props, or costumes.

Once a play is up and running, the stage manager becomes the production stage manager, or PSM. The director usually leaves and the PSM takes over. The PSM, often with the help of several **assistant stage managers** (ASM), conducts the technical rehearsals, authorizes when an understudy goes on instead of a primary cast member, calls for brush-up rehearsals, and continually gives friendly reminders to everyone about where they have to be and when.

During a performance the PSM sits in the control booth and calls all the cues: instructing the light board operator when to change the lights, the sound board operator when to play music, and the backstage crew when to move scenery. At the end of a performance, the PSM gives notes to the actors and crew and also writes a detailed **performance report** that includes any problems that occurred and what needs to be fixed before the next performance.

In short, the stage manager is the conduit and facilitator of the whole process, something akin to a conductor or maestro. Stage managers must be well organized, know how to communicate with artists as well as backstage crews, and possess the rarest of all qualities—the ability to stay calm in a crisis.

William Missouri Downs

A stage manager typically has so many responsibilities that she or he will often need one or two assistants. Here, stage manager Danielle Fullerton and assistant stage manager Leean Kim Torske go over a checklist before an evening performance.

wide. Some flats are plain wall units, whereas others are built to accommodate doors, windows, and fireplaces. Other scenery units include platforms, steps, and staircases, fake fireplaces, doors, and window frames.

In many small theatres, designers are forced to build their own designs, but in larger professional theatres like the Springfield Ensemble Rep the designers turn over their drawings, paintings, blueprints, scale models, and sketches to the **technical director**, or TD. The TD supervises the construction crews, which include painters, carpenters, electricians, stitchers, wig makers, and others who are often collectively known as the "tech crew." The technical director has authority over all the crew chiefs, such as the master carpenter and the chief electrician, and answers only to the director, the designers, the budget office, and the artistic director. Depending on the size of the production, the tech crew can be made up of a few people or dozens.

NOON: Fund-Raising, Designing, and Sewing

At a local restaurant, the artistic director is having lunch with a wealthy business owner, trying to subtly convince her that supporting the Springfield Ensemble Rep is good for the community and her company. Most theatres make only about 50 percent of their budget from ticket sales, so fund-raising goes on seven days a week (see Chapter 2).

Meanwhile, back in the costume shop, drapers and stitchers are making the costumes for the play that opens in two weeks. A **draper's** job is to study the costume designer's drawings and renderings (see Chapter 9) and then find a way to cut fabric into patterns that realize the design. A few feet away the **stitchers** sew the fabric patterns together creating the full costumes. They also build or find **rehearsal costumes**, used temporarily during rehearsal so that the actors get a feel for the actual costumes long before they are ready. For example, if an actress must wear a long Victorian skirt in a play, then the costume shop sews a long rehearsal skirt of plain muslin. Actors seldom get to put on the real costume until just days before a play opens.

In a nearby shop, the **prop master** is busy working on the props for the next production. **Prop** is theatre lingo for "properties" and includes hand props or any objects actors handle while on stage, such as pens, fans, cigars, and umbrellas. There are also set props, which include sofas, chairs, beds, etc. Prop masters find and buy props for productions, and they often design and build them. The prop master is also in charge of **rehearsal props**. Just

The technical director supervises the various construction crews to ensure the designer's visions are realized. Here, tech director Larry Hazlett guides traffic as various construction crews work.

William Missouri Downs

William Missouri Downs

Typically, actors don't wear their costumes in rehearsal until just days before a play opens. In order to get a feel for the costume, the costume shop often builds rehearsal costumes. Here, actors Megan Antles, Katrina Despain, and Rachel Rosenfeld model their rehearsal skirts and corsets. The corsets are worn on the outside during rehearsal so that they can be easily removed during breaks.

About ten days before opening night the lighting designer begins setting the light cues including levels, fades and colors. In this photo a lighting designer works on cues for the musical comedy *Angry Psycho Princesses* while set crews paint the set.

as with rehearsal costumes, these props are used during rehearsals to represent the real property that the actors will not be able to use until the last week of rehearsals.

1 PM: More Rehearsing

Back in the rehearsal halls, work on the next production is slowed due to problems with space allocation. The next play is to be a musical that takes place during the Restoration, which will require several simultaneous rehearsals. In one rehearsal hall, the musical director is teaching the actors their songs. The **musical director** supervises all aspects of a musical and conducts the orchestra during performances. In another hall, the **choreographer** has created new dance numbers and is teaching the steps to the dancers. In still another, the **movement coach** is showing the actors how people moved during the Restoration—a time when graceful mannerisms were the norm. Starved for space, the **fight director** is forced to hold his rehearsal in a hallway. Fight directors are experts at staging safe, realistic, make-believe fights. Stage combat, such as fistfights and swordplay, must be carefully choreographed and can be time-consuming to create. Every 30 seconds of a staged fight can take many hours to rehearse. Finally, upstairs the voice and dialect coach has found an unused office for her rehearsal. The **vocal coach** helps the actors with speech clarity, volume, and preservation of their voices for the long run of a show. If the character requires a particular accent, the coach will also give the actors lessons on how to speak realistically with that accent.

William Missouri Downs

2 PM: Creating Sets and Sounds, and Advising the Director

In the sound booth, the **sound designer** is working with various effects recordings as she synthesizes the sounds, so that everything from the pre-show music to the sound of a doorbell is exactly right (for more on sound design see Chapter 9). In a nearby office, the **set designer** boots up his computer and uses a CAD (computer aided design) program to design a set for a production that will not be needed for several months. Designers often work many months in advance and on several sets at a time (see Chapter 9).

Back in the literary department, the director of the next play is meeting with a dramaturg for advice on the production. The duties of a **dramaturg** can be difficult to define because no two theatres use them in exactly the same way. In some theatres, the dramaturg is a literary advisor and expert in theatre

Prop masters spend their days researching, designing, and building properties. Properties are built to endure the run of the show and must often be historically accurate. In this shot, Rachel George builds miniature dolls for an opera at the Festival Theatre in Edinburgh, Scotland.

Drew Farrell/ArenaPAL/Topham/Image Works

There are many types of rehearsals, including fight, dance, blocking, and singing. At this movement rehearsal, students from Point Park University practice for Bill Nunn's experimental dramatization of African folktales.

AP Images/Keith Srakode

history who helps the director understand specifics about a play's performance history, the historical period in which the play is set, as well as the play's style and verse. At other theatres they serve as a literary manager, whereas in others they assist with a play's development by setting up workshop productions and staged readings to help the play find its final form. A common joke is that dramaturgs often spend a significant portion of their time responding to the question "What is a dramaturg?" Dramaturgs are still relatively rare in the theatre, and only a few theatre organizations can afford the help of a dramaturg (for more on dramaturgy, see Chapter 8).

3 PM: Attending Meetings and Creating a Mission Statement

The various crew chiefs now take a moment for a **production meeting**. In this meeting, all aspects of the production are discussed and evaluated. The director, stage manager, and technical director are all present along with the heads of the various crews. Every aspect of the next production is discussed, including lights, set, props, and costumes. The purpose of the meeting is to report on the progress of the crews and make sure any small problems are circumvented.

In his office, the artistic director has just finished a meeting concerning next year's season and is writing a new mission statement. A theatre's **mission statement** declares in clear and concise terms the theatre's purpose and key objectives. These objectives can include quality, diversity, and accessibility. It can also state what type of theatre is to be produced—from comedies and classics to thought-provoking, socially relevant plays or perhaps even new plays by up-and-coming playwrights. A theatre might state, for instance, that its goal is to bring cultural enrichment to the community or give a voice to a wide range of artists and visions.

4 PM: Publicizing a Play and Fitting Costumes

The **publicity department** is working on promoting the next play. Today, they are setting up an interview with the director at the local radio station. They are also arranging times for actors to tour area schools as a part of the theatre's outreach program. Additionally, they must design print, radio, and television ads. Advertising is expensive and budgets are limited, so they must decide which venues will give them the best return on the investment. Not only do they want to entice their patrons to see a play, but they also hope to reach out to people who generally do not attend the theatre in order to further build the audience.

A few doors down, the costume shop manager is doing fittings. One at a time, the actors come in and try on their new attire while a stitcher pins and tucks the fabric to make sure everything fits just right. One costume might require several fittings, so the costume shop is always busy.

5 PM: Brainstorming a Concept

The various shops are cleaning up for the day and getting ready for the evening performance. But before they can head home, the designers are called to a concept meeting for a play that will be produced three months from now. A **concept**

Strictly speaking, there is only one creative artist in the theatre. It is the playwright, the one who makes something out of nothing. The rest of us—directors, designers, actors—are interpretive artists. We take what the playwright has created and demonstrate to the audience what we think the playwright's creation looks and sounds like.

Terry McCabe, Director

Long before a play goes into rehearsal, there are numerous production meetings. Here costume designer Sarah Varca and set designer Casey Kearns look over costume renderings for the musical *Angry Psycho Princesses* with director Lou Anne Wright and director/writer Sean Warren Stone.

William Missouri Downs

meeting is an artistic gathering held long before the play is cast or the sets and costumes designed. During this meeting, the director and designers brainstorm, research, and experiment with different set, costume, and light possibilities as they interpret the playwright's script. There can be dozens of concept meetings in which the director synchronizes all the aesthetic elements and talents needed to produce theatre.

6 PM: Preparing for the Evening Performance

As the literary staff, bookkeepers, and administrative assistants head home through the front doors of the theatre, the actors arrive for the evening performance via the stage door. The **stage door** is usually located behind the theatre and has a little lobby where there is a notice board. Here the actors can check for any messages and sign in, letting the stage manager know that they are in the building. The time the actors arrive at the theatre is known as their **call**, and the time the play starts is called **curtain**. If they have a lot of makeup to apply, the actor's call might be several hours before curtain; if they have little hair or makeup to apply, call may be as little as 45 minutes beforehand. Actors spend the time before the performance warming up their body and voice, doing their hair, and putting on makeup and costumes.

Backstage the prop master is making sure that all the props needed that night are on the prop table. The **prop table** has each prop laid out and clearly labeled. Few things can be more disastrous than an actor losing a prop, so actors are not allowed to leave the backstage area without putting the props back on the table. The prop master is also making sure each prop is in working order: if a production requires a gun, for example, it must be test fired. If food is needed during a play, a prop crew must prepare it.

On stage, the light crew begins checking each light to make sure that it is working. The high-intensity bulbs used in theatrical lighting can burn out at any time, even when they aren't being used, so each light, one at a time, must be raised and lowered while a technician checks that it is still properly aimed. Meanwhile, the **sound board operator** is running various sound cues and making sure all the speakers, mixer, amplifiers, backstage monitor, and intercom are working.

The sound designer selects or creates every sound you hear during a performance. Here, sound engineer Gabriele Nicotra works the sound mixing board at the Little Sicily Stage in Malmesbury, England.

Louise Wilson/Getty Images

Hanging theatrical lights often requires a large crew. Each light must be individually hung, circuited, focused, and aimed. Once the lights are flown into position, the crew must make dozens more adjustments before opening night. Here, lighting designer Larry Hazlett works with Michael Earl and Jessi Sundell to hang the lights.

© Don Turner. Property of Cengage Learning.

7 PM: Opening the House

It is now getting busy backstage. All the actors have arrived. The costume shop, dressing rooms, and makeup rooms are buzzing with people. The stage manager calls out, "One hour until curtain." That means that the house will open in 30 minutes. The **house** is theatre lingo for the place where the audience sits. Once it opens the actors will no longer be allowed to walk on stage, so if they want to warm up in the theatre they must do it now. The actors make their way to the stage to do a **prop check** just to ensure everything is where it needs to be. Tonight's play also has a fight sequence, so two actors practice their fight choreography one last time. They rehearse on stage because they want to recreate exactly what they will do tonight.

Nearby, the house manager is making final checks before letting the audience enter the theatre. The **house manager** is in charge of all the ushers. It is his job to deal with any seating problems and to make sure the audience find their seats and that the play begins on time. If the ushers encounter a problem seating people, the house manager may tell the stage manager over a headset or intercom that they need to "hold" until the audience is ready.

© Don Turner. Property of Cengage Learning.

Modern computer-operated lightboards can control hundreds, if not thousands, of lights and generate an incredible variety of effects with a touch of a button. However, every cue must be painstakingly loaded into the computer. Here, a lighting technician tests to make sure the lights are ready for opening night.

Half an hour before curtain, the stage manager orders the actors off the stage. Sound and light checks are finished and the house opens. Backstage, the stage manager walks through the dressing and makeup rooms announcing, "The house is now open." The theatre's microphone system is turned on so that everything that happens during the play will be broadcast in the dressing rooms, makeup rooms, and even the bathrooms backstage. This way the actors can hear the performance and not miss their entrances. It also means that the actors who are not on stage can clearly hear the audience entering, talking, or laughing.

The stage manager announces, "Ten minutes to curtain!" The actors now make the final adjustments to their costumes and makeup. Nerves can be a real problem, even for experienced actors; many of them are doing deep breathing or relaxation exercises. Moments later the stage manager shouts, "Places!" This is the actors' final warning. Those who enter at the top (beginning) of the show now take their places backstage, while others gather in the greenroom. The **greenroom** is the place where actors wait before their entrances. The term *greenroom* has been around for about 300 years and there are several theories as to its origin. Some say that it comes from the green color this room used to be painted in order to soothe the actors before they made their entrance. Others think it comes from the old fashioned practice of calling the stage "The Green," hence the room that's just off stage is the "green room." However, no one really knows where the term comes from. Some modern greenrooms have television monitors allowing the actors to watch the production, but one thing they usually all have in common is that greenrooms are seldom fancy and rarely painted green.

Because theatre is live, a lot can *and will* go wrong. As a result, several theatrical superstitions have developed over time (see Spotlight, "If It Can Go Wrong, It Will"). It is considered bad luck, for example, to wish an actor "good luck" before a

Prior to curtain can be a hectic time backstage, with actors warming up, dressing and, of course, applying makeup. Here actors Landee Lockhart, Lana Percival, and Kathryn Demith ready themselves an hour before taking the stage.

William Missouri Downs

SPOTLIGHT ON If It Can Go Wrong, It Will

Murphy's law is alive and well in the theatre, proving the old adage true: "If it can go wrong, it will." And because theatre is a live medium, when something goes wrong it generally happens in front of the audience. Often mistakes are minor. For example, an actor stumbles on a line, a bulb burns out, a doorknob falls off, etc. But there have been times when a performance turned into a disaster, as in the Broadway musical *Spider-Man: Turn Off the Dark*, in which several actors sustained serious injuries.

Apocryphal stories abound, including the actor who got hungry during a performance of a Stephen Sondheim musical so he decided to order a pizza and have it sent to the greenroom. Coming in the back door of the theatre, the delivery person made a wrong turn and ended up walking on stage in the middle of a tender love ballad. At another theatre, the stage manager mistakenly called for the phone to ring just moments before the end of the play. The stunned actors didn't know what to do. So one of them answered the phone, turned to the other actor on stage and said, "It's for you."

In another case, during a production of the musical *West Side Story*, the gun that Chino uses to kill Tony failed to fire. The poor actor pulled the trigger over and over—nothing but "click, click, click." The audience began to snicker. Finally, the actor ran over and kicked Tony, who fell down, playing dead. Chino then turned to the audience and said, "Poisoned shoes." That night the prop master worked for hours to make sure the gun would never fail again. He cleaned and oiled it to ensure it would fire with the slightest touch. During the next performance the gun went off without a hitch and the prop master breathed a sigh of relief. But moments

before the end of the play, when Maria points the gun at the Jet and Shark gang members, the gun accidentally fired. It was pointed at one of the members of the Jet gang . . . so he fell and played dead. That night the play ended with Maria being taken away in handcuffs, charged with murder.

Unlike a movie, when things go wrong on stage there is no second take. As actor Willem Dafoe said, ". . . acting for film is like a musician playing in a recording studio and acting in the theatre is like playing live in concert. . . ."

When things go wrong in the theatre, it happens live. The actors know it, and sometimes the audience too. Here Brikai Cordova, in the musical *Angry Psycho Princesses*, acts out her worst nightmare—a trap door failing.

William Missouri Downs

performance. Instead, actors wish each other bad luck by saying "break a leg." There are several theories as to where this expression originated. One of the most popular theories comes from Shakespeare's day, 400 years ago, when the audience would sometimes throw money at the actors' feet during the curtain call. The actors would then have to kneel down to pick up the money—in other words, bend or "break" their legs to pick up the tips, which meant that their performance was good. Another theory goes back 2,500 years to the ancient Greeks. In those days, some scholars think that the audience didn't clap at the end of the performance but stomped their feet instead. Thus, "break a leg" meant that the performance was so good that audience members would break their legs while stomping.

8 PM: Performing the First Act

The Springfield Ensemble Rep's stage manager now arrives in the control booth to work beside the light and sound board operators. It is from here that the SM will call all the cues and run the show. The house manager pops in to say that the audience is seated and the doors are closed. It's time to start the play. The sound board and light board operators, as well as the backstage crews, are now on headsets. Nowadays, these headsets are wireless, which allows crews to move around freely. Over headsets the stage manager says, "House lights to half." The light board operator brings the house lights halfway down for a few moments to let the audience know the play is about to start. "Fade out pre-show music, house lights out, go." The house is plunged into darkness. "Lights 1, sound 1, go." The play begins. During the show there is very little talking over the headsets. Most of the time there is only one-way communication from the stage manager to the assistant stage manager, the light board operator, the sound board operator, and the stage crews. Usually the only time anyone else speaks is when there is a question or problem.

Meanwhile, in the greenroom there is also little talk. Most actors are listening to the play over the speakers (or watching it on a monitor) and judging the audience's reaction. Other actors waiting for their entrances are reading the newspaper, relaxing, playing cards, running their lines, etc. One actor comments on a joke that always gets a laugh but didn't tonight. "It's a dead audience," he says. "We'd better pick up the pace." Actors always talk about the audience during the performance. If it is going well they might say, "We're killing them." If the play is going poorly they might say, "Let's just run for curtain." The latter comment means that there is no hope for a positive response to the play, so they may as well get the play over with as fast as possible.

About five minutes before their entrance, the actors leave the greenroom and go backstage. Here they are met by the assistant stage manager. It is the assistant stage manager's job to make sure that everything runs smoothly during the scene. Getting around backstage is an obstacle course. The actors must find their way around braces holding the walls of the set, electrical cables taped to the floor, as well as backstage crew and other actors waiting to make their entrances. Even though light from the performance spills off the stage, it is still quite dark. To help actors and crew find their way, dim red or blue running lights have been clamped to the prop table and set braces. During blackouts in the play, moving can be an even bigger problem, so obstacles have been marked with glow-in-the-dark tape to give actors and crews a faint reference point to guide them through the shadows. To make sure the audience can't hear the actors moving around backstage, crews have screwed strips of old carpeting to the floor.

> What you don't see backstage is what really controls the show.
>
> **Sarah Sutton,**
> Actress of stage and screen,
> (Doctor Who, 1981–1983)

During a play, the backstage area can be a dark and dangerous place. Performers take great care to keep talking to a minimum and concentrate on the performances. Here, two actors await their entrance during a production of *La Bohème* at the New Israeli Opera. Behind them sits the assistant stage manager.

O. Rotem/Lebrecht/The Image Works

> We are also artists and give a performance every night.
>
> **Cindy Toushan,** Stage manager

During a play anyone helping out backstage is a part of the **running crew**, which includes **stagehands** who shift scenery and generally set up the play for the next scene. Moving scenery around in the dark is one of the most potentially dangerous things in the theatre, and each crew member must be well rehearsed in order to avoid accidents. Stagehands can move scenery using wagons, platforms on casters, a revolve (a large turning platform often powered by electric motors), or elevators that raise and lower segments of the stage. The running crew also includes **dressers** who help actors make quick costume changes. When actors must change in a great hurry in order to make it back onstage, they will have an appointed dresser just offstage; when the actor leaves the stage, they will work with the dresser in quick and well-rehearsed movements to change from one costume to the next. Modesty is not allowed. The running crew usually has some **riggers**, also known as "flymen," who mount and operate all curtains, sets, and anything else that must move via the fly system above the stage. Most theatres also have a variety of curtains that can be used to frame the set and conceal offstage spaces. The curtains used on the sides are called **legs**, and those that frame the top of the stage are referred to as **teasers**. Open-mesh gauze curtains, called **scrims**, are used to make the stage appear opaque when a scene downstage (in front) of it is lighted, and transparent or translucent when a scene upstage (behind) the scrim is lighted. The **cyclorama**, often shortened to *cyc* (pronounced "psych"), is a large, stretched curtain suspended from a U-shaped rod. It makes a background that curves around the back of the stage to suggest unlimited space. Cycloramas are usually neutral in color, but lighting designers can turn them into almost anything, from a symbolic collage of colors to a starry sky.

9 PM: Performing the Final Act

During intermission, the actors make their way back to the dressing and makeup rooms. Here they often compare notes on how the play is going, change costumes, touch up their makeup, and drink lots of water. Acting under the hot lights can take its toll and actors must keep their vocal cords moist.

When the play begins again, the stage manager watches the performance and calls every cue from the control booth. Each theatre has its own protocol as to how cues should be called, but generally it's done by calling "warning," "standby," and "go." The SM gives a "warning" over the headsets to alert crews a few minutes before the cue to make sure everyone is where they need to be. The SM calls "standby" just before the cue and "go" the moment the cue is to be executed. To reduce confusion, each cue is numbered. Talk over the headsets might sound something like this: "Standby lights 32. And go." The light board operator presses a button on the light board, and the computer automatically changes the lights. "Standby sound 15 and lights 33; warning scene change." The sound board operator makes sure that sound cue 15 is ready and set to the correct volume. The light board operator checks to make sure the light board computer has the correct cue up, while backstage crews take their places for the next scene change. Sometimes there can be so many warnings, standbys, and cues given that the stage manager must double up by saying something like, "Standby lights 25 through 28, standby sound 15 through 18. Lights 25, go. Lights 26, go. Sound 15, go."

Mike Goldwater/Alamy Stock Photo

During a production, the assistant stage manager sits in the wings to ensure that everything backstage runs smoothly. Communication with all of the other members of the stage crews is maintained through headsets. Generally, it is an uneventful job punctuated by moments of panic.

10 PM: Clearing Out

After the curtain call, the actors work their way up to the dressing rooms and begin hanging up their costumes and removing makeup. Usually the stage manager stops in to share a few notes and make any announcements, such as the need for a brush-up rehearsal.

Even before the audience has left the theatre, backstage crews are cleaning up. The prop master begins putting away the props. The running crews are stowing equipment. When the last audience member has left the house, the theatrical lights shut down and the bland white work lights pop on. Crews clean the stage and check for any damage or problems, which are reported to the stage manager. The stage manager then writes the performance report that is e-mailed to the entire artistic staff and crew, informing them of any problems or concerns.

Twenty minutes after the show is over, the actors are out of makeup and heading home. At the stage door they meet a few friends and fans. Meanwhile, the folks in the box office are adding up tickets and receipts as they account for every seat. As the last audience member leaves the lobby, the ushers head home after them.

11 PM: Bringing Out the Ghost Light

The last of the running crews are finishing up. Everything is now powered down. The last person to leave the theatre rolls the ghost light out on stage, and the theatre is locked. Once again, as the famous set designer Robert Edmond Jones said, "the stage is lonely, and forlorn and as silent as midnight."

After the play, some audience members will gather at the stage door in the hope of meeting the stars. Here Academy, Tony, and Emmy Award winner Gregory Rush signs autographs after performing on Broadway in Eugene Ionesco's absurdist comedy *Exit the King*.

William Missouri Downs

Making a living in the theatre requires hard work and grueling hours, and the pay is often very limited. However, for theatre people the joy of doing a job they really love outweighs the drawbacks. Playwrights, actors, directors, stage managers, artistic directors, and designers seldom see their work as just a job, but rather as a creative outlet. Their work is intensive, but for them, there is nothing more satisfying. Nothing beats a life in the theatre.

Curtain Call

When theatre, or almost any work of art for that matter, is at its best, it appears to be almost effortless. In the theatre, this effortlessness is an illusion. From inception to fruition, theatre requires thousands of hours of labor and the talents of many trained, creative, and hard-working individuals. When theatre succeeds, it does so because every member of the ensemble understands his or her duties, yet is also allowed to solve problems, express opinions, use the techniques of his or her trade, and be creative. On the other hand, the director or artistic director who micromanages a production, just like the corporate executive who micromanages a company, will limit the potential for creativity and in the end produce a well-controlled but sterile product. As director Terry McCabe says, a good director sees the creative team "as valuable colleagues precisely because they might enlarge the director's own sense of the play."

SUMMARY

In the theatre, as in many other professions, creativity often occurs within an ensemble. The key to working within an ensemble is to ensure that all the members of the group are allowed to be creative but that they also work in unison toward the same artistic vision. A theatre's ensemble can be divided into four categories: administrative, creative, construction, and production. The administrative team includes accountants, box-office staff, administrative assistants, fund-raisers, grant writers, publicity personnel, and producer(s) who run the business aspects of any theatre. The creative team is the artists who invent the play and stage the production, specifically the playwright, the director, the actors, and the designers. The team can also encompass assistant directors, dramaturgs, musical directors, conductors, vocal coaches, understudies, dancers, and choreographers. The construction team includes the technical director(s) and crew chief(s) who supervise a company of stitchers, contractors, and laborers who hang the lights, build the sets, fabricate the props, and stitch the costumes. The production team includes stage manager(s), house manager(s), and ushers, as well as the lighting, set, and costume crews who work behind the scenes during the performances. In fact, large productions can have far more people behind the scenes than on stage: the Broadway musical *Titanic* needed seven prop people, fourteen carpenters, three follow-spot operators, two computer operators, three riggers, and four stage managers for every performance. At nearly any time of the day, members of the ensemble are hard at work on the elements that create contemporary professional theatre.

MindTap

Test your knowledge with online printable flashcards and online quizzing.

KEY TERMS

Chapter 6

THE ART OF PLAYWRITING

Playwriting is often called the "lonely profession", and takes thousands of hours of contemplation. Pictured is playwright Arlene Hutton in her New York City study.

© Aaron Lee Fineman

MindTap®

Start with a quick warm-up activity and review the chapter's learning objectives.

I created *Tracers* with a group. In the workshop process I pushed for "Truth" more than anything else. Most of my writing tends to be autobiographical with poetic license—Hopefully unmasking, honest, and most importantly theatrical. I think of it as mythologizing my life.

John DiFusco, Playwright

MindTap°

Read, highlight, and take notes online.

In the case of the text, in theater (unlike the movies) the writer is the final arbiter.

Tom Stoppard, Playwright

Many theatres in the United States specialize in the development of new plays. One of the most famous is Playwrights Horizon in New York City. Hundreds of playwrights have had their new scripts developed here and the theatre boasts numerous world premieres.

Theatre begins with the playwright, the artist who conceives the theme, the characters, the dialogue, and the story. The root word *wright* in playwright comes from the Middle Ages and means "one who builds." A shipwright was someone who built ships; a wheelwright was someone who built wheels. It follows that a playwright is someone who builds plays. Playwrights are so important to the process that many theatre professionals call them the "primary artist." The playwright Moss Hart said, "The writer is the person who was there when the paper was white." Yet when a play is produced, it is unlikely that the director, actors, or designers will ever meet the playwright. In fact, the playwright is the only member of the ensemble of a production who can be long dead.

In this chapter, we will look at the artists who build plays and the techniques they use to express themselves. We will also examine the elements that make up a play and how playwrights combine these elements to craft a script. Studying the elements of playwriting will help you better analyze performances and the written words upon which the contributions of all other theatre artists depend.

The Playwright's Life

Unlike the other artists in the theatre, who usually work within the ensemble, the playwright typically works alone for months, if not years, to write a play (which, incidentally, accounts for why a playwright didn't make an appearance at the Springfield Ensemble Rep, featured in Chapter 5). In fact, playwriting is the most time-consuming of all the arts of the theatre. The combined number of hours it takes the actors to rehearse, the designers to design, and the director to direct does not come close to the amount of time it takes the playwright to conceive and write the play. This, along with the fact that playwrights are the primary artists, is why playwrights get top billing in the program, even above the director, in contrast to Hollywood movies, where the director gets top billing.

As we mentioned in Chapter 2, playwrights do not sell their copyright. Consequently, they retain control of the script and technically no director, actor, designer, producer, or anyone else can change the script without permission from the playwright or the playwright's lawyer, publisher, or estate. We say "technically" because sometimes members of the ensemble do change the script without seeking the playwright's permission. They just slip the changes in and hope that the playwright doesn't find out. (For more on copyright, see "Copyright Law: Infringement, Public Domain, and Parody" in Chapter 2.)

Owning the copyright means that playwrights retain a lot of power over their plays, but they do not necessarily make a lot of money from them. One of the reasons they don't make much money is that they are not employees of the theatre and so are not allowed to form closed-shop unions and strike for better compensation. A **closed-shop union**, sometimes called a union shop, is a union to which all employees *must* belong and which the employer formally recognizes as their sole collective bargaining agent. The advantage to closed-shop unions is that the employees can call a strike if their demands go unmet. Television and screenwriters have a powerful

William Missouri Downs

closed-shop union called the **Writers Guild of America (WGA)**. As a result, staff writers on television shows can earn $5 to $10,000 or more a week, and a single screenplay can sell for hundreds of thousands if not millions of dollars. Screen and television writers are allowed to form a closed-shop union because they sell their copyright, giving up their power to control the script, the production, or the final product. This makes them "writers for hire" (in other words "employees"). Their scripts can be cut and changed by the director or producers, and sometimes even the actors without permission. As writer Thomas McGuane said, "Aspiring to be a screenwriter is like aspiring to be a co-pilot." The exception to this would be screenwriters who direct their own work, make independent films, or write small films that are seen only online. These writers often retain their copyright and thus creative control. For example, Woody Allen (*Annie Hall, Midnight in Paris*) writes and directs his own movies and is not a writer for hire.

Playwrights, because they retain the copyright, are not writers for hire. Instead, they are considered "management," and U.S. law does not allow managers to form closed-shop unions. Playwrights' only option is a weak **open-shop union**. In an open shop, membership is optional, so meaningful strikes are impossible. The playwrights' union, the **Dramatists Guild of America (DGA)**, can champion the rights of playwrights but can do little to demand higher pay. Because of this, few playwrights make a living from their art.

Even well-known playwrights have trouble making a living. Tony Kushner, famous for writing the Pulitzer Prize winning play *Angels in America* said, "I make my living now as a screenwriter! Which I'm surprised and horrified to find myself saying, but I don't think I can support myself as a playwright at this point. I don't think anybody does." Inadequate compensation is one of the major reasons playwrights must find outside employment, such as higher paying writing jobs in Hollywood, to make ends meet. But most seem to return to the stage. Why write plays if the pay is so low? It's simple, they love it, they love the live audience and thrill of hearing their words said without being edited, rewritten or changed—something so

Unlike playwrights, screen and television writers have a closed shop union called the Writers Guild of America (WGA), which means they can band together and demand better wages. Playwrights have an open shop union Dramatists Guild of America (DGA) so they cannot strike for better pay. Pictured here is the 2007 WGA strike.

AP Images/Reed Saxon

many screen and television writers must endure. Playwright Terry Teachout said it best, "If you want to make money, get a job. The pay is better, and so are the hours. Just don't expect anyone to clap for you when the five o'clock whistle blows."

The reward for low pay and long hours is that playwrights, unlike most screenwriters, see their work presented as written. Their unique voices remain pure and their ideas about how the world is or should be are communicated to audiences without alteration. When it comes down to it, all that playwrights have are their words, and to playwrights, their words are far more valuable than any paycheck. Playwright Sir Tom Stoppard wrote in his play *The Real Thing* (1982) that words build bridges across incomprehension and chaos. Words, he said, "deserve respect. If you get the right ones in the right order, you can nudge the world a little." And all playwrights, rich or poor, want to nudge the world. (See Spotlight "The Life of a Playwright: Sarah Ruhl.")

SPOTLIGHT ON The Life of a Playwright: Sarah Ruhl

Growing up in Chicago, Sarah Ruhl loved to read. Her favorites were short stories by Virginia Woolf and Katherine Mansfield, and poems by Elizabeth Bishop and Wallace Stevens. She also loved to read plays by Maria Irene Fornes and William Shakespeare. She went on to earn her MFA (Masters of Fine Arts) from Brown University, and it was there that she fell in love with playwriting. When her first play was produced at Brown's new play festival she remembers thinking, "Oh, there's no turning back at this point. I'm completely in love with this job, vocation, hobby, whatever you'd like to call it."

When she works on a new play Ruhl often gets her story ideas from ordinary incidents in everyday life. "I mean, of course work emerges out of extraordinary moments of loss and ecstasy and all that," Ruhl said, "but it also emerges from day-to-day observations." For example, one of her most famous plays came from a chance comment she overheard during a dinner party. A doctor said, "My cleaning lady is depressed and won't clean my house. So I took her to the hospital and had her medicated. And she still won't clean!" That one remark gave birth to the comedy *The Clean House*, the story of a Brazilian maid looking for the perfect joke while working for an obsessive family. *The Clean House* was produced all over the world and was a Pulitzer Prize finalist.

Ruhl's other plays often celebrate what she calls "the pleasure of heightened things." For example, her play *Dead Man's Cell Phone* is about a woman who repeatedly asks a man sitting next to her in a coffeehouse to answer his ringing cell phone, only to discover that he is dead. This event leads to a play about love and death in the digital age. "Cell phones, iPods, wireless computers will change people in ways we don't even understand," Ruhl said. "We're less connected to the present. No one is where they are. There's absolutely no reason to talk to a stranger anymore—you connect to people you already know. But how well do you know them? Because you never see them—you just talk to them. I find that terrifying."

Ruhl often writes quirky comedies about deeply serious subjects. She feels that one should have the ability to step back and laugh "at horrible things even as you're experiencing them."

Joseph Marzullo/WENN Photos/Newscom

Playwright Sarah Ruhl

Sara Krulwich/The New York Times/Redux Pictures

Sarah Ruhl's *Passion Play* follows three different communities in different historical periods who are mounting different productions of plays concerning Christ's death and resurrection. The New York production pictured here featured Kate Turnbull, front, and Dominic Fumes.

The Playwright's Art

The playwright's job is to grapple with the lives of human beings and to boldly try to find solutions and/or significance by imaginatively translating real life into stories. They take the raw chaos of life and find or add structure in order to create meaning. All writers do this, but what makes playwriting unique, and difficult to do, is that it is a very limited form of storytelling. A playwright can only use dialogue, stage directions, and an occasional parenthetical to build a story. **Dialogue** is the spoken text of the play, the words the characters say. Finding the right words for each character takes many rewrites and an acute sensitivity to how people express themselves. To help the actor or the reader interpret a particular line of dialogue, a playwright sometimes adds **parentheticals**, short descriptions of how a line of dialogue is to be performed. The playwright also writes the **stage directions**, which are notes that indicate the physical movements of the characters. Within these limited parameters, a playwright builds a play using the basic tools of playwriting, including theme, characters, conflict, language, and plot.

> I believe that whatever a character says is true. So I write down everything the character says— pages and pages. Then, the trick is weeding through all that and finding the story that is really buried in there. And sometimes you really have to dig.
>
> ***August Wilson,*** Playwright

Theme

Playwrights are philosophers in that they search for meaning in the world and attempt to understand human nature. Their search results in a statement about life, a central idea, or a moral; this is the play's **theme**. The French poet

Andre Breton said, "A work of art has value only if tremors from the future run through it." In other words, a work of art must speak to many generations, it must convey meaning that stands the test of time. The theme of a play is more often implied than directly stated, because playwrights rarely sit down to write a play about a particular theme. Instead, the theme usually reveals itself during the writing process. American playwright Arthur Miller said that he often didn't know what his plays were about until the second or third draft. Even then, playwrights rarely state the theme, because themes that are explicitly stated are less powerful than those that are revealed through action. Consequently, the theme is often open to interpretation by audiences and readers.

> Drama cannot deal with people whose wills are atrophied, who are unable to make decisions which have even temporary meaning, who adopt no conscious attitude toward events, who make no effort to control their environment.
>
> **John Howard Lawson,**
> Playwright, screenwriter, and author

Action

A playwright's ability to write good characters is based on an ability to examine and understand people's motivations and emotions. For this reason, playwrights often write about people they know and understand, including themselves. Yet not all characters are good material for the stage. Stage characters are different from those written for novels, poems, or short stories, because they must be able to express themselves and take action. For thousands of years, playwrights have used the word *action* to define character and story. **Actions** are the characters' deeds, their responses to circumstances, which in turn affect the course of the story. In other words, the situation of a play is what happens but action is what the characters *do* with what happens. Characters in plays come to life not by what they *feel* and *think* but by what they *say* and *do*.

In real life, most of us rarely take action. We receive an unjust parking ticket and we pay it rather than fight it in court; our boss treats us unfairly and we bear it rather than file a complaint; a huge corporation or the government cheats us and we accept it rather than deal with the red tape. Most of us would make for weak characters in a play because dramatic characters must be willing to take substantial action. If there is no action, there is no story because there is no conflict.

Plays are based on stories that contain conflict. No one wants to see a play about the land of the happy people. Pictured here is the comedy *The Exit Interview* at the Interact Theatre in Philadelphia.

© Kate Raines

Conflict

Unfortunately, conflict is one of the constants of human existence. Hardly a day goes by that we are not involved in some major or minor conflict with ourselves or each other; this is true for individuals, families, societies, and nations. Historians Will and Ariel Durant write in their book *The Lessons of History* (1968) that in the last 3,420 or so years of recorded history, only 268 have seen no war. And in all those thousands of years, there has never been *one single day* without conflicts among individuals, families, and societies. A play is essentially the history of a particular conflict. Plays are not about people who have idyllic lives; they're about people who have unfulfilled needs and desires and the obstacles or opponents preventing them from obtaining what they want. The result is conflict. It's a simple equation: desire + obstacle + lack of compromise = conflict. For example:

> *Desire:* Romeo loves Juliet and Juliet loves Romeo.
>
> *Obstacle:* Their families will not allow them to see each other, let alone marry.
>
> *Reason compromise is not an option:* They can't live without each other.

Notice that the third element, the reason compromise is not an option, is what makes the story possible. The playwright can write a play because the characters are not willing to compromise and must take action. In the process, they cause conflict. Once playwrights know what the conflict is and why the characters must take action, they must write characters who express themselves with language. Language helps audiences comprehend what characters are thinking, feeling, wanting, or intending to do. Characters use language as action or to promote or enhance action. They use language to drive the story forward.

Language

Words are the playwright's paint. When mixed properly, they can glance or glaze, collide or clip to reveal the heart of a character. Yet dialogue does not begin with words; it begins with the need to talk. We talk because we want. If we want nothing, we say nothing. Even small talk about nothing in particular can be traced to our need for companionship. As infants, we cry when we want to be fed or changed. As we grow, our needs become more complicated and we learn language in order to communicate. The need for a bottle or a fresh diaper is replaced by the needs for friendship, for justice, and for protection of our ego. As we mature, our strategies to get what we want through speech become more complicated. We learn to manipulate language in order to provoke, settle scores, find love, defeat enemies, and satisfy our wants without announcing them directly. Sometimes, when our deepest wants go unfulfilled, they seep into our subconscious, coloring our speech with secondary meanings and concealed desires. Dialogue is a combination of what the character needs to say and what the character is compelled to say. It's simple communication colored by the character's environment, history, emotions, and situation. Let's look at a few of the tools playwrights use to write dialogue: subtext, imagery, rhythm, tempo, and sound.

Subtext

A line of dialogue has two levels: what the character says (the text) and what the character consciously or subconsciously means (the subtext). **Subtext** is the hidden

People may or may not say what they mean . . . but they always say something designed to get what they want.

David Mamet, Playwright

meaning behind the words, the real reason a character chooses to speak. In other words, dialogue is like an iceberg; only part of the meaning can be seen above the waterline. For example, when a playwright adds subtext, the simple line "I hate you" can take on any of hundreds of possible meanings, from "I love you" to "I miss you" to "I wish I were you." When King Lear speaks the famous line "Blow, winds, and crack your cheeks. Rage, blow!" he is not talking about the weather but about his own troubled life and madness. The subtext makes the line memorable.

Another way of looking at subtext is to realize that playwrights are psychologists in that they are constantly analyzing human character. One way to understand a character, or another person for that matter, is to understand *how* they hear, because what is said and what is heard can be very different. More often than not, people filter what they hear through their own needs, emotions, and prejudices. People ignore, misinterpret, or read special meanings into just about everything. We project our own thoughts and emotions onto other people. For example, look at a simple exchange between two people:

BETH:	Honey, where's the coffee?
SHANE:	In the cabinet near the fridge.
BETH:	And the sugar?
SHANE:	Right beside it, on the left.

This is boring dialogue because both characters hear each other perfectly and respond obviously. But look what happens when the characters hear something different from what the other is saying. In this next example, simple questions are heard but misinterpreted, adding depth and subtext to an otherwise mundane exchange.

BETH:	Honey, where's the coffee?
SHANE:	You don't think I know, do you?
BETH:	And the sugar?
SHANE:	Are you testing me?

Obviously, what Shane hears is quite different from what Beth is saying, so we learn something about Shane's psychological makeup. Playwrights know that how someone listens and responds reveals a lot about who they are and what they are thinking.

Imagery

In a movie it's easy to show images. What the screen can show is almost limitless, so screenwriters love to write scenes that let the audience see all manner of things first-hand. Playwrights, on the other hand, are limited by the confined space of the stage and small budgets. So they must be more like poets and write dialogue that allows the audience to see things in the mind's eye. They do this by writing dialogue full of imagery, picture-making words that allow the audience to see into their imaginations. A classic example comes from Eugene O'Neill's *Long Day's Journey into Night*, when the character Edmund recounts his days at sea.

EDMUND: I was on the Squarehead square rigger, bound for Buenos Aires. Full moon in the trades. The old hooker driving fourteen knots. I lay on the bowsprit, facing astern, with the water foaming into spume under me, the masts with every sail white in the moonlight, towering high above me. I became drunk with the beauty and singing rhythm of it, and for a moment I lost myself—actually lost my

Joan Marcus

In contrast to movies, plays create imagery with words rather than photography, special effects, or action sequences, so playwrights work hard to find the right words for each character and scene. For example, in Eugene O'Neill's classic *Long Day's Journey into Night*, Edmund's monologue about his days at sea is necessarily as powerful as any movie scene. This 2003 production featured Robert Sean Leonard and Brian Dennehy. Directed by Robert Falls, Plymouth Theatre, New York.

life. I was set free! I dissolved in the sea, became white sails and flying spray, became beauty and rhythm, became moonlight and the ship and the high dim-starred sky! I belonged, without past or future, within peace and unity and a wild joy, within something greater than my own life, or the life of Man, to Life itself! To God, if you want to put it that way. Then another time, on the American Line, when I was lookout on the crow's nest in the dawn watch. A calm sea, that time. Only a lazy ground swell and a slow drowsy roll of the ship. The passengers asleep and none of the crew in sight. No sound of man. Black smoke pouring from the funnels behind and beneath me. Dreaming, not keeping lookout, feeling alone, and above, and apart, watching the dawn creep like a painted dream over the sky and sea which slept together.

Then the moment of ecstatic freedom came. The peace, the end of the quest, the last harbor, the joy of belonging to a fulfillment beyond men's lousy, pitiful, greedy fears and hopes and dreams!

If this were a scene from a movie, the scriptwriter could take us to the crow's nest and show us the flying spray and the black smoke. One shot might be enough to convey the thoughts and feelings of the character. But the playwright is limited by the stage and must verbally communicate the thoughts and images critical to the story.

Rhythm, Tempo, and Sound

Playwrights love the music of language; they write dialogue that has a particular rhythm, tempo, and sound. By not only choosing the character's words carefully but also adjusting the sounds, a playwright can reveal a character's feelings. For example, in Tennessee Williams' *Cat on a Hot Tin Roof* (1955), Maggie describes her sister-in-law, her rival for Big Daddy's money, as a former "Cotton Carnival Queen." The hard sound of each of the first letters gives the character a chance to show jealousy and contempt without being too obvious. Sounds are combined to create "rhythm." As in music, *rhythm* in dialogue is a variation of sounds that creates a pattern, which prompts an emotional response. The characters each have their own rhythm, which manifests itself in the dialogue. The rhythm of dialogue is much more subtle than the rhythm of poetry. It's a gentle adjusting of the lines' sounds and stresses. Given the needs of the moment, dialogue should pulsate or flow, jingle or swing, oscillate or tranquilize. To understand rhythm, look at the following line:

The right word in the right place.

Its rhythm comes from the repetition of the *r* sound juxtaposed with the soft ending word, *place*. Now compare the following lines, which have the same meaning but different rhythms:

The perfect word perfectly placed.

An accurate word in its correct location.

A proper expression placed with perfection.

Many films have been based on plays, but on rare occasion a play is based on a film. Such was the case of the musical *Dirty Rotten Scoundrels*, which was originally a film and later remade into a musical (lyrics by David Yazbek and a book by Jeffrey Lane). This production was staged at the Arvada Center in Colorado.

Patricia Switzer

Rhythms and sounds convey particular *tones* and evoke particular character types. The first line, "The perfect word perfectly placed," is dominated by the percussive sound of the *p*'s but also contains the soft consonants *th* and *w*. This gives the line what some might call a comfortable sound—perhaps we see a young woman saying the line as she laughs in her lover's arms. "An accurate word in its correct location" is more formal and harder sounding with the *c*'s and *t*'s; it might bring to mind a business executive praising a subordinate. "A proper expression placed with perfection" is dominated by a rhythmic pattern of soft *p*'s; we might envision a retired English professor describing a favorite line of poetry. No two people talk the same way or use the same rhythms. A playwright adjusts each line so that the words reveal each character's inner rhythm.

Dialogue is also designed to be spoken at a particular speed, or *tempo*. A good line of dialogue has an internal clock that makes the tempo unmistakable to the reader or actor. For example, Shakespeare masterfully uses Leontes' tempo and rhythm to expose Leontes' true nature in *The Winter's Tale*:

> Is whispering nothing?
> Is leaning cheek to cheek? Is meeting noses?
> Kissing with inside lip? stopping the career
> Of laughter with a sigh? (a note infallible
> Of breaking honesty). Horsing foot on foot?
> Skulking in corners? Wishing clocks more swift,
> Hours minutes, noon, midnight? And all eyes
> Blind with the pin and web but theirs; theirs only
> That would unseen be wicked? Is this nothing?

Here, Shakespeare gives the usually even-tempered King Leontes a fervent, fanatical tempo as he wonders whether his wife has committed adultery. The many short, almost half-asked questions reveal thoughts tumbling out at breakneck speed, suggesting a jealous temper.

Plot

Playwrights are always trying to plot the stories of life. Although we often use the words *plot* and *story* interchangeably, there is a difference between the two. *Story* is everything that happens, and **plot** is how it all fits together. The plot gives the story a particular focus. For example, "the king died and the queen died" is a very basic story. But "the king died, and the queen died of grief" is plot. This example comes from the novelist and critic E. M. Forster, who, in his book *Aspects of the Novel* (1927), said that story is the chronological sequence of events and plot is the causal and logical structure that connects events. A play generally has only one story but may have a main plot and a subplot or a multitude of plots. Playwrights may start developing a play with the characters and the conflict, but soon they must get down to plotting the story.

Plotting the story means finding its structure. Real life is raw and disorganized; a play structures life into a unified whole. **Plot-structure**, as it is sometimes called, is the playwright's selection of events to create a logical sequence and as a result to distill meaning from the chaos of life. Even a play written to

The narrative impulse is always
with us; we couldn't imagine
ourselves through a day without
it. . . . We need myths to get
by. We need story; otherwise
the tremendous randomness
of experience overwhelms us.
Story is what penetrates.

Robert Coover, Novelist

argue that life is meaningless must be logically structured. Plotting the structure of a story is not easy, because thousands of factors can change the sequence of events. Although no two stories are the same, they generally fall into two categories: formula and non-formula.

Formula Plots

Playwrights don't come up with a new plot every time they tell a story. Sometimes they depend on formula plots. A formula plot is one that follows a blueprint. Today, formula plots prevail in most big Hollywood movies and many plays. Formula is nothing new; it is, in fact, as old as humanity. In his book *The Hero with a Thousand Faces*, Joseph Campbell examines myths and storytelling throughout the ages. He found that most myths have a similar structure no matter what country, culture, or century they come from; they all follow similar formulaic plotlines. Storytellers from ancient Greece to Kenya to China to Hollywood often use the same formula. In fact, the first bedtime story you were told as a child was probably a formula story. The basic sections of a formula plot are beginning, middle, and end. By pinpointing the moment one section of the story ends and the next begins and by defining the components of each section, we can discover the mechanics of a formula plot.

Beginning

In the beginning of most plays, the playwright sets up the characters and the basic situation, which includes the time and location, character relationships, and some exposition. **Exposition**, sometimes called **back story**, lets the audience in on what happened to the characters before the play began and what happens between the scenes and offstage. For example, if two characters talk about what happened the night before, that's exposition.

At the beginning of a play, the playwright also introduces the protagonist and antagonist. The **protagonist** is the central character who pushes forward the action of the play. The protagonist can be a hero or a severely flawed soul, as long as the audience can identify with, care for, and even root for him or her. The **antagonist** is what the ancient Greeks called the "opposer of action." It's the adversary who stands in the way of the protagonist's goals. An antagonist may be a one-dimensional villain, a complex character, an element of nature such as a storm or a huge whale, or even an aspect of the protagonist's own character such as alcoholism or self-doubt.

This information about setting and characters is conveyed through the structural components of the beginning of a formula plot: event, disturbance, point of attack, and major dramatic question.

Most plays begin with an **event**, an unusual incident, a special occasion, or a crisis in the characters' lives. This unique moment could be a wedding, a funeral, a homecoming, or preparation for a party. With the event, the playwright draws the audience into the play. At the beginning of a play, the basic situation often has equilibrium. In other words, the lives of the characters have achieved a certain stasis, or balance—a balance that must be disturbed if there is to be conflict. The **disturbance** is an inciting incident that upsets the balance and gets the action rolling by creating an opportunity for conflict between protagonists and antagonists.

The disturbance causes the situation to deteriorate to the point where the protagonist must make a major decision that will result in conflict. This moment is called the **point of attack**. It is the moment in the plot when the fuse is lit. This decision defines what the play is about; it states the protagonist's goal. It's the core action of the play, sometimes called the *through line*, for at that moment we know what the play is about.

The disturbance and the point of attack cause a **major dramatic question**, sometimes called **MDQ**. This is the hook that keeps people in the theatre for two hours because they want to know the answers. It is the major dramatic question, not the theme of the play, that causes curiosity and suspense. For example, if the major dramatic question in *Romeo and Juliet* is "Will love triumph over hate?" then the theme would be a broader statement about the nature of love.

Middle

The middle of a formula play is full of conflicts, crises, and complications, which are the hurdles that the protagonist must clear to achieve the goal. **Conflict** is the struggle of opposing forces in the play; **crises** are events that make it necessary for the characters to take action; and **complications** are roadblocks that stand in the way of success. Conflicts, crises, and complications are what make a story interesting. As film director Alfred Hitchcock said, "Drama is life with the dull parts left out." All of this unrest is governed by **rising action**, which means that each conflict, crisis, and complication is more dramatic and more serious than the ones before. In other words, the middle of a play follows *the path of most resistance*. Any moments of apparent success always lead to an even greater undoing. The middle of a formula play ends with the **dark moment**, when the protagonist fails, the quest collapses, and the goal seems unattainable.

End

The dark moment is followed by **enlightenment**, which occurs when the protagonist figures out how to defeat the antagonist. Enlightenment can come in many forms: the protagonist may join forces with someone; a revelation may shed light on the problem; or the protagonist, after falling into an emotional abyss, may now see the error of his or her ways. The enlightenment is often closely tied to the theme of the play, because the manner, the cause, and the type of enlightenment often reveal the playwright's philosophy.

Enlightened, the protagonist is ready to defeat the antagonist. For the first time the protagonist is able to resolve the conflict with the antagonist. The **climax** is the moment the antagonist is defeated. The climax doesn't have to be violent or horrible. It can be quiet, even subtle. Whatever its quality, the climax must be a direct result of the protagonist's actions.

The **denouement** is the final outcome of the play, a short final scene that allows the audience to appreciate that the protagonist, because of the preceding events, has learned some great or humble lesson. The scene also often hints at the future for the characters, as balance returns. This new balance enables the protagonist to comprehend why he or she suffered and take charge of or accept destiny. The denouement also allows audience members to feel catharsis, or purging of emotions. They may leave the theatre believing, if only for a moment, that someday their lives too might include a moment of understanding, forgiveness, or triumph. (See Spotlight, "Formula Story Telling—*Star Wars* compared to *Romeo and Juliet*.)

SPOTLIGHT ON Formula Storytelling—*Star Wars* compared to *Romeo and Juliet*)

To study formula storytelling let's have a little fun by comparing two very different stories, *Romeo and Juliet* by William Shakespeare and the original *Star Wars* movie. As unlikely as it may seem, these stories share a similar formulaic structure, just as a grand cathedral and a plain box-like office building can share the same skeletal design. The first column lists the standard structural elements of a formula story. As you can see, although they're different stories, they do follow the same structural order.

Andy Bradshaw/UPPA/Photoshot/Newscom

Corbis

Structural Element	Romeo and Juliet	Star Wars
Event	Young men from the warring Capulet and Montague families engage in a street brawl.	Luke Skywalker meets the Jedi master Obi-Wan Kenobi.
Disturbance	Romeo, of the house of Montague, and Juliet, of the house of Capulet, fall in love, despite their families' feud.	Luke's family is killed.
Point of Attack (decision)	Romeo and Juliet decide to marry, despite the obstacles they face.	Luke decides to join Obi-Wan, become a Jedi knight, and fight for good.
Conflict Crises Complication	Tybalt, Juliet's beloved cousin, challenges Romeo to a fight, but Romeo refuses to fight back—until Tybalt kills Romeo's friend. (Tybalt is now Romeo's kin because Romeo and Juliet have secretly married.)	Luke must join forces with the less-than-trustworthy Han Solo; they are caught by the evil Death Star and wind up facing death again and again, such as when they are nearly crushed by an enormous garbage compactor.

© 2018 Cengage Learning

Structural Element	Romeo and Juliet	Star Wars
Dark Moment	Romeo kills Tybalt and is banished from the city.	Han Solo refuses to help. As part of the Republic's fighting force, Luke attacks the Death Star. Many fellow fighters are killed. The evil Darth Vader is about to kill Luke.
Enlightenment	Friar Laurence mixes a potion that causes Juliet to fall into a deep sleep. Her parents, thinking she's dead, transport her to the family tomb, where Romeo goes to save her.	Han Solo comes to Luke's rescue.
Climax	Thinking his love dead, Romeo commits suicide. Juliet awakens and, finding her lover dead, also takes her life.	In another attack on the Death Star, Luke feels the Force and is able to blow the Death Star to pieces.
Denouement	The grief-stricken Montagues and Capulets promise to end their long feud.	Princess Leia rewards Luke and Han Solo for their service and bravery.

© 2018 Cengage Learning

In a formula story the fundamental elements—event; disturbance; point of attack; major dramatic question; conflict, crisis, and complications; dark moment; enlightenment; climax; and denouement—all occur in exactly the same order. This formula can be used in full-length plays or ten-minute plays (see Spotlight "How Many Acts? How Many Intermissions?") and in big Hollywood action-adventure flicks or small independent films. In fact, formula storytelling is so common that there are even software programs to help writers build their stories. But not all plays or Hollywood movies follow the formula. Sometimes playwrights use nonformulaic structures.

Non-Formula Plots

When playwrights or screenwriters abandon formula, they allow the story to grow naturally from the characters' actions, motivations, and needs. Writers who abandon formula are often trying to look at life the way it *is*, or as they perceive it, rather than trying to fit it into a standard structure. Many writers who create character-driven stories believe that formula plots do the audience a disservice because they don't require them to confront the chaotic and ineffectual parts of life. In real life we seldom defeat our antagonists, confront our problems, risk it all, refuse to compromise, or have enlightening experiences.

A good example of a nonformulaic movie is Quentin Tarantino's *Pulp Fiction* (1994), starring John Travolta and Samuel L. Jackson, which cleverly interweaves the stories of several characters involved in varying degrees of criminal behavior. This movie is unique in the highly fragmented telling of its stories, whose ties are revealed only at the end. An example of a nonformulaic play is Marsha Norman's

The very impulse to write, I think, springs from an inner chaos crying for order, for meaning, and that meaning must be discovered in the process of writing or the work lies dead as it is finished.

Arthur Miller, Playwright

SPOTLIGHT ON How Many Acts? How Many Intermissions?

Modern plays can be anywhere from a few seconds to many hours long. Most long plays are divided into sections called *acts*, which are separated by short breaks called *intermissions*. The practice of taking an intermission originated about 400 years ago during the Italian Renaissance, when indoor theatres were introduced. At the time, theatres were lit with candles; performances had to be halted at regular intervals so that the spent candles could be replaced and lit. For most plays the candles had to be replaced four times, so plays were divided into five acts. When you read a Shakespeare play, you'll notice that they have five acts. Interestingly, the division into acts was added after Shakespeare's day—his plays were performed outdoors during the daytime, so he included no intermissions. Later, as candle technology improved, four-act plays with three intermissions became the norm. Today, indoor theatres are no longer lit by candles, but most long plays still have at least one intermission as a relic of the Italian Renaissance and a chance for audience members to stretch their legs. Most plays today are staged in one of the following formats.

Three-act full-length play: The three-act format is not as common today as it was 50 years ago. The double intermission makes the play longer and more formal. Tracy Letts' Tony Award–winning play *August: Osage County* (2007) is an example of a contemporary three-act play.

Two-act full-length play: This is the most common way to divide a full-length play. The intermission is generally taken just after the middle of the story. Most modern plays, such as Caryl Churchill's *Top Girls* (1982), follow this format. However, when directors stage older plays, they often break for only one intermission. For example, today Shakespeare's plays are often staged as two-act plays.

Full-length one-act play: There is no intermission in this type of play, so the beginning, middle, and end flow without interruption, much like a movie. Because people cannot sit for too long without a break, full-length one-act plays are generally shorter than two- or three-act full-length plays (usually between 1 hour 20 minutes and a maximum of 1 hour 35 minutes). *Art* (1996) by Yasmina Reza is an example of a full-length one-act play.

Short one-act plays: These plays can be anywhere from several seconds to about an hour long. Often, several short one-acts are produced on a single night with an intermission after each play. Some playwrights even write several short one-act plays as *companion pieces*, designed to be performed on the same night. By doing this, the playwright doesn't have to share the evening with other short one-acts. Companion pieces can have related or unrelated themes and stories. Examples of related one-acts are *Lone Star* (1979) and *Laundry & Bourbon* (1980) by James McLure. Examples of unrelated one-acts are Christopher Durang's *Sister Mary Ignatius Explains It All for You* (1979) and *The Actor's Nightmare* (1981).

Ten-minute plays: Ten-minute plays are a relatively new format and are growing in popularity. Theatres that produce these tiny plays will stage as many as ten in one evening. Often there is no formal intermission between ten-minute plays, but there may be a short pause while the set is changed. The Actors Theatre of Louisville, a major regional theatre, is often credited with pioneering this format as a way to introduce new voices in playwriting during their new-play festival each year.

Pulitzer Prize–winning '*night, Mother* (1982). It is about a woman, Jessie, who explains to her mother, Thelma, why she's decided to kill herself as she goes through the house tying up the loose ends of her life. The play has no clear-cut protagonist or antagonist, nor is there an opening event or disturbance. Jessie's decision was made before the play begins and not as a reaction to any event that happens on stage. There is a great deal of crisis and conflict as Thelma tries to talk Jessie out of

Joan Marcus

her decision, but there are few complications and nothing makes Jessie reconsider. The play ends at the point of its greatest dramatic tension; there is no denouement.

Russian playwright Anton Chekhov neatly alluded to the power of nonformulaic plays when he said, "Let everything on the stage be just as complicated and at the same time just as simple as it is in life. People eat their dinner, just eat their dinner, and all the time their happiness is being established or their lives are being broken up." When you attend a nonformulaic play, expect the playwright to take you on a journey that, just like real life, is unpredictable.

When playwrights abandon formula, they allow stories to grow naturally from the characters, often presenting a "slice of life." Marsha Norman's Pulitzer Prize–winning play *'night, Mother* is one such nonformulaic play. This 2004 revival starred Brenda Blethyn and Edie Falco. Directed by Michael Mayer, Royale Theatre, New York.

Curtain Call

Playwrights are philosophers, psychologists, poets, and storytellers all rolled into one. They write because they have a deep desire to tell stories that change or entertain the world. They are often solitary people who search their life experiences for interesting stories and characters with the hope that they reveal a bit of truth about human nature. They are also opinionated and want to express themselves. So great is their need to communicate their thoughts about how life is or should be that they often accept low pay in order to find an audience. But in return for their low pay and hard work, they can create worlds and can try to find truths about our relationships and our problems as well as our successes. An old saying in the theatre is "Playwrights write to get well." If they are well, so is the world.

We're one of the last handmade art forms. There's no fast way to make plays. It takes just as long and is just as hard as it was a thousand years ago.

Steven Dietz, Playwright

SUMMARY

MindTap®

Test your knowledge with online printable flashcards and online quizzing.

The playwright is the artist who conceives the theme, characters, conflict, dialogue, and plot of a play. So important to the theatre are playwrights that they are often called the primary artist. Yet playwrights are often not a part of the theatre ensemble; in fact, most members of an ensemble never meet the playwright whose play they are producing. Playwrights often have trouble making a living because they are self-employed artists. They can join a union that will champion their rights, but because theirs is an open-shop union, they cannot strike to negotiate better compensation. However, because they own the copyright for their work, they are able to control how their plays are presented and they get top billing in the program. A playwright's life may be difficult, but each one knows the joy that lies at the heart of sole authorship and finds great satisfaction in communicating his or her ideas without alteration.

In a sense, playwriting is a very limited form of writing. Plays consist only of dialogue, stage directions, and parentheticals. But playwrights do have many tools with which to construct a play, including theme, character, conflict, language, and plot. With these tools, playwrights can create stories of dramatic power, full of action and insight.

Playwrights may create unique plots or use formula plots, which are based on myths and stories that have been told for centuries. The basic elements of a formula plot are event; disturbance; point of attack; major dramatic question; conflict, crisis, and complications; dark moment; enlightenment; climax; and denouement. When playwrights create their own structures, the plot grows naturally from the characters' motivations and needs, not from a formula's predetermined requirements.

KEY TERMS

Chapter **7**

THE ART OF ACTING

Actors often use substitution to perform feelings from their own experiences that parallel the emotions called for in the script. Here actors perform a powerful scene from *A Man for All Seasons* at the Arvada Center for the Arts and Humanities.

Patricia Switzer

Outline

MindTap®

Start with a quick warm-up activity and review the chapter's learning objectives.

The actor has perhaps the most romantic role in the theatre. On the opening night of a new play, the playwright goes unnoticed, nervously pacing the lobby; the director sits unseen in the audience; and backstage dozens of stage-hands labor incognito. Unlike these offstage members of the theatre ensemble, the actor takes center stage on opening night and is the play. Who among us hasn't dreamed of being an actor or a movie star? It would be a charmed life, speaking great speeches, commanding the attention of admiring audiences, and winning critics' hearts—in fact, even actors dream of such a life. Yet for all its rewards, acting is hard work. The applause comes only after months of rehearsal and years of training. And actors rarely land a role before they have failed tens of dozens of auditions and struggled for months if not years with little or no income. (See Spotlight "The Life of an Actor: Terri White.")

SPOTLIGHT ON The Life of an Actor: Terri White

A life in the theatre is easier said than done. Employment seldom lasts more than a few months so actors are continually auditioning, trying to find their next "gig." The on-again-off-again lives of actors mean that one moment they are taking a bow in front of hundreds of adoring fans, and the next they might be counting their tips after a long night of waiting on tables. No actor's life demonstrates the harsh realities of a career in the theatre more than that of the Broadway actor and singer Terri White.

Ms. White was born into a family of traveling performers, and took to the stage herself when she was only eight years old. She learned to tap-dance and

Terri White takes a bow on Broadway.

often performed to her theme song "Nobody Knows When You're Down and Out." Soon she was acting on Broadway, singing with Liza Minnelli, and, between gigs, performing at nightclubs around New York City. She even acted with five-time Academy Award nominee Glenn Close in the Tony-nominated musical *Barnum* (about P. T. Barnum, the great showman of Barnum & Bailey Circus fame). But then her luck ran out.

After several years of not being able to find work, Ms. White was evicted from her apartment and forced to sleep on a friend's couch. When her money ran out, not wanting to burden her friends, she began sleeping on a bench in Washington Square Park near NYU. "I didn't go to a shelter because there was a certain pride in myself," Ms. White said. "I didn't want to take a pity home." She never mentioned to her fellow homeless that she had once been a star on Broadway.

One night she was recognized by a police officer who helped her find a place to live and get her life back on track, and soon thereafter, her luck began to change. A year later, Ms. White was cast in the Broadway musical *Finian's Rainbow* at the same theatre she had last performed with Glenn Close many years before.

Asked about her future as an actor she said, "I didn't dream I was going to be homeless, and a year ago, I didn't think that I was going to be back on Broadway, so I can't figure out what's happening after *Finian's*." A life as an actor can be highly rewarding, but it is a life filled with nonstop competition, heartbreak, and few safety nets. It is not a life well suited to a fragile ego, those who are easily daunted, or those lacking great personal discipline and devotion.

In this chapter, we will examine the training and life of actors. We'll also look at the techniques actors use to analyze and play characters, especially the techniques that apply to everyday life as well as the stage. Basically, acting is performing a part, something we all do. As Shakespeare said, "All the world's a stage and all the men and women merely players." You may never direct or write a play, but at some point in your life you'll need to play a part.

Training to Be an Actor

Some people just have a natural talent for acting. They have the charisma and stage presence that make them interesting to watch. They can even make the art of acting appear effortless. However, good acting on stage or in film or television requires a lot of training. Yet for most of theatre's history there were no acting schools. The only way to learn acting was by becoming an apprentice at a theatre. Apprentices helped out backstage and sometimes played what are jokingly called "spear-carrier roles." These are the small roles such as servants, attendants, or soldiers that seldom have any lines. After years of service to a theatre, if the apprentice had proven himself, he might be allowed to take a larger role. Today, actors in the United States and Canada usually start their training in a conservatory, university, or college. Undergraduates can earn a **BFA (Bachelor of Fine Arts)** in acting, and many graduate schools offer an **MFA (Master of Fine Arts)** in acting. An MFA in acting takes two to three years and includes intense training in voice, dialects, movement, singing, dancing, auditioning, characterization, theatre history, dramatic literature, acting styles, and much more. (BFAs and MFAs are also available in directing, design, playwriting, and other theatre arts.)

Once an actor leaves academia, it takes determination, imagination, and most of all stamina to live the actor's life, but it is seldom the end of the training. When actors are not struggling to find an acting job or working a second job to make ends meet, they are often taking classes to improve their body, voice, and mind—what actors call their "instruments."

MindTap®

Read, highlight, and take notes online.

Patricia Switzer

Occasionally, actors have the opportunity to play a character beyond their emotional knowledge and life experience. In this situation, they rely on the technique of substitution, replacing the character's emotions with unrelated emotions of their own. This production of *Christmas Carol* was produced by the Arvada Center in Colorado and stars Stephen Day and Richard White. Directed by Rod Lansberry.

Training the Body

Actors, like athletes and dancers, train for years in order to learn greater physical control. This training can include dance, martial arts, and yoga to enhance movement and relaxation; gymnastics, fencing, and stage combat to prepare for realistic-looking fight scenes; and even circus-arts training such as clowning and juggling to prepare for physically demanding roles in broad comedies. They also learn to reduce body tension as they focus on the physical characteristics, mannerisms, and body language of a character or of a particular style of acting.

Training the Voice

An actor's vocal training can be divided into two broad categories: breathing and speaking. At its most basic, the act of breathing simply ensures an adequate supply of oxygen to the blood. But actors must learn to allow the body to breathe in the most tension-filled moments. No matter what is happening on the stage, the actor must know how to permit the body's air pressure to support the voice so that it can be heard at the far corners of the theatre. To do this without amplification takes training—years of rigorous exercises and techniques designed to allow speech without rigid shoulders, braced knees, a tense back, or any of the other posture problems that can make nonactors appear ill at ease when they speak in front of crowds.

Like singers, actors take years of voice training in order to learn to control their pitch, volume, and resonance. They must also learn to project their voices night after night without becoming hoarse. In addition, actors may learn a variety of dialects so that they can be cast as a character who speaks with a French, Italian, Southern, or other accent on a moment's notice. In order to learn an accent and to speak clearly, actors often use the **International Phonetic Alphabet (IPA)**. IPA is a system for transcribing the sounds of speech; it is independent of any particular language but applicable to all languages.

With training an actor can build a flexible, dynamic, articulate voice with which to flesh out a character, focus on the sounds and images of the playwright's words, and sound natural show after show while being heard by thousands of people.

Training the Mind

It takes concentration and discipline to perform in the theatre. Actors train their minds to memorize thousands of lines of dialogue in a short period of time, as well as to think on their feet. They must be involved with the needs of their characters but never forget that they are acting in imaginary situations. This duality means that actors must have unwavering focus but also be aware of everything going on around them. In fact, acting may be the ultimate multi-tasking. In order to train their minds, actors use improvisation, game-like acting exercises, and even yoga to help build their self-confidence and ability to concentrate even in the most difficult situations. (See Spotlight "An Actor's Nightmare—Forgetting Lines.")

Acting is simply my way of investigating human nature and having fun at the same time.

Meryl Streep,
Stage and screen actor

The actor's basic problem has remained the same throughout the ages. He is the only artist whose basic raw material is himself; he uses his own muscles, brain, emotions, voice, speech, and gestures to identify with and create another human being.

Lee Strasberg,
Acting teacher

SPOTLIGHT ON   An Actor's Nightmare—Forgetting Lines

When actors forget their lines it is called "going up" or "blanking" and it can be a nightmare. Unlike movie and television where actors only need to memorize a few lines at a time, or have cue cards waiting just off camera to assist them, stage actors must memorize thousands of lines of dialogue and get them right night after night. Some stage actors swear that it is best to memorize just before they go to bed at night, claiming that their subconscious works on the lines while they sleep. Others seek out assistants to "run" their lines with them. In addition, directors occasionally hold special rehearsals where the actors "speed-through" their lines in an attempt to implant the words in their brain.

During rehearsals in the first few weeks the actors carry "the book"—which is the script, whether in booklet form or photocopied pages—with them on stage. But within a week or two the director will instruct the actors to go "off book," and leave the script behind. At this point the stage manager will follow along in the script waiting for the actors to forget a line, or to "go up" on a line. When she goes up, the actor simply says, "line" and the stage manager cues her by speaking the first few words of the dropped line until the actor again takes over. Knowing their lines perfectly is often considered the benchmark of professionalism for actors, but sometimes even the best have difficulty. A hundred years ago theatres often used a prompter, a stagehand who would sit near the stage during the performance, to feed the actors their lines should they go up.

Today prompters are rarely used, but when they are they're often high tech. For example, the Academy Award nominated and five-time Tony Award–winning actress Angela Lansbury once used a tiny wireless earpiece during a performance. But this does not always work. When the stage legend Mary Martin, famous for playing Peter Pan, tried the same trick she found that the earpiece not only picked up the voice of the prompter, but also taxi radios from the street. Actors have also been known to write their problem lines on the stage furniture, or hide it in the brim of their hat, but this is considered highly unprincipled, and in some cases such actors have been fired. Using earpieces and hiding lines are rare exceptions. Far more often actors have no help: if they go up, they are on their own. The stage is a risky business.

William Missouri Downs

When an actor forgets her lines—it's often called "going up" in theatre lingo—it can be a terrifying moment in which time seems to stand still. Here actress Rosie Frater has a momentary lapse in memory.

Gurus and Mentors: Acting Teachers

The need for actor training has given birth to countless acting schools and teachers who each expound particular methods for helping actors tap into their creativity and train their body, mind, and voice. Some of the most famous acting teachers are Stella Adler, Sanford Meisner, Uta Hagen, Michael Chekhov, and

> An actor lives, weeps, laughs on the stage, but as he weeps and laughs he observes his own tears and mirth. It is this double existence, this balance between life and acting that makes for art.
>
> **Konstantin Stanislavsky,**
> Acting teacher and director

Lee Strasberg. Some acting teachers have created actor-training methods for the needs of their own styles of theatre; these teachers include Jerzy Grotowski, Bertolt Brecht, and Tadashi Suzuki. Almost all modern actor-training methods trace their heritage, at least in part, to one of the greatest of all acting teachers, Konstantin Stanislavsky (1863–1938). Often called the father of modern acting, Stanislavsky was the cofounder of the world-famous Moscow Art Theatre. He also wrote several books that revolutionized the world of acting, including *An Actor Prepares* (1926) and *Building a Character* (1949). Throughout his life, Stanislavsky advocated many different approaches for training actors. One of his most famous techniques taught actors to be more natural onstage by recalling their own emotions and transferring those feelings to their characters, thereby finding a detailed emotional identification with the characters they played. This individualized, psychological approach to acting became known as the **Stanislavsky system**, or **method acting**.

In January 1923, members of the Moscow Art Theatre arrived in America for a tour. By the time they left in the spring of 1924, they had changed U.S. acting forever: in their productions even the tiniest spear-carrying role was fully thought out and played as a multidimensional individual with deep motivations. Shortly thereafter, Stanislavsky's ideas about acting would revolutionize the American theatre.

American acting gurus such as Stella Adler (1902–1992) and Lee Strasberg (1899–1982) developed Stanislavsky's methods, and new theatres such as the Group Theatre and the Actors Studio, both in New York City, promoted variations of Stanislavsky's methods. Marlon Brando, James Dean, Rod Steiger, Geraldine Page, Dustin Hoffman, Jane Fonda, Robert De Niro, Paul Newman, Jack Nicholson, Christopher Walken, Gene Wilder, Anne Bancroft, and Al Pacino are some of the actors trained in Stanislavsky's methods at the Actors Studio. Even Marilyn Monroe studied there when she got tired of playing the ditzy-blonde roles that had made her famous. Today, Stanislavsky's influence in the United States still predominates; nearly all actors and actor-training programs borrow from his system. One of the few actor-training methods that does not is the one devised by Tadashi Suzuki. (See the Spotlight "Tadashi Suzuki.")

Acting teacher Konstantin Stanislavsky is best known for his revolutionary approach to acting, which advocated that actors identify emotionally with their characters rather than simply playing "types."

Bettmann/Corbis

Acting Techniques We All Can Use

Acting is not limited to actors. Every day we are confronted with situations that call for acting: The professor looks at us during a lecture and we stifle a yawn and feign interest; we're pulled over for speeding and try to act remorseful; we attend our cousin's wedding and heartily congratulate the bride even though we're convinced she is making a colossal mistake. Although we are told honesty is the best policy, we all learn how to act and hide our emotions at an early age—in fact, acting may even have been one of the reasons for our survival

SPOTLIGHT ON Tadashi Suzuki

Not all modern actor-training methods trace their heritage to Konstantin Stanislavsky. One exception is Tadashi Suzuki's actor-training system, which became popular in the United States in the early 1980s. Suzuki was enthralled with the traditional Japanese forms of theatre, Noh and Kabuki. Noh acting and its more popular version, Kabuki, take years of training and discipline to master. In fact some Japanese Kabuki actors train from childhood. Others learn the art from their fathers, who learned it from their fathers in a process that goes back many generations. Some Kabuki actors in Japan are even declared "national treasures," in the same way that important sites and structures in the United States are put on the National Register of Historic Places. (For more on Noh and Kabuki see Chapter 11.)

Suzuki decided to form his own theatre that would embody the stamina and concentration of traditional Japanese theatre. He began training actors in techniques ranging from modern Western ballet to Indian Kathakali dancing (a traditional form of folk drama) in order to develop their ability to control their body. Suzuki said that his rigorous training was designed to temper and shape the body so that the actor can bring to the stage a "brilliant liveliness" that takes into account the "tiniest details of movement." He wanted to free the actors to express the character in every way possible.

An example of Suzuki's attention to the details of movement is his work with actors' feet. Traditional Japanese plays are performed in tabi, white divided-toe socks that put a focus on the feet and thus make them an important part of the performance. Suzuki developed complex exercises so that actors could discover how their feet could express character. He even named a chapter in his book *The Way of Acting* "The Grammar of the Feet." By putting so much attention on a part of the body that is often ignored by modern Western actors, he teaches actors that there is more to characterization than just circumstances, objectives, and character analysis. In fact, sometimes the most complex understanding of character comes when actors free their body and thus find power and control.

Wu Ching-teng/Xinhua Press/Corbis Wire/Corbis

Acting coach Tadashi Suzuki

as a species. After all, human beings are woefully unprepared compared to other animals; our strength is meager, our skin is thin, our eyesight is below average, and our sense of smell is poor. Prehistoric hunters would have gone hungry if they had been honest with their prey. Instead, they used stealth to sneak up on a deer: they moved downwind, wore a costume made of deerskin, and acted as a member of the herd. By the time the deer knew an impostor, an actor, was in their midst, it was too late. Because acting, on some level, is common to all humans, we're going to look at acting techniques not only from the actor's point of view but also at how nonactors can use these techniques in everyday life.

Changing How You Feel

Actors have known for thousands of years the two basic methods of controlling one's emotions. These methods go by many names, but, for simplicity, we'll label them "outside/in" and "inside/out." If you change yourself physically—in other words, on the outside—you can change how you feel on the inside, and if you change how you feel on the inside, you can change what other people see. The mind and body connection is a two-way street: change your body and you can affect your emotions; change your emotions and you can cause your body to react. For example, when you get ready to take part in a formal wedding, you clean yourself up, put on a fancy dress or tux and, as a result, feel more confident and attractive. The physical adjustments change how you feel.

The same principle is true for people who have makeovers on television shows; often participants say that their new look makes them feel more alive, sexy, or in control. In fact, the purpose of makeovers is not to change people's appearance but to change how they feel—in other words, to make them *act* differently. Changing your appearance is an obvious way to change how you feel, but you can also alter how you feel by manipulating the shape of your body or by, say, changing what you hold in your hand. You feel very different cradling a bouquet of flowers than you do when you clutch a gun. Actors have been doing this for thousands of years. In 400 BCE, a Greek actor named Polus performed the title role in Sophocles's *Electra*. (Men played women's roles in ancient Greek theatre.) In the play, Electra grieves the death of her brother Orestes. In her hand is an urn, which she believes contains his ashes. In order to

The art of acting takes many years of training and experience to master. Pictured here are Jonathan Groff and Alfred Molina in the Tony Award-winning Best Play *Red* by John Logan.

Gina Ferazzi/Los Angeles Times/Getty Images

feel the true, deep emotions of the character and give a convincing performance, Polus put the ashes of his recently deceased son in the urn and held it on stage.

You may also be able to change how you feel by making a small physical change—try it yourself. The next time you feel upset, tired, or bored, force yourself to smile. It may take a few minutes, but if you're sensitive to it, the forced smiling may make you begin to feel better. The opposite is also true. Sometime when you are feeling good, force yourself to frown. After a few minutes, your emotions may follow the physical cue and you may start feeling a little sad.

This outside/in technique can be quite useful for nonactors. For example, several years ago a newly graduated law student was going to interview with a fancy law firm in Switzerland. The first round of interviews was to be held over the phone, and then the company would fly the three final candidates to Switzerland for face-to-face interviews. The new lawyer desperately wanted the job, or at least the free trip to Switzerland. The lawyer sat there in his apartment in tattered shorts and a frayed tee shirt waiting for the phone to ring, but he didn't feel right for the job; even though he passed the bar examination, he didn't feel like a lawyer. So he pulled out his best suit, shirt, and tie. He shaved, showered, and dressed for the interview as if it were to be face-to-face. He made himself feel the part of a capable young law-school graduate. Changing himself physically brought out that part of his personality that was good enough to get the job. During the phone interview, he easily played the part of the competent young lawyer because he felt like one.

An actor can also change himself or herself physically by changing what they are feeling. This technique might be called inside/out. By simply producing an emotion, they change their outward appearance. But it is not as easy as it sounds. How do you harness emotions? One method used to do this is what the acting teacher Stanislavsky called **emotional memory**—also known as sense memory or affective memory. The idea is to think back over a certain incident and remember it well enough to relive the accompanying emotions. This process occurs all the time in daily life; we can get so caught up in telling a story that we relive the emotions. For example, as you are telling a friend about how your significant other dumped you and get to the moment when "good-bye forever" was said, suddenly the tears start flowing again. Your memory causes you to relive the emotions accompanying the event. Acting from the inside out is no different. We have all fallen in love, felt anger, or suffered the death of someone close. These emotions, if they can be recalled and controlled, allow an actor to make genuine connections with how the character feels and responds.

> Emotional power is maybe the most valuable thing that an actor can have.
>
> **Christopher Walken,**
> Stage and screen actor

Nonactors can also make good use of this inside/out technique. Let's go back to our law school graduate who used the outside/in technique for the phone interview. A few weeks later he found himself in Switzerland awaiting the face-to-face interview. As he looked at the elegant brass and leather decor of the lobby, he was overtaken by a sense of inadequacy. He thought he wasn't good enough to work in such a fancy office. So he searched his emotional memory for a time when he felt confident and recalled his game-saving home run in college. He concentrated on the sights and smells of the ball field. He could almost see the stern look on the pitcher's face and then the fastball and hear the thwack of the bat as he connected. Rounding first, he looked up and saw the ball soar over the fence—the fans were going wild and his teammates were running out from the dugout. As he recalled the details of the event, he felt a sense of confidence come over him; soon his breathing calmed and his shoulders relaxed. During the interview, the trepidation returned a few times, but all he had to do was think "thwack!" and he felt, and therefore acted, confident. Was this job applicant lying to his future employers? No. His confident feelings were real, just as an actor's emotions can be real. He simply chose which emotions he was going to play rather than letting his emotions control him. In short, he was a good actor. By the way, he got the job.

An actor working from the outside in, concentrating on physical details, is often said to be using a **technical approach** to acting. An actor working from the inside out, finding the right memories to relive the needed emotions, is often said to be using method acting. Whichever system is used, and actors often use both, the intended result is feeling the needed emotions rather than being dominated by whatever emotions are naturally occurring. In short, acting isn't always *acting*; it is also *being*.

Acting is more than controlling emotions. It is also the ability to see ourselves in someone else's shoes. One of the highest forms of intelligence is the ability to see life from someone else's point of view. An actor playing a part must not only control emotions but also needs to understand life. Sometimes this means seeing life from the point of view of a character that has very different values and perceptions. Two methods actors often use to achieve this empathy are the "magic *if*" and substitution.

Empathy and the Magic If

Sympathy is concern for another person, but empathy is more. **Empathy** is the ability to understand and identify with another's situation, feelings, and motives so completely that you feel you are experiencing that situation and those emotions. In other words, when you feel empathy, you're feeling yourself in the place of another. Empathy is as close as people can come to a shared experience. Many believe that actors cannot truly know a character without empathy. But this doesn't mean that actors must have experienced the death of a loved one before they can understand a character who is in mourning, or face death to understand how a terminal patient feels, or commit a murder in order to know the inner thoughts of a killer. Empathy is also possible when an actor vicariously stands in the shoes of another, builds a vivid image of the situation, and reacts.

Stanislavsky used a technique that he called the **magic *if*** to stimulate the imagination toward empathy. This technique is based on one question: "What would I do *if* I were this character in these circumstances?" The magic *if* is a springboard to the imagination; it allows actors to find similarities between themselves and the character and to explore the resulting emotions and thoughts. Of course, in order for the magic *if* to work, actors must spend many hours researching a character's motivation, situation, and back story. Empathy and the magic *if* can lead to a deep personal understanding or to a flash of tolerance that can be mined for greater insight into the character. Stanislavsky said, "We must study other people and get as close to them emotionally as we can, until sympathy for them is transformed into feelings of our own." In other words, the actor must study the character until the actor has empathy. Needless to say, here is a great lesson that many nonactors—as well as many countries, races, and cultures—could stand to learn.

> The most important thing in acting is honesty. If you can fake that, you've got it made.
>
> ***George Burns,***
> Actor and comedian

Michal Daniel

Substitution

Of course, no actor has the personal experience and understanding to quickly slip into every role. Occasionally, a play demands a character with which the actor has no experience or emotional bond. The solution is sometimes the actor's technique of **substitution**. When actors have little or no emotional bond with a character, they replace the character's emotions with unrelated but personal emotions of their own.

Robert Lewis tells a wonderful story about substitution in his book *Method—Or Madness*. Many years ago, an actor named Ben-Ami was in a Yiddish play in New York City. In one scene, Ben-Ami's character had to act out a scene in which he takes his own life. He stood at the edge of the stage staring into the audience with a revolver to his head. During every performance, sweat would break out on his face and his eyes would seem to pop out of his head. Ben-Ami could keep the audience on the edge of their seats for well over a minute without saying a word and hardly moving, as he debated whether he should pull the trigger. Finally he would say, "Ikh ken nit!" (I can't do it!), and the audience would bring down the house with cries of relief and applause. Night after night, he created such an emotional reality that soon he became the hit of Yiddish theatre. A young actor in the play asked him how he did it, but Ben-Ami said, "It's better for people not to know. . . . It'll spoil the show." On the closing night, Ben-Ami finally

Fully understanding a character such as Richard III requires understanding his circumstances and objectives. What are his given circumstances? Born with a deformity that affects others' perceptions of him, he has learned to manipulate people to gain their sympathy; he is in line for the throne of England, but many are before him. What is his superobjective? He feels he deserves power—and the love that comes with it—as a reward for the bad hand that life has dealt him. This 2004 production of Shakespeare's *Richard III* features Peter Dinklage. Directed by Peter DuBois, Public Theater, New York.

told the young actor how he pulled it off—he used substitution. Here is his explanation:

> My problem with this scene was that I personally could never blow my brains out. I am just not suicidal, and I can't imagine ending my life. So I could never really know how that man was feeling, and I could never play such a person authentically. For weeks I went around trying to think of some parallel in my own life that I could draw on. What situation could I be in where, first of all, I am standing up, I am alone, I am looking straight ahead, and something I feel I must do is making me absolutely terrified, and finally that whatever it is I can't do it? . . . I finally realized that the one thing I hate worse than anything is washing in cold water. So what I'm really doing with that gun to my head is trying to get myself to step into an ice-cold shower.

Ben-Ami found an emotional parallel that worked for him, one that allowed him to play the moment and to some extent find empathy. Through the use of empathy, the magic if, and substitution, it is possible to understand the emotions of another, even a character who is quite unlike yourself.

Plays are often about imperfect characters whose unfulfilled desires lead to inner conflict. In August Wilson's *Fences* (1987), patriarch Troy Maxson feels he has been "fenced in" by discrimination. He once had a shot at playing major-league baseball, but now he toils at a dead-end job. He still dreams of being a ballplayer, but he is well past his prime. His broken dream colors every interaction with his family. In this photo from the original Broadway production, James Earl Jones plays Troy Maxson. Directed by Lloyd Richards, 46th Street Theatre, New York.

1987 Ron Scherl/StageImage/The Image Works

Understanding a Character

Centuries before the invention of psychology, actors were studying people's mental states and the motivations behind their behavior; playing a convincing character requires the ability to analyze personality. One key to analyzing stage characters is to treat them as if they were real people. Understanding character can also be of great help to nonactors; compassion can make our jobs and relationships more fulfilling. One way to start analyzing a character is to make a list of the character's traits by answering a series of questions about general, physical, sociological, and psychological traits:

General Information

What is the character's education?

What is the character's career or occupation?

What is the character's financial situation?

What are the character's talents?

What are the character's hobbies?

What are the character's tastes?

Physical Traits

What is the character's age and sex?

What is the character's appearance?

What does the character wear?

What is the character's health status?

What are the character's mannerisms?

Sociological Traits

What is the character's nationality?

What is the character's religion?

What is the character's class or status?

What are the character's family relationships?

What are the character's political views?

Psychological Traits

What is the character's temperament?

What kind of childhood did the character have?

What are the character's hopes and ambitions?

What are the character's disappointments?

What are the character's fears and phobias?

What are the character's inhibitions?

What are the character's obsessions?

What are the character's superstitions?

What are the character's morals and philosophy of life?

This list of questions could go on for pages, but every single aspect of a character is too much for an actor, or a psychologist for that matter, to totally comprehend. A simpler method is to look at basic elements such as these: circumstances and objectives, public and personal sides, internal conflicts and character flaws, and motivation.

Circumstances and Objectives

When trying to analyze characters, or people for that matter, a good place to start is with the circumstances of their life: their situation, their problems, and the limits life has placed on them. Actors often call this approach to character analysis the **given circumstances**. It can include broad topics such as upbringing, religion, and social standing, but it can also include what happened to the character the moment before he or she entered the stage. For example, if the character has been fighting with a spouse, that particular given circumstance will certainly affect the character's emotional state and behaviors, such as tone of voice.

Next, it is important to understand the character's objective: what does he or she desire? Because characters may desire many things during the course of a play, a good actor often singles out the most important want, or the driving force that governs the character's actions throughout the entire play. This driving force is called the character's **superobjective**. For example, the character of Hamlet has many objectives during the course of Shakespeare's great tragedy—he wants to find his father's killer, he wants justice—but his superobjective, at least according to Stanislavsky, is to find God. Knowing the superobjective and given circumstances can take you a long way toward understanding a stage character, another person, or even yourself.

Public and Personal Images

There are two ways to view a character—or a person. One is from the public side, or what other people see. The second is from the personal side, or how we see ourselves. For example, from the outside, or the public image, a character might be described as:

- Irritating
- Perfectionist
- Hypercritical
- Anxious
- Work-centered
- Domineering
- Fault-finding

You may recognize this description. It's the classic definition of an obsessive-compulsive. Here is another description:

- Fears disapproval
- Self-doubting
- Anticipates catastrophe

- Wants to be admired for ability
- Feels wounded when others don't value helpful hints
- Feels there is a right way and a wrong way
- Rarely feels support

Although this second set of characteristics sounds completely different, it is also a description of an obsessive-compulsive, but viewed from the inside, the personal image. To develop a strong, unique character, an actor must always look from both the public and personal images. How people or characters perceive themselves and how others perceive them is seldom harmonious and often results in conflict. This discrepancy between the personal and public views happens because stage characters, like people, have limited self-awareness. To make this point, playwright Arthur Miller used the story of *Oedipus*, the ancient Greek tragedy about a king who gouges out his eyes when he discovers he has unknowingly killed his father and married his mother (for more on *Oedipus*, see Part 3). If Oedipus had more self-awareness, he would have seen that "he was not really to blame for having cohabited with his mother, since neither he nor anyone else knew she was his mother. He would have decided to divorce her, provide for their children, firmly resolve to investigate the family background of his next wife, and thus deprive us of a very fine play." Because Oedipus doesn't have clear, perfect knowledge of himself, discovery, growth, and a great tragedy are all possible. Limited self-awareness often causes some sort of flaw, vice, error in judgment, or internal conflict.

Inner Conflicts and Character Flaws

Another way to understand a character is to identify internal conflicts and character flaws. Powerful characters are often in conflict not only with others but also with themselves. This **inner conflict** can be a ghost from the past or some sort of unfinished business that is so compelling that it handicaps the character until it is confronted. In *Hamlet*, there is a literal ghost—the ghost of Hamlet's father. But Hamlet is also torn by the conflicts between his desire to seek revenge, his gentle nature, and his need to find an elusive God. A character's inner conflict can be an unresolved disagreement, a lost opportunity, a sense of inadequacy, or some other debilitating factor that preoccupies the character over the course of the play until he or she is able to put it to rest.

If this inner conflict is powerful enough to affect the character's good judgment and cause the character to make unfortunate choices, then it's a **character flaw**, sometimes called a **fatal flaw** or **tragic flaw**. This personality imperfection cripples the character and prevents him from achieving his superobjective. Knowing a character's inner conflicts and flaws, as well as the given circumstances, superobjective, and public and personal images, will take you a long way toward understanding one of the most defining elements of character: motivation.

Motivation

Motivation is the reason a character takes a particular action. It is embodied in the character's conscious or subconscious personality. It can come from some dark part of the character's past or simply be the desire to do the right thing.

> Actors are responsible to the people we play. I don't label or judge. I just play them as honestly and expressively and creatively as I can, in the hope that people who ordinarily turn their heads in disgust instead think, "What I thought I'd feel about that guy, I don't totally feel right now."
>
> ***Philip Seymour Hoffman,***
> Stage and screen actor

> I think very few people are interested in the craft of acting, which is actually to demask, to reveal what it is to be human.
>
> ***Cate Blanchett,***
> Stage and screen actor

Wherever they come from, the motivations of characters are seldom complicated; the character may be complicated and the motivation may be hidden, but once it appears, it can usually be stated in a single sentence. For example, Juliet's motivation is that she is in love with Romeo and will do anything to be with him.

The key to understanding a character's motivation is to look at it from the character's point of view. A well-drawn character is always attempting to change negatives into positives—from his or her perspective. Characters, like people, may be misguided, even totally wrong, but they seldom see their motivations or the resulting actions as negative or evil. For example, if an actor studying the character of a father who abandons his child concludes that the father is "hateful" and "uncaring," he is not doing his homework. "Hateful" and "uncaring" are negative ideas coming from an external image and lead to a shallow interpretation of the father's motivations. Instead, the actor must find the positive motivation, the character's own reasons, for doing such a terrible thing as abandoning a child. After deeper analysis, the actor may discover that the father must think his actions are best for the child—perhaps he cannot provide for the child or he sees himself as too emotionally unbalanced to care for him or her. These would be reasons for thinking that abandoning the child would be best for the child; they are examples of positive motivations. A character can commit an evil act based on a strong "positive" motive. To truly understand a character, or another human being, you must find their positive motivations. Using your own morals or values to judge a character or a person seldom leads to true understanding.

These are just a few ways that actors analyze a character in order to gain a greater understanding. Good acting is far more than simple imitation. It is the ability to understand why characters think what they think, feel what they feel, and do what they do. Only when an actor can see life from someone else's point of view can he or she play a life on stage convincingly.

The Actor's Life

Like professional sports, acting is a business and, like athletes, actors need agents to help them find jobs, promote their careers, and negotiate contracts. There are also several labor unions that fight for actors' rights, including fair wages and safe working conditions. The union that represents stage actors is the **Actors' Equity Association**, often shortened to "Actors' Equity" or simply "Equity." The **Screen Actors Guild (SAG)** represents movie and television actors, and the **American Federation of Television and Radio Artists (AFTRA)**, which is affiliated with the AFL-CIO, represents talk-show hosts as well as announcers, singers, disc jockeys, newscasters, sportscasters, and even stunt people. Many actors join all three unions because they never know which medium their next job may come from.

The general public often assumes that actors are highly paid. This certainly can be true for big screen and television stars, who can make millions a year. But fat paychecks are the exception; the vast majority of actors take home very little money for their efforts. There is so little money to be made at acting that a majority of actors do something in addition to acting to make ends meet—they are servers, administrative assistants, and delivery people. They take jobs that allow for a flexible schedule so they can attend acting classes and go to auditions. Their intermittent employment and lack of job security can make mortgages, insurance, and credit cards difficult to obtain.

Once actors land a job, seldom does it last more than a few weeks or months, after which they are back on the street auditioning for a new job. Competition at these auditions is fierce. There can be dozens if not hundreds of actors battling for the same part. Acting jobs are so scarce that Actors' Equity has created the **Equity waiver**, a loophole that allows its members to work for free in small productions. There are so few paying jobs that many actors act for free in order to sharpen their skills and in the hope of being discovered. Equity-waiver productions have to meet many qualifications. For example, the theatre must be fully insured, the play cannot have a long run, and the theatre must have fewer than 100 seats. As a result, many Equity-waiver theatres have 99 seats.

Auditions

There are as many types of auditions as there are plays, theatres, and directors. A common type of audition is the **cattle call**, also known as the "open call." Call is theatre lingo for "audition." During a cattle call, actors are generally given only about one minute to strut their stuff. If the director is impressed, the actor's name is placed on a **callback list** and allowed to come back for a second and perhaps a third and fourth audition as each callback narrows the field of candidates. Other auditions consist of **cold readings** of a script; in other words, the actors are not given a chance to prepare. For other auditions, actors can bring prepared scenes or monologues, or they might be asked to improvise, dance, or sing. The director can take the actors through a myriad of tests to look for vocal clarity, energy, stage presence, talent, and personal chemistry. Auditions are so important that some actors take more classes on how to audition than on how to act.

Rehearsals

Once the actors are cast in a play, they begin rehearsals. Normally rehearsals last from three to five weeks, but there are exceptions. Rehearsals for complex or experimental plays can last much longer—Stanislavsky once rehearsed a play for nearly a year—whereas rehearsals for a simple summer-stock play might be crammed into one week. However long the rehearsal process is, actors seldom rehearse on the stage until just a few days before a play opens. Most rehearsals take place in a rehearsal hall, which is an empty room approximately the same size as the stage. In the rehearsal hall, actors must use their creative

Escada/Getty Images Entertainment/Getty Images

Few actors make a living at their art. In fact, 95 percent of actors must supplement their income by taking second jobs. Waiting tables is popular because the hours are often flexible, enabling actors to attend auditions and rehearsals.

Auditioning for a play can be stressful. An actor might be asked to cold read from the script, present prepared monologues, or sing and dance. The process can take days, and more often than not ends in failure for the actor. But for those lucky few who make it, a life in the theatre can be very rewarding.

Emmanuel Faure/The Image Bank/GettyImages

imaginations because there is no finished set. They have to use simple rehearsal furniture and props. A plain folding chair can represent a grand throne, or a simple piece of wood may stand in for a king's jeweled staff. Costumes aren't generally ready until just a few days before the play opens.

Here is an approximately chronological list of the kinds of rehearsals:

- **Table work:** Some directors start rehearsals by having the cast read aloud through the play while seated around a table. After the reading, the director and actors discuss their thoughts about the characters and motivations and about the play in general. Sometimes the director invites the designers to the first table reading to make presentations about what the set, lights, and costumes will look like.

- **Blocking rehearsals:** This is a series of rehearsals during which the director and actors work out the basic movements, a process that is called "blocking."

- **General working rehearsals:** During these rehearsals the director and actors work on individual scenes and concentrate on understanding the characters' motivations, emotions, and personalities.

- **Special rehearsals:** If a play has fight scenes, musical numbers, or dance numbers, or if the characters have dialects, the director can call special rehearsals for each.

- **Off-book rehearsal:** During this rehearsal, the actors must have their lines memorized. It's called "off book" because the actors no longer have the script, or the "book," on stage with them.

- **Run-throughs:** During these rehearsals, the actors go through the entire play from beginning to end with as few interruptions as possible. A run-through gives the actors a feel for how the play works as a whole.

- **Tech rehearsals:** By this point, rehearsals have moved from the rehearsal hall to the stage. During tech (short for *technical*) rehearsals, the lights, sounds, props, and set are added.

- **Dress rehearsals:** These are the final rehearsals, only a few days before the play opens, when the costumes and makeup are added.

- **Final dress rehearsal:** This is the last rehearsal before an audience is invited. Ideally, the play is run as if it were a real performance.

Performances

After the opening night, the actors settle in for the run of the play. A short run can be just a few performances, as is often the case with smaller theatres and university and community theatres; a long run can last for months or even years, as is the case in big Broadway theatres. In the professional theatre, plays are traditionally performed six nights a week. Actors may also have one or two matinee performances a week; on those days, they face the exhausting task of performing the play twice in one day. The only day actors have free is Monday, when theatres are generally closed. In theatre lingo, Mondays or any day a theatre closed is called a **dark night**.

Musicals require dozens of special rehearsals for the actors to learn their parts. Here, musical director Robert Bass works with actors Dwayne Croft and Emily Pulley.

Damon Winter/The New York Times/Redux Pictures

Curtain Call

Perhaps the ability to act is in our genes. Children seem to pick the talent up quite early and practice it often. As adults, where would teachers, doctors, lawyers, salespeople, clerics, administrative assistants, servers, or, indeed, politicians be if they could not act? American playwright Arthur Miller said in *American Playhouse: On Politics and the Art of Acting*, "The fact is that acting is inevitable as soon as we walk out our front doors and into society."

But what happens when acting takes over every aspect of our lives? Some believe that with the invention of television we are so inundated with constant acting that we know few sincere moments. Miller points out that one of the oddest things about the lives of contemporary individuals is that today, as never before in human history, we are surrounded by acting. He said that "when one is surrounded by such a roiling mass of consciously contrived performances it gets harder and harder to locate reality. . . ." At its most innocent, acting is found in a child's game of make-believe; at its most important it's an instrument of survival; at its most sinister it is all the lies we tell each other and ourselves.

SUMMARY

MindTap®

Test your knowledge with online printable flashcards and online quizzing.

It may look easy, but becoming an actor takes dedication and years of training. That training usually begins at a conservatory, a university, or a college, but most actors go on to train for years after that in order to perfect their voice, body, and mind, or what they call their "instrument." The need for actor training has led to many acting schools and teachers who teach various acting systems. Most of these systems trace their heritage to the father of modern acting, Konstantin Stanislavsky, the founder of the Moscow Art Theatre and the Stanislavsky system, or what is often called method acting. Stanislavsky taught his actors to recall their emotions and then transfer those feelings to their characters in order to find a detailed emotional identification with them.

Actors use many techniques that can be useful to nonactors. These include outside/in acting, or changing physically in order to change emotions, and inside/out acting, or changing emotions in order to change physically. Outside/in acting is often referred to as the technical approach. Inside/out acting is often referred to as method acting. Other techniques actors use are empathy, the magic *if*, and substitution. In order to understand the characters they play, actors study the character's physical, sociological, and psychological traits. They also examine the character's public and personal images and the character's inner conflicts, flaws, and motivation.

An actor's life can be full of auditions, rehearsals, and performances. But it is also full of unemployment because paying acting jobs are scarce. The vast majority of actors work second jobs to make ends meet. Even when they find a job, they aren't always well paid. In order to protect their interests, performers have formed three unions to help win fair wages and safe working conditions: Actors' Equity, the Screen Actors Guild, and the American Federation of Television and Radio Artists.

KEY TERMS

Actors' Equity Association *142*

American Federation
of Television and Radio Artists
(AFTRA) *142*

BFA (Bachelor of Fine Arts) *129*

Blocking rehearsal *144*

Callback list *143*

Cattle call *143*

Character flaw *141*

Cold reading *143*

Dark night *145*

Dress rehearsal *145*

Emotional memory *135*

Empathy *136*

Equity waiver *143*

Fatal flaw *141*

Final dress rehearsal *145*

General working rehearsal *144*

Given circumstances *140*

Inner conflict *141*

International Phonetic Alphabet
(IPA) *130*

Magic *if* *136*

Method acting *132*

MFA (Master of Fine
Arts) *129*

Motivation *141*

Off-book rehearsal *145*

Run-through *145*

Screen Actors Guild (SAG) *142*

Special rehearsal *145*

Stanislavsky system *132*

Substitution *137*

Superobjective *140*

Table work *144*

Technical approach *136*

Tech rehearsal *145*

Tragic flaw *141*

Chapter 8

THE ART OF DIRECTING

The director of a play is a jack-of-all-trades, knowledgeable in acting, design and script analysis. Pictured are Corinne Landy, Hannah Kipp and Dustin Petrillo in the musical comedy *Angry Psycho Princesses*. Directed by Sean Warren Stone, William Missouri Downs and Lou Anne Wright.

William Missouri Downs/UW Archive

Outline

MindTap®

Start with a quick warm-up activity and review the chapter's learning objectives.

American playwright Tennessee Williams said that a play script is only the "shadow of a play and not even a clear shadow of it. . . . The printed script is hardly more than an architect's blueprint of a house not yet built." The **director** turns the printed script, the blueprint, into a production. To do this, the director must have the artistic vision and the talent to coordinate dozens of theatre artists, technicians, and other personnel to work toward that vision with a singleness of purpose. This coordination allows a production to speak with the unique voice of an individual artist. The director also represents the audience members, because the director frames each moment of the play by deciding exactly what the audience will see. In order to turn these decisions into reality, the director must guide and persuade every member of the theatre ensemble and oversee all the artistic and technical aspects of the production. The director must synthesize the work of the playwright, the designers, and the performers into a unique theatrical event.

Although many major universities offer a Master of Fine Arts in directing, most directors start their theatre career as an actor, designer, playwright, choreographer, or critic. For example, one of America's most renowned directors, Elia Kazan, who directed the first production of Arthur Miller's *Death of a Salesman* as well as such great films as *On the Waterfront*, was an actor long before he started directing. Similarly, Robert Brustein, founder of both the Yale Repertory and American Repertory Theatres, started as a drama critic; Harold Prince, director of such Broadway productions as *The Kiss of the Spider Woman* and *The Phantom of the Opera*, was a producer; and Susan Stroman, director of the Broadway smash hit *The Producers*, began as a choreographer. Directors come from these many backgrounds because directing takes many talents. Directors must know how to inspire and coach actors, they must know how to communicate complex aesthetic ideas to designers, and they must understand the playwriting process. Directors must also know how to create a cohesive, pleasant working environment. Moreover, an effective director has the ability not only to lead but also to inspire everyone involved with the play to be creative, to make decisions, and to add their talents to the production. The director must have the sensitivity of an artist, the fortitude of a good teacher, and the skills of an efficiency expert. (See Spotlight "The Life of a Director: Tisa Chang.") And yet, as important as directors are to the process today, they are relatively new to the history of the theatre.

> It's our job to create an atmosphere of creativity that will stimulate the best work from the actor, to be a mirror, tell them what they are doing and what we see. Both for the playwright and for the actor, the director is the surrogate audience until the actual audience arrives.
>
> **Marshall Mason,**
> Director

The Birth of Directors

For thousands of years, the role of director was not filled by a single person. The director's functions were simply tacked on to the duties of playwrights and actors. In ancient Greece, around 400 BCE, playwrights staged the plays they wrote. The term for these playwright-directors was **didaskalos**, or "teacher," because they not only wrote the play but also instructed the performers and advised the designers and technicians. Two thousand years later, in Shakespeare's day, directing was quite simple, at least compared with today. Elizabethan plays were staged outdoors in the midday sun, so there was no need for a lighting designer. The actors wore costumes appropriate to their character's station and profession, but no one took into account the overall look or historical accuracy, so there was little need for a costume designer. And the stage set was virtually the same for every play, so there was no need for a set designer. Consequently, there was little need for a director to coordinate the designs. Playwright Ben Jonson, Shakespeare's contemporary, complained

MindTap

Read, highlight, and take notes online.

SPOTLIGHT ON The Life of a Director: Tisa Chang

Born in China, Tisa Chang grew up in New York City, where as a child she learned to play piano and perform traditional Chinese dances and ballet. She attended the High School of Performing Arts and Barnard College at Columbia University. Soon she was dancing and acting in successful Broadway plays, including *Pacific Overtures*, *The Basic Training of Pavlo Hummel*, and *Lovely Ladies*. Then she started working at the Chinese Theater Group at La MaMa, an experimental theatre group in the East Village neighborhood of Manhattan, where she staged a bilingual adaptation of Shakespeare's *A Midsummer Night's Dream* set in China in 1000 BCE.

In 1977, she founded the Pan Asian Repertory Theatre in New York City. The goals of the Pan Asian Rep are to celebrate professional Asian American artists and to present "Asian American masterpieces, adaptations of American classics, and . . . new work by Asian American writers, which reflect[s] the evolution of Asians in America." The Pan Asian Rep fast became one of the most influential Asian American theatres. Other Asian theatres in the United States include the East West Players in Los Angeles and The National Asian American Theater Company in New York.

Chang has directed intercultural productions such as *Return of the Phoenix*, which was adapted from the Peking Opera, as well as a Shogun *Macbeth*, Cambodian and Tibetan plays, and what Chang calls "the canon of Asian-American classics." "Beyond language and playwriting as the source . . . our theatrical production relies a great deal on the articulation. . . . We're talking about incorporating direction and design [that can] absolutely alter a script," says Chang. "I think that I would probably never direct a two-person play where people are sitting on chairs and talk to each other and expound. . . . I really love the magic and the latitude that we can have with direction and design and music and poetry."

About her directing style Chang says, "I don't like directors who over-impose or superimpose things onto a play. I just think all we [as directors] are doing is making the play clear and engaging." One of Chang's latest projects was to direct Elizabeth Wong's *China Doll*, a play that tells the life story of Anna May Wong (1905–1961), a Chinese American actress who starred in such early Hollywood movies as *The Thief of Bagdad* with Douglas Fairbanks, Sr., and *Shanghai Express* with Marlene Dietrich. Wong acted in Hollywood at a time when the vast majority of Asian roles were played by white stars in "yellowface." She spent her life trying to achieve stardom as she fought against Hollywood stereotypes. Chang, whose own work is often geared toward challenging stereotypes, has said, "I think the best theatre has a cohesive concept and a solid ensemble, and speaks to people on many different levels. And hopefully, the audience members leave the theatre thinking about what they saw."

Corky Lee/Courtesy of the Pan Asian Repertory Theatre

Director Tisa Chang

that directing a play was an exhausting job for which one did little more than prompt actors and yell at musicians. The job was so trivial that programs of the day have no mention of the position. When the first indoor theatres were built, they were lit with candles. The lighting was so inadequate that the actors would just try to find the brightest spot to stand in when the time came to speak their lines. Most of the directing at that time was done by an actor-manager, often the play's star, who told the other actors where to stand so that he could be seen in the best light.

The modern concept of a director did not come about until the nineteenth century, when a new genre of theatre called *realism* became popular. Realism called for psychologically complex characters, honest acting, and natural-looking sets. Realism also played off the worldwide scientific, social, and philosophical movements of the day. At the end of the century came the invention of electric lights, which made sophisticated lighting effects possible. Theatre was becoming a complex illusion, so there was a need for one person, a master coordinator, to oversee the various elements of production.

Georg II, the Duke of Saxe-Meiningen (1826–1914), the ruler of a small German state, is often credited as the first modern director. Being a wealthy monarch gave him the freedom and the resources to construct his own theatre and to organize and direct a resident company of actors and other artists. He was in a total leadership position, for he was the actors' literal ruler as well as their director—a power, no doubt, some modern directors wish they had. Duke Georg organized his actors, his subjects, into an ensemble in which there were no stars. He insisted on long rehearsal periods and ordered his actors to explore every psychological aspect of their characters. He also made many advances in staging. His crowd scenes were famous for looking like paintings, and his costumes, scenery, and props were fully integrated and authentic. Once he even used a real stuffed horse on stage in order to make a battle scene waged among fallen horses seem more real. One critic said that his production of Shakespeare's *Julius Caesar* was so real and so well directed that "one could believe that one was actually present at the beginning of the revolution."

From 1874 to 1890, the duke and his acting company toured Europe and gave more than 2,600 performances of 41 plays. In the audience for one of these productions was Russian acting teacher Konstantin Stanislavsky (see Chapter 7). So impressed was Stanislavsky by the duke's staging that he used many of his directing techniques at the new **Moscow Art Theatre**. When Stanislavsky directed, he, like the duke, was concerned with every detail of the production, from the accuracy of props to the timing of special effects such as birdcalls and cricket chirps. He made copious notes about the characters, as well as detailed diagrams of the actors' movements. He also insisted on a rehearsal process that lasted for months rather than

The director is in charge of everything the audience sees. Here director Julie Taymor directs an actor during a rehearsal of the *Lion King* at Pretoria's National Theater in Pretoria, South Africa. Ms. Taymor is the first woman to win the Tony Award for directing a musical.

AP Images/Jerome Delay

days or weeks, which was the norm for most theatre in that day. Like the duke, he spent a long time in rehearsals for even the smallest bit parts.

These early directors created the modern idea of the director as the person who interprets, organizes, and coordinates all the elements of a play into a meaningful, integrated whole. Today, directors are an indispensable part of the theatre ensemble. In Hollywood, movie directors have become so important that theirs is always the final name in the credits before the movie begins. In the theatre they receive top credit in the program—only the playwright is listed higher.

Before Rehearsals Begin

The director's job can be split in two phases: pre-rehearsal and rehearsal. Pre-rehearsal might be called the "paper phase" of the job because everything is on paper: designs drawn on paper, scripts written on paper, research in books, and notations in notebooks. During the paper phase, the director must discover what the play means and how the theatre ensemble might convey that meaning to the audience. The paper phase often lasts longer than the rehearsal phase. The paper phase includes script analysis, structural analysis, concept meetings, production meetings, and casting.

It All Starts with the Script

The director's pre-rehearsal preparation begins with script analysis. Although studying a play can be as simple as using Goethe's play-analysis formula (see Chapter 4), in order to direct a play, every character and every word of the script must be scrutinized. The director's analysis might include working with the playwright (if the playwright is alive and available) as well as spending countless hours rereading the script, and researching the history and criticism of the play. The director's intensive analysis includes finding the script's strengths and weaknesses. For example, if a particular character is underdeveloped, the director may note that a particularly strong actor is needed to flesh out that part. The director must understand each character's motivations, desires, and given circumstances (see Chapter 7) as well as the play's mood and atmosphere and the moral and philosophical statements made by the playwright.

However, a director's analysis does not end with the script. In order to have a comprehensive understanding, a director must research previous productions—for it is a good idea to know how other directors have staged the play—and what the critics said about them. The director may also study the playwright's life. Often playwrights write about personal events and emotions, so knowing about the playwright can lead to a greater understanding of the play. The play's location, period, and historical background must also be carefully investigated, including the political trends and the social and moral codes that were in effect when the play was written.

Not doing this research can lead directors to mistaken interpretations of the characters. For example, a director who has not done the historical research might assume that Hedda in Henrik Ibsen's *Hedda Gabler* (1890) is a bit of a spinster. After all, she is in her mid- to late twenties and only recently married. But research would reveal that 25 was the average age of marriage for women in 1890 Norway. Without the research, the director might read into the character something the playwright never intended. This little bit of investigation could change the director's concept of Hedda, which in turn would affect the director's casting and staging decisions.

All this script analysis and research can be very time-consuming. For example, when Konstantin Stanislavsky directed Anton Chekhov's *The Seagull,* he spent a month and a half alone in a tower in the Ukraine studying. For help with the research process, some directors work with a **dramaturg**, a literary advisor and theatre-history expert. Dramaturgs can assist a director or theatre company in many ways. They can aid with the selection of plays, work with the playwright to help fully realize the script, and research the historical or literary background of a play in order to help directors, designers, and actors better understand the text. Armed with a strong background in theatre history, literature, and criticism, the dramaturg can serve as an information resource or as an integral part of the director's decision making. The dramaturg can make sure that the director's concepts and style stay within the standards of the theatre or are consistent with the ideas a theatre company wishes to express in a particular season of plays. Although common in other parts of the world, dramaturgs are still rather rare in U.S. theatre. Some directors feel that dramaturgs are an important part of the process, but others feel that what dramaturgs do is really part of the director's job. (For more on dramaturgy, see Chapter 5.)

Structural Analysis

While accumulating social, historical, and critical knowledge of the play, the director also studies the script's structure. This analysis often includes all the elements covered in Chapter 6, such as theme, characters, language, and plot, but it can also lead to the study of the smallest structural units within a play: french scenes and beats.

A **french scene** begins whenever a character enters or exits and continues until the next entrance or exit. For example, let's say a father and daughter are arguing and then Mom enters. Mom's entrance marks the beginning of a new french scene. If the father or mother or daughter exits, a new french scene begins. The length of each french scene varies, as does the number of french scenes within a play, act, or scene. A fast-paced farce may have dozens, but a play with no entrances or exits has only one. The idea of french scenes originated in, of course, France, when the printing press was still a novelty and quite expensive. To cut costs, actors were given only the pages on which they had lines rather than the full script. The most cost-efficient way of dividing a play was from one entrance or exit to the next entrance or exit. Although this did little to help the actors with character analysis and continuity, it did save a few precious pages. If you ever read a French neoclassical tragedy such as *Phaedra*, you'll notice that the script is split into french scenes. However, this antiquated method of dividing a play would have been long forgotten had it not been such a help in playwriting and directing. Because a french scene deals with only certain characters at a particular point in the play, it divides a play into small, workable units. The director treats each french scene as a mini-play that has the structural elements of a full play: beginning, middle, and end. With each entrance or exit, the play changes, the characters' attitudes shift, and the story moves forward.

A **beat** is the next smaller structural unit; it is a single unit of thought. It's a section of dialogue about a particular subject or idea. A change in subject or idea means the beginning of a new beat. A beat can be anywhere from a single word to several pages long. Beats are similar to paragraphs in other kinds of writing, but they are not signaled by indentations or any other typographical device. As an illustration, the

Patricia Switzer

Beats and french scenes combine to form scenes and acts. For example, in the Tony Award–winning play *Equus*, a psychiatrist attempts to treat a young man who has a pathological fixation on horses. This play has hundreds of beats, dozens of french scenes but only 35 scenes and 2 acts. The photo is from a production staged by the National Theatre Conservatory.

following scene is divided into beats—but remember, beats are never indicated in a real script. This scene, which has four beats, is about a woman who has returned home to take her elderly father to the hospital for what she thinks is a hernia operation.

BEAT ONE

DARLA: We gotta go. Where is she?
HENRY: Moonpie? She's out.
DARLA: Wish you wouldn't do that. Cats that wander don't live as long. How long she been missin'?
HENRY: She's not missin'. She killed a warbler two hours ago. Feathers everywhere.
DARLA: *(yelling out the window)*: Moonpie! Moonpiiiie!
HENRY: Absolute carnage. Apocalypse in the back-yard. So she can't be far.
DARLA: M. P.! M. Peeee!
HENRY: If the cat don't know its name, what the hell makes you think it'd know its initials?

BEAT TWO

DARLA: You're feelin' better.
HENRY: Me? I feel terrible.
DARLA: Where the blazes is a double hernia anyway?
HENRY: I'd show you, but I'd be arrested.
DARLA: Are you sure it's a hernia?
HENRY: What do I know; pain is pain.

BEAT THREE

HENRY: I cancelled the papers and I'm havin' my mail forwarded to you.
DARLA: Why can't Mom pick up your mail?
HENRY: Your mother'll just lose it. Besides I think she sneaks over here and opens my mail. Tries to find out if I got a lover. I can't prove anything, but my Sears bill is missin'.
DARLA: I can only stay two days. I think it'd be better if she picked up your mail. She could read it to you in the hospital.

BEAT FOUR

HENRY: She can't read my mail.
DARLA: Why not?
HENRY: She had her cataract surgery.
DARLA: What? When? *(dialing the phone)* Why didn't you tell me?!
HENRY: I told her not to dilly dally. Told her, one eye at a time. Did she listen? Course not.
DARLA: She never lets it ring more than twice.

HENRY:	Waited too long, so she had to get both eyes done at once. Got some nurse with her twenty-four hours a day.
DARLA:	Did you send flowers?
HENRY:	Why should I? She can't see 'em.
DARLA:	Daddy, you should've told me.
HENRY:	She's fine. Blind but fine. Got two huge silver patches on her face. Makes her look like some kinda massive gnat.

The word *beat* is misleading. It usually refers to a rhythmical unit. So why do theatre people use the word *beat* instead of *unit* or *section*? The explanation dates from the time when the disciples of Stanislavsky came to the United States to teach. Americans were supposedly confused by the Russians' thick accents, so they mistook the word *bit* for *beat*. If you say, "First you must split the play into little bits" with a Russian accent, you'll find some truth to this theory. Whether it's true or not, looking at "beats" as "bits" makes sense. A director, as well as actors and playwrights, divides dialogue into bits/beats to understand moment-by-moment changes in the characters' actions, conflicts, and motivations. This process is seldom as obvious as shown in Table 8.1, because directors often go through this process subconsciously, but the table illustrates how each beat reveals the moment's action, conflict, and motivation. Try it yourself—take a scene or a french scene from your favorite play and break it into beats.

Table 8.1 Action, conflict, and motivation beat by beat

BEAT	ACTION	CONFLICT	MOTIVATION
1	Darla must find the cat before she locks up the house and takes her father to the hospital.	Her elderly father doesn't seem to care about the cat or the hospital.	Darla's parents are divorced, so she feels she must take care of them, including little details like the cat.
2	Darla asks her father about why he's going into the hospital.	He doesn't want to tell her the truth about his medical condition. He's dying.	Henry feels that a real man doesn't complain. Darla feels that real men are too secretive.
3	Darla and Henry disagree about who will pick up his mail.	Darla wants her parents to get back together and will do anything to make them have contact. Henry doesn't want to talk about his medical condition, so he changes the subject.	Darla feels that her parents are lonely and need each other. Besides, she wants some time for herself. Henry knows he has cancer and doesn't want anyone to know.
4	Darla learns that her mother is also in the hospital.	Darla must find out about her mother. She feels guilty because she hasn't called her in a few days. Henry is thrilled that the attention is off him.	Darla loves her mother, perhaps more than she loves her father. Henry wants Darla to know that there is no chance of his getting back together with her mother.

In doing so, you will find a deeper understanding of how the play was constructed and learn how the scene works moment by moment, just as a director does.

The Production Concept

After spending weeks and even months researching and analyzing a script, the director gains a deep understanding of all the elements of the play. The next step is to devise a **production concept**. This is the metaphor, thematic idea, symbol, or allegory that will be central to the whole production. A director without a production concept is like a driver without a road map. However, for all the work that goes into it, the production concept is usually quite simple. For example, a director working on Ibsen's *A Doll's House*, a play about a woman who breaks free of her domineering husband, could envision the lead character, Nora, as a woman trapped in a beautiful birdcage. During the course of the play, Nora could come to see this birdcage as a terrible dungeon. With this concept, the director would be making a statement about how we allow ourselves to be trapped by our lives, seldom questioning our premises, rarely realizing that we are entangled by our own limited point of view. Once the director has a concept, it must be communicated to the designers through a series of production meetings. During these meetings the designers and director also discuss the play's philosophy, interpretation, theme, physical demands, history, and style. Between meetings, the designers attempt to realize the director's production concept by drawing sketches of possible sets, costumes, and other designs. There can be dozens of production meetings held over a period of weeks, even months, before final designs are agreed upon. Only after the homework and production meetings are done is the director ready to cast the play and begin rehearsals. (For more on production concepts and meetings, see Chapter 9.)

Casting the Right Actors

Casting the right actors is critical for the success of a play. A common theatre adage is that 90 percent of directing is casting. In fact casting is so important that some directors hire **casting directors**, who specialize in finding the right actor to fit the part—a practice that is common with Hollywood movies.

Actors are usually hired because they are stars and can draw an audience or because they have the talent to play the role, or a combination of the two. There is no fairness-in-casting law. Directors have the right to cast whomever they feel is the best person for the job; they don't have to give everyone a fair chance.

Directors can **cast to type**, or hire an actor who physically matches the role. In other words, if they are looking for a 70-year-old Italian mother, they cast someone who looks just like, or is, a 70-year-old Italian mother. Casting to type can also mean finding an actor who has a deep understanding of the character's emotions and motivations. Directors can also **cast against type**, or deliberately cast actors who are the exact opposite of, or very different

What does the director do? He bears to the preparation of a play much the same relation as an orchestra conductor to the rehearsal of a symphony. But the symphony is performed by the conductor with each member of the orchestra playing under his leadership. He does not play the leading part. He does more. He interprets, shapes, guides, inspires the entire performance.

Tyrone Guthrie, Director

from, what is expected. For example, the director might choose to cast an older-than-usual pair as the lovers in *Romeo and Juliet*, thereby making a statement about how love is right for all people, not just the young and beautiful. Directors also sometimes use **gender-neutral casting**, or casting without regard for the character's gender, and **cross-gender casting**, or intentionally casting men to play women's roles and women to play men's in order to study societal perceptions of gender identity. One of the most controversial forms of casting is **color-blind casting**, or choosing actors without regard for their race or ethnic background; ignoring skin color often makes for unbelievable interpretations and fundamental changes in the text and denies the racial conflicts in our society.

Joan Marcus

The choice of Whoopi Goldberg to play Prologus, a Greek actor, in a 1997 Broadway revival of *A Funny Thing Happened on the Way to the Forum* is an example of color-blind (as well as gender-blind) casting. This practice has generated much controversy, although it is gaining popularity. Some feel it a fair way to ensure all actors are considered equally for a role, and others feel it masks the scarcity of roles for people of color in U.S. theatre.

The Director's Role during Rehearsals

Once the paper phase is over, the director is ready to begin rehearsals. In a large production with a big cast, the director may have an **assistant director** to lend a hand. The first few days of rehearsal are critical because this is when the director must unite all the actors into an ensemble with a common goal. No two actors are alike; they have different methods and personalities. Some actors need reassurance, while others need a firm foundation. Some actors approach their roles through intellectual analysis, while others thrive on nothing but inspiration. Early in the rehearsal process the director must present a game plan and clear goal to all the actors. Initial rehearsals may be taken up with reading and analyzing the script, as well as improvisation. Then the director, with the help of the actors, begins blocking. **Blocking** is the movement of the actors on stage. At its most basic, blocking is simply making sure the actors don't bump into each other or the furniture, but it quickly becomes a complex set of movements that express the characters' emotions, thoughts, and relationships. Blocking is also how the director achieves focus and reinforces the story with stage pictures.

Focus

Achieving **focus** in a movie is easy. Directors can simply point the camera at whatever they want the audience to look at. Close-ups and lingering camera angles can emphasize a tiny drop of incriminating blood on a killer's hand or a character's fleeting glance of guilt. On stage, focus is much more difficult because the audience is free to look wherever they like. The stage director must gain the audience's attention and direct their gaze to a particular spot or actor. This can be accomplished through lighting, costumes, scenery, voice, and

When I create something, I usually have it completely created in pre-production. But then I go in and I feed off of the actors also, because that ultimately gives me the best result.

Susan Stroman,
Director and choreographer

movements. Focus can be gained by simply putting a spotlight on one actor, by having one actor in red and everyone else in gray, or by having one actor move while the others remain still. All these techniques will quickly draw the audience's attention to the actor whom the director wants to be in focus. There are also more subtle ways to lead the audience's eyes and pull focus. A few of these are body position, stage area, level, contrast, and triangulation.

One of the most basic ways a director achieves focus is through actors' body positions. For example, in Figure 8.1 (A) the actors are **sharing focus**. They both have a shoulder thrown back (a position sometimes called "one-quarter" because the actors are turned a quarter away from the audience). Because the audience can see the actors equally, this position is used when what both actors are saying is of equal importance. In (B) the actor on the right takes focus because the actor on the left is standing in **profile**, or "half" away from the audience. The audience's eyes naturally go to the actor on the right because he is in the most "open" position. Perhaps at this moment in the play the character on the right is talking about how he knows his wife is cheating on him. The director feels that this speech is very important to the story and doesn't want the audience to miss a word of it, so she has the actor on the left "close" himself by standing in profile. In (C) the actor on the right is standing in "three-quarters," an even more closed position than profile, so the actor on the left naturally demands a great deal of focus. Perhaps the character on the left is having an affair with the other character's "loyal" wife and the director wants the audience to see his guilty reaction, so the actor on the right gives the focus to the actor on the left.

Of course, all movements must be justified and fit into the action of the play. Actors mechanically turning to give and take focus would look silly, so motivated reasons for each individual movement must be found. During rehearsals actors are often asked to "open" themselves, to "share focus," to "give focus," or to "close" themselves in order to fit the focal demands of the moment. Actors who take focus when they aren't supposed to are said to be **stealing focus** or **upstaging** the other actors.

A director can also achieve focus by using different **stage areas** (see Figure 8.2). Each area is labeled from the actors' point of view as they face the audience; for example, "stage right" is to the audience's left. Using these labels,

Figure 8.1 Achieving focus through the actors' body positions.

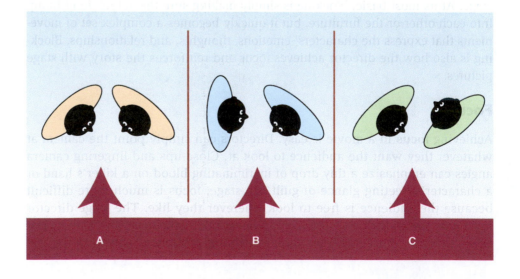

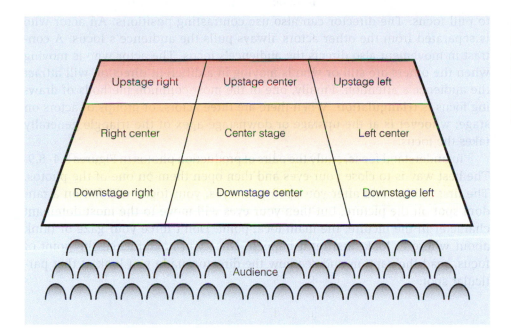

Upstage right	Upstage center	Upstage left
Right center	Center stage	Left center
Downstage right	Downstage center	Downstage left

Audience

Figure 8.2 Stage areas. To help with blocking, the stage is split into a grid and each area is labeled. Using these labels, directors can easily ask the actors to move to a particular place or look in a particular direction.

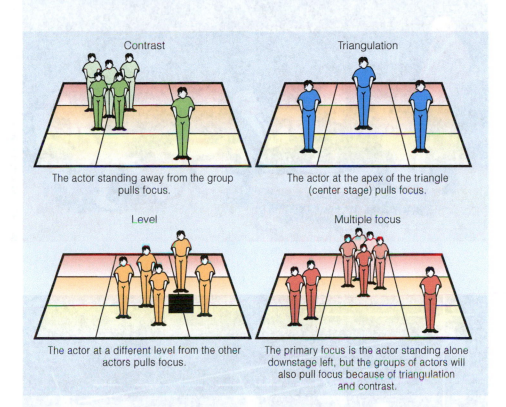

Contrast

The actor standing away from the group pulls focus.

Triangulation

The actor at the apex of the triangle (center stage) pulls focus.

Level

The actor at a different level from the other actors pulls focus.

Multiple focus

The primary focus is the actor standing alone downstage left, but the groups of actors will also pull focus because of triangulation and contrast.

Figure 8.3 Achieving focus through contrast, triangulation, and level.

directors can easily ask the actors to move to a particular part of the stage or look in a particular direction. An actor who is center stage or downstage tends to draw the audience's attention more than actors in other areas.

Focus can also be achieved through level (see Figure 8.3). An actor who is at a different elevation than the other actors, either because he is on a platform of some kind or because he is standing while others are seated, tends to pull focus. The director can also use contrasting positions. An actor who is separated from the other actors always pulls the audience's focus. A contrast in movement also directs the audience's focus. The actor who is moving when the others are still or who is moving in a different direction will attract the audience's attention. Finally, one of the most common methods of drawing focus is **triangulation**. When there are three actors, or groups of actors on stage, whoever is at the upstage or downstage apex of the triangle generally takes the focus.

To understand focus, study the pairs of production photos in Figures 8.4–8.9. The best way is to close your eyes and then open them on one of the photos. The first millisecond after you open your eyes, your focus will fall on a random spot on the picture, but then your eyes will move to the most dominant character in the picture, the main focal point. Don't force your gaze or think about where to look; just let it happen. Once you have picked the point of focus, read the caption and see how the director made you look at that particular spot.

Figure 8.4

Figure 8.5 Drawing focus with level, gaze, and contrast. From a University of Wyoming production of Edward Albee's *Who's Afraid of Virginia Woolf?* directed by Rebecca Hilliker.

Figure 8.6

Figure 8.7 Drawing focus with triangulation. From a University of Wyoming production of Henrik Ibsen's *A Doll's House*, directed by William Downs.

Figure 8.8

Figure 8.9 An example of double or triple focus. From a University of Wyoming production of Arthur Miller's *Death of a Salesman*, directed by William Downs.

In Figures 8.4 and 8.5, the director is using several techniques to pull focus. The first is level: Only one actor is standing, so he pulls focus. Second, the other actors are giving focus by looking toward the standing actor. The audience has a tendency to look where the actors look. It's rather like the chain reaction created by a person on a crowded street corner looking up at the sky—curious passersby will also look up. The third technique is contrast: The three seated actors are leaning back at the same angle, giving the standing actor focus by virtue of his contrasting position.

In Figures 8.6 and 8.7, the director is using a triangle to pull the focus to the downstage character. Even though all the actors are in open positions, the focus is still taken by the downstage actor because he is at the downstage apex of the triangle. Also, the two upstage actors are looking at the downstage actor. The secondary focus is on the woman because she is the best lit.

In Figures 8.8 and 8.9, there is a double focus, perhaps even a triple focus. The two actors on the right are the first focus. The secondary focus is on the young woman sitting stage right, and then focus goes to the actor standing with his arms around the young women. Notice that if you look where any actor is looking and then to whom that actor is looking, and so on, your eyes eventually come to the man with his hand raised. Therefore, he takes the main focus.

Reinforcing the Story with Pictures

Words are a fine method of storytelling, but directors often go a step further by composing pictures with the actors that reinforce the story. This technique is called **picturization**. It uses many of the visual-art principles of painting and photography in order to express the characters' relationships, psychological situations, and moods at a glance. In real life people move without regard for where others are around them, groups of people seldom arrange themselves to tell a story, and there is randomness to crowds. For example, from a random photo of a bankruptcy auction on a farm in Iowa, we could probably tell that an auction was being held. The auctioneer might be in focus and around him would be dozens of farmers, but we'd know little else about the people or the situation. If the same scene were being shown on stage, the director would create pictures to help tell the story. From a single stage picture, we would be able to identify the members of the unlucky farm family. We'd know that this person is the mother, this is the father, and here stands the best friend. If a picture is well staged, we should even be able to tell what the characters' relationships are. We would know which of the farmers in the crowd had a vested interest in the proceedings and who were merely onlookers. We would also understand the mood of the moment, the sense of loss, and how the auction is the end of a way of life. A director arranging the actors to make these pictures is concerned not just with which characters are in focus but also with telling the story.

If it is well staged, showing the purpose of the scene, the characters' objectives, and the mood of the moment, the picture can be given a title, like the title of a painting. One moment might be titled "True Love," the next moment "The Betrayal," and the next moment "The Confession." This title identifies

> The director must be the master of theatrical action, as the dramatist is the master of the written concept.
>
> **Harold Clurman,**
> Director and theatre critic

Harper Point Photography

Figure 8.10 Well-placed actors create a composition that tells a story. In this scene from the comedy *Kosher Lutherans* staged at the Bas Bleu Theatre, the director has created a stage picture that demonstrates the energy and mood of the scene without any need for dialogue.

the moment's main thrust or principal purpose. For example, in Figure 8.10, in a scene from a production of the comedy *Kosher Lutherans*, the placement of the actors creates a picture that tells a story. Without knowing any of the dialogue we could write a title such as "The show off" or "I win, you lose." Most of the time, the audience is unaware that they are seeing a succession of deliberate images. Yet when these stage compositions are well done, the audience might be able to understand the play even if the dialogue was in a foreign language.

> The director builds a bridge from the spectator to the actor. Following the dictates of the author, and introducing onto the stage friends, enemies, or lovers, the director with movements and postures must present a certain image which will aid the spectator not only to hear the words, but to guess the inner, concealed feelings.
>
> *V. E. Meyerhold,*
> Director and designer

Different Types of Directors

Today, there are as many styles of directing as there are directors. Some directors are authoritarian leaders who micromanage every aspect of the play. Others are more like creative coaches who guide and inspire as they orchestrate the play in a democratic style. Every director has unique philosophies and methodologies about this highly individual process. But when it comes to working with an existing script, directors all fall somewhere in the spectrum between interpretive and creative.

Interpretive Directors

Interpretive directors attempt to translate the play from the page to the stage as accurately and faithfully as possible. They are not slaves to the playwright, but they make every attempt to realize the playwright's words and actions in a style that is true to the script. Directors inevitably impose their individual style on a production, but interpretive directors attempt to stage the play in a manner that they feel would please the playwright. Of course, an exact translation from page to stage is impossible—every line an actor speaks is an interpretation of the playwright's words, every movement an actor makes is an interpretation of the script, and every design is an interpretation of the playwright's wishes.

Creative Directors

Creative directors often add concepts, designs, or interpretations atop the playwright's words that were never intended by the playwright. Their plays are sometimes called **concept productions**, because the director's artistic vision, or concept, dominates. In 1937 American director Orson Welles (1915–1985), famous for writing, directing, and starring in the movie *Citizen Kane*, directed one of the most celebrated concept productions. For a production of Shakespeare's *Julius Caesar*, he placed the action in pre–World War II Rome. He made the character of Caesar into the dictator Benito Mussolini and replaced the Shakespearean music with the anthem of Mussolini's fascist regime, thereby making a statement about the politics of the day. English director Peter Brook staged another famous concept production in 1970 when he turned Shakespeare's *A Midsummer Night's Dream* into a circus, with magic tricks, trapeze artists, and actors spinning plates on sticks. Brook and his designer, Sally Jacobs, set the play within a roofless white box with ladders, swings, and catwalks. The result was an athletic, acrobatic performance that did not look like anything Shakespeare originally intended. Today, concept productions are common, with directors staging *Hamlet* in Chicago during the gangland wars of Prohibition and *The Taming of the Shrew* in the Wild West. Creative directors stage concept productions in order to capture the spirit of the play, modernize the play, or simply create a unique evening of theatre.

Some creative directors go so far as to almost discard the playwright's words, using the script as only a loose outline. These directors believe that the script should mutate to fit the needs of an individual director or production. Of course, the main problem for these directors is the small number of plays they can direct, because playwrights own the copyright to their plays and have the right to deny production to any director who does not properly follow the script. Directors who wish to alter a playwright's intention must gain the playwright's permission or wait until the play is in public domain, as are Shakespeare's plays. (For more on copyright and public domain, see Chapter 2.) There have been several famous battles between playwrights and directors over who controls a play. One of the most famous took place in 1984 during a production of Samuel Beckett's *Endgame* at the American Repertory Theatre. (See Spotlight "Playwright versus Director.")

Contemporary Trends

Traditionally, theatre artists were divided into *creative artists*, the playwrights who create the scripts, and *interpretive artists*, the directors, actors, and designers who work within the parameters the playwright has set. This dividing line between creative and interpretive artists is now being questioned by many directors as well as playwrights and actors. They are blurring the traditional assignments and creating and staging plays that allow all the members

SPOTLIGHT**ON** Playwright versus Director

n 1984, JoAnne Akalaitis directed Samuel Beckett's *Endgame* at the American Repertory Theatre. Samuel Beckett is one of the world's most famous absurdist playwrights. *Endgame* is the story of two clown-like characters, Hamm and Clov, one of whom is partially paralyzed and the other acts as his servant. Other characters are Hamm's parents, who live in trash cans. Beckett's stage directions state that the play takes place in a room with two windows and little else. But Akalaitis saw the play differently. She set the action in a New York City subway station after a nuclear holocaust, which changed the meaning of the play. When Beckett heard about the production, he went to court to shut it down. In the end, they settled out of court. The production was allowed to go forward, but the program included a note, written by Beckett, condemning the production. The note says that the American Repertory Theatre's production is a "complete parody" of his work, and that anyone who cares for the play can't help but be "disgusted" by what Akalaitis did to it. The theatre's artistic director responded in a program note that reads in part, "To insist on strict adherence to each parenthesis of the published text not only robs collaborating artists of their interpretive freedom but threatens to turn the theatre into a waxworks."

This exchange defined one of the greatest problems of the relationship between the director and the playwright: Who has the power? Is the play set in stone when the playwright writes it, or can it be adjusted to fit the director's artistic vision? Some directors have attempted to solve the problem by saying that the playwright should be in charge of only the dialogue and the director in charge of the staging. This division of labor doesn't solve the problem because playwrights also write the stage directions that describe the physical aspect of the play, and both are copyrighted. With Hollywood films, screenwriters have lost this battle. Writers for movies are secondary characters whose vision is seldom realized. In the theatre, the battle has just begun. However, unlike screenwriters, playwrights have a powerful advantage because they own the copyright, so they may not be so quickly defeated. Recently some better known directors have been contending that their blocking and production concepts should also be copyrighted and are filing lawsuits to ensure that no one can replicate their staging without permission and payment. Concerning the mess, the playwright and screenwriter Paul Rudnick (*I Hate Hamlet*) said, "From now on I'm only going to have my plays directed by lawyers." Needless to say the battle over creative control and copyrights in the theatre will be hotly debated on the stage and in courts for many years to come.

Richard Feldman

In recent years, playwrights have sometimes threatened legal action to stop directors from altering their work. Examples include a production of Edward Albee's *Who's Afraid of Virginia Woolf?*, in which a man in drag was cast as Martha, and a play by an experimental theatre company that incorporated a portion of Arthur Miller's play *The Crucible*. One of the most famous cases of a playwright intervening to stop a production of one of his plays involved JoAnne Akalaitis's 1984 production of Samuel Beckett's *Endgame* (pictured here).

of the ensemble to be creative artists and share in the development of the play. Plays have always been developed; seldom does a playwright labor in total isolation and then suddenly put forth a finished script. Most plays go through an extensive process of readings and workshop productions that help the playwright rewrite. But now many directors and actors are getting involved in the development process much earlier, even at the moment of conception. So instead of the production being an interpretation of the playwright's script, the production is the creation of an ensemble of playwright, designers, actors, and director.

Playwright Caryl Churchill often workshops her plays using a communal method of development that allows actors to help create the script through improvisation and the director to co-determine the direction of the final script. Such was the case with Churchill's play *Cloud Nine*, the story of several generations of a family and how they are governed by class, race, and gender—a play, by the way, that features cross-gender casting. Instead of writing in a secluded study, she spent several weeks working with the director on the idea and setting for the play. Then actors were brought in to improvise as they jointly workshopped the idea. Churchill took what she learned and wrote a tentative script with rudimentary dialogue. This first script was again workshopped with the director and actors to refine the dialogue, and this collaboration resulted in the final production. Another famous example of this new method of directing is Moisés Kaufman's play *The Laramie Project*, a docudrama about the murder of a gay university student. The play was researched by a company of actors who conducted personal interviews with people who lived in the town in which the student was murdered. Kaufman acted as both director and playwright as he worked with the actors to develop the final production.

Curtain Call

In the end, all directors are judged by process and product. The process is everything that leads up to opening night; the product is opening night and beyond. A good process doesn't always lead to a good product, but occasionally a good product is born of bad process. The acid test for the process is if all the members of the ensemble have clearly seen and added to the production. Did the environment allow meaningful creativity for all the members? The acid test for the product is far more subjective, because more people are involved, including the audience and critics. But, as director Peter Brook says in *The Empty Space*:

> I know of one acid test in the theatre. It is literally an acid test. When the performance is over, what remains? Fun can be forgotten, powerful emotions also disappear and good arguments lose their thread. When emotion and arguments are harnessed to a wish from the audience to see more clearly into itself—then something in the mind burns. The event scorches onto the memory an outline, a taste, a trace, a smell—a picture. It is the play's central image that remains, its silhouette, and if the elements are rightly blended this silhouette will be its meaning, this shape will be the essence of what it has to say.

So the acid test for a production is whether its meaning stays with the audience. The playwright's words will be forgotten or paraphrased, the actors' names will disappear, the designer's colors will fade, and the set will be discarded, but the director knows that the production was successful if the thought remains.

SUMMARY

In order for a production to succeed, dozens of artists, technicians, and other personnel must work together with a singleness of purpose seldom found outside the theatre. The director is the leader and coordinator who takes the playwright's words and frames them into a production. The job requires many skills: The director must know how to work with and inspire actors, designers, and playwrights, and how to coordinate all the elements that make up a production. Yet the director is one of the newest positions in the theatre. For thousands of years playwrights and actors essentially functioned as directors. It wasn't until about 150 years ago, when realism became popular, that the duties of the director were separated into a single job. Two early directors who helped define the position were the Duke of Saxe-Meiningen and Konstantin Stanislavsky.

The director's job can be split in two parts: pre-rehearsal and rehearsal. Pre-rehearsal is spent evaluating and researching the script, conceiving a production concept, and working with designers. To analyze a play, a director often breaks it into french scenes and beats. Dividing the play into these small units helps the director discover the structure and understand the play moment by moment. Once the director has done careful analysis and research, it is time for meetings with the designers in order to find a production concept, or central metaphor, that unites all the elements of the production. Only after weeks or months of work does the director finally cast the play.

The director has many casting options, including casting to type, casting against type, gender-neutral casting, cross-gender casting, and color-blind casting. During rehearsals the director blocks the play to lead the audience's eyes and achieve focus. The methods the director can use to pull focus include body position, stage area, level, contrast, and triangulation. Directors also use picturization to tell the play's story.

The director's job is so complex that it often requires several assistants, such as an assistant director and a stage manager. Additionally, some productions also need a movement coach, a voice and dialect coach, and a fight director. Musicals need a musical director and a choreographer to work with the musicians and teach the actors the songs and dance numbers (for more on these additional ensemble members, see Chapter 5).

No two directors have the same working methods. But they can be divided into two broad, nonexclusive categories: interpretive directors who are loyal to the playwright's intentions, and creative directors who often impose upon the script their own concept that is independent of the playwright's intentions. Some directors are now challenging traditional ideas by staging plays that allow actors, playwrights, and directors to work on a play from its inception to the opening night.

MindTap®

Test your knowledge with online printable flashcards and online quizzing.

KEY TERMS

Assistant director *157*

Beat *153*

Blocking *157*

Casting against type *156*

Casting director *156*

Casting to type *156*

Color-blind casting *157*

Concept production *164*

Creative director *164*

Cross-gender casting *157*

Didaskalos *149*

Director *149*

Dramaturg *153*

Focus *157*

French scene *153*

Gender-neutral casting *157*

Interpretive director *163*

Moscow Art Theatre *151*

Picturization *162*

Production concept *156*

Profile *158*

Sharing focus *158*

Stage area *158*

Stealing focus *158*

Triangulation *160*

Upstaging *158*

Theatrical designers create everything from the ground plan of a set, to the costumes and the lights. Here, Annaleigh Ashford, Kristine Nielsen and Fran Kranz star in *You Can't Take It With You* at the Longacre Theatre. Production set design by David Rockwell, costume design by Jane Greenwood, lighting design by Donald Holder, sound design by Jon Weston and hair and wig design by Tom Watson.

Chapter 9

THE ART OF DESIGN

Sara Krulwich/The New York Times/Redux

Outline

The house lights dim, the curtain rises, and we see a solitary actor standing in the center of a bare stage. There is almost nothing to support the actor—simple work lights, no costume, no set, nothing but a blankly lit empty space. Could this be theatre? Absolutely. Yet theatre often uses designers to assist the actors, playwright, and director by setting the stage. When sets, lights, sounds, and costumes are added, the audience is immersed in the world of the play even before the first line is spoken. Theatre is intended to be experienced by our eyes, our ears, our mind, our whole being, so theatre has always had designers in one form or another to help create the experience.

MindTap®

Start with a quick warm-up activity and review the chapter's learning objectives.

Today, most plays have set, lighting, and costume designers, but some also have sound and makeup designers. All these artists must work together to create the visual effects of a dramatic production—in other words, the play's environment. Environment is integral to any story.

Every plot, conflict, and character would change if they were moved to new surroundings. Imagine the Christmas movie *Miracle on 34th Street* transported to the steamy South or the chilly moral fable *Fargo* set in sunny Hawaii. Their stories, characters, and possibly themes would be transformed. Even the most well-known plays by Shakespeare seem new and different when they are set in unexpected periods and locations, such as when the feud between families in the early Renaissance Italy of *Romeo and Juliet* is transformed into a contemporary gang war in the Leonardo DiCaprio movie version. The plots and dialogue are unchanged, but the shift in environment drastically alters the tone and the characters. Whether the set is complicated or simple, familiar or novel, the designer's duty is to create a virtual environment that will remind the audience who the players are and where they're supposed to be. Design can communicate the spirit and soul of the play to the audience.

From Page to Stage

MindTap®

Read, highlight, and take notes online.

There are as many methods of designing a virtual environment as there are designers and productions, so this will be a sweeping look at what might be called a typical design process: taking the play from the page to the stage. "My approach, after reading the script," says Ming Cho Lee, one of the United States' premier set designers, "is to question the director about an overall production scheme, discussing choices: Should it be realistic or abstract? Should it be period or not? Should the material be metal, wood, granite? Then I do a rough sketch for the director to find out if I'm going in

Every element of a theatrical design, including lights, costumes and set, must blend together in order to form one unified whole. Notice in this photo how the lights, set, and costumes form a perfect unity for this production of *Blithe Spirit*. Lighting design by Jon Olson, set design by Brian Mallgrave, and costume design by Chris Campbell. This production was directed by Rod Lansberry.

Patricia Switzer

the right direction. Then I make a one-half-inch scale model and paint it up. All this takes time." In fact, the process can take so much time that designers must begin their work many months before the actors start rehearsal.

Doing the Homework

Long before the rehearsals begin, the designers begin work by studying the script. The playwright has created the blueprint for a production; in order for the play to exist, the words on the page must be transformed into action and environment on the stage. The designer's analysis of the script is as detailed and comprehensive as any director's or actor's. A complete understanding of the characters is essential because the characters define the environment and the environment reveals the characters, especially their personal surroundings—their home, office, or room. Characters' tastes, lifestyles, incomes, jobs, educations, and temperaments are reflected in the environment they've created, just as the décor of your dorm room and how you dress reflect your character.

Understanding the characters and script, however, is only the beginning. In order to create an accurate virtual environment, set, lighting, sound, costume, and makeup designers must often do detailed investigations into the location and historical period. They may need to study the architecture, the color schemes, and the styles. They might also study the customs, manners, and cultures. This research helps the designers answer dozens of critical questions, including:

- How does the play's environment affect and reflect the story and characters?
- How do the story and characters affect and reflect the environment?
- What significant details of the environment will define and individualize the characters?
- How do the characters feel about their environment?
- How does the environment relate to the play's theme?
- Is the personal environment in or out of harmony with the characters?

There are also historical considerations:

- What is the time period of the play?
- What was the religious, social, and political climate of that period?
- What was the religious, social, and political climate when the play was written?

Designers also consider practical questions, such as these:

- What are the mechanical requirements, such as the number of doors needed for exits?
- What are the budgetary limitations?
- What are the deadlines?
- What are the physical limitations of the stage?
- What are the physical dimensions of theatre in which the play will be performed?

Like baseball parks, no two theatres are exactly the same. The size, seating arrangement, and layout can directly affect the design. (See the Spotlight "Theatre Spaces.")

Design is an act of transformation. In working with a director, a designer transforms words into a world within which actors are engaged in human action. It might be a metaphoric world, an emotional world or an architectural world, but it is a process of bringing design ideas into a place where they can be executed.

Ming Cho Lee,
Theatre designer

SPOTLIGHT ON Theatre Spaces

Environment begins with the theatre itself. Theatre can take place just about anywhere, from stages to street corners. For much of its history, theatre has not been performed in theatre buildings but in what are called **found, or created, spaces**. Typically, these have been parks, churches, and town squares, but they can also be basements, warehouses, gymnasiums, jails, or subway stations. Theatre can take place just about anywhere an audience can gather. Set designer Robert Edmond Jones said, "In its essence, a theatre is only an arrangement of seats so grouped and spaced that the actor—the leader—can reach out and touch and hold each member of his audience. Architects of later days have learned how to add conveniences and comforts to this idea. But that is all. The idea itself never changes." The standard types of theatres today are proscenium arch, thrust, arena, and black box.

The most common type is the **proscenium arch**. The word *proscenium* comes from the ancient Latin word for "stage." The proscenium arch originated in Italy in the 1500s. Proscenium arch theatres are a little more formal than the other types because the audience is separated from the actors. As in a movie theatre, the audience sits safely in the dark, looking through a picture frame at the actors on the other side. In fact, proscenium arch theatres are sometimes called "picture frame" theatres. In some theatres, the separation between actors and audience is made even greater with the addition of an orchestra pit between the audience and stage. However, in modern proscenium arches the actors can come closer to the audience on what is called a **lip** or **apron**, a part of the stage that extends into the audience's side of the picture frame. Some aprons are on a hydraulic or manual elevator and can be raised and lowered; at stage level they are an extension of the stage, and when lowered they become the orchestra pit. Above the stage, a traditional proscenium arch hides an elaborate network of pulleys, riggings, and counterweights called a **fly system** that raises scenic pieces out of the audience's sight. Fly systems can tower 80–100 feet above the stage and are usually manually operated, although some modern proscenium arch theatres have computerized fly systems. At the sides of a proscenium arch stage are the **wings**. Out of the audience's sight, the wings are areas from which actors make their entrances and where set pieces can be stored or moved onto the stage.

A **thrust stage** has a lip (apron) that protrudes so far into the auditorium that the audience must sit on three sides of the stage. This "peninsula" or "runway" type of stage reduces the distance between the actors and audience. Even from the back rows, the distance is small. This allows for a more intimate style of acting. Occasionally called "three-quarters-round," many thrust theatres have passageways or tunnels called **vomitories**, or "voms," that run into and under the audience to allow actors quick access to the stage. Vomitories are just like the stadium tunnel a football team disappears into at halftime.

In order to answer all these questions, designers must have well-rounded educations in history, dramatic structure, art, art history, and criticism. Many universities offer an MFA (Master of Fine Arts) degree in set, costume, light, and sound design. Designers must also have a great deal of imagination, because, in the words of Robert Edmond Jones (1887–1954), one of the United States' foremost set designers, they need to "immerse themselves in [the play]" and even "be baptized by it." Only then can they begin their work on the design.

Design Team Meetings

Once the designers have researched and studied the play, they are ready for the artistic and production meetings. The director, stage manager, and designers begin by reviewing practical issues: the physical limits of the theatre, safety concerns, budget limitations, and scheduling. Soon they get down to finding, understanding, and communicating the production concept. As you read in Chapter 8, the production

Historically, it is unclear how the word vomitory came to be used for a theatre space, but the word comes from the Latin verb *vomere*, which means to "spew out"; literally, actors are "spewed out" from the stage down these tunnel-like exits.

The thrust stage is much older than the proscenium arch theatre. Twenty-five hundred years ago, ancient Greek tragedies were performed on a version of the thrust stage. Four hundred years ago, Shakespeare's plays were first performed on a thrust stage.

Arena theatres are far less common than proscenium arch or thrust theatres. Often called "theatres-in-the-round," arenas have the stage in the center, like an island, surrounded on all sides by audience. Arena theatres resemble sports stadiums, boxing arenas, and circus rings. Like thrust theatres, arenas have vomitories to allow actors easy access to the stage as well as a close relationship with the audience. Arena productions may cost the least to stage because elaborate scenery is not possible. Walls, doors, and large furniture pieces would only block the audience's view, so sets are kept simple. Although this keeps expenses low, it limits the number of plays that can be effectively produced. The major challenge for productions on arena stages is the audience's **sight lines**, because there are few places the actors can stand or sit without blocking someone's view. To solve this problem, actors often try to keep their backs to the vomitories so they are open to a majority of audience members. Another solution is to keep moving. Some directors make the actors move, shift, or turn every 30 seconds or so to ensure that no one audience member's view is blocked for too long. Arena stages are probably the oldest type of theatre, for whenever people gather for an outdoor event, whether a tribal ceremony, a sporting event, or a rally, a circle seems to be our natural method of gathering.

Most **black box theatres** seat fewer than a hundred people. The audience sits close to the actors, making these theatres ideal for small, intimate plays. Sometimes called "studio," "flexible," or "experimental" theatres, most black boxes have no permanent seating arrangement. They are bare spaces that allow seats to be arranged differently for every production. The space can be set up as a proscenium arch, a thrust, or an arena, or it may be configured in some experimental, nontraditional actor/audience arrangement. In some black box productions, audience members have sat on stage with the actors or followed the actors from location to location or looked down into a pit where the action was taking place. Black box theatres are often in found spaces, such as converted warehouses or storefronts. They are called "black boxes" because the walls are usually painted black to de-emphasize them, and the space is often square. However, no two black box theatres are exactly alike.

Michael Earl

Stage designers today often use computer design software like AutoCAD, 3D Studio Max, Sketchup, Maya, ZBrush, as well as Illustrator and Photoshop (the same programs used by big Hollywood production companies like Pixar and Industrial Light & Magic) to create their set design. This design by Michael Earl for the play *The Spitfire Grill* is early in the process. Once the director is happy with the design, Earl will add color and other graphics.

Proscenium arch theatres are sometimes called "picture frame" theatres because the arch resembles the frame of a picture. Today proscenium stages, like this one in Canada's Avon Theatre, are the most common type of stage in North America, but they originated in Italy during the Renaissance.

Terry Manzo/The Stratford Festival of Canada

Thrust stages, like that of the Festival Theatre in Canada, protrude into the auditorium so that the audience sits on three sides. Like the proscenium arch, thrust theatres have been around for hundreds of years. In fact, William Shakespeare's plays were first performed on a thrust stage.

Terry Manzo/The Stratford Festival of Canada

concept is the master symbol or allegory that the director, playwright, and designers conceive as the central metaphor. The director and designers use this metaphor to physically express the mood, tone, theme, and philosophy of the script.

It can take many meetings for the director and designers to agree on a production concept. During these meetings they talk about how they see the play, how they feel about each scene, and how they hope to affect the audience. The director may tell personal stories that connect to the play's theme or discuss reasons for staging the play. Some directors use models, sketches, photos, paintings, and even music, as

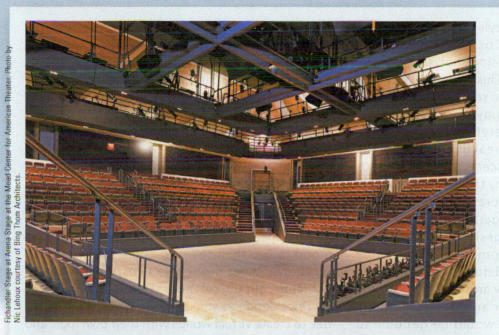

In arena theatres, or theatres-in-the-round, the audience surrounds the stage, as in a sports arena. Performing on an arena stage can be a challenge because actors must often shift positions to remain open to the audience. This example is the Fichandler Stage of Arena Stage in Washington, DC.

Black box theatres are also known as studio, flexible space, or experimental theatres and they come in all shapes and sizes. They are called black box theatres because their walls are almost always painted black and they often have a boxlike shape.

well as words to communicate their ideas about the production concept. "Designing is something that you don't approach in a linear way like you approach climbing a ladder, one step at a time," says set designer Ming Cho Lee. "It's actually a constant exploring of ideas. It's about how you connect with a play, how you live the life of the play." During these meetings the director and designers also talk about mood, pace, atmosphere, and colors, as well as character and story. The director also talks about the production's style—perhaps realism or expressionism or some combination of "isms." (For more on style, see the Spotlight "Theatrical Styles.")

SPOTLIGHT ON Theatrical Styles

All plays have a style. Style is the way in which a work is expressed or performed. Some plays, like most television shows, are lifelike imitations of nature. This is a style known as **realism**. To design realistic sets, lights, makeup, and costumes, designers pay close attention to details that will make everything appear to be a genuine duplication of real life, whatever the period. For example, if a scene is about a 1950s housewife in her kitchen, then the designers would use historically accurate faucets, running water, and a working refrigerator from the postwar era. They would also design natural-looking light that seems to be coming from a source onstage, such as a ceiling fixture or sunlight flowing in through the window and bouncing off the 1950s flowered wallpaper and linoleum floors. The housewife's costume would be genuine to the period, as if it came off a department-store rack, and the dinette set would look as if it came from the time Eisenhower was president. The only difference from real life would be that one wall of the kitchen is missing so that the audience can peek in on the action.

For some plays, **simplified, or suggested, realism** is appropriate. For this style, designers suggest rather than duplicate the look of a period. What the audience sees is not a carbon copy but a suggestion of a 1950s kitchen, whose details they must fill in with their imagination. This style is sometimes called **selective realism** because some design elements appear authentic, but other elements are stylized. For example, our 1950s kitchen might appear real, but the lights may express the mood rather than seem to come from a source on stage. Or our housewife's costume might be authentic, but the set more symbolic.

Once designers step away from realism, they are free to create virtual worlds with their own logic and rules. They can pursue a metaphorical, symbolic, or stylized look. Stylization can take several forms; one of the most common is **expressionism**. With

Designers sometimes combine diverse elements into a single design as is the case with the play *Linda* by Penelope Skinner. This set of an ultra realistic modern kitchen also has nonrealistic elements such as no walls. This production was staged at the Royal Court Theatre in London. Set design by Es Devlin.

Donald Cooper/Photostage

expressionism, the audience sees the story through the mind of one character. Settings may be distorted by the character's conscious or subconscious phobias, prejudices, or psychoses. Instead of photographic reality, the audience sees the character's inner reality. With an expressionistic style, our 1950s kitchen might have slanted walls leaning in on our housewife showing her feelings of claustrophobia and being trapped in her marriage. The TV shows *Scrubs* and *That 70s Show* have used expressionism to illustrate the mindset of a character, such as someone literally drowning in a cup of coffee or the walls closing in on an office worker.

When stylization is taken to an extreme, little or no attempt is made to re-create reality; instead, oversized symbols and fantastic dreamlike or nightmarish images dominate the stage. With **surrealism**, the subconscious

of the characters is emphasized in the design—now our 1950s kitchen is located in Hell. With **symbolism**, a certain piece of scenery, a costume, or light may represent the essence of the entire environment: our 1950s kitchen might have huge faucets that torture the housewife with their incessant dripping.

Finally, some sets contain little that looks real. The purpose of these sets is to remind the audience that they're watching a play. Now our 1950s kitchen has only a sink, and no walls. Instead, advertising posters are hung around the stage with smiling 1950s housewives looking down on our character and extolling the marvels of a modern kitchen.

Few designs have only one style. Designers often mix styles to fulfill their aesthetic goals for an environment that fits the production concept and the needs of the play.

Whereas realism aims for authenticity, expressionism attempts to re-create the world as the characters see and feel it—subjectively, with their emotions and unconscious thoughts made visible. This 2001 production of Elmer Rice's expressionist play *The Adding Machine* at the University of Colorado, Denver, featured a set by Richard Finkelstein, lights by Scott Hay, and costumes by Jane Nelson-Rudd.

Inspired by psychoanalysis and the workings of the human mind, surrealist playwrights attempted to break down the barriers between the conscious and the unconscious. In this 2005 production of August Strindberg's *A Dream Play*, adapted by Caryl Churchill, we see inside the mind of the main character as he dreams of his past. Directed by Katie Mitchell and designed by Vicki Mortimer, National Theatre, London.

Designers in the theatre communicate the production concept—the central metaphor of the play—through lights, sound, sets, and costumes. They make a play's ideas more clear and complete than they would be in real life. Nothing on stage is arbitrary. Everything, from a costume's button to the color of the light to the angle of a door, is chosen to communicate the production concept.

The designers' opinions may change the entire look of the play. For example, when Julie Taymor designed the costumes for the Broadway hit *The Lion King: The Musical*, she wanted race to be an important part of the story. "What I love about *The Lion King*," says Taymor, "is that this is a show with a predominantly nonwhite cast that is not about race. On the other hand, it's all about race—and that should be acknowledged, because there are very powerful traditions . . . and that fact shouldn't be ignored." The producers, on the other hand, did not think the theme of race was particularly important, but Taymor persisted. During a production meeting, she convinced them to agree to the design for African-inspired clothes. The result was a change in the whole production concept.

Filling the Empty Space

Once the designers understand the production concept, they need to make the leap from words to images. They create drawings, renderings, thumbnail sketches, models, and plans of the sets, costumes, makeup, and lights. After each production meeting, the designers combine the play's needs, their research, the style, and the concept, and let them "bake." Designers may contemplate these issues for weeks to allow their training and their creative mind to conceive ideas that will express the production concept. No two designers work the same way. But they all must take into account the demands of the play and the limitations of the theatre while transforming abstract ideas into concrete designs that convey the central metaphor of the play.

The **basic elements of design**—the designer's toolkit, in a sense—are line, dimension, balance, movement, harmony, color, and texture. If the master symbol of the play is the need to get back to nature, the designers might choose earth tones, the colors of growing plants, and natural textures. If the master concept is to glorify humankind's great achievements as represented in our cities, then straight lines and massive forms that reflect the sun might be used. If the master concept is to show a world out of balance, then the designers might use odd-shaped masses that seem to teeter unsteadily or defy the laws of gravity. The designer's choices are limitless because there are infinite possibilities that could meet a play's production needs. To understand more about the design process, let's look at each of the major design areas: sets, lights, sound, costumes, and makeup.

Designing the Set

Twenty-five hundred years ago in ancient Greece, designers painted screens, sewed costumes, and built masks to help create the characters and suggest the play's virtual environment. During the Italian Renaissance, designers constructed elaborate stage settings using two-dimensional flats that were painstakingly painted to appear as if they were three-dimensional throne rooms, landscapes, and dungeons. At other times in theatre's long history, the set design has been simple. For example, for hundreds of years Chinese opera was performed outdoors on bare platforms. Instead of complex designs, settings were indicated with simple symbolic gestures by the actors or with minimal set pieces. If the story required a character to climb a tall mountain, the actor would pantomime it using only a small stepladder; a plain wooden stool could represent a grand golden throne. This worked for the Chinese opera because the audience knew they had to use their imagination to "see" the set. Today, set designs can be simplistic or complicated. The only limitation is the theatre's budget and the designer's talent and imagination.

Designers often have trouble describing exactly how they do their job. The set designer John Lee Beatty says, "One of the fun things about being a designer is that you don't know where the designs come from—they just come out." Simply put, they take the words of the playwright and the ideas of the director and turn them into visual imagery. Set designers have a strong background in interior design, architecture, and art history, as well as theatrical conventions of various periods. But above all, designers must be artists. They draw and draft their art by hand, although now the use of **computer aided design (CAD)** programs is more common.

Designers who draw their designs by hand often make numerous thumbnail sketches in an attempt to realize the production concept, taking into account the locations, environment, and historical background of the script. This doodling can be done in pencil, pen, or charcoal. Figure 9.1 shows an early drawing by designer Michael Earl for a production of *My Fair Lady*. After this rough sketch, he decided that the set had to be more open, so he eliminated the pillar on the right and showed more of the city's skyline in the background (Figure 9.2).

Once the director approves the sketch, the designer paints a color rendering (Figure 9.3). After that is approved the designer moves on to blueprints. Like architectural drawings for a building, these blueprints include scale drawings of every part of the set. The view from above is called the **floor plan**; the views from front and back are called the **elevations** (see Figure 9.4). These drawings must be rendered exactly to scale and show the placement

I'm looking for a connection with the world we live in, a passion for seeing that [connection] translated in visual terms. What I'm trying to train [students in] is the ability to translate text or music into meaningful images.

Ursula Belden,
Theatre designer and professor

Michael Earl/University of Wyoming Archives

Figure 9.1 Early rough sketch of a set from a production of *My Fair Lady*. Design by Michael Earl.

Figure 9.2 The later rough sketch.

Michael Earl/University of Wyoming Archives

Figure 9.3 The final color rendering.

Michael Earl/University of Wyoming Archives

of every door, window, and platform, as well as furniture, light switches, and baseboards. They also include the wallpaper patterns, shading, and texture. Once the blueprints are complete, the set-construction crew gets to work, using the designer's exact specifications to build the set. The complete process from production meeting to final design often takes months. Figure 9.5 shows the final set for the production of *My Fair Lady*, generated from the sketches shown in Figures 9.1, 9.2, and 9.3.

Sometimes, if the director wants more help visualizing the set before building it, the designer also crafts handmade three-dimensional scale models of the setting. The preliminary model is called the "white model" because it is made of heavy white paper and white foam board (Figure 9.6). After the director and designer study the white model and agree on changes, the designer now makes a second, more detailed color model. The second model includes every aspect of the set in detail (Figure 9.7). Figure 9.8 shows the final set for a production of *All My Sons*, generated from the models shown in Figures 9.6 and 9.7.

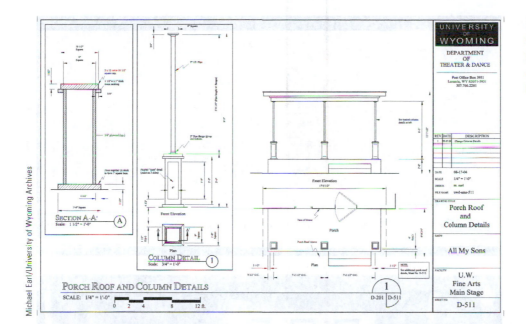

Michael Earl/University of Wyoming Archives

Figure 9.4 Elevation of a set from a University of Wyoming production of Arthur Miller's *All My Sons*, drawn by designer Michael Earl.

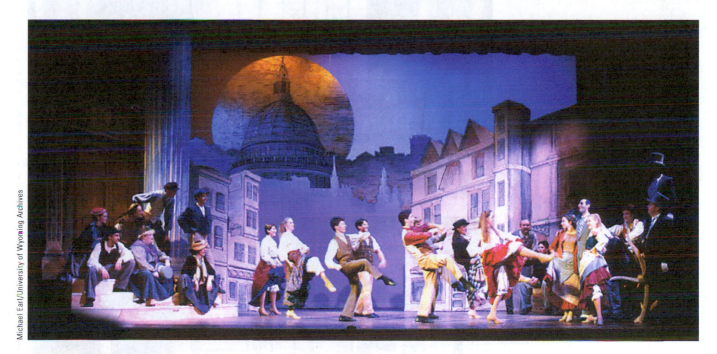

Michael Earl/University of Wyoming Archives

Figure 9.5 The final set for *My Fair Lady* at the Struthers Theatre in Warren, Pennsylvania.

Designers who use CAD follow a similar process but use computers instead of paper, paint, and physical models to produce exact blueprints. CAD was originally developed to help engineers and architects draft buildings and bridges but was quickly adapted to theatre sets. Sophisticated modeling programs can also show the design three-dimensionally from almost any angle. This allows the designer to let the director walk through a virtual reality set (much like a computer game). Computer modeling has changed the way set designers design because it allows almost unlimited changes and creative experimentation.

Figure 9.6 A white model from a production of *All My Sons*, prepared by designer Michael Earl.

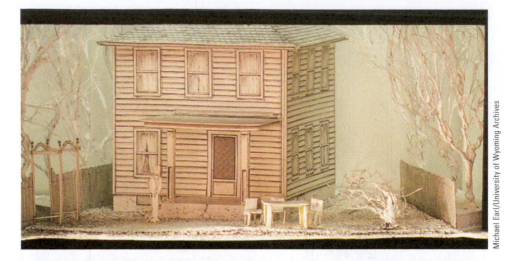

Michael Earl/University of Wyoming Archives

Figure 9.7 The second model in full color. Both the white and color models must be built exactly to scale so that the director can visualize blocking and anticipate any problems before the set is built. This model and the white model shown in Figure 9.6 are quite small, only about 18 inches wide by 12 inches tall.

Michael Earl/University of Wyoming Archives

Figure 9.8 The final set for *All My Sons*.

Michael Earl/University of Wyoming Archives

Whether set designers work by hand or with a computer, or both, they must turn out exact designs that take into account durability and safety, as well as the length of time available for construction. Budget is also a concern, as are the physical needs of the play and the structural limitations of the theatre. (For more on set design, see the Spotlight "The Life of a Designer: Ming Cho Lee.")

SPOTLIGHT<u>ON</u> The Life of a Designer: Ming Cho Lee

Ming Cho Lee has been called the "dean" of American scene design. Born in Shanghai, Lee's parents divorced when he was six and, as was common in China at the time, he lived with his father. "I had weekend visits with my mother, and those were the great moments of my life," he recalled. His mother took him to the theatre, movies, and Chinese opera. She also allowed him to study drawing and watercolor painting. In 1949, he came to the United States and studied art, design, and theatre at Occidental College and UCLA before moving to New York City, where he became the principal designer for the New York Shakespeare Company, the Juilliard Opera Theatre, and the Peabody Arts Theatre in Baltimore.

Lee became known for his minimalist sets that used basic colors and geometric shapes to create "environments" rather than realistic-looking settings. He did not, however, limit himself to minimalism. One of his most famous sets was for Patrick Meyers' play *K2*. Although he made the rocky face of the world's second tallest mountain (Everest is the tallest) from sculpted Styrofoam covered with layers of tissue and paint, the audience could believe that the actors were really hanging hundreds of feet in the air. Lee won the 1983 Tony Award for best set design for *K2*. Other famous shows he has designed include the original production of the rock musical *Hair*, a revival of Arthur Miller's *The Crucible*, Ntozake Shange's *For Colored Girls Who Have Considered Suicide/When the Rainbow is Enuf*, and Michael Cristofer's *The Shadow Box*.

In 1969, Lee became a professor of design at Yale School of Drama, where he trained many of today's important set designers, including John Lee Beatty, Heidi Landesman, Michael Yeargan, Marjorie Bradley Kellogg, Adrianne Lobel, and Douglas Schmidt. "Teaching," says Lee, "forces a teacher to always go through a process of self-evaluation." And self-evaluation is at the heart of all art.

Lee is a strong supporter of multiculturalism and laments the lack of it in U.S. design today. He believes its absence is "linked to the lack of visibility of designers and production people. A black child can see black actors and say, 'I want to do that.' He or she can read about black directors. But if that child sees a set or a lighting design, there's no sense of who is responsible for it. It's almost as if it came into being completely on its own somehow." Lee feels the only way to combat the problem is for designers of color to become more visible. "We must let young people know, and I mean young Asian, black, Latino, and Native American boys and girls, that this kind of expression is available to them, that they can survive in this field, and they don't have to give up who they are to do so."

Theatre designer Ming Cho Lee

This set design by Ming Cho Lee for Eugene O'Neill's *Ah! Wilderness* illustrates his characteristically spare use of color and shapes to suggest a more substantial environment. This 2001–2002 production by the Guthrie Theater was directed by Douglas C. Wager.

> A good design . . . is one that takes on significance and that resonates at the end of the show. It needs to unfold and take on meaning, and become imbued with emotion and importance; it needs to connect with the piece in a way that keeps surprising, and that keeps allowing the audience to have ideas and revelations as the evening goes on.
>
> **Adrianne Lobel,** Set designer

> Light is the most important medium on the stage. . . . Without its unifying power, our eyes would be able to perceive what objects were but not what they expressed. . . . What can give us this sublime unity which is capable of uplifting us: . . . Light!
>
> **Adolphe Appia,** Lighting designer

Designing the Lights

For thousands of years theatre was performed outdoors, so the sun provided the light. Many of these pre-electricity civilizations built their theatres so that the afternoon sunshine would hit the stage. The first indoor theatres were built about 500 years ago and used chandeliers filled with sputtering candles to illuminate the stage. In 1545, Sebastiano Serlio (1475–1554) published *Architettura*, a book on Italian set design, in which he described how to change the quality of the light by placing reflectors behind the candles and globes of colored water in front. A hundred years later, Nicola Sabbatini (ca. 1574–1654) published the *Manual for Constructing Theatrical Scenes and Machines*, which told how oil lights could be dimmed by lowering tin cylinders over the flames. But these early lighting design techniques were complicated and their effects modest. Because the light in the theatre was so dim, the auditorium and audience had to be lit as well as the stage. The actors resorted to painting their faces with cosmetics so that their expressions could be seen.

By the 1840s gas-lit theatres were common. There were even gas-powered spotlights, in which jets of hydrogen and oxygen were ignited with small bits of lime; this is the source of the word **limelight** and the phrase "to be in the limelight." Needless to say, all that gas made theatres prone to fire. For example, the Paris Opéra used 28 miles of tubing to carry the highly flammable gas to all its lights. In 1856, the magazine *The Builder* stated that it was the fate of all theatres to eventually burn down. In the nineteenth century, over 10,000 people died in theatre fires in England alone. That fate changed in 1881 with the advent of electric lights. For the first time in theatre's history, lighting designers could adequately light the stage and allow the audience to sit in the dark. Soon there were master lighting designers, such as Adolphe Appia (1862–1928), who used light, shadows, and color to create complex lighting effects. However, lighting design as an art form continued to be unrecognized until 1970—when the first Tony Award was given for lighting design. Today, theatrical lighting has become a refined art. Designers have a wide range of instruments and effects at their disposal, and new inventions continue to improve the art.

One of the most important advances in lighting design was the invention of computerized lighting, which allows an entire lighting design, including hundreds of exact levels and cues, to be controlled by a computerized light board called a **dimmer**. The first Broadway play to use a computerized light board was the musical *A Chorus Line* in 1975, which was lit by Tony Award–winning lighting designer Tharon Musser. Using computer-controlled dimmers, said Musser, means that a designer can "have consistency and smoothness. You get the same show every night." Today, with a touch of a button, computerized light boards allow the lighting designer to set exact light levels and program fade-ins and fade-outs for hundreds of lights. There are even dimmers that allow audio coordinated light cues to be precisely synchronized with music and sound effects. And when the lighting designer's work is done, an entire lighting design can be stored on a flash drive or in the cloud.

The latest advances in lighting design are software programs that allow designers to create three-dimensional designs and perform simulated lighting effects on their computers. Before the advent of this technology, their only option was to make simple renderings to demonstrate what the final lighting design would look like. This meant that their design could not be shown to the director until after the lights were actually hung and aimed—just days before a play

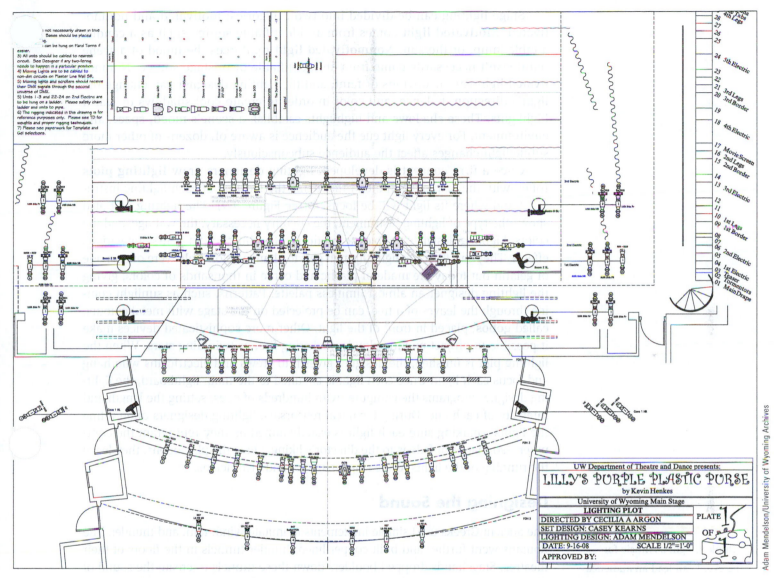

Figure 9.9 A light plot is a detailed drawing that shows the locations of lighting instruments, wattage, color, and other details necessary to the lighting design. A light plot is a record of the designer's vision and a map that guides the crew in hanging and positioning the lights. The light plot pictured here was created by Adam Mendelson for the children's play *Lilly's Purple Plastic Purse*.

opened. But today, with the help of these powerful software programs, lighting designers can make photorealistic pictures and real-time lighting computer simulations that allow everyone involved with the production to know exactly what the final results will be, long before the set is built or the costumes stitched.

Before lighting designers sit down with their dimmers or computers, however, they study the script and meet with the director and other designers to discuss the overall look of the production. The most central role of the lighting designer is to evoke mood. Because of this they need more than just knowledge of computer software, lighting instruments, and circuitry. They must also understand art and human emotions. As a result, lighting designers often study painting, optics, and art. The great designer Robert Edmond Jones said, "At rare moments, in the long quiet hours of light-rehearsals, a strange thing happens. We are overcome by a realization of the *livingness* of light. As we gradually bring a scene out of the shadows, sending long rays slanting across a column, touching an outline with color, animating the scene moment by moment until it seems to breathe, our work becomes an incantation. We feel the presence of elemental energies."

Adam Mendelson/University of Wyoming Archives

Stage lighting can be divided into two categories: motivated and nonmotivated. **Motivated light** comes from an identifiable source such as a candle, a table lamp, or the sun. **Nonmotivated light** reinforces the mood of a scene but doesn't necessarily come from an identifiable or onstage source. Nonmotivated light can be obvious or faint, and the lighting designer can change the light's direction, balance, and color in order to create cool shadows or warm highlights. These shadows and highlights establish a scene's mood, space, and environment. For every light cue the audience is aware of, dozens of other more subtle light changes affect the audience subconsciously.

Once a firm concept is developed, lighting designers draw **lighting plots** (often with the help of computers) that detail the location of each lighting instrument and where its light will be focused (see Figure 9.9). The lighting plot also shows the type of lighting instrument, the circuitry necessary, the wattage, and the colors. Lighting designers employ a multitude of techniques for achieving various effects. They can filter the light through gels to change color. **Gels** were once made of gelatin but today are made of plastic and come in thousands of colors, giving the lighting designer an almost limitless palette. Patterns, such as sunlight coming through the leaves of a tree, can be projected on the stage with metal cutouts, called **gobos**, placed in front of the light. Other more sophisticated devices make it possible to project moving clouds, flickering fire, or twinkling stars. When the lighting plot is finished, the designer gives it to crews and electricians who hang and focus each light. Once each light is circuited to the main lightboard, the lighting designer programs the computer with hundreds of cues, setting the length and intensity of each cue. During technical rehearsals, lighting designers often refine the lights—making sure each light is exactly aimed as they reprogram the computer—so that each fade is to the director's liking. Once the play opens, they leave the running of the lights to the stage manager and electricians.

Designing the Sound

The ancient Greeks used simple implements to imitate wind, rain, and thunder. The Romans went further and built copper-lined thunder tunnels in the floors of their theatres. Stagehands dropped boulders down these tunnels to create the sound of distant thunder or, if the boulders were large enough, an earthquake effect. Some 1,500 years later, Shakespeare's plays included the sound effects of trumpet fanfares and cannon fire to thrill the audience and help set the scene. In fact, one of these sound effects was the reason that Shakespeare's theatre burned to the ground in 1613: a spark from one of the cannons lit the roof on fire. In minutes the wooden theatre was engulfed in flames, creating a special effect a little more spectacular than the one Shakespeare intended. Many forms of non-Western theatre also use sound effects. For example, Japanese Kabuki theatre uses special floor resonators to amplify the sounds of the actors' feet as they dance.

Today's sound designers can record, mix, filter, reverberate, modulate, amplify, and cue up sound effects exactly when they are needed. They record sounds from real life, and they use sounds from vast sound libraries that contain everything from distant foghorns to birds singing in the morning, and from crickets chirping on a calm night to deadly gunfire. Sound designers in the theatre and in film can also digitally sculpt sounds in order to get the right ring of a doorbell, and they can synthesize sounds for the exact tone needed to convey a particular emotion or meaning. Sound designers may take extraordinary steps to get the perfect sound. The sound of Luke Skywalker's land speeder in *Star Wars* (1977)

I think of light as music for the eye. I can lead an audience fluidly from one place to another, from one feeling to another. . . . It tells you where to look; it tells you how to feel about what you see.

Jennifer Tipton,
Lighting designer

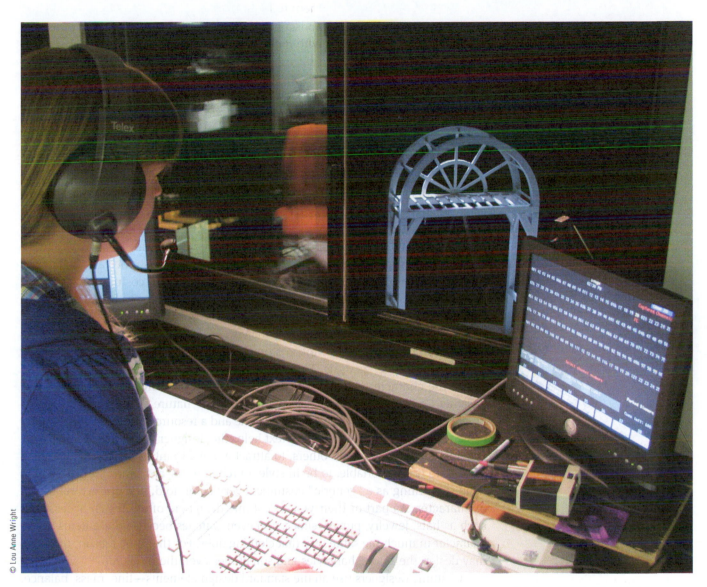

© Lou Anne Wright

was made by recording Los Angeles freeway traffic through a vacuum-cleaner tube. The sounds of torpedoes firing in *The Hunt for Red October* (1990) were layered with animal growls, a Ferrari engine, and a screeching screen-door spring.

Theatrical sound designers, like their film counterparts, spend hours trying to synthesize and record the exact sounds needed because the right sound can often express things that words cannot. They also design systems to amplify an actor or singer's voice to make sure they can be heard. Yet their hard work often goes unrecognized—it wasn't until 2008 that Broadway presented Tony Awards for best sound design of a play and of a musical, which went to *The 39 Steps* and *South Pacific*, respectively. Speaking about the lack of recognition, sound designer John Gromada once said, "Often critics credit the directors with the work that we do. . . . I've written to these critics to say, 'I don't care if you like my work or don't like my work. Just mention my name.'"

Sound designers must have a detailed knowledge of acoustics, electronics, digital music editing programs, audio mixing boards and signal processing equipment, microphones, effects processors, and amplifiers. They must also know exactly where to place speakers to get the desired effect. In addition, some

Modern, computerized light boards can be found in almost every theatre's light booth. Here, light board operator Danielle Fullerton makes a few adjustments prior to a technical rehearsal. Through the light booth's window she can see the lighting effects on the stage below.

sound designers are also composers or musicians: they write and play transition music or underscore scenes with mood music.

Designing the Costumes

As long as there has been theatre, there have been costumes. In precolonial African theatre, masks and costumes were an integral part of the performance. Four hundred years before the birth of Christ, the Greeks used costumes in their tragedies to reveal the characters' mood and enhance their performances. In Shakespeare's day, wealthy lords and ladies donated their worn gowns and leggings to the local theatre so that actors might have a variety of outfits to choose from. Costumes can be exaggerated like those in the Japanese Kabuki theatre or understated, as is often the case in modern realistic plays. Whether they are larger than life or subtle, all costumes reflect and establish the character's social and economic status, lifestyle, age, country, occupation, education, and geographical origin. The costumes also reflect the historical period, season, and even the time of day. Further, costumes must fit the needs of the script, the budget of the theatre, the style of the set, the color of lights, and the production concept. Therefore the costume designer must be a visual artist, fashion designer, historian, and psychoanalyst.

Like all other designers, the costume designer is an expert at play analysis, especially character analysis. This is why most costume designers begin with the words the characters say. "I start with the text," says Tony-nominated costume designer Constance Hoffman, "No matter what the nature of the project is, that's where I begin and what I use as a touchstone and a resource for everything that the design becomes." Starting with the text helps the designer determine if a character is going to dress to impress others, to attract a mate, to intimidate, to celebrate, to imitate, to be comfortable, to be in style, to rebel, or for any other purpose. There is no such thing as a "generic" costume; every color, fold, and cut is a reflection of character. As part of their work, costume designers often design accessories such as hats, jewelry, purses, shoes, and even watches because these items reveal character in much the same way that clothing does. For the same reason, they also may design the actors' hairstyles and sometimes even their makeup.

Costume designers use all the standard design elements—line, mass, balance, harmony, composition, movement, texture, and color. Choosing the right colors for a costume not only requires artistic judgment but also an understanding of the psychological effects each color has on an audience, as well as how each color will appear under tinted theatrical lights. Costume designers must also take into account how the costume will fit the body type and shape of the actor cast for the role. In addition, they appreciate the movement of different fabrics—some are flowing and others stiff—and the various effects they can create. Designers must also consider how the costume will work during the performance. If the costume has a large hoop skirt, it must be made to fit through doorways. If there is a fight sequence, then they must build a durable costume that can take wear and tear.

Not all costumes are designed and built from scratch. Sometimes costume designers buy outfits off the rack at local department stores, and other times they will shop for pieces at thrift stores. A theatre can also borrow costumes from patrons or rent them from large costume rental companies. Renting costumes is always a compromise, because what the costume rental companies have in stock is unlikely to fit the production concept. And, although it saves time, renting can be expensive: the rental, insurance, cleaning, and shipping fees add up to a substantial amount. Another option is to "pull" a show, or take the costumes from the theatre's storage vaults. Most college and professional

> The only time a sound designer is mentioned in a review is when the critic doesn't like what you're doing. "The tinny, loud sound," they'll write. Or 'the excruciatingly distorted sound." They rarely say anything positive about your sound reinforcement.
>
> **Scott Lehrer,** Sound designer

theatre companies have huge costume vaults where they store thousands of costumes of various styles, sizes, and historical periods that were either created for other productions, donated, or purchased. Pulling costumes for a show can save the theatre a great deal of time and money; however, unless the vault contains exactly what the play or director requires, numerous alterations must be made.

Like all other designers, costume designers attend production meetings and use drawings to communicate what the designs will look like. The first costume renderings are tentative sketches, which can go through many variations before the final design is set in stone. Once the designs are agreed upon, the costume designers decide which costumes they will buy, borrow, rent, and build.

In order to build a costume, a designer paints or sketches detailed **costume plates** that the costume construction crew will use to assemble the costumes. These sketches indicate how each costume is shaped, where seams and folds are, how the costume flows, and what fabrics should be used—some designers even attach fabric swatches to the plates. (See Figures 9.10 and 9.11.)

At smaller theatres, the costume designer sometimes doubles as head of the costume-construction crew. But at larger and professional theatres, the designer leaves the constructing of the costumes to patternmakers, cutters, tailors, and fitters. Depending on the size and type of show, the building of the costumes can take weeks. Once the costumes are done, a **dress parade** is held. The actors

Tina Haatainen-Jones

Tina Haatainen-Jones

Figure 9.10 & 9.11 Costume designers often draw costume renderings which help the cutters and stitchers to realize the design. These renderings were created by Tina Haatainen-Jones for a Disney compilation of Broadways hits, including a tap dancer in a scene from *Guys and Dolls* and for the character of Mama Rose in *Gypsy*.

try on their costumes and parade in front of the costume designer and director, who confer on changes needed before opening night.

Designing the Props

One of the rarest designers in the theatre is the prop designer. As discussed in Chapter 5, "prop" is theatre lingo for theatrical property or just property. Properties generally mean **set props**, or anything that sits on the set including sofas, chairs, and beds, and **hand props**, or any objects actors handle while on stage, such as pens, fans, cigars, money, and umbrellas. Prop designers are responsible for envisioning, building, finding, and, if necessary, renting the props. They also find, rent, and design set decorations. **Set decorations** are similar to props except that they are items that are not touched by actors. For example, if an actor touches a picture on the shelf, it is a prop; if they don't touch it, then it is considered set decoration. Generally, a prop designer builds props only when they cannot be found. They will often spend their time looking through antique stores, junk shops, and bargain stores trying to find exactly what the play needs. If they can't find it or if the prop is something that doesn't exist in real life, such as the huge man-eating plant in the musical *Little Shop of Horrors*, then the prop designer designs and builds it. Prop designers work much like set designers. They make a series of sketches or use CAD programs to design props. If a theatre doesn't have (or can't afford to hire) a prop designer, oftentimes the set designer must design the props as well.

> As a costume designer, you don't get credit for a great performance, but rarely do you have a great performance with a terrible costume.
>
> **Susan Hilferty,**
> Costume designer

Makeup design is often the responsibility of the costume designer, but makeup artists are hired for complicated makeup designs, as in the musical *Cats*. Makeup effects can be achieved by painting the face with color, shadows, and highlights or by using three-dimensional pieces such as beards, wigs, false noses, scars, or, in this case, whiskers.

Reuters/Corbis

Makeup, Wigs, and False Noses

Around the world and over the centuries, actors have used makeup to disguise and to exaggerate their features. Japanese Kabuki theatre is known for its striking, stylized makeup that exaggerates the actors' features. In the West, there are two categories of makeup. **Straight makeup** does not change the actors' looks, but makes their faces look more three-dimensional and therefore more visible to the audience because the bright theatrical lights wash out their facial features. Actors also wear makeup so they will look more like the character they are playing and less like themselves. **Character makeup** is an attempt to transform the way actors look—for example, by adding gray hair, wrinkles, and shadows to a youthful actor who must play an old man. The type and the amount of makeup actors need changes with every production. For a realistic play in a small theatre, the actors might wear no makeup. For a realistic play in a large theatre, the actors might wear lots of powder and rouge to add shadows and highlights so that they can be seen from the back row. For a nonrealistic or highly stylized play, they may have to come in many hours before curtain so that an artist can apply layers of special makeup. Actors who are playing a character much older, younger, or different from themselves might also need to wear a beard or a wig. These are often designed by the costume designer and constructed by a specialized wig maker.

If the play requires only straight makeup, the actors often do it themselves. All actor-training programs include classes in how to create and apply a makeup scheme. But more complicated makeup often requires a makeup designer. The musicals *Cats* and *Beauty and the Beast* needed a makeup designer to design exactly how each character should look and to make renderings of the design much like those of costume and set designers. If a special prosthetic piece, such as a scar, a false nose, or a wart, is needed, the makeup designer makes a plaster cast of the actor's face and casts the prosthesis in synthetic rubber. An exact fit allows the prosthesis to be held on with just a dab of nontoxic theatrical glue.

Curtain Call

Once the designs are finished, they are turned over to the technical director (or TD in theatre lingo). The TD turns the designers' drawings, paintings, blueprints, models, and sketches into fully realized sets, lights, and costumes. The TD usually presides over large construction crews who build the set, stitch the costumes, and hang the lights. For a small or simple production these crews may consist of only a few people, but most plays have dozens of crew members and they almost always outnumber the actors. (For more on the ensemble that makes theatre work, see Chapter 5.)

In the end, just days before the play opens, everything comes together with the technical rehearsals. The first tech rehearsals combine sound and lights with the set. These rehearsals are often called so that the crews can ensure they have everything covered. Next come the dress rehearsals when the actors get to rehearse in costumes for the first time. The night before the play opens is the final dress rehearsal. At this point, the only thing missing is the audience—even the curtain call is run to a mostly empty house and

> In the last analysis the designing of stage scenery is not the problem of an architect or a painter or a sculptor or even a musician, but of a poet.
>
> ***Robert Edmond Jones,***
> Theatre designer

the only people sitting in the dark are the designers. (For more on the various types of rehearsals, see Chapter 7.) Although the designers aren't part of the curtain call, their work is onstage for all to applaud.

About the challenges of being a designer, Robert Edmond Jones said:

> The designer is forced to work and think in a hundred different ways—now as an architect, now as a house-painter, now as an electrician, now as a dressmaker, now as a sculptor, now as a jeweler. He must make idols and palaces and necklaces and frescoes and caparisons. As he works, he may be all too well aware of the outward limitations of the play he is to decorate and the actors he is to clothe. But in his mind's eye he must see the high original intention of the dramatist and follow it.

SUMMARY

MindTap

Test your knowledge with online printable flashcards and online quizzing.

Designers have been a part of the theatre for thousands of years. Whether plain or complex, their job is to remind the audience of where the characters are supposed to be—in other words, to create the play's environment. To do this, designers must do a lot of homework. They must research and analyze the play's dramatic structure, period, history, location, mood, characters, and theme. They must also take into account the budget and the physical configuration and size of the theatre: proscenium arch, thrust, arena, or black box.

All designers work with a director to create the production concept, which is devised from the master symbol or allegory and becomes the central metaphor for the production. The director and designers must also decide what style the play will reflect: naturalism, realism, selective realism, expressionism, surrealism, or symbolism.

Once they have a production concept, the designers make numerous drawings, renderings, thumbnail sketches, models, and plans of the sets, costumes, and lights. Many, if not most, designers have a strong background in art and history as well as interior design, architecture, and theatre. They must know how to paint, draw, and draft. The process of designing a set can take months as the designers move from thumbnail drawings, rough drawings, and final drawings to models and blueprints. Once the designs are done, the technical director and construction crews turn them into fully realized sets, lights, and costumes. Technological advances have had a great effect on design methods, and therefore on the theatre as a whole. From acoustic modeling of auditoriums and computer-controlled lights to automatic fly systems, the theatre is quickly catching up with the modern world.

KEY TERMS

Apron *172*

Arena theatre *173*

Basic elements of design *178*

Black box theatre *173*

Character makeup *191*

Computer aided design (CAD) *179*

Costume plate *189*

Dimmer *184*

Dress parade *189*

Elevations *179*

Expressionism *176*

Floor plan *179*

Fly system *172*

Found, or created, space *172*

Gel *186*

Gobo *186*

Hand props *190*

Lighting plot *186*

Limelight *184*

Lip *172*

Motivated light *186*

Nonmotivated light *186*

Proscenium arch *172*

Realism *176*

Selective realism *176*

Set decoration *190*

Set props *190*

Sight lines *173*

Simplified, or suggested, realism *176*

Straight makeup *191*

Surrealism *177*

Symbolism *177*

Thrust stage *172*

Vomitories *172*

Wings *172*

Chapter **10**

A CREATIVE LIFE

A life in the theatre is a life spent being creative. With every production, actors, designers, playwrights and directors are faced with new challenges and fresh problems to solve. Here, James Earl Jones and Cicely Tyson perform in the two-person show *The Gin Game* at the Golden Theatre in New York.

Sara Krulwich/The New York Times/REDUX

Outline

MindTap®

Start with a quick warm-up activity and review the chapter's learning objectives.

In his book *The Big Questions*, philosopher Lou Marinoff says, "if you regularly experience hallucinations—that is, if you see and hear things that no one else sees and hears—you might be called "psychotic," and diagnosed with a psychiatric disease. Then again, if you see things that no one else sees and turn them into movies, or hear things that no one else hears and turn them into symphonies, then possibly you are a director or composer." Yet creativity is more than just imagination. It is the adrenaline rush and "aha!" that happens when we find an answer that has not been found before. It is a moment of enlightenment that solves a problem, thereby adding value to our lives. The creative moment may happen in a flash, but it almost always follows years of hard work, research, and thinking. The desire to live a creative life is one of the main reasons people go into the theatre, but creativity is hardly limited to the arts.

Creativity

Mihaly Csikszentmihalyi (pronounced "Chick-sent-me-high-ee"), a leading researcher on creativity, wrote in his book *Creativity*, "Most of us assume that artists—musicians, writers, poets and painters—are strong on the fantasy side, whereas scientists, politicians, and businesspeople are realists. This may be true in the terms of day-to-day routine activities. But when a person begins to work creatively, all bets are off—the artist may be as much a realist as the physicist, and the physicist as imaginative as the artist." Let's clear up some of the many fallacies surrounding creative thinking as we attempt to answer an important question: how can you be more creative, whether as an artist, business person, astronaut, or physician's assistant—in whatever endeavor you pursue?

In order to answer the question, we must first define what creativity is. **Creativity** is discovery. It is the moment someone invents something that is new or transforms something extant, thereby adding value to our culture, society, or lives. It can be a major flash of inspiration that changes the world, or a moment of insight into just about anything—big or small. For example, David Perkins of Harvard University (co-director of Project Zero, a research project studying cognitive skills among scientists and artists), recalled a story of a friend who stopped to have a picnic while traveling in France. He had all the ingredients needed for a fine lunch: cheese, bread, and wine. But he lacked one key item, a knife with which to slice the cheese. He thought for a moment, took out his credit card, and set out to slice the cheese. Perkins points out that this is a great example of small, everyday creativity. He feels that we should not conceptualize creativity as something that only happens in elitist circles, artistic endeavors, or in ivory towers. Creativity is all around us, and we are all capable of being creative.

Because creative work depends on a certain level of specialized knowledge, some people think that artists must be extremely intelligent people. However, studies have found that an extremely high IQ (intelligence quotient) is not necessarily a great advantage when it comes to being creative. Having an IQ over 120, which is "high-average intelligence" according to the Stanford-Binet Intelligence Scale, doesn't seem to make people more creative. What does matter is the *type* of intelligence an individual has. (For more on this subject, see the Spotlight "Identify Your Intelligences and Cultivate Your Creativity.") As a result, a person of slightly above-average intelligence can often be just as creative as one with a very high IQ. More important to creativity than raw intelligence are technique and talent.

MindTap

Read, highlight, and take notes online.

SPOTLIGHT ON Identify Your Intelligences and Cultivate Your Creativity[1]

One of the keys to discovering our talents and being more creative is to identify the types of intelligences in which we excel. In recent years, the theory of multiple intelligences has become popular among educators because it allows us to account for an expanded range of human potential. Formulated by Howard Gardner, professor at the Harvard Graduate School of Education, the theory states that we all possess different types of intelligence, not just the kind measured with a standard IQ test. It is our unique combination of these intelligences that makes up our talents.

We've all heard stories of geniuses who had trouble with tasks that seem elementary to the rest of us. British playwright, critic, and essayist George Bernard Shaw could write great stories, unforgettable characters, and powerful criticism, but he had trouble spelling. Similarly, American statesman, inventor, and philosopher Benjamin Franklin had trouble with simple math. Because we all possess different degrees of the various kinds of intelligences, we all have areas in which we struggle and ones in which we shine. Often we are unaware of our particular gifts—our talents just seem natural to us. The first step in discovering and cultivating our talents is to find out which types of intelligence are our strengths. In his book *Frames of Mind: The Theory of Multiple Intelligences*, Gardner identifies six forms of intelligence: linguistic, musical, logical-mathematical, spatial, bodily kinesthetic, and personal.

- **Linguistic intelligence.** This kind of intelligence is the understanding of how language works and the ability to use language to convince others and express ideas. According to Gardner, "In the poet's struggle over the wording of a line or stanza, one sees at work some central aspects of linguistic intelligence." Not only poets but also playwrights, writers, political leaders, actors, and legal experts possess a high level of linguistic intelligence. Its characteristic is a great technical facility with words and language.

- **Musical intelligence.** This is the ability to recognize, remember, and organize tones and musical patterns. The musical mind is concerned with pitch, melody, rhythm, and harmonic elements of sound. We say of these people that they have a "gifted ear." Gardner notes, "Of all the gifts with which individuals may be endowed, none emerges earlier than musical talent." People who have a strong musical intelligence are often also gifted in math. People who possess a high degree of musical intelligence include composers, musicians, singers, music critics, and recording engineers.

- **Logical-mathematical intelligence.** This is the ability to order and unify structures and to perceive patterns and causal relationships. This ability can be related to material objects but

[1] Adapted from Howard Gardner, *Frames of Mind: The Theory of Multiple Intelligences*, 1983. Perseus Books Group.

Creativity and Technique

Imagine a talented actor playing the role of Shakespeare's Hamlet. The audience is enthralled, the performance is winning the hearts of the critics, but is the actor being creative? He may be having an adrenaline rush, but has he come up with unique answers about the role of Hamlet? Is he solving problems, thereby adding value to the role of Hamlet? More than likely, during a performance, the actor is not being creative, but is instead relying on technique. **Techniques** are procedures that have been proven to work repeatedly. They are methods by which a complex task can be accomplished, such as raising a child, fixing a heart valve, or playing a Shakespearean character. Technique is what we learn from being creative. The actual creativity for our Hamlet actor more than likely occurred during the rehearsal process, not during his performance.

Many of us, just like our Shakespearean actor, depend on technique. We learn techniques that are based on other people's creativity; Einstein's equation $E = mc^2$

> Creativity consists of 1 percent inspiration and 99 percent perspiration.
>
> **Thomas Edison,** Inventor

it more often takes an abstract form, as with mathematics. People with a high degree of this type of intelligence look for order in what may appear to be chaos. They can perceive and define the relationship between parts of a whole. Philosophers, scientists, and mathematicians often possess a high level of logical-mathematical intelligence.

- **Spatial intelligence.** This is the ability to sense and retain visual images and to mentally manipulate them. It includes the abilities to transform two-dimensional images into three-dimensional objects and to make mental models, which are the key to understanding many scientific concepts. Sculptors, architects, football coaches, and theatre directors must have a high degree of this type of intelligence. It is also important to anyone who must read maps or create diagrams.

- **Bodily kinesthetic intelligence.** At first the idea of body movements as a form of intelligence may seem strange but our brain controls our muscles and allows us to judge the timing, force, and extent of our movements. When certain parts of the brain are injured, motor movements can be impaired even though the muscles are fully capable. This type of intelligence also includes eye-hand coordination and fine motor movements. Athletes, dancers, pianists, and actors need a high level of bodily kinesthetic intelligence.

- **Personal intelligences.** Intrapersonal intelligence is the ability to understand one's own feelings. This talent can also be turned outward in the form of interpersonal intelligence, or the ability to understand the moods, motivations, and intentions of others. Those who need this ability to "read" other people include political and religious leaders, parents, teachers, therapists, counselors, doctors, nurses, and social workers.

To illustrate these various intelligences, Gardner points out that "Sigmund Freud was the exemplar of intrapersonal intelligence; Albert Einstein represented logical-mathematical intelligence; Pablo Picasso, spatial intelligence; Igor Stravinsky, musical intelligence; T. S. Eliot, linguistic intelligence; Martha Graham, bodily kinesthetic intelligence; and Mahatma Gandhi, interpersonal intelligence." However, most activities require more than one form of intelligence. Dancers combine bodily kinesthetic, spatial, and musical intelligences. Journalists use interpersonal and linguistic intelligences. Portrait photographers combine spatial and personal intelligences to fully capture their clientele. Engineers need spatial and logical-mathematical intelligence to create their products and linguistic intelligence to explain them. Our unique combination of intelligences forms the building blocks of our talents, and when we discover our unique talents, we are better able to cultivate our creativity.

was originally his creative solution to understanding energy and mass, but today it is part of the standard technique that all students learn in physics class. Only when students master a given subject can they begin to have spontaneous moments of creativity about it. And mastering a subject takes time. In most fields of study, including the theatre, achieving technical expertise can take decades. The French playwright Alexandre Dumas *fils* (1824–1895) ("*fils*" is the French word for son—he was the son of a famous writer of the same name) once said, "Technique is so important that it sometimes happens that technique is mistaken for art."

> It takes at least five years of rigorous training to be spontaneous.
>
> **Martha Graham,** Dancer and choreographer

Creativity and Talent

Talent is natural ability. One of the key tests of talent is time. For example, if 100 people spent ten hours learning to play baseball, all of them would probably understand the game but some would be better players than others. We would say that these players have a talent for playing baseball. A common question is, are we born with talent or can it be developed? The answer is both.

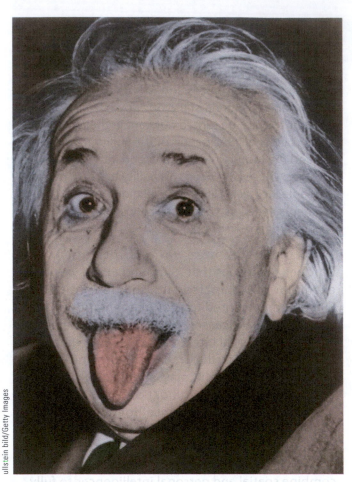

ullstein bild/Getty Images

Creativity and imagination are related. Einstein said that one of the keys to his creativity was that he could imagine the problem he was working on and then translate it to the language of mathematics. He developed his special theory of relativity when he imagined he was riding through the universe on a beam of light.

Our environment is one of the chief factors that helps us develop our talents. Even though we are all born with particular talents, environment can dictate whether we develop or deny them. For example, many people who play the piano come from a home where at least one parent played the piano or was interested in music. Drew Barrymore, producer and star of the movie *Charlie's Angels* and a veteran of over 80 other films and TV shows comes from a family of famous actors going back to her grandfather, John Barrymore. Naturalist Charles Darwin's grandfather was interested in early theories of evolution. Physicist Albert Einstein's father studied math. Our culture, religion, and society, as well as our home environment, can also affect talent. For instance, you may have the talent to be a great dancer, but if you grow up in a cultural environment that forbids dancing, you're less likely to develop that talent.

Different talents develop at different ages. Musical, mathematical, and acting talent can appear at an early age, but talent for playwriting, philosophy, and poetry seldom emerge until people are in their mid or even late twenties. However, even child prodigies can improve upon their natural talent by gaining technique through practice. For example, Austrian composer Wolfgang Amadeus Mozart began studying music at the age of four and wrote his first symphony at the age of eight. But only 12 percent of his compositions were written in the first ten years of his career and few of them are popular today. Yes, Mozart was a child prodigy and he had natural talent, but he needed to develop his technique to produce the works that have made his creativity legendary. In his book *Creativity: Genius and Other Myths*, Robert Weisberg points out that only three major composers produced masterworks before they had at least ten years of musical practice and preparation. Talent is an important part of creativity, but one must develop technique for talent to be fully revealed.

Creative People

Talent and technique are essential to creativity, but creative people also share certain characteristics. Many researchers, including David Perkins of Harvard University, Mihaly Csikszentmihalyi of Claremont Graduate University, John Dacey of Boston College, and Kathleen Lennon of Framingham State College, have attempted to define these common traits. They have found that creative people have a hopeful outlook when facing complex or difficult tasks, are resourceful when unusual circumstances arise, are less afraid of their own impulses, and enjoy being playful. Creativity and play often go hand in hand. (See Spotlight "Playfulness: The First Quality of Genius.") Researchers have also found that creative people are exceptionally curious, able to concentrate, skilled at finding order and options, and willing to take risks. Many of these characteristics describe theatre people, but they also describe creative people in all walks of life. The more you can indulge these sides of your own personality, the more you can bring creativity into your life.

> Talent is like the marksman who hits a target which others cannot reach; genius is the marksman who hits the target others cannot even see.
>
> **Schopenhauer,** Philosopher

SPOTLIGHT ON   Playfulness: The First Quality of Genius

Playfulness has long been associated with creativity. As Donald Newlove says in his book *Invented Voices*, "Playfulness is the first quality of genius—without it we're earthbound." Not only is playfulness an important part of creativity, but many studies have shown that art can foster creativity in young people and can also improve their ability to succeed in school. A study by the Arts Education Partnership found that students with high levels of arts participation outperform "arts-poor" students by virtually every measure. Shirley Brice Heath of the Carnegie Foundation for the Advancement of Teaching found that disadvantaged youth involved in after-school arts programs do better in school than those who spend their time in after-school sports or community involvement programs. The National Research Center on the Gifted and Talented at the University of Connecticut found that students involved in the arts have greater motivation to learn; instead of just studying to get the right answer, they enjoy learning for the experience itself. Finally, researchers at Harvard University's Project Zero, an educational research group headed by Howard Gardner, found that students whose education includes art often become passionately engaged by subjects that students with less arts education find "boring," such as classical works and Shakespeare.

Theatre is a great way to expose children to the arts because it often includes many different art forms, such as instrumental music, singing, storytelling, dance, and art. Unlike television, children's theatre does not allow children to watch passively; instead they must often join in. The first children's theatre in the United States was founded in 1901. Today, there are hundreds of children's theatre companies across the United States that recognize the connection between children, the arts, and creativity. Many of them have theatre-arts training classes in which children gain greater concentration, coordination, communication skills, and self-confidence, as well as increase their creativity and intelligence. Theatre classes can also enhance children's literacy, develop their storytelling abilities, expand their imaginations, and broaden their cultural and individual identities as it opens their minds to alternative perspectives.

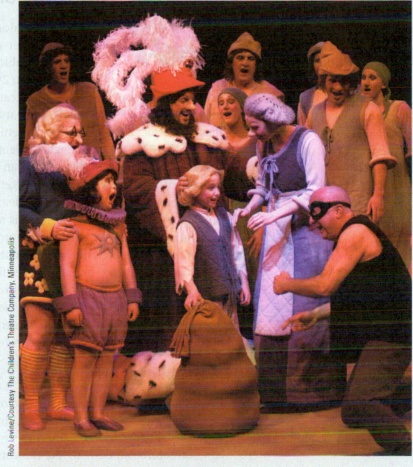

Rob Levine/Courtesy The Children's Theatre Company, Minneapolis

Children's theatre provides kids with a fun opportunity to express their creativity.

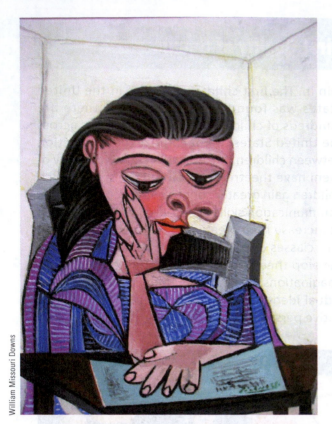

William Missouri Downs

Picasso said, "Action is the foundational key to all success." A creative life is a life of trial and error, experimentation and hard work. "Inspiration exists" said Picasso, "but it has to find you working."

A Burning Curiosity

Creative people have a deep desire to understand the world and how it works. As a result, they are open to new experiences and are seldom satisfied with the standard authoritative answers offered by governments, corporations, religions, science, or society. In order to search out new answers, creative people must ask questions that others overlook. Our education system is designed to fill us with answers but is less focused on teaching us how to ask questions. As Wendell Johnson said in his book *People in Quandaries,* "Probably the most impressive indictment that can be made of our educational system is that it provides the students with answers, but it is poorly designed to provide them with skill in the asking of questions that are effectively directive of inquiry and evaluation." Or, to repeat an old adage, a fool knows all the answers, but none of the questions. Creative people ask questions—questions to which there may be no answer, at least not yet.

The Power of Concentration

Creativity is seldom as spontaneous as it looks. It typically comes only after months, years, or decades of hard work. For example, Pablo Picasso produced 20,000 works of art in 75 years, Einstein 248 publications in 53 years, Darwin 119 publications in 51 years, Freud 330 publications in 45 years, and Shakespeare 37 plays and more than 150 sonnets in 24 years. Creative people are often so focused that they make social errors such as forgetting names or appointments. Sir Isaac Newton (1642–1727) the great English scientist, astronomer, and mathematician, would sometimes not arrive to dinner until an hour after he was called. His concentration was so great that he would simply forget to eat. Other times, while entertaining company, Newton would jot down an idea and become so engrossed in what he was doing that he would disappear into his room and forget that visitors were waiting.

Malcolm Gladwell, a regular contributor to *The New Yorker* and best-selling author, has popularized the "**10,000-hour rule**" in his recent book *Outliers: The Story of Success*. The "10,000-hour rule" specifically suggests that all masters of creativity—from Bill Gates to Mozart to Helen Mirren—spent a minimum of 10,000 hours practicing in their respective fields before they rose to significant and consistent success. If you find yourself well suited to concentrating on particular tasks for long stretches of time, take note: those tasks might reveal important areas of creativity for you.

The Ability to Find Order

Creative people have the ability to find or create order where others see chaos. Order is created when we make analogies, find similarities, connect ideas that have not been previously connected, uncover new possibilities, and discover or invent structure. Structure can be real, like the composition of an atom, or imagined like the design of a play. Both are important because we not only have the ability to ascertain the world in which we find ourselves, but to recreate it. Structure is essential because, as we mentioned in Chapter 1, when we find or create it, we also discover meaning. Many cultures, governments, societies, and religions have attempted to stifle the never-ending quest for new structures, but the urge is always alive and well as long as a creative individual dares to say, "There must be a better way."

Mental Agility and the Ability to Find Options

Creative people have the ability to let their minds roam as they search for new perspectives and new approaches to problems. They use both convergent and divergent thinking. **Convergent thinking** is measured by IQ and involves well-defined rational problems that have only one correct answer. **Divergent thinking** involves fluency and the ability to generate a multitude of ideas from numerous perspectives. However, creative people do not come up with different questions and answers just for the sake of being different. For example, when a creative person is given a psychological examination such as the Rorschach inkblot test (a clinical personality test that uses splotches of ink on a piece of paper), their answers show originality but are not "weird." ("Weird," in this case, means answers that do not have any stimulus from or basis in the inkblot itself.) For instance, if the inkblot looks vaguely like a monkey, a creative person might answer that it looks like Richard Nixon. In other words, the creative person's answer is rooted in some stimulus from the inkblot: if you think about it, Richard Nixon, from the right angle, did have some simian traits. Creative people have mental mobility and the ability to find options based in reality.

The Willingness to Take Risks and Accept Failure

It is not enough to have a good idea; creative people test their ideas. They seek criticism and they accept failure. Failure is the difference between what we expect and what we get. For many of us, failure is not an option in our jobs or in our lives. But if failure is not an option, then creativity is not an option, because the vast majority of creative work ends in failure. Thomas Edison conducted 2,004 experiments before he found the right filament for the electric light—that means he had 2,003 failures. Pablo Picasso produced 20,000 works of art but many of them were mediocre. Ludwig van Beethoven's musical sketchbooks contain more than 5,000 pages of music that failed to make it into his symphonies. Even Shakespeare wrote plays that might be considered failures; have you ever seen a production of *Timon of Athens*

> Most of all, forget those romantic myths that creativity is all about being artsy and gifted and not about hard work. They discourage us because we're waiting for that one full-blown moment of inspiration. And while we're waiting, we may never start working on what we might someday create.
>
> **R. Keith Sawyer,** Psychologist

> Failure is unimportant. It takes courage to make a fool of yourself.
>
> **Charlie Chaplin,** Actor

Pavel L Photo and Video/Shutterstock.com

Failure is a part of creativity. Even great works of art sometimes start as failures. When Tchaikovsky premiered *The Nutcracker* ballet in St. Petersburg Russia in 1892 both the critics and the audience considered it a huge failure. It is now one of the most popular ballets in the world.

or *King John*? Hans Bethe, winner of the Nobel Prize in physics, said two things are required for creativity: "one is a brain. And second is the willingness to spend long times in thinking, with a definite possibility that you come out with nothing." Creative people have the ability not only to learn from their failures but also to accept failure as an important part of the creative process. They know that the odds of finding a creative answer to a problem are directly related to the number of attempts.

Enhancing Your Creativity

Too often we think of creativity as happening by chance. Or we assume that creativity is something that happens to only talented people. Certainly, luck is involved with being in the right place at the right time, and talent does make it possible to take advantage of opportunities, but as scientist Louis Pasteur (1822–1895) said, "Chance favors the prepared mind." Or as the lawyer Johnnie Cochran (1937–2005) put it a century later, "Luck is the residue of preparation." In other words, with appropriate techniques and developed talents, we all have the potential to be creative. Let's look at a few basic ways to increase creativity.

Consider Your Environment

Greece in the fifth century BCE, Florence in the fifteenth century, and Paris in the nineteenth century were all centers of creative activity. The mingling of different lifestyles and beliefs and the freedom to express them encouraged people in each of these places to exchange ideas and solve problems in new ways. But there have been many more times in history when the environment limited creativity. Conformist cultures and rigid regimes are not as likely to produce creativity as are those where new voices and ideas can be heard and appreciated. Nor is creativity likely in societies or groups where adherence to tradition limits new ideas. Sir Ken Robinson, an expert on creativity, wrote in his book *Out of Our Minds: Learning to Be Creative,* "Creativity prospers best, under particular conditions, especially where there is a flow of ideas between people who have different sorts of expertise." If you seek out places where creativity is allowed, and spend time with people who have different expertise, you will begin to find that elusive creative environment.

Temper Your Criticism

Creative people are always interested in criticism and feedback, but one roadblock to creativity is allowing yourself to be too critical of your new ideas. People are often more creative when they imagine as many solutions as possible and hold off critical judgment until later. (This process, called *brainstorming*, is discussed in detail later in this chapter.) A recent scientific study placed a group of researchers in a closed conference room with a problem to solve. They were told that they should all analytically judge every suggestion as soon as it was offered. After a day of thinking and judging, they failed to solve the problem. The next day they were given an equally difficult problem to solve, but this time they spent the morning pitching possible solutions without judging them or even considering plausibility. That afternoon, the scientists were asked to critically judge each possible solution. It worked—one of their morning pitches solved the problem. By withholding criticism, they succeeded in increasing creativity.

If you constantly censor your ideas, you will stifle your creativity. The next time you have a problem to solve, write down every solution that comes to mind, without censoring any of them. Soon you'll have a list of possible and improbable solutions.

It hinders the creative work of the mind if the intellect examines too closely the ideas as they pour in.

Friedrich Schiller, Playwright, poet, and historian

Later, come back to the list and evaluate each solution. Nothing is more detrimental to the creative process than censoring every idea you have the moment it's created; this only causes creative gridlock.

Assess Your Motivation

Experts have found that the reason for wanting to be creative can affect the extent of creativity. If a person's primary motivation is a goal outside the creative act itself, he or she will generally be less creative. For example, Konstantin Stanislavsky (1863–1938), the Russian acting teacher and director, observed that actors' creativity is significantly stifled if they are thinking of the audience rather than concentrating on the artistic task. He said that an actor must be able to develop a "circle of his own attention" where other motivations such as wealth, critical praise, or success are unimportant. Beginning artists who dream of becoming wealthy or a star tend to drop out of art if they are not immediately successful. On the other hand, beginning artists who focus only on the creative process tend to stick with it for years and have more opportunities to be creative—and thus have a greater chance of becoming wealthy and a star. The same is true in all fields. If the product is more important than the process, you will generally be less creative.

Adjust Your Schedule

Creativity takes time. People whose lives are totally booked with family and work obligations—dashing from school to soccer practice to piano lessons to a part-time job—seldom have much time to be creative. This is true of many Americans. According to a recent report of the International Labour Organization, the United States has surpassed Japan as the nation whose workers put in the most hours in the advanced industrial world. The average American works eight weeks more per year than the average Western European. All this work can be good for personal wealth, the company, or the country, but it can be dangerous for creativity, especially if it is mindless, follow-the-rules work. Creativity requires time to let the mind wander.

Let Your Mind Wander

If your mind wanders while you are trying to take a final exam, you could be in trouble, but there are times when "zoning out" can be quite helpful. Modern researchers find that on average we do a lot of daydreaming. According to two leading researchers, Jonathan Schooler and Jonathan Smallwood of the University of California, Santa Barbara, our minds wander as much as 30 percent of the time. "People assume mind wandering is a bad thing, but if we couldn't do it during a boring task, life would be horrible," Dr. Smallwood insists. Such

In the theatre, creativity is often a group activity. One artist's creativity is inspired by another's. Here, Anne Louise Briggs rehearses a scene from Aaron Posner's *Stupid Fu*&king Bird*, which was inspired by Anton Chekhov's 1896 play *The Seagull*. This production was directed by William Missouri Downs and produced by the Salt Lake Acting Company.

William Missouri Downs

mind wandering can help foster imagination and creativity. Psychologist R. Keith Sawyer, in his book *Explaining Creativity: The Science of Human Innovation*, says: "In creativity research, we refer to the three Bs—for the bathtub, the bed and the bus—places where ideas have famously and suddenly emerged. When we take time off from working on a problem, we change what we're doing and our context, and that can activate different areas of our brain." It is heartening to know that allowing our minds to wander in appropriate situations can make us more imaginative, productive, and help to incubate new ideas. (For more, see the Spotlight "Creativity Is More Than Imagination.")

SPOTLIGHT ON Creativity Is More Than Imagination

One of the great modern thinkers on creativity is Sir Ken Robinson, who is internationally recognized as an expert on how to enhance creativity. Not only is he a consultant to many Fortune 500 companies, but Queen Elizabeth II knighted him for his service to the arts.

In his book *Out of Our Minds: Learning to Be Creative*, Sir Ken writes that creativity involves *doing*, not just imagining. We all—more or less—have the ability to imagine. Asked to imagine a blue-eyed dog with three legs, you can picture such a likeness in your mind's eye with relative ease. Our imagination can take us on flights of fancy as we generate mental representations of just about anything. But creativity, says Sir Ken, is more complex than simple imagination, because it involves taking action. Creativity involves doing something like mathematics, writing, music, acting, engineering, building a multimillion-dollar business, or any one of a thousand activities.

Furthermore, Sir Ken says that creativity produces outcomes that are original in some form. For example, creativity may result in something novel on a personal level, or unique to a particular community, or original to humanity as a whole. But uniqueness is not enough. In addition to originality, creativity must also be of *value*. Unlike imagination, creativity advances, changes, or improves an individual, a society, or humanity. Creativity, according to Sir Ken, is "*imaginative processes with outcomes that are original and of value.*"

In order to make something that is both original and of value we must be able to perceive and judge the ideas and beliefs through which we frame our understanding of the world, and then make connections that previously went unconnected. So creativity is not a chance event but a conscious effort. The "aha" moment may happen in a second, but taken as a whole, creativity is a process, not an event.

For more on how to be more creative and teach creativity, read Sir Ken Robinson's books.

Brian To/FilmMagic/Getty Images

Sir Ken Robinson

The Need for Solitude

One of the keys to letting your mind wander is solitude, which can be hard to find in this modern world full of noise and distractions. Contemporary thinking on productivity suggests that collaboration is the most essential element to success. Consequently, schools group students into teams and demand that they work together, and businesses commonly design offices without walls to maximize collaboration. However, many people are often more creative when they work alone. In many cases, the level of creativity often goes down as group size increases. In addition, the creative answers groups come up with are often less interesting. Hollywood director Darren Aronofsky has suggested that if you put ten people in a room trying to come up with their favorite ice cream, they are going to agree on vanilla. Steve Wozniak, co-founder of Apple computer said, "Most inventors and engineers I've met are like me. . . they live in their heads. They're almost like artists. In fact, the very best of them are artists. And artists work best alone. . . I'm going to give you some advice that might be hard to take. That advice is: Work alone. . . Not on a committee. Not on a team." Creativity often requires alone time.

Change Your Life

One of the best ways to enhance creativity is to get regular exercise and plenty of sleep. Pulling all-nighters is not a good way to come up with creative answers. Scientists have shown that people whose lives or jobs make too many demands on their sleep are generally less creative than people who get their full seven or eight hours. After sleeping a full night, according to neuroscientist Candace Pert of the National Institute of Mental Health, the body is capable of releasing more endorphins. Endorphins are chemicals that control the brain's perception of, and response to, pain and stress and can help promote a feeling of well-being. Obviously, a feeling of well-being is more conducive to creativity than the state of feeling stressed out.

One simple way to release endorphins in the brain is through exercise. When you exercise, you put yourself into an "endorphinergic state" that can last for hours or days and can increase creativity.

> Without great solitude, no serious work is possible.
>
> *Picasso,* Painter

> The principal goal of education in the schools should be creating men and women who are capable of doing new things, not simply repeating what other generations have done; men and women who are creative, inventive, and discoverers, who can be critical and verify, and not accept, everything they are offered.
>
> *Jean Piaget,* Psychologist

Creativity Is about Problem Solving

Without the ability to solve problems, your creativity will be limited. In order to solve a problem, you must first detect a problem. Mihaly Csikszentmihalyi says, "Many creative individuals have pointed out that in their work the formulation of the problem is more important than its solution and that real advances in science and in art tend to come when new questions are asked or old problems are viewed from a new angle." Once you perceive a problem, you need to look for a creative solution.

Here are steps that artists as well as scientists often use when trying to solve a problem:

- **Specify the problem.** The first step in problem solving is to identify the problem in specific terms. In his book *People in Quandaries,* Wendell

Johnson recalls a psychiatrist who was often sent patients who had been diagnosed as seriously maladjusted. He noticed they weren't necessarily more maladjusted than the average patient, but they all had one thing in common: "They were unable to tell him clearly what was the matter." They had not been able to tell their doctors what the problem was, so their doctors had been unable to suggest solutions. Johnson goes on to say, "By far the most important step toward the solution of the laboratory problem lies in stating the problem in such a way as to suggest a fruitful attack on it. Once that is accomplished, any ordinary assistant can usually turn the cranks and read the dials. . . . There cannot be a precise answer to a vague question."

- **Break the problem into manageable components.** Most problems are made up of dozens of smaller problems. We need to unravel the strands of the problem to begin to analyze it. Break the problem into manageable components, and there is a good chance you can solve them one at a time. For example, when actors rehearse a play, they stop, go back, and try it again, over and over, in order to solve one little problem at a time; they don't take on the entire play all at once. Inability to solve a problem is often due to trying to solve too many problems at once.

- **Brainstorm possible solutions.** Often brainstorming can be considered a group activity, but it can also be an individual act. Once you have identified the problem and broken it into manageable components, you can start coming up with possible solutions. Recall the example from the previous section about the scientists pitching solutions to a problem. Their brainstorming helped stimulate their creativity, which resulted in a number of good ideas for an effective solution. Sometimes brainstorming yields ideas about how to solve a problem by using existing techniques. In these cases, it may seem that free-association didn't stimulate any creativity because it did not result in a brand-new technique. However, it did generate a moment of insight into the fact that an appropriate technique to solve the problem already exists.

- **Test the solution to see if it works.** Here is where you use critical thinking skills to see if the first three steps have in fact provided a solution. Testing the answer is often the longest step, particularly in the

Every production is filled with hundreds of problems that must be solved in order to ensure a smooth performance. Here director Rachel Rosenfeld and playwright Jaime Cruz work to resolve script problems long before rehearsal begins.

William Missouri Downs

sciences, where collecting data can take years. Testing the solution in the theatre also requires data. For example, most new plays are "workshopped," or read in front of an audience numerous times before the official premiere; the playwright evaluates audience reaction to new scenes as the work continues to evolve through development.

At the end of the process, if the most likely solution fails, it's time to start over with step one—did you clearly specify the problem?

If these steps sound similar to the scientific method, they should. In many ways, art and science are closely related. They both rely on experimentation, research, free speech, curiosity, originality, intellectual examination, and creativity. So the next time you attend a jazz concert, watch a ballet, or go to the theatre, think of all the problems the artists had to solve in order to create an evening of entertainment and art. As they express themselves, they realize that art is about more than expressing emotions; it is also about finding those moments of insight that make a live performance communicate ideas and provide a magical experience.

Curtain Call

The Intellectual Property Association in Washington, D.C., a trade association for owners of patents, trademarks, and copyrights, estimates creative ideas in the United States to be worth around 360 billion dollars a year. Such a huge resource generates more income than agriculture, automobiles, or aerospace.

In the theatre, creativity often depends on the interaction of individuals who must not only work together but also build on each other's creativity. The finished product is not only limited by time and money but also by the egos, techniques, and collaborative creativity of the ensemble. Most people who go into the theatre do not do it for the money but rather the hope of living a creative life. Many factors lead to creativity, but most people who work in creative fields would probably agree that the best way to live a creative life is to just do it. As Anne Bogart writes in her book *A Director Prepares*:

> Do not assume that you have to have some prescribed condition to do your best work. Do not wait. Do not wait for enough time or money to accomplish what you think you have in mind. Work with what you have RIGHT NOW. Work with the people around you RIGHT NOW. . . . Do not wait for what you assume is the appropriate stress-free environment in which to generate expression. Do not wait for maturity or insight or wisdom. Do not wait till you are sure that you know what you are doing. Do not wait until you have enough technique. What you do now, what you make of your present circumstances will determine the quality and scope of your future endeavors. And at the same time be patient.

> Creative activity involves a combination of control and freedom, conscious and unconscious thought, and intuition and rational analysis.
>
> **Sir Ken Robinson,** Writer and arts education adviser

SUMMARY

MindTap

Test your knowledge with online printable flashcards and online quizzing.

Creativity can be defined as a moment of insight. Closely tied to creativity are technique and talent. Technique is composed of the lessons learned from creativity, and talent can often be developed or denied by our environment. To be more creative, it is important to examine and emulate the traits of creative people. Creative people have a burning curiosity, strong concentration, and a mental agility that allows them to find order where others see only chaos. They also have the ability to accept failure, because more often than not creative solutions fail. IQ is a factor in creativity, but studies have found that an extremely high IQ does not make people more creative. The key is to find the kinds of intelligence in which you excel. Howard Gardner's theory of multiple intelligences identifies linguistic, musical, logical-mathematical, spatial, bodily kinesthetic, and personal intelligences.

In order to enhance your creativity, you need adequate amounts of exercise and sleep as well as an environment that nourishes creativity and allows time for you to be creative. It is also important to examine the reason you want to be creative; if your motivation is too far removed from the creative act itself, you will probably not be very creative. Another important aspect of being creative is to generate ideas without immediately censoring them. One of the best ways to enhance your creativity is to learn to solve problems. The steps of problem solving include specifically defining the problem, breaking the problem into manageable components, brainstorming possible solutions, and testing to see if the most likely solution works.

KEY TERMS

10,0000-hour rule *200*

Bodily kinesthetic intelligence *197*

Convergent thinking *201*

Creativity *195*

Divergent thinking *201*

Linguistic intelligence *196*

Logical-mathematical intelligence *196*

Musical intelligence *196*

Personal intelligences *197*

Spatial intelligence *197*

Talent *197*

Technique *196*

Chapter 11

THE MUSICAL

The musical has been a mainstay of American theatre for well over a hundred years and has been called the only uniquely American art form. Here, Jill Paice and Robert Fairchild perform in *An American in Paris*, at the Palace Theater in New York.

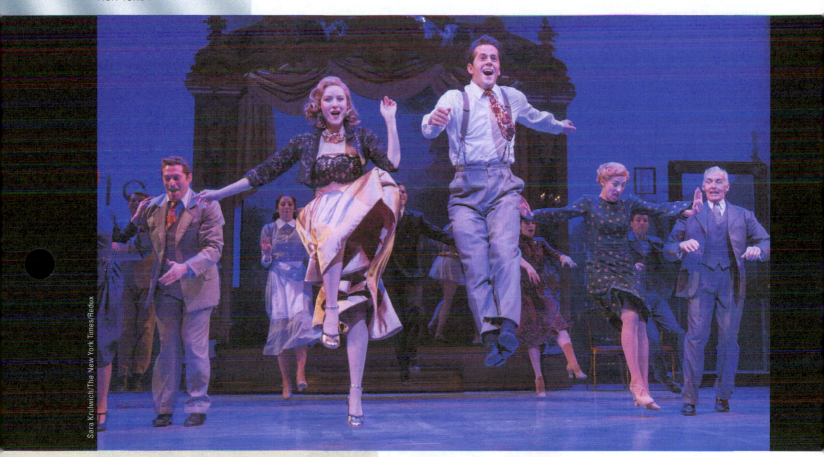

Sara Krulwich/The New York Times/Redux

Outline

No doubt about it, Americans love musicals. From Broadway theatres to high schools, from cruise ships to casinos—musicals are everywhere. Not only are they often big box office hits, but some of the longest running shows in the history of the theatre have been musicals. For example, *The Phantom of the Opera* ran on Broadway for over 11,000 performances. Broadway shows sell over $1 billion worth of tickets annually, and the majority of those seats are for musicals. Why are musicals so popular? Perhaps it's because music—from deafening car stereos, to telephone-hold Muzak, to our favorite tracks that get us through the day—is a constant for most of us. Perhaps the rhythmic repetition of our heart

MindTap°

Start with a quick warm-up activity and review the chapter's learning objectives.

> American musical theatre is our indigenous art form. We can't claim drama, ballet, or opera, but musical theatre is our very own. . . . Musicals are in our blood and in our bones, are part of our collective personality.
>
> **Molly Smith,** Artistic director of the Arena Stage

MindTap°

Read, highlight and take notes online.

Avenue Q represents a new twist on the traditional musical comedy, where irreverence and racy humor take center stage. Featuring puppets manipulated by bunraku-like handlers, this innovative musical tells the story of Princeton, an eager college graduate who comes to New York City with big dreams and little money. He settles into a slightly shady neighborhood populated by a motley host of characters in search of work, love, and a reason to be. A sort of *Sesame Street* for adults, *Avenue Q* showcases songs such as "I'm Not Wearing Underwear Today," "Everyone's a Little Bit Racist," and "What Do You Do with a B.A. in English?" Book by Jeff Whitty, lyrics and music by Robert Lopez and Jeff Marx. Directed by Jason Moore, John Golden Theatre, New York, since 2003.

beating inside of us gives music its power. Researchers have shown that music can intensify our emotions, increase our blood pressure, cause our pupils to dilate, and raise our heart rate. Music can make us dance with joy or trigger depression; it can inspire us to make love or to make war. French emperor Napoleon Bonaparte summed up the power of music when he said, "Give me control over he who shapes the music of a nation; I care not who makes the laws." In this chapter, we will examine one of the oldest forms of theatre, the play that combines music and drama, and its popular modern variation, the American musical.

The Many Types of Musicals

There are two categories of theatre: plays with music and plays without. Plays without music are sometimes called **straight plays**. Plays with music come in all shapes. Let's make a quick survey of the various forms before we look at the elements and the history of musical theatre. **Opera**, such as Giacomo Puccini's (1858–1924) *Madama Butterfly* (1904), is a drama that is set entirely to music; all the lines are sung, usually to grand classical music. **Operetta**, or light opera, such as *The Mikado* (1885) by Gilbert and Sullivan, differs from "grand opera" because it has a frivolous, comic theme, some spoken dialogue, a melodramatic story, and usually a little dancing.

A musical, unlike most operas, combines both singing and dialogue, and comes in a variety of forms. A **musical comedy**, such as *Guys and Dolls* (1950), is characterized by a light-hearted, fast-moving comic story, whose dialogue is interspersed with popular music. A straight **musical**,

Ethan Miller/Getty Images Entertainment/Getty Images

such as *West Side Story* (1957), has a more serious plot and theme. A **rock musical** uses rock music—the rock and roll of the 1950s (*Grease*, 1972), the psychedelic rock of the 1960s (*Hair*, 1967), or contemporary pop and rock (*Rent*, 1996). A program of sketches, singing, dancing, and songs pulled from the same author or authors is called a **revue**, or musical review; a program of unrelated singing, dancing, and comedy numbers is called a **variety show**. Variety shows and revues descend from **vaudeville**, a popular form of stage entertainment from the 1880s to the 1940s. An evening of vaudeville included a dozen or so slapstick comedy routines, song-and-dance numbers, magic acts, and juggling or acrobatic performances. Vaudeville descends from **burlesque**, a form of musical entertainment featuring bawdy songs, dancing women, and sometimes striptease. Burlesque began in the 1840s as a parody of the pretentiousness of opera—and of the upper class who could afford to attend it.

Whether opera, rock musical, or burlesque, no matter what your taste, you are sure to find a type of musical theatre to your liking. Now let's take a closer look at the structure and music of most forms of musicals.

The Script

Musical scripts have three components: book, music, and lyrics. The **music** is the orchestrated melodies, the **lyrics** are the sung words, and the **book** is the spoken lines of dialogue as well as the plot. Unlike most straight plays, musicals often need several writers. The **book writer** writes the dialogue, the **composer** writes the music, and the **lyricist** writes the lyrics. For example, Joseph Stein wrote the book for *Fiddler on the Roof* (1964), Jerry Bock wrote the music, and Sheldon Harnick wrote the lyrics. Occasionally, a versatile writer, such as George M. Cohan (*Fifty Miles from Boston*, 1908) and Meredith Willson (*The Music Man*, 1957), can write all three, but the duties for most musicals are shared. And these creative teams don't appreciate it when only one member of the team is credited for the entire work, as often happens. The wife of lyricist Oscar Hammerstein, a famous name in musical theatre, once overheard someone at a party say, "I just love Jerome Kern's 'Ol' Man River'" (from the musical *Show Boat*). She indignantly corrected the guest by pointing out that her husband had written the lyrics and that all Kern wrote was "Dum, dum, dum dum; dum, dum, dum dum."

Musicals with a particularly well-developed story and characters, such as *Fiddler on the Roof*, are sometimes called **book musicals**. *Fosse* (1998) and other **dance musicals** feature the work of a director-choreographer such as Tommy Tune, Michael Bennett, or Bob Fosse. Musicals that feature a particular band's songs are called **jukebox musicals**, like *Mamma Mia!* (2001), which was built around the music of Abba. Musicals that are mostly singing and have less spoken dialogue, such as *Les Misérables* and *Evita*, are known as **operatic musicals**. Operatic musicals are similar to operettas, but their tone is often much darker and more dramatic. For example, Steven Sondheim's operatic musical *Sweeney Todd: The Demon Barber of Fleet Street* features a story of betrayal, seduction, and revenge, subjects that are far too serious for light operettas. (For more on Sondheim and *Sweeney Todd*, see the Spotlight "Steven Sondheim.")

> One difference between poetry and lyrics is that lyrics sort of fade into the background. They fade on the page and live on the stage when set to music.
>
> **Stephen Sondheim,** Musical theatre lyricist and composer

SPOTLIGHT ON Stephen Sondheim

One of the most accomplished lyricists and composers of contemporary American musicals is Stephen Sondheim (b. 1930). Sondheim wrote his first musical at the age of fifteen, but his remarkable career officially began when he became a protégé of legendary lyricist and producer Oscar Hammerstein II (1895–1960). Sondheim's Broadway credits begin with the lyrics for *West Side Story*, including the famous "I feel pretty / Oh, so pretty / I feel pretty and witty and bright!" He went on to write the lyrics for the golden-era musical *Gypsy* (1959) and was lyricist and composer for the ever-popular *A Funny Thing Happened on the Way to the Forum* (1962).

Sondheim has also written less traditional musicals like *Company* (1970), *Follies* (1971), *A Little Night Music* (1972), and *Pacific Overtures* (1976). These musicals are known as "concept" musicals because they focus on a particular event rather than a more traditional cause-and-effect story plot. For example, *Company* follows

Robbie Jack/Corbis

One of Stephen Sondheim's most famous musicals, *Sweeney Todd* is the tale of a murderous barber who wreaks havoc in eighteenth-century London to avenge his unjust imprisonment. Supposedly based on a real case, the story of *Sweeney Todd* fascinates audiences as much as the mystery of Jack the Ripper. Music and lyrics by Stephen Sondheim, book by Hugh Wheeler. Royal Opera House, Covent Garden, London, 2003.

the main character, a single guy named Bobby, through a series of dinners with his somewhat neurotic friends. *Follies* tells the story of a condemned theatre building in which a series of vaudeville-like *Follies* had run many years ago. Because the theatre is due to be demolished to make room for a parking lot, all of the old "follies girls" return to the theatre for a reunion. The story runs in both the present and the past, showing the audience the younger versions of these characters. *Pacific Overtures* (1976), which was staged Kabuki style, portrays the ways in which Japan's culture was affected when the United States forced the isolated islands to open up to international trade in 1853.

One of Sondheim's most famous musicals is *Sweeney Todd: The Demon Barber of Fleet Street* (1979), which combines a conventional plot structure with an operatic score. *Sweeney Todd* explores a subject that is highly unusual for musicals: revenge-based serial murder and cannibalism. The musical is the story of Benjamin Barker, a barber who has led a beautiful life until a corrupt and depraved judge convicts him on trumped-up charges. After serving his time on a prison island, Benjamin returns, assumes the name Sweeney Todd, and sets out on a mission of revenge, slitting the throats of men who come to his shop for a shave, and then giving them to his neighbor, Mrs. Lovett, who turns the bodies into meat pies. Sondheim has even reimagined his musical as a Hollywood movie starring Johnny Depp. The film version, with more dialogue and less singing, is more of a book musical, whereas the original was an operatic musical. Other popular Sondheim musicals include *Sunday in the Park with George*, loosely based on the life and loves of French neo-Impressionist painter Georges Seurat; *Into the Woods*, which combines classic fairy tales into a story that shows that life seldom ends happily ever after; *Assassins*, which explores the history of presidential assassins in America, from John Wilkes Booth to John Hinckley, Jr.; *Passion*, which was adapted from Ettore Scola's film *Passione d'Amore*.

Sondheim's work proves that a musical can be about any subject. As Sondheim's mentor, Oscar Hammerstein, once said, "It is nonsense to say what a musical should or should not be. It should be anything it wants to be, and if you don't like it you don't have to go to it. There is only one absolutely indispensable element that a musical must have. It must have music."

From Ballads to Showstoppers

A traditional musical begins with an **overture**—a medley of the show's songs played as a preview. The overture lets the audience know that it's time to stop talking because the performance is about to begin; it can also provide time for latecomers to take their seats. At one time, overtures were the standard opening for all musicals. *The King and I, My Fair Lady*, and *Gypsy* all had overtures. But in 1975 the musical *A Chorus Line* cut out the overture; one was written but cut before the show opened because the show's creators felt that it might destroy the illusion that the audience was watching a real chorus line audition. Since then the overture has become optional. Musicals like *The Producers, Wicked, Spamalot*, and *The Color Purple* have traditional overtures. Other musicals, such as *Chicago* and *The Drowsy Chaperone*, have short mini-overtures, whereas *Rent* and *Spring Awakening* dispense with the overture altogether.

During the show, different types of songs are used for different dramatic and theatrical purposes. Leonard Bernstein and Stephen Sondheim use a large variety in *West Side Story*, a retelling of *Romeo and Juliet* set on the streets of New York. "Tonight" is a **ballad**, a love song for Tony and Maria. "Gee, Officer Krupke" is a **comedy number** that provides comic relief. "A Boy Like That," a sung conversation between Maria and her best friend, advances the story line. And "America" is a big production number called a **showstopper** because of the torrent of applause that such numbers often receive, literally stopping the show.

Songs are placed strategically within the story, usually at points where dialogue is not sufficient, so the characters must break into song to fully express what they are feeling. Some songs are followed later by a **reprise**, a repetition of the song, sometimes with new lyrics, sometimes with the same lyrics but with new meaning or subtext in order to make a dramatic point.

> A song without music is a lot like H_2 without the O.
>
> **Ira Gershwin,** Musical theatre lyricist

Perhaps the most famous of Stephen Sondheim's works is *West Side Story*. He was only 26 years old when he wrote the lyrics for this classic retelling of Shakespeare's *Romeo and Juliet*. The revival pictured here, produced at the Palace Theater in New York, starred George Aram, Karen Olivo, and Cody Green.

Sara Krulwich/The New York Times/Redux Pictures

Musicals: Then and Now

Although it's often said that the musical is an American invention (and that may be true), music, dance, and song have been a part of the theatre since its beginnings. Traditional African dramas and ritual plays have always incorporated music and dance. Twenty-five hundred years ago, Greek tragedies depended on a chorus of singing and dancing men. Aristophanes may have been creating musical comedy when he combined parody, satire, wit, and music in his plays. Then, for hundreds of years the Roman stage was filled with bawdy song and dance, and during the Middle Ages traveling bands of performers offered popular songs mixed with stories full of slapstick comedy. Elizabethan plays often included folk songs—Shakespeare's *The Tempest* alone includes nine songs. Japanese Kabuki plays depend on dance, music, and song. Musical masques, operas, burlesques, minstrel shows, variety shows, and music hall revues are all ancestors of the modern American musical. Though Americans were not the first to add song and dance to the theatre, they did make a unique form of musical theatre by borrowing from and combining earlier forms. Let's take a closer look at musicals throughout history.

Opera: High Art and Comic Relief

In opera, there is no spoken dialogue. Instead, the actors sing and sometimes chant their speeches and conversations. Opera developed 500 years ago during the Italian Renaissance. Its creators were attempting to imitate ancient Greek tragedies; many scholars of the time thought the plays of Aeschylus, Sophocles, and Euripides were intended to be sung rather than spoken. In the end, they created

Modern American musicals are sometimes based on movies with which the audience is familiar. There have been musical versions of *Legally Blonde, The Lion King, The Producers,* and many others. One of the latest is Mel Brooks' musical version of his movie *Young Frankenstein,* pictured here.

Sara Krulwich/The New York Times/Redux Pictures

a hybrid of music and drama, an art form in which the actors sang all their lines. The word *opera* comes from the Latin for "work"; the Italians may have originally called these singing plays "works in music" or "musical works for the stage." The first operas were staged in Italy in the late 1500s, and the first public opera house was built in Venice in 1637. Opera proved to be so popular that by the end of the century Venice alone had 11 opera houses. Opera hit its peak in the nineteenth century. Notable opera composers include Richard Wagner (1813–1883), Giacomo Puccini (1858–1924), Wolfgang Mozart (1756–1791), Gioacchino Rossini (1792–1868), and George Frideric Handel (1685–1759).

Today, traditional opera is not as common as it once was. It's also often considered an elitist form of entertainment enjoyed primarily by the wealthy and well educated. But other forms of opera are still quite popular. **Comic opera**, including operetta, developed out of *intermezzi*, or comic interludes performed during the intermissions of operas. This style of opera became widely popular with the work of Sir William Schwenck Gilbert (1836–1911) and Sir Arthur Seymour Sullivan (1842–1900), including *The Pirates of Penzance* (1879), *The Mikado* (1885), and

Michal Daniel

Gilbert and Sullivan's *The Pirates of Penzance* is the story of Frederic, a child mistakenly apprenticed to a band of kindhearted pirates. In his 21st year, Frederic has fulfilled his apprenticeship and is eager to return to respectable society. However, the pirates inform him that he was bound until his 21st birthday, and since he was born in a leap year on February 29, technically he has celebrated only five birthdays. When Sir Arthur Sullivan was working on *Pirates*, he wrote to his mother, "I think [the opera] will be a great success, for it is exquisitely funny, and the music is strikingly tuneful and catching." He was right—*The Pirates of Penzance* was an instant hit and is still performed regularly. This 2004 production featured Dan Callaway as Frederic and was directed by Joe Dowling, Guthrie Theater, Minneapolis.

> Nothing takes you inside the
> soul of a human being like a
> musical does.
>
> **Lisa Kron,** Tony Award–
> winning writer

H.M.S. Pinafore (1878). When Gilbert and Sullivan's *H.M.S. Pinafore* was staged in the United States in 1879, it was a triumph. Soon, American theatres added song and dance wherever possible in their shows.

Early American Musicals

The earliest American musicals were **ballad operas**, brought from England and popular during the colonial period. These comic operas mixed popular songs of the day with spoken dialogue. About a hundred years later, around 1840, burlesque was all the rage. It featured songs, skits, and plenty of racy dancing girls in a "leg-show"; later burlesque shows also included striptease acts. The original purpose of burlesque was to lampoon high society's operatic tradition by turning it into a kind of sexy caricature. Today, burlesque lives on in The Pussycat Dolls, an all-female group of dancers, whose lineup has included Carmen Electra and guest stars Britney Spears and Gwen Stefani. These modern acts no longer satirize high art, but they continue the tradition of striptease's sly humor and sexual innuendo.

By 1890, vaudeville had replaced burlesque as the dominant form of American musical entertainment. It was designed to be more respectable, wholesome, and family oriented. It added acts by ventriloquists, acrobats, jugglers, magicians, male and female impersonators, and monologists (early stand-up comedians) to the toned-down song and dance numbers. Vaudeville shows could also include animal acts; ballroom dancing; demonstrations of scientific discoveries; famous criminals recounting their lurid past; comic skits featuring actors playing Irish, Jewish, Italian, or "blackface" stereotypes; and sing-alongs of "Camptown Races," "Swanee River," "Oh! Susanna," and other popular songs.

Most vaudeville companies were small and traveled the rails from town to town putting on one-night shows in local theatres. Big-time vaudeville was the

In the late nineteenth century, vaudeville was the dominant form of musical entertainment in the United States. Intended as a family-friendly alternative to burlesque, vaudeville often featured family acts such as *The Three Keatons* (who, incidentally, shared the stage with escape artist Harry Houdini and his wife, Beatrice). The Keatons' shtick included skits that showed their audiences how to "properly" raise a child, but included throwing the youngster though fake walls and scenery. The youngest member of this act grew up to become one of America's greatest silent film stars: Buster Keaton, the great stone face.

Bettmann/Corbis

Ziegfeld Follies (1907–1931), a series of lavish musical reviews on Broadway, featuring Will Rogers, Fanny Brice, and other popular stars. (In many ways, the *Follies* live on in today's Las Vegas stage shows.) Many early movie stars got their start in vaudeville, including W. C. Fields, Al Jolson, Buster Keaton, Fred Astaire, and the comedy team George Burns and Gracie Allen. The vaudeville circuit was also a popular subject of early American movies. On television, the *Ed Sullivan Show*, the *Sonny and Cher Comedy Hour*, and the many other variety shows from the 1950s through the 1970s were descendants of vaudeville. Today, shows like *America's Got Talent*, *So You Think You Can Dance*, and *American Idol* are descendants of this tradition, recreated within a reality-TV format.

Another popular form of musical theatre in the nineteenth century was the **minstrel show**. Unique to the United States, these shows came to prominence in the late 1840s and lasted well into the twentieth century. The shows included comic scenes, dance interludes, and sentimental ballads, all based on white stereotypes of black life in the South. These shows flourished for a couple of reasons. First, black music was very popular, but it was considered improper for whites to go to a theatre to hear black musicians play, so white performers put on black makeup—called *blackface*—and performed what was supposedly black music, such as Thomas Rice's song "Jump Jim Crow" (ca. 1828). (For more on blackface, see the Spotlight "Blackface, Redface, Yellowface" in Chapter 3.) Second, minstrel shows provided Northern white audiences with an idea of what the lives of the slaves were like, albeit in a highly distorted and romanticized way. These early minstrel shows were nothing but entertainment and they never challenged white audiences to think about the atrocities of slavery.

As the shows became more popular, their structure became standardized. The first part had musical numbers with bits of comic dialogue; the second was full of songs, dance, and standup routines; and the third segment typically featured a one-act play. The skits in the minstrel shows often contained illiterate and foolish exchanges that made fun of blacks. Yet, because the blackface makeup provided a kind of mask, some performers felt free to incorporate social commentary about abolition and women's rights into the skits. This was particularly true of shows in the 1860s, the Civil War years, when some black performers also painted their faces black and formed their own minstrel troupes. In fact, the most famous minstrel performers in the late 1800s and early 1900s were black.

When Hollywood got into the act, the faces under the black makeup were once again white. The first "talkie" movie, *The Jazz Singer* (1927), featured white actor Al Jolson in blackface performing in a minstrel show, and later the famous stars Fred Astaire and Judy Garland portrayed minstrel show performers in blackface. Not until the 1950s and 1960s brought the civil rights movement did minstrel shows fall into total disrepute.

The Black Crook, a melodrama about black magic staged in New York City in 1866, is often called the United States' first modern musical. The story was a Faust-like melodrama about a crook-backed practitioner of black magic (hence the title) who makes a pact with Lucifer that allows him to live one extra year for each soul he delivers to hell. His first victim is the virtuous Rudolphe, who has been imprisoned by an evil count. However, Rudolphe escapes, frees a trapped fairy queen, discovers buried treasure, and saves the day. In the end, the sorcerer fails to deliver any souls and is carted off to Hell himself. By most accounts the play was poorly written and doomed, but just before it opened, the producers had an odd stroke of luck when the nearby New York Academy of

Shuffle Along (1921) was a wildly popular all-black musical review and a first in many respects: it introduced jazz dancing to Broadway, premiered such notable black entertainers as Paul Robeson and Josephine Baker, and featured the first realistic African American love story at a time when onstage love scenes between blacks were taboo. The show's catchy music included "I'm Just Wild about Harry," which years later became Harry Truman's presidential campaign song. Here, Noble Sissle poses with some of the *Shuffle Along* showgirls. Sissle and Eubie Blake, a team made famous on the vaudeville circuit, wrote the music and lyrics. Another famous vaudeville team, Flournoy Miller and Aubrey L. Lyles, wrote the book.

Baltimore, Maryland/The Maryland Historical Society

Music caught fire, stranding a troupe of Parisian ballet dancers. The enterprising producers of *The Black Crook* hired the dancers and quickly restaged the play, combining the melodrama with music and dance into a production described as an "extravaganza" that included demons and sprites and "bare-armed" women. *The Black Crook* opened September 12, 1866, and was a massive success, running for 475 performances and making over $1 million on an investment of only $25,000—a considerable profit even today. It would be revived on Broadway an unprecedented eight times and have more than 200 performances in London.

The success of *The Black Crook* spawned a host of similar extravaganzas that were, by today's standards, just musical reviews containing unrelated but toe-tapping songs by a number of composers, chorus girls dancing in elaborate production numbers, and plenty of spectacular costumes and magnificent sets without regard for the story or characters. The joke-filled dialogue was only an excuse to get from one song to the next. These early musical plays lacked strong plot and believable characters, but both were deemed unnecessary because entertainment was the primary purpose, not drama.

African American Musicals

The success of *The Black Crook* also opened the door for the first full-length musical comedy conceived, written, produced, and performed by African Americans in New York. Composer and producer Bob Cole, along with lyricist Billy Johnson, formed a production company and opened *A Trip to Coontown* at the Third Avenue Theater in 1898. The story of a con man, the musical used minstrel stereotypes and spoofed *A Trip to Chinatown*, a popular musical comedy. But one of its songs challenged the racist policies of the day: a young black man sings about how he and his date were denied entry to a nightclub because of the color of their skin. *A Trip to Coontown* played to both whites and blacks and had two long runs in New York and a successful tour.

That same year, the ragtime musical *The Origin of the Cakewalk* (1898) became the first all-black show to play at a top Broadway theatre. But getting onstage required some ingenuity. The play's black composer, Will Marion Cook, went to the theatre and confidently informed its manager that the white owner had sent the troupe to perform that night. They were such a success that the manager immediately signed them for a long run. Only later did he find out that the theatre owner had known nothing about Cook's players.

By the 1920s there were a host of black musicals and revues including *Runnin' Wild* (1923), *Dixie to Broadway* (1924), and *Blackbirds* (1926). They had black casts and many had black writers, but blacks and whites acting together on stage was still considered improper, at least by whites. Broadway had opened its door a crack for black librettists, book writers, composers, and actors, but not until 1959 did a straight play by a black playwright make it to Broadway—Lorraine Hansberry's *A Raisin in the Sun*. Of course, blacks were not the only ones discriminated against. Women also encountered discrimination. (See the Spotlight "Unsung Heroines of the American Musical.")

Railroads, War, and Jazz

In 1869 the Union Pacific met the Central Pacific Railway at Promontory Point, Utah, completing the first transcontinental railroad across the United States. By 1900, nearly 300 touring theatre companies were taking advantage of this new, relatively fast form of travel. All the larger towns along the tracks built a theatre where these companies could play one-night or one-week stands. Most of the plays were melodramas, but there were also plenty of musicals, which were fast becoming America's favorite form of entertainment. Even today, successful musicals usually spawn one or more road companies that travel around the country.

By World War I, the music of George M. Cohan (1878–1942) and Irving Berlin (1888–1989) was dominating Broadway. Their big-ticket musical comedies, such as Cohan's *Hello, Broadway* (1914), were patriotic and sentimental. They had cardboard characters and flimsy stories in which the guy always got the girl, good always triumphed over evil, and life was all ice cream, apple pie, and the American way. The plots never stood in the way of giving audiences an evening of pure entertainment and plenty of catchy tunes such as Cohan's "You're a Grand Old Flag" (1906) and "Yankee Doodle Dandy" (1904) and Berlin's "God Bless America" (1918).

After the war, jazz began influencing the American musical. Brothers George and Ira Gershwin (1898–1937 and 1896–1983) wrote a string of successful musical comedies whose songs are still popular today: *Lady, Be Good!* (1924) with the song "Fascinating Rhythm," *Strike Up the Band* (1930) with "I've Got

SPOTLIGHT ON Unsung Heroines of the American Musical

Women have always sung, danced, and acted in musicals on the U.S. stage, but for a hundred years, almost all the composers, book writers, and lyricists have been men. In spite of their lack of recognition and opportunity, some women have been successful writers for musicals. Dorothy Fields (1905–1974) wrote the lyrics for *Sweet Charity* (1966) and the book for *Annie Get Your Gun* (1946). Betty Comden (1919–2006), with her partner Adolph Green (1915–2002), wrote lyrics for *On the Town* (1944), *Wonderful Town* (1953), *Subways Are for Sleeping* (1961), *Hallelujah, Baby* (1967), and the screenplay for the movie *Singin' in the Rain* (1952). In 2013 Cyndi Lauper made history when she won the Tony for writing both the music and lyrics for the musical *Kinky Boots*. But it wasn't until 2015, 69 years after the first Tony Awards were held, that the all-female writing team of Jeanine Tesori and Lisa Kron won the Tony for writing the music, lyrics, *and* book for the musical *Fun Home* based on a 2006 graphic coming-of-age memoir by well-known cartoonist Alison Bechdel. Concerning the lack of diversity in

the field, Lisa Kron said, "I think theatre is not actually about looking at people who are like you. Theatre is about what happens when people unlike each other [collide]—that's what happens on a stage. That's what drama is made of—when people unlike you reach across that divide."

In 2015, *Fun Home* wins five Tony Awards, including Best Musical.

Sara Krulwich/The New York Times/Redux Pictures

---

a Crush on You," and *Girl Crazy* (1930) with "But Not for Me," "Embraceable You," and "I Got Rhythm." Playing in the orchestra for these shows were soon-to-be-famous big band leaders Glenn Miller and Benny Goodman.

These early musicals had simple stories about charming princes, gallant young men, romantic swashbucklers, and wealthy gentlemen, all of whom were looking for love. Happy endings and no mention of the dark side of life were a must; the few plays that ended unhappily always did so for the good of humanity. For example, at the end of Sigmund Romberg's *The Student Prince* (1924), the kind young heir to the throne sacrifices his personal happiness for the good of the kingdom when he sorrowfully pulls himself away from his true love, a beer-hall girl, in order to marry a princess whom he does not love. The characters and stories of these sweetheart musicals may have been simple, but most of the musical comedies we enjoy today follow the same formula.

The Show Boat Revolution

In 1927, lyricist-librettist Oscar Hammerstein and composer Jerome Kern (1885–1945) revolutionized musical theatre with *Show Boat*. It combined musical comedy and serious drama to create what we recognize today as the quintessential American musical. The story begins aboard the show boat *Cotton Blossom* in 1880s Mississippi. Gaylord Ravenal, a riverboat gambler, comes aboard and falls for Magnolia, the daughter of the ship's captain, Cap'n Andy. When the star of the *Cotton Blossom*'s show, Julie, is forced out by the local sheriff because she is a mixed race

The Ronald Grant Archive

Today we are used to seeing realistic relationships between black and white characters portrayed on stage and screen, but when Hammerstein and Kern's *Show Boat* premiered in 1927, such portrayals were a revelation. *Show Boat* was based on a book by novelist and playwright Edna Ferber, who was well known for strong female protagonists and strong secondary characters who managed to rise above racial or other discrimination. Adapting *Show Boat* for the stage is a testament to the courage of Hammerstein, Kern, and producer Florenz Ziegfeld; they took a huge chance staging a story of such depth for audiences accustomed to much lighter fare. This photo from the 1936 film version of *Show Boat* features Paul Robeson (center), who sang one of the musical's signature songs, "Ol' Man River."

woman married to a white man, Magnolia and Gaylord fill in. Years later, Gaylord and Magnolia are married and have a daughter, Kim. After Gaylord racks up sizable gambling debts and leaves Magnolia, she looks for a singing job to support herself and Kim. She runs into Julie at a club, and the kindhearted Julie lets Magnolia take her own singing job. At a New Year's Eve show, Cap'n Andy comes to the club and is surprised to see Magnolia on stage. When she is almost booed off stage, he brings the crowd around in a magnificent sing-along. He then convinces her to return to the *Cotton Blossom*, where a contrite Gaylord is waiting to be reunited with his family.

Unlike the musicals that came before, *Show Boat* had a consequential story, powerful dialogue, three-dimensional characters, and songs and dances that tied directly into the plot. Instead of a line of pretty dancing girls, the chorus consisted of black dockworkers, and they portrayed real people rather than the black stereotypes common at the time. The theme was more serious and dealt with, among other subjects, racial issues. Moreover, black and white actors performed on stage at the same time, which was still a rare occurrence. Yet old attitudes and customs don't reverse themselves overnight; in the original production the role of Queenie was played in blackface by a white actress named Tess Gardella (1897–1950), who was famous for playing "Aunt Jemima" or "mammy" characters in vaudeville.

In spite of its shortcomings, *Show Boat* was the first production to combine dancing, choruses, toe-tapping melodies, and huge spectacle with a strong plot and plausible characters. In 1932, following on the heels of *Show Boat*'s tremendous success, Ira Gershwin and George S. Kaufman's musical *Of Thee I Sing*, a biting satire of Washington politics, became the first musical to win the Pulitzer Prize—the highest award given for American drama. Although frothy love stories didn't disappear from Broadway, more musicals featured complex characters: the professional gambler who can't turn down a bet, Sky Masterson, in *Guys and Dolls* (1950); the bombastic but vulnerable king of Siam in *The King and I* (1951); the self-important but charming Professor Higgins in *My Fair Lady* (1956); and the kindhearted con man, Harold Hill, in *The Music Man* (1957). The American musical was becoming a serious art form, and more musicals won the Pulitzer, including *South Pacific* (1950), *Fiorello!* (1960), *How to Succeed in Business without Really Trying* (1963), *A Chorus Line* (1976), *Sunday in the Park with George* (1985), and *Rent* (1996).

Thoroughly Modern Musicals

During the 1927–28 season, Broadway had more than 70 theatres with a total of 264 productions, including 46 musicals—a record that has never been broken. The great stock market crash of 1929 drastically reduced their numbers. George and Ira Gershwin's operatic musical *Porgy and Bess* (1935), Marc Blitzstein's (1905–1964) labor parable *The Cradle Will Rock* (1938), and other musicals of the Great Depression took on the tone of the times. After the United States entered World War II at the end of 1941, musicals returned for a while to flimsy plots with a patriotic flair. But in

> I know the world is filled with troubles and many injustices. But reality is as beautiful as it is ugly. I think it is just as important to sing about beautiful mornings as it is to talk about slums. I just couldn't write anything without hope in it.
>
> **Oscar Hammerstein,**
> lyricist and producer

The 1950s and 1960s produced some of the most beloved Broadway musicals of all time. These "golden age" musicals not only told entertaining and exciting stories, but also featured perennial favorites, such as "There's No Business Like Show Business" *(Annie Get Your Gun)* and "Luck Be a Lady" *(Guys and Dolls)*. One of the most popular golden age musicals was *The Sound of Music,* which recounted the adventures of the singing von Trapp family, featuring the timeless songs "Do-Re-Mi" and "My Favorite Things," and was made into an Academy Award–winning movie starring Julie Andrews. In the original Broadway production (1959–1963), Mary Martin played the plucky governess, Maria Rainer. Music by Richard Rodgers, lyrics by Oscar Hammerstein II, book by Howard Lindsay, Russel Crouse, and Maria Augusta Trapp. Directed by Vincent J. Donehue. Lunt-Fontanne Theatre, New York.

Photofest

1943, Richard Rodgers (1902–1979) and Oscar Hammerstein's *Oklahoma!* came to Broadway. Like *Show Boat*, it had well-developed characters, song-and-dance numbers integrated into the story, and some serious plot elements, including a murder. It even incorporated classical ballet. The story of *Oklahoma!* is simple—it is the tale of a cowboy and a farmhand competing for the affections of a farm girl in Oklahoma Territory in 1906. However, it was influential because it incorporated storytelling techniques new to musicals, and the use of dance to develop the plot and the characters.

At the end of the war, Americans seemed filled with optimism, believing that they had saved the world for democracy and that the American dream of prosperity, order, and happiness was within everyone's grasp. This optimism led to the two decades that many consider the golden age of American musicals. Broadway was filled with great musicals: *Carousel* (1945), *Annie Get Your Gun* (1946), *South Pacific* (1949), *Guys and Dolls* (1950), *The King and I* (1951), *My Fair Lady* (1956), *West Side Story* (1957), *The Sound of Music* (1959), *Fiddler on the Roof* (1964), and *Man of La Mancha* (1965). All provided more than just light entertainment; they combined powerful, often serious stories with musical numbers that advanced the plot. Stephen Sondheim recalls a man walking out of *West Side Story* when it was first produced: "He wanted a musical—meaning a place to relax before he has to go home and face his terrible dysfunctional family. Instead of which he got a lot of ballet dancers in color-coordinated sneakers snapping their fingers and pretending to be tough. His expectation had been defeated." Today, a golden age of musicals exists not in the United States but in India; although "Bollywood" musicals don't have the robust stories of America's golden age musicals, they are just as rich in spectacle and song—and they are as immensely popular as U.S. musicals once were. (See the Spotlight "Hooray for Bollywood!")

The most expensive Broadway play ever produced was *Spider-Man: Turn Off the Dark*. With music and lyrics by Bono, this comic book musical cost over 75 million dollars to stage and required over 180 previews before it finally opened.

Sara Krulwich/The New York Times/Redux Pictures

SPOTLIGHT ON Hooray for Bollywood!

The term *Bollywood* blends "Hollywood" and "Bombay" and is often used in the West to refer to the cinema of India. Some consider the term pejorative slang, but others take it as a compliment. An average of 800 films are made every year in India, and many of them are musicals. That's more than twice the number of films Hollywood produces per year, making India not only the top producer of movies around the world but also the top producer of musicals. Movies are India's sixth largest industry and employ more than 300,000 people.

Indian movie stars such as Madhuri Dixit, Shilpa Shetty, Aishwarya Rai, and Karishma Kapoor are mobbed everywhere they go and, just like Hollywood stars, must hire bodyguards to protect them from admiring fans and overzealous paparazzi. Bollywood directors such as Rakeysh Omprakash Mehra, Raj Kapoor, Guru Dutt, Mehboob Khan, and Bimal Roy are as famous in India as Alfred Hitchcock and Steven Spielberg are in the United States. Every year the Bollywood version of the Academy Awards is watched by a half a billion people in 110 countries.

Since the first Indian talkie in 1931, song and dance have been an integral part of Indian films; even many nonmusicals include a few songs. Bollywood musicals typically have stock love stories, heroes, heroines, love affairs, song-and-dance sequences, and happy endings. Here's how the Bollywood musical goes: A young man and woman fall in love. After their first meeting, the man sings a love song rhapsodizing about his beloved's beauty. However, some obstacle keeps the lovers apart, and they sing in a split-screen duet about their painful separation. In the end, they are reunited and celebrate their love with a huge song-and-dance number as flamboyant as any 1940s Broadway musical. Although most Bollywood musicals follow this formula, audiences are satisfied as long as the songs are fresh and exciting.

It is not surprising that musicals are so popular in Indian cinema. For thousands of years, song and dance have been an integral part of ritual, religious, and social life in India. Modern Indian theatrical music traces its roots to the Urdu Parsee theatre of the 1930s, which drew its inspiration from classic Indian literature and its staging techniques from nineteenth-century British melodrama. Bollywood movies and musicals have helped to define the national character of this huge country with 17 major languages, 5,000 gods, and 6 primary religions. Now Bollywood films are becoming popular around the world. Every year 3.5 billion people see Bollywood movies. By contrast, approximately 2.5 billion people a year see Hollywood movies. Bollywood musicals have even begun to inspire Hollywood movies (*Moulin Rouge!*, 2001) and Broadway musicals (*Bombay Dreams*, 2005). There are now more than 100 cinemas in the United States that show Bollywood movies.

Photostage

A tongue-in-cheek homage to the musicals of Indian cinema, *Bombay Dreams* tells the typically Bollywood story of a poor Bombay tour guide, Akaash, who becomes a superstar with the help of Priya, an independent filmmaker, and Rani, a glamorous movie star. As Akaash gains money, fame, and the attentions of Rani, he wonders if these things can take the place of his family, friends, and relationship with the girl-next-door Priya. This 2002 production at the Apollo Victoria Theatre in London featured Ayesha Dharker as Rani. Book by Meera Syal, music by A. R. Rahman, and lyrics by Don Black.

Musical theatre in the 1960s and 1970s broke even more expectations and took more risks. *Cabaret* (1966) showed Germany's period of political freedom and cultural experimentation just before the Nazis came to power. *Hair* (1967) introduced rock music, hippies, and nudity to the musical. *The Wiz* (1975) retold the story of the Wizard of Oz from the perspective of an African American schoolteacher and her streetwise companions, who travel through an Oz with an urban flavor in search of happiness. *A Chorus Line* (1975) dealt with homosexuality in a matter-of-fact way. These plays once again challenged the traditions of the American musical and brought a new strain of intellectual complexity to this fun-loving form of theatre.

Modern musicals can be about any subject. Some even make fun of musicals, as is the case with the comedy *Angry Psycho Princesses* written by William Missouri Downs and Sean Stone. Pictured here is Brikai Cordova as the Evil Queen Badassery with (L-R) Daniel Daigle, Riley Wisler, Justen Glover, Charles Johnson, Colter Schmidt and Cody Mock.

The End or a New Beginning?

During the 1920s, an average of 40 musicals per year were produced on Broadway. During the depression years of the 1930s the annual average fell to about 18. During the war years of the 1940s the average was 16. By the 1990s the number had fallen even farther, to only about five musicals per year. In the 1994–95 Broadway season, only two new musicals were produced. Over those decades, musicals also fell out of favor in Hollywood. Even though the brilliant composer-lyricist Stephen Sondheim had been writing such notable musicals as *Company* (1970), *Sweeney Todd* (1979), and *Into the Woods* (1987), many felt that the golden age of the American musical had passed.

The main problem for musical theatre today is the cost. Unlike straight plays, Broadway musicals almost always cost big money. For example, *Phantom of the Opera* had 36 actors, more than 50 crew members, and 30 musicians. It needed 120 wigs, 260 costumes, and a massive set—not to mention the 20,000 AAA batteries it used each year. When it opened on Broadway in 1988, the cost was $375,000 a week. In comparison, the entire Broadway run of *The King and I* (1951–1954) cost $360,000. Even taking inflation into account, production costs have skyrocketed from decade to decade. In 1956 *My Fair Lady* cost $401,000 to produce; in 1975 *A Chorus Line* cost $1,145,000; in 1986 *Phantom of the Opera* cost over $7 million. Today, a Broadway musical can cost $5–$15 million on average to produce. The most expensive musical ever—perhaps the most expensive play ever—is the spectacle *Spider-Man: Turn Off the Dark*, which originally cost over $75 million to stage.

As production costs have increased, so have ticket prices. When *A Chorus Line* opened on Broadway in 1975, the best seats sold for $15.

Sara Krulwich/The New York Times/Redux Pictures

Because big Broadway musicals can be so expensive to produce, smaller musicals such as *The 25th Annual Putnam County Spelling Bee* are becoming increasingly popular. This musical takes an affectionate look at the mortifications of middle school via six misfits who compete for a spelling bee trophy. Because *Spelling Bee* has a small cast, a simple set, and cost a mere $3.5 million to produce, it broke even after only 18 weeks on Broadway. As long as the public clamors for musicals—and they always do—producers will find innovative ways to keep this fun-loving art form alive. This production of *Spelling Bee* premiered in 2005 and was directed by James Lapine at the Circle in the Square Theatre, New York. Book by Rachel Sheinkin, music and lyrics by William Finn.

Fifteen years later, when it closed, the price of a ticket was $50. Today, a ticket to a Broadway musical typically costs $100. (For more on production costs, see the Spotlight "Theatre Can Be Expensive" in Chapter 2.)

Today, usually only Walt Disney and other huge corporations can afford to foot the bill for new mega musicals. Consequently, some Broadway producers have turned to staging revivals of popular older musicals that have a greater chance of making back their investment. Others are trying to ensure success by basing "new" musicals on well-known movies, such as *Big, Footloose, The Producers, Hairspray, Legally Blonde, Young Frankenstein, The Addams Family,* and *Shrek.* Expensive musicals such as *Phantom of the Opera* and *Miss Saigon* are still popular, yet there still seems to be room for smaller musicals *The Fantasticks, I Love You, You're Perfect, Now Change,* and *Fun Home* that have small casts and can be produced on a shoestring. Whenever people say the American musical is on its way out, the art form always seems to stage another comeback. Today, new musicals such as *Urinetown, Avenue Q, Wicked, The 25th Annual Putnam County Spelling Bee, Monty Python's Spamalot, Spring Awakening, The Visit,* and *Hamilton* are keeping the art form alive and pushing it to new levels. Another method of creating hit musicals is to build stories around popular music the audience already knows, as is the case with *Mamma Mia!* and *Jersey Boys.*

Curtain Call

Depending on whom you talk to, the American musical is alive and well or on its deathbed. Musical theatre historian Denny Martin Flinn is one who has sounded the death knell for the musical: "When *A Chorus Line* gave its final Broadway performance fifteen years after it opened, the last great American musical went dark, and the epoch was over." Stephen Sondheim, who gave us such great musicals as *Sunday in the Park with George* and *Sweeney Todd,* recently told critic Frank Rich that only two types of Broadway musicals exist today: "revivals" and "the same kind of musicals over and over again." In his opinion, most musicals today are nothing more than "spectacles" and "stage versions of a movie." "We live in a recycled culture," said Sondheim. "I don't think the theatre will die per se, but it's never going to be what it was. You can't bring it back. It's gone. It's a tourist attraction."

However, this kind of pessimism is common each time there is a new turn or major development in musical theatre. There may be good years and bad, but the American musical is far from dead. It is simply in another transition as it evolves to become what culture and business require of it, just as it evolved

American Musicals are popular worldwide. This billboard in Shanghai, China advertises a production of *Hairspray*.

to allow blacks and whites together on stage with *Show Boat* in 1927. Music and theatre have been traveling hand in hand for thousands of years, and even though the shape of the musical can't be predicted, there will be musicals as long as people like a story told with song.

> It is clear that the musical theatre is changing. No one knows where it is going. Perhaps it is going not to one place but to many. That would be healthy, I think, just as the search in itself can be healthy. . . . Thus it was for Shakespeare in Elizabethan times; thus it was for writers of musicals after Rodgers and Hammerstein; and thus it will be again.
>
> **Tom Jones,** Lyricist

SUMMARY

MindTap®

Test your knowledge with online printable flashcards and online quizzing.

Musical scripts are made up of three parts: book, music, and lyrics. The **librettist** writes the book, the composer writes the music, and the lyricist writes the lyrics. Musicals that feature a well-developed story and characters are called book musicals. Musicals that emphasize dance are called dance musicals, and musicals in which singing dominates are known as operatic musicals.

Music, dance, and song have been a component of theatrical traditions around the world for thousands of years. The modern American musical has evolved from a number of musical traditions, including opera, operettas, musical reviews, variety shows, vaudeville, and burlesque. The distinction of the first modern American musical is often given to *The Black Crook*, a melodrama about black magic staged in New York City in 1866. In 1898 the ragtime musical *The Origin of the Cakewalk* was the first all–African American show to play at a top Broadway theatre.

By World War I, big-ticket, sentimental musical comedies dominated Broadway. They seldom told complex stories or featured well-developed characters. The first big revolution in the American musical came in 1927 when Oscar Hammerstein and Jerome Kern wrote *Show Boat*, which combined aspects of musical comedy and serious drama to create what today we consider the quintessential musical. Sixteen years later, another well-rounded musical advanced the form: Richard Rodgers and Oscar Hammerstein's *Oklahoma!* Like *Show*

Boat, Oklahoma! featured serious plot points, well-developed characters, and songs and dances used to develop the plot.

The musicals of the 1960s, 1970s, and 1980s brought a new round of innovation by taking on a wide variety of social and political issues. Today, there are musicals to fit every taste: rock and roll musicals, musicals based on movies, and traditional revivals of Broadway classics.

KEY TERMS

Perhaps one of the most theatrical forms of Global theatre is the modern Chinese opera (sometimes called the Peking Opera) which combines elaborate costumes, colorful makeup, and stylized movement with dance, music, and acrobatics.

Chapter **12**

THEATRE AROUND THE WORLD

William Missouri Downs

MindTap®

Start with a quick warm-up activity and review the chapter's learning objectives.

Outline

ost of theatre's early history was not recorded or was lost, so we can only speculate about its origins. Where did theatre come from? What spark created it? The most common theory is that theatre grew out of religious ritual and myth. The word *ritual* comes from the Latin *ritualis*, a ceremonial act connected with human life and all that sustains it. Many thousands of years ago people used rituals to help them understand and deal with their environment. Because they did not have scientific methods with which to grasp the causes of plagues, floods, droughts, earthquakes, volcanic eruptions, and eclipses, they developed ceremonies to try to influence the intangible forces that they believed controlled the cosmos. The goal of these rituals was not the act itself but a particular effect: adequate rainfall, an end to sickness, a bountiful harvest, a successful hunt, victory in battle, or favor from gods. Rituals were also a means to pass on traditions and knowledge of a society's history and heroes; thus the sophisticated storylines called myths were born. Soon people discovered that these rituals and myths could also teach and entertain. In this way, ritual was for early humans what art is for us today.

Ritual still plays an important part in our lives. We have religious rituals such as baptism, communion, bar and bat mitzvahs, and last rites. We have legal rituals such as marriage and divorce; governmental rituals such as presidential inaugurations; rites of passage such as graduation ceremonies; and rituals commemorating historical events such as the fireworks on the Fourth of July. Rituals, according to Dr. Barbara H. Fiese of Syracuse University, are "events or acts that evoke emotions or conferred meaning." Her findings, published in the *Journal of Family Psychology*, show that rituals have a significant effect on a person's emotional health and that families with strong rituals often have a stronger sense of self and produce happier marriages.

But at what point do rituals become theatre? Scholars have debated this question for decades. Some divide the answer into three stages: ritual, ritual theatre, and theatre. **Ritual theatre** is an early form of theatre; it used theatrical techniques such as song, dance, and characterization, but it was still firmly rooted in religion. This three-stage approach makes sense, because there probably

Ritual rooted in religion and tradition is a fundamental aspect of culture all over the world. Rituals are performed to honor deities, affirm group identities, and foster the continuation of a particular way of life. In the United States, one of the most long-lived forms of ritual is Native American traditional dance. Here, the Tewa-speaking Pueblo of Santa Clara in New Mexico perform the cloud dance. It's easy to see how ritual evolved into theatre—many elements of ritual can be seen in theatrical performance, such as set "dialogue" in the form of chants and songs; prescribed physical action; and the use of costume, makeup, and masks.

Ira Block/National Geographic

wasn't one defining moment when ritual turned into theatre. The transformation took thousands of years.

Many scholars agree on two traits that distinguish theatre from ritual. First, theatre has an actor who plays a character, a person who takes on a role portraying another human being or even an object, animal, or embodied idea. A priest doing what a priest does may be theatrical and the religious ritual may be dramatic, but it is not theatre. Theatre is artificial. To paraphrase Aristotle, a play is an imitation of an action, not the action itself. Second, theatre usually has a story with a conflict. Conflict is the key to all drama. Many religious or social rituals have a prescribed order of events, but they usually do not act out a story that includes scripted conflict. (*Scripted* doesn't necessarily refer to a written play; it can also refer to a simple outline, scenario, or improvisation "written" in the memory of a group of people.) When these two traits are present—actors playing characters and stories with conflict—we have drama. Looking at theatre this way, we can see that a play can be a ritual (ritual theatre) but not all rituals are plays.

When was the transition from ritual to theatre complete? No one knows, of course, but historical clues allow us to make an educated guess that theatre has existed for thousands of years. In Africa, long before the development of written alphabets, ritual plays were passed down through generations. In India during the Bronze Age (4000–1500 BCE), there were mythological dramas full of song and dance, and the Indus Valley civilization (2700–1500 BCE) even had a god, named Siva, of actors and dancers. In China during the Zhou dynasty (1122–256 BCE), there were ritual performances with singing, dancing, and impersonators. And there are records in hieroglyphics of what may have been theatrical activity in Egypt during the Early Dynastic Period (3100–2686 BCE). Later, around 1800 BCE, a man named Ikhernofret wrote of his participation in a ritual play in Abydos about the death and resurrection of Osiris, the god of fertility and the underworld. He describes how he put on "regalia," or a costume, and ceremonially "overthrew the enemies of Osiris," that is, participated in a scripted conflict. But we do not know if this was a play or a traditional ritual because we do not know if there were actors playing characters.

We do know that theatre in one form or another has been performed in every part of the world for thousands of years—from the Khon theatre of Thailand, the Kamyonguk theatre of Korea, and the Wayang Wong dance-drama of Java, to the Creole theatre of Sierra Leone and the masked theatre of Nigeria. For thousands of years, the Aborigines in Australia have staged performances that fuse music, dance, and drama. Even in some Muslim countries, where prohibitions on theatre have stifled the art, performers present shadow plays and puppetry. There are as many types of theatre as there are peoples, creeds, faiths, and cultures.

> The theatre of every age has something to teach us, if we are sensitive enough and humble enough to learn from it.
>
> **Robert Edmond Jones,**
> Theatre set designer

African Theatre

Most experts agree that human beings came into existence in Africa, so there is little doubt that theatre was born on the African continent. However, the wealth of theatre that has been a tradition in Africa for thousands of years has not always been recognized as theatre by Westerners. In fact, the only way to understand African theatre is to free yourself from Western conventions and accept a broader definition—some even argue, a more accurate definition—of *theatre*. For most ancient Africans, theatre was seamlessly tied into the myths, rituals,

MindTap

Read, highlight and take notes online.

rites, and communal celebrations of everyday life. Today, historians often divide African theatre into three periods: the precolonial times when African theatre was in its purest form, the colonial period when Western-style drama was introduced to Africa, and the postcolonial period.

Precolonial Forms

Precolonial African theatre grew out of ritual. It incorporated acting, music, storytelling, poetry, dance, costumes, and lots of masks to create a theatre that combined ritual and ceremony with drama. But, unlike Western theatre where the audience sits quietly and watches actors perform, precolonial African theatre seldom separated the audience and the performers. Instead, African ritual theatre encouraged the audience to sing and dance as they formed a circle of participants that fused the two most important institutions of precolonial Africa: religion and community. Because the performers often used masks, the audience could be part of the performance and yet look different from the performers. (For more on masks, see the Spotlight "Masks and Theatre.") Some label precolonial African theatre "nonliterate drama" or "pre-drama," as if it were incomplete. Yet it might be argued that **Western drama** is the one that's lacking because it is less connected to its original ritual inspiration. We might even suggest that perhaps, someday, Western theatre will regain its ritual heritage, the heritage that traditional African theatre has never lost. Even today ritual and theatre are closely related in Africa. Nigerian playwright Ola Rotimi (1938–2000) said, "It is not uncommon to observe at the end of a ritual ceremony an afterpiece in the form of a play with a clear entertainment intent."

Another common form of precolonial African theatre was storytelling. Storytellers did more than relate stories; they were also actors who mixed narrative with impersonation and mime into a highly theatrical presentation. Some also sang their stories and accompanied themselves with musical instruments. As they related myths, religious legends, and folktales, these actors performed with few props on a stage that was often little more than a circle drawn on the ground. In some countries, this type of storytelling theatre is named for the performance space, as in Morocco, where it is called *Halqa*, or "circle." Such simple staging meant that the actors had to paint detailed verbal images. This "verbal scene painting," a technique Shakespeare also used, invited the audience to "see" the play with their mind's eye. African storytellers were a solo act; if they needed other actors, they often invited members of the audience into the circle to play the parts. In this way, the storytellers were directors because they told the audience-actors what to say and do. Storytellers are still popular today in Africa and often perform in open-air markets and other public places.

Invaders: Colonial Forms

Traditional African theatrical art was interrupted by Arab and European invasions, which brought foreign religions and customs to the continent. Early European travelers and missionaries who witnessed African ritual theatre dismissed it because it was so unlike anything they knew. In the parts of Africa invaded by Muslims in the seventh century, such as Morocco, Algeria, and Tunisia, Islam's antagonistic view of theatre often reduced theatrical activity. Later, in the rest of the continent, sixteenth-century European and Christian

SPOTLIGHT ON   Masks and Theatre

Although actors today in the West rarely wear them, masks have been important in ritual, religion, and theatre for thousands of years. Archeologists have found 20,000 year-old cave paintings depicting people wearing masks. There is evidence of masked rituals in prehistoric Africa, Europe, Asia, and in the Americas from the Andes to Alaska. Masks can help wearers enter an altered state or at least allow them anonymity as they take on the qualities of a different person, an animal, or a mythical being. On Halloween, children and adults who might otherwise feel inhibited put on masks and in doing so assume the qualities of the mask. Children suddenly become little devils or princesses, and adults do things they would never consider if they were not masked: once you change your face, you can change who you are. In fact, as historian Will Durant points out, the word *persona* signified the actor's mask. It later came to mean the part played by human beings in life and finally to mean human beings themselves. Today, some theatres still use the words *dramatis personae* to list characters in the program. *Dramatis personae* means "masks of the play."

In the theatre, masks have been used for many reasons; some are decorative, but others provide complex symbolic meanings. Masks can help actors play characters, and they can help the spectators identify the characters. In some countries, masks are considered a higher form of characterization than an actor's facial expressions, because a mask embodies a character in its purest form. When masks are regarded this way, their function is not to hide expressions but to amplify them. For example, in traditional African theatre, the mask allows the wearer to identify with and assume the spirit of a mythical ancestor or a supernatural being. In Japanese Noh drama, the masks are so important that they have been handed down from father to son for centuries. Noh masks have even been declared national treasures. In ancient Greek drama, masks that covered the entire head not only helped actors play different characters but may also have helped them to be heard, for some had large mouth openings that served as megaphones.

Today in Indonesia, India, China, Japan, and Africa, masked theatre is still regularly performed. Masks encourage and empower us to transform ourselves as they permit us to replace our reality—if only temporarily—with that of another. Masks are as old as the theatre itself and as modern as *The Lion King*.

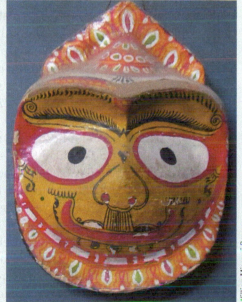

William Missouri Downs

William Missouri Downs

From ancient Greeks to eastern drama, masks have been a mainstay of performance. These masks are from the Indian theatre.

> The saddest thing about theatrical development in . . . Africa has been the fact that the theatre of Europe came to Africa and established itself in complete ignorance of and indifference to [our] traditions. It did not even try to superimpose itself onto the traditions, but rather led an isolated existence related only to the needs of a few who fell within its ambit.
>
> **Robert Serumaga,** Playwright

invaders tended to stifle traditional African theatre and establish Western theatrical forms. As the slave trade turned state against state and tribe against tribe, these internal wars weakened Africa and opened the doors to foreign domination. In the nineteenth century, Great Britain, France, Portugal, Belgium, Germany, Spain, and Italy divided Africa into territories. These occupying countries imposed their languages, customs, religions, and theatre on Africa in what became known as the colonial period. By the early twentieth century, the colonization of Africa was essentially complete.

As European settlements were established in Africa, Catholic and Protestant missionaries brought Western-style theatre to dramatize Bible stories in order to win converts, and the occupying governments used drama to promote their political views. In 1801, in the Cape of Good Hope in what would become South Africa, the British opened the first European-style theatre on the African continent. A short time later, European theatre companies began traveling to Africa to entertain the colonists, and soon there were a host of local imitators. The first report of a European-style play performed by Africans appeared in 1866. But these plays did not assimilate traditional African theatre. During the colonial period, traditional African theatre was devalued and even suppressed, while theatres with Western-style stages, curtains, and proscenium arches were considered indispensable.

Postcolonial Forms

During the 1960s, the majority of African nations won their independence from European rule. With independence came calls for cultural renewal and the revival of traditions that had been banned or discouraged by the European occupiers. Soon, traditional African theatre became an important means of reestablishing native culture and transmitting common experiences, but there were also new forms of theatre that mixed traditional African ritual theatre and Western-style drama into what is called **total theatre**. Total theatre has encouraged African nationalism, glorified Africa's past, and advanced African customs, rituals, and culture. This type of drama has also dealt with serious political themes and applauded, questioned, or discredited European influences.

One of the most common types of plays written in Africa during the postcolonial period is what in Hollywood is called a "fish-out-of-water story," such as John Sayles's *The Brother from Another Planet* (1984). This is a story in which the protagonist is thrown into a new and completely unfamiliar environment. The best known of these plays is *Sarzan* (1955) by Senegalese poet Lamine Diakhaté (1927–1987). *Sarzan* is the story of a black French army officer (*sarzan* is African-French pidgin for "sergeant") who has been away from Africa for 15 years and is now totally assimilated into French culture. When he returns to his native village, he is confronted with traditional African ceremonies that he now considers "barbaric." He criticizes his people, but eventually goes mad as he imagines himself persecuted by the wisdom of his ancient ancestors. Plays such as *Sarzan* cut to the core of the conflict many people in Africa felt, and still feel, as they were forced to reconcile Africa's cultural past with outside influences.

The struggle for African independence brought internal revolutions and war. Soon, African playwrights were criticizing white rule, apartheid, and African dictators. Plays began calling for political consciousness, social awakening, and revolution. The political tone of African drama was not appreciated by the repressive regimes in several countries; they felt that theatre was only spreading dissent. Several playwrights, including Ken Saro-Wiwa (1941–1995) of Nigeria, were executed for their outspoken views. In 1995 Saro-Wiwa attempted to protect the Ogoni people against encroachments of Shell oil company, but Nigeria's brutal dictator Sani Abacha stopped him. Saro-Wiwa was imprisoned, tortured, brought to trial on trumped-up charges, and executed. (See the Spotlight "The Life and Death of Ken Saro-Wiwa" in Chapter 1.) Another famous African playwright who endured imprisonment for his ideas is Wole Soyinka, considered by many to be Africa's greatest living playwright.

The son of an Anglican priest, Soyinka (b. 1934) was born in Nigeria when it was still a British colony. His plays are deeply rooted in African myths, dance, and rituals. But he is also influenced by Western drama, including ancient Greek theatre, Shakespeare, and European nonrealistic plays. Soyinka's plays combine symbolism, mysticism, and beautiful dialogue, and they make strong political points. His play *Dance of the Forest* (1966) celebrates Nigerian independence but also warns against returning to Nigeria's violent past, the "recurrent cycle of stupidities," chronic dishonesty, and abuse of power he feels were caused by European colonialism. His many other plays parody tyranny and corruption in post-independence Africa and attack African dictators, including Uganda's Idi Amin and Zaire's Mobutu Sese Seko.

Soyinka once said, "The greatest threat to freedom is the absence of criticism," and his outspoken political plays and criticism often got him into trouble. At the beginning of Nigeria's civil war in the late 1960s, Soyinka wrote an article appealing for an end to hostilities and was arrested and held for nearly two years in solitary confinement. While in prison he continued to write, making his own ink and writing on toilet paper and cigarette packages. In 1986 he became the first African to win the Nobel Prize for Literature. In his acceptance speech, he said, "There is a deep lesson for the world in the black races' capacity to forgive, one which, I often think, has much to do with ethical precepts which spring from their worldview and authentic religions, none of which is ever totally eradicated by the accretions of foreign faiths and their implicit ethnocentrism."

Today, African theatre is some of the most diverse in the world. There are plays performed in plush, acoustically perfect European-style theatres that rival any in the world, and plays performed in open-air venues, not confined by walls. Western plays are popular, but so are anti-colonial plays that protest Western influences, as well as plays that are rooted in ritual, religion, and community celebrations. In *African Theatre Today*, Martin Banham observes, "Theatre in Africa, today, is more alive, more positive, more functional, and more assertive than its counterpart in Europe or America."

> A book if necessary should be a hammer [or] a hand grenade which you detonate under a stagnant way of looking at the world.
>
> **Wole Soyinka,** Playwright

> Theater is revolutionary when it awakens the individual in the audience. . . . [P]eople who never believed that they even possessed the gift of self-expression become creative, and this in turn activates other energies within the individual. I believe the creative process is the most energizing. And that is why it is so intimately related to the process of revolution within society.
>
> **Wole Soyinka,** Playwright

Indian Theatre

Like Africa, India has an ancient civilization and some of the oldest theatre traditions. There is evidence of ritual theatrical dance performance existing in India as far back as 2500 BCE. Some scholars believe that modern theatre in India began when the army of Alexander the Great staged Greek-style plays during its invasion in 326 BCE. (See Chapter 13 for a discussion of classical Greek theatre.) Other scholars argue that theatre existed in India long before Alexander's invasion and that the Greeks only influenced it. Whether or not it predated the Greek invasion,

The Sanskrit play *Ramayana* (ca. 300 BCE) chronicles the life and adventures of the virtuous king Rama, an incarnation of the god Vishnu. In this modern production, Rama battles the evil, multi-headed king Ravana, who kidnapped Rama's wife, Sita. This ancient story provides Hindus with a code of ideal conduct, much as the Bible does for Christians, and has long been popular in India—when it was made into a 78-episode TV series in the 1980s, India almost came to a standstill every time it aired.

Dinodia Photo Library

Indian theatre was at least transformed by ancient Greece. Evidence includes the name for the curtain used in some ancient Indian plays: "the Greek."

One of the most valuable historical records of Indian theatre is the **Natyasastra**, an encyclopedic book of dramatic theory and practice written sometime between 200 BCE and 200 CE. The *Natyasastra* has 37 chapters and covers every aspect of classical Indian drama, including costume design, theatre layout, playwriting, directing, acting, music, and philosophy. It even teaches actors how to dance and select stage gestures. But the *Natyasastra* is not just a how-to book; it is also a treatise on dramatic theory and philosophy. It states that theatre is a form of religious enlightenment and that the bliss of the aesthetic experience is a portal to nirvana, the ultimate bliss. According to the *Natyasastra*, the divine forces that sustain the universe wanted theatre to be "religion for those who are religious-minded, love for those who are amorous-minded, knowledge for the ignorant, criticism for the learned, a delight for the Gods, and a solace for the afflicted." All these qualities were present in India's oldest form of drama, Sanskrit drama, which dominated theatre in India for a thousand years.

Sanskrit Drama

Sanskrit drama is named for the ancient Indian language in which its plays are performed. For over a thousand years, professional touring companies performed Sanskrit drama in courts, temples, palaces, or temporary theatres on special occasions. Unlike many forms of early Western and Eastern theatre, women have always been a part of India's theatre and scholars believe there may have been acting troupes made up entirely of women. Sanskrit plays, based on Indian myths, combine the natural and the supernatural, the believable and the unbelievable. These productions include comic and serious themes, fables with poetry, heroism, mythological characters, and love stories in which the righteous triumph and virtue is rewarded.

One of the most famous Sanskrit plays is *Shakuntala* (ca. 400), a love story in seven acts written by the playwright Kalidasa (ca. 373–415 CE). The play opens with a prologue in which the audience is invited to enjoy the beauty of nature. The setting is a forest, where a hermit lives with his adopted daughter, Shakuntala.

Oh, gone! Gone are all of them! Shakuntala has robbed me of all my desire to return to the capital. Well, I will set up a camp with my companions in the vicinity of this grove. Oh, how impossible it is to punctuate, even for a moment, the stream of my thoughts that flows towards only one destination it has known— Shakuntala. Oh, Shakuntala! Shakuntala! My body has an apparent movement. But my heart? Oh, it only turns back like a silken pennon, borne against the gale.

King Dushyanta,
in Shakuntala, by Kalidasa

Their peaceful existence is interrupted by King Dushyanta, who arrives in a chariot. King Dushyanta instantly falls in love with Shakuntala and marries her, but after consummating the marriage, he is called back to court. He gives Shakuntala a ring and assures her that he will return to her as soon as possible. Soon Shakuntala discovers she is pregnant, so having heard nothing from the king, she decides to travel to court to find him. A holy man tells Shakuntala that the king will remember her only as long as she keeps the royal ring he gave her. She loses the ring while bathing in a river during her journey, and when she arrives in court, indeed the king does not recognize her. A despondent Shakuntala is lifted into the air and carried off to a forest, where she gives birth. Meanwhile, in another part of the wood, a fisherman finds the king's ring in the belly of a fish. Before he can explain how he came to have it, he is charged with stealing it. He is taken before the king, and, when the king sees the ring, his memory of Shakuntala is restored. Stricken with remorse, he sets out to find her. He flies over the Himalayas, where he discovers her and their son. He begs forgiveness, wins her heart, and everyone lives happily ever after.

Sanskrit plays always end happily and never deal with death or violence. The scenery is scant, but the costumes and makeup are elaborate. The performances are always accompanied by music from tambourines, lutes, flutes, and zithers. Each act of a Sanskrit play follows the structure of a musical movement or sonata that is full of love, laughter, pathos, anger, energy, fear, disgust, wonder, and finally serenity. Sanskrit plays have magical imagery and fantastic stories in which animals and trees can speak. They are also longer than Western plays, taking up to six hours to perform.

The characters in Sanskrit drama were standardized types, and the acting was anything but realistic. Instead of learning how to conjure real emotions, actors of Sanskrit drama studied for many years to learn representations of emotions through highly stylized gestures. They had to master 24 head gestures, 6 glances of the eye, 6 movements of the brow, 4 movements of the neck, 5 leaps, and 10 gaits. To top it off, they had to learn dozens of hand gestures with one hand and dozens more with both hands, all of which have precise meanings.

By the tenth century CE, Sanskrit drama was no longer an active force in Indian theatre. Writers were freeing their creativity from the stranglehold of the *Natyasastra*'s rules, and a succession of invasions by Huns, Muslims, and Afghan armies were weakening the ancient kingdoms of India. As the kingdoms died, so did Sanskrit drama.

One Hundred Thousand Verses

The traditional Indian folk theatre performed today traces its practices back to Sanskrit theatre. Although its beginnings were in the second century CE, the contemporary form, known as **Kathakali**, dates from the seventeenth century, and is a dramatized version of the Hindu epic poems *Ramayana* and *Mahabharata*. With 24,000 verses, the *Ramayana* dates from around 300 BCE and is about Rama, a human form of the god Vishnu. Rama serves as an example of the ideal Hindu man: he is brave, handsome, and devoted to his wife. Sita, his radiant wife, represents the ideal Hindu woman. The poem was made into a 78-part television miniseries in India, watched by over 100 million people. In the United States, Virgin Comics (now Liquid Comics) made the *Ramayana* into the comic book *Ramayan 3392 A.D.*, which placed the Indian classic in a post-apocalyptic future. A Hollywood movie version of the comic book is in the works.

The epic poem *Mahabharata*, which is more than 2,500 years old, has 100,000 verses and roughly 1.8 million words; that makes it ten times longer than the Bible. The *Mahabharata's* story is so long and complicated it would be equal to all of Shakespeare's 37 plays rolled into one story. *Mahabharata* is said to have been dictated by the god of wisdom, for it illustrates the futility of war. In India it was made into a 94-part television miniseries. The Kathakali plays get their themes from these ancient epic poems, including peace rather than war, righteousness defeating evil, and courage overcoming weakness.

Kathakali performances are highly stylized and are similar to the tradition of gesture and dance described in the *Natyasastra*. The words are sung to the sounds of percussion instruments and cymbals. Actors paint their faces with stylized, intensely colored makeup that identifies their characters. For example, noble male characters have green faces; evil and angry characters wear red makeup; and women have yellow faces. The elaborate costumes are topped with large, crown-like headdresses. Actors train from childhood to learn the precise gestures, distinctive footwork, and stylized eye and eyebrow movements for each performance. Kathakali plays can be performed in temple grounds and indoor halls, and are traditionally performed with no scenery.

Kathakali is one of the oldest types of theatre in the world. A form of Indian folk drama that traces its traditions back to Sanskrit theatre, it features dramatized versions of the Hindu epic poems *Ramayana* and *Mahabharata*. Kathakali is notable for its elaborate makeup, extraordinary costumes, and highly stylized dance and gestures.

Hideo Haga/The Image Works

The British Invasion

European-style theatre was introduced to India during the British occupation, which began in the 1700s. At first, these plays were simply to entertain the troops, but soon Western-style plays were being used to educate Indians in British ideas, tastes, and morals. By the nineteenth century, hundreds of Indian plays imitated Western models, including proscenium arches and realistic acting. In the twentieth century, European theatre in India continued to grow, although some playwrights began to use Western-style theatre to protest the British occupation. Censorship of such plays did not stop the protests; Indian playwrights simply masked their political points in the guise of historical or mythological stories. In 1947, after a long struggle, India won its independence from England, but its theatre continued to be influenced primarily by Western models.

Today, India has thousands of theatre companies—Calcutta alone has 3,000 registered theatre groups—producing every conceivable style of theatre from Western-style comedies and dramas to traditional Kathakali and Sanskrit plays. Well-known playwrights write about modern Indian life and clashes with tradition. Mahesh Dattani's (b. 1958) *Bravely Fought the Queen* (1991) tells the story of two married couples who harbor dark secrets while pretending to live the "Indian dream." Traditional forms remain popular but sometimes tell Western stories—Shakespeare's *King Lear* and the biblical story of Mary Magdalene have both been converted to Kathakali scripts. Of course, Bollywood films dominate the Indian performing arts scene, attracting even theatre actors to Bombay (now Mumbai) in search of quick stardom.

The modern Chinese opera (sometimes called the Peking Opera) has little in the way of sets, but does have spectacular costumes. Pictured here are actors in Shanghai rehearsing a sword dance.

William Missouri Downs

Chinese Theatre

China has another of the world's oldest civilizations. Archeologists have found the remains of Stone Age societies that are 10,000 years old, as well as pottery and beautifully carved jade from 5000 BCE. Records of early Chinese theatre are fragmentary, but we do know that it grew out of regional religious rituals related to Confucianism, Taoism, and Buddhism, and ritual dances performed during the Shang dynasty (ca. 1500–1027 BCE). The first known theatre building in China was constructed in 610 CE, but Chinese actors traditionally date their drama to 714 CE, when Emperor Ming-Huang (712–755) created a school of the arts. According to legend, the emperor dreamed that he made a trip to the moon and was most impressed with the singers and actors there. Upon awakening, he founded a school known as the Pear Garden where musicians, dancers, and actors could be trained. To this day, actors in China sometimes refer to themselves as the Children of the Pear Garden.

Theatre in the form of "music drama" was well established in China by the reign of Chen-Tsung (998–1022), but it didn't blossom until the 1200s, after Mongol warriors led by Kublai Khan swept into China from the north, establishing the Mongol Yuan dynasty (1280–1369). During this period there may have been as many as 500 playwrights turning out thousands of plays. After the Mongols were defeated, the Ming dynasty (1368–1644) introduced more literary forms of theatre that were designed for the elite members of society. Then, in the Qing dynasty Emperor Ch'ien-lung (1736–1795) brought to Beijing the best performers from all over China and created the *ching-hsi*, or "opera of the capital"—what Westerners call the Peking or Beijing opera.

The Opera of Peking

Peking opera is a synthesis of music, dance, acting, and acrobatics. It was first performed by strolling players in markets, temples, courtyards, and the streets. Although it is called *opera*, all it has in common with Western-style opera is singing and musical accompaniment. Because they originally performed outdoors, Peking opera actors had to develop a piercing style of singing their lines in order to be heard over boisterous crowds. The orchestra—made up of gongs, cymbals, lutes, rattles, drums, castanets, and a two-string violin—also had to turn up the volume. The sets had to be kept simple so that the stage could be quickly set up and struck. Because there was little scenery, audience members had to use their imaginations. Scenes could be changed rapidly because they were indicated by a song, dance, pantomime, or symbolic movement. For example, by circling the stage, an actor signified that he was on a long journey; by running across the stage holding a piece of flowing cloth, the actor showed that it was windy; if the story required the character to enter on horseback, the actor pantomimed a stylized gallop while swinging a riding whip.

Like actors in Indian Sanskrit theatre, actors in the Peking opera made no attempt to portray natural emotions. Instead, they learned numerous precise, stylized gestures. For example, one manner of trembling indicates extreme anger, and another type indicates that the character is cold. Flicking a sleeve in one way expresses disgust; flicking it another way shows astonishment. Performers also had to learn to sing and speak according to rigid conventions. Each role had tone and pitch requirements and a delivery that followed fixed

Dance, dialogue, song, and extravagant costumes are at the heart of Chinese Opera. Based on ancient folktales, these plays are still staged and are an honored part of Chinese traditional theatre.

William Missouri Downs

rhythmic patterns—when they were not singing, the actors half-chanted, half-spoke their dialogue. It could take more than 20 years of rigorous training to master all the gestures, facial movements, and vocal techniques needed to be an actor in the Peking opera.

As in many other forms of Eastern drama, the characters in the Peking opera were not individuals but types. Standard roles included scholar, lover, hero, maiden, old woman, coquette, virtuous wife, and acrobatic warrior-maiden. Elaborate geometrical designs were used for the **painted-face roles**, which included supernatural beings, warriors, and bandits. With the painted-face roles, the color of the actor's makeup indicated the character's personality. Red makeup indicated loyalty; blue indicated vigor and courage; yellow showed intelligence; black showed honesty; and brown symbolized stubbornness or obstinacy. In addition, almost all plays had a clown who wore white makeup. The clown's purpose was to keep the audience laughing, even during tragic scenes, by improvising malicious comments about the other characters.

The two types of plays of the Peking opera are based on history, mythology, folklore, and tales of romance. Civil plays feature plots about imperial concubines, conniving palace eunuchs, chivalry, and romance. Military plays are often set during the Three Kingdoms period (220–265 CE) when China was divided into three rival kingdoms. Although this was a period of great turmoil, it was regarded as a time that exemplified the highest ideals of chivalry and honor. An example of a military play is *Yang Ping Pass*, the story of two warlord-emperors. Emperor Cao Cao seeks revenge on rival Emperor Liu Bei for the death of one of his generals. Cao Cao's troops are poised to attack at Yang Ping Pass. Discovering the planned attack, one of Liu Bei's chief staff officers wants someone to burn Cao Cao's store of grain to force him to withdraw. An old general agrees to set the fire although the other officers feel it's a suicide mission. Undaunted, the old general succeeds in burning the grain but he is then surrounded by Cao Cao's troops. The old general seems doomed, but at the last moment, Liu Bei's troops come to his aid. A chorus of actors stages a glorious battle, using swords, javelins, and spears as they fill the stage with elaborate, acrobatic, swashbuckling action, deafening percussion, and triumphal tableaus. In the end, the old general is rescued.

The Peking opera was dramatically altered when Communists took control of the government in 1949. Communist officials denounced the Peking opera, saying that it preserved superstition, perpetuated the backward laws of a feudal society, reinforced old-fashioned Confucian philosophy, and encouraged a class system of servants and masters. At the beginning of the Cultural Revolution in 1966, Mao Tse-tung organized students into units of "Red Guards," whose purpose was to wipe out every vestige of the old bourgeois culture, including the Peking opera. No longer allowed to perform traditional plays, the Peking opera created new plays with pro-Communist themes. The Cultural Revolution ended in 1976, and in 1978 traditional Peking opera was once again allowed. However, by that time the traditional plays seemed out-of-date to audiences, and the art began to die. Today there are efforts to revive Peking opera in China, though audiences for these performances often primarily consist of tourists.

Western Influences on Chinese Theatre

In the nineteenth century, Westerners brought their economics, customs, and theatre to China. Western-style theatre was often called "talking" or "spoken" drama, for it lacked the dancing, singing, and spectacle that the Chinese were used to in the Peking opera. By the late 1800s, Western theatre was recognized in China but wasn't always welcomed by the general public. However, students in urban areas were intrigued by the Western focus on ideas and realism, and they began translating and staging plays by European playwrights Bertolt Brecht and Henrik Ibsen in an effort to shed light on China's social and political problems. Over the years, traditional Chinese theatre borrowed more from Western theatre. By the 1950s, for instance, the Peking opera's simple platform stages had been replaced with Western-style proscenium arches including curtains and an orchestra pit.

Prior to World War II, many Chinese playwrights took a leftist political stance and wrote plays about daily life that criticized the old order. For example, *Leiyu (The Thunderstorm)*, written in 1934 by Cao Yu (1910–1996), tells the story of the disintegration of a rich family as a result of corruption in old China. However, during the Cultural Revolution, spoken drama was restricted—the government favored dance-dramas that appealed to rural audiences and emphasized Communist ideology and propaganda. Since the late 1970s, China has once again opened up to the West, and many American and European theatre artists have visited to collaborate with the Chinese theatre community. Realism is still the dominant form of Western theatre performed in China today, but younger playwrights have begun exploring more contemporary works and techniques. Although spoken drama continues to grow in China, it is often associated with political and social causes and, as a result, is often censored.

Japanese Theatre

Although Japanese civilization can be traced back almost as far as Chinese civilization, theatre that is uniquely Japanese evolved more slowly, primarily because for many centuries Japan was under foreign domination. Fifteen hundred years ago, Chinese society, government, and art predominated. The Japanese copied Chinese poetry and ritual dance. Then, around 1200 CE, Japanese feudal lords, called shoguns, began a 200-year battle to control the islands and to limit Chinese influence. But just as the shoguns were making progress against China, a new outside force appeared: the Europeans. Initially, the shoguns tolerated the Westerners, and they gladly traded goods with Portuguese, Spanish, English, and Dutch sailors. With trade came Western commodities, but it also brought Western belief systems including Christianity. At first, Christian missionaries made many converts in Japan, but at the end of the sixteenth century, Japanese authorities expelled the missionaries in an effort to gain more control over the populace. In 1603 a shogun named Tokugawa Ieyasu took power and condemned all outside influences—including Christianity. (Hundreds of Japanese converts and European priests were executed before Christianity became legal in Japan in 1873.) Huge numbers of foreigners were expelled and Japanese people were forbidden to leave the country; any who left were not allowed to return. For the next 250 years, the Japanese people lived in isolation from the rest of the world. During this period forms of theatre unique to Japan began to flourish.

At its earliest stages, however, Japanese theatre can be traced back a thousand years. It was greatly influenced by Buddhism and Shinto, a religion native to Japan. Shinto does not divide existence into a physical world and a supernatural world; Shintoists worship the life force in rivers, rocks, trees, and other elements of nature from which they believe creativity, healing, and even disease originate. In the sixth century, Buddhism, a religion that stresses spiritual enlightenment through meditation, proper conduct, and wisdom, joined Shinto as a strong influence on Japanese society.

Japanese theatre, like that of most other cultures, originates in ritual. More than a thousand years ago Buddhist missionaries from China developed dance-

Koichi Kamoshida/Getty Images News/Getty Images

Noh plays are performed on a bare stage whose only adornment is the *kagami-ita*, a painting of a pine tree at the back of the stage. The tree symbolizes eternal life, a meaning that may derive from Shinto ritual—according to myth, deities descended to earth via the pine tree. To the left of the Noh stage is the *Hashigakari*, a narrow bridge that the principal actors use to make their entrances.

like dramas related to Buddhist and Shinto festivals. They were intended to drive away demons, bring health, celebrate the harvest, and deliver prosperity. Japanese theatre began when Buddhist priests added choral songs to these ritual dances. Like the Japanese tea ceremony, Japanese drama emphasizes mood, serenity, contemplation, and simplified movements. To fully appreciate the Japanese theatre, one must prepare to receive the dreams, poetic vision, and beauty that are derived from simplicity and restraint. There are two types of traditional Japanese theatre: Noh drama and Kabuki.

Noh Theatre

Japanese **Noh** drama developed during the 1300s from the dance-prayers of Buddhist priests, who danced, sang, and prayed at religious shrines. It is said that in 1374 a shogun named Yoshimitsu saw one of these early dance-prayers and was so impressed that he invited the performers to his court; there he set about joining poetry, acting, singing, and dance into a new form of theatre called *Noh*, which means "talent" or "skill." By the middle of the fifteenth century, Noh was the favorite theatre of the shoguns and their aristocratic patrons. Noh performances, like the Japanese tea ceremony and sumi-e paintings, were understated and refined. Everything redundant was pruned. The actors—men only—moved in a stately manner with a deliberate tempo that allowed every step, gesture, and word to be dignified and fully contemplated. The stage was a simple raised platform with a floor of highly polished wood that reflected the actors' brightly colored embroidered kimonos, expressive masks, or stylized makeup. (See the Spotlight "Masks and Theatre.") Under the floor were special resonators that amplified the sounds of the actors' feet when they danced. Painted on the back wall of the stage was a pine tree symbolizing eternal life.

Noh stories have five possible subjects: the deities, the deeds of heroic samurai, women (these are known as "wig plays" because men who played women wore a wig), insanity, and famous legends. Each play has three parts: a *Jo*, a *Ha*, and a *Kyu*. The *Jo* is usually a chance meeting between two characters, often a wandering Buddhist monk and someone who in the West would be called the protagonist (i.e., the central character who pushes the action forward). This character is usually a tormented figure such as a dishonored warrior, an emperor's jealous wife, an abandoned courtesan, or even a god or ghost. In the *Jo*, introductions are made and the characters engage in a question-and-answer sequence that reveals the protagonist's concern. In the second part of the play, the *Ha*, the protagonist performs a dance that expresses his or her concern. In the third part, the *Kyu*, the protagonist appears as a new self, and the cause of the torment is resolved. For example, in *Sotoba Komachi (Komachi at the Grave)*, one of the most famous Noh dramas, the *Jo* begins when a monk stumbles upon a tragic old woman near a grave. She is tortured by choices she made in her youth. The *Ha* takes us back to the time when, as a young woman, she demanded that a suitor swim across a lake 100 times before she would consider his marriage proposal. On his 99th crossing, the young suitor drowned. In the *Kyu*, the woman is once again old, but through the catharsis of reliving past events, she realizes her cruelty and pride and is emancipated from her suffering.

An evening of Noh drama often included several plays with small farces between them. Some of these farces parodied the serious plays on the same program, much as the ancient Greek satyr plays parodied the tragedies performed the same day. The similarities between Noh and ancient Greek drama have led some scholars to speculate that Alexander the Great and Hellenistic theatre may have had a more

> Noh is the inexpressible beauty of doing nothing.
>
> **Zenchiku,** Noh actor

far-reaching effect on world theatre than is generally believed, but others conclude that the only relationship between the two is the human tendency to develop theatre from ritual (for more on Greek and Hellenistic theatre, see Chapter 13).

Noh theatre reached its present form in the 1600s and has remained practically unchanged ever since. Today, the Noh actors' stylized performance techniques have become living traditions that are handed down from father to son. Every detail of the performance, every movement and vocal intonation, even the costumes and makeup are strictly regulated and cannot be altered. Even the language of fourteenth-century Japanese shoguns has been retained, which makes Noh plays largely unintelligible to modern Japanese audiences. Audience members who wish to understand the dialogue must bring a translation. But understanding all the dialogue is not a problem, for the meaning of a Noh play transcends the story or words. Today in Japan, the Noh tradition is popular even though virtually no new Noh plays have been written since the 1600s.

Kabuki Theatre

Noh drama was designed for aristocrats and shoguns; there were few performances for the general public. But by the seventeenth century, a robust and spectacular version of Noh was created for the masses. It was called **Kabuki**, from the characters for "song" (*ka*), "dance" (*bu*), and "skill" (*ki*). A woman named Okuni created Kabuki in the seventeenth century. The owner of a brothel, she began holding Noh theatre imitations in front of her shop in order to drum up business. Her female Kabuki players were a sensation; after each performance men lined up to purchase the ladies' services. But when the samurai began fighting duels over the women, the

Kabuki theatre began in the early 1600s as a popular form of Noh drama. Kabuki is known for stylized movements, singsong speech, and energetic characters. Over the years, Kabuki has gone in and out of fashion in Japan; it was briefly banned by occupying U.S. forces after World War II, but today it is the most popular form of traditional theatre. It has long influenced Western theatre and film artists, and elements of Kabuki can even be seen in contemporary TV cartoons—when called to action, the Mighty Morphin Power Rangers strike mie poses.

Michael S. Yamashita/Encyclopedia/Corbis

shogun prohibited his men from attending the performances. When this failed to end the civil disorder surrounding the performances, the shogun issued a decree in 1629 forbidding women from performing in Kabuki plays. Kabuki plays were then performed by companies of boys. Ironically, the change in actors did not solve the problem, for the samurai were soon demanding sexual favors from the boy actors and fighting over them. As a result, in 1659, boys were also forbidden to be Kabuki actors. This left Kabuki theatre to adult male actors, as it remains today. (For more see the Spotlight "Men Playing Women.")

SPOTLIGHT<u>ON</u> Men Playing Women

Theatre's male-dominated religious origins have often meant that women were barred from performing. This was certainly the case in Western theatre. The women of ancient Greece were not allowed on stage, and in Rome there were only a few female performers. Not until the 1500s did women begin appearing on stage in the West, and they didn't become commonplace until the 1600s. Today, men still occasionally play female characters—Robin Williams played a man who disguises himself as a woman in the movie *Mrs. Doubtfire* and Tyler Perry plays the strong grandmother figure Madea in his movies *Diary of a Mad Black Woman* and *Madea's Family Reunion*.

Outside the West, women actors have fared better. For thousands of years, women have been performing in the Chinese theatre. They were briefly banned from the stage in the late eighteenth century, by a decree of Emperor Ch'ien-lung (1736–1795). When the Qing dynasty was overthrown, women returned to the stage, although men playing female characters remained popular. For example, in 1924, Mei Lanfang, what Westerners would call a female impersonator, was voted the best actor in China. In India women have always been part of the theatre. In Africa the participation of women has varied from one country to another.

Today prohibitions against women on stage are rare. One holdout is Japan's Kabuki theatre, where women have been banned for more than 350 years. In the Meiji period (1868–1912), the suggestion that women be allowed to act in Kabuki plays was quickly rejected, because many felt that women playing female characters would be too real. Today, although the ban has been lifted, there are still no female Kabuki actors in Japan. The men who play female roles are called **onnagata**. Like all Kabuki actors, they train from childhood. *Onnagata* performers take their study of female characters very seriously. In the early to mid 1800s they often lived as women offstage in an attempt to perfect female movements and manners, and even today no *onnagata* is considered to be at the peak of his abilities until he has been playing women's roles for at least 20 years. After a lifetime of studying and imitating women, according to Kabuki expert Shutaro Miyake, *onnagata* often feel that they know women better than women know themselves. As they see it, only a man can *objectively* understand a woman. Of course, many in the West would argue this point.

Monika Graff/The Image Works

Men have played women's roles in theatre for thousands of years, often because of social or religious restrictions placed on women in public. In Kabuki theatre, men continue to play women, training for many years to act, dance, and move like women.

Over the centuries, Kabuki has become a popular form of mass entertainment. Although it borrowed a great deal from Noh, Kabuki is decidedly less restrained. It has a greater variety of characters, contains more battle scenes, and enacts many melodramatic moments. Kabuki actors wear the colorfully embroidered, gold-lined kimonos and elaborate makeup and wigs of Noh theatre, but Kabuki adds spectacular scenery, including revolving stages, trapdoors, and breathtaking special effects. Even Noh's pine tree painted on the back wall of the stage is exaggerated. Another notable difference is the audience. Unlike Noh theatregoers, Kabuki audience members are expected to be active participants. They call out an actor's name if they like a particular moment, or, if they don't like an actor, they might cry out *Daikon*, or "radish," the Japanese equivalent of calling an actor a "ham." Or audience members might yell out "You are better than your father," referring to the Kabuki tradition of passing roles down from father to son for generation after generation. Such audience participation during the performance stands in for the Western tradition of the curtain call, which does not exist in Kabuki.

Kabuki acting is so highly stylized that the movements are almost puppet-like. In fact, Kabuki borrowed many of its movements from **Bunraku**, the Japanese puppet theatre (see the Spotlight "Bunraku Puppets"). In Kabuki every movement of the body or limbs is exaggerated. At particularly intense or profound moments in the drama, the actors perform what is known as a *mie* **pose**. This is a sudden, striking pose accompanied by several powerful beats of wooden clappers known as the **Ki**. During a classic *mie* pose, the actors strike a fierce posture, with their eyes crossed, chin sharply turned, and big toe pointed toward the sky, while the *Ki* sounds with several sharp blows or accelerates to a crescendo. As in Noh plays, the dialogue is sung or shouted in a highly stylized and theatrical manner.

There are three kinds of Kabuki plays: history plays about major political events of the past, domestic plays about the loves and lives of merchants and townspeople, and dance-dramas about the world of spirits and animals. A typical Kabuki story is quite simple. *Kanjinchō*, a history play that was first staged in 1840, is one of the most popular in the Kabuki repertoire. The play tells the story of the famous Japanese warrior Yoshitsune (1159–1189 CE) who was forced to flee because of unjust accusations of disloyalty by his half-brother, the shogun. At the suggestion of his loyal servant Benkei, they disguised themselves as traveling Buddhist monks in order to get past roadblocks. As the play begins, Togashi, the chief officer at a border crossing, explains that the barrier has been erected to capture the fugitive Yoshitsune. Moments later, the disguised Benkei, Yoshitsune, and his men enter, but they are immediately stopped. They don't have identification papers and are about to be arrested, when the quick-witted Benkei, acting as head of the group, tries to convince Togashi that they are collecting donations for a local Buddhist temple. Suspecting a trick, Togashi asks Benkei to read his list of donors (*Kanjinchō*). In one of the most famous scenes, Benkei takes out a blank scroll and pretends to read. Togashi is so impressed with Benkei's loyalty that he decides to let the party go even though he sees through their disguises. It appears they will get away, but suddenly one of Togashi's guards becomes suspicious. He picks out the disguised Yoshitsune for questioning. Just when it looks as if all is lost, Benkei begins flogging his master, Yoshitsune, and ordering him to get back in line. No servant would ever strike his master in such a way, so the guard is convinced that it can't possibly be Yoshitsune. Once past the barrier, Benkei begs forgiveness for striking his master, but Yoshitsune praises his resourcefulness.

SPOTLIGHT ON Bunraku Puppets

Bunraku is Japan's professional puppet (or doll) theatre. Developed in the seventeenth century, its roots go back to the eighth century. At the height of its popularity, Bunraku nearly put Kabuki out of business. The Kabuki theatre was forced to win audiences back by building more elaborate scenery, stealing Bunraku stories, and incorporating more stylized movements.

Bunraku puppets are about one-third life size and have remarkable dexterity, including flexible joints and movable eyes, mouths, and eyebrows. When in the hands of a master, these puppets can seem remarkably lifelike. During performances, a narrator tells the story in a sing-song chant and does all the voices, while the puppets pantomime the story. Hundreds of years ago, these puppets were controlled by a single operator, but today's more complex puppets require three operators. The most senior of the puppet masters controls the right hand and the head; the second in seniority controls the left hand, and an apprentice controls the feet. Only the senior puppet master is allowed to show his face during the performances; the other puppeteers are required to dress in black, including black hoods to hide their faces. It takes approximately ten years of training to move from apprentice to senior puppet master.

Jack Fields/Documentary Value/Corbis

Although Bunraku puppet masters are visible during performances, they are often so skilled that audiences are completely absorbed by the story and focus only on the puppets. The puppets themselves are quite intricate and sophisticated. For example, some puppets are constructed so that their faces can quickly transform into the faces of terrifying supernatural beings.

> When the components of art are dominated by restraint, the result is very moving.
>
> **Chikamatsu Monzaemon,**
> Playwright

There are also farcical Kabuki plays. One of the most famous is *Migawari Zazen* (1911), about an adulterous husband who plots to slip out of the house so that he can spend the night with his mistress. He tells his wife that he is going to spend the evening meditating under a large robe and that she must not disturb him, but when she isn't looking, he puts his servant under the robe and escapes. When the wife finds out that her husband is gone, she slips under the robe and waits for his return. When he does, he tells the "servant" of his exploits, unaware that the person under the robe is really his wife. At the height of his drunken merriment, his wife emerges from the cloak. Needless to say, the rest of the story is not one of marital bliss.

The Japanese Shakespeare: Chikamatsu

One of the most popular Kabuki and Bunraku playwrights was Chikamatsu Monzaemon (1653–1725), who, like Shakespeare in the West, wrote crowd-pleasing plays that combined poetry and prose in dramatic tales of comedy, tragedy, love, and war. In fact, Chikamatsu is often called the Japanese Shakespeare—perhaps someday we in the West will know enough about Japanese theatre to call Shakespeare the English Chikamatsu. The author of over 100 plays, he often based his stories on actual events and scandalous gossip. One of his most famous plays, *The Love Suicides of Amijima* (1721), is based on a report of a real double suicide. In the play, Jihei, an apprentice clerk, refuses to marry the girl chosen for him because he is in love with a prostitute. Jihei manages to get the dowry back from his mother, but before he can return it, he is cheated out of the money by a close friend. Rather than face the humiliation, he and the prostitute decide to kill themselves so that they can be united in death.

> Art is something which lies in the slender margins between the real and the unreal.
>
> **Chikamatsu Monzaemon,**
> Playwright

Western Influences on Japanese Theatre

In 1853 a small fleet of U.S. naval vessels commanded by Matthew C. Perry sailed to Japan. Perry wanted the shogun to open his ports to international trade. At first he was snubbed, but after years of intense negotiations, Japan signed a treaty of commerce and once again the island nation was open to Western-influence. A few years later, the shoguns were overthrown and an emperor once again controlled Japan. At the beginning of the 1900s, a modified form of Kabuki theatre, called *Shimpa* ("New School of Movement"), began to emerge. *Shimpa* toned down the spectacle of Kabuki and allowed a bit of Western realism into the performances. *Shimpa* plays moved from the melodrama of Kabuki to stories of everyday life, particularly those of women. And for the first time in hundreds of years, women played women's parts, but only in *Shimpa* plays. Kabuki plays remained all male.

Today, Kabuki theatre is still the most popular form of traditional Japanese drama. Some Kabuki theatres seat more than 2,000. Western-style drama is also popular, such as the works of Shakespeare and Broadway musicals. As in other societies with a strong traditional culture, many modern playwrights in Japan seek to reconcile traditions and history with contemporary culture. Novelist and playwright Hisashi Inoue's *Chichi to Kuraseba (The Face of Jizo)* (1994) portrays the relationship between a father and daughter and their quest for happiness after the bombing of Hiroshima. Modern Japanese drama also focuses on social issues, such as the oppression of women, the suppression of individualism, and the intersection between technology and humanity.

Islamic Theatre

In the ancient Muslim world, theatre was not seen as being of value to society, so plays were not an important part of Islamic culture. The Koran, Islam's holy book, contains a warning about "graven images," similar to the one in the Bible (Exodus 20:4) (see Chapter 14). This prohibition applies to dolls, statues, portraits, and people playing a character. As a result, art in many Islamic countries was limited to abstract ornamentation. This ban is still in effect in some countries today. For example, in 2001, Taliban leaders in Afghanistan ordered massive, 2,000-year-old statues of Buddha to be blown up.

The idea of theatre was so unfamiliar in many Islamic lands that when Arab translators discovered *Poetics*, Aristotle's treatise on dramatic theory, they were quite perplexed by it. Theatre as we know it in the West never developed in some Islamic countries or was slow to arrive. There were two forms of theatre extant in the Muslim world before it came into cultural contact with the West. The first was Shadow Theatre and second was the Ta'ziyeh religious dramas of Iran.

William Missouri Downs

Storytellers got around Islamic laws forbidding "graven images," including acting, by staging shadow plays with puppets. The puppets were generally made from the hides of camels or cows and were brightly painted. A puppeteer manipulated the puppets behind a transparent white curtain; lit from behind with candlelight, the shadows of the puppets were thrown onto the curtain.

Shadow Theatre

Shadow theatre, which probably originated in China around 100 BCE, is created by lighting two-dimensional figures and casting their shadows on a screen. The audience watches the silhouettes while a narrator tells a story. In some ways this theatre might be compared to a primitive television set. The first records of shadow plays in Islamic lands appear in the seventh century, but it wasn't always accepted. One of the first shadow-theatre artists was a man named Batruni. During one performance in a mosque, he showed the South Arabian king riding on a horse. The image so frightened the audience that Batruni was accused of being a magician and executed. By the eleventh century, shadow plays were popular in Islamic Spain, and by the thirteenth century they had spread throughout North Africa and into what today is Turkey.

Some shadow plays tell stories about Allah and his prophets and about historical events; others had comic plots about people who think highly of themselves. An example of a comic play is *Taif al-Khayal (The Spirit of the Shadow)* by Muhammad Ibn Daniyal (ca. 1248–1311), the story of a man who is appointed to be "king of the lunatics." Proud of his new status, the man starts dressing as a soldier and describing himself as a heroic warrior who is "more cunning than a serpent" and "more thirsty than the sand." He decides that with his new power he should take a wife, but because of his low position and lack of money, the matchmaker can only find him an unattractive spouse. In the end the man sees the error of his prideful ways and goes on a pilgrimage to atone for his sins.

The Ta'ziyeh religious dramas of Iran are performed outdoors and use live horses and camels. Here, actors perform in a play that memorializes Imam Hussein, the grandson of Muhammad, who died in the battle of Karbala in 680 CE. This 2008 performance took place in Noushabad, south of Tehran.

Majid/Getty Images News/Getty Images

Religious Drama

Another form of Islamic theatre is the Ta'ziyeh religious drama of Iran, which allowed for actors, both professional and amateur, and has been performed in open-air playing spaces and on some occasions in specially constructed indoor stages for hundreds of years. Scholars have compared Ta'ziyeh plays to the religious dramas that existed in Europe during the Middle Ages (see Chapter 14). Ta'ziyeh plays enact the suffering and death of Imam Hussein, grandson of the Prophet of Islam, who was killed in battle in 680 CE just outside of Baghdad. Later Ta'ziyeh plays contain other religious themes, including stories about Moses and the Pharaoh and Solomon and the Queen of Sheba. There were even comic Ta'ziyeh plays. Ta'ziyeh plays have persisted, even though religious leaders sometimes condemn them because of the ban on graven images.

Ahmad al-Rubaye/AFP/Getty Images

Western-style theatre is very popular in many Middle Eastern countries, and with few exceptions (such as Saudi Arabia), women are allowed to act and direct. Here, Awatif al-Salman, a veteran star of Iraqi stage and television, talks to the press after a performance of *Baghdadi Love Circle* at the National Theatre in Baghdad in 2008.

Western Influences on Islamic Theatre

In the 1800s, colonization by Britain, France, and Italy introduced Western theatre to many Islamic countries. But the idea of people rather than puppets acting was so foreign that it had to be explained to the audience before the play began. Soon, Western-style theatres caught on in many Islamic countries. But these early performances were mostly private productions and not seen by the general public. In 1847 Marun al-Naqqash (d. 1855) wrote the first European-style play in Arabic. It was based on French playwright Molière's *The Miser* (1668). By the late nineteenth century, hundreds of European plays had been adapted and translated to Arabic. Molière, Racine, and Shakespeare were favored by Islamic audiences, but soon there were plays that told stories from a purely Islamic point of view. Today, shadow theatre is still popular, but there are also hundreds of theatre festivals and thousands of Western-style productions in Islamic lands. In some countries, the modern Islamic theatre even includes important female artistic directors and playwrights.

Because of their subjugation in many Islamic countries, women traditionally have not been allowed to be part of the theatre. One of the first references to a woman in a Western-style play comes from Alexandria in 1876. A local newspaper reported that a woman was part of a private performance, but there is little information. There is also a report of a young woman appearing on stage in a play in Istanbul in 1919; because of audience complaints, the play closed after only one performance. In 1915 Munira al-Mahdiyyah became one of the first Muslim women to appear on stage in Egypt. She went on to become the first female artistic director in the Muslim world when she formed her own theatre company.

Rob Elliott/AFP/Getty Images

As in many other parts of the world, theatre in Arab and Islamic regions manages to survive despite restrictions and outright bans. During the Taliban's rule in Afghanistan (1995–2002), theatre was outlawed and actors were often imprisoned. And yet, soon after the fall of the Taliban, the Afghanistan National Theatre returned to the ruins of the Kabul theatre and staged a play about life under the Taliban regime. Roya Naquibullah, dressed as a bride, symbolizes the return of peace.

Today, although still rare, women are a part of the Islamic theatre. One of the most well-known Muslim playwrights is Algerian-born French playwright Fatima Gallaire-Bourega (b. 1944), who uses her plays not only to express herself but also to prompt discussions about such topics as violence against women, religious fanaticism, and female sexual desire. Her play *You Have Come Back* (1986) is about a woman named Lella who returns to her native Arab village after living in France for 20 years. At first, Lella is welcomed home, but, within a day, her family finds her ideas about men, life, and love are just too different. The women of the village are so outraged by Lella's Western point of view that they decide to put her on trial. Found guilty of being a blasphemer who has deserted Islam, Lella is clubbed to death by the women of the village. Throughout the violent clubbing, Lella protests and accuses the women of having been "dead for ages." The play ends with women of the village being called to evening prayer. They leave behind Lella's lifeless body. Because of its subject matter, this play cannot be performed in Gallaire-Bourega's native Algeria, but it has been produced internationally.

East Meets West

For thousands of years, Eastern and Western theatre developed independently of each other. Yet some scholars believe that Eastern forms of theatre are direct descendants of ancient Greek (Western) theatre. We know that Alexander the Great staged Greek plays during his invasion of India in 326 BCE and that they

In Sanskrit drama, the natural and the supernatural blend to create a fantastic universe. A particularly ambitious Western retelling of a Sanskrit story was Peter Brook's 1985 production of *The Mahabharata*. This cycle of three plays about an epic battle between two sets of cousins in an ancient Indian dynasty took 12 hours to stage and featured performers from all over the world. In this scene from the 1989 filmed version of the play, the Hindu god Ganesh communes with the poet Vyasa, the mythic composer of the *Mahabharata*. Directed by Peter Brook and adapted by Jean-Claude Carrière.

had some effect on Indian theatre. But could this effect, over centuries, have traveled all the way to Japan? There is no way to be sure, but there are tantalizing clues. For example, early forms of Japanese ceremonial plays contained celebrations of the phallus, just as in the ancient Greek plays. Both ancient Greek plays and Japanese Noh plays use masks, as do many other forms of drama around the world, but some masks from ancient, pre-Noh dance-dramas have Aryan features, which suggests that they might come from India or the Mediterranean. In addition, Noh drama uses a chorus and limits the number of actors, just as ancient Greek tragedies do. But for most scholars, these similarities are not enough to prove a direct link. In fact, some scholars believe that the golden age of Greek drama was inspired by forms of Eastern theatre coming from central Asia, and still others believe the influence flowed in both directions.

When Westerners finally discovered Eastern drama, it made an impact. In 1789 Sir William James translated the Indian Sanskrit play *Shakuntala* into English. Sanskrit drama so impressed German playwright Johann Wolfgang von Goethe that he borrowed its staging techniques for his masterpiece *Faust* (see Chapter 16). Eastern drama's emphasis on feeling rather than scientific analysis appealed to the Romantics, whose work was quite popular at the time (see also Chapter 16). Eastern theatre became even more influential during the revolt against realism. In the twentieth century, many Western directors cited Eastern theatre as a major influence in their work. The German playwright Bertolt Brecht imitated the Peking opera by having the actors perform on a bare stage and making no attempt to hide the fact that it was a performance. He also crafted his plays to be epic in proportion, much like Sanskrit drama (for more on Brecht, see Chapter 17)

Today, Western playwrights, directors, and designers continue to draw inspiration from Eastern theatrical traditions. French director Ariane Mnouchkine (b. 1939) is well-known for her Kathakali and Kabuki-inspired productions of Greek tragedies and Shakespeare's plays. The productions of English director Peter Brook (b. 1925) use myth, fables, and history from all over the world to explore universal human experience—notable is his 1985 production of *The Mahabharata*, which featured a multicultural cast. American director and designer Julie Taymor (b. 1952), most recently in the public eye for her work on the Broadway production of *The Lion King*, is heavily influenced by puppetry and masks, drawing on African, Asian, Mayan, and Indian traditions.

Curtain Call

Many differences often prevent Westerners from fully appreciating non-Western theatre. For example, much traditional theatre outside the Western tradition relies on established conventions and has remained relatively unchanged for centuries, in contrast to the ever-changing "isms" of Western drama (see Chapter 17). Much non-Western theatre is more stylized, theatrical, and visual than Western theatre. Many non-Western plays are accompanied by continuous music, dance, and highly traditional stylized acting, the particulars of which have been polished for hundreds of years. Non-Western actors are also likely to wear bright costumes with symbolic colors and masks. The stories of modern Western theatre are usually ones about everyday people, whereas the stories of Eastern theatre are often based on folk history, ancient religions, and myths. And adding to the differences, non-Western plays often appeal more to the senses than to the intellect; they take the audience through meandering fairy tales in contrast to the streamlined, cause-and-effect stories of Western theatre. But even with these differences, Westerners can enjoy non-Western theatre as long as they open their minds to a broader, perhaps more accurate, definition of theatre.

SUMMARY

MindTap

Test your knowledge with online printable flashcards and online quizzing.

No one knows for certain where theatre and drama originated, but many scholars believe that it grew out of religious rituals, ceremonies, and storytelling. Theatre is different from ritual, because it has actors who play roles, not themselves, and because it involves a conflict. Theatre can be divided into two broad categories: Western and non-Western. Western drama came from Athens and spread through the Mediterranean region to Rome and Western Europe. Non-Western drama includes all other forms, from the ancient ritual theatre of Africa to the traditional theatre of Asia.

African theatre can be divided into three periods: precolonial, colonial, and postcolonial. Precolonial African theatre was not limited by a physical structure, which allowed for mass participation in the performance. It also was closely tied to ritual. During the colonial period, European invaders brought Western-style theatre to Africa and either discouraged or ignored traditional African theatre. Postcolonial theatre mixes Western-style theatre with traditional African ritual theatre to create "total theatre." Modern African theatre encourages African nationalism and glorifies Africa's customs, rituals, and traditional culture. It can also contain serious themes that call for political and social revolution.

India also has an ancient civilization and some of the oldest theatre traditions, though scholars debate its origins. Some believe that theatre in India began when the army of Alexander the Great staged Greek-style plays during their invasion. For more than a thousand years, Sanskrit drama was performed by touring professional companies in courts, temples, palaces, and temporary theatres. The actors in Sanskrit plays use stylized gestures to convey fancies, sentiment, sweet poetry, heroism, mythological forces, and love stories in which the righteous triumph and virtue is rewarded. European-style theatre was introduced to India during the British occupation and still is very popular, along with traditional Kathakali and Sanskrit plays.

Chinese theatre grew out of the religious rituals related to Confucianism, Taoism, and Buddhism. The most famous type of Chinese theatre is the Peking opera, which uses chanting, dancing, and symbolic pantomime to tell the stories based on history, mythology, and folklore. In China, Western-style drama is known as "talking" or "spoken" drama, for it lacks dancing, singing, and spectacle.

Japanese theatre was greatly influenced by Buddhism and Shintoism. Like the Japanese tea ceremony, it stresses simplicity and discipline. Japanese Noh drama developed during the 1300s from the dance-prayers of Buddhist priests. It was the favorite theatre of the shoguns. Noh has remained practically unchanged since the 1600s. Kabuki is a popular form of Noh. Created by a woman named Okuni in the seventeenth century, Kabuki uses stylized movements from Bunraku, the Japanese puppet theatre.

In some Islamic countries, theatre was forbidden. As a result, Western-style theatre was slow to arrive. To get around the Koran's ban against people acting roles, shadow theatre with puppets became popular. In Iran, religious dramas known as Ta'ziyeh plays were also popular, even though their use of actors was controversial. European-style theatre was first introduced to Islamic lands by Napoleon and other Westerners.

KEY TERMS

Bunraku *247*

Kabuki *245*

Kathakali *237*

Ki 247

Mie pose *247*

Natyasastra 236

Noh *244*

Onnagata 246

Painted-face roles *241*

Peking opera *240*

Precolonial African theatre *232*

Ritual theatre *230*

Sanskrit drama *236*

Shadow theatre *250*

Total theatre *234*

Western drama *232*

Chapter **13**

THE GREEKS TO THE RISE OF CHRISTIANITY

The 2000 year-old Roman theatre in what is now Merida, Spain, is one of the best-preserved ancient theatres. A large section of the skene is still intact.

William Missouri Downs

Outline

MindTap

Start with a quick warm-up activity and review the chapter's learning objectives.

Around 500 BCE, Greece was made up of over 150 independent city-states, including Sparta, Corinth, Thebes, and Athens. They seldom united except against foreign invaders. In the early years of the fifth century BCE, they joined to fight two massive invasions by the Persians, who ruled a vast empire that today would include Iran, Afghanistan, Pakistan, parts of Central Asia, Asia Minor, Iraq, and northern Saudi Arabia. In the Battle of Marathon (490 BCE) Athenians defeated the Persian army even though they were outnumbered five to one. A few years later in the Bay of Salamis, the small Athenian navy sank over 300 warships, roughly half the Persian fleet. As the Greeks basked in the glory of their underdog victories, the great age of the city-state of Athens began. Over the next 90 years there would be remarkable literary, philosophical, and artistic accomplishments. This was a period of power and prosperity known as the golden age of Greek theatre. The Athenians seemed to know that they were living in a special time; Pericles (ca. 490–429 BCE), the great Greek statesman responsible for building the Parthenon, said, "Our city is an education to Greece. . . Future ages will wonder at us, as the present age wonders at us now." (See the Spotlight "The Cradle of Western Civilization.")

SPOTLIGHT ON The Cradle of Western Civilization

Athens is often called the cradle of Western civilization because so many modern Western forms of government, theatre, art, and philosophy originated there. In your education so far, you've probably encountered ancient Greek ideas about these topics, particularly philosophy. The word *philosophy* comes from the ancient Greek words for "love" and "wisdom," and philosophy is considered exactly that: a love and a pursuit of wisdom. The Athenians called philosophy *logos*, which referred to reasoned, verifiable, and logical explanations as well as freedom of speech. *Logos* was the opposite of *mythos*, which referred to beliefs, such as myths about the gods, that could not be verified. Using a combination of logos and mythos, the ancient Greeks began to ask profound and perhaps unanswerable questions:

- What is the nature of reality?
- What is real and what is illusion?
- What is knowledge?
- What is justice?
- What is virtue?
- What is the meaning of life?
- What does "to know" mean?

Philosophers of earlier civilizations had asked these questions, but the Greek philosophers approached these questions with a great deal of skepticism that led to innovative ways of looking at the world. Ancient Greece's fertile ground for free thought and discourse gave birth to the first known democracy

in the history of the world. But Greek democracy was limited: it applied only to free men, or *citizens*, and did not include slaves or women. Of the 300,000 inhabitants of Athens, only about 43,000 qualified as citizens, which meant that the vast majority of the people were not represented in government. This inequity was seldom questioned. As Steven Kreis of Florida Atlantic University says, "The Athenians would have had some difficulty understanding the statement, 'We the People.' This would have had to be modified to read, 'We the Citizens.'" Clearly, universal human rights were not a high priority in ancient Greece.

Built in the fifth century BCE atop the Acropolis, the Parthenon is located about a hundred yards from the Theatre of Dionysus. Its Doric columns and colonnade of friezes—now over 2,500 years old—are a testament to the strength and wealth of the Athenian democracy.

The Birth of Tragedy

MindTap°

Read, highlight, and take notes online.

It can't be coincidence that Western drama was born in ancient Athens at exactly the same moment as democracy, because theatre and democracy germinate from the same idea: that it's good for people to put their differences aside and pool their talents and experiences, so that out of mutual collaboration something fine—maybe something brilliant, maybe something lasting—can be made.

David Ives, Playwright

Although there are many theories about how theatre began in Athens, many scholars accept Aristotle's claim that theatre grew out of a ritual called the **dithyramb**. The dithyramb was a hymn sung at the altar of the god **Dionysus**, the god of wine and fertility, and it was accompanied by dancing, singing, and perhaps improvisations by a chorus that may have numbered as many as 50 men. The god of wine and fertility had been honored in many regions of the ancient world for well over a thousand years. Depending on the locality and period, the celebration took different forms. In some countries naked women spent a day running wild in the hills surrounding the town. The Athenian festivals included a rowdy procession, which today would be rated NC-17 because some of the participants carried huge phalluses. These bawdy parades included city officials, wealthy citizens, sacrificial animals, and drunken men. During this festival all business was suspended, courts of law were closed, and prisoners were given "get out of jail free" passes so that they could attend. Evidently these celebrations often got out of hand—two days after many festivals, an official assembly was convened to consider charges of misconduct.

The parade was followed by a competition of dithyrambs. All-male dithyrambic choruses often competed for prizes and awards for the best presentation at one of two religious festivals held in Athens each year to honor Dionysus. Although scholars are uncertain how dithyrambs evolved into plays, it is known that by the sixth century BCE the dithyrambic competition had been replaced by a play competition. In 534 BCE an actor named **Thespis** wrote and acted in a play that won the competition. According to tradition, Thespis created theatre by stepping from a dithyramb chorus and playing an individual role. In other words, he moved from being one of a group of men performing a ritual to an individual performing a character. (The word *thespian*, meaning "actor," derives from Thespis's name.) Early Greek plays, like the dithyrambs before them, were performed with all-male casts; women were not allowed to perform, and men played women's roles.

Playwrights may have auditioned for these competitions by reading parts of their scripts and pitching the story line to city officials. Three plays were selected, and each

Actors mosaic, House of the Tragic Poet, Naples National Archaeological Museum, Naples, Italy.

This mosaic from the first century CE shows actors, surrounded by their masks, getting ready to rehearse a comic satyr play. Satyr plays provided comic relief after the gravity of trilogies. The only satyr play that has survived from antiquity is *Cyclops* by Euripides, which parodies the story of the *Odyssey*.

playwright was assigned a wealthy citizen, called a **choregos**, who financed the production. The duties of the choregos included paying for special effects, costumes, and salaries. The playwright was also assigned a chorus and actors. For several months, the playwright supervised every aspect of rehearsals and often played the lead role. To win a competition was considered a great honor. The winner often received a cash award and had a monument erected in his name.

Built into the side of a hill below the Parthenon in Athens, the **Theatre of Dionysus** could seat as many as 17,000 people. The main features of ancient Greek theatres were a circular playing area called the **orchestra**, or "dancing place," and a seating area called the **theatron**, or "seeing place." This is the source of the word *theatre*. There was also a building behind the orchestra called the **skene**. The skene held dressing rooms and storage spaces, and its front façade was used as a backdrop for productions (the word *skene* is the source of the words *scene* and *scenery*). At first, the skene was most likely a simple tent put up for performances (*skene* comes from the Greek word for "tent"). Later it became a wooden structure and then a permanent stone building.

The theatre of Dionysus was used for theatrical productions for over a thousand years. It was also reported that Socrates lectured here.

Much of the theatre of Dionysus used wooden seats but the seats were made of marble toward the front. Special chairs such as these were reserved for the most important citizens.

Before Acts and Intermissions

Modern Western plays have a simple framework of acts and intermissions. Ancient Greek plays have a slightly more complicated framework consisting of five elements: a prologue, a parodos, alternating episodes and stasimons, and an exodos. Performances begin with a **prologue**, a short speech or scene by one or more actors that sets the location and time and provides the necessary mythological exposition. Greek plays are based on myths and occasionally on historical events, so their original audiences were familiar with the basic stories of the plots. The prologue told the audience which myth or historical event was the basis for the play; however, plays did not have to follow the myth exactly. Playwrights could interpret, change the theme, or alter the parable in order to explore current political or social issues.

The prologue is followed by the parodos. **Parodos** means "entrance" and that's exactly what it is—the entrance of the **chorus** to the orchestra. The parodos contains many songs and dances as the chorus tells the audience who they are in the play and provides background information. Greek plays were filled with songs and dances, but unfortunately all the music and choreography have been lost, so we can only guess what the parodos was like. The chorus may have included as many as 50 dancing and singing men. Some scholars argue that, as the individual actors became more important, the chorus may have been reduced to as few as 12 members. The chorus serves many purposes during the course of a performance: it can portray crowds of warriors, citizens, or mythological characters; it can chant the playwright's comments; or, through choral songs, it can debate the play's moral themes. The parodos is followed by the first episode.

In the first **episode**, the actors step from the skene building and play a scene. Back in the days of Thespis, only one actor was allowed in each play, but in later decades, a second and then a third actor were permitted. The main actor is called the **protagonist**, the second actor is the **deuteragonist**, and the third actor is the **tritagonist**. The Athenians limited the number of actors because this was a competition and no playwright was allowed an unfair advantage. However, they did not limit the number of characters an actor could play, so an actor could change his mask and costume and play more than one part.

Each episode is followed by a **stasimon**, which contains more songs and dances by the chorus as it comments on the action of the play thus far. During the stasimon, the actors exit into the skene to change masks and costumes and prepare for the next episode. The play follows this basic pattern—episode followed by stasimon followed by episode—until the **exodos**, which is a summation by the chorus on the theme and wisdom of the play. The play ends in a processional song as the chorus leaves the orchestra.

Ancient Greek plays were extravagant—brimming not only with song and dance but also a lot of spectacle. The skene could be adorned with paintings to help set location or mood, and special effects were achieved with devices such as the **periakto**, a pivoting device that allowed all the paintings to be changed in a flash, and the **mechane**, a crane that could fly actors in over the skene. These actors, usually playing gods, could gently land in the orchestra, on the skene, or perhaps even hover overhead. This special-effect crane is the source of the Latin phrase **deus ex machina**, or "god from a machine," used today to describe a contrived or unimaginative ending during which an implausible twist, such as a god flying in, solves all the problems of the plot. There was also the **ekkyklema**, a platform that could be rolled out from the skene to reveal a tableau. But

William Missouri Downs

one spectacle these plays didn't include was blood or murder, at least seldom on stage. If a character was murdered, it happened in the skene building, from which the audience could hear his terrifying cries. Then the ekkyklema would be rolled out to show the frozen, deadly aftermath of the bloody event. This must have horrified audiences, but more than likely the dead body was only a dummy, as the playwright could not afford to let a real actor play dead if he was needed for the next episode.

Masks were an important part of Greek and Roman plays. Masks allowed one actor to play many roles but also limited facial expressions and vocal inflections. As a result, subtle character portraits were rare in the Dionysian theatre. In this frieze a young actor holds a comedy mask.

From Hubris to Catharsis

Today the word *tragedy* means an unfortunate or disastrous turn of events. To the Greeks, however, the subject of a tragic play was serious but not necessarily sad or disastrous. In fact, *tragedy* comes from the ancient Greek word *tragoīdia*, which means "goat song," and may refer to the fertility rites from which the Dionysian festivals grew; the Greeks considered the goat a sexually potent animal. For the ancient Greeks, tragedies were about the meaning of life and were designed to help the audience understand the reasons for the suffering and daily dilemmas they faced. They were based on the idea that virtue can grow out of hardship, and wisdom from suffering. These plays ask powerful questions: What is humankind's purpose? Are we at the mercy of fate or can we rise above our destiny? Which moral code is more important, honoring our family or obeying the state? Can we recognize our character flaws before they destroy us? The purpose of these plays was not to make the audience feel somber but rather to enable them to experience an intense, twofold feeling of pity and fear known as **catharsis**. Catharsis occurs when one truly encounters life and confronts its many riddles.

The Greeks felt that tragedy does not happen to lower-class people or the poor. A **tragic hero** is an extraordinary person of noble birth or a person who has risen to great political or social heights, yet is someone with whom the audience can empathize. Simply being the object of an accident or a catastrophe over which one has no control does not make one a tragic hero. Rather, tragic heroes are characters who are able to make choices, take action, bring trouble upon themselves, and ultimately take responsibility for their choices. At the beginning of a play, the tragic hero is often successful and happy but makes an error in judgment or has a character flaw (sometimes called a tragic or fatal flaw), a personal failing that leads to his or her downfall. The Greeks called this flaw **hamartia**. A common hamartia is **hubris**—overbearing pride or arrogance. The tragic hero's hamartia leads to **peripeteia**, or a radical reversal of fortune. This reversal is followed by **anagnorisis**, in which the hero goes through a process of self-examination to recognize his or her true identity. In the end, the hero suffers the terrible consequence of committing the tragic error. This consequence is often death or a life worse than death. The punishment the hero suffers always seems undeservedly harsh, which leads to purgation and catharsis as the audience members feel great pity and fear: pity for the hero's misfortune and fear that they also might possess the same tragic flaw. If a tragedy was done well, as the exodos was occurring, the audience members had a catharsis that purged them of their hamartia. (For an example of how these principles and the ancient Greek framework are applied to a play that is still performed today, see the Spotlight "*Oedipus Rex*.")

Tragic Trilogies and Satyr Plays

Tragedies were presented in trilogies. During the Festival of Dionysus, playwrights presented three plays that might have related themes. The *Oresteia* (458 BCE), written by Aeschylus, is the only extant trilogy, so it gives us an idea of how the plays within a trilogy were connected. The three plays are *Agamemnon, The Libation Bearers*, and *The Eumenides*. In the first play, Agamemnon, king of Argos, returns home after winning the Trojan War. His wife, Queen Clytemnestra, welcomes him, but during the years that he has been away she has taken a lover. She had grown bitter toward Agamemnon because he had sacrificed their daughter to the gods so that his fleet would have favorable winds as they sailed to Troy. To make matters worse, Agamemnon returns accompanied by his concubine. Seeking revenge, Clytemnestra lures Agamemnon into the palace, where she stabs him to death.

In the second play, *The Libation Bearers*, Orestes, the son of Agamemnon and Clytemnestra, is ordered by the god Apollo to avenge his father's death or face terrible consequences. Orestes murders his mother and her lover, but now

ArenaPal/The Image Works

Sophocles' Oedipus is the quintessential Greek tragic hero. His fatal flaw, or hamartia, is his hubris, or his arrogance, which prevents him from seeing his flaws and acting in a way that spares him terrible suffering. This 1992 production of *Oedipus* played at the Royal Shakespeare Company featured Gerard Murphy as Oedipus (bottom), shown with Tiresias, the blind seer who predicts Oedipus' fate (top).

> I have nothing but contempt for the kind of governor who is afraid, for whatever reason, to follow the course that he knows is best for the State; and as for the man who sets private friendship above the public welfare—I have no use for him, either. Let every man in mankind's frailty consider his last days; and let none presume on his good fortune until he find life, as his death, a memory without pain.
>
> **Creon,** in Antigone, by Sophocles

SPOTLIGHT<u>ON</u> Oedipus Rex

Oedipus Rex was first presented in the Theatre of Dionysus around 430 BCE. Written by the playwright Sophocles, it, like most Greek tragedies, is based on a myth. This myth starts with Laius and Jocasta, the childless king and queen of Thebes, an ancient city-state in central Greece. Wanting an heir, the king seeks the advice of the oracle of Apollo at Delphi. In Greek society, oracles housed mediums (both the place and the medium are known as *oracles*), considered soothsayers of wise counsel who could foretell the future by interpreting dreams, reading the stars, or examining the entrails of dead animals. The oracle tells the king that if he has an heir, his son will grow up to murder him and marry his own mother. Naturally, the king is upset when the queen announces she is pregnant.

When his son is born, the king gives the infant to a shepherd with the order to leave it on the slopes of Mt. Cithaeron. (Exposure to the elements was a common way to get rid of an unwanted child in those days.) But the shepherd takes pity on the baby and gives him to some passersby who happen to be servants of King Polybus and Queen Merope of Corinth. The king and queen adopt the boy and rear him as their own. When the child, Oedipus, is about eighteen, a drunken guest informs him of his adoption. Oedipus travels to the oracle at Delphi to ask about his identity. Instead of revealing his lineage, the priest simply repeats the grim prophecy given to Laius about a son who kills his father and marries his mother. Overwhelmed by the prediction, Oedipus vows to get as far away from Corinth as possible, determined to prevent the prophecy from coming true.

At a crossroads near the city-state of Thebes, Oedipus argues with a man in a chariot about who has the right of way. The war of words escalates, and the young Oedipus kills the man in self-defense. When Oedipus approaches Thebes, he finds that a Sphinx—a monster usually depicted as a winged lion with a woman's head—is terrorizing the city. Sitting atop a cliff over the road into the city, she asks each passerby a riddle and kills those who fail to answer correctly. The Sphinx asks, "What walks on four legs in the morning, two legs in the afternoon, and three legs in the evening?" Oedipus, confident in his wisdom, answers, "Man, for when he is born, he crawls on all

fours; as he grows older, he stands on two feet; and at the end of his life, he uses a cane as a third leg." The Sphinx is furious that Oedipus has the correct answer, and she plunges off the cliff to her death. Oedipus is rewarded by being crowned king of Thebes, and he marries the queen Jocasta, whose husband has just been murdered. Everything is going well for Oedipus until a plague strikes the city.

This is the place in the myth where Sophocles begins his play. Greek tragedies usually present only the climactic final part of the myth on which they are based. Here is how Sophocles' play unfolds.

The prologue: King Oedipus learns of the plague and how an oracle has foretold that it will not end until the murderer of former King Laius is found and punished.

The parodos: The chorus enters. It represents a crowd of elderly men who pray that the gods will end the horrible plague.

First episode: King Oedipus proclaims that he will investigate the murder, find the person responsible, and punish him. He prays that the murderer's life be "consumed in evil and wretchedness." Oedipus sends for a blind prophet to help find the murderer, but when the old man refuses to help, Oedipus accuses him of conspiring with Creon (Jocasta's brother) in the murder. The prophet professes ignorance, but suggests that Oedipus is the guilty party, which sends Oedipus into a rage.

First stasimon: This choral song expresses great doubt about Oedipus having anything to do with the murder.

Second episode: Creon defends himself against the charges, but Oedipus still wants him executed for treason. Jocasta tells Oedipus to ignore the oracle because this same oracle predicted that Laius would be killed by his son, yet he was reportedly killed at a crossroads by thieves. Oedipus begins to doubt himself.

Second stasimon: The choral song expresses doubts about Oedipus's innocence and condemns his hubris, or pride, arrogance, and vanity. The chorus is beginning to turn against

(Continued)

Oedipus as it warns the audience members to remember their place and to accept their fate.

Third episode: A messenger arrives with the news that the king of Corinth has died of natural causes. Jocasta is thrilled because this means that the oracle was wrong, that life is governed by chance, not destiny. But then the messenger, in an attempt to add some good news, announces that the king of Corinth was not Oedipus's father but that Oedipus was adopted.

Third stasimon: The chorus warns that any human who has the audacity to question the powers of the gods will be tangled in a web of pain.

Fourth episode: Fearing the worst, Oedipus sends for the shepherd who had found him on Mt. Cithaeron and forces him to tell the story of what happened, so many years ago, when he was ordered to expose the baby. Learning the truth, Oedipus rushes into the palace (the skene).

Fourth stasimon: The choral song bemoans the downfall of Oedipus.

Final episode and exodos: A messenger reveals Jocasta has hanged herself and that Oedipus removed a pin from her dress and has stabbed himself in the eyes. Blind, Oedipus begs Creon to forgive him and asks to be let out of the city to wander until the end of his days.

the Furies—terrible, winged goddesses of vengeance with serpentine hair—attack the grief-stricken Orestes. The final play of the trilogy, *The Eumenides*, questions the idea of revenge killing. Orestes' fate is taken away from the gods, and the final judgment is given to a court of citizens who find Orestes not guilty. This third play makes a statement about how human reason must replace the unyielding rule of the gods. The *Oresteia* was produced in 458 BCE, a few years after a coup almost overthrew the Athenian government—the play was definitely a political statement and an endorsement of the Athenian system of democracy.

Trilogies were followed by a short comic-relief play called a **satyr play**. Often burlesque, these plays parodied the myths, gods, heroes, and characters in the tragedies. Satyrs were filled with wild dancing, indecent language, and obscene gestures and were named for the half-beast, half-human creatures who were said to be companions of the god Dionysus. The word *satire* is derived from satyr plays.

Playwrights of the Golden Age

Dozens of Greek playwrights wrote plays during the fourth and fifth centuries BCE, and over 2,000 plays were produced, but the majority of their scripts have been lost. Of the few scripts remaining, only three tragic playwrights are represented: Aeschylus, Sophocles, and Euripides. Fortunately, these three were considered the best playwrights of the age. Together these playwrights wrote more than 300 plays, yet only 10 percent of their work has survived. Because these few remaining works intrigue us so, it's hard not to wonder what we're missing. As U.S. astronomer and educator Carl Sagan said, "It is a little as if the only surviving works of a man named William Shakespeare were *Coriolanus* and *A Winter's Tale*, but we had heard that he had written certain other plays, unknown to us but apparently prized in his time, works entitled *Hamlet, Macbeth, Julius Caesar, King Lear*, and *Romeo and Juliet.*"

Aeschylus: The Warrior Playwright

Aeschylus (ca. 525–456 BCE), often called the father of tragedy, is the earliest writer of Greek tragedy whose plays still exist. He was born into a prominent family near Athens and fought in the battles of Marathon and Salamis, which crushed the Persians. His first play was produced at the Theatre Dionysus in 499 BCE, and during the next 40 years he wrote some 90 plays, of which six, or perhaps seven, have survived. Many of Aeschylus's plays are about profound spiritual and moral issues expressed through sharply defined characters and powerful dramatic situations. For example, the *Oresteia* examines the ethical and political chaos that results when opposing forces, each claiming to have justice on their side, depend on irrational emotions to seek revenge rather than looking for rational solutions. Aeschylus is often considered the most "theatrical" of the ancient playwrights, because his plays have huge casts, lavish costumes, and lots of special effects. Ancient critics said that the special effect used at the entrance of the Furies in his play *The Libation Bearers* was so powerful that pregnant women in the audience miscarried. After his death, he became almost a mythical figure. (There was even a legend that he died when an eagle mistook his bald head for a rock and dropped a tortoise on it in order to crack its shell to get at the meat inside.) On his epitaph, however, Aeschylus suggests that fighting in the battles of Marathon and Salamis, not being one of Athens's greatest playwrights, was the crowning achievement of his life.

Sophocles: The Wise and Honored One

The son of a wealthy merchant, Sophocles (ca. 496–406 BCE) was well educated and became a highly respected citizen of Athens. His name means "the wise and honored one." As a young man, known for his grace and handsome features, he was chosen to lead a victory choir during a celebration of Athens's victory over the Persian fleet at Salamis. He served as the city's treasurer and was appointed to important government committees. As a playwright, his first victory at the Theatre Dionysus occurred in 463 BCE, when he defeated Aeschylus. He went on to write more than 120 plays, of which seven have survived. He won the Festival of Dionysus 24 times, and he never came in less than second. His plays are known for their complex characterization, harmonious lyrics, and effective dialogue. Whereas Aeschylus's plays often dealt with long time spans and several generations of a family, Sophocles' plays concentrated on a few critical moments within a character's life. He also often depicted humans as beings trapped by fate. Fate, he said, is not predetermined by the gods but is rather a result of our inflexible personalities. (See the Spotlight *"Oedipus Rex"* about one of Sophocles' most famous characters.)

Euripides: Never Afraid to Speak His Mind

Named for the straits of Euripus, Euripides (ca. 480–406 BCE) was born on the island of Salamis, just about the time and only a few miles away from where

> When good men die their goodness does not perish, But lives though they are gone. As for the bad, All that was theirs dies and is buried with them.
>
> ***Euripides,*** Playwright

Richard Termine Photography

Euripides is famous for writing some of the most powerful female characters of Greek tragedy, including Electra, Medea, and Hecuba. *Hecuba* (ca. 425 BCE) is the story of the former queen of Troy, now a prisoner of war, who takes revenge for the sacrificial death of her daughter. This play provides a timeless examination of the psychology of the victor and the victim in time of war. This 2005 production starred Vanessa Redgrave and was staged by the Royal Shakespeare Company performing at the Brooklyn Academy of Music.

the Athenians destroyed the Persian fleet. Born to an influential family, he was taught by such learned philosophers as Anaxagoras, the first person to explain solar eclipses. Euripides was an award-winning gymnast and his father wanted him to be an athlete, but he preferred the arts. He soon became known as a playwright who was never afraid to speak his mind, for he filled his plays with stinging indictments against war and the savagery of Athenian warriors. In *The Trojan Women* (415 BCE), he questions the use of the army. During the **Peloponnesian War** between Athens and Sparta and their allies, the Athenian army demanded that the people of the island of Melos, who were neutral in the war, surrender. When they did not, the Athenian army murdered all the men of military age and sold the women and children into slavery. In *The Trojan Women*, Euripides dramatizes a similar event and points out that such events are not caused by the gods, or natural right, but rather by human cruelty. In his plays he made the gods petty and uncaring and his characters flawed, but fully rounded. In addition, he was one of the first writers to treat women as major characters.

Euripides stood out among his peers because he denounced the oracles, described soothsayers as "men who speak few truths but many lies," and questioned the existence of the gods. His lost play *Melanippe* was reported to have begun with the line, "O Zeus, if there be a Zeus, for I know of him only by report . . . ." Because of his views, he was indicted on a charge of impiety and seldom won popularity contests such as the one held at the Theatre of Dionysus. In fact, he did not win that contest until he was in his forties and took the top honor only four times. Of the 90-some plays he is said to have written, 19 have survived, and he is now the most often produced of the ancient Greek tragic playwrights. His most popular play today is *Medea* (432 BCE), the story of a woman who is divorced by her husband and seeks revenge by destroying his life and killing their children. Unlike other Greek tragedies, there is no retribution—no Furies that pursue Medea. Instead she is rewarded and rides away, unharmed, in a golden chariot.

Greek Comedies

The last day of the festival at the Theatre of Dionysus was devoted to comedies, at least after 486 BCE. These comic plays had a loose structure that directly or indirectly lampooned society or the political landscape of the day—much as a *Saturday Night Live* skit satirizes government figures and current events. But ancient Greek comedies went even further. Not only were they full of sight gags, obscene humor, and outrageous political banter, but the actors also wore thickly padded costumes, grotesque masks, and abnormally large leather phalluses that hung down between their legs and mocked the male genitalia. Scholars now call these early comic plays **Old Comedy** because they were written before the end of the Peloponnesian War, when there was a relatively high degree of freedom of speech in Athens.

Aristophanes (ca. 448–380 BCE) wrote 40 comedies, of which 11 have survived. Aristophanes was famous for caricatures of Greek leaders and stinging attacks on society. He was daring enough to lampoon politicians, generals, and other celebrities sitting in the audience. No subject was off limits to his scornful wit. His play *The Wasps* was a satire of democracy, and in *The Frogs* he accuses Euripides of spreading skepticism. Two of his most famous comedies were *The Clouds* (419 BCE) and *Lysistrata* (411 BCE). In *The Clouds* Aristophanes mocked the philosopher Socrates and sophists. Sophists were well-educated men who, for a fee, taught critical thinking, rhetoric, and debate to the Athenian upper class. The story of *The Clouds* centers on a lower class farmer and his playboy son, who has gone deeply in debt. The father advises his son to take lessons from Socrates on logic and argumentation so that he can outfox his creditors. The son goes to Socrates' school, which is lampooned as "The School of Very Hard Thinkers." Here he finds the students engaged in preposterous experiments while Socrates hangs in a basket studying the clouds. Aristophanes' parody portrayed Socrates as being so busy thinking that he didn't have time to bathe as he contemplated such important questions as "Do gnats hum through their mouths or their anuses?" Soon, the son learns how to weasel his way out of his debts and how to use clever arguments to question everything and make the most absurd acts appear logical. When the son returns he gets into an argument with his father over which playwright is better, Euripides or Aeschylus. Then he gives his father a whipping, all the while logically arguing his right to do so. In the end the father sets fire to Socrates' school, sending the philosopher and his students running.

> Tragedy is a representation of an action that is heroic and complete and of a certain magnitude, by means of language enriched with all kinds of ornament . . . it represents men in action, and does not use narrative; and through pity and fear it brings relief to these and similar emotions.
>
> **Aristotle,** Philosopher

> In the last war we were too modest to object to anything you men did—and in any case you wouldn't let us say a word. But don't think we approved! We knew everything that was going on. Many times we'd hear at home about some major blunder of yours, and then when you came home we'd be burning inside but we'd have to put on a smile and ask what it was you'd decided to inscribe on the pillar underneath the Peace Treaty. And what did my husband always say, "Shut up and mind your own business!"
>
> **Lysistrata,** in Lysistrata by Aristophanes

William Missouri Downs

Monuments like this were once awarded to the choregoi (theatre sponsors) by the city of Athens as awards for the best plays presented at the Theatre of Dionysus. This monument, one of the few still in existence, today stands on a side street in Athens.

Aristophanes' most famous work is the anti-war comedy *Lysistrata* (411 BCE). Written in the 21st year of the Peloponnesian War, it is about a woman named Lysistrata who organizes the women of Athens and Sparta into staging a sex strike; the women lock themselves in the Acropolis and deny their husbands sex until the men stop the war. This bawdy comedy, like his others, is full of sexual innuendo and overtly crude references concerning everything from digestion to various bodily excretions. In his plays, Aristophanes used more than 70 different words, modifiers, and metaphors to describe male genitalia and more than 70 others to describe their female counterparts.

What makes such anti-war comedies extraordinary is that they were written during the long and bloody Peloponnesian War. This was a horrible time to live in Athens. The 27-year-long war had killed tens of thousands and the Spartans had burned Athenians' crops, so food had to be shipped in. With the shipments came a plague that killed one-third of the population of Athens. In his book *A War Like No Other*, Victor Davis Hanson estimates that 100,000 Athenians died because of the Peloponnesian War. That would be as if 44 million Americans had died during World War II. Yet Athenian audiences were willing to endure the playwrights' attacks on their motives and on their belief in the greatness of Athens.

Aristotle and Alexander the Great

The period of relatively liberal influence and innovation in ancient Athens came to a close when Athens surrendered to Sparta in 404 BCE, ending the Peloponnesian War. Athens's city walls were torn down and its navy burned. The 140-year-old Athenian democracy was over, but the city itself was spared. The generals of Sparta, as they conquered Athens, were reportedly so moved by a chorus singing from one of Euripides' plays that they decided not to burn down the city. However, the Athenians were forced to give up democracy and adopt Sparta's more autocratic form of government. Spartan men were raised to be strong, sober soldiers. They were also said to be great lovers, and young men were permitted to indulge, without prejudice of gender, in many relationships. But their pragmatic lifestyle produced few poets, artists, actors, or playwrights.

During this turbulent period, political issues became too dangerous to discuss openly, civil liberties disappeared, and freedom of speech was strictly controlled. This was the period when the philosopher Socrates was put on trial for "corrupting the youth." In *Apology*, Plato's version of the speech given by Socrates when he defended himself, Socrates indirectly blames Aristophanes' *The Clouds* for turning public opinion against him. In 399 BCE Socrates was found guilty and forced to drink hemlock.

Comic playwrights, denied freedom of speech, turned from personal and political satire to what scholars now call **New Comedy**. Its safe themes and mundane subject matter steered clear of insulting those in power.

The subjects included young lovers, meddling mothers-in-law, and marital misunderstandings—themes shared by many modern sitcoms. One of the most popular playwrights of New Comedy was Menander (342–292 BCE), who wrote more than 100 plays. The title of his only extant play gives an idea of the sorts of topics his plays addressed: *The Curmudgeon*. His plots revolved around humorous situations and made fun of domestic life, romantic love, and marriage. He is famous for the line, "In marriage, there are no known survivors." Menander's comedies were popular for 700 years and were often imitated.

Fifty years after Athens was defeated in the Peloponnesian War, Greek tragedy also lost its brilliance. The plays were shallow; the writers lacked the talent or the freedom to write great scripts; and performances were seldom noteworthy. The philosopher, educator, and scientist Aristotle (384–322 BCE) called the playwrights of his day "hacks." In an attempt to remind playwrights how to construct a proper tragedy and to rebut Plato's condemnation of theatre in *The Republic* (ca. 378 BCE), Aristotle wrote **Poetics**, the first known treatise about how a dramatic story is constructed. He called the work *poetics* because playwrights were known as *poets* in ancient Greece. (Aristotle also wrote a treatise on comedy, but it has been lost.) With typical Greek rationalism, Aristotle approached dramatic storytelling as a science. He sought the universal guidelines that characterize a dramatic story. He broke plays into basic elements, much as scientists today identify compounds according to the elements listed in the periodic table. According to Aristotle drama has six essential elements: plot, character, diction, thought, spectacle, and song (see Chapter 4). When *Poetics* was rediscovered during the Renaissance, these guidelines became hard-and-fast rules. Today, many consider *Poetics* to be the single most influential work in all of literary criticism. It is used as a how-to book in many playwriting and screenwriting classes. In fact, it is required reading at every major film school in the United States. (For more on *Poetics*, see Chapters 1, 4, and 15.)

Had it not been for Aristotle's most famous pupil, **Alexander the Great** (356–323 BCE), Greek theatre might have been a footnote to history. Alexander often said that he cherished Aristotle no less than if he was his own father. At the age of eighteen, Alexander became king of Macedonia in northern Greece. By the time of his death at the age of thirty-two, he was one of the greatest military generals in history. Not only did he defeat the Persians, which led the Egyptians to express their gratitude by crowning him a pharaoh, but he also built an empire that stretched from the Mediterranean to modern-day India and from Egypt to the Arabian Sea. While on military campaigns, he loved to read books on science and history as well as the plays by Euripides, Sophocles, and Aeschylus. As he concentrated power, Alexander spread Greek culture, including Greek art, philosophy, science, and theatre to the far corners of his empire. The Romans copied the Greek theatre they encountered on the western flank of Alexander's empire.

It was in Egypt that Alexander championed the **Library of Alexandria**—one of the first universities. So vast was this library that it had entire wings devoted to poetry, astronomy, mathematics, and theatre. Its lecture halls could hold hundreds of students and its library stacks held 400,000 papyrus scrolls. This is where Euclid (325 BCE–ca. 265 BCE) wrote *Elements*, his treatise on geometry and algebra; Archimedes (ca. 287–212 BCE) discovered pi; and Eratosthenes (275–194 BCE) calculated the distance around the earth to within 185 miles of its true circumference. Alexandria was the home of many useful inventions, including

> Alexandria was the greatest city the Western world had ever seen. People of all nations came there to live, to trade, to learn. . . It is probably here that the word cosmopolitan realized its true meaning—citizens, not just of a nation, but of the Cosmos. To be a citizen of the Cosmos. . .
>
> **Carl Sagan,** Astronomer

William Missouri Downs

Egyptian archaeologists recently uncovered lecture halls from the sister campus of the great Library of Alexandria. It was here, hundreds of years before the birth of Jesus, that scientists discovered that Earth revolved around the sun, Euclid wrote his treatise on geometry, and Archimedes discovered pi. Notice that this lecture hall imitates the basic layout of a Greek theatre.

a hydraulic clock, the odometer, a fire-engine pump with pistons and valves, and early versions of the steam engine. Also in Alexandria, the astronomer Aristarchus (ca. 270 BCE) discovered that the earth revolved around the sun, thereby predating Copernicus's "discovery" by 1,800 years. The Library also gave us female doctors such as Metrodora (second century CE) who wrote a treatise on disease of the womb, and female astronomer/mathematicians like the great Hypatia (ca. 370–415 CE). And it was in Alexandria that much of the world learned of the great Greek playwrights. The original manuscripts of Euripides, Aeschylus, and Sophocles were first owned by the city of Athens, which was reluctant to lend them to the Library of Alexandria. As insurance, the library paid 15 talents as a cash deposit. That would be the equivalent of about $3.5 million today. Athens sent the manuscripts, but once the library received them, it forfeited the deposit, kept the originals, and, to the dismay of Athenians, returned only copies.

Alexandria became the most prominent cultural, intellectual, political, and economic metropolis of the Western world. The city, perfectly located for trade on that great mass transit system known as the Mediterranean Sea, exported Greek ideas, theatre, and culture throughout the rest of the known world. The two centuries between Alexander's death in 323 BCE and the Roman conquest of Greece in 146 BCE became known as the **Hellenistic period**, from the Greek word meaning "to imitate the Greeks." Greek theatre spread to many societies and civilizations around the Mediterranean and beyond. So great was the reach of Hellenism that Greek theatre may have influenced theatre in India. (For more on Indian theatre, see Chapter 12.)

During the Hellenistic period, every town of any size around the Mediterranean had a theatre. Yet this period boasts few celebrated playwrights and no scripts that are now considered classics. As the years went by, fewer plays were tied to the Festivals of Dionysus. Instead, plays were produced primarily to honor military victories or merely for the sake of entertainment. The farther theatre went from its ritual roots, the less need it had for the dithyrambic chorus or the orchestra in which the chorus performed. New Hellenistic theatres were built and old theatres modified, with smaller semicircular orchestras, and the skene was moved forward to become the main performance area. Actors were becoming popular entertainers rather than people involved in religious rites. Soon traveling companies of actors trekked all around the Mediterranean and even established the first actors' union, called the **Artists of Dionysus**.

The Romans built over a hundred theatres—the remains of this one lie within the Sicilian city of Catania. After it fell into disuse, houses were built atop the area. Today, the Italian government is excavating the site.

Roman Spectacles

Around 800 BCE a people called the Etruscans ruled the area that would come to be known as Rome—*Roma* comes from the Etruscan word for "river." Under Etruscan rule, the small farming village on the marshy banks of the Tiber River grew into a prosperous city. In 509 BCE the people of Rome rebelled against the sometimes cruel Etruscan rule, overthrew the king, and drew up laws that stated that anyone who proclaimed himself king could be killed without trial; thus began the Roman Republic, which would last almost 500 years. For 200 years, the republic was involved in almost continuous warfare as it defeated the remaining Etruscans, the Gauls, the Samnites, and several Greek colonies. By 275 BCE the Romans ruled the Italian Peninsula and set out to pick up the pieces of Alexander's empire, which by now was disintegrating. In the second century BCE, they took control of Greece, and some 150 years later, the Roman Republic was replaced by a dictatorship and empire. At this point, Rome was the most powerful nation on earth, with a territory so vast that the Mediterranean was virtually its lake. Roman armies were known for their deadly efficiency. When the Mediterranean city of Carthage challenged Rome it was utterly destroyed, and the ground near the city plowed with salt so that nothing could grow there. When the Jews stood up against Rome the destruction was so vast that ancient historian Josephus numbered the total of Jewish dead at 1.2 million.

The city of Rome did not produce any goods; instead it became wealthy by plundering countries for a thousand miles around. Slaves, gold, and precious stones

The Roman theatre Odeon of Herodes Atticus was built in Athens in 161 CE and held more than 5,000 people. In the 1950s the theatre and orchestra were restored; the ancient skene building is original. This theatre is still used to stage plays.

William Missouri Downs

were carried back to Rome, but the Roman armies also brought back the cultures of the countries they defeated. The Greeks in particular fascinated the Romans. "It was no little brook that flowed from Greece to our city," said Roman statesman and philosopher Marcus Tullius Cicero (106–43 BCE), "but a mighty river of culture and learning." Ten thousand Greek words slipped into the Latin vocabulary. Roman military commanders shipped tens of thousands of Greek manuscripts, statues, and other works of art back home. Huge numbers of educated Greeks were made slaves by the conquering Roman legions and carried off to tutor the youth of Rome. As the Roman poet Horace said, "Captive Greece took captive her rude conqueror." Romans soon assimilated Greek culture and with that culture, of course, came Greek theatre.

The Las Vegas of Ancient Times

Two thousand years ago, Rome was the wealthiest city in the world. Its avenues were lined with marble-clad arches and domes. There were hundreds of palaces, temples, estates, villas, libraries, reading rooms, art galleries, and dozens of public baths with hot and cold running water, some of which could accommodate 1,800 bathers at a time. There were over 1,000 miles of aqueducts channeling hundreds of thousands of gallons of water to the city each day; the chief architect of Rome's water delivery system is reported to have said, "Who will venture to compare with these mighty conduits the idle pyramids. . .?" There were bankers everywhere—Rome even had interest-bearing checking accounts and travelers checks. Beneath the city streets was the most advanced sewer system the world had ever known, and above, every type of entertainment imaginable. Rome was the Las Vegas of the ancient world.

Roman politicians knew that if they spent enormous sums on entertainments like chariot races, athletic contests, musical concerts, triumphal processions, mortal combats, and the theatre, the general population would not trouble themselves with things like politics. This political diversionary tactic is still known today as **bread and circus**. The underlying idea was that if you give the general population enough food (bread) and entertainment (circus) they will not question the government and do pretty much as they are told. When two

> Whoever wished to see all the goods of the world must either journey throughout the world or stay in Rome.
>
> ***Aelius Aristides,***
> Ancient Greek orator

William Missouri Downs

The Coliseum in Rome was the site of brutal "entertainments" for hundreds of years. During the middle ages, many Christians believed it to be the entrance to Hell. It stands today as a major tourist attraction.

Roman actors, Bathyllus and Pylades, created a public rivalry about who was more talented, the Emperor Augustus (63 BCE–14 CE) said, "It's better that the citizens should quarrel about them than about Pompey and Caesar."

Roman leaders built huge structures to hold massive entertainments. The Circus Maximus had a chariot racetrack 2,200 feet long and 700 feet wide in a stadium that could hold 180,000 spectators. The Coliseum, which could hold 50,000 spectators, had an arena 287 feet by 180 feet where gladiators battled to the death for the crowd's amusement. There were even gladiator schools where the captives from conquered lands and condemned criminals learned to fight and kill. During the Coliseum's 100-day dedication in 80 CE, 9,000 animals and 2,000 people were slaughtered in sport.

The Romans took these bloody entertainments at the Coliseum to a new level when they started dressing the condemned in costumes so that they could act out roles before they were killed. A condemned person might be dressed up as the princess from *Medea* and then, as happens in the play, he would be burned to death in a live-action retelling of the story. Another might be dressed as Atys who, as the myth goes, was castrated by the gods. One unfortunate slave was tricked into playing Orpheus, the musician in Greek and Roman mythology whose songs were so beguiling that animals followed him and rivers stopped flowing to listen. A special set, complete with flowing streams and trees, was built in the Coliseum expressly for this show. As the unsuspecting man played the lyre (a stringed instrument of the harp family) and sang for the crowd's amusement, the lions were released.

During the Roman Republic, theatres were temporary structures designed to honor many different gods and to celebrate such events as the dedication of a new temple. These temporary theatres were built facing a particular god's temple and then torn down and reassembled across from another god's temple. Some of these structures must have been massive because there are records of special insurance that contractors had to take out against damaging the underground sewers as they carted the heavy framing through the streets.

I come home more greedy, more cruel and inhuman, because I have been among human beings. By chance I attended a midday exhibition, expecting some fun, wit, and relaxation. . . . But it was quite the contrary. . . . In the morning they throw men to the lions; at noon they throw them to the spectators. The crowd demands that the victor who has slain his opponent shall face the man who will slay him in turn; and the last conqueror is reserved for another butchering. . . . Man, a sacred thing to man, is killed for sport and merriment.

Seneca, Roman playwright, commenting on gladiators

Lou Anne Wright

In 1709, an Italian woman was digging in her garden when the earth gave way. In the gap she found ancient stonework, which turned out to be one of the two theatres from the Roman city of Pompeii. Pompeii was destroyed when Mount Vesuvius erupted in 79 CE. Seen here is the larger of the two theatres. This theatre has exceptional acoustics. An actor whispering from the orchestra can be heard in the last row of the theatron.

The first permanent theatre was built in 55 BCE in Rome by the general and statesman Pompeius Magnus—the self-styled "Pompey the Great" (106–48 BCE). Pompey's theatre sat 17,000 people and had a huge curved portico, an engineering marvel over 600 feet long. The stage was roofed and the theatron covered with a linen awning that protected the audience from the strong Mediterranean sun. Construction of such huge theatres was possible because of Romans' engineering genius and their invention of concrete. It was in this theatre that Julius Caesar was assassinated in 44 BCE. It has often been reported that he was killed in the senate, but the senate building was actually closed for repairs at the time, so the legislators were meeting in the Theatre Pompey instead. The Pompey remained in use for more than five centuries. In the Middle Ages, long after it had been closed, it was a tourist site. Later it was destroyed by fire, and the remaining bricks and stones were stolen and used in other structures. Today, all that remains of this great theatre is the elegant curve of the street that follows the shape of what was once the great portico. The Theatre of Pompey no longer exists, but nearly 100 other Roman theatres built in Rome, Italy, Spain, France, North Africa, Greece, and Asia Minor have survived.

Roman theatres were designed to give the audience a great deal of comfort. Some theatres air-conditioned the audience with streams of cool water that ran down between the seats, and in others, slaves sprayed the audience with perfume. But we know that audience members were not always well behaved because in the prologues of many plays, the actors beg for proper manners and

William Missouri Downs

The influence of ancient Greek culture can still be seen throughout the Mediterranean. The Theatre of Marcellus, which uses elements of Greek architecture, was completed in Rome in 11 BCE and held approximately 14,000 people. The theatre was abandoned around 300 CE after the Christians came to power. During the Middle Ages it was used as a fort, and in the sixteenth century a private home was built atop it. Today, only the lower columns of the theatre exist. It is the only one of the four major theatres of ancient Rome that still stands.

for mothers to leave their crying babies at home. The attitude of Roman audiences toward theatre was much like our attitude toward television; if a show was not to their liking, or if they thought the gladiator contest next door might be more interesting, they did the equivalent of changing channels by simply walking out. As a result, the theatres tried hard to amuse the audience, including using lots of special effects. Some theatres were equipped with copper-lined tunnels cut beneath the seats so that boulders could be rolled through them to create an "earthquake" effect that would shake the entire theatre. On other occasions, theatre engineers flooded the orchestra so that sea battles, complete with miniature warships and slaves fighting to the death, could be staged.

Roman Mimes

One of the most popular forms of entertainment was that of the **Roman mimes**, whose shows were filled with jugglers, acrobats, comic skits, buffoonery, and plenty of vulgar language, indecent songs, and nudity. These plays had stereotypical characters like doddering old fathers, sentimental lovers, and crafty slaves, and most of the stories were about drunkenness, greed, adultery, and sex. One popular play was called *Grandpa Takes a Wife*. Needless to say, these plays had little literary value. Women were allowed onstage but usually only as scantily dressed sex objects. According to some historical accounts, when audiences grew bored with a performance, they sometimes demanded that the players stop the play, take off their clothes, and perform sex acts onstage; most mime troupes were happy to oblige. Originally, mime performers were not silent—unlike Marcel Marceau and other modern pantomimes—but had dialogue and plenty of improvised comic ad-libs. As the empire grew and the population of Rome became more diverse, with many native languages, the mimes became wordless and depended more on music, action, gesture, dance, and mimicry.

Mime performances often contained satire, even though satire was against the law in Rome. To play it safe, the actors set most of their skits in Greece

Robbie Jack/Encyclopedia/Corbis

The Roman playwright Plautus filled his plays with boisterous indecencies, seductions, and cheap gags. Like many Roman playwrights, he populated these plays with Greek characters, thus limiting the chance that any Roman would take offense. His stories have retained their popularity throughout history. This scene from the musical *A Funny Thing Happened on the Way to the Forum*, which is based on the comedies of Plautus, illustrates the bawdy silliness that marked his work. This 2004 production featured Desmond Barrit as Pseudolus, a slave trying to buy freedom from his owner. Music and lyrics by Stephen Sondheim, book by Burt Shevelove and Larry Gelbart. Directed by Edward Hall, National Theatre, London.

and made fun of Greek characters and customs, cloaking their jokes in double entendres. Once in a while a mime attempted a joke about the emperor, but this was risky. Emperor Caligula ordered one actor burned alive onstage for making an insulting jibe. However, the mime troupes' audacity seemed undiminished, for later that same year another troupe mocked the murdered actor's death by staging a play with a performer pretending to be a charred cadaver. In another case an actor humorously suggested that Emperor Nero had poisoned his father and drowned his mother (Nero did, in fact, have his mother killed). As he said the line "Hail Father, Hail Mother" he pantomimed drinking and swimming. Nero took pity on the actor and had him banished from Italy.

However, not everyone was entertained, particularly the new religious group known as Christians. At the time thousands of different deities were worshipped in Rome. Never before had there been such a variety of religious beliefs concentrated in one place. Religion was so important to the Romans that they assumed that other people's religions were equally important to them, so they were highly tolerant of other people's deities and beliefs. The only catch was a law that required all religions to include in their rituals some brief homage to the emperor's "genius" and "divinity." To the Romans, one's religious devotion was indistinguishable from loyalty to the state. This is where the Christians got into trouble; they, unlike the other religious groups, refused to proclaim their patriotism to Rome, took a pacifistic view toward military service, renounced pagan pleasures, skirted Roman laws, preached that the meek and not the imperial family were the inheritors of the earth, and voiced loud moral objections to

Roman entertainments such as gladiator contests and the theatre. As a result many emperors saw Christianity as a dangerous, unpatriotic cult whose aim was to overthrow the government—a charge not too far off the mark.

The earliest record of Christian writing against the theatre comes from Tatian (ca. 160 CE), who denounced theatre as "a chronicler of adultery" and "a storehouse of madness." Other Christian leaders like Tertullian of Carthage (160–225 CE) described theatres as "citadels of obscenity." He concluded that when the end came and the earth was consumed in flames, actors would be "more than ever vocal in their own tragedy." Saint John Chrysostom (ca. 347–ca. 407 CE) called theatre a "plague" and preached its destruction. The reaction of the Roman mimes was typical: they made pious Christians a favorite target for parody—a choice that did little to win favor from the Christians when they took power a few hundred years later.

By the late Empire, the obscene mimes were the most popular form of theatre in Rome, but the actors themselves had no basic rights. A few performers became quite wealthy and were able to buy their freedom, but most remained slaves. Roman law deprived actors of all civic rights; there were even laws forbidding government officials from marrying actresses. (See the Spotlight "Theodora: The Mime Who Became an Empress.") Similar laws would remain in effect in many parts of Europe for well over a thousand years.

2,000-Year-Old Sitcoms

Roman playwrights never reached the level of sophistication achieved by the ancient Greeks. In fact, most Roman plays were translations loosely based on Greek comedies. Comedy in both the Roman Republic and the empire was far more popular than tragedy, yet the Romans never developed the advanced sense of humor necessary to relish satire as the Greeks did. As a matter of fact, satirizing someone, through plays or otherwise, was considered libelous and a crime punishable by death. The earliest known Roman playwright, Livius Andronicus (ca. 284–204 BCE), is often called Rome's Thespis, because he is said to have introduced tragedy to Rome in 240 BCE. Unfortunately, there is no evidence to confirm this. Livius Andronicus was a Greek living in the city of Tarentum when it was sacked by the Romans. Most of the citizens were slaughtered, but he was enslaved and taken to Rome. As a slave, Livius Andronicus wrote several tragedies and comedies based on Greek models. He performed at public festivals and was well liked, but when he wrote an Old Comedy play in the style of Aristophanes, satirizing the Roman government, he was thrown in jail. After he was released, he wrote another satirical play and was banished from Rome. Only a few fragments of plays by Livius Andronicus, Rome's first known playwright, remain. Two comedic playwrights we do know more about are Plautus and Terence.

Plautus (254–184 BCE) was one of the most popular playwrights during the Roman Republic. His plays gave Roman audiences just what they wanted: pure entertainment full of gags, rollicking puns, improbable coincidences, love stories, and slapstick. Plautus was so popular that many theatre managers replaced other playwrights' names with his in order to increase attendance. More than a thousand years later, Shakespeare (1564–1616) used Plautus's play *The Twin Menaechmi*, a farce about identical twins, as the basis for his play *Comedy of Errors* (1591). And Plautus's play *The Pot of Gold* (ca. 194 BCE), about a man who is driven berserk by an elusive buried treasure, was the basis for Molière's

Returning home from the theatre, your house seems to you to be too simple, your wife ceases to be attractive, since she is not as beautiful as the actress whom you applauded, and you take out your ill humor on your immediate family.

Saint John Chrysostom,
Early church father

SPOTLIGHT ON The Mime Who Became an Empress

The most powerful actress of the Roman world was Theodora (ca. 502–548 CE). Born into a destitute family, she became a mime and acted in Roman theatres around Constantinople. Theodora was a favorite of audiences not only because of her staggering good looks and comic abilities but also because of her crude performances, often done in the nude. Roman mimes frequently performed skits that by today's standards would be rated NC-17, and Theodora was no exception. Because of such performances, the word *actress* in the Roman world was often synonymous with *prostitute*—a charge that was often true.

Her talents caught the eye of the patrician Justinian, who was in line to become emperor of the Byzantine Empire (reign 527–565 CE), which until the fall of Rome in 476 had been the eastern half of the Roman Empire and now was all that was left of it. Justinian wanted to marry Theodora, but Roman law forbade government officials from marrying actresses. However, Justinian was determined, and in 525 he overturned the law. Theodora gave up acting, became a Christian, and they were married. Two years later Justinian and Theodora were crowned emperor and empress of the Byzantine Empire.

Theodora proved her worth as she shared the throne's responsibilities and power. During her 20 years as empress she was known for her compelling speeches that helped unite generals to defend the sovereignty of the empire. Scholars suggest that the emperor frequently subordinated his judgment to that of his wife. She used her influence to protect women's rights, challenged the pope by protecting heretics, and secretly encouraged the rise of an independent Eastern Church. However, in addition to her benevolence toward some members of society, she was also known for her cruelty—those who offended her were likely to disappear without a trace.

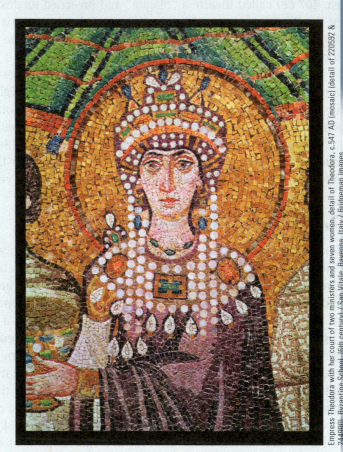

Empress Theodora, from a sixth-century mosaic in the Basilica of San Vitale, Ravenna, Italy.

comedy *The Miser* (1669). Even today his plays and characters are still being recycled. Stephen Sondheim's musical *A Funny Thing Happened on the Way to the Forum* (1962) is based on the comedies of Plautus.

Terence (ca. 195–159 BCE) was another popular Roman comic playwright. His full name was Publius Terentius Afer; "Afer" most likely indicates that he was from Africa and was black. One of his most famous plays was *The Self-Tormentor* (163 BCE), a comedy about a son who marries a girl his father has forbidden him to wed. Unlike Plautus, whose plays were essentially translations of Greek comedies, Terence adapted the stories and added his own perceptions. His scripts had the refined sentiment lacking in most popular Roman plays, which were elaborate spectacles interspersed with crude jokes.

The Singing, Acting Emperor

Not all Roman playwrights wrote comedy. Lucius Annaeus Seneca (ca. 4 BCE–65 CE) was perhaps Rome's greatest tragic playwright. His dramas reflected the Stoic belief that disaster results when passion overtakes reason; he believed it was important to detach ourselves from everything we do not have the power to control. Because many of his scripts called for wild special effects, such as the walls of Troy falling or a cow being slaughtered to reveal a calf inside, some modern scholars believe that Seneca's plays were written to be read rather than publicly performed. However, there is evidence that serious plays were performed in Rome, although they drew a smaller, more sophisticated audience. The Roman rhetorician Marcus Fabius Quintilianus (ca. 35–ca. 100 CE) reported seeing tragic Roman actors playing their parts with such conviction that they left the stage weeping.

In 48 CE Emperor Claudius made Seneca the tutor to his 11-year-old adopted son Nero (37–68 CE). This was a logical choice because Seneca was not only a playwright but also a scientist: his book *Quaestiones Naturales* was a popular science text well into the Middle Ages.

Seneca taught the young Nero about theatre, and by the time he became emperor at the age of sixteen, he saw himself as a talented poet, singer, and actor, and often performed in Roman theatres. Nero did not play the violin as has sometimes been depicted; rather, he played the lyre, an instrument more closely related to the harp or the guitar. During his lifetime, Nero received generally good reviews of his work as a performer, but it is hard to know if these were honest assessments or forced opinions; after all, he was emperor. We do know that Nero had a prodigious repertoire and that his performances, including countless curtain calls, could last for many hours. The length of his performances, rather than a lack of talent, may have been the reason some people tried in vain to exit the theatre early. It was reported that women faked labor pains and men pretended they were dying so that they could get out of the theatre without retribution. Nero took his art so seriously that he tried to improve the strength of his voice by performing breathing exercises with weights on his chest. On certain days he ate nothing but garlic and olive oil, which he believed improved his singing voice. In 66 CE he went on a two-year concert tour around the Mediterranean. By the time he returned to Rome he had won 1,500 singing awards and delighted audiences all over the northern Mediterranean region.

Nero fancied himself such a friend of the performing arts that he required his troops to take at least one wagon packed with musical instruments and theatrical effects whenever they left for war. In the end, Nero suspected many people, including his old tutor, of plotting against him. He ordered Seneca to kill himself. Seneca protested but was compelled by his Stoic beliefs to obey. Three years later Nero was overthrown and fled Rome; when troops closed in on him, he took his own life. His last words were reported to have been "Oh, what an artist dies with me!" Today, Nero is often thought of as a terrible emperor, largely because of his callous persecution of Christians after the great fire of Rome. Many believe that this persecution was not due to religious differences but rather the common suspicion that Christians had started the fire. Whatever the truth about these events, it still can be said that Nero was one of the greatest supporters of art and theatre in Western history.

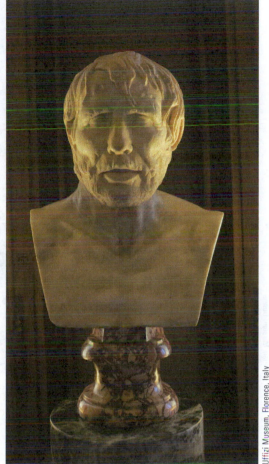

Uffizi Museum, Florence, Italy

The great Roman playwright Seneca was tutor to the Emperor Nero and tried to reign in some of Nero's tendencies toward excess. This bust is located in the Uffizi Museum in Florence, Italy.

William Missouri Downs

One of the largest structures for live performance in the ancient world was the Roman theatre at Ephesus (today part of Turkey). This massive theatre sat over 25,000 people. To get an idea of its size, compare it to the modern 20-story crane that sits beside it in this picture.

Curtain Call

The Western Roman Empire fell about 400 years after the time of Nero and Seneca. In 410 CE Rome was sacked by the Goths, then again in 455 by the Vandals and again in 474 by the Barbarians. By 500 CE the aqueducts had been cut, large parts of the city were deserted, and the Western Roman Empire lay in shambles. The Eastern Roman Empire, with its capital in Constantinople (today's Istanbul), would continue for another thousand years, but Rome was a defeated city.

As Christians took control of the remains of the Western Roman Empire, as well as Constantinople, they set about creating a state that persecuted their former persecutors—anyone not a member of the Christian religion. Pagan temples and statues were destroyed throughout the empire, and pagan rituals were forbidden under punishment of death. In the fourth century CE, Christian mobs attacked a branch of the Library of Alexandria, burning its books and murdering the librarians. Its manuscripts on science, mathematics, astronomy, art, philosophy, and medicine were viewed as worthless pagan gibberish. Other universities in Athens and Constantinople were ordered closed as faith and obedience to the church were rated a greater human achievement than empirical observations. Around 500 CE, the Parthenon in Rome was turned into a church. In 526 the last Egyptian temples dedicated to the goddess Isis were closed. In 529 the Academy, Plato's school of philosophy in Athens, was also shut. It had been in existence for more than 900 years but the Christians, now in power, considered it a pathway to paganism.

As the Christians rose to power, they stepped up their attacks on the one institution they found most obscene and insulting: the theatre. In 401 CE the fifth Council of Carthage decreed excommunication for all who attended the theatre rather than church on holy days. Later, actors were forbidden from taking the sacraments unless they renounced their profession. And in 438 the Theodosian Code, an update of all Roman law at the time, deprived actors of all rights, even the right to salvation. In 530 the Eastern Roman Emperor Justinian ordered that everyone without exception must go to their local church and convert to Christianity. He also decreed that baptism would be a prerequisite to owning property or any possessions. Non-Christians were to be "stripped of everything and reduced to extreme poverty." This was certainly a problem for actors because the Church refused to baptize anyone involved in the theatre. Shortly thereafter, theatre was forced out of existence. The last known reference to theatre in Rome is in a letter written in 533; after that, the historical record goes dark.

SUMMARY

Greek theatre grew out of religious rituals that celebrated the god Dionysus. Five hundred years before the birth of Christ, the Greeks built enormous theatres and performed tragedies and comedies. Through their drama, they were searching for the meaning of life and asking powerful questions about humankind's purpose. The most famous of tragic playwrights were Aeschylus, Sophocles, and Euripides. Aristophanes is the only Greek comic playwright whose plays have survived. Greek plays do not follow the modern framework of acts and intermissions; instead they have five elements: prologue, parodos, episode, stasimon, and exodos. The main part of a tragedy's plot is made up of hamartia, hubris, peripeteia, and anagnorisis.

In 404 BCE the Peloponnesian War ended the golden age of Greek theatre. As liberties decreased and freedom of speech was limited, Greek theatre faded. Aristotle wrote *Poetics* in an attempt to teach the playwrights of his day how to construct a proper tragedy. His most important student was Alexander the Great, who began the Hellenistic Age by spreading Greek culture and theatre throughout the Mediterranean and beyond on the point of his sword.

The expanding Roman Empire consumed the Hellenistic empire and appropriated Greek culture and theatre. As time went by, Roman theatre became less associated with religious ceremony and more about amusement, and Rome became the entertainment capital of the ancient world. The major Roman playwrights were Plautus, Terence, and Seneca. One of the most popular forms of theatre in Rome was mime. Its actors packed the theatres with obscene plays, vulgar language, and buffoonery. With the fall of the Roman Empire, Christians took control. Christians despised the theatre and eventually had it banned.

MindTap
Test your knowledge with online printable flashcards and online quizzing.

THEATRE

THE RESTORATION, THE ENLIGHTMENT, AND ROMANTICISM

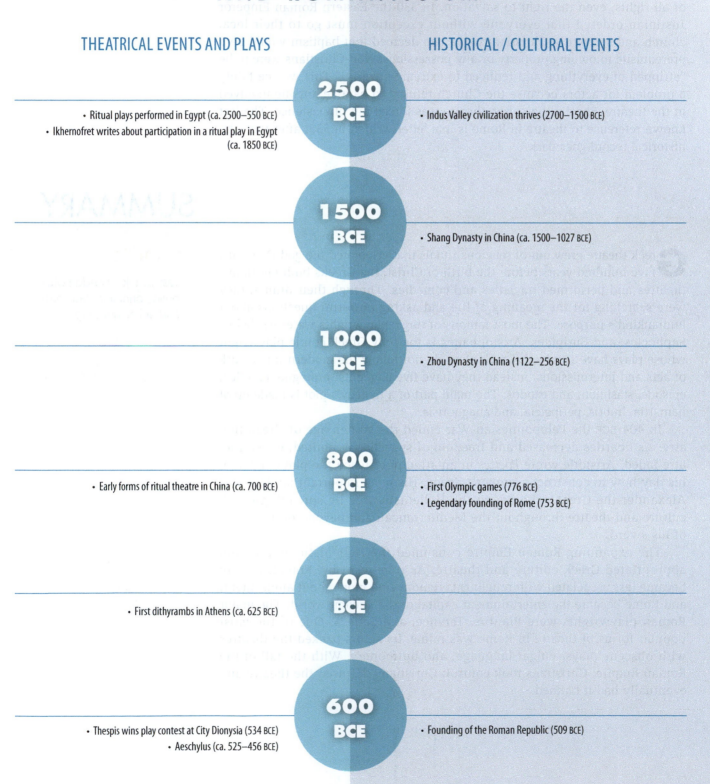

THEATRICAL EVENTS AND PLAYS

HISTORICAL / CULTURAL EVENTS

2500 BCE

- Ritual plays performed in Egypt (ca. 2500–550 BCE)
- Ikhernofret writes about participation in a ritual play in Egypt (ca. 1850 BCE)

- Indus Valley civilization thrives (2700–1500 BCE)

1500 BCE

- Shang Dynasty in China (ca. 1500–1027 BCE)

1000 BCE

- Zhou Dynasty in China (1122–256 BCE)

800 BCE

- Early forms of ritual theatre in China (ca. 700 BCE)

- First Olympic games (776 BCE)
- Legendary founding of Rome (753 BCE)

700 BCE

- First dithyrambs in Athens (ca. 625 BCE)

600 BCE

- Thespis wins play contest at City Dionysia (534 BCE)
- Aeschylus (ca. 525–456 BCE)

- Founding of the Roman Republic (509 BCE)

THEATRICAL EVENTS AND PLAYS

HISTORICAL / CULTURAL EVENTS

500 BCE

- Comedy added to City Dionysia (486 BCE)
- Lysistrata, Aristophanes (411 BCE)
- Oresteia, Aeschylus (458 BCE)
- Sophocles (ca. 496–406 BCE)
- Aristophanes (ca. 448–380 BCE)
- Medea, Euripides (431 BCE)
- Euripides (ca. 480–406 BCE)
- Oedipus the King, Sophocles (430 BCE)

- Battle of Marathon (490 BCE)
- Plato (427–347 BCE)
- The Peloponnesian War (431–404 BCE)

400 BCE

- Poetics, Aristotle (ca. 330 BCE)
- First theatrical performance in Rome (ca. 364 BCE)
- Menander (ca. 342–292 BCE)
- Livius Andronicus (284–204 BCE)

- Socrates tried and executed (399 BCE)
- Plato condemns theatre in Republic (ca. 373 BCE)
- Aristotle (384–322 BCE)
- Alexander the Great (356–323 BCE)
- Elements, Euclid (ca. 300 BCE)

300 BCE

- Plautus (254–184 BCE)

- Construction of the Great Wall of China begins (214 BCE)

200 BCE

- Terence (195–159 BCE)

- Ptolemy (ca. 90–168 BCE)

100 BCE

- First permanent theatre in Rome, built by Pompey (55 BCE)

- Julian calendar instituted (46 BCE)

1 CE

- Lucius Annaeus Seneca (ca. 4 BCE–65 CE)
- Theatre of Marcellus built in Rome (11 BCE)

- Traditional year for Jesus' birth (ca. 1 to 3 CE)
- Fire destroys Rome (64)
- Nero, Emperor, actor and musician, overthrown (68)
- Romans crush rebellion in Jerusalem (70)
- Coliseum constructed in Rome (ca. 80)

100 CE

- Shadow theatre starts in China (ca. 100)
- Tatian condemns the theatre (ca. 160)

THEATRICAL EVENTS AND PLAYS

HISTORICAL / CULTURAL EVENTS

200 CE

- Tertullian writes that Christians should have nothing to do with theatre (ca. 200)
- Natyasastra, classic treatise on Sanskrit drama (ca. 200 BCE–ca. 200 CE)
- Livius Andronicus (284–204 BCE)

300 CE

- Kalidasa, Sanskrit playwright (ca. 373–415)

- Constantine converts to Christianity (312)
- Constantinople, capital of eastern Roman Empire, founded (330)

400 CE

- Shakuntala, Kalidasa (ca. 400)
- Theatregoers excommunicated by the Church (401)

- Fall of Rome (476)

500 CE

- Last known theatre performance in Rome (533)
- Theodora, Empress of Eastern Roman Empire (527–565)

- Plato's Academy is closed (529)

KEY TERMS

Alexander the Great *269*

Anagnorisis *262*

Artists of Dionysus *271*

Bread and circus *272*

Catharsis *262*

Choregos *259*

Chorus *260*

Deus ex machina *260*

Deuteragonist *260*

Dionysus *258*

Dithyramb *258*

Ekkyklema *260*

Episode *260*

Exodus *260*

Hamartia *262*

Hellenistic period *270*

Hubris *262*

Library of Alexandria *262*

Mechane *260*

New Comedy *268*

Old Comedy *267*

Orchestra *259*

Parodos *260*

Peloponnesian War *266*

Periakto *260*

Peripeteia *262*

Poetics *269*

Prologue *260*

Protagonist *260*

Roman mimes *275*

Satyr play *264*

Skene *259*

Stasimon *260*

Theatre of Dionysus *259*

Theatron *259*

Thespis *258*

Tragic hero *262*

Tritagonist *260*

Chapter **14**

THE DARK AGES TO THE DAWN OF THE RENAISSANCE

Passion plays descend from the liturgical plays performed during the Middle Ages. Still popular today, they are performed throughout the world during Lent and Easter to commemorate the suffering, death, and resurrection of Jesus. Passion plays are often a community affair and are staged at both the amateur and the professional levels, by anyone from congregants of local churches to large professional casts. This passion play, with its particularly artful costumes and staging, was performed in 2000 by professional actors and the townspeople of Oberammergau, Germany.

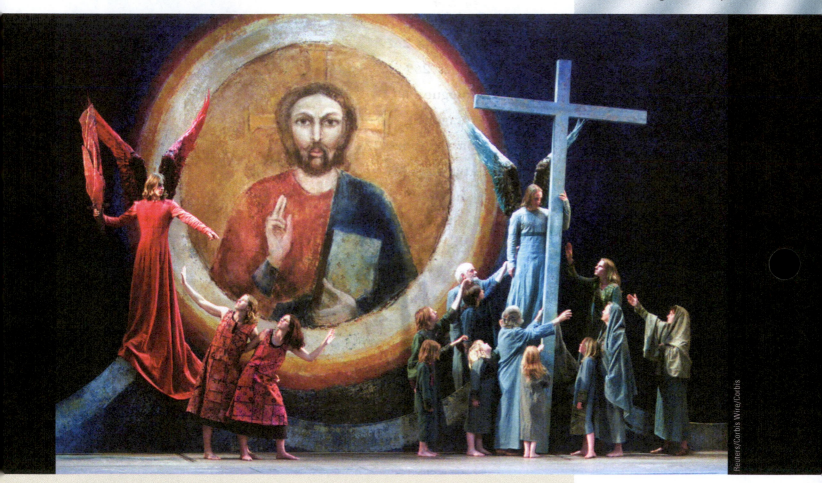

Reuters/Corbis Wire/Corbis

Outline

A Dark Age for Theatre

The Middle Ages
From the Churches to the Streets
The Fall of Lucifer and Other Entertainments
Pride, Lust, Sloth, and Gluttony: Allegories

Aristotle Rediscovered

A More Secular Theatre

The Renaissance Begins
The Printing Press and Subversive Ideas
Humanists
The Demise of Religious Theatre

Curtain Call

MindTap®

Start with a quick warm-up activity and review the chapter's learning objectives.

Scholars and historians often speculate about what caused the demise of the Western Roman Empire. Some attribute it to a failed economy, others to political corruption, while still others blame the rise of Christianity. Whatever the cause, in 476 AD Rome fell to a series of barbarian invasions. At the time of its demise, Rome and the Empire were largely Christian, and as Christians, they set about converting their conquerors. As they continued to gain power and prominence, both before and after the fall of Rome, Christians also focused on destroying the one art they most despised: the theatre. The rise of Christianity meant that the Theatre of Dionysus in Athens, which existed as one of the most important stages for presenting plays for over a thousand years (regardless of whether it was in Greek or Roman hands), fell into disuse. Hundreds of theatres built by the Romans themselves, from Africa to England, were also abandoned. This was the beginning of the Dark Ages.

The millennium that followed the fall of the Western Roman Empire can be divided into several historical periods, including the Dark Ages (from the end of the Western Roman Empire to around the year 1000 CE), the Middle Ages (1000–1200 CE), and the High Middle Ages (1200–1450 CE). During the Dark Ages in Europe, except in Muslim Spain, there were few new inventions and fewer innovative thinkers. Disease and repeated barbarian invasions depleted Europe's population. The primeval forests, many of which had been laboriously cleared for cultivation by the Romans, began to grow back, and the great Roman roads fell into disrepair. Astrology, superstition, and a strong belief in the supernatural guided the lives of most people. For example, many believed that angels guided the stars and that invisible demons lurked everywhere—especially in one's bed, and even in one's body. A sneeze at the wrong time was a bad omen and had to be disarmed with an immediate "God bless you." People believed that witches were real and could summon swarms of locusts or dry up a mother's milk.

Literacy and learning became the province of monasteries, and formal education was reserved for clergy, lords, and kings. During this period, hundreds of years before the invention of the printing press, books were rare and expensive. In today's dollars, a single, hand-copied volume would cost around $1,700. Only monasteries had Bibles. The common people were taught that everything they needed to know about the world began and ended with those appointed by God to

During the Dark Ages in Europe, all theatres had long been closed and professional actors were banned from performing. However, the public still craved entertainment. Traveling entertainers provided "acceptable" diversions, such as storytelling, animal tricks, and music, much as street performers around the world do today.

Mary Evans Picture Library

look after their souls: church officials. The Roman Catholic Church's teachings were the final word on geography, political science, history, ethics, philosophy, psychology, and even hygiene. The public walked a fixed path, preoccupied with salvation and the world to come. Morals were unambiguous—consisting only of strict obedience to God's will as interpreted by the Pope and his emissaries, the local priesthood. Understanding came only through faith. Happiness could be achieved only by obedience to the Church in this life in order to gain admittance to the next. There was no need to understand or explain the natural causes of the world, because the earth was simply a "vale of tears" that one could escape through earning salvation.

A Dark Age for Theatre

In the centuries after the fall of Rome, memories of the classical world faded. Ruins of ancient Greek and Roman theatres dotted the European landscape—some were looted for their marble, others were devastated by erosion and earthquakes, and still others were rebuilt as fortresses to protect against invasions by Huns, Vikings, Turks, and Mongols. One of the few structures left largely untouched was the Coliseum, but only because it was widely believed to be the entrance to Hell.

The art of theatre, shunned by a rigid society and outlawed by the Church, barely survived in memory or in practice. Yet scholars have been able to piece together hints that "theatrical" entertainments did occasionally turn up in the Dark Ages. New Comedy may have survived in Greek-speaking lands in the form of puppet plays. In Constantinople, ancient tragic plays may have been used to teach Greek. Scholars have even found curious fragments of plays by Euripides, rewritten to incorporate Christian themes. Some playwrights wrote dramas with biblical storylines (see the Spotlight "Hroswitha: The Nun Who Wrote Plays"). Companies of jugglers, storytellers, dancers, animal trainers, acrobats, and musicians traveled around Europe, entertaining the public. We can imagine these artistic descendants of the Roman mimes performing slightly cleaned-up versions of their unruly skits. For the most part, theatre had gone underground, and its players had become shady vagabonds who performed wherever they could find an audience and whenever the authorities blinked.

The Middle Ages

The Middle Ages began in the late tenth century and are marked by economic recovery; stronger, centralized governments; and longer periods of peace. Even so, because many of the roads built during the Roman Empire had decayed, travel was rare, many societies had become isolated, and the Latin of the Roman Empire was evolving into separate Romance languages: French, Italian, Portuguese, Romanian, and Spanish. (The word *Romance* comes from the Latin *fabulare romanice*, which means "to speak in the Roman way.") Latin existed only as a language of diplomacy, commerce, law, science, philosophy, and the Church. Mass was still given in Latin, even though the vast majority of people no longer understood it. The copies of the Bible and other books that did exist were handwritten and locked away in monasteries, and

MindTap

Read, highlight and take notes online.

To understand the Middle Ages we must forget our modern rationalism, our proud confidence in reason and science, our restless search after wealth and power and an earthly paradise; we must enter sympathetically into the mood of men disillusioned of these pursuits, standing at the end of a thousand years of rationalism, finding all dreams of utopia shattered by war and poverty and barbarism, seeking consolation in the hope of happiness beyond the grave, inspired and comforted by the story and figure of Christ.

Will Durant, Historian

Representation of a Mystery Play

From a drawing by David Jee in Sharp's " Coventry Mysteries," 1825

North Wind Picture Archives

During the late Middle Ages, plays with biblical themes were staged on wagons in town squares. These theatre festivals often lasted several days and some are still held in several European countries.

few ordinary citizens were literate enough to read them. The Vatican (papal government), sensing that it was losing the common people, began to allow theatrical elements into the Mass for the purpose of "fortifying" the faith of the general populace. In the early tenth century, priests were permitted to act as "living impersonators" of biblical figures in short plays on religious topics. These living impersonations were acted in the vernacular, not in Latin like the rest of the Mass.

The earliest surviving text of one of these liturgical impersonations comes from 923 CE, 400 years after the last mention of theatre in Rome. These brief plays, called *playlets*, were first performed during Easter services and were most likely a variation of tropes. **Tropes,** which had been part of religious services for centuries, are chanted or sung phrases incorporated into Mass as an embellishment or commentary on a religious lesson. In the first playlet, a priest dressed in white in order to represent an angel was joined by three choirboys who represented the three Marys—Christ's mother, her sister Mary, and Mary Magdalene—who visited Christ's empty tomb on Easter morning.

This tiny playlet was performed directly on the church's altar, which represented Christ's tomb and was therefore a perfect setting. Soon priests began staging Biblical playlets in other parts of the church. At that time, churches did not have pews (a luxury that was still a few hundred years in the future). Because

SPOTLIGHT<u>ON</u> Hroswitha: The Nun Who Wrote Plays

The earliest liturgical dramas were written by priests and monks whose names are now long lost. One of the few Dark Age dramatists whose name we do know is Hroswitha (ca. 935–ca. 1001 CE). She is not only the first known woman poet in Germany but also the first known woman playwright in Europe. A Benedictine mother superior in Gandersheim, Saxony (a region in the eastern part of today's Germany), Hroswitha wrote six short dramas in Latin about the lives of saintly women, using the plays of the Roman comic playwright Terence as a model. She mimicked Terence not because she thought his work superior and worthy of emulation, but rather because she believed that many Christians were overly delighted by his bawdy comedies. She copied his style in order to entice Terence's Christian audience but replaced sexual innuendo and titillation with themes of Christian values and morals.

Her play *Abraham* was about a religious recluse caring for his orphaned niece. One day, the niece runs away and marries a handsome seducer who then abandons her. Alone on the streets, she becomes a prostitute. Abraham sets out to find his niece. When he does, he disguises himself and enters her bedroom. Thinking he is a client, she kisses him. When he takes off his disguise, she recognizes him and is paralyzed with guilt. In the end he convinces her to return home and give up her life of sin. Hroswitha's other plays depict the battle between Christianity and paganism and tell stories about heroic but frail women who victoriously defend their virtue against strong men. In the end most of these protagonists suffer horrible martyrdoms but are rewarded with heavenly bliss.

Most scholars believe that Hroswitha intended her plays to be read rather than performed, but there is some evidence that at least one of her scripts may have been staged for a visiting abbot. However, Hroswitha was an anomaly. Formal theatre reviving the work of Roman playwrights was still hundreds of years in the future. During her lifetime there were merely simple, religious plays based on stories from the Bible and very few original storylines.

AKG London

Tenth-century poet and dramatist Hroswitha.

the congregation stood, they could easily move about the church and gather around a new setting. These settings—called *houses*, or **mansions**—are much like the Stations of the Cross that later became standard in Catholic churches. Within a hundred years, every area of the church building was being used as a theatre, with priests, altar boys, and sometimes even nuns as the actors.

By 1060, nativity plays during Christmas festivals had become popular. Later, scenes were added about Herod, the massacre of the innocents, and the flight into Egypt. These liturgical playlets were even accompanied by stage directions detailing how actors should manage special effects. One read, "Abel shall have a saucepan beneath his garment against which Cain shall knock when he pretends to kill Abel, who shall then lie full out as if he were dead."

Carol Pratt

Mystery plays like *The Second Shepherd's Play* mixed buffoonery and light entertainment with biblical teachings. This modern production was staged by Theatre at the Shakespeare Library in Washington D.C.

By the late 1100s, these modest church plays were becoming popular throughout Europe. But church officials still had concerns about the propriety of clergy dressing in costumes and acting. Exodus 20:4 states, "Thou shall not make unto thee any graven images, or any likeness of anything that is in heaven above, or that is in the earth beneath, or that is in the water under the earth." A similar warning exists in Deuteronomy 4:15. But during the long history of the Church this commandment has been interpreted many different ways. During some centuries, monks who refused to plaster over painted representations of Christ were imprisoned, tortured, and beheaded. At other times images, murals, sculptures, icons, and frescoes were outlawed, but the rules were only loosely enforced. For hundreds of years this commandment was also used to ban the theatre because actors were thought of as living versions of graven images. The same commandment exists in Islam and prevented the growth of theatre in Muslim lands for a thousand years. (See Chapter 12.)

Yet the popularity of the theatre could not be denied. To the dismay of Church leaders but to audiences' delight, some bawdy bits were working their way into the performances. The Mass had become a sideshow to the main event: a play. In 1210 Pope Innocent III took steps to bring order to the services and restore dignity to the clergy. He decreed that plays should be moved outside the church and townspeople should be encouraged to take over the acting.

From the Churches to the Streets

In 1264 Pope Urban announced that plays would be allowed on the Thursday following Trinity Sunday, or the **Festival of Corpus Christi**. (He warned, however,

William Missouri Downs

When Islamic armies in the 12th century moved through India, they often chiseled the faces off temples as they did with this temple in Udaipur. They did this in order to follow the graven image warning in the Koran.

that priests should no longer take part in the staging.) In the years following, other dramatic festivals were held on Easter, Christmas, and special occasions, such as deliverance from plague. (See the Spotlight "The Black Death Takes Center Stage.") Nevertheless, theatre was still tolerated only as a teaching tool. Not everyone was thrilled by the rekindled popularity of drama, and there were still many ecclesiastical

SPOTLIGHT ON The Black Death Takes Center Stage

In December 1347, a ship from Caffa (on the Black Sea) landed in Marseille, a port on the Mediterranean. The sailors were sick and soon died. Little did the people know that this seemingly small event was the beginning of "the plague." The sailors' infection had come from rotting corpses that had been tossed over the walls of Caffa when it was under siege by Mongols. The corpses had attracted rats infected with the *Yersinia pestis* bacterium. The rats were bitten by fleas, which ingested the bacteria and passed it to humans.

The disease shows up as painful lumps or "buboes" in the groin or armpits—hence, "bubonic" plague. Soon after infection the body is racked with fever, chills, headache, cough, and finally pneumonia. In this time period, which predates the use of antibiotics by over 500 years, death usually arrived within three to five days. Highly contagious, the Black Death spread quickly. Doctors were powerless. (It wasn't until 1894 that the *bacillus* of bubonic plague was even discovered.) By 1351, approximately one-third to one-half of Europe's approximately 75 million people had died of plague. Some cities were so badly ravaged that there are reports of people digging their own graves and then lying down in them to die.

Without scientific knowledge, people often made the plague worse. For example, many Christians killed off the cats that could have helped control the rat population, thinking they were representatives of the devil. They also blamed the Jews for spreading the plague, and more than 500 Jewish communities were exterminated across Europe. During the same period, countless typhus epidemics killed tens of thousands of people and flu outbreaks killed tens of thousands more. Many people attributed the diseases to an untimely conjunction of Mars, Jupiter, and Saturn; the modern word "flu" comes from the word *Influenza*, a shortened version of "celestial influences." As Flagellants (part of a radical Christian movement) marched through the

streets beating themselves with sticks and preaching that the Last Judgment was at hand, a few people did try to get away from plague-filled cities by taking refuge in the countryside. However, a surprising number made no attempt to save themselves because they were sure that the plague was a punishment from God.

The plague significantly affected the arts. For many years afterward, an image called the "dance of death" was common in paintings and frescoes; it was usually comprised of a procession of the living, from pope to pauper to child, being led to the grave by mocking, dancing skeletons. For the next 300 years, periodic outbreaks of plague closed theatres all over Europe, sometimes for up to a year. In some cases, theatre itself was even blamed for causing the dreaded disease.

Dance of Death (colour lithograph) / Private Collection / Bridgeman Images

A sixteenth-century painting of the dance of death, a compelling subject for artists in the decades following the Black Death in Europe.

doubts. Some clergy argued that acting, even in a play about the Bible, was a form of demonic possession. Other clergy maintained that plays, in which actors *pretend* to be punished for transgressions they are *pretending* to have committed, might give the public the wrong impression about the wages of sin. Yet most clergy felt that theatre, along with paintings and music, had the power to awaken devotion. In the end theatre was permitted as long as it was not idle amusement but education.

Although theatre had now officially moved outside the churches, the performances didn't move far. At first they were staged on the church's front steps, but this interfered with foot traffic. A new method of staging was needed. The answer was horse-drawn wagons, called **pageant wagons**, which were pulled up in front of the audience in the town square and used as the stage for performances of short religious plays. Some of these wagons were quite complicated. Reports of the day describe wagons that were two stories tall and had trapdoors, cranes from which God and angels could descend, and hell-mouths that opened to belch clouds of smoke as they swallowed up townspeople acting out the fate of the damned. The costumes were usually just the dress of the day, but additions could be made to create animal-headed demons, divinities with golden hair, and winged angels. As is true for most of theatre's history, women were seldom permitted on stage, so the actors in these playlets were mostly men.

The Fall of Lucifer and Other Entertainments

These outdoor liturgical plays were called *Geistspiele* in German-speaking lands, *autos sacramentales* in Spain, and *sacre rappresentazioni* in Italy. In English-speaking countries, they became known as **mystery plays**. The word *mystery* here has nothing to do with the modern meaning of "enigma" or "puzzle," but comes from the Anglo-French word for "occupation," *mesterie*, because these liturgical plays were often performed by guilds, the labor unions of the day. For example, the shipwrights might stage a play about Noah's ark, the goldsmiths might stage the story of the Magi, and the bakers might stage the Last Supper. A series of several mystery plays performed in biblical chronological sequence from Creation to the Day of Judgment was called a **mystery cycle** and was often named for the town where the performances took place. For example, the Wakefield Cycle had 32 mystery plays, including *The Fall of Lucifer*, *The Anti-Christ*, and *Doomsday*. Performances started at sunrise and lasted, with the help of torchbearers, until after sunset. One cycle in London reportedly took seven days to perform.

Mystery plays seldom had a single author, and the writers rarely put their names on the scripts because that would show pride, one of the seven deadly sins. The performers in the cycles often copied and rewrote each other. If someone from Wakefield was traveling through Coventry and liked a particular play in Coventry's cycle, he would simply rewrite it to suit Wakefield's needs—there were no copyright laws. As a result, there were dozens of versions of each play and only a few authors' names have survived.

The one element almost all mystery plays shared was comic relief. Audiences in the Middle Ages, just as today, wanted to be entertained. However, the Bible provides little light entertainment, so comedy had to be added to the plays. Because tampering with stories from the Bible could lead to charges of blasphemy, the players got around the rules by filling in the blanks of biblical stories with comic scenes. For example, the Bible says that Noah got on the ark with his wife, but it doesn't specify the particulars; so boarding the ark becomes a comic episode in which Noah's wife at first refuses to budge unless she can take along her "gossips."

Another example of comedy added to a biblical story is in ***The Second Shepherd's Play***. This play asks what the three shepherds might have been doing

Belyal the devil must have burning gunpowder in pipes in his hands, ears, and arse when he goes into battle. The four daughters—Mercy, Peace, Truth, and Righteousness—wear mantles; Mercy, white; Peace, black; Truth, sad green; and Righteousness, red. Stewards must control the crowds who are to be separated from the action by a ditch.

Stage direction in **Castle of Perseverance,** Early morality play (ca. 1425)

EVERYMAN: Death, if I should this pilgrimage take, And my reckoning surely make, Show me, for saint charity, Should I not come again shortly?

DEATH: No, Everyman; and thou be once there, Thou mayst never more come here, Trust me verily.

EVERYMAN: O gracious God, in the high seat celestial, Have mercy on me in this most need; Shall I have no company from this vale terrestrial Of mine acquaintance that way to me lead?

DEATH: Yea if any be so hardy That would go with thee and bear thee company.

Everyman, English morality play

before the angel came to tell them that Christ had been born and they decided to go to Bethlehem bearing gifts (Luke 2:8–18). As one might guess, the shepherds had been involved in a comic farce. At the beginning of the play, Col, Gib, and Daw, the three shepherds, are minding their flocks and complaining about taxes and nagging wives when Mak, a comic villain, arrives. He is known as a petty thief, and the shepherds don't trust him with their sheep. Mak casts a magic spell over the shepherds, putting them to sleep, and makes off with one of their lambs, which he takes to his wife. Mak's wife is thrilled to have the lamb, but reminds him that stealing is punishable by hanging. They hide the lamb in a baby's crib, and Mak returns to the shepherds so that they won't suspect anything. When the shepherds awake, Mak tells them that he's had a dream in which his wife gave birth and leaves to find out if it's true. The shepherds count their flock and discover one is missing. They immediately suspect Mak and rush off to find him. Arriving at Mak's house, they find the crib and Mak's wife acting as though she just gave birth. The lamb's braying while Mak defends himself must have been the high point of the comedy. The jig is up when the shepherds inspect the crib. This is the moment when the angel appears to tell them that a child is born in Bethlehem. The play's mood abruptly changes: the shepherds' bickering ends, Mak and the lamb are abruptly forgotten, and the rest of the play follows the Bible to the letter.

Pride, Lust, Sloth, and Gluttony: Allegories

The popularity of these dramatizations of scripture led to the development of other types of religious drama. **Miracle plays** told stories about the lives of the saints, and **morality plays** were about how we should conduct our life. The emphasis was now on created characters facing moral choices between vice and virtue. Some of these plays had simple points, such as the attack on poor hygiene and gluttony in *Condamnation de Banquet* (1509). Other morality plays are *Money Is the Root of All Evil* and *Everyman*.

An interesting facet of medieval morality plays were allegories, characters and actions that represented abstract concepts. In *Everyman* each character is an allegory, and the journey Everyman takes represents the journey we all make from birth to death. Here Everyman (center) is accompanied by (l to r) Strength, Five Wits, and Beauty, portrayed as a circus troupe who, in the end, desert him before he meets Death. This 1996 Royal Shakespeare Company production featured Joseph Mydell as Everyman. Directed by Kathryn Hunter and Marcello Magni at The Other Place Theatre, Stratford-upon-Avon, England.

Donald Cooper/Photostage Ltd.

One common element in these plays was allegory. An **allegory** is a dramatic device in which an actor represents or symbolizes an idea or a moral principle. Early morality plays had characters representing the seven deadly sins: Pride, Lust, Sloth, Gluttony, Hatred, Avarice, and Anger. Soon the allegorical characters proliferated, and morality plays included the likes of Death, Life, Wine, Beauty, Discretion, Fellowship, Winter, Summer, Good, Evil, Folly, Wisdom, Sobriety, Bad Luck, Hypocrisy, and Snobbishness. The most famous morality play, **Everyman** (ca. 1495), makes abundant use of allegorical characters. At the beginning of the play, Death summons Everyman to a reckoning before God. Everyman, taken by surprise, exclaims, "Oh Death, thou comest when I least had thee in mind!" To buy more time, Everyman sets out to find someone to accompany him on his journey. He goes to Good Fellowship and Worldly Goods and begs them to join him. They refuse. Next he goes to Good Deeds, Knowledge, Beauty, Strength, Five Wits (the five senses), and Discretion and begs them to journey to the grave with him. Some agree at first but then they panic and desert him. In the end only Good Deeds agrees to travel with Everyman. Having learned a great lesson, Everyman's soul ascends into heaven.

In the United States today, some fundamentalist churches stage morality plays on Halloween in what are called "Hell Houses." The rooms contain scenarios that are supposed to lead to Hell, such as drunk driving, abortion, drugs, homosexuality, and the occult—each showing a battle between angels and demons. These plays differ very little in theme from the morality plays of 500 years ago.

Mystery, miracle, and morality plays soon became so popular that in England, Ireland, and Scotland alone more than 100 towns were producing some type of play at any given time. In France, some towns transformed the whole central plaza into an outdoor theatre during religious festivals. The townspeople might build a beautiful castle to represent heaven at one end of the plaza; at the other, a massive, mechanical, smoke-belching hellmouth; and between them dozens of settings such as Judas's hanging tree and Bethlehem. As the all-day performance moved from one set to the next, the audience followed on foot or viewed the entire "theatre" from balconies and rooftops.

Aristotle Rediscovered

The High Middle Ages is sometimes called the twelfth-century Renaissance or the mini-Renaissance. This period of great change, when the seeds of the Renaissance were planted and the first cracks in the medieval way of life began to show, began with the fall of Muslim Spain and the rediscovery of Aristotle.

Without a powerful Roman Empire to impede its progress, Islam, unlike Christianity, spread rapidly. It was founded around 610 by the prophet Muhammad (ca. 570–632 CE). Over the next century, Islam spread east from Mecca to the border of China and southwest through Upper Egypt. Muslim armies defeated Jerusalem in 638, Alexandria in 641, and Persia in 652. By 711,

Muslim armies had spread Islam through North Africa into Spain. For the next 700 years the Iberian peninsula (Spain and Portugal) was predominantly Muslim. There they built great cities such as Granada and Córdoba, which grew to populations of nearly half a million. When London was a tiny mud-hut village, Córdoba had 113,000 houses, 700 mosques, 300 public baths, and 21 suburbs. In addition, it was said that one could walk through its streets for ten miles at night and always have lamps to guide the way. For four centuries, from 800 to 1200, Islam led the world in standards of living, religious tolerance, literature, science, mathematics, medicine, and philosophy, but because the Muslim view excluded theatre as a viable social entity, plays were not an important part of the early Islamic world (see Chapter 12). Rather, the artistic and intellectual achievements of Muslim Spain were represented by its libraries. Fed by manuscripts taken from the Library of Alexandria in Islam's conquest of Egypt, every Muslim city in Spain had an impressive library. Spain had become the intellectual center of Europe.

The reconquest of Spain, spurred by the pope and by Christian royalty in neighboring kingdoms, began around 1085. The attacks continued intermittently until 1492 when the last Muslim stronghold surrendered to the armies of King Ferdinand and Queen Isabella—the same king and queen who funded Christopher Columbus's expeditions. Most of Spain had been in Muslim hands for over 700 years, but it now became largely Catholic. During the Christian attacks, many Muslim libraries were burned, but the few that survived drew scholars from all over Europe. As they read the Arabic translations of ancient Greek texts, they were staggered by what they found. Here were stacks of forgotten knowledge: books on science, medicine, and the greatest collection of astronomical data in the world at that time. Soon more of these ancient books began turning up in monasteries, church catacombs, and small private libraries. By the middle of the thirteenth century, French and Italian scholars had gathered hundreds of ancient texts on math, astronomy, and philosophy. The Spanish Inquisition drove the last Muslims out of Spain, but they left behind the seeds of the Renaissance and a different way of looking at the world.

Among all the ancient manuscripts that were rediscovered, those of Aristotle had an enormous effect on the Church. The synthesis of Aristotle's philosophy with the doctrines of the Roman Catholic Church was called **Aristotelian Scholasticism**. Saint Thomas Aquinas (1225–1274), an Italian Dominican priest, was among the earliest—and certainly the most historically successful—at joining Aristotle's ideas with Christian theology. He referred to it as Aristotle's philosophy in "Christian dress." Although this synthesis was initially scorned, Aristotelian Scholasticism dominated Church thought and the curricula at Europe's universities by the late thirteenth century. Aristotle's philosophies became so important that some Church fathers even suggested he had been sent by God to prepare the way for Jesus Christ. Many medieval scholars believed that Scripture and Aristotle were the total sum of all necessary knowledge. For example, the official charter of Trinity College at Cambridge University stated, "All students and undergraduates should lay aside their various authors and only follow Aristotle and those who defend him." (See the Spotlight "Aristotle and Aristotelian Scholasticism.")

SPOTLIGHT ON Aristotle and Aristotelian Scholasticism

Aristotle's theory of causality had an enormous impact on Christianity and on the theatre during the High Middle Ages. According to this theory, four causes brought order to the world: material, formal, efficient, and final.

- *Material cause* is physical material whose potential is not yet realized. An example is a block of marble that is to be made into a statue.

- *Formal cause* is physical material whose potential has been actualized, such as the finished statue.

- *Efficient cause* is the agent that actualizes the material, such as the artist who carved the statue.

- *Final cause* is the end in mind, such as the statue's ultimate purpose.

To Christians of the time, Aristotle's philosophy reinforced the idea that everything has a purpose and all things are connected. Therefore, everything is a sign of God's pleasure or wrath—or possibly the work of Satan. For example, comets and meteors are fireballs hurled by an angry God, earthquakes are God's way of showing His displeasure, and floods are the result of sin. If a person dies of a mysterious disease, there must be a witch nearby, and a plague is a sure sign of God's displeasure and the need to reform. Aristotle's four causes had a critical influence on theatre. Until the late nineteenth century, the study of psychology didn't exist. An actor playing a role or a playwright writing a character would never think to ask, "What is this character's motivation?" Deep character analysis that included upbringing, environment, motivations, and subconscious desires was still hundreds of years in the future. During the Middle Ages, the answer to the question "Why does this character decide to do this evil deed at this particular moment?" was that it was the result of a fight between God and the Devil. In other words, behaviors were attributed to the efficient causes that were perceived as controlling the world at the time. This is why the characters of morality plays are allegorical. They represent efficient causes in the universe, so they were real characters in the medieval mind, not mere symbols.

Louvre Museum, Paris, France

The great philosopher Aristotle was also a critic of theatre. His book Poetics is still used to teach playwrights and screenwriters the basics of their craft. This bust is located in the Louvre in Paris.

A More Secular Theatre

Despite the Church's control of the arts, secular theatre had most likely never entirely disappeared in the centuries after the fall of Rome. In the High Middle Ages, small secular plays called **interludes** became popular. The term *interlude* comes from the Latin *ludus*, which means "play," and *inter*, which means "between." Thus, an interlude was a play between other forms of entertainment. It may have started as a short nonreligious play slipped between mystery plays or inserted into a larger entertainment, such as a musical concert. Interludes were first performed at court for royal banquets, marriages, birthdays, and other celebrations, or to entertain visiting dignitaries. The subject may have been a historical event, a comic episode, or a particular lesson. One interlude used song, dance, and allegories from the morality plays to present the marriage of Wit and Science.

From a historical perspective, *interlude* is the perfect name for these plays because they represent the transition between medieval plays, whose only purpose was to moralize and teach biblical lessons, and the wholly secular plays of such soon-to-be-born playwrights as William Shakespeare. Not long after the great Greek tragedies of Aeschylus, Sophocles, and Euripides and the Roman comedies of Plautus, Terence, and Seneca had resurfaced, university students were performing these classics for their fellow pupils and small invited audiences. However, the transition from the dominance of religious plays to the preference for secular plays in Europe took hundreds of years.

The Renaissance Begins

On Tuesday, May 29, 1453, after a six-week siege, Constantinople [called Istanbul today], the head of the Eastern Roman Empire, fell to the Ottoman Turks. The body of the last Roman emperor of the Eastern Empire, Constantine XI, was found among tens of thousands who had died defending the city—his purple robes embroidered with eagles set him apart. The victor, Mehmet II, ordered Christian sanctuaries to be made into mosques. Although the conquerors allowed Christians to continue to practice their faith, this was the end of the Christian city of Constantinople. It became, as it remains today, the Muslim city of Istanbul. As the Turks ransacked the city, they burned Constantinople's libraries, which contained thousands of manuscripts from classical Greece. Countless critical texts were lost, but once again, a few were saved by fleeing scholars. Among their meager belongings, they salvaged a few of the plays of Aeschylus, Euripides, and Sophocles. These plays, in combination with the manuscripts that survived the fall of Muslim Spain, would contribute to the growth of knowledge during the Renaissance.

The **Renaissance** (ca. 1350–1650) was an extraordinary period in European history. During the Middle Ages, the overwhelming concerns had been God, redemption, and life after death. But the weakening Church and the flood of ancient Greek and Roman knowledge changed every aspect of life in the West: commerce, agriculture, politics, and science, as well as the theatre. During the Renaissance, the foremost concerns of society shifted to humankind, ancient wisdom, and life in the present. The Renaissance's focus on individualism and creativity led to the emergence of Michelangelo and Leonardo da Vinci and hundreds of other great artists. During the Renaissance, Christianity, which had dominated every aspect of people's lives for almost a thousand years, was divided into dozens of warring denominations. Many Europeans began to step away from a life spent in preparation for Judgment Day into a life of secular reason, intellectual curiosity, and creativity. In many ways, the Renaissance was a time of rebellion and rebirth—in fact, the word *renaissance* means "rebirth." To understand what happened in the theatre during the Renaissance, we need to look at some of the major changes that occurred in Europe: the invention of the printing press, the humanist revolution, and the Reformation.

The Printing Press and Subversive Ideas

Before the printing press, books were hand-copied, usually in monasteries by the monks. It took so long for information to be distributed that most authors could not find a wide audience during their lifetimes. A prominent scholar or physician might own a handful of books, and a famous professor or wealthy merchant might own two or three. Charles V of France (1338–1380) had a library that was renowned for its size: 910 books. In 1300 the largest library outside the Islamic world was the Library of Christ Church Priory at Canterbury, with almost 2,000 books. Books were so rare and expensive that students couldn't afford them; the texts were chained to lecterns at universities, and professors read from them while students listened. (The word *lecture* comes from the Latin word meaning "to read.") The printing press was the beginning of mass media and the popularization of ideas. Much like the World Wide Web today, it increased the output of written works and decreased their cost; in so doing, the printing press made literacy and learning available to millions. Scholars estimate that more books were printed in the 50 years after the invention of the printing press than scribes had been able to copy by hand in the previous 1,000 years. By 1515, all the known works of ancient Greek authors had been translated and printed.

However, not everyone was happy with the new technology. The clergy generally distrusted the printing press and thought it might become a vehicle for subversive ideas—they were right. The wealthy had misgivings about it because they thought mass printing would lower the value of rare works in their libraries—it did. Many copyists feared they would be thrown out of work—they were. Authors were upset when the printing press increased plagiarism. With few copyright laws, printing companies pirated each other's works and tried to undermine their competitors by offering the same book at a lower price. Still other opponents pointed out that any idea, no matter how frivolous, could now be widely disseminated. When the first printing press came to Florence, Politian, an Italian scholar and poet, wrote, "Now the most stupid ideas can, in a moment, be transferred into a thousand volumes and spread abroad." Soon pamphleteers were using the printing press to air complaints against feudalism, taxes, and the Church.

Humanists

The word **humanist** first appeared in fifteenth-century Italy, where it was used to describe university students who rejected the traditional curriculum of theology and instead studied the classical subjects of rhetoric, literary criticism, history, poetry, painting, architecture, music, and classical literature. Through *studius humanitatis*, Latin for "studies of humankind," humanists worked to

AS400 DB/Bettmann/Corbis

With the invention of the printing press, information was more readily disseminated than it had been in the Middle Ages. The subsequent rise in literacy rates and shared knowledge brought about immense cultural and political change in Europe. Some argue that printing changed the way Europeans thought about the world. Medieval books were expensive and, because much of the population couldn't read, heavily illustrated. In contrast, printed books focused on the written word and the author's line of reasoning. This shift from images to words led scholars and scientists to leave medieval metaphor behind and adopt the scientific method.

strengthen the awareness and claims of the individual. In other words, they were interested in self-development, not pious passivity. They wanted to make humans the measure of all things. Their motto was the statement of the Roman playwright Plautus: "I am a man. Nothing human is alien to me." They felt that the key to changing the present and the future lay in the philosophies and art of the classical world. The humanists' manifesto was to be healthy in mind and in body, to seek virtue, to live the good life, and to explore all potentialities. The humanist movement gained momentum in the fifteenth century and was a significant force throughout the next.

Humanists idolized the ancient Romans and Greeks. They Latinized their names, revered Socrates as their "patron saint," and even burned candles before busts of Aristotle and Plato. For humanists, the present was disappointing, so they traveled to Rome to study ruins of classical buildings, statues, and monuments in an attempt to learn the secrets of the past. Rome was no longer much of a city, as barbarian invasions, erosion, and a thousand years of neglect had done significant damage. The population was a tenth of what it had been during its heyday. The aqueducts had fallen into disrepair, leaving the city with an unreliable water supply. The streets were muddy, and most of the fields had turned into swamps. The marble of ancient Rome had been thrown into furnaces to make lime or used for building material. St. Peter's Basilica was constructed almost entirely from marble plundered from ancient Roman buildings. Many humanists set out to save the last remaining classical buildings in Rome. They also called for a new theatre that followed the guidelines of Aristotle's *Poetics*. (We discuss *Poetics* further in Chapter 15.)

The Demise of Religious Theatre

At noon on October 31, 1517, a monk named Martin Luther (1483–1546) used the front door of All Saint's Church at Wittenberg as his personal complaint box by nailing up a list of 95 complaints against the Roman Catholic Church. His action might have gone down in history as an isolated act of defiance, but within a month, the newly invented printing presses in three German towns were rolling out copy after copy of his declaration. This heralded the end of a unified Christendom and the beginning of the Protestant Reformation.

Catholic means "universal"; the Roman Catholic Church defined itself as the sole and universal church. *Protestant* comes from the Latin word *protestans*, which means "one who protests." The Protestants rebelled against Church corruption and demanded an end to penance pilgrimages, indulgences, selling of relics, and all hypocrisies. An indulgence was a form of penance. In return for a monetary payment to the Church, a priest wrote an indulgence, a certificate of absolution for past sins or release from purgatory after death. According to a popular saying, "just as soon as the silver tinkles into the alms box, the soul will take wing from the burning heat of purgatory." Indulgences were even available for acquittal from future sins. Indulgence could be bought for oneself or for friends, lovers, or relatives who had died. Luther also attacked the sale of relics. The Church claimed to have all sorts of holy relics, some of which could be purchased, whereas others were put on display in the hopes of creating pilgrimages to attract religious tourists and the money that they brought with them. For example, one could buy a speck of wood that a priest claimed was from the actual cross on which Jesus was crucified, a bit of cloth that baby Jesus was wrapped in, straw from the manger, or bread crumbs and fish bones from the Last Supper. A church in Paris claimed to have Christ's actual crown of thorns on display; another in Constantinople said they had the lance that pierced Christ on the cross, whereas five different churches in France said they had the "one authentic relic of Christ's circumcision." Of course, none of these were genuine, but the Church made a lot of money by selling them or allowing unwitting believers—who believed the relics had healing or other powers—to view them. The Protestants also wanted the clergy to be allowed to marry and to celebrate Mass in the vernacular. At first, Pope Leo X did not take Luther seriously, saying that he was "some drunken German who will amend his ways when he sobers up." But later he ordered that the rebellious priest be excommunicated and his pamphlets burned. He even declared Luther an outlaw, which meant that anyone could kill him without fear of punishment.

The result of the protests was not just a single schism in the Church, but dozens of fractures. Puritans, Lutherans, Anglicans, Presbyterians, Huguenots, Quakers, Millenarians, Antinomians, Brownists, Separatists, Seekers, Ranters, Anabaptists, and other Protestant groups began gaining ground throughout Europe. In 1525 Luther wrote, "There are nowadays almost as many sects and creeds as there are heads." An English pamphleteer listed 29 sects of Christianity in 1641. By 1649 another list included more than 180 denominations. The next century was one of the most violent in history. There were sacks, sieges, assassinations, massacres, and seesaw battles as Christian sects battled over alternative interpretations of the Bible and the new boundaries of Europe. Before the turmoil was over, there were calls for a stable, secular political order and for a more secular theatre.

The great crisis within Christianity ended liturgical drama in many parts of Europe. The fundamental problem was that each play had its own interpretation of the stories and lessons of the Bible. In 1539 the Roman Catholic Church decreed that church officials could produce no liturgical drama without prior approval. In Protestant countries, religious plays were often viewed as a relic of Catholicism and their performance was forbidden. Soon, monarchs all over Europe were curbing liturgical plays. In Paris, religious plays were forbidden in 1548, and shortly thereafter they were banned in England. By 1550, religious plays had almost disappeared from Italy. (However, Spain, dominated by Catholicism, did not forbid religious dramas until 1765.) As theatre became more secular, it became safer to perform and thus began to grow. Even the pope got into the act: Pope Leo X had a ballroom theatre built at the Vatican and was said to laugh "heartily" at secular plays.

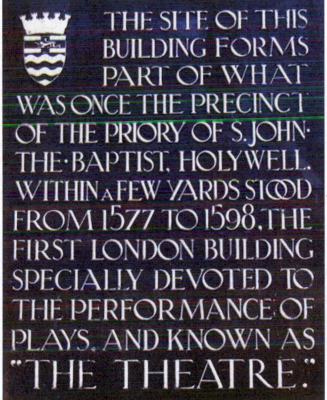

Plaque outside The Theatre, 1920, Shoreditch, England.

The first permanent theatre building to be erected in London in the post-Roman era was constructed in 1577 and was simply called, "The Theatre." In 1598 it was torn down, but its timbers were reused in the construction of Shakespeare's Globe. Today, on the spot where The Theatre once stood, there is only this small plaque hanging on the side of an office building.

I remit to you all punishment which you deserve in purgatory on their account, and I restore you to the holy sacraments of the Church . . . and to that innocence and purity which you possessed at baptism; so that when you die the gates of punishment shall be shut, and the gates of the paradise of delight shall be opened; and if you shall not die at present, this grace shall remain in full force when you are at the point of death.

A standard indulgence,
Associated with St. Peter's Basilica, Rome, ca. 1500

Curtain Call

By the 1400s, mystery, miracle, and morality plays still dominated, but secular plays ruled in court and at universities. By 1450 interludes were no longer short plays stuck in between other entertainments but had evolved into full-length plays. As the trickle of ancient knowledge became a flood, the plays of Roman and Greek playwrights were widely translated into the vernacular and imitated. Much had been lost—of the 123 plays of Sophocles once housed in the Library of Alexandria, only seven survived. Of Aristotle's two books on playwriting, only one remained. Of the thousands of books on science, philosophy, astronomy, and medicine, only a fraction had escaped destruction. Yet it was enough, for Europeans now stood on the cusp of the Renaissance and seemed to know it. The Italian poet Francesco Petrarch (1304–1374) wrote, "We must awake or die!"

SUMMARY

MindTap®

Test your knowledge with online printable flashcards and online quizzing.

The early Roman Catholic Church was not fond of theatre. As it gained power after the fall of the Roman Empire, it threatened excommunication for all who attended the theatre and deprived actors of all rights, even the right to salvation. During the Dark Ages, the Church virtually ended theatre. In the Middle Ages it used plays to educate the illiterate masses in their faith. These early liturgical plays most likely grew out of tropes and brief plays on Biblical themes that were acted by priests and choirboys. However, when these little plays began interfering with religious services, they were moved outside the church and priests were forbidden to act. Soon trade-guild members took over the acting, and liturgical plays were staged on movable pageant wagons during religious festivals and special public occasions. Three types of plays became popular during the Middle Ages: mystery plays, miracle plays, and morality plays.

During the High Middle Ages, the rediscovery of ancient knowledge led to a resurgence of interest in the ideas of Aristotle. Aristotelian Scholasticism, the synthesis of Aristotle's philosophy with the doctrine of the Roman Catholic Church, had an enormous impact on European thinking and society. Aristotle's theory of causality marked a critical turning point in theatre. Centuries before the birth of the study of psychology, the theory of causality provided a rudimentary analysis of a character's motivation. During this time, theatre began moving back to the secular realm with interludes, brief nonreligious plays performed between cycles of mystery plays, as a part of other entertainments, or at court for special occasions.

At the dawn of the Renaissance, people began looking back and embracing the philosophical, scientific, and artistic accomplishments of antiquity. The invention of the printing press helped spread this ancient knowledge, and the humanist revolution called for a new form of theatre that modeled Aristotle's classical teachings. The Protestant Reformation was another blow to liturgical drama as different denominations warred over interpretations of the Bible stories of the plays. Theatre began moving toward secular themes, and religious plays were banned in many areas of Europe.

THEATRE
THROUGH THE MIDDLE AGES

THEATRICAL EVENTS AND PLAYS

HISTORICAL / CULTURAL EVENTS

500

• Theatre is all but extinct in medieval Europe (533–900)

550

• Buddhism introduced to Japan (ca. 552)
• Mohammed (ca. 570–632)
• Block printing introduced in China (ca. 590)

600

• First theatre in China is built (610)

650

• Muslims conquer Syria, Persia, and Egypt (636–651)

700

• Pear Garden theatricals of Emperor Ming Huang of China (714)

800

THEATRICAL EVENTS AND PLAYS

HISTORICAL / CULTURAL EVENTS

900

- Sanskrit drama begins to decline (900)
- Liturgical playlets incorporated into Easter Mass (923)
- Hroswitha (ca. 935–ca. 1001)

1000

- Reconquest of Spain begins (1000)
- Crusades (1095–1270)

1100

- Simple plays in religious services are popular in Europe (ca. 1150)

1200

- Sanskrit drama ceases (1206)
- Pope Innocent III bans plays in religious services (1210)
- The Church allows plays during Feast of Corpus Christi (1264)
- Flowering of theatre in China (1280–1368)

- Muslims conquer central and northern India (1206)
- Magna Carta drafted (1215)
- St. Thomas Aquinas (1225–1274)
- Inquisition begins (1231)
- Yuan (Mongol) dynasty in China (1280–1368)

1300

- Cycle plays begin (ca. 1300)

- Bubonic plague strikes Europe (1348–1353)

1350

- Mystery and miracle plays popular in Europe (ca. 1350–1575)
- Noh drama begins in Japan (ca. 1374)
- *The Second Shepherd's Play* (ca. 1375)

- Kingdom of Ayutthaya (Thailand) established (1350)
- Filippo Brunelleschi, inventor of perspective painting (1377–1446)
- Papal Schism (1378–1417)

THEATRICAL EVENTS AND PLAYS

HISTORICAL / CULTURAL EVENTS

1400

- Morality plays popular in Europe (ca. 1400–1550)
- Zenchiku, Noh actor (1405–1470)

- Construction of Forbidden City begins in Beijing (1406)
- Inca Empire in western South America (1438–1533)

1450

- Noh theatre is popular in Japan (ca. 1450)
- *Everyman* (ca. 1495)

- Johannes Gutenberg invents printing press (ca. 1450)
- Constantinople falls to the Ottoman Turks (1453)
- Sistine Chapel is built in Rome (1473)
- First ballet danced as entertainment for Duke of Milan (1489)
- Christians "reconquer" Spain from Muslims (1492)

1500

- *Mona Lisa,* Leonardo da Vinci (1503)
- Martin Luther launches the Reformation (1517)

KEY TERMS

Chapter **15**

THE RENAISSANCE

One of the few surviving Renaissance theatres is the Teatro Olimpico in Vicenza, Italy. Notice the perspective scenery located within the doors, which was installed in 1585 and is the oldest surviving stage set in existence.

William Missouri Downs

Outline

MindTap®

Start with a quick warm-up activity and review the chapter's learning objectives.

The Renaissance was a time of great contrasts. In many countries the right to put children to work was protected by the law. Imprisonment for debt was common. Capital crimes often included murder, treason, heresy, witchcraft, robbery, counterfeiting, perjury, adultery, rape, homosexuality, and attempted suicide. What today might be called pornography was commonly seen, as street vendors sold erotic drawings on corners. Everyone was armed with at least a dagger. In many countries the legal age for marriage was fourteen for boys and twelve for girls (Romeo and Juliet are fourteen and twelve). And yet this was also a time when the ancient books of Archimedes were rediscovered, stimulating the study of math. The words of the great Roman orator and philosopher Cicero were being read again. Plato and Aristotle were becoming available in a small number of local libraries. The numbers of universities were growing and, although knowledge of the world was often limited by the church, there were still more intellectuals who were attempting to broaden their minds.

During the Renaissance, theatre in Europe fell into three broad categories. *Popular theatre* consisted of simple comedies and dramas for the common people, performed on the streets or in makeshift theatres, temporary structures, or found spaces such as arenas and courtyards. Later, with the establishment of permanent theatres, the work of such famed playwrights as Shakespeare, Calderón, and Molière became popular with the masses. *Humanist theatre*, which slavishly imitated ancient Greek and Roman plays, was popular with sovereigns, aristocrats, and intellectuals. The third category was *liturgical drama*, which continued to thrive in Spain after it had been outlawed in many other parts of Europe. Most Renaissance theatre was some variation or combination of these three types.

The Italian Influence

Although the intellectual and artistic thinking that typified the Renaissance appeared at different times in different parts of Europe, most scholars agree that the Renaissance first took hold in fourteenth-century Italy. Many theatrical movements that influenced theatre throughout Europe originated in Italy, including commedia dell'arte, humanist theatre, perspective scenery and the proscenium arch.

The Rebirth of Slapstick

As liturgical drama became less popular, the theatre of the common people morphed into simple comedies that were actually loose imitations of Plautus, Terence, and the Roman mimes (see Chapter 13). Traveling companies searched for crossroads, squares, and fairs where they could set up a makeshift platform and attract an audience. The most successful form of this theatre was the **commedia dell'arte**. It originated in Italy in the 1500s and became popular throughout Europe between 1550 and 1750. Its troupes of wandering players were not the amateur actors of the mysteries but professional actors who performed impromptu farces. It is from the commedia dell'arte that we get the word *slapstick*, which is comedy that stresses farce and horseplay. In commedia dell'arte, a slapstick is a device made of two pieces of wood hinged together so that they "slap." When the slapstick is applied to an actor's behind, it makes a

MindTap

Read, highlight and take notes online.

This 1657 painting by Karel Dujardin depicts the transitory nature of commedia dell'arte performances. Commedia troupes were a bit like traveling carnivals, setting up wherever they could attract an audience. Skilled professionals, commedia actors could often sing, dance, and play musical instruments as well as act and improvise. Notice the mask that the seated player is wearing. Stock masks and costumes cued audiences in to what characters the actors were playing. Most commedia masks were caricatures of human faces, but some of them depicted animal faces that represented the traits of a specific character.

Erich Lessing/Art Resource, NY

loud crack, as if the actor really were getting a painful licking; in fact the victim is in no pain.

Common subjects of commedia dell'arte plays are slaves tricking their masters, misunderstandings between lovers, and peasants who are smarter than aristocrats. There were no scripts, so the players improvised on basic scenarios, and no two performances were exactly the same. During parts of the performance, the actors may have improvised scenes based on suggestions from the audience, much like Drew Carey's televised comedy contest *Whose Line Is It Anyway?*

A company of commedia actors numbered from 5 to 25, and many included a few women. Each actor specialized in playing one particular stock character based on a common stereotype. These stock characters were distinguished not only by their roles but also by their costumes and masks. For example, the crafty **Arlecchino**, or **Harlequin**, is a servant of **Pantalone**, a stingy, retired Venetian merchant who often makes a fool of himself by courting young girls. The multicolored lozenges on Harlequin's costume represent the old rags he used to patch his pathetic, threadbare clothing. Other stock characters include **Scapino**, a servant and acrobat who is smarter than his master; **Innamorata** and **Innamorato**, a leading lady and leading man who are lovers; and **La Ruffiana**, a gossipy old woman who meddles in the affairs of the lovers. Once an actor mastered a particular role, he or she would play that role for life; one well-known actor was said to have played the "young lover" well into his seventies. Some of the actors even gave up their own names and took the names of their characters. Similar character types are found in the early twentieth-century slapstick of the Keystone Kops, Charlie Chaplin, and

The Theatro Olimpico in Vicenza Italy opened in 1585. Notice how it was built to imitate an ancient roman theatre, including an orchestra and curved theatron.

William Missouri Downs

the Three Stooges, as well as in modern sitcoms and movies such as *Gilligan's Island*, *Two and a Half Men*, *The Breakfast Club*, and *Meet the Parents*.

As the popularity of commedia dell'arte grew, even royal courts hosted performances to celebrate victories and marriages. In 1571 a troupe of commedia actors was summoned to Paris to perform on the occasion of the marriage of Charles IX; for the next 200 years, commedia dell'arte was a favorite of the French monarchs and spread throughout Europe. However, the Church looked upon these vagabond players as rogues and a public nuisance, so the lives of actors tended to be paradoxical: one day they were performing for kings, and the next they were being run out of town. One famous commedia player was a woman named Isabelle, an actress who took her stock character's name. It was said that she spoke three languages, played many musical instruments, and was well educated. She was highly respected, even by royalty. In 1604, while her company traveled between Paris and Italy, she fell ill and died. Her company of actors took her to the local church for burial, and the priest accorded her with full honors, including torchbearers and banners. However, because she was an actor, he would not allow her to be buried in consecrated ground, despite her talent and popularity.

Classical Correctness

By the sixteenth century, after the surviving plays of Aeschylus, Sophocles, Euripides, Plautus, Terence, and Seneca had been rediscovered, translated, and published, the humanist movement had become a powerful force in the theatre. Humanist theatre sought to mimic—even duplicate—the ideas, style, structure, and staging of ancient Greek and Roman theatre. For the humanists, imitation was the highest form of flattery. Two basic elements of humanist theatre were adherence to Aristotle's unities and declamatory acting.

In 1531 the first complete edition of Aristotle's writings was published. Included was the now famous *Poetics* (see Chapters 1, 4, and 13). Soon, humanists began to demand that Aristotelian dramatic principles be applied to drama of the day. Aristotle, they argued, was obviously an authority on philosophy, religion, and the natural sciences, so how could anyone question his wisdom when it came to writing a play? This was the beginning of what became known as the **three unities**, which were rigid rules for playwriting. The unities became the absolute form of classical correctness, even though they were in fact a misinterpretation of Aristotle's writing by Renaissance scholars. The unities require that the action of a play take place within a period of 24 hours (unity of time), that comedy and tragedy never commingle (unity of action), and that all the settings in a play can be reached within 24 hours (unity of place)—although this last requirement was in fact an embellishment of Aristotle's theories. Theatre critics' compliments and condemnations of plays were based solely on the three unities. In fact, in France plays were censured if they failed to observe the unities. It might seem strange that the innovative artists of the Renaissance would be so rigid about artistic expression in the theatre, but one of the hallmarks of the period was its adherence to the authority of the ancient scholars.

In France and Italy, theatre artists also sought to imitate ancient Greek plays and acting. A host of theatres revived the classical plays, and playwrights emulated the scripts of Aeschylus, Sophocles, and Euripides. An oratorical, elocutionary method called **declamatory acting** also became popular. In this style, actors delivered their lines directly to the audience in a rhetorical manner typified by order, harmony, and decorum. The actors were relying on the word of humanist scholars who believed this must have been how acting was done in the days of the ancient Greeks. In fact, the scholars were only guessing, for there is no record. Other humanist scholars believed that ancient Greek plays were entirely sung. This led to a new type of theatre at the end of the sixteenth century called *opera*. (For more on the humanist movement, see Chapter 14.)

> What can be more absurd than the introduction in the first scene of a child in swaddling clothes, who in the second appears as a bearded man?
>
> **Miguel de Cervantes,** Author of Don Quixote, advocating the three unities

The Baroque Theatre of the Krumlov Castle complex in the Czech Republic is still used as a theatre and is lit by candlelight, just as it was during the Renaissance. However, because of its age, performances are allowed only once a year.

Pavel Slavko

Italian Perspective Scenery

In 1414 *De Architectura,* an encyclopedic text by the Roman architect Vitruvius (ca. first century BCE) was rediscovered. One of its volumes dealt with theatre design. Soon Italian humanists were using Vitruvius's guidelines and their knowledge of the ruins of ancient Roman theatres to build new theatres throughout Italy. These theatres copied the Roman semicircular *theatron,* the curved *orchestra,* and the *skene* building. The major difference was that the Italian theatres were indoors and lit with candles. This architectural change required the addition of intermissions so that the candles could be relit. Although theatres are no longer lighted with candles, we keep the intermission as a relic of the Italian Renaissance and those first indoor theatres.

The Italians also gave the theatre **perspective scenery.** Filippo Brunelleschi (1377–1446), the first important architect of the Italian Renaissance, is credited with inventing perspective painting. This type of painting relies on converging lines and a vanishing point to create the illusion of three-dimensional reality on a flat, two-dimensional surface. The innovation of perspective made medieval art seem flat and cartoonish. In contrast, Renaissance art depicted depth, motion, and realism. In order to make perspective painting work in the theatre, designers added a picture frame known as the proscenium arch. Then they angled, or "raked," the stage floor up toward a vanishing point. The resulting three-dimensional set became all the rage. Today, even though stage floors are no longer raked, the area farthest from the audience is still called **upstage** and the area closest to the audience is called **downstage.**

Most indoor theatres during the Renaissance were lit by candles but the Teatro Olimpico was also lit by oil lamps. Here is a 500-year-old example of theatre lighting technology.

Teatro Olimpico, Vicenza, Italy

Spanish Theatre

Due to the reconquest and the Inquisition, Spain was now strongly and almost entirely Catholic and did not have many struggles with conflicting Christian sects. This gave Spain a certain stability, which allowed it to have a larger empire in the New World than any other European country, but it also delayed the coming of the Renaissance to this country. The Spanish failed to embrace humanism and the flood of ancient Greek and Roman knowledge. In the theatre, the unities never caught on and the Church remained fully in control. Religious dramas called *autos sacramentales* were still being performed in Spain 200 years after liturgical plays had lost popularity in the rest of Europe. While Italians were building theatres with proscenium arches and perspective scenery, Spanish drama was still being performed on pageant wagons or on crude platform-stages called *corrales,* temporary structures built in the courtyards of inns. Secular plays were allowed, but they often had liturgical themes and were flavored with patriotism. The Golden Age of Spanish theatre arrived in the seventeenth century with two influential playwrights: Lope de Vega and Calderón.

Félix Lope de Vega y Carpio (1562–1635), commonly known as Lope de Vega, is considered one of the most influential Spanish playwrights and was certainly the most prolific. He claimed to have written over 2,200 plays, but the number is probably closer to the 400 or so that have survived. He once boasted that he wrote ten plays in one week and an entire play before breakfast. In any case, he wrote hundreds of *autos sacramentales* as well as historical dramas, intrigues, and "cloak-and-sword" plays, with fast-moving plots about love, honor, and vindication. His most popular work, *The Sheep Well* (1614), was about the murder of a tyrannical feudal lord by humble villagers. Under torture by authorities, the villagers stand strong and refuse to confess or name names. In the end, they are saved by the intervention of a good king. In his plays, Lope de Vega was an idealist: God inspires kings, common people should obey the

400 years after his death, Lope de Vega is still one of the most popular Spanish playwrights. His home in Madrid is a museum visited by tens of thousands of people every year.

William Missouri Downs

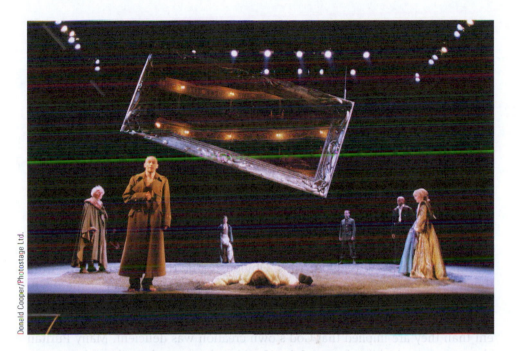

Donald Cooper/Photostage Ltd.

Although more than 30,000 plays may have been written during the Golden Age of Spanish drama, most were about a narrow code of honor, which limited their historical significance. One exception is Calderón's *Life Is a Dream*, which explores destiny, free will, and complex human motivation. Because of its universal appeal, this play is often produced today. This 1998 production featured George Anton (foreground) as Sigismund. Directed by Calixto Bieto, Lyceum Theatre Company, Edinburgh.

king as well as the Church, and personal honor must not be betrayed. He also wrote comedies, such as *Dog in the Manger* (1615), which is about a common man who loves and is loved by both a princess and her lady-in-waiting.

Pedro Calderón de la Barca (1600–1681) also wrote hundreds of *autos sacramentales* and secular "cloak-and-sword" plays that reflected the Spanish values of love, honor, revenge, and religious servitude. But Calderón's plays had more symbolism and depth than Lope de Vega's. Of all Calderón's works, *Life Is a Dream* (1635) is regarded as having the most universal theme. The play explores the mysteries of human destiny and the conflicts between free will, predestination, and human motivation. The story is about a king of Poland who imprisons his son Sigismund at birth because the stars have told him that his son will lead a rebellion against him. Sigismund grows up chained in a dank dungeon. Cut off from human contact, he, of course, becomes a savage beast. But then his father, suffering the guilt pangs of old age, relents and allows his son to join him in the castle. When Sigismund is taken from his dungeon to court, he proves to be a violent, thoughtless, and ruthless being. The king drugs Sigismund and banishes him back to his cell. When Sigismund awakes, he finds himself back in chains. He isn't sure if his journey to the castle was real or a dream. Sigismund vows to change and become a just human being. In the end he defeats his cruel father and becomes king. *Life Is a Dream* was a play ahead of its time because it attempted to explain the human character as being shaped by environmental and psychological causes rather than predetermined by fate or dictated by "final cause" (see Chapter 14 for information on Aristotle's theory of causality).

Elizabethan Theatre

In England the first secular theatre grew out of the universities, where students studying the ancient Greek and Roman playwrights formed clubs to stage private performances of classical plays. These students and their professors wrote plays that replicated those of the ancients. One student thespian group, the **University Wits**, included such soon-to-be-famous playwrights as Thomas Kyd (1558–1594) and Christopher Marlowe (1564–1593). Even grammar schools were producing translations and imitations of classical plays. It wasn't long before **boy companies** were also producing classical plays. These boy companies were not amateur groups but professional, organized companies of boys who competed with adult acting troupes in the temporary theatres erected all over London.

When Elizabeth I became queen of England in 1558, there wasn't a single professional theatre in London. By the time of her death in 1603, London had been transformed into one of the theatre capitals of the world. Actually, the theatres were not *in* London but in its suburbs, because after 1574 theatre was banned within the city limits due to the protests of a religious group called the **Puritans.** The Puritans got their name from their zeal to "purify" the church. The only way to escape the fires of hell, according to the Puritans, was through hard work, abstinence from all profane amusements and sensual pleasures, and careful observance of religious rites. Obviously, the theatre kept people from their work, so the Puritans condemned theatre as a temptation of the devil. In addition, they felt that enacting stories spun from one's imagination placed one in a blasphemous rivalry with God—to wish that things should be different than they are implied that God's own creation was deficient. Many Puritan clergymen attacked the theatre. John Northbrooke wrote that all one learns at a theatre is how to "deceive your husband, or husbands their wives, how to play the harlot to obtain anyone's love, how to ravish, how to beguile, how to betray, flatter, lie, swear, foreswear, how to allure to whoredom, how to murder, how to poison . . . blaspheme, to sing filthy songs of love and speak filthy."

To avoid the London magistrates and the Puritans, theatre managers built their theatres outside the city limits. Two types of permanent public playhouses began appearing around London: small indoor theatres such as the Blackfriars, which catered to wealthy clientele, and huge outdoor theatres such as the Rose and the Globe, which were open to the general public.

In 1576 London's most famous indoor theatre (Blackfriars Theatre) was built by James Burbage (1531–1597), a carpenter and part-time actor. He skirted the anti-theatre laws by locating his theatre in an old Dominican friary called **Blackfriars**, which meant that technically the church owned the land, not the city. Many years earlier King Henry VIII had confiscated the land from the Catholic Church and no one had updated the laws; so Blackfriars was still not legally part of London. This loophole allowed Burbage to open his theatre, but he immediately ran into trouble. The citizens of Blackfriars petitioned the government saying that the theatre would gather together "vagrants and lewd persons" and that the "playhouse is so near the Church that the noise of the drums and trumpets will greatly disturb and hinder both the ministers and parishioners in time of divine service and sermons." In the end Burbage lost the battle and was forced to turn his theatre over to a boy company, which was considered both safer and quieter.

A year later, James Burbage also built London's first permanent outdoor theatre. This time he played it safe and built just outside the London city limits in an area known as Shoreditch. The structure was simply called "the Theatre." Shoreditch was a rundown neighborhood about as romantic as the name suggests. This first theatre proved to be so popular that there were soon a host of imitators. These theatres all followed the same basic design, like that of the Spanish *corrale*, with a platform stage jutting into the middle of an open courtyard encircled by tiers of gallery seats; on the floor around the stage was an area where people could stand and watch the show.

One of the most famous outdoor theatres was the Rose, built on the south side of the Thames in an area famous for such dubious attractions as brothels, prisons, gunpowder storehouses, lunatic asylums, unconsecrated graveyards, and bear-baiting arenas. Bear-baiting involved tying a bear to a stake at the center of the arena and unleashing packs of dogs; the bear killed dozens of dogs, but eventually the dogs overwhelmed the bear. Here, among such less than desirable "entertainments," the Rose and several other theatres were built. The Rose was known for its clogged drainage system, which sometimes smelled so bad that a performance had to be cancelled. When Shakespeare's *Romeo and Juliet* was performed in the nearby Globe, Juliet's line "What's in a name? That which we call a rose by any other name would smell as sweet" most likely brought down the house with gales of laughter because the audience knew it was a reference to the Rose's less-than-pleasant odor.

By the late 1500s, every Londoner was within two miles of a theatre of some kind, and all theatres were doing a profitable business. Wanting in on some of the action, the owner of the land on which the Theatre stood decided to triple his rental fee. Rather than pay, Burbage moved his theatre out of Shoreditch. He found a plot of land on the south bank of the Thames, only "97 paces" from the Rose, and set about pulling down the Theatre and carting the timbers several miles to the new location. At the new site, rather than simply reconstructing the Theatre, the company built a fancier playhouse using parts from the old one. The new theatre's sign contained the image of the mythological Atlas bearing the weight of the world on his shoulders. Perhaps it symbolized the effort it had taken to move the timbers to the new location, or perhaps it simply illustrated the theatre's new name, the Globe.

William Missouri Downs

In 1989 crews working on a new ten-story office building on Southwark Bridge Road in London discovered the buried remains of the Rose Theatre. In order to preserve the ruins, the building was redesigned. Today, in the basement of the "Rose Court" office building you can find the foundations of the Rose Theatre, the first theatre in which Shakespeare acted.

The World of the Globe

Performances at the Globe and the other outdoor theatres began at about two in the afternoon when daylight flooded the stage and lasted until about five.

[N]either at their standing in the streets, nor before the comedy begin, nor all the time there, any rude or immodest exclamations be made; nor any humming, hawking, whistling, hissing, or laughing be used, or any stamping or knocking, . . . nor that any clapping of hands be had . . . except his Majesty, the Queen, or others of the best quality here, do apparently begin the same.

Rules for audience conduct at a Cambridge University play put on for the king, 1632

This schedule led to criticism from the Puritans because the theatre was obviously causing people to idle away their afternoons when they should be working. The Puritans, in their attempt to close all theatres in the London area, managed to get laws passed that forbade anyone from advertising a production. So theatre owners found ingenious ways to publicize their product. One method was with flags—a black flag over the theatre meant that the day's performance would be a tragedy, a white flag signified a comedy, and red signified a history play.

A trumpet fanfare proclaimed that the performance was about to begin, and the audience, as many as 2,800 people, entered the doughnut-shaped theatre through a narrow office where a box was located. The theatregoers dropped payment into the box—hence the modern phrase **box office**. The cheapest tickets were for the main floor, where about 800 people stood elbow-to-elbow in a mob known as the **groundlings**. A ticket for a groundling was cheap, costing only about as much as a quart of ale at a local pub. For an extra charge, one could climb the stairs to the galleries on the second and third floors, from which about 2,000 patrons could look down on the production from the comfort of cushioned benches. The population of London at that time was approximately 200,000, so if the Globe was filled to capacity it meant that one out of every 70 Londoners was sitting or standing in its playhouse.

Once inside the Globe, the audience found themselves amidst multi-colored flags, curtains, and ribbons. The wooden pillars and banisters were painted to simulate marble. It was all for show, however. In reality the accommodations were quite rudimentary. For example, there was no privy—men simply relieved themselves on stones out back, and women just had to wait. During the performance vendors sold ale, water, gingerbread, oranges, and apples, all of which were occasionally used as ammunition if the audience didn't like the play or players. The behavior of an Elizabethan audience was poor by today's standards. Not only did people talk and eat

When the puritans outlawed theatre advertisements within the city of London, theatres such as the Globe and the Rose (shown here) used flags to promote the type of play to be shown that day. A white flag meant comedy, a black flag signified tragedy, and a red flag denoted a history play.

William Missouri Downs

during the performance, but reportedly prostitutes and pickpockets often worked the crowds. A pamphlet written at that time warned London newcomers to avoid the theatres. It closes with this amusing story about pickpockets in the crowded theatres:

> A tradesman's wife of the Exchange, one day when her husband was following some business in the city, desired him he would give her leave to go see a play; which she had not done in seven years. He bade her take his apprentice along with her, and go; but especially to have a care of her purse; which she warranted him she would. Sitting in a box, among some gallants and gallant wenches, and returning when the play was done, returned to her husband and told him she had lost her purse. "Wife (quoth he) did I not give you warning of it? How much money was there in it?" Quoth she, "Truly, four pieces, six shilling and a silver tooth-picker." Quoth her husband, "Where did you put it?" "Under my petticoat, between that and my smock." "What (quoth he,) did you feel no body's hand there?" "Yes (quoth she) I felt one's hand there, but I did not think he had come for that."

Plays at the Globe moved fast and aimed to please. Because the unities never caught on in England, the locations of scenes were limited only by the playwright's imagination. Storylines moved freely from location to location just as modern motion pictures do. Shakespeare's *Antony and Cleopatra*, for example, shifts smoothly between ancient Egypt and Rome. Because the theatres were outdoors, there were no candles to relight and no need for intermissions. The five-act structure of Shakespeare's plays was added after his death.

The scenery of Elizabethan theatre was minimal; the plays used what is called **verbal scene painting**. English playwrights, like their Spanish counterparts, let their words paint pictures so that the audience could "dress" the stage in their imagination. For example, in Shakespeare's *Macbeth*, the king paints the scene of a large manor in a picturesque rural landscape when he says, "This castle hath a pleasant seat; the air nimbly and sweetly recommends itself unto our gentle senses." The Elizabethan audience needed nothing more.

What these productions lacked in sets, they made up for in costumes, which were often extravagant affairs of gold, lace, silk, and velvet, donated to the theatre by aristocratic patrons. There was no attempt, however, to make the costumes historically accurate. Actors performing Shakespeare's *Julius Caesar* (1598) wore Elizabethan costumes, not togas. Their aim was not to give a history lesson but to entertain. Performances had music and plenty of special effects and realistic swordplay. Actors hid bladders filled with sheep's blood under their costumes so that during fight sequences, when they were "stabbed," real blood would ooze out. The stage was filled with trapdoors so that actors playing ghosts and spirits could mysteriously appear and disappear. Above the stage were cannons filled with blanks that could be fired to create realistic battle sequences.

Actors had little time to learn their parts, for theatres often put on a different play every day—except when bad weather or a plague closed the playhouses. Instead of weeks or months, as is often the case today, actors

In 1949, American actor Sam Wanamaker set out to find the spot where Shakespeare's Globe Theatre had stood. He was shocked to find that the only memorial was a blackened bronze plaque on the wall of a brewery. Determined to create a better monument, he began a campaign to raise millions of dollars to build a faithful replica of the Globe. It took decades and, although Wanamaker did not live to see the completion of his dream, Shakespeare's Globe stands again through his efforts, only a few blocks from its original site. The exterior (top) and interior (center & bottom) were painstakingly researched for authenticity, but no one knows for sure exactly what Shakespeare's Globe looked like.

Lou Anne Wright

William Missouri Downs

William Missouri Downs

often had only hours to figure out their blocking, rehearse fight sequences, stage dance numbers, and learn their lines. To make preparing even more difficult, the actors were not given a full script but only their lines handwritten on a roll of paper. This is the source of the theatre terms *part* and *role*, for the actors were given only a *part* of the script, and their lines were written on a *roll* of paper.

A company of actors in Shakespeare's day consisted of 8 to 15 players. Some of the actors, such as Shakespeare himself, were shareholders who divided the company's profits or losses, and others were hired to act in a single production and paid a set fee or a percentage of the box office. Each company would also have two or three boy apprentices who were trained to play women's parts because women were not allowed on the stage (although some women did appear). Boys played the role of Juliet and other young women, and mature men played older female characters, such as Juliet's nurse. The practice of men and boys dressing up as women was typically condemned by clergy and was one of the many reasons actors were often damned as scoundrels and scourges.

During the outdoor productions of Shakespeare's day, audiences did not see complex stage sets. Instead, actors used verbal scene painting to describe the play's various settings. Only a few simple props were used to hint at the location and situation. A potted sapling might represent a dark forest; a royal chair might indicate a golden throne room; or, as in this production of *The Tempest*, a ship's wheel could represent the entire vessel. This production featured Geraldine Alexander as Ariel, the spirit helper to the play's protagonist, Prospero. Directed by Lenka Udovicki, Shakespeare's Globe, 2000.

Rogues and Vagabonds

Religious leaders frequently condemned the theatre in Shakespeare's time because it was deemed obscene, morally lacking, and thought to contain adulterous scenes, all of which aroused dangerous passions in the youth. The Puritans particularly hated the theatre. They labeled all who attended drunkards, thieves, prostitutes, and criminals. But they saved their worst condemnation for the actors, whom they labeled scoundrels doomed to everlasting hellfire. One of the many books published at this time that rebuked the theatre was *The Anatomy of Abuses* (1583), which said that actors were ordained by the devil, and consecrated by "Heathen Gods to draw us away from Christianity and towards idolatry."

Women were not allowed on stage in Shakespeare's England, although on occasion a few managed to sneak on. (See Spotlight "Women on Stage.") Men and boys had to dress up as women; this led to even more condemnation because the Bible expressly calls such cross-dressing an "abomination" (Deuteronomy 22:5). It was also considered wicked for anyone to dress outside their rank in society, which actors had to do in order to play kings, lords, and ladies. It was a very great insult to the Puritanical belief system for actors to

SPOTLIGHT ON Women on Stage

Women were not allowed to act on the English stage during Shakespeare's day; however, there are records of women surreptitiously making appearances—as portrayed in the 1998 movie *Shakespeare in Love*. In 1611 an ecclesiastical court charged Mary Frith (or Moll Cutpurse, as she was known) with appearing in a play called *The Roaring Girl* at the Fortune theatre. The word "Roaring" was used in Shakespeare's day to mean any person who was noisy, showy, or antisocial. Not only did she appear onstage, but she also played the role of a man, and had done so for several months before she was discovered. According to court records, during a performance she "sat upon the stage in the public view of all the people there present in man's apparel and played upon her lute and sang a song." A witness to her trial wrote that she wept before the judge, but he wasn't sure if this was an act or not because she "tippled some three quarts of sack before she came to her penance." She was sentenced to six months in the notorious Bridewell Prison where she was urged to contemplate her sins.

A few years later King Charles I (1600–1649) invited a French theatre to perform in London. In France, women were a common sight in the theatre, but their presence on the English stage was too much for the locals. The actresses were hissed off the boards. Women would first legally appear on the English stage in 1661. (See Chapter 16.)

One hundred years later, after women were legally allowed on stage in Europe and America, there were still many people who condemned them for performing; it was typical of religious leaders at the time to believe that women should not display themselves in public. Acting in a play was considered unnatural, immodest, and unwomanly. Further complicating the issue, by the 1800s, several women had risen to become managers of theatre companies. This put significant power in the hands of the "weaker sex." Reverend Robert Turnbull wrote that such power could cause women to develop "distaste for simple and home born enjoyments, as well as for sober everyday duties." It wasn't until the mid 1800s that women began to be generally accepted as a part of the Western theatre.

Donald Cooper/Photostage Ltd.

Although women are allowed on most stages today, the notion of men playing women's roles and vice versa intrigues many directors. Mark Rylance, past managing artistic director of Shakespeare's Globe Theatre, is well known for playing around with gender roles. He's played Cleopatra in *Antony and Cleopatra* and has staged an all-female production of *The Taming of the Shrew* and an all-male production of *Twelfth Night*. In *Twelfth Night* he played Olivia, the woman who has fallen in love with Cesario, the young man who is actually Viola, a young woman who decided to make her way in the world by dressing as a man. This production featured Michael Brown (right) as Viola/Cesario. Directed by Tim Carroll, Shakespeare's Globe, 2002.

parade around the stage in the finery of aristocracy when God had placed them in a lowly societal position.

Actors and playwrights sometimes made the situation worse by attacking those who were critical of them. One of those playwrights who made fun of the Puritans' pious pontifications was William Shakespeare. In his play *Twelfth Night* (ca. 1600) Shakespeare includes the character of Malvolio, a loathsome Puritan busybody who lectures the other characters about principles during the rowdy Christmas holiday of Twelfth Night. In addition Ben Jonson had great fun parodying the Puritans in his play *Bartholomew Fair* (1614).

Prodded by the Puritans, the English government passed the "Vagabond Act," which stated that any person, including entertainers and actors, who were caught roaming the countryside "masterless" would be deemed rogues and vagabonds. Such lowlifes could be branded on the chest with the letter "V," and taken into slavery for two years. If the rogue was found a second time roaming the country without a job, he could be branded on the cheek with the letter S and condemned to servitude for life.

To protect themselves, acting companies sought legal immunity. They found that the best protection was the patronage of a lord or other noble, preferably a member of the royal family, who often enjoyed the theatre. If they had the patronage of a lord, earl, or king, a theatre company could wear its noble master's colors and take his name. The actors at the Globe became "the Lord Chamberlain's Men." The Lord Chamberlain was Queen Elizabeth's cousin and was responsible for the conduct of theatres and the presentation of plays at court. An acting company could not have much safer patronage than that. After Queen Elizabeth's death, the Globe's players became "the King's Men" under King James I (1566–1625). With this new notable title they became the premier acting company in London. The King's Men performed for King James 187 times, but they were still never totally safe from prosecution.

John Quincy Adams Ward, William Shakespeare, 1870, New York City, New York.

This statue of Shakespeare in New York City's Central Park was unveiled in 1872. It was funded by the famous American actor Edwin Booth, older brother to the Assassin John Wilkes Booth.

Shakespeare and His Contemporaries

Most would agree that William Shakespeare was the most influential writer of the Elizabethan theatre, but he was certainly not the only, or even the best known, playwright of his time. Between the end of the sixteenth century and the beginning of the seventeenth, England turned out a number of noted playwrights. Before we look at the Bard, let's take a look at two of the playwrights whose work now lives on in the shadow of Shakespeare's.

Christopher Marlowe: A University Man

Born two months before Shakespeare, Christopher Marlowe (1564–1593) was the son of a shoemaker (Shakespeare was the son of a glove maker). Unlike Shakespeare, Marlowe was formally educated at the University of Cambridge, where he received a bachelor's and a master's degree and was a member of the University Wits. When Shakespeare was a mere actor and had not yet written a play, Marlowe was already a leading member of the Lord Admiral's company at the Rose theatre and one of the top playwrights in London. He was also living a mysterious life as a spy for the Protestant Queen Elizabeth, who kept an eye on the Catholics. In many ways, Marlowe was a true Renaissance man. He loved scholarship, hated ignorance, and wrote plays that were filled with classical allusions and about characters who were seeking knowledge. Among his most famous are *The Jew of Malta* (1590), a tragedy about a hero who seeks limitless wealth, and *The Tragical History of Doctor Faustus* (1589), about a scholar in Germany who desires limitless knowledge at any cost. Faustus has grown bored with the traditional forms of gaining knowledge and decides to sell his soul to Lucifer so that he may learn all there is to know about the nature of the world. Lucifer provides Faustus with a devil, Mephastophilis (Marlowe's spelling of Mephistopheles), who serves him for 24 years, helping him gain knowledge, riches, and fame. Despite occasional misgivings about his deal with Lucifer, Faustus never repents and his soul is eventually delivered to hell—through the trapdoor at the center of the stage. So powerful was this play, in this age of religious superstition and fear of evil spirits, that the lead actor always wore a cross around his neck and ecclesiastical garments under his costume—just in case.

In many ways, *Faustus* is autobiographical, for Marlowe was a scholar who yearned to know the unknown. He even joined a group of freethinkers led by soldier, explorer, and writer Sir Walter Raleigh that studied astronomy, philosophy, and secular rather than sanctified ways of looking at Scripture. In 1593 Marlowe made the mistake of publicly pointing out some inconsistencies in the Bible and was charged with heresy. The authorities couldn't find him, so they arrested his roommate, the playwright Thomas Kyd, best known for *The Spanish Tragedy* (1589), a bloody tale of ghosts, revenge, and so many homicides that hardly a character was left standing at the end (this play inspired Shakespeare to write *Hamlet*). Kyd was taken to a prison near the Tower of London and tortured on the rack, a crude device that stretched the victim's body until it dislocated his joints. He finally gave in and acknowledged that his roommate had made the offending remarks. He said that Marlowe was "irreligious, intemperate, and of cruel heart" and that he would often "jest at the divine Scriptures." Punishment for such an offense was a long imprisonment in one of London's dark dungeons or, if one were lucky, just having both ears cut off. But Marlowe would never find out which punishment awaited him; before he could be arrested the 29-year-old playwright was murdered during a fight over a bill at a restaurant. Some were not entirely sorry about his death—the Church claimed that God had punished him for his atheism, and Queen Elizabeth was probably pleased to avoid a scandal concerning one of her spies. Thomas Kyd, a broken man, died a year later.

Ben Jonson: The First Poet Laureate

Another of the talented playwrights of Shakespeare's day was his friend Ben Jonson. As a youth, Jonson (1573–1637) had worked for several years as an apprentice bricklayer, but the trade did not agree with him. We do not know exactly when he became an actor and playwright, but by 1597 he was in trouble with the censors. In that year Jonson co-wrote the play *The Isle of Dogs*, a satiric comedy that was labeled "lewd and slanderous." As a result, the Rose theatre, where the play had been staged, was closed for three months and Jonson and several other actors were imprisoned. Upon his release, Jonson joined

Donald Cooper/Photostage Ltd.

Christopher Marlowe's *The Tragical History of Doctor Faustus* is based on a medieval legend of a German doctor who decided to sell his soul to Lucifer. The story of Faustus has inspired dozens of works over the centuries, including Queen's song "Bohemian Rhapsody" (1975) and the movie *Bedazzled* (1967; remake, 2000). In this 2002 production of Marlowe's play at London's Young Vic Theatre, Jude Law (right) played Faustus and Richard McCabe (left) played Mephastophilis.

Nature that framed us of four elements,
Warring within our breast for regiment,
Doth teach us all to have aspiring minds:
Our souls whose faculties can comprehend
The wondrous Architecture of the world:
And measure every wandering planet's course,
Still climbing after knowledge infinite,
And always moving as the restless Spheres,
Will us to wear ourselves and never rest,
Until we reach the ripest fruit of all,
That perfect bliss and sole felicity,
The sweet fruition of an earthly crown.

Christopher Marlowe, in
The Tragical History
of Doctor Faustus

Shakespeare's company as an actor. The following year he got into a quarrel with an actor named Gabriel Spencer and killed Spencer during a duel.

Jonson once again found himself in prison, this time charged with murder. At his trial he managed to escape execution by pleading "benefit of clergy," a legal loophole that exempted clergy from common punishments. Jonson was not a member of the clergy, but he could do something that few outside the clergy could do in those days: He could read, and furthermore, he could even read Latin. All a felon had to do in order to claim "benefit of clergy" and avoid the gallows was to read Psalm 51:1–2 in Latin. "Have mercy upon me, O God, according to thy loving kindness: according unto the multitude of thy tender mercies blot out my transgressions. Wash me thoroughly from mine iniquity and cleanse me from my sins." It was reported that some Elizabethans who could not read memorized these lines in Latin just in case they should ever need them. Because of his learning Jonson was granted a reprieve. However, all his property was confiscated and he was branded on the thumb with the letter *T* that stood for "Tyburn," the place near London where executions took place. The branding

The British Library/HIP/The Image Works

Ben Jonson started as an apprentice bricklayer, but soon became an actor, playwright, and good friend of William Shakespeare. He wrote many plays, including *The Isle of Dogs* and *Every Man in His Humour*. Known for his temper, he once killed an actor in a duel. He was spared the gallows only because he could quote (in Latin) Psalm 51:1–2, which are known as the "hangman's verses."

was not only a warning to Jonson but would allow authorities to know that he was a second-time offender should he be arrested again. For the rest of his life, Jonson was a marked felon.

The following year Jonson wrote his first big hit, *Every Man in His Humour* (1598). Not only was the play produced by the Globe theatre but Shakespeare was in the cast. The following year he wrote *Every Man out of His Humour*. For Elizabethans, *humour*, which comes from the Latin word for "fluid," referred to the concept of four bodily humours that control temperament. The four humours are blood, phlegm, black bile, and yellow bile—a nice way of saying urine. Depending on the relative proportions of these humours, a person could be sanguine (cheerful and optimistic), phlegmatic (sluggish or unemotional), melancholic (depressed and withdrawn), or choleric (easily angered). Jonson's "humour" plays mocked human shortcomings and foibles. A few years later Jonson wrote his masterpiece *Volpone (or the Fox)* (1605), about a rich merchant who pretends to be near death in order to acquire sympathy gifts from three fortune hunters who hope to be his sole heir. Later in his life, Jonson wrote lyrical poetry and court masques (discussed in the next section of this chapter) that so pleased King James I that he was made the first poet laureate of England. Thereafter he was patronized by the rich and famous, although he was never wealthy himself.

At the end of his life, Jonson wanted to be buried in Westminster Abbey, but he lacked the money to buy a full-length burial site, so they took his limited funds and buried him standing up. This was confirmed in the nineteenth century when workers digging a new grave came upon his upright coffin. Today you can find his two-foot by two-foot grave in Westminster Abbey. It reads simply, "O Rare Ben Jonson."

William Shakespeare: The Bard

Very little is known about William Shakespeare (1564–1616). We do know that he was born in the small town of Stratford-upon-Avon, about 75 miles northwest of London; that his mother came from a prominent local family; and that his father, a man who had climbed Stratford's political ladder, fell on hard times and managed to spend his wife's entire inheritance. Shakespeare attended a well-respected elementary school, and then at the age of thirteen or fourteen, he dropped out in order to work full time in his father's tannery. At the age of eighteen, records show that Shakespeare was forced to make a hasty marriage to Anne Hathaway, who was eight years his senior and pregnant with his child. Six months later, Anne gave birth to a daughter, Susanna, and in 1585 twins, Judith and Hamnet, were born. When he was 28 he was living in London, apparently without his family, where he worked as an actor. By the age of 30 he was writing plays. By the age of 49 he had retired from writing and moved back to Stratford, where he died three years later after an alleged hard night of drinking with Ben Jonson. Other than that, there is frustratingly little information about one of the most influential writers of all time. From his birth to his death there are fewer than 50 historical references to Shakespeare, and most of these are documents about minor lawsuits and business dealings in addition to church registries and his will. Other than his plays, sonnets, and poems, there is also little evidence of a literary life. There are no Shakespeare letters, diaries, or other manuscripts. This lack of solid information has opened the way to speculation that Shakespeare was not the true author of the plays attributed to him but was just an actor who was a front man for some lord or duke. These skeptics are now called Anti-Stratfordians (see the Spotlight "The Most Famous Whodunit in Theatre").

Shakespeare seems to have arrived in London in 1592, when his name first appeared as that of an actor with the Lord Chamberlain's company. By 1598, he was a well-known performer; his name tops a list of actors in Ben Jonson's *Every Man in His Humour*. It's believed that he had begun writing plays around 1591. Most likely he had started as a play doctor—one who helps edit, fix, and adapt other playwrights' words. In 1592, when a plague hit London, the playhouses were forced to close, and many actors left the city to join companies of traveling players. However, according to many scholars, Shakespeare probably waited out the plague at the estate of Henry Wriothesley, the Earl of Southampton, a patron of the arts. It was here that he most likely wrote his first poems and sonnets, many of which celebrate his passionate relationships with a beautiful young man and a mysterious "dark lady."

After the playhouses reopened, Shakespeare quickly became popular as a playwright because he gave audiences what they wanted. He often started his plays with an event, a jolting moment to get the audience interested, just as many Hollywood screenwriters do today. He intensified his tragedies with comic

Shakespeare's plays have been adapted for countless operas, dance performances, and films. Baz Luhrmann's movie adaptation of *Romeo and Juliet*, starring Leonardo DiCaprio, is one of the most popular. Luhrmann retains the original Shakespearean dialogue but, in one modern twist, has the Capulets and the Montagues engage in gun fights rather than swordplay.

20th Century Fox Film Corp/Everett Collection

SPOTLIGHT ON The Most Famous Whodunit in Theatre

Anti-Stratfordians (sometimes called anti-Shakespeareans) are people who question whether Shakespeare really wrote all those wonderful plays. They don't deny the existence of William Shakespeare, but they simply can't bring themselves to believe he wrote the plays and poems attributed to him. They ask how a man with a limited education, an ordinary actor, the son of an illiterate glove maker, could write some of the greatest plays and most exquisite dialogue the world has ever known. They contend that only a well-educated, sophisticated, well-traveled aristocrat with an impressive vocabulary could have created the plays and that Shakespeare, a common actor, was nothing more than a front man.

Much has been made of Shakespeare's signature. Some suggest that he couldn't have been that literate because he spelled his name so many ways—Willm Shaksp, William Shakespe, William Shakspere, and William Shakspeare—sometimes even using different spellings on the same document. But we must remember that spelling was flexible in Elizabethan England. The first dictionaries didn't come out until 1604, and they were rare. It may well be that Shakespeare simply never decided exactly how he wanted to spell his name or was using shorthand. Anti-Stratfordians also point out that not a single letter in Shakespeare's hand has survived. One would think that a great literary playwright such as Shakespeare would have written hundreds of letters in his lifetime, and yet not one remains. Additionally, there is no record of Shakespeare ever attending college. How could someone without a college education write plays with detailed references to law, medicine, history, botany, astronomy, mythology, theology, literature, and court life as Shakespeare did? But Louis B. Wright, the great Shakespeare scholar, said, "The anti-Shakespeareans base their arguments upon a few simple premises, all of them false. . . . They forget that genius has a way of cropping up in unexpected places and that none of the great creative writers of the world got his inspiration in college or a university course."

Anti-Stratfordians have put forward several claims about the identity of the "real" author: The list includes Roger Manners, the fifth Earl of Rutland; William Stanley, the sixth Earl of Derby; Edward de Vere, the seventeenth Earl of Oxford; Sir Henry Nevill, the diplomat; and Sir Walter

relief and filled his plays with implied sex, overt violence, and conflict. He paid no attention to the restrictive unities so popular in Italy and France, but instead jumped, as modern screenplays do, from location to location. He also stole from other writers, borrowed plots, and even on occasion pilfered lines, passages, and phrases from other plays. Between 1599 and 1608 Shakespeare wrote many of the plays that made him famous, including the comedies *Much Ado about Nothing* (1598) and *Twelfth Night* (1600), the history *Henry V* (1598), and the tragedies *Romeo and Juliet* (1595), *Hamlet* (1600), *Othello* (1604), *King Lear* (1605), and *Macbeth* (1606). By the time he reached his late forties, Shakespeare was a wealthy man—he owned a 12.5 percent stake in the Globe Theatre. *The Tempest* (1611) was the last play he wrote before retiring to his boyhood home of Stratford.

Almost 400 years after his death, Shakespeare is one of the most staged playwrights in the world. Additionally, over 300 movies and television shows have been based on his plays, including the musical *West Side Story* (1961) and the science fiction movie *Forbidden Planet* (1956). A few of the recent movies based on his plays include *A Midsummer Night's Dream* starring Calista Flockhart, Michelle Pfeiffer, and Kevin Kline; a musical adaptation of *Love's Labour's Lost* starring Alicia Silverstone; a version of *The Taming of the Shrew* called *10 Things I Hate about You*, which starred the late Heath Ledger; and a small-budget independent movie, *Romeo*

Raleigh, the explorer. Other Anti-Stratfordians suggest that Christopher Marlowe was not killed in a bar fight, but staged his own death to evade charges of atheism, and wrote the plays while in hiding. Scholars who feel Marlowe was the real Shakespeare point out that Shakespeare never mentions in his plays locations near his home town of Stratford but often mentions places near Marlowe's home district of Kent. At one point in *Henry IV* Shakespeare even mentions a tavern that was owned by Marlowe's sister. Others say that Sir Francis Bacon, the English philosopher who helped develop a scientific method for solving problems (see Chapter 16), was the real author. Some have even suggested that Queen Elizabeth I penned all the plays.

Famous Anti-Stratfordians included Walt Whitman, Mark Twain, Sigmund Freud, Charlie Chaplin, and Orson Welles. Mark Twain said, "When Shakespeare died, in Stratford it was not an event. It made not more stir in England than the death of any other forgotten theatre-actor would have made. Nobody came down from London; there were no lamenting poems, no eulogies, no national tears—there was merely silence, and nothing more."

William Missouri Downs

The final resting place of William Shakespeare (1564–1616). Because he gave a great deal of money to a church in Stratford-Upon-Avon, he (unlike many of his peers) received a consecrated burial. Many people today wonder whether the man buried here was a great playwright or just a great front man. The world may never know for sure.

& Juliet vs. The Living Dead. Perhaps the most popular contemporary movie version of a Shakespeare play is Australian director Baz Luhrmann's version of *Romeo and Juliet* called *Romeo + Juliet* starring Leonardo DiCaprio. Luhrmann's adaptation is a music video–style story set in the mythical, gang-plagued city of Verona Beach. In reference to his chic adaptation of the 400-year-old script, wherein the young aristocrats at the center of the story carry pistols instead of swords and perform Shakespeare's lines over a soundtrack that includes popular bands such as Radiohead, Garbage, and the Butthole Surfers, Luhrmann said, "What people forget is that Shakespeare was a restless entertainer. When he played the Elizabethan stage, he was basically dealing with an audience of 3,000 drunken punters who were selling pigs and geese in the stalls. He played to everyone from the street sweeper to the Queen of England. And his style was to have stand-up comedy one moment, a song, and then the highest tragedy right next to it. . . . He was a rambunctious, sexy, violent, entertaining storyteller, and we've tried to be all those things."

Shakespeare used one of the largest vocabularies of any English writer: almost 30,000 words. By comparison the average college student today has a vocabulary of about 20,000 words. And when he could not find the right word, Shakespeare often made one up. Today, many of Shakespeare's words and phrases have become part of our everyday speech. He coined over 1,600 common English words and

> [Y]ou are here to learn about the human condition . . . and there's no better way than embracing Shakespeare.
>
> ***Captain Picard,*** to Lt. Commander Data, in Star Trek: The Next Generation

phrases by changing nouns into verbs, verbs into adjectives, and by combining words that had never previously been connected. For example, among the words he invented are *assassination, eventful, dwindle, courtship,* and *lonely.* And he is the source of the phrases "to catch a cold," "fair play," "foregone conclusion," "as luck would have it," "too much of a good thing," "in one fell swoop," "cruel to be kind," "play fast and loose," "good riddance," "vanish into thin air," and "in the twinkling of an eye." In addition, Shakespeare is one of the most quotable writers of all time. In *Bartlett's Familiar Quotations*—the single most important reference source of famous quotes before the Internet came along—Shakespeare alone takes up 47 pages, which is significantly more than any other writer.

From Extravagant Masques to Puritan Abstinence

At court, the **masques** were the most popular form of theatre. They originated in the early 1500s as a form of entertainment written especially for the monarch and an invited audience. Usually staged in banquet halls, court masques were characterized by grand dances, extravagant costumes, lavish spectacle, poetry, and florid speeches, all hung on a thin story line praising the monarch and demonstrating the need for loyalty. The characters often came from myths and allegories. Women played goddesses, nymphs, the "Beauties," and the "Graces," and men played mythological gods, heroes, and the "Sons of Peace." In England, women were allowed to perform in the private court masques even though they were not allowed to perform on public stages. The fanciful and ornate costumes included masks—hence the name *masque,* from the French spelling of the word. These elaborate productions were staged for important occasions and holidays and for important guests of state. They were also staged on such holidays as Mardi Gras and Twelfth Night, which marked the end of the Christmas season 12 days after Christmas. Most of the actors were amateurs, but professional actors were often hired from local playhouses to play the more difficult parts. Some masques even featured cameo performances by aristocrats, royal children, and other members of the royal family.

Ben Jonson wrote many of the masques for the English court in the seventeenth century, and they were staged by Inigo Jones (1573–1652), the first major architect of the English Renaissance. He studied under Italian masters of staging and brought back ingenious stage machinery and special effects—moving clouds with sky-borne chariots and simulated starlight, earthquakes, and shipwrecks—along with Italian perspective scenery and controllable lighting with candles. One masque during the reign of King James I cost more than 4,000 pounds—more than the cost of all the other plays at court during his entire reign.

The extravagant frivolity of the masques offended the growing religious movement led by the Puritans, who objected to their tax money going to pay for such entertainments. However, Puritan attacks on the theatre sometimes backfired. In 1632 a Puritan named William Prynne (1600–1669) published a pamphlet titled *The Players Scourge* in which he attacked the theatre as sinful, lewd, and an ungodly spectacle of corruption. He labeled actors and playwrights "whore-masters, ruffians, drunkards and godless." He wrote that the theatre had been invented by Satan and was a form of devil worship. He went too far, however, when he called actresses "whores." He didn't know that the queen was to play a role in the next masque. For unintentionally implying that the queen was a whore, Prynne was fined, had both ears cut off, and was sentenced to life in prison.

In 1643 civil war broke out in England. The Puritans, led by soldier and statesman Oliver Cromwell, took over the government. In 1649 they convicted the reigning king, Charles I, of treason and beheaded him. When the Puritans took power, ordinances were passed in an attempt to legislate a new morality. Adultery became a felony punishable by death, and horse racing, gambling, playing dice, swearing, drinking, and bear-baiting were outlawed. In order to make sure that the bear-baiting ban was carried out, the Puritans had all the bears living in the woods near London killed.

The Puritans took revenge on the theatre, blaming it for every catastrophe, including a rare earthquake that hit in 1580. Theatres were called a hotbed of homosexuality, which was a capital offense at that time. On February 8, 1648, they ordered all theatres in London, including the Globe, demolished. England's theatres would remain dark for the next 18 years. Acting companies, fearing persecution, soon followed the remnants of the royal household into exile in France. Yet theatre in England wasn't quite dead. Illegal productions were still staged, mostly in courtyards of inns, but the consequences were dire if the players were caught. In one case, troops raided a performance, seized the costumes, arrested the actors, and drafted audience members into the army. The Puritans brought these anti-theatre sentiments with them when they crossed the Atlantic (see the Spotlight in Chapter 16: "Puritans and the Little Church around the Corner").

French Theatre

In 1600, while theatres were flourishing in Italy, England, and Spain, Paris had only one theatre and no permanent acting company. That single theatre, a rather crude affair called the Hôtel de Bourgogne, was a long, narrow hall with a platform at

William Missouri Downs

> I am persuaded that Satan hath not a more speedy way and fitter school to work and teach his desire, to bring men and women into his snare of concupiscence and filthy lusts of wicked whoredom, than those plays and theatres are; and therefore it is necessary that those places and players should be forbidden and dissolved, and put down by authority, as the brothels and stews are.
>
> **John Northbrooke,** Puritan clergyman, 1577

The Globe Theatre was torn to the ground when the Puritans outlawed the theatre. Today, an apartment building graces the original site. Nearby, the site of the Rose Theatre has been partially excavated. It is currently located in the basement of a 20 story office building called The Rose Court.

one end. A second theatre wasn't built in Paris until 1629, more than a decade after Shakespeare's death. Because of the scarcity of permanent theatres, plays were often performed in indoor tennis courts. A proscenium arch and stage would be built at one end and seats placed on the other. Most tennis courts also had observation galleries running around the top, which could be conveniently made into a balcony. Once the performance was over, the stage would be torn down and the room converted back into a tennis court. There may have been few theatres but there was no shortage of tennis courts; by the sixteenth century the sport was so popular in Paris there were more than 250 indoor courts. King Charles IX loved the sport so much that he had two tennis rackets added to his royal portrait.

French tragic playwrights wrote in **Alexandrine Verse**, which had 12 syllables to a line. An actor would lift his voice for the first six syllables and lower it for the last six. Each line was then followed by a slight pause. David Bodanis, in his book *Passionate Minds* about the playwright Voltaire, gives a perfect example of how Alexandrine Verse worked. Read the following 12 syllable lines raising your voice and lowering your voice and taking a slight pause after each:

> One sentence must rise and, from that peak it must fall
>
> This may happen quickly, or it may then be slow
>
> But it must keep on thus, however dull the rush

The problem with Alexandrine Verse is that it can sound rather staid, even boring to modern ears. In Paris, however, it was the accepted method of writing dialogue and few French playwrights questioned it. Also strictly followed were the unities, which, along with the use of perspective scenery, gave them something in common with the Italians. Three of the most important French playwrights of the Renaissance were Pierre Corneille, Jean Racine, and Molière.

Pierre Corneille: The Rule Breaker

Pierre Corneille (1606–1684) was the son of a distinguished magistrate. At twenty-one, after he fell in love and was rejected, he consoled himself by writing poetry. This soon led to writing plays. One of his most famous plays is *Le Cid* (1637), the story of the young lovers Chimène and Rodrigue. When Chimène's father insults Rodrigue's elderly father, Rodrigue is bound by honor to challenge

When it was written in 1636, Corneille's *Le Cid* was denounced by many French critics because it was not completely faithful to neoclassical principles. During the Renaissance, French critics, audience members, and artists often complimented or condemned plays based solely on how well they measured up to the yardstick of the three unities. Today these outdated rules are ignored, and *Le Cid*, considered a masterpiece of Renaissance theatre, is produced often. This 2005 production was directed by Gervais Gaudreault at the Théâtre du Trident, Québec City, Canada.

Louise Leblanc Photography

Chimène's father. The duel ends in the death of Chimène's father. Chimène is still in love with Rodrigue, but feels she must ask the king to either kill her lover or banish him forever. Rodrigue offers Chimène his sword and invites her to kill him, but she is too tortured by what has happened and refuses. Rodrigue leaves to fight the Moors. He returns a great hero, with all of Seville singing his praises, but Chimène still cannot forgive him and she again calls for his death. The king will not order the death of a war hero, so Chimène announces that she will marry any man who will kill Rodrigue. A gentleman named Sancho takes up the challenge, but Rodrigue refuses to defend himself. After Chimène begs Rodrigue to take up arms, he does so; he soon gets the better of Sancho but refuses to kill him. With this, the code of honor is satisfied, and the lovers are together at last.

Le Cid was denounced by many critics and playwrights but loved by general audiences. The controversy became so big that soon l'Académie française (the French Academy), an exclusive club of writers founded in 1634 to maintain standards of literature and language, made an official ruling. It praised the playwright for following many neoclassical doctrines but criticized him for slight deviations from the classical unities. Stunned by the criticism, Corneille did not write another play for four years. But the litmus test for French plays had been codified: in order to win praise, playwrights had to become strict practitioners of neoclassic drama and follow the unities to the letter.

Thus began a period of French drama marked by an artificial formality. Plays were hampered by arbitrary laws of composition, and playwrights could not write a word without pondering the likely critical reception of the play. In French neoclassical theatre, as in French society, symmetry, balance, decorum, and harmony were the ideal. There was now a "correct" method to set a table and to stage a play.

Jean Racine: The Rule Advocate

The great French playwright Jean Racine (1639–1699) was raised cloistered within an unorthodox Catholic faction called the Jansenists who denied all earthy pleasures, including reading. One of his religious instructors caught him reading a book and threw it into a fire. Defiant, Racine smuggled in another copy. When he was finished reading it, he handed it to his instructors and said, "Here, now you can burn this one, too." As a young man he showed promise for a literary career but was counseled against becoming a playwright. One of his teachers wrote, "In the eyes of right-minded people such an occupation is in itself not a very honorable one; but, viewed in the light of Christian religion and Gospel teaching, it becomes really a dreadful one . . . [D]ramatists are poisonmongers who destroy not men's bodies but their souls." Racine wasn't deterred by such attacks. He was fascinated by the plays of Sophocles and Euripides, and he went on to write many plays that were adaptations of Greek tragedies. His most famous work, *Phaedra* (1677), is based on *Hippolytus* (428 BCE) by Euripides. In the story, Phaedra, wife of the king of Athens, is in love with her stepson, Hippolytus. One day word arrives that her long-absent husband has died, so Phaedra reveals her deep, forbidden love to Hippolytus. Horrified by her admission, Hippolytus spurns Phaedra. Then word arrives that the king is not in fact dead. To cover her transgression, Phaedra accuses Hippolytus of rape. The king returns home, learns of Phaedra's charge, and confronts Hippolytus. He denies the accusation, but his father does not believe him and calls upon Neptune to kill his son. Learning of her stepson's death, Phaedra confesses her guilt and poisons herself. *Phaedra*, like all of Racine's plays, compressed dramatic action by strictly following neoclassical rules and adhering to the unities.

Racine's fame did not last, for he had a hot temper and didn't care for critics. At the height of his success, Racine had made so many enemies that, in order to bring him down, rival theatre companies would find out what he was writing and open a play with the same theme or title on the same day. In 1677 his enemies managed to spoil the premiere of *Phaedra* by having the play hissed off the stage. Bitterly disappointed, Racine quit the theatre. Louis XIV was unmoved by the public's verdict, however, and he asked Racine to be the royal historiographer.

Molière: The Risk Taker

Molière (1622–1673) was France's comic writer. Born Jean-Baptiste Poquelin, he took the stage name Molière at the age of twenty-four. His father was the superintendent of the royal upholstery, a prosperous position that allowed the young Molière to attend college and study law, but his heart wasn't in it. Instead he rented a tennis court and started his own theatre company, which promptly went bankrupt. Three times Molière was arrested and thrown in jail for debt, and each time his father paid his expenses with the hope that the young man would come to his senses. But a burning desire to make theatre, not upholstery, drove the young Molière. Having failed in Paris, Molière spent the next 12 years traveling through France and Italy as an actor, playwright, and manager of an insignificant theatre company. Then in 1658, Molière's luck changed when his company was invited to perform for King Louis XIV. Unfortunately, Molière had an odd hiccup that rendered him a terrible tragic actor—the king was unimpressed. Molière saved the day, however, by performing a short comedic after-piece that impressed the king.

With the king's blessing, Molière began writing highly political farces, comedies, and comic-ballets that satirized French life. When incompetent doctors killed Molière's son by prescribing a powder made of antimony—a metallic element used today as a flame retardant, a paint pigment, and a component of car batteries—Molière wrote a number of satires about the medical profession. The most famous were *The Doctor in Spite of Himself* (1666) and *The Imaginary Invalid* (1673). But Molière saved his boldest attacks for the Church.

Often considered his greatest play, *Tartuffe, or the Imposter* (1664) is about a religious hypocrite. A wealthy gentleman named Orgon brings Tartuffe, who claims to be extremely pious, into his home to attend to his family's spiritual needs. Tartuffe professes to be interested in saving souls but is really a swindler and seducer. In the face of mounting evidence, Orgon refuses to believe that Tartuffe is really a con man. As a result, Tartuffe manages to cheat the family of its fortune and seduce Orgon's wife before the king steps in at the last moment and sets everything right. This ending pleased King Louis XIV, but almost immediately the Church attacked the play. The vicar of St. Barthèlemy called Molière "a demon in flesh" and "the most notably impious creature and libertine who ever lived." He went on to say that Molière should be burned at the stake as "a foretaste of the fires of hell." But Molière wasn't finished with religion. In 1665 he wrote *Don Juan*; in his version of the story about the legendary ladies' man, the hero is a freethinker who doesn't believe in heaven, hell, or devils. When one of the characters asks Don Juan what he does believe in, he answers, "I believe that two and two are four, that four and four are eight!" This was just too much. The play was banned, never to be produced again during his lifetime. Eight years later Molière died. Because French law prohibited actors from being buried in sacred ground, his

---

[I]f the plays that are according to the rules are not liked, and if those that are liked are not according to the rules, then the rules must necessarily have been badly made. So let's laugh off this chicanery which they want to impose on the public's taste, and consult nothing about a play but the effect it has on us. . . . [L]et's not seek out arguments to keep ourselves from having pleasure.

Molière, in The School for Wives

Today, this statue of Molière is in the lobby of the Comédie-Française, one of the most famous French theatres.

Comédie-Française, Paris, France.

Donald Cooper/Photostage Ltd.

Molière's plays are filled with stock commedia dell'arte characters: the henpecked husband, the miser, self-absorbed lords and ladies. These characters were immediately recognizable to his audiences, which freed their attention so that they could more fully absorb his stinging attacks on the hypocrisy and pretentiousness of French society. Inspired by the death of his son at the hands of incompetent doctors, Molière wrote *Le Malade Imaginaire* (*The Imaginary Invalid*, or *The Hypochondriac*), a sparkling satire about the medical profession. Ironically, Molière collapsed while playing the hypochondriac Argan and died a few hours later. This 1981 production at the National Theatre, Olivier, in London, featured Daniel Massey as Argan (kneeling).

body was bound for an unmarked grave. Impassioned pleas from Molière's wife won the heart of the King who tried to allow an exception. But the church would not relent, so Molière was buried in a cemetery reserved for unbaptized infants.

Curtain Call

The Renaissance was a time of contradictions. The rediscovery of ancient wisdom, art, and science led to great advances, and to this day, calling someone a "Renaissance" person is an immense compliment. Yet during the Renaissance, Europeans were seldom able to free themselves from the presumptive authority of the past. Most people still believed in devils and witches. In 1487 Jacob Sprenger, a Dominican inquisitor, published a guide for the detection of witches in which he said that maleficent women "can summon swarms of locust and caterpillars to devour a harvest; they can make men impotent and women barren; they can dry up a woman's milk, or bring abortion, by a look alone they can cause love or hatred, sickness or death. Some of them kidnap children, roast them, and eat them." During the Renaissance, however, there were also intellectuals who coexisted with these inquisitors and who tested new ground and developed new scientific methods. The important thinkers of the age are now celebrated, yet during the Renaissance they were often afraid to reveal their discoveries. In 1609 inventor Galileo Galilei improved the newly invented telescope and was able to see the sun's spots and Jupiter's moons. Soon he confirmed the 1530 theory of Nicholas Copernicus that, contrary to the teachings of Aristotle and the Roman Catholic Church, the sun was at the center of the solar system. And yet he kept silent, at least at first, for fear of persecution. His fears were well founded. Questioning Church teachings often led to a horrible death or imprisonment, and those who questioned Aristotle didn't fare much better.

Theatre during the Renaissance was also full of contradictions. It had moved away from its liturgical roots, yet it was now rooted in rules even older than those imposed by the Church—in many countries a misunderstood Aristotle became the unquestioned authority on how to write a good play. And although the Church allowed theatre, theatre professionals and religious authorities never enjoyed a comfortable relationship. During the Renaissance some of the world's greatest writers, actors, and designers were honored and enjoyed, but they were also often forced to live on the periphery of society. However, a new age was coming—a time when Europe finally moved away from established authority and cultivated a skepticism necessary to usher in the age of Enlightenment.

SUMMARY

MindTap

Test your knowledge with online printable flashcards and online quizzing.

The word *renaissance* means "rebirth." During the Renaissance, secular theatre once again became popular in the West. Liturgical theatre declined because of the Protestant Reformation, a time when different denominations warred over interpretations of the Bible. As a result, three kinds of theatre dominated Renaissance Europe: popular, humanist, and, in some areas, liturgical.

In Italy, popular theatre included commedia dell'arte, which brought back the slapstick farces of the Roman mimes. Commedia plays were improvised farces featuring stock characters. The humanists sought to imitate the classical theatre of ancient Romans and Greeks, using Aristotle's *Poetics* as a touchstone. Humanist plays were shaped by the three unities, a set of dramatic rules about a play's time, place, and action. These plays also featured a declamatory style of acting, a rhetorical approach thought to imitate the style of ancient Greek drama. Italian theatres were built with the elements of ancient Greek theatres but included the newly invented perspective scenery and proscenium arch.

In Spain, a fiercely Catholic nation, religious plays such as *autos sacramentales* still dominated. They were performed in courtyards and open-air theatres, and they often had themes of valor, chivalry, and patriotism. Two of the most notable Spanish playwrights during the Renaissance are Lope de Vega and Calderón.

In England, popular secular theatre thrived. The Puritans' objections to the theatre kept theatre buildings outside London's city limits and gave actors the reputation of rogues and vagabonds. The two types of permanent public playhouses in England at the time were outdoor theatres (such as the Rose and the Globe) and indoor theatres (such as Blackfriars), which were similar to the theatres of Italy. William Shakespeare came to prominence during this era. Christopher Marlowe and Ben Jonson are two of his contemporaries who have also remained famous.

A popular form of court entertainment was masques. Written especially for monarchs and an invited audience, they featured grand dances, extravagant costumes, lavish spectacle, and poetry and florid speeches praising the monarch and demonstrating the need for loyalty. Elizabethan theatre came to a screeching halt when the Puritans took over the government of England. The Puritans who came to America brought their hatred for the theatre with them.

In France, professional theatre took a little longer to catch on. Theatre buildings were often temporary, built within existing tennis courts. In order to gain the favor of critics, most French playwrights followed the three unities without question. Three French playwrights who came to prominence during the Renaissance are Corneille, Racine, and Molière, the latter best known for his satirical attacks on the professions and the Church.

THEATRE
THE RENAISSANCE

THEATRICAL EVENTS AND PLAYS		HISTORICAL / CULTURAL EVENTS
• Italian translation of Aristotle's *Poetics* (1549)	**1525**	• Erasmus publishes complete edition of Aristotle's writings in the original Greek (1531)
• Commedia dell'arte flourishes (ca. 1550–1750) • Golden Age of Spanish theatre (ca. 1550–1650) • Lope de Vega (1562–1635) • Christopher Marlowe (1564–1593) • William Shakespeare (1564–1616) • Queen Elizabeth bans religious dramas (1570) • Ben Jonson (1572–1637) • Inigo Jones, architect and stage designer (1573–1652)	**1550**	• Elizabeth I becomes queen of England (1558) • Francis Bacon, "father of the Enlightenment" (1561–1626) • Galileo Galilei (1564–1642)
• Blackfriars Theatre opens (1576) • First professional public theatre in Spain (1576) • The Rose is built outside London (1576) • *The Tragical History of Doctor Faustus*, Christopher Marlowe (1589) • First opera, *Dafne*, by Jacopo Peri (1597) • *Every Man in His Humour*, Ben Jonson (1598) • Globe Theatre opens (1599)	**1575**	• Pope Gregory XIII eliminates ten days from the calendar (1582) • Virginia Dare is first English child born in American colonies (1587)
• Pedro Calderón de la Barca (1600–1681) • Kabuki begins in Japan (ca. 1603) • Pierre Corneille (1606–1684) • Globe Theatre burns and is rebuilt (1613)	**1600**	• Galileo improves design of telescope (1609) • *Mayflower* drops anchor near Cape Cod (1620)
• Molière (1622–1673) • Women banned from performing Kabuki in Japan (1629) • Jean Racine (1639–1699) • Aphra Behn (1640–1689) • Puritans ban theatrical performances and close all theatres in England (1642)	**1625**	• Taj Mahal constructed in India (1630–1653) • First coffeehouse in Europe opens in Venice (1640) • Qing Dynasty, last imperial dynasty of China (1644–1912)
• *Tartuffe*, Molière (1664)	**1650**	

KEY TERMS

One of the most popular restoration comedies produced today is Goldsmith's *She Stoops to Conquer*, a lively satire on class differences and hypocrisy. Pictured are Cush Jumbo, David Fynn, and Sophie Thompson in a production at the Royal National Theatre in London.

Chapter **16**

THE RESTORATION, THE ENLIGHTENMENT, AND ROMANTICISM

Nigel Norrington/CameraPress/Redux

MindTap®

Start with a quick warm-up activity and review the chapter's learning objectives.

Outline

The Puritans ruled England from 1642 to 1660. When their leader Oliver Cromwell died, civil war once again loomed. Then, on May 8, 1660, Parliament announced that Charles II, son of the beheaded Charles I, had the inherent legal right to the throne, and the rule of the Puritans—who had been inflexible in their demonization of theatre—ended. Thousands celebrated as Charles II touched English soil for the first time since he fled into exile years before. In response, Charles II said, "It must surely have been my fault that I did not come before, for I have met with no one today who did not protest that he always wished for my restoration." Thus began the period of English history known as the **Restoration**.

The Restoration was a period of licentious gaudiness inspired by the elaborate styles that Charles brought with him from the French court. The Puritans' close-cropped hair, which had earned them the label "roundheads," was replaced with French powdered wigs and simple leggings were discarded for silk stockings. But the Restoration was also a time of scientific discovery, new philosophical concepts, improved economic conditions, and a return of the theatre—in the French style.

The Restoration

During the Restoration, theatre did not return to the open-air, public theatres of Shakespeare's day. Because Charles II had spent his exile in France, proscenium arches, neoclassical rules, plush costumes, and upper-class patrons shaped the new drama of London. The most popular type of theatre during this period was the **comedy of manners**. These plays often featured great wit and wordplay and told stories about sexual gratification, bedroom escapades, and humankind's unrefined nature when it comes to sex. One of the great playwrights of this age was William Congreve (1670–1729), whose comedy *The Way of the World* (1700) laughed at the hypocrites, fools, and aging coquettes of the day. This line from the play shows the flavor of its humor: "You should have just so much disgust for your husband as may be sufficient to make you relish your lover."

MindTap˙

Read, highlight and take notes online.

Once the strict rule of the Puritans ended in England, Restoration theatre rebounded with ribald comedies that exposed the social follies of the upper class. Known as the comedy of manners, the most popular plays of this period were rife with marriages of convenience, sexual confrontations, marital infidelities, and coy lovers. A classic example of the comedy of manners is William Congreve's *The Way of the World*, the story of shallow, deceitful aristocrats who plot to prevent two lovers from marrying. Complex and funny, this play is notable for its witty and well-written conversations. This 1992 production featured Tom Hollander, Emma Piper, and Barbara Flynn. Directed by Peter Gill, Lyric Hammersmith, London.

Donald Cooper/Photostage Ltd.

The Restoration also brought another innovation: in 1661, thanks to Charles II, women could legally appear on stages in England for the first time. One of the first English actresses was a woman named Margaret Hughes, but the most famous was the pretty and irreverent Nell Gwynn (1650–1687). (See the Spotlight "Nell Gwynn.") Women on stage were a novelty and most audience members found them "delightful," but some still considered them indecent. One pamphleteer noted that women are forbidden by "apostolic prohibition" to speak in church, but in the theatre they "sing, discourse, and

> All women together ought to let flowers fall upon the tomb of Aphra Behn, for it was she who earned them the right to speak their minds.
>
> **Virginia Woolf,** Novelist

SPOTLIGHT ON Nell Gwyn

Perhaps the most flamboyant of the early English actresses was the outrageously entertaining Nell Gwyn (1650–1687). Born into poverty, she earned a living by singing in taverns and selling oranges at the Drury Lane Theatre, the King's playhouse. At an early age she began playing small parts and quickly became the darling of the London theatre. Her specialty was "breeches roles," in which she wore men's clothing and delivered humorous prologues and epilogues, and became a star of restoration comedies. In his famous diary, Samuel Pepys reported that Nell was such a comic genius that he saw one of her plays three times. She had a succession of wealthy lovers, but soon caught the eye of King Charles II and became his mistress, a position that paid a nice allowance.

Nell's sardonic wit has long been celebrated in the theatre. For example, one day a crowd, believing that Nell's passing carriage belonged to one of the king's Catholic mistresses, jeered at her, calling out, among other things, "Catholic Whore". Nell took this in stride, lowered the window and yelled back at the crowd, "Be silent, good people; I'm the *Protestant* whore." When Charles II failed to give his out of wedlock son a royal title, she openly referred to the child as a "little bastard," which so horrified the King that he immediately rectified the situation. In addition, she often aimed her jesting at her rival mistresses, calling one of them who suffered from a twitchy eye "Squintabella." The King so loved her outrageous personality that, years later, as he lay dying he begged his heir, the Duke of York, "not to let poor Nellie starve." Three years later Nell died of a stroke, most likely brought on by syphilis. She was 37 years old. She was buried at St. Martin-

in-the Fields, a church that is today located near Trafalgar Square; sadly, the exact location of her grave has been lost. She and King Charles II today have 1,700 descendants.

John Hammond/NTPL/The Image Works

Perhaps the most famous actress of the English Restoration was Nell Gwynn. Her ability to sing and dance not only won over audiences but also captured the heart of King Charles II. Nell used her star power to help others, and her heart of gold was legendary. Upon seeing sick and disabled ex-soldiers wandering the streets of London, she insisted that the king open one of the first hospitals for veterans. Some would prefer not to give Nell credit for this act of kindness—after all, she was the king's mistress—but to this day the soldiers at the Royal Hospital Chelsea raise a glass and toast the generosity of Nelly Gwynn.

are often the principal entertainment. Which is certainly inconsistent with the modesty of their sex."

The Restoration also brought the first professional female playwrights. The most famous Restoration-era woman to make her living by writing was Aphra Behn (1640–1689). Before becoming a playwright, she had been a spy for the English government in Antwerp. Her first big hit was *The Forced Marriage* (1670); before her career ended, she wrote nearly 20 more plays full of sexual intrigue, loveless marriages, and satire. Her best-known play was *The Rover, or the Banished Cavalier* (in two parts, 1677 and 1681), for which she had to endure charges of plagiarism by critics who were shocked that a woman could write a successful play. All of Behn's plays were about subjects considered inappropriate for a woman to think about, much less write about, and she was often labeled a "smutty writer." Defending one of her plays, she wrote, "It was bawdy, the least and most excusable fault in the men writers, to whose plays they all crowd, as if they came to no other end than to hear what they condemn in this, but from a woman it was unnatural." Today, Behn is seen as a trailblazer who challenged the established roles of women.

Complaints against the theatre were not limited to allowing women on stage. The theatre in general continued to be denounced in pamphlets and from pulpits. The anti-theatre contingent chastised dramatists and performers for encouraging idleness, perverting the youth, and promoting impiety. During the Restoration dozens of books played on the public opposition to the theatre. Jeremy Collier's *Short View of the Profaneness and Immorality of the English Stage* (1698) listed three decades' worth of improprieties. *The Stage Condemn'd* (1698) traced the evils of the theatre to the shortcomings of English education. The *Evil and Dangers of Stage-Plays* (1706) catalogued nearly 2,000 "abominations" in plays in just the two preceding years. The book with the best title was *A Serious Remonstrance in Behalf of the Christian Religion, Against the Horrid Blasphemies and Impieties which are still used in the English Play-House, to the Great Dishonour of Almighty God, and in Contempt of the Statutes of this Realm Shewing their plain Tendency to overthrow all Piety, and*

In 1688 Restoration-era playwright Aphra Behn published what she called a memoir and travel narrative titled *Oroonoko: or The Royal Slave*. It is the story of an African prince who is first betrayed by a rival king and then by English slave-owners after he is tricked into slavery. Circumstances force him to lead an army of ex-slaves in a rebellion against his masters, and he is subsequently executed. In this 1999 production by the Royal Shakespeare Company, Nigerian playwright Biyi Bandele's adaptation and director Gregory Doran's staging resulted in a play that preserves Aphra Behn's vision but brings the story up to date. Shown here are Ewart James Walters as Kabiyesi, the heartless king, and Geff Francis as Orombo, the king's deceitful vassal.

Donald Cooper/Photostage Ltd.

advance the Interest and Honour of the Devil in the World; from almost Seven Thousand Instances, taken out of the Plays of the present Century, and especially of the five last years, in defiance of all Methods hitherto used for their Reformation (1718). There is little need to describe what this book was about—the title says it all.

By the early 1700s, theatre all over Europe seemed to be marking time. The theatres where humanists had set out to blaze new trails in hopes of making the ancient classics live again were now confined by the unities and other neoclassical rules. For Restoration audiences, which consisted primarily of the upper classes, going to the theatre had more to do with socializing than with seeing a performance. They even brought their waitstaff to serve banquets during the performance and used their servants to exchange messages. The theatre had become a place to conduct business and show off one's wealth and finery. In fact, in France and England, being seen became so important that some audience members were not content to sit in the candle-lit audience. They wanted to sit on the stage, where they could show off their fine threads and establish their place in the social strata. Theatre owners were more than happy to comply. Soon the most expensive seats were onstage, next to the actors. As many as a hundred patrons might be sitting and standing on the far edges of the stage during a performance. Soon the stage became so crowded that in one case a police officer was needed in order to part the crowds and allow an actor to make his entrance. Playwrights and actors protested, but this practice was a great moneymaker, so it persisted until the 1760s. The theatre of the Renaissance was dead. However, the West was on the brink of a dramatic transformation.

Restoration audiences were comprised primarily of members of the upper class, who were more interested in socializing with fellow theatergoers than watching the play. Much to the frustration of the playwrights and actors, performances were given with as many as 100 patrons crowded onto the stage alongside them. Later, the artists prevailed in pushing wealthy audience members off the stage and into enclosed seating areas, or boxes, near the stage. This 1818 colorized woodprint clearly shows the wealthy audience sitting in boxes beside the stage at the Royal Court theatre in London.

William Missouri Downs

The Age of Reason

The Italians called the period from around 1670 to 1800 the Illuminismo; the French called it les Lumières; the Germans, the Aufklärung; and the English, the Enlightenment, while the American founding father Thomas Paine (1737–1809) called it the "Age of Reason." The **Enlightenment** glorified humans' power to reason and analyze. It was a period of great philosophical, scientific, technological, and political revolutions. In fact, some scholars call the Renaissance the "false Enlightenment," because although the West moved beyond the strict confines of medieval hierarchy, it was still firmly grounded in the dogma of organized religion and the ancient philosophies of Aristotle. During the Enlightenment, intellectuals broke free from the influence of the church and the presumptive authority of Aristotle. As Vincenzo Galilei, father of Galileo, wrote, "It appears to me that those who rely simply on the weight of authority to prove any assertion, without searching out the arguments to

During the Enlightenment, travel novels became best sellers as Europeans desired to know more about the people and cultures of the world. A highly popular parody of these novels was Jonathan Swift's *Gulliver's Travels*, the fanciful tale of a traveler to "several remote nations of the world." The book satirizes human nature via Gulliver's encounters with a number of exotic peoples. Here, he tangles with the Lilliputians, tiny men with enormous egos. *Gulliver's Travels* also makes fun of Enlightenment philosophers by satirizing scientific societies— Gulliver tells of the Grand Academy of Lagado, whose members work on inane projects, such as trying to get sunshine from cucumbers and building houses from the roof down.

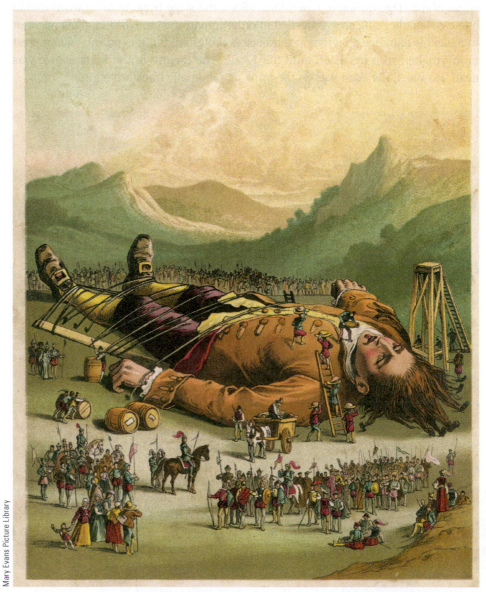

Mary Evans Picture Library

support it, act absurdly." Intellectuals began to believe that science and secular reasoning could conquer fear, superstition, ignorance and lead to social transformation including new forms of government that would embody the philosophies of the Enlightenment, which included life, liberty, and the pursuit of happiness.

The seeds of the Enlightenment had been planted when the explorers brought back stories of distant and exotic lands and cultures. The public had a voracious appetite for tales of travel to Asia, Africa, and the New World. Social satire even took the guise of travel books, such as Montesquieu's *Persian Letters* (1721), Jonathan Swift's *Gulliver's Travels* (1726), and Voltaire's *Candide* (1759). The exposure to foreign ideas took a toll on Europe's ordered worldview. Some Europeans began to wonder, for example: If the world was only 6,000 years old, how could the Egyptians claim that their culture went back 13,000 years? How could the Brahmins in India claim the earth had existed 326,669 "ages," each many centuries long? If the Creation had occurred "at the beginning of the night before Monday, the 23rd of October, 4004 BC," as Anglican archbishop James Ussher had determined after much study of biblical texts, what could explain the records of a fully developed civilization in China at that same time? And according to the Bible, the Great Flood had covered the entire earth, so why were there not historical records of it in every part of the world? Even more confusing was that many of these newly discovered peoples had never heard of the pope or Jesus but they had laws, morals, and concepts of right and wrong—ones that in some cases were more just than those in place in Europe. These questions cast doubt not only on the credibility of church teachings, but also on the knowledge European scholars had taken from Aristotle.

By the early 1700s, biblical explanations of the cosmos no longer satisfied many European intellectuals. Scholars began thinking that Aristotle might be wrong about a lot of things. For example, they questioned his concept of final cause (see Chapter 14). If everything had a final cause, then all events, from the everyday to the cosmic, were the result of God shaping nature to fit a particular purpose. But now scientists and mathematicians were discovering the mathematical order of the universe. For example, mathematics could be used to accurately predict the arrival of comets and eclipses and the rise of the sun and the moon. If science and mathematics could explain these events, then what role did God have in them? These scientific discoveries fostered a skepticism that permeated all aspects of society, including theatre. But before we explain the Enlightenment's influence on theatre, let's take a quick look at its effect elsewhere.

Science: A Faith in Reason

At the dawn of the Enlightenment, most universities were still controlled by organized religion and classical thought, so some intellectuals considered them hopelessly outdated. John Milton (1608–1674), the English poet, said that all the University of Cambridge offered him was an "asinine feast of sour thistles and bramble." There was no such thing as academic freedom; the Church and the State controlled what professors taught. So, by 1730, Enlightenment philosophers and free thinkers throughout Europe had formed scholarly societies and intellectual salons where they could exchange ideas. In the colonies, American statesman and scientist Benjamin Franklin (1706–1790) founded the American Philosophical Society. The charter of France's Académie des Sciences summed

Enlightenment is man's leaving his self-caused immaturity. Immaturity is the incapacity to use one's intelligence without the guidance of another.
Immanuel Kant, Philosopher

The application of science to nature will constantly grow in scope and intensity, and we shall go on from one marvel to another. The day will come when man will be able to fly by fitting on wings to keep him in the air [and] one day we shall be able to fly to the moon.
Bernard Fontenelle, Scholar, in 1702

Lastly, there are idols, which have migrated into men's minds from the various dogmas of philosophers. . . . These I call Idols of the Theatre, because in my judgment all the received systems of the philosophy are but so many stage-plays, representing worlds of their own creation after an unreal and scenic fashion. . . . And in the plays of this philosophic theatre you may observe the same thing which is found in the theatre of the poets, that stories invented for the stage are more compact and elegant, and more as we should wish them to be, than true stories out of history.

Francis Bacon, Philosopher

The Panthéon, Paris, France.

Located in the heart of Paris, the Pantheon was built as a church. During the French revolution, it was converted to a shrine to human reason. Here you'll see the resting places of such luminaries as Voltaire, Rousseau, and Madame Curie.

up the purpose of these groups: to "disabuse the world of all those common errors that have long passed for truth." Many of these societies attacked religious dogma and proclaimed that theirs was a new faith—a faith in reason.

This emphasis on reason led to revolutions in mathematics, physics, botany, chemistry, geology, and zoology. It was the Enlightenment that brought us dictionaries, scientific journals, compasses, factories, fountain pens, museums, fire extinguishers, and the flushing toilet. It was during the Enlightenment that Anton van Leeuwenhoek (1632–1723) improved the microscope and began studying microorganisms; Benjamin Franklin experimented with electricity and invented the lightning rod; Antoine-Laurent Lavoisier (1743–1794) developed modern chemistry; and Edmund Halley (1656–1742) claimed that comets recorded in 1456, 1531, and 1607 were actually the same one and predicted that it would return in 1758 (he was right). When Halley's comet showed up on time, it helped dispel the belief that comets were a sign from God of a coming disaster—in other words, that they had a final cause.

Philosophy: Embracing Doubt

Enlightenment philosophers dared to reason for themselves as they cast off metaphysical thought based on intuition and imagination. Instead, they relied on empirical evidence based on repeatable observations of nature and tested scientific proofs. One of the first of this new breed was English philosopher Francis Bacon (1561–1626), who attacked Aristotelian Scholasticism. He called for acquiring knowledge via the scientific method rather than relying on what he called the four "idols of knowledge," or false notions that hinder critical thinking. The four idols are "idols of the tribe," or humans' innate tendency toward wishful thinking and perceiving more order in phenomena than exists; "idols of the cave," or individuals' inclination to interpret experiences according to their own cultural beliefs and prejudices; "idols of the marketplace," or society's use of jargon and loosely defined, abstract words rather than specific terms to explain the world; and "idols of the theatre," or humans' tendency to believe eloquently phrased speculation, skimpy evidence, and superstition that seldom stand up under empirical reasoning. Bacon maintained that if one "begins with certainties, he shall end in doubts, but if he will be content to begin with doubts, he shall end in certainties." This statement is the essence of Enlightenment thought.

Other important Enlightenment philosophers are Thomas Hobbes (1588–1679), a friend of the playwright Ben Jonson, who questioned the existence of good and evil in the world; René Descartes (1596–1650), who said that skepticism is a virtue; and John Locke (1632–1704), who said that in government there should be a division of power, a system of checks and balances, and separation of church and state. Thomas Jefferson used many of Locke's ideas when he wrote the Declaration of Independence. Locke also wrote extensively on human psychology. He attacked the common idea of his day that we have certain ideas programmed into our brains. He said that the mind at birth is a *tabula rasa* (blank slate) and that all our knowledge comes from the senses. In other words, we are a product of our environment, and nothing can be known independent of experience.

Religion: Is Nothing Sacred?

All this new thinking and skepticism had a profound effect on religion. During the Renaissance, bloody wars had raged over which type of Christianity was God's revealed path, but during the Enlightenment, the authority and accuracy of Christianity itself was questioned. Books and pamphlets critical of Christianity began to appear. Some, such as *Miracles—No Violations of the Laws of Nature* (1683), postulated that many events the Bible called miracles had natural causes and could be explained logically. Others, such as John Toland's *Christianity Not Mysterious* (1696) and *Treatise on the Three Imposters* (1719), attacked the Holy Trinity, Jesus, Moses, and Muhammad. Most of these books and pamphlets were published anonymously because criticism of Christianity still brought a death sentence in many countries. Many of the leaders of the Enlightenment were agnostics, some were atheists, and others regarded themselves as "reasonable Christians" and attempted to explain that rationalist thought was compatible with Christianity. But most called themselves Deists. They believed in a god, though they did not call it *God*; instead they referred to the *Creator* or *The God of Nature*. Deists viewed the Creator as a great non-intervening watchmaker who set the cosmos into motion and let it run on its own. The Creator also endowed humans with the gift of reason with which to know the cosmos. For Deists, the Creator had made a logical, mathematical world, and so, to understand the Creator, one must understand mathematics and the laws of science.

During this period attacks on Christianity became so common that the French playwright Voltaire (discussed in detail in the following pages) predicted that it would not exist within a hundred years. In 1731 the French philosopher Montesquieu pointed out that with French aristocrats, "If religion is spoken of, everyone laughs." The ranks of religious leaders declined. Between 1766 and 1789 the number of monks in France fell from around 26,000 to less than 17,000. This decline also happened in England and the American colonies, where church attendance was very low. Modern scholars estimate that less than 5 percent of the population in the American colonies consisted of regular churchgoers (it was only at 10 percent by 1800, the first year records exist). It was during this time that Thomas Jefferson published his own version of the Bible in which he cut out all references to miracles, because he felt they were contrary to enlightened thought.

Though it trended away from organized religion for the most part, the Enlightenment also gave birth to the beginnings of modern religious tolerance. The seeds of religious tolerance were planted by Enlightenment scholars, some of whom were the politicians and government officials of the time. During this period, countries such as England and the United States began to legally allow for the free exchange of ideas, faith, and philosophies. As the historian Will Durant has said, "Traditions and dogmas rub one another down to a minimum in such centers of varied intercourse; where there are a thousand faiths we are apt to become skeptical of them all."

Donald Cooper/Photostage Ltd.

The Marriage of Figaro by French playwright Pierre Beaumarchais is a classic example of an Enlightenment-era play. Although it is a comedy, it includes well-reasoned attacks on the clergy, the state, and censorship. Figaro, a wit with a strong sense of justice, says, "Provided in my writing I mention neither the authorities nor the state religion, nor politics, nor morals, nor the officials, nor finances . . . nor any person of consequence, I may print whatever I like, subject to inspection by two or three censors." This, of course, highlighted the playwright's dilemma—the play, banned during the reign of Louis XVI (1774–1792) for its skewering of the elite, couldn't get past the censors. This 1991 production featured Kate Buffery (left), Sarah Payne (right), and Simon Schatzberger as Figaro. Translated and adapted by Ranjit Bolt. Directed by Lou Stein, Palace Theatre, England.

Theatre during the Enlightenment

The revolutions in philosophy, astronomy, science, and religion had a profound effect on the theatre. The revolution in philosophy changed how playwrights viewed character. A rationalistic empiricism slowly took over as actors and playwrights began to look at the characters' environment in order to understand why they make particular decisions. In the past a character was evil simply because he was evil or was controlled by the devil, but now playwrights began to look at a character's motivation, circumstances, and upbringing, using an early form of what today we call psychology. The revolution in astronomy caused people to question religion and led to political plays that disputed the church's power and the divine rights of kings. But the most profound revolution was in the sciences, which caused a dramatic leap in technology and industry. People could control and manipulate nature in ways that had never been possible. This resulted in the Industrial Revolution, greater productivity, greater wealth, and a strong "bourgeoisie," a middle class composed of small business owners and manufacturers who wanted a theatre of their own.

As the middle class gained power, theatres began to turn to them for patronage and playwrights began writing plays with middle-class heroes who spoke in prose—everyday language without metrical structure. The new types of middle-class plays came to be known as **domestic tragedies** and **sentimental comedies**. Unlike the tragic plays of ancient Greece or the French Renaissance, whose heroes were of noble birth, domestic tragedies told stories about common people who felt grand emotions and suffered devastating consequences. Unlike the Roman comedies that caricatured common people or the Restoration comedies that poked fun at the well-to-do, sentimental comedies showed middle-class characters finding happiness and true love. These new comedies and tragedies showed that all people experience the same emotions, despite income level or social standing. These plays marked a major change in the theatre, for no less than Aristotle had said that tragedy could be only about "extraordinary" people and comedy only about "lesser" people. Domestic tragedies and sentimental comedies are still with us. The movie *American Beauty* (1999), with Kevin Spacey and Annette Bening, is a perfect example of a **domestic tragedy**.

During the Enlightenment, theatre began to fracture. Some playwrights held on to the old neoclassical rules, but others questioned and broke those rules. *She Stoops to Conquer* (1773), by Oliver Goldsmith (1730–1774), is a Restoration comedy free of ambiguous moral tones; *The Critic* (1779), by Richard Brinsley Sheridan (1751–1816), is a comedy that makes fun of stale neoclassical writing; and *The London Merchant* (1731), by George Lillo (1693–1739), is the tragic story of a man who succumbs to a depraved woman and murders his uncle. However, Lillo's tragic character is not a king or a person of high rank, but a man from the middle class. Other Enlightenment playwrights began voicing revolutionary sentiments against the clergy, corruption, and despotism and calling for religious tolerance and democracy. Diderot, Lessing, Beaumarchais, and Voltaire were four who led this revolution.

Diderot: The Playwright Who Wrote the Encyclopedia

Denis Diderot (1713–1784) was one of the most important French philosophers of the Age of Reason. Between 1751 and 1772, he compiled, wrote, and edited the first Western encyclopedia, the 28-volume *Encyclopédie*. It included hundreds of articles and detailed drawings on a wide range of subjects, including commerce, anatomy, minerals, fossils, glaciers, earthquakes, volcanoes, the mechanical arts, and agriculture, as well as art and theatre. The *Encyclopédie* heralded the supremacy of the sciences, championed tolerance, denounced superstition, attacked dogma, and held as "truth" only that which could be verified and proven empirically. It included articles by European scholars such as Bacon, Descartes, Hobbes, and Locke and from the American colonists Benjamin Franklin and Thomas Jefferson. In his other writing, Diderot argued, as did many Enlightenment philosophers, that morality could be independent of divine origin and that it should be emancipated from theology. As a result, the Vatican routinely placed Diderot's works on its *Index of Forbidden Books* and ordered his writing burned. In Paris in 1751, several of Diderot's editors were imprisoned and Diderot went into hiding. Their salvation came a few weeks later when during dinner King Louis XV and a guest got into a royal quarrel over the exact composition of gunpowder. In order to end the squabble they sent a footman out to search the streets for a copy of the forbidden *Encyclopédie*, where under the letter *G* they found the correct answer. After winning the argument, the King ruled that such secular reference books weren't so bad after all and the editors were released. But they still had to fear persecution from the Church.

> They say an actor is all the better for being excited, for being angry. I deny it. He is best when he imitates anger. Actors impress the public not when they are furious, but when they play fury well. In tribunals, in assemblies, everywhere where a man wishes to make himself master of others' minds, he feigns now anger, now fear, now pity, now love, to bring others into these diverse states of feeling. What passion itself fails to do, passion well imitated accomplishes.
>
> **Denis Diderot,** in The Paradox of Acting

> Whoever reasons rightly, invents, and whoever desires to invent must be able to reason. Only those who are not fitted for either believe that they can separate the one from the other.
>
> **Gotthold Ephraim Lessing,** German Enlightenment playwright

Diderot was also a dramatist who penned books on the techniques of acting. In the theatre, just as in his philosophical writings, he called for a break with the past and proposed startling reforms. He felt that the neoclassic unities were restrictive and out of date and said, "Forget your rules, put techniques aside; it is the death of genius." He wrote two plays, *The Natural Son* (1757) and *Father of the Family* (1758)—both influential works, for they introduced domestic tragedy and sentimental comedy to France. *The Natural Son* is the story of Dorval, a middle-class man who knows very little about his background, save that he is illegitimate. Dorval's problems begin when he falls in love with Rosalie, the fiancée of his best friend, Clairville. Even though he believes that Rosalie has feelings for him, he cannot ruin his friend's wedding and resolves to leave. On his way out of town, he sees Clairville being attacked by armed bandits. He fights them off and saves his friend. Dorval then learns that Rosalie's father, a wealthy merchant, has lost his fortune and cannot give his daughter a dowry. He comes to his friend's rescue a second time by secretly paying the dowry from his own pocket. The madly-in-love Dorval soon discovers that Rosalie's father is his own long-lost father, which, of course, makes Rosalie his sister. The play ends with the marriage of Clairville and Rosalie; Dorval marries Clairville's sister, and everyone cries tears of joy. The play surprised French audiences with the idea that middle-class life was worthy of serious art and that common folk could hold an audience's interest just as well as pedigreed characters.

Diderot also authored *The Paradox of Acting*, a book that attacked the pompous declamatory style of acting that had dominated European stages. During most of the 1700s, becoming an actor had required little more than studying clichéd gestures and inflections. Diderot called for a new type of acting that used natural speech and movement, carefully controlled by the intellect, to express genuine feelings. He said, "Imagine a huge wall across the front of the stage, separating you from the audience and behave exactly as if the curtain had never risen."

Lessing: The Philosopher of the Three Rings

Gotthold Ephraim Lessing (1729–1781) was the German equivalent to Diderot. He was a playwright, critic, and Enlightenment philosopher who wrote tragedies and comedies about the middle class. While a university student, he fell in love with the stage and wrote his first play. When his parents discovered his interest in the theatre, his mother wept uncontrollably, and his father, a prominent Lutheran pastor, demanded that he immediately return home for a stern lecture. Lessing responded, "The Christian faith is not something which one should accept on trust from one's parents." In spite of this impertinence, he managed to convince his parents that he was not a lost cause. He returned to school, where he became a Deist and devoted himself to free thought and the theatre.

Lessing's greatest play was *Nathan the Wise* (1779). Set in Jerusalem during the Fourth Crusade, the story is about a Jewish merchant whose wife and seven sons are massacred by the Christian Crusaders. A few days later a friar brings to Nathan a Christian infant whose mother has died and orders him to raise it as a Christian. Instead, Nathan takes the child and teaches her only those religious doctrines on which Jews, Christians, and Muslims agree. Years later, the child, now a young woman, is saved by a knight who discovers that she was born Christian but not raised as one. The knight betrays Nathan to the authorities.

Nathan is taken before a sultan who asks him which of the three religions is best. Nathan uses an analogy of three rings, each representing one religion, to show that each faith is true only insofar as it makes its believer virtuous. The play was a grand plea for religious tolerance, yet the Church condemned it, and Lessing was attacked as an atheist. The play could not be produced during his lifetime. When Lessing died, a theological journal announced that Satan had taken him away to the fires of hell. Lessing, like so many Enlightenment writers and actors, was denied consecrated burial. His body was dumped into a public grave.

Beaumarchais: The Barber Who Started a Revolution

The French Enlightenment playwright Pierre-Augustin Caron de Beaumarchais (1732–1799) was an inventor and thinker who spent countless hours at the leading intellectual salons of France, where he met Diderot and other philosophers and became inspired by the concepts of democracy and liberty. His most famous plays are *The Barber of Seville* (1775) and its sequel, *The Marriage of Figaro* (1784). Both star the character of Figaro, a witty barber, surgeon (barbers often served as surgeons), and philosopher who is willing to tackle any problem or injustice. Wolfgang Amadeus Mozart promptly wrote an opera based on *The Marriage of Figaro* (1786), and Gioacchino Rossini later wrote one based on *The Barber of Seville* (1816). Beaumarchais's plays reflect the attitudes of the Enlightenment, and Figaro's lines are full of audacious criticism of aristocrats. For example, in *The Marriage of Figaro*, he asks what aristocrats have done to deserve their good fortune. His answer: "You gave yourselves the trouble to be born, and nothing more; for the rest you are sufficiently ordinary." The play goes on to attack politicians and the sale of public offices as well as the poor treatment of women in the male-dominated society. Not surprisingly, *The Marriage of Figaro* was immediately banned and Beaumarchais imprisoned for a time.

King Louis XVI of France called the play a "dangerous folly" and said that the Bastille, the great Paris prison, would have to be torn down before he would allow it to be performed. Later he reluctantly relented and allowed a single reading of the script in a private theatre. It was unseasonably hot that day, and the windows of the theatre were painted shut. Soon audience members were fainting due to the heat, so Beaumarchais smashed the windows with his cane to let in fresh air—certainly a symbolic gesture. The reading was a triumph. A year later the play was produced at the Comédie-Française. Before the play, the gates outside the theatre collapsed from the push of the crowds trying to get in. During the performance the audience applauded almost every line—as a result, it lasted over five hours. In the middle of the performance someone in the audience threw a rotten apple core at a duchess sitting in one of the boxes reserved for royalty. Some scholars have seen this act as the start of the French Revolution, which began in earnest only a few years later.

Just like the character of Figaro, Beaumarchais set out to fight despotism. An avid supporter of the American Revolution, he recruited French officers to lead colonial soldiers into battle and loaned the American Congress his own money to help fight the war. In November 1776, the Congress wrote that the United States was more indebted to the "generous, indefatigable, and

Comédie-Française, Paris, France.

The great French playwright Beaumarchais aided the American Revolution by spying on England, loaning money to the American Continental Congress, and recruiting talented French soldiers to lead American troops into battle.

SPOTLIGHT ON Puritans and the Little Church around the Corner

Theatre got off to a rocky start in America when the very first actors to stage a play were arrested. On August 17, 1665, three amateur actors at Cowle's Tavern in Virginia performed a play called *Ye Bear and Ye Cubb*. They barely finished the curtain call before local Puritans—often referred to as "pilgrims" in our history books—had the trio thrown in jail. Puritans often objected to the theatre, calling actors "ministers of the devil." In *A Testimony Against Prophane Customes* (1687) one such Puritan wrote that the theatre originated with "Devil-Gods" and was "displeasing and dangerous to the souls of men." At that time it was widely rumored that half of all condemned murders admitted before their execution that it was going to the theatre that led them to ruin.

Puritans later evolved into Congregationalists, Methodists, Baptists, Quakers, and Presbyterians, which as a group would continue to make life difficult for theatre people for the next hundred years. They not only damned the profession from their pulpits, but also pushed local governments to pass laws condemning it. The Pennsylvania Assembly prohibited plays in 1700, but the British government later repealed the law. The same happened in New York in 1709. In 1750 the Central Court of Massachusetts banned the first attempt to present a play in Boston and threatened to levy heavy fines on anyone who attended subsequent productions. It would not be until the British occupied Boston during the Revolutionary War that another play would be produced there.

In October 1774, on the eve of the American Revolution, the First Continental Congress passed a resolution to discourage "every species of extravagance and dissipation, especially all horse-racing, and all of gaming, cock-fighting, plays and other expensive diversion and entertainment." Four years later, during the Revolutionary War, the Continental Congress passed a resolution to suppress theatrical entertainments because they caused "idleness, dissipation, and general depravity of principles and manners." These laws against the theatre were later repealed, but the anti-theatre sentiment persisted. When a yellow-fever epidemic hit Philadelphia in 1792, Quakers blamed the outbreak on the presence of a theatre in their community.

For protection some theatres took to calling themselves "museums" and labeled their performances as "educational" programs, but this seldom worked. In some cities actors could not find housing, nor were they allowed to rent hotel rooms. Other communities passed licensing laws that required theatres to pay outrageous fees in order to perform; few theatre companies could afford the tax. In Springfield, Illinois, a young attorney named Abraham Lincoln fought against the licensing fees and won. Decades later when he was assassinated in Ford's Theatre (1865) by an actor, some said his death was God's warning against the theatre. At that time,

intelligent" playwright Beaumarchais "than to any other person on this side of the ocean." Although Beaumarchais was a great supporter of the Revolution, his plays were seldom performed in the United States, for theatre in the States had the Puritans to contend with. (See the Spotlight "Puritans and the Little Church around the Corner.")

Voltaire: Honored Philosopher Who Teaches Men to Think!

One of the most influential thinkers of the Enlightenment was French poet, essayist, novelist, and playwright Voltaire, the pen name of François-Marie Arouet (1694–1778). Voltaire's writing often got him into trouble with the Church, and his satirical verse and sharp wit occasionally landed him in the Bastille. In his early years Voltaire was in love with the famous French actress Adrienne Lecouvreur, but in 1730 she died of typhoid. Theatre people in France were celebrated on the stage but accorded little respect in real life.

Albert Palmer, a successful theatre manager, estimated that seven out of ten Americans felt that attending the theatre or acting in a play was "almost a sin." As late as 1877 the Methodist Episcopal Church was still excommunicating members of its congregation who attended the theatre.

Things began to change in 1870 when a New York City reverend refused to allow the funeral of a comedian/actor named George Holland to take place at his church because of Mr. Holland's profession. Shortly thereafter, New York newspapers were full of editorials condemning the reverend's actions. Even the great Mark Twain weighed in, calling the reverend a "crawling, slimy, sanctimonious, self-righteous reptile." This did not change the reverend's mind, but a little church around the corner from the reverend's agreed to hold Holland's funeral. Following this public outcry, treatment of actors began to change.

Today, the little church around the corner still stands at the corner of 29th and 5th Avenue in New York City. Some of its stained glass windows depict actors rather than saints. And to this day theatre people sometimes say "the little church around the corner" in reference to any house of worship that opens its doors to *all* people, even actors.

The Church of the Transfiguration in New York City is known in the theatre community as the Little Church around the Corner for its longstanding tolerance toward theatre artists.

Because Mademoiselle Lecouvreur failed to renounce her life in the theatre, she was denied a church burial and her body was thrown into a shallow grave in an open field where no headstones were allowed. Voltaire said, "Actors are paid by the king and excommunicated by the church. They are commanded by the king to play every evening and by the church forbidden to do so at all. If they do not play, they are put in prison. If they do, they are spurned into a kennel. We delight to live with them and object to be buried with them. We admit them to our tables and exclude them from our cemeteries."

Even though Voltaire was the most celebrated French playwright of the age, he wasn't treated much better than the actors. From 1726 to 1729, the king of France exiled Voltaire to England. Not long after he had arrived, he attended the funeral of the great mathematician Sir Isaac Newton (1642–1727). Newton had discovered the mathematical laws governing gravity, invented the calculus needed to explain those laws, and provided irrefutable evidence that the laws governing the universe were systematic, rational, and comprehensible. Newton was a national hero, and his funeral at Westminster Abbey was

Imagno/Hulton Fine Art Collection/Getty Images

One of the greatest playwrights of The Enlightenment was Voltaire. A prolific author, he wrote plays, poems, philosophical novels, histories, and political and religious criticisms. He also helped translate the works of Sir Isaac Newton into French. In fact it was Voltaire who first chronicled the story of Newton and the apple.

People who believe in absurdities will eventually commit atrocities.

Voltaire, Playwright

fit for a king. Voltaire was astonished, for only bishops and aristocrats received such honors in France. But the Enlightenment had taken hold of England, and it inspired Voltaire. He became a Deist and preached that there were no miracles in the universe, only fixed laws. In fact, Voltaire is credited with the oft repeated notion, "If God did not exist, it would be necessary to invent him."

When Voltaire was allowed to return to France he lived with Emilie du Chatelet, the French mathematician, physicist, and author who was the first person in France to translate the works of Newton. Together they attempted to build on Newton's discoveries. In fact, it was Voltaire who first published the story about Newton and the apple. Even so, Voltaire found that his literary mind was no match for Madame Chatelet's scientific intellect and rather than compete with her he returned to the stage to attack religion, superstition, and the government. In his play *Zaire* (1732) he wrote about a young slave caught between Islam and Christianity in which he said, "Our thoughts, our manners, our religion, all are formed by custom, and the powerful bent of early years." In *Mérope* (1742) he criticized hereditary aristocracy, saying "He who serves his country worthily needs no ancestry." His play *Fanaticism, or Mahomet the Prophet* (1741), is still so controversial that almost three centuries later modern productions have met with protest and cancellations. All this, of course, got Voltaire in trouble with the censors, the Church, and the king. After the death of Emilie du Chatelet, Voltaire was once again forced to flee France.

In 1759, Voltaire purchased an estate in the village of Ferney near the Swiss border, only a few miles from Geneva. Ferney became an intellectual and cultural mecca—a site to which philosophers, actors, playwrights, and free thinkers traveled in order to have an audience with one of the greatest leaders of the Enlightenment. To entertain his guests, he built a 300-seat theatre on his estate; he often invited his visitors, servants, and any professional actors who stopped by to perform. He even took the stage himself. For the next 20 years, safe on his estate, Voltaire used his vast wealth to fight legal battles against the Church and won several lawsuits, forcing the State and the Church to pay retributions to the families of people they had tortured and executed for heresy. He also wrote dozens of books, plays, and pamphlets promoting religious tolerance, making fun of religious superstitions, and calling for a theatre of ideas. In short, Voltaire was one of the first to fight for what today we might call "human rights."

Late in his life, even though the clergy were still calling for his arrest, Voltaire decided to tempt fate and return to Paris. At the gates of the city, officials asked if he had any contraband in his carriage. He answered, "I believe there is nothing here that is contraband except myself." He was now 84 years old and the five-day, 300-mile trip had been hard, but his homecoming was a triumph. There were parades and meetings with dignitaries, including Benjamin Franklin, and people filled the theatres to see his plays. At one theatre only days before his death, the audience leapt to its feet and shouted, "Hail Voltaire! Honored philosopher who teaches men to think!"

English playwright Joanna Baillie (1762–1851) typified the Romantic sensibility in that her tragic heroes inevitably allowed their emotions to overwhelm their reason, leading them either to destruction or to a strengthening of their identity. In her *Count Basil* (1798), a military leader is detained from joining his troops because he is infatuated with the beautiful Victoria. Basil's enemy, Victoria's father, takes advantage of Basil's emotions and manipulates the innocent Victoria and her ladies-in-waiting into using their "powers of seduction" to keep Basil preoccupied. In the meantime, Basil's troops win a critical battle and, shamed because he did not accompany his troops to victory, Basil commits suicide. This 2003 production was directed by Leslie Jacobson, Horizon Theatre, Arlington, Virginia.

Andrew Linden Photography/Horizons Theatre

Romanticism

The Enlightenment philosophers and scientists changed human thought forever. Before the Enlightenment the secrets of the cosmos were explainable only by miracles and theology. Now it was a "giant clock" known as the Newtonian universe where everything was logical and reasonable. But cold reason and hard logic seldom make for great theatre—theatre is about emotions. Some poets, novelists, and playwrights began to question the Scientific Revolution's obsession with logic. These writers, known as **Romantics**, felt that science was not adequate to describe the full range of human experience, and their writings stressed instinct, intuition, and feeling. They wanted to go beyond reason to a transcendent realm of emotion where experience cannot be rationally explained. The English Romantic poet John Keats (1795–1821) wrote, "O for a life of sensations rather than of thought"; William Wordsworth (1770–1850) said that "all good poetry is the spontaneous overflow of powerful feelings"; and William Blake (1757–1827) admonished us to "bathe in the waters of life."

The French philosopher Jean-Jacques Rousseau (1712–1778), who said, "I am not here to think, but to be, feel, live," is sometimes called the father of the Romantic movement because he rebelled against the rationalists of the Age of Reason. Rousseau argued that people could find happiness in a "state of nature" and that they should learn from nature rather than the artificial and corrupted teachings of society or civilization. Romantic writers shared Rousseau's appreciation of nature and could lose themselves in contemplation of the landscape. For the Romantics, being close to nature was unquestionably good, so any character on stage that was "of nature" was inherently better than a character hindered by civilization. Blaise Pascal (1623–1662), the French physicist, mathematician, and philosopher, expressed the essence of Romanticism when he said, "The heart has its reasons that reason does not know." In short, the romantic age was a celebration of love, emotion, and chivalry, and an attack against tradition, corruption, and Alexandrine verse. Romantic plays were overflowing with an uncompromising optimism that celebrated uncorrupted, nostalgic, deeply earnest, self-assured, rosy-cheeked heroes, who revolted against authority because they knew in their heart they were right. It is from this age that we get the idea of artists being obsessive, moody, and lovesick. In 1839 the Spanish artist Leonardo Alenza y Nieto (1807–1845) made fun of this when he painted "Satire on Romantic Death," which portrays a temperamental artist leaping to his death from a cliff. Behind him two artists have already done themselves in, one by hanging, another with a gunshot.

Romantic playwrights set out to break all the neoclassical rules. The Romantics attacked the three unities, saying that compressing a story into a 24-hour period was affected and absurd. At the time, all plays were supposed to have five acts, but the Romantics said that a play should be only as long and contain only as many acts as are needed to tell the story—or as long as the writer's passions hold out. As a result, Romantic plays tended to be very long. When one of them is produced today, the director often has to make substantial edits to keep the production from lasting past midnight. The Romantics also transformed stage design by calling for more realistic sets. Because they wanted to imitate nature, they gave many of their plays a pastoral setting. Painted flats were abandoned and new sets were designed to incorporate picturesque forests, mountains, and gardens.

The Night Romanticism Won

Perfect examples of Romantic plays are Friedrich von Schiller's (1759–1805) *The Robbers* (1778) and Edmond Rostand's (1868–1918) *Cyrano de Bergerac* (1897). The best-known Romantic play today is *Les Misérables*, based on a novel by the French playwright Victor Hugo (1802–1885), who also wrote *The Hunchback of Notre Dame* (1831). So popular is Hugo's *Les Misérables* that the modern musical version has been performed almost continuously on various stages around the world since 1980, and the novel has been adapted to the screen more than 40 times, including a 2012 movie starring Hugh Jackman, Russell Crowe, Anne Hathaway, and Eddie Redmayne. But perhaps the most notorious production of a Romantic play was Victor Hugo's *Hernani*, performed in 1830 at the Comédie-Française in Paris. It was a riot, literally.

At the time Romantic plays were still rare in France and largely unaccepted. The old guard in the audience believed that plays must always be written in verse and that the neoclassic unities must always be obeyed. On the other side, a band of Romantics wanted more plays like *Hernani* as well as realistic dialogue and an end to arbitrary structural laws. It wasn't a fair fight—the old guard stamped their feet, whistled, and cried "Murder!" in an attempt to halt the production, while the Romantics lowered fishhooks from the balcony to lift off the wigs of the

Laurie Lewis/Lebrecht

Romanticism was a literary, artistic, and philosophical movement that originated in the second half of the nineteenth century. In the theatre, Romanticism gave birth to plays such as Edmond Rostand's *Cyrano de Bergerac*, the story of a brave and gifted poet whose love for Roxanne is thwarted by his extremely large nose. There have been operas, plays, ballets, and movies based on *Cyrano de Bergerac*. One of the most recent movie versions was the film comedy *Roxanne*, starring Steven Martin.

aristocrats below. Add this to the fact that the ushers had arrived late and failed to unlock the lavatories until just moments before the curtain—it's no wonder everyone was in a foul mood. For three nights the audiences argued, and their debate often drowned out the actors. Soldiers with bayonets had to be called in to protect the players from all the debris being thrown on the stage by the old guard. The arguments grew so unruly that one audience member was reportedly bayoneted. Finally, on the fourth night, the squabble ended. The Romantics had won.

Goethe: The Bard of Berlin

One earlier playwright had used all the ingredients of the perfect Romantic play. His panoramic dramas paid no attention to the unities; his sprawling stories seemed almost formless in comparison to the neoclassical theatre. His name: William Shakespeare. He became popular all over Enlightenment Europe, particularly in Berlin. In Germany the Romantic movement was called **Sturm und Drang** ("storm and stress"), which had been the title of a play written by Friedrich M. Klinger in 1776. Sturm und Drang plays exalted nature, emotions, and individualism. Johann Wolfgang von Goethe (1749–1832) was the greatest of the Sturm und Drang playwrights. Goethe was not only a playwright but also a critic, a journalist, a painter, a biologist, a statesman, a poet, a novelist, a philosopher, a scientist, and the manager of the Duke of Weimar's playhouse. As a scientist, he organized meteorological observation stations all over Germany, published books on optics and botany, and was one of the first to argue that the fossils imbedded in geological strata might indicate their age. Meanwhile,

> One ought, every day at least, to hear a little song, read a good poem, see a fine picture, and if it were possible, to speak a few reasonable words.
>
> ***Goethe,*** Romantic playwright

he filled more than a hundred volumes with his novels, plays, and letters. His writing is credited with the power to touch its readers deeply. In the novel *The Sorrows of Young Werther* (1774), the lovelorn protagonist kills himself. Not long after it was published, a string of lovesick young men and women took their own lives; in their pockets were found copies of Goethe's romantic novel.

Goethe's most famous Romantic play is *Faust*, an immense work that contains two prologues and two parts. Part 1 (1808) cannot be produced on a single night without editing, and Part 2 (1832) requires so many sets that most theatres cannot produce it. The story differs from Christopher Marlowe's *Tragical History of Doctor Faustus* (see Chapter 15), written more than 200 years earlier. Goethe's Faust is searching for personal fulfillment and ideal loveliness, so his dealings with the devil are quite different from those of Marlowe's Doctor Faustus. Rather than searching for unlimited knowledge, Goethe's Faust agrees that Mephistopheles can take his soul should Mephistopheles introduce him to something he wishes would never end. A true Romantic hero, Faust believes that this would be the moment of ultimate fulfillment,

SPOTLIGHT ON Traveling Stars and Ira Aldridge

I n 1869 the Union Pacific met the Central Pacific Railway at Promontory Point, Utah, completing the first transcontinental railroad across the United States. Ten years later there were more than 150,000 miles of track worldwide, and by 1900 there were more than three hundred traveling theatre companies in the United States alone. Every town of any size built a theatre where traveling acting companies could play one-night or one-week stands before moving to the next town fifty miles down the tracks.

Soon, actors were traveling around the world on railroads and steamships and becoming international stars. Two of the biggest were Sarah Bernhardt and Edwin Booth. Bernhardt (1844–1923) was celebrated for her graceful manners, personal charisma, and the rich clarity of her voice. It was reported that thousands of men had crushes on her, including the famous psychologist Sigmund Freud. Booth was one of America's first bona fide "stars." His elegant, naturalistic style made him a matinee idol from Honolulu to London. Unfortunately, it was his younger brother, John Wilkes Booth, who would make the Booth name live in U.S. history forever.

One of the earliest traveling stars was Ira Aldridge. Born in 1807, when slavery was still legal in much of the United States, Aldridge was the son of working-class African Americans known then as "Free Negroes." It was said that his father was an African prince who had been kidnapped into slavery but later won his freedom. Aldridge began acting at an early age at the African Theatre in New York City, the first African American theatre company in the United States.

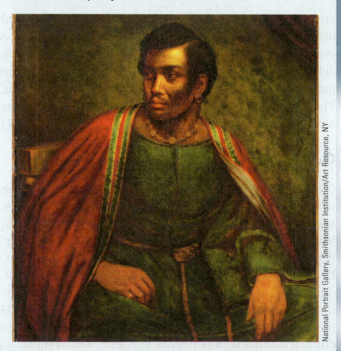

National Portrait Gallery, Smithsonian Institution/Art Resource, NY

Celebrated nineteenth-century actor Ira Aldridge, the first black actor to play Othello.

after which there would be no point in existing. Faust uses Mephistopheles to aid him in his philosophical and spiritual development, but in the end works out his own salvation and is redeemed, unlike Marlowe's Faustus. Some see the play as the epitome of the Romantic philosophy and the individual's search for truth, which is at the core of all Romantic plays.

Melodrama

In the end, the Romantic movement succeeded where the Enlightenment had failed: the rigid unities were finally eliminated from the theatre. But for all the turmoil it caused, Romanticism was merely a flash in the history of the theatre. Soon, cheap imitations of Romantic plays were stealing the stage—imitations that lacked the soul of the Romantic writers but exploited their excesses. These new cut-rate plays came to be called melodramas and were made popular by the traveling actors who were crossing the United States and Europe with the help of the newly invented locomotive (see the Spotlight "Traveling Stars and Ira Aldridge").

Founded in 1821, the African Theatre was run by James Brown, who is believed to be the first African American playwright. That an African theatre existed in the United States at that time is extraordinary because there were so few places where "free" blacks were allowed even to assemble. As it was, white audience members frequently interrupted performances by throwing firecrackers on the stage and making derisive remarks. In 1823, Brown wrote and Aldridge acted in *King Shotawa*, a play about a slave insurrection on St. Vincent Island in the Caribbean. That year the theatre was forced to close its doors after white hoodlums nearly destroyed it. According to a report in a local newspaper, "The ebony-colored wags were notified by the police that they must announce their last performance, but they, defying the public authority, went on and acted nightly. . . . The police finally disrupted a performance by arresting the actors. . . . They were released on the promise 'never to act Shakespeare again.'"

Faced with such bigotry, Aldridge left the United States in 1825 and sailed for London, where he experienced far less prejudice. That year, at the Royal Theatre, Ira became the first black actor to play in Shakespeare's *Othello*. Because black actors had not been allowed on stage in much of the Western world, the part of Othello was traditionally played by a white actor wearing dark makeup (see the Spotlight "Color Consciousness" in Chapter 3). Aldridge became one of the greatest Shakespearean actors of the day, taking on traditionally white roles such as Macbeth, King Lear, and Shylock. Soon he was famous throughout Europe. Newspaper accounts called him "a star of the first magnitude" and "the most beautiful male artist that one can imagine." He was known for his restrained realism and understated body language, which made one critic say, "You listen, it seems, to every beat of his heart." Following his performances, Aldridge often stepped before the curtain and appealed to the audience for "respect for his African race." He performed all over Europe, including Belgium, Germany, Austria, Hungary, Switzerland, France, Sweden, Russia, and the Ukraine. Late in his life, Aldridge made arrangements to return to New York City, but took ill while acting in Poland and died on August 7, 1867. He was buried there with full state honors. Today, Aldridge's grave is a national shrine cared for by the Society of Polish Artists of Film and Theatre. A thousand miles away, at the Shakespearean Memorial Theatre in Stratford-upon-Avon in England, a chair is dedicated to Aldridge's memory as one of the greatest Shakespearean actors of all time.

Bigotry and fanaticism have excited themselves in all possible shapes to annoy the professors of the dramatic arts; but, fortunately, for the honor of the stage and dignity of human nature, it has found patrons and friends in the persons of the greatest and most learned men in the most enlightened periods of the world's history. . . .

Ira Aldridge, Actor, from an address given in England

The word **melodrama** is a blend of *melody* and *drama* and refers to the background music often played during these performances. Just as modern movies have a sound track, these plays are accompanied by a small orchestra. Like Romantic plays, melodramas are often about a working-class protagonist who sets out on a great adventure, but melodrama's writers mix in sensational subjects, stock characters, virtuous heroes, dastardly villains, and striking spectacles such as earthquakes, battles, and floods. The plots are formulaic, filled with unbelievable coincidences, disguises, mistaken identities, and oversimplified moral dilemmas. Unlike Romantic plays, melodramas seldom question authority and they usually lack depth. Melodrama never makes audience question their morals, beliefs, or values. Its carefully calculated plots are devoid of philosophical skepticism and always leave the audience feeling good because they support the values of marriage, God, and country.

One of the most prolific writers of melodrama was the Frenchman Eugene Scribe (1791–1861), who wrote nearly 400 plays (with the help of assistants). Scribe was the king of formula writers and turned out play after play with the

Enormously popular, melodramas dominated nineteenth-century stages. Audiences loved them because they included a sympathetic protagonist who suffered at the hands of an evil antagonist, lots of exciting action, thrilling suspense, and a happy ending that promoted middle-class values. This poster depicts an eventful evening in the life of the long-suffering heroine of Theodore Kremer's *For Her Children's Sake* (1902). It's easy to see from this scenario how modern soap operas evolved from melodrama.

Library of Congress, Prints and Photographs Division [LC-USZC4-12468]

Everett Collection

Melodrama and Romanticism are still with us. For example, the space epic *Star Wars* is a modern example of Melodrama structure, and Obi-Wan Kenobi's line "May the Force be with you" is a modern take on Romantic philosophies.

same simple structure. The sympathetic protagonist suffers at the hands of an evil antagonist in the course of intense action, suspense, and contrived plot devices. The ending is always happy and the loose ends are neatly tied up. All this "neatness" earned his melodramas the sarcastic label **well-made plays**. Today, Scribe is considered one of the worst playwrights to have ever made a living on the stage, and the term *well-made play* is synonymous with a bad formula plot. In the modern theatre it is unlikely that you'll ever see one of his plays, but had you lived during the mid-nineteenth century, you could not have avoided them. Middle-class audiences loved him even though his fellow artists condemned him. When the German poet Heinrich Heine was on his deathbed, his breath failing, a doctor asked him if he could make a hissing sound. Heine softly answered, "No, not even for a play by Scribe." Melodrama and Scribe are still with us today in the form of television soap operas and popular movies such as the *Star Wars* and the *Fast and Furious* film franchises.

Curtain Call

Theatre seems to go through cycles: A change begins when someone creates a new way of looking at the art. Some artists wish to keep an old style alive, but new artists are always inspired to provide innovations and creative ways of doing theatre. Later, imitation and complacency will creep in, followed by outright stagnation. Then someone upsets the cart once again and the cycle begins anew. Denis Diderot said it best:

> We are the slaves of custom. Let a man with a spark of genius appear in our midst with a new work. First of all he dazzles us and causes discord among the thinking minds; gradually he gathers them together; soon after, imitations follow; they are studied; rules are formulated, art is born again, and limits fixed to it, and it is maintained that everything that does not fall within the scope of these limits is bizarre and bad: they are the veritable Pillars of Hercules, beyond which none can venture but at his peril.

The Enlightenment upset the Renaissance world, and Romanticism upset the Enlightenment, but then it stagnated as melodrama. As the nineteenth century drew to a close, the world of theatre was about to be reinvented once again, this time in a radical new form called "realism."

SUMMARY

MindTap

Test your knowledge with online printable flashcards and online quizzing.

The Restoration ended the Puritans' restrictions on the theatre. The most popular type of theatre during this period was the comedy of manners, which often had themes about sexual gratification and the bedroom escapades of the rich. Also during the Restoration, women first became accepted as actors and playwrights. But there were still many complaints against the theatre by religious groups.

During the Enlightenment, philosophers and playwrights changed human thought: Bacon called for a new inductive science, Newton reduced the natural world to a mathematical equation, and Beaumarchais supported revolutionary politics. They all demanded tolerance and an end to superstition. Before the Enlightenment, the secrets of the cosmos were explainable only by miracles and theology; now the universe was mathematical and logical. Enlightenment plays included domestic tragedies and sentimental comedies, in which common people felt deep emotions and their stories were just as tragic as those of any emperor or king. Some of the greatest playwrights of the age were Denis Diderot, Gotthold Lessing, Pierre Beaumarchais, and Voltaire.

The Enlightenment had done much to advance human reason, but some poets, novelists, and playwrights began to question the Scientific Revolution's obsession with logic. These writers, known as Romantics, felt that science was inadequate to describe human experience, and their writings stressed instinct, intuition, and feeling rather than logic. Philosopher Jean-Jacques Rousseau is often called the father of the Romantic movement, and perhaps the greatest Romantic playwright is Goethe. But soon the Romantic movement was pushed aside in favor of what we call melodrama today. Melodramas borrowed heavily from Romantic plays, as they were often about a working-class hero who set out on a great adventure. They had simple plots that left the audience feeling good because their stories praised traditional values and institutions.

THEATRE

THE RESTORATION, THE ENLIGHTENMENT, AND ROMANTICISM

THEATRICAL EVENTS AND PLAYS

HISTORICAL / CULTURAL EVENTS

1650

- Nell Gwynn (1650–1687)
- Theatre returns to England (1660)
- First professional actress performs in London (1661)
- *Ye Bear and Ye Cubb*, William Darby (1665)
- Voltaire (1694–1778)

- Puritan rule is ended in England (1660)
- Isaac Newton formulates his law of gravitation (1665)
- Salem witch trials (1692)

1700

- *Love Suicides at Sonezaki*, Chikamatsu (1703)
- Denis Diderot, encyclopedist and playwright (1713–1784)

- Jean-Jacques Rousseau (1712–1778)

1725

- Gotthold Lessing (1729–1781)
- Pierre Beaumarchais (1732–1799)
- Licensing Act (1737)
- Johann Wolfgang von Goethe (1749–1832)

- *Gujin tushu jicheng*, an encyclopedia, printed with movable copper type in China (1726)
- *Encyclopédie*, Denis Diderot (begun in 1745)
- Ruins of Pompeii excavated, beginning of archaeology (1748)

1750

- *Peking* Opera begins (ca. 1750)
- William Brinsley Sheridan (1751–1816)
- *Candide*, Voltaire (1759)
- Audience members banned from the stage in France (1759)

- Melody of "Twinkle, Twinkle, Little Star" is published in France (1761)
- James Watt makes first practical steam engine (1765; patented in 1769)

1775

- *The Barber of Seville*, Pierre Beaumarchais (1775)
- *Nathan the Wise*, Gotthold Lessing (1779)
- *The Marriage of Figaro*, Pierre Beaumarchais (1784)

- U.S. Declaration of Independence ratified (1776)
- U.S. Constitution ratified (1787)
- French Revolution begins (1789)

1800

- Victor Hugo (1802–1885)
- Ira Aldridge (1807–1867)
- *Faust*, part one, Johann Wolfgang von Goethe (1808)

- World population reaches an estimated one billion (1802)
- Explorers Lewis and Clark reach Pacific Ocean (1805)

KEY TERMS

Theatre continues to challenge its audiences to think about our world and to confront ideas that are not portrayed in the mainstream media. *Disgraced* confronts Muslim-American identity and buried prejudices. This production featured Gretchen Mol, Hari Dhillon, Josh Radnor and Karen Pittman at the Lyceum Theater in New York.

Chapter 17
MODERN THEATRE

Sara Krulwich/The New York Times/Redux

MindTap

Start with a quick warm-up activity and review the chapter's learning objectives.

Outline

The 1800s were a century of invention and expansion. The telegraph (1844), the phonograph, the telephone (both in 1876), and the jukebox (1889) astounded the masses. In 1885 German inventor Gottlieb Daimler constructed the first high-speed internal combustion engine. In the same year, German engineer Karl Benz built the first primitive automobile. Only 16 years later, English poet Wilfrid Scawen Blunt described the "exhilarating experience" of riding in an automobile at the amazing speed of 15 miles per hour. The public delighted in the new creations of chewing gum, ice cream, Kodak cameras, synthetic fibers, and Coca-Cola. At the same time, the Industrial Revolution brought immense political, social, and environmental changes. In 1895, Svante August Arrhenius, a Swedish scientist, published the first paper on the effect of carbon dioxide on the climate, what would a hundred years later be called global warming and climate change.

The Advent of Realism

MindTap
Read, highlight and take notes online.

The French theatre designer Louis Daguerre (1787–1851) was known for his lifelike sets. He used hand-painted screens and gas-powered lighting effects to stage realistic sunrises and storm clouds. But it is for his invention of the *daguerreotype*, in 1829, an early form of photography, that he is best known today. Around 1840, English physicist William Fox Talbot (1800–1877) improved upon Daguerre's daguerreotype and created modern photography. The invention of photography changed the way people looked at the world. Now, a boy in London could see an actual photo of the battlefield of Bull Run in Virginia, not an artist's depiction. A mother in Michigan who wanted to see the U.S. president's face could study his photograph, not a drawing. Soon "real" was all the rage, especially in the theatre. There was a call for sets to be more "genuine," acting to be more "honest," and dialogue to be modeled after everyday speech. But this call for reality quickly became more than a desire to mirror the world; it became a hunger to uncover the basic forces of human nature and to show people as they really are. This was the birth of **realism**.

Contributing to the rage for theatrical realism was Thomas Edison's invention of the incandescent light bulb in 1879. By 1880 the first electric streetlights were installed in New York City, and not long after there were so many glowing streetlights in the Broadway theatre district that it was nicknamed "The Great White Way." In 1885, the New Lyceum on Fourth Avenue was the first theatre in the world to be lit with electric lights. For the first time in the history of the theatre, every kind of lighting effect—from an eerie, stormy night to a warm summer day—could be realistically presented and controlled. Because of electric lights, the audience could sit in total darkness for the first time, like peeping toms spying on the action of a play. But more than just electric lights and photography influenced this new form of theatre; it was also inspired by the writings of Charles Darwin, Sigmund Freud, and Karl Marx.

Influences: Darwin, Freud, and Marx

English naturalist Charles Darwin (1809–1882) is, of course, famous for his book *On the Origin of Species by Means of Natural Selection* (1859), which states that all the animals on earth evolved from a common ancestry over millions of years

Michal Daniel

Playwrights who wrote in the Realistic style sought to portray not only events and settings realistically but also characters who reflected the circumstances they were born into. George Bernard Shaw's comment on English class warfare, *Pygmalion*, tells the story of Eliza Doolittle, an uneducated flower seller who continually clashes with the smug professor Henry Higgins. Eliza's Cockney accent, disheveled clothing, and defiant attitude reveal her lower-class upbringing, and Henry's haughty arrogance pegs him as an upper-class English gentleman. This 2004 production featured (l to r) Barbara Bryne as Mrs. Pearce, Henry's housekeeper; Bianca Amato as Eliza Doolittle; and Daniel Gerroll as Higgins. Directed by Casey Stangl, Guthrie Theater, Minneapolis.

and that the primary mechanisms for evolution are environment and natural selection. Darwin's ideas not only contradicted the biblical account of Creation, but they also, in many ways, contradicted the Newtonian idea of a logical universe set into motion by a great rational creator. Darwinism described a wasteful and irrational, or at least mistake-prone, world in which most species are failures. Darwin's observations implied that from an evolutionary standpoint, humans are animals, not divine creations placed on earth to rule *over* animals. This theory had an enormous impact on the theatre. Now, in order to write or portray a realistic character, the playwright or actor had to understand the character's environment and heredity. Whereas Romantic heroes had been a force to be reckoned with—complete, if perhaps simple, beings who knew right from wrong—*realistic* protagonists were products of their environment, upbringing, and psyche.

After Darwin equated humans with all other animals, the Viennese psychologist Sigmund Freud (1856–1939) revolutionized ideas about how our animal minds worked. Freud said that the human unconscious plays a major role in shaping behavior. These unconscious motivations, he said, might be memories from early childhood or traumatic events blocked out of our conscious awareness. Freud theorized that people spend vast amounts of energy forming defense mechanisms to cope with such memories and that these often end in neuroses. He argued that our basic instincts can be controlled only through socialization, yet socialization can cause us to suppress natural desires and urges. When such urges are suppressed long enough, they become part of the unconscious mind, which reveals itself through slips of the tongue, jokes, and dreams. Freud wrote numerous books on these topics. One of his most famous texts is *The Interpretation of Dreams* (1899), in which he analyzes the characters of Oedipus and Hamlet. Freud's deep, detailed analysis of the human mind began to take over literature and the theatre. There was now a desire to show characters who were

> As the poet brings the guilt of Oedipus to light by his investigation, he forces us to become aware of our own inner selves, in which the same impulses are still extant, even though they are suppressed.
>
> **Sigmund Freud,**
> Psychoanalyst

complete and whole and whose conscious and unconscious motivations were well justified.

German philosopher and social scientist Karl Marx (1818–1883) founded two of the most influential mass movements in modern history: democratic socialism and revolutionary communism. Marx wrote about the negative aspects of capitalism and the Industrial Revolution and expressed moral indignation over the economic plight of the working class. In *The Communist Manifesto* (1848), he studied the history of class conflict. In *Das Kapital* (1867), he said that the free enterprise system is seriously flawed and is a cause of great human misery because it exploits the poor. He felt that as long as the bourgeoisie and the upper class were making profit (surplus value) off the laborers (the proletariat), there would be social conflict, which would eventually lead to serious economic crises.

Influenced by Marx's arguments, playwrights began writing realistic stories that spotlighted human oppression. Romantic plays popular earlier in the century were being replaced by drama that questioned society's values and discussed the social and domestic problems of the middle class. Along with economic injustice, such subjects as divorce, euthanasia, women's rights, sexual double standards, venereal disease, religious hypocrisy, unregulated capitalism, blind patriotism, the plight of the poor, and the grim realities of everyday life—all taboo subjects in most plays before Marx—were now placed center stage. In short, Marx's ideas made the theatre of the past seem like frivolous entertainment that purposely avoided addressing the problems of a world dominated by a class system. More playwrights began to believe that their purpose was to improve society. They wanted to cause changes in the state, the community, the church, and even the family, and lead the way to a new social order.

As plays became more political, playwrights often attached a lengthy preface, appendix, or manifesto to explain the political theme of a play. Some of these realistic plays simply pointed out the social problem without offering a solution. These **problem plays** were based on the idea that before a problem can be solved, society must first understand that the problem exists. This new breed of playwrights felt that if audience members were distressed by what they saw in a play, they should try to remedy that social ill rather than complain about the play—attack the message, they said, not the messenger. Swedish playwright August Strindberg (1849–1912) said that the commercial dramatist had been "peddling the ideas of his time in popular form, popular enough for the middle classes, the mainstay of theatre audiences, to grasp the gist of the matter without troubling their brains too much." Now the playwrights of realism were purposely troubling the audience's brains. These plays of social indictment seem to have a common theme: "We have met the enemy and he is us."

Box Sets and Fourth Walls

With the advent of realism, set design also changed. It now seemed necessary to show how people were directly affected by their environment. Theatres began building sets that authentically replicated a character's surroundings. The forestage, or *apron*, was used less because electric lights allowed the action to take place behind the proscenium arch, where a realistic setting, often one of the newly invented box sets, could be built. A **box set** is a true-to-life interior containing a room or rooms with the **fourth wall** removed so that the audience has the feeling of looking in on the characters' private lives.

One of the first theatres to have box sets was the Olympic Theatre in London, which was managed by actor and singer Lucy Elizabeth Bartolozzi Vestris (1797–1856), the first female theatre manager in London. Not only did plays at her theatre have historically accurate costumes and real properties, but her box sets also had working doors, real windows, real trim, and ceilings. To playgoers of the nineteenth century, seeing a scene taking place in an ordinary living room was remarkable. In 1852 the British actor Charles Kean's (1811–1868) production of Shakespeare's *King John* had realistic costumes, set, and props that he had researched to make sure they were historically correct.

Local Flavor and Real People

Along with realistic sets, darkened theatres, and themes that questioned society, dramas also had realistic characters, whose speech and manners were much like those of everyday people. Characters onstage did the sorts of things that people do in everyday life. Not only did these characters have specific psychological motivations, but they also came from a particular place, which affected what they believed and how they acted. Some playwrights of realism attempted to capture "local color" and regional dialects. For example, John Millington Synge (1871–1909) wrote plays about the rugged lives of Irish peasants, using their dialect; the most famous are the tragedy *Riders to the Sea* (1904) and the comedy *The Playboy of the Western World* (1907). Fellow Irishman Sean O'Casey (1880–1964) went so far as to record conversations of slum dwellers in Dublin and use their words verbatim in his plays.

Realistic playwrights did away with heightened or poetic speech in favor of natural dialogue; they also discarded asides (actors' comments to the audience) and soliloquies, and they took pains to hide exposition. Dialogue became so natural that it even, on occasion, included obscenities. Realism was led by a host of innovative playwrights, including Henrik Ibsen, George Bernard Shaw, and Anton Chekhov. Another great playwright of the time was Oscar Wilde, whose comedies forced Victorian society to reexamine its hypocrisies (see the Spotlight "Oscar Wilde").

Henrik Ibsen: The Father of Realism

The most famous realistic playwright is Henrik Ibsen (1828–1906), often called the father of realism. Ibsen wrote his first play in 1850, the year many historians choose as the beginning of realism, but his first plays were hardly realistic. Initially, he was a Romantic writer and his early plays were verse dramas largely based on Norwegian history and folk literature. It was not until he left Norway and lived in Italy and Germany that he seriously considered writing the realistic plays that eventually earned him an international reputation. The turning point came when he saw a production of one of his historical plays staged by the Duke of Saxe-Meiningen (1826–1914), one of the first modern directors. (For more on the Duke of Saxe-Meiningen, see Chapter 8.) Ibsen was impressed by the Duke's revolutionary methods of staging scenes so that they looked real. Afterward, Ibsen set out to write realistic plays that would present the audience with ordinary people speaking in everyday language. He said, "We are no longer living in the age of Shakespeare. . . . What I desire to depict [are] human beings, and

SPOTLIGHT ON Oscar Wilde

rish playwright Oscar Wilde (1854–1900) is famous for such comic plays as *Lady Windermere's Fan* (1892), *A Woman of No Importance* (1893), and *An Ideal Husband* (1894). Wilde was quite the character, advocating "art for art's sake" and known for aesthetic idiosyncrasies such as wearing his hair long and often having a huge flower in his lapel. He was also known for his wit. In 1881, when he arrived in the United States for a lecture tour, a customs official asked him if he had anything to declare. Wilde answered, "I have nothing to declare but my genius." His plays were filled with witty repartee that forced Victorian society to reexamine its hypocrisies and the arbitrariness of its moral and social taboos.

In 1895 Wilde wrote his most famous play, *The Importance of Being Earnest*. But just a few months later, Wilde's plays were considered unproduceable, because he had been publicly humiliated and was facing a two-year prison term: his crime was his sexuality. Wilde was in love with Lord Alfred "Bosie" Douglas. Douglas's father, Sir John Sholto Douglas, Eighth Marquess of Queensbury (famous for creating rules for boxing), was livid about his son's relationship with Wilde and left a calling card at Wilde's club calling him a "Somdomite" [*sic*]. In turn, Wilde charged the marquess with libel but lost the case. Only a few days later, Wilde was charged with violating Section 11 of the Criminal Law Amendment Act which, when broadly interpreted, made homosexuality a crime. After three trials, Wilde was found guilty and sentenced to two years in prison at hard labor. He was released on May 18, 1897, but he was a broken man. Wilde died three years later at the age of 46. On his deathbed, he still retained his wit: "My wallpaper and I are fighting a duel to the death. One or the other of us has to go." Today, Wilde is one of the most produced playwrights of the Victorian age, and several of his plays have been made into movies. In 1999 *An Ideal Husband*, the story of a successful politician threatened with blackmail, starred Minnie Driver, Cate Blanchett, Rupert Everett, and Julianne Moore; and in 2002 *The Importance of Being Earnest*, a comedy of manners and mistaken identity, featured Rupert Everett, Colin Firth, Reese Witherspoon, and Dame Judi Dench.

Historical/Corbis

Playwright, novelist, poet, and wit Oscar Wilde.

therefore I [will] not let them talk the language of the gods." His plays also began to present complex, sometimes disturbing, views of human society, which he said was important because "man shares the responsibility and the guilt of the society to which he belongs."

One of Ibsen's most important realistic plays was *A Doll's House* (1879), the story of Nora, a pretty housewife who is expected by her banker husband and the patriarchal society to be cheerful, obedient, and mindless. Ibsen's intent is not to condemn Nora but to make a statement about a society that limits women

Michal Daniel

Norwegian playwright Henrik Ibsen wrote many plays about the moral failings of modern society. In *Hedda Gabler*, the title character, a bored and destructive young woman, amuses herself by gossiping, engaging in almost-adulterous relationships with her husband's acquaintances, and manipulating the actions and emotions of those around her. Her aristocratic contempt for her husband's bourgeois family and friends leads to tragedy. This 2000 production featured (l to r) Sean Haberle, Christina Rouner, Laila Robins as Hedda, and Stephen Yoakam. Directed by David Esbjornson, Guthrie Theater, Minneapolis.

by sheltering them. In the course of the play, the petted and spoiled Nora begins to examine her life. She realizes that she has always been dominated by men, first by her father and now by her husband. In the end, she leaves her husband and children and strikes out on her own to redefine her identity. When *A Doll's House* was first performed, the audience was outraged because the play did not reinforce their family values. A riot took place outside the theatre. Playhouses in Hamburg and Vienna threatened to withhold royalties unless Ibsen rewrote the ending so that Nora stayed with her husband.

Ibsen went on to write *Ghosts* (1881), which examines incest and the devastating effects of incurable venereal disease; *Hedda Gabler* (1890), a psychological study of a sexually repressed and destructive woman; and *Enemy of the People* (1882), about an idealistic doctor who tries to save a resort city from its polluted waters only to discover that the community is more interested in capitalism than in the safety and health of its citizens. Ibsen's plays hammered away at society's institutions, encouraging audiences to question their habits and values. In fact, Ibsen's gravestone depicts a hand wielding a hammer—the perfect symbol for his life and the realistic plays for which he is most remembered.

George Bernard Shaw: Cerebral and Socially Relevant

Victoria became queen of Great Britain in 1837. Her reign, the second longest in English history, lasted until 1901. The Victorian age was a time of rigid morals, inflexible conventions, prudish behavior, and, above all, punctilious good taste. Darwin's ideas on evolution were perverted into "social Darwinism," or socioeconomic "survival of the fittest." It justified a *laissez-faire* economic system in which profit was a divine right, and the conditions of its victims, the poor and the working class, were of little concern. Soon the working class formed unions and made alliances with liberal intellectuals such as British playwright George Bernard Shaw.

Whereas Ibsen wrote grim dramas that directly confronted society, George Bernard Shaw (1856–1950) wrote what might be called "high comedies," cerebral, socially relevant plays that had an intellectual scope so vast they forced audiences to reassess their values. Shavian comedies are filled with characters who cannot resist an argument about social issues. No character is exempt from talking politics and theorizing about moral, artistic, or religious reform. For example, in *Man and Superman* (1903) bandits discuss rival systems of government while waiting for an attack. In his plays, Shaw commented on poverty, corruption, and romantic ideas about love and war. He sought to correct popular misconceptions about historical figures and pushed for social reforms including women's rights and the agenda of the Fabian Society, a British intellectual movement that believed socialism could be achieved through gradual reform. (Their work laid the foundations of the modern British Labour Party.) In his book *The Quintessence of Ibsenism* (1891), Shaw argued that the prime function of playwrights is to expose the social and moral evils of their time.

Anton Chekhov: The Lazy Chaos of Life

Anton Chekhov (1860–1904) was another famous realistic playwright. After growing up mostly in poverty, Chekhov put himself through medical school and set up free clinics in provincial Russia to help the poor. By the time he was in his mid-twenties he was the primary support for his family, but he still found time to write over 600 short stories, mostly comedies. He said, "The artist should not be the judge of his characters and what they talk about, but only an impartial witness. . . . A writer should be as objective as a chemist." Encouraged by friends, he tried his hand at playwriting, but his first play *The Seagull* (1896) went so poorly that Chekhov ran from the theatre at intermission. He later joined one of the greatest theatres in the world, the Moscow Art Theatre, run by the father of modern acting, Konstantin Stanislavsky. (See the section in Chapter 7, "Gurus and Mentors: Acting Teachers.") Stanislavsky restaged *The Seagull* and the second time around it became a great success. Chekhov went on to write three more plays that are considered classics, including *Uncle Vanya* (1899), *The Three Sisters* (1901), and *The Cherry Orchard* (1904). Chekhov placed on stage the lazy chaos of lives crushed by life's absurdities and missed opportunities. Most of Chekhov's characters are decent and sensitive people, who dream of improving themselves, but haven't the vaguest idea of how to do it. He called his plays "comedies," which has led to great debates in the theatre community. How can plays about stagnant and helpless people be considered funny? And yet they can be. Chekhov felt that playwrights do a disservice by showing protagonists who win against impossible odds. Such things, Chekhov argued, rarely happen in real life. In Chekhov's plays, the protagonists pass the time by talking about nothing of consequence while little happens. In this respect, the TV sitcom *Seinfeld* might be called "Chekhovian."

Chekhov's last play, *The Cherry Orchard*, is often considered his best. This play has no clear protagonist. Instead, it deals with a family of characters who tell many stories at once—just as in real life. At the center of this comic drama are Lyubov Ranevskaya and her daughter Anya; they were once wealthy but now have no money left. As the play begins, they return from France to their heavily mortgaged estate near Moscow. They are told that their estate and its cherry orchard are to be sold to pay back taxes. Lopakhin, a self-made millionaire, suggests that they cut down the cherry orchard and rent the land for summer cottages. This would provide the funds they so desperately need, but Ranevskaya

> [I]n real life people don't spend every minute shooting each other, hanging themselves, and making confessions of love. They don't spend all their time saying clever things. They're more occupied with flirting, eating, drinking, and talking stupidities. . . . Let everything on the stage be just as complicated, and at the same time just as simple as it is in life. People eat their dinner, just eat their dinner, and all the time their happiness is being established or their lives are being broken up.
>
> **Anton Chekhov,** Playwright

does nothing. In the end the estate is sold at auction. The new owner of the estate turns out to be Lopakhin, who sets out to cut down the cherry orchard, and the family is forced to leave. In one last gesture of absurdity, they accidentally lock their ancient butler in the abandoned mansion, where he dies, forgotten. The audience's reaction to such frustrating inaction is often laughter, just as Chekhov wanted. But also, after seeing the characters on stage take no action, audience members may be motivated to do the opposite in real life.

In 1923, the Moscow Art Theatre performed Chekhov's *A Cherry Orchard* in the United States. American audiences and critics were amazed by the intense psychological realism that resonated from the Russian actors. Sitting in the audience for almost every performance was the American actor Lee Strasberg, who said that the performance seemed to be filled with living, breathing people, not actors. Strasberg was so impressed that he went on to found The Actors Studio, which still teaches American actors the lessons learned from the Moscow Art Theatre. (For more, see the Spotlight "Chekhov, Stanislavsky, and the Birth of Modern Acting.")

SPOTLIGHT ON Chekhov, Stanislavsky, and the Birth of Modern Acting

The birth of modern, realistic acting can be traced to the opening night of Anton Chekhov's *The Seagull* on December 17, 1898. The play had been a total disaster when it was first staged two years earlier in St. Petersburg, but Konstantin Stanislavsky (1863–1938) and Vladimir Nemirovich-Danchenko (1859–1943), the co-founders of the Moscow Art Theatre, decided to stage the play with a realistic set, natural staging, and acting characterized by psychological realism. These elements had been tried before, with varying degrees of success, but Stanislavsky and Danchenko wanted to bring them together into a completely realistic production. Stanislavsky had the actors draw on their own experiences and emotions to shape how their characters spoke and moved, thereby creating a complex human being with well-motivated feelings and desires.

Chekhov was so nervous about the opening night that he did not attend. At the end of the first act, the audience sat silently. Backstage, most of the actors were convinced that the new realistic acting and the play were a failure. Actress Olga Knipper, who later became Chekhov's wife, fought back tears. Then "like the bursting of a dam, like an exploding bomb," as one audience member later wrote, "a sudden deafening eruption of applause broke out." Stanislavsky was said to be so happy that he danced a jig. The Moscow Art Theatre became one of the most influential theatres in the world, and Stanislavsky became the father of a new, realistic approach to acting and a new kind of actor training. (For more on Stanislavsky's ideas on acting, see Chapter 7; for more on Stanislavsky and directing, see Chapter 8.)

William Missouri Downs

Anton Chekhov tried to be an objective observer of life. He said, "The artist should not be the judge of his characters and what they talk about, but only an impartial witness . . . A Writer should be as objective as a chemist." This University of Wyoming production of Chekhov's *Uncle Vanya* featured Megan Antles, Katrina Despain, and Kenneth Stellingwerf.

Naturalism: A Slice of Life

Naturalism often represented the seedy side of life in order to show the audience life as it is rather than as we would like it to be. Perhaps the best example of naturalism is Maxim Gorky's *The Lower Depths,* a study of wretched derelicts in a horrible tenement run by greedy landlords. Konstantin Stanislavsky directed this original 1902 production at the Moscow Art Theatre. It later toured Western Europe and the United States.

For some, however, realism was not real enough. A few directors, actors, and playwrights began calling for an even more extreme form of realism, an accurate "documentary" of everyday life, including its seamy side. French novelist Émile Zola (1840–1902) named this new "photographic" realism **naturalism**, and his phrase "slice of life" is an often-quoted description of it. Naturalistic plays exposed the squalid living conditions of the urban poor and explored such scandalous topics as poverty, venereal disease, and prostitution. This earned naturalism the designation "sordid realism." Naturalism placed the underbelly of life on stage in order to expose social ills and repressive social codes without preaching about them. The hope was that showing an appalling situation on stage would shock the audience into calling for social reform. Two proponents of naturalism were the Russian playwright Maxim Gorky (1868–1936), whose play *The Lower Depths* (1902) took a stark look at people living in the cellar of a Moscow flophouse, and the French director André Antoine, who staged the play *The Butchers* (1888) with real sides of beef infested with maggots.

The period of realism and naturalism was also a time of important social change. Women's rights became an important issue in Europe and the United States. In England the 1882 Married Women's Property Act abolished a husband's grip on his wife's inheritance, Oxford and Cambridge universities both started colleges for women, divorce laws were changed to allow women more freedom, and there were attempts to make public schooling for boys and girls equitable. Even so, as the turn of the century approached, women still did not have the right to vote in the United States and most of Europe. The old morals and sexual prejudices, however, were crumbling. Many argued that one reason was the criticism from realism and naturalism. However, even as the great drama critic William Archer proclaimed that realism was the ultimate dramatic style, realism and naturalism were facing challenges.

Sovfoto/Universal Images Group Editorial/Getty Images

The Rise of the Avant-Garde

In 1895 Auguste and Louis Lumiere opened the world's first movie theatre in Paris. Unlike Thomas Edison, who was working on devices that allowed only one person at a time to watch a movie, the Lumieres projected the image on a screen, allowing hundreds and later thousands of people to watch. At first these movies were simple. The very first was called *Workers Leaving the Lumiere Factory*, a one-minute shot of workers walking out of the factory. As unsophisticated as these first motion pictures were, the general public was fascinated and lined up night after night to see such thrilling one-minute movies as *The Arrival of a Train* and *Boat Leaving the Harbor* (You can find these movies on YouTube). Within a few years, stories and characters were added and the modern motion picture industry was born. In the United States these new movie theatres were called "nickelodeons" because they only cost a nickel. By 1910, there were more than 10,000 nickelodeons in the United States. By 1911, 1,400 legitimate stages in the United States had been converted to movie houses. By 1915, the number of touring theatre companies had dropped from 300 to 100, and soon the number fell to less than ten. It certainly looked as though theatre was being killed off by the movies. Many playwrights and directors believed that the biggest problem was realism and naturalism. For example, depicting a sunset on stage takes a battery of lights plus a crew of stagehands, and even then it doesn't look completely real. For a movie to show a real sunset, all that's needed is a camera at the right location at sundown.

Soon there were calls for theatre to "re-theatricalize" itself by doing what the camera could not do. Many theatre artists began to reject naturalism and realism, and a variety of new styles began to emerge. Unlike previous periods, when one style dominated for a while and then was replaced by another style, now several styles flourished simultaneously. New perspectives on the human experience led to avant-garde theatrical styles, each with its own systems and theories. The word **avant-garde** can describe any artist or work of art that is experimental, innovative, or unconventional. Symbolism, expressionism,

Sovfoto/UIG/Getty Images

One of the most significant directors of the twentieth century was Vsevolod Emilevich Meyerhold (1874–1940). Originally a member of the Moscow Art Theatre, Meyerhold lost interest in realism and struck out on his own as a director. Declaring that theatre should present something different from everyday reality, he began exploring avant-garde, alternative, and abstract methods of staging. In this production of Russian playwright Vladimir Mayakovsky's political satire *The Bedbug* (1929), Meyerhold used symbolist staging to tell the story of a man who comes back to life after being frozen for 50 years, only to discover that the world has become a sterile place filled with dehumanized beings.

futurism, Dadaism, surrealism, and absurdism are some of the avant-garde styles, or "isms," that playwrights, directors, and designers created in order to rebel against realism and naturalism and draw audiences back to the live stage.

Symbolism to Expressionism

In the theatre, an "ism" is a set of ideas about the style, purpose, and scale of a production. Some critics and artists feel such labels help the audience understand a particular performance. Others feel that these labels limit art by creating arbitrary rules that artists must follow—as the Aristotelian unities did during the Renaissance (see Chapter 15). Given these perspectives, let's look at a few of the isms that became popular early in the twentieth century, some of which are still popular.

One of the first isms in the rebellion against realism and naturalism was **symbolism**. Symbolists argued that the realists' objective observation of the world using the five senses was not the best way to show inner truth. They believed that such truths could be hinted at only through symbols. Whereas conventional theatre mirrored images of common life, the symbolists searched for truth beyond the physical world. Symbolist drama sought to replace the specific and concrete with the suggestive and metaphorical. Symbolist plays had rapturous moments of silence representing communion between two souls, doors and windows that mysteriously opened and closed, and lamps that dimmed on their own—all of which gave the plays mystery or spirituality or whatever truth lurks below the surface of things. Symbolist theatre did not last long because the plays had little plot or action and tended to baffle the audience. But traces of symbolism have been incorporated into almost every type of theatre in the form of symbolic acts, gestures, designs, and dialogue that hint at deeper truths. Among the isms that followed were expressionism, Dadaism, surrealism, and absurdism.

The only theatre worth saving, the only theatre worth having, is a theatre motion pictures cannot touch. When we succeed in eliminating from it every trace of the photographic attitude of mind, when we succeed in making a production that is the exact antithesis of a motion picture, a production that is everything a motion picture is not and nothing a motion picture is, the old lost magic will return once more.

Robert Edmond Jones,
Theatre set designer

In 1922 New York's Provincetown Players staged the original production of Eugene O'Neill's expressionist play *The Hairy Ape.* The Provincetown Players was formed by avant-garde theatre artists who re-belled against the big Broadway productions of light musicals and other flimsy entertainment. The Players' no-star policy reflected their support of socialist causes, and their willingness to experiment supported many different forms of drama outside thea-tre's mainstream.

Gwen Watford Collection/Lebrecht Music & Arts/Corbis

Expressionism started in Germany around 1910 as a reaction to a new kind of painting called Impressionism. Monet, Renoir, Cezanne, and other Impressionist painters were interested in how reality appears to the eye at a particular moment—in other words, a subjective account of an objective perception. With expressionism the artist imposes his own internal state onto the outside world itself; therefore, expressionism is a subjective account of a subjective perception. For example, if a person who is drunk says that he sees pink elephants on the walls, he isn't describing objective reality—there are no pink elephants on the walls. Rather, he is revealing his own internal state. Unlike a realistic play, an expressionist play shows the audience those pink elephants, so they can see what the character feels, because reality is partially created by our perceptions of it.

Expressionist plays often use deliberate distortion—walls slanted inward to make the room feel claustrophobic, wallpaper striped like prison bars, or trees having the form of huge strangling hands. Similarly, some characters may not be portrayed as real people, but as the protagonist perceives them—perhaps as cogs in an industrial machine or mindless puppets acting out a grotesque parody.

Expressionism gained impetus on June 28, 1914, when a Serbian terrorist assassinated the heir to the Austro-Hungarian throne, Archduke Franz Ferdinand, and sparked World War I. At the beginning of the war, generals talked of gallant cavalry charges and grandly announced that it would all be over "within three months." But it lasted more than four years and was one of the bloodiest wars in history. The battle lines stretched 475 miles from Belgium to France. In the first month of fighting 260,000 French troops were killed. In a single afternoon in 1916 50,000 British soldiers were mowed down by machine gun fire. When the war finally ended on November 11, 1918, nearly 9 million soldiers were dead, and another 21 million wounded. And yet the destruction was not finished; that same year a great flu pandemic hit the world. Before it was over one-fifth of the earth's population came down with the flu, and 50 to 100 million people died as a result. In the United States nearly 600,000 perished in the pandemic. That is more than the total number of Americans killed in combat during World War I, World War II, and the Vietnam and Korean Wars. In 1918 alone, more Americans died of the flu than have died of AIDS in the last 20 years.

Following the "great war" and the flu pandemic, the "roaring twenties" gave way to a massive worldwide economic downturn known as the Great Depression. In the United States 33 percent of banks failed (compared with only 1 percent in the 2008–09 recession), the stock market lost 85 percent of its value (compared to a 53.8 percent drop in 2008–2009), and the unemployment rate hit 25 percent (compared to 10.1 percent in 2009). A graduating college senior in 1930 stood little chance of finding a job for five to ten years. (See the Spotlight "The Revolt of the Beavers.")

These difficult times brought on a new cynicism and apathy. Many began to believe that the German philosopher Friedrich Nietzsche (1844–1900) had been right when he proclaimed, "God is dead . . . and we have killed him." Nietzsche felt that the absence of God was a tragedy, but also believed human beings needed to accept the tragedy and move forward in a world that was unjust and meaningless.

The way to expressionism in the theatre had been opened by works such as *A Dream Play* (1902) by Swedish playwright August Strindberg (1849–1912)—a 14-act play that follows the disconnected logic of a dream. However, after World War I, expressionist plays became political and often supported socialist and pacifist causes. An example is Elmer Rice's (1892–1967) *The Adding Machine*

SPOTLIGHT ON The Revolt of the Beavers

During the Great Depression, as part of Roosevelt's New Deal, the government formed the Works Progress Administration (WPA) to help put Americans back to work. The WPA included the Federal Theatre Project, which was designed to employ thousands of actors, directors, designers, and musicians who could not find work.

With so many Americans suffering unemployment, some of the plays produced by the Federal Theatre Project had themes that concerned the working class. For example, one of the musicals funded was *The Cradle Will Rock*, which was directed by Orson Welles (1915–1985), famous for later directing the movie *Citizen Kane* (1941), and produced by John Houseman (1902–1988), who many years later won an Oscar for best supporting actor in the movie *Paper Chase* (1973).

The Cradle Will Rock was a political story about steelworkers who want to unionize for representation at the huge corporations, which in the play controlled the press, the universities, and churches. The production was set to open on June 17, 1937, but bowing to right-wing pressure groups, the government locked the doors on the play before it opened. When Welles and Houseman tried to use the props and costumes to stage the play at another theatre, U.S. government agents surrounded the theatre. Not letting this stop him, Houseman rented an even larger theatre where they intended to perform the play for free. Thousands of people showed up. But before the curtain could rise, Actors' Equity (the union that represents stage actors—see Chapter 8)

refused to let the actors act on the stage without being paid. It looked as if the play would never open.

Then, an actress named Olive Stanto had a brilliant idea. The union said they could not act without being paid "on the stage." It said nothing about acting for free in the auditorium. She began to sing. Soon the other cast members joined in. That night the entire musical was performed in the auditorium, with no costumes, no props, no set, and no orchestra. Archibald MacLeish, the American poet and writer, called it the most moving theatrical experience of his life. After the performance the government fired John Houseman and Orson Welles quit.

Congressional critics continued to attack the pro-worker ideas presented by the Federal Theatre Project artists. Another government target was the children's play *The Revolt of the Beavers*, which they claimed disseminated communist propaganda. Congressional hearings were called. During one of these hearings, a defender of the Federal Theatre Project described it as having "Marlowesque madness," referring to Christopher Marlowe, the great Elizabethan playwright (see Chapter 15). To which Representative Joseph Starnes of Alabama asked: "Who is this Christopher Marlowe, is he a Communist?"

The Federal Theatre was the first of the WPA projects to have its funding cut. It existed for only four years, but in that short time over 30 million people attended its plays. It was certainly a high point of creativity in American theatre. And it is a reminder of the power of the theatre and the deep desire of some to silence it.

(1923), about a man named Mr. Zero, who is fired from his job and replaced by an adding machine. Another common expressionist theme was the conflicts between truth and illusion, life and art, reality and appearance. The classic *Six Characters in Search of an Author* (1922) by Luigi Pirandello (1867–1936) embodies this approach—in this play, six characters take on a life of their own when the playwright fails to complete the play in which they were supposed to appear.

One of the most famous expressionist playwrights is Eugene O'Neill. O'Neill (1888–1953) was the first American playwright to win the Nobel Prize for literature (1936). Many of his plays in Romantic and realistic styles are considered American classics—*A Touch of the Poet* (1935), *The Iceman Cometh* (1939), and the autobiographical plays *A Long Day's Journey into Night* (1956) and *A Moon for the Misbegotten* (1952), in which he wrote about his mother's drug addiction and his father's alcoholism. But he was also known for expressionist plays such as *The Hairy Ape* (1922), the story of Yank, a stoker in the engine room of an ocean liner. At the beginning of the play, Yank thinks that his life is important and useful because he is one of the men who make the great ship move. But when the shipowner's daughter visits the engine room, she is shocked by what she sees. To her, the room seems like a steel cage, and the stokers look like Neanderthals. Overwhelmed by the sight, she faints. Because of her reaction, Yank begins to question his point of view. When he visits New York City, his perception is that the city is a slave to grotesque commercialism and inhabited by identical puppets with simpering, toneless voices. When these "puppets" ignore him, Yank lashes out and lands in jail. He decides to seek revenge by destroying the complex social machine that is controlling his life, but he can find no support. He goes to a zoo, where he finds a gorilla that seems to understand him. When Yank frees the beast, it crushes him and throws him into the cage. In the end, Yank dies bewildered and humiliated, realizing that he had no power over the massive machine that dominated his life.

Like expressionism, **Dadaism** and **surrealism** were founded in opposition to realism. For Dadaists, life has no purpose, and they confused and antagonized their audiences by refusing to adhere to a coherent set of principles, thereby mirroring the madness of the world. The performances of the late stand-up comedian Andy Kaufman are as close to Dada as one can find in contemporary popular culture. Like Dadaism, surrealism attacked the evils and restrictions of society. But, unlike the Dadaists, the surrealists tried to reveal the higher reality of the unconscious mind with fantastic imagery and contradictory images. They felt that if the subconscious could avoid the conscious mind's control, it would rise to the surface, where it could be used to find truth. Surrealist performances were often violent and cruel as they tried to shock the audience into the realization that "normal" realities are arbitrary.

One of the most famous surrealists was the French writer and director Antonin Artaud (1896–1948), who studied Asian religions, mysticism, and ancient cultures; he spent part of his life with the Tarahumara Indians, an indigenous people of northwest Mexico. Artaud wrote several manifestos and the book *The Theatre and Its Double* (1938), in which he declared that theatre, above all, should wake the nerves and heart. Artaud called for a **Theatre of Cruelty**, which would agitate the masses, attack the spectators' sensibilities, and purge people of their destructive tendencies. Artaud and the surrealists rejected Stanislavsky's methods of teaching acting. They wanted stylized, ritualized performances, not realism, which they felt restricted the theatre to the study of psychological problems and society's dilemmas. Artaud argued that proscenium arch theatres create a barrier between the audience and actors and that performances should instead be staged in found spaces, such as warehouses and airplane hangars.

> [Absurdism] is that which is devoid of purpose. . . . Cut off from his religious, metaphysical and transcendental roots, man is lost; all his actions become senseless, absurd, useless.
>
> **Eugène Ionesco,** Absurdist playwright

Absurdism: Beckett, Ionesco, and Pinter

The devastation and genocide of World War II led many playwrights to conclude that humans face a cold, hostile universe and that our existence is futile. Relationships seemed ineffective, language was imprecise, and the traditional structure of plays failed to reflect the ridiculousness and anxiety of a cosmos without

Realism, whether it be socialist or not, falls short of reality. It shrinks it, attenuates it, falsifies it; it does not take into account our basic truths and our fundamental obsessions: love, death, astonishment. It presents man in a reduced and estranged perspective. Truth is in our dreams, in the imagination.

Eugène Ionesco, Absurdist playwright

cause or fate. They also had no use for characters with detailed motivations that completely and logically explain their actions, because humans act in baffling, contradictory, and unexpected ways. Thus **absurdism** was born. It is sometimes useful to view absurdism as loosely divided into three broad categories that often overlap: fatalist, hilarious, and existentialist. Fatalistic absurdism suggests we are trapped in an irrational universe where even basic communication is impossible. Hilarious absurdism highlights the insanity of life in a comical way. Existential absurdism holds that human beings are naturally alone, without purpose or mission, in a universe that has no God. The absence of God means that humans have no fixed destiny, but, for the existentialists, this is not a negative, for without a God humans can create their own existences, purpose, and meaning. Existentialists feel that we can escape from the chaos of the world only by making significant decisions, taking action, and accepting complete responsibility, without excuses, for our actions.

Perhaps the most famous of the absurdist playwrights was Samuel Beckett (1906–1989). Beckett could best be considered a fatalist, though his work is sometimes hilarious and can ask existential questions as well. His plays include *Endgame* (1957), *Krapp's Last Tape* (1958), and *Happy Days* (1961). As a young man Beckett was an assistant to and disciple of the novelist James Joyce. When World War II broke out in Europe, he was trapped in Paris where he joined the French Resistance and saw many of his close friends murdered by the Nazis. After the war, he began writing plays that dramatized moral and social uncertainty. His most famous work is *Waiting for Godot* (1953): Vladimir and Estragon, two clown-like tramps, meet each day on a barren plain, a dreamlike vacuum that some critics say is the aftermath of a nuclear holocaust, and wait for someone named Godot. They try to break the monotony of waiting by bickering, doing comic routines, and contemplating suicide, but Godot never shows up. The play is about our inability to take control of our existence and the absurdity of wasting our lives hoping to know the unknowable. The Irish literary critic Vivien Mercier famously described *Godot* as a two-act play "in which nothing happens, twice."

Samuel Beckett's *Happy Days* is an absurdist play about a husband and wife. The wife, played here by Felicity Kendal, spends the duration of the play half-buried in a pile of dirt. As time goes slowly by, she finds occasional happiness in chatting with her husband and engaging in petty rituals such as brushing her hair. In true absurdist fashion, her predicament is never explained. Absurdist playwrights would agree with Scottish psychiatrist Ronald D. Laing (1927–1989), who said, "Madness is a sane response to an insane world." This 2003 production was directed by Peter Hall, Arts Theatre, London.

Robbie Jack/Corbis Entertainment/Corbis

Another well-known absurdist is Romanian-born French playwright Eugène Ionesco (1912–1994), who might best fit into the category of hilarious absurdism. His play *The Bald Soprano* (1949) is a parody of the middle class. Mr. and Mrs. Smith and Mr. and Mrs. Martin, polite but empty people, spend a social evening together and engage in silly small talk, full of clichés. Often in a very comical way, his plays convey the seeming uselessness of trying to find meaning in a universe ruled by chance and irrational values. One of his most famous plays is *Rhinoceros* (1959), in which the characters are slowly transformed into horned, thick-skinned mammals; although this vision of humanity is certainly fatalistic, chilling, and insightful, it is also hard not to laugh when we see and hear this transformation from human to beast.

Harold Pinter (b. 1930), winner of the 2005 Nobel Prize in literature, is another influential absurdist playwright that might best be categorized as hilarious. Pinter writes "comedies of menace" that both frighten and entertain. One of his most popular plays is *The Dumb Waiter* (1957), about two hired killers, Ben and Gus, employed by an enigmatic organization to murder an unknown victim. The two hit men wait for instructions in a dingy basement room that contains a dumbwaiter (a tiny elevator used to convey food from one floor to another). All they know is that instructions will soon arrive; they'll make the hit and drive off, as they always do. Then an envelope with matches is mysteriously pushed under the door. Ben and Gus become nervous. Next the dumbwaiter moves, and someone from above orders "two braised steaks and chips, two sago puddings and two teas without sugar." Fearing that they will be discovered, Ben and Gus attempt to placate whoever is above by sending up bits of food. It doesn't work, for the dumbwaiter comes back down with requests for Greek and Chinese dishes. When Gus goes out for water, Ben gets instructions on the dumbwaiter to kill the next person who enters the room. Moments later, Gus is pushed in. He's stripped of his jacket, tie, and gun. He is the next victim, and the play ends. Pinter is famous for his dialogue, which captures the incoherence, broken language, and pauses of modern speech but also has a **Kafkaesque** quality, meaning that it is marked by surreal distortion and impending danger. (This term comes from the writing of Franz Kafka [1883–1924], whose books described an often unintelligible and hostile world.) Perhaps the most renowned playwright of existential absurdism is Jean-Paul Sartre.

Jean-Paul Sartre: Existentialism

Another philosophical approach to grow out of the atrocities of World War II was existentialism. As we've mentioned, **existentialism** is a philosophy that ties in to the absurdist movement, though it does add a certain ray of light to the picture. Existentialists hold that human beings are naturally alone, without purpose or mission, in a universe that has no God. The absence of God means that humans have no fixed destiny, but, for the existentialists, this is not a negative, for without God humans can create their own existences, purpose, and meaning. Existentialists feel that we can escape from the chaos of the world only by making significant decisions, taking action, and accepting complete responsibility, without excuses, for our actions. For existentialists, humans are earth-bound and can define themselves only by what they do with their lives. For example, right after World War II many Nazis were brought to trial, and one of their common defenses was that they had had no choice but to obey orders. Existentialists would argue that individual moral standards are more important than a society's arbitrary and often absurd rules. They would say that there is no difference between German officers blindly following orders and people who blindly follow religious laws without thinking for themselves. Existentialism

> Man is fully responsible for his nature and his choices.
>
> **Jean-Paul Sartre,** Philosopher and playwright

teaches that humans have free will, but that there are no alibis, no gods to thank, no devils to blame, no original sin to account for our situation and that existence precedes essence. For example, a pair of scissors is created to cut paper—to cut paper is the essence of the scissors. According to existentialists, however, humans do not have a predetermined essence, or purpose; instead, they must use their minds and their existence to create their essence (see the Spotlight "Absurdism and Aristotle's Final Cause" and the discussions of "final cause" in Chapters 14, 15, and 16). This

SPOTLIGHT ON Absurdism and Aristotle's Final Cause

To understand the absurdist playwrights we must go all the way back to Aristotle (384–322 BCE), who wrote in his book *Physics* that there were four "causes" he believed explained how the world worked. You might remember from Chapter 14, "The Dark Ages to the Dawn of the Renaissance," that "material cause" was simply the physical stuff of the world. For example, the material cause of a statue would be raw marble. The next was "formal cause," which was physical stuff whose potential has been actualized—for example, a finished, carved statue. The third was the "efficient cause," the being or thing that caused the material to become formalized, in this case, the artist. The "final cause" was that which brought it all together, the purpose, meaning, or "end in mind"—or the statue's point, theme, or intent. The most important cause is final cause, for it implies that everything has a purpose. But what if everything doesn't have a purpose?

Today, most people are Aristotelians, whether they know it or not. They live their lives believing—or at least hoping—that everything has a purpose, a final cause. For example, when terrible things happen to us we often justify it by saying, "It's all part of God's plan." As the American historian Will Durant said, most of us long to believe that the great drama of our lives, "has a just author and a noble end." Absurdist playwrights actively reject this belief. If "final cause" is a reality, the absurdists contend, then what is the purpose of childhood diseases, or random floods, tornados, hurricanes, hailstorms, volcanic eruptions, tsunamis, earthquakes, and flu pandemics? Philosopher, mathematician, and historian Bertrand Russell wrote in his book *Mysticism and Logic*, "Man is the product of causes which had no prevision of the end they were achieving; that his origin, his growth, his hopes and fears, his loves and his beliefs, are but the outcome of accidental collo-

cations of atoms. . . ." Following this line of logic, the absurdist playwrights suggest that it certainly would be absurd to look for some sort of implied meaning in universe. If there is no final cause, then would it not be intelligent for human beings to invent their own final cause?

The absurdist playwrights eliminated final cause and created plays where human beings had to laboriously survive the careless brutalities of nature, the bloodshed of human aggression, and the tribulations of existence—both trivial and extreme—without the assurance of dogma or the hope of a divine purpose. They felt that they were portraying the true reality of human life, and that it is only in dealing directly with that reality that we can begin to improve the human condition. It was their hope that human beings would no longer be slaves to external metaphysical and theological purposes imposed upon them by culture or society, but rather create our own unique final cause and maintain integrity and honesty with the self from moment to moment.

Waiting for Godot by Samuel Beckett is perhaps the most famous absurdist play. This production was directed by Sean Mathias and featured Patrick Stewart and Ian McKellen.

Geraint Lewis/Alamy Stock Photo

idea contradicts what many religions teach, that essence precedes existence, or that we are all created with a preconceived purpose.

A notable existentialist is French philosopher and playwright Jean-Paul Sartre. His plays included *The Flies* (1943) and *No Exit* (1944). *No Exit* was first performed in France in May 1944, just before the liberation of Paris and a year before the end of World War II. It is the story of a man and two women, who find themselves in Hell, which just happens to be a living room decorated with Victorian furniture. For Sartre, existence is the will to create our future, and the opposite of existence is not having the power to create our future or giving that power away—whether through law, religion, or government. Sartre said, "Man is nothing else but what he proposes, he exists only in so far as he realizes himself, he is therefore nothing else but the sum of his actions, nothing else but what his life is." In *No Exit*, the character of Garcin is more succinct: "You are nothing else but your life."

Bertolt Brecht: Appealing to the Intellect

Bertolt Brecht (1898–1956) was a German poet, director, and playwright who also challenged traditional ideas about theatre. In 1929, after watching policemen shoot unarmed civilians during a protest, Brecht became a communist. Four years later he was forced to flee Germany because of his outspoken criticism of Hitler. Brecht also began to rebel against the commercial theatre, which he felt catered only to the wealthy and privileged. He set out to write and stage plays that would force the audience to think about the social issues of the day. His great innovation was **epic theatre.** An *epic* is usually a story, play, or poem that has a large cast, covers a long period, and includes a large number of sometimes unrelated incidents. Although epic theatre has been around for centuries, the term is now most often associated with Brecht's theories. The cycle plays of the Middle Ages could be considered epics (see Chapter 14). And today Tony Kushner's sweeping two-part *Angels in America* (1993; I: *Millennium Approaches* and II: *Perestroika*) could also be called an epic (see Chapter 3).

Brecht viewed the grand scope of epic theatre as a perfect mechanism to confront the numerous social and political troubles of his day, but was worried that the theatre could also be used to brainwash the masses. Rather than being lulled into the illusion of the play, Brecht wanted his audience to remain alienated from the performance so they could critically consider the play's themes. He called this *Verfremdung*, or "estrangement," what we refer to today as the **alienation effect.** For example, have you ever become so totally immersed in a play, or movie, or so completely sympathized with a character that during the performance you lost track of time? When you were so acutely immersed, did you stop and think about the political, social, and economic implications of the story? Most likely you did not. Such total immersion, Brecht felt, was dangerous because it opens the audience to mindless manipulation. People who are constantly manipulated in a theatre, Brecht said, were also more susceptible to being brainwashed outside the theatre by dictators, corporations, and religions. Certainly Brecht's concerns would apply to average

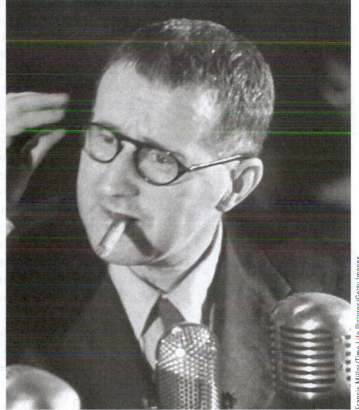

Francis Miller/Time Life Pictures/Getty Images

Best-known for his plays *The Life of Galileo* (1938), *Mother Courage and Her Children* (1939), and *The Caucasian Chalk Circle* (1945), Bertolt Brecht was one of the most influential playwrights of the twentieth century. Brecht believed that theatres should be more akin to political lecture halls. He wanted his audiences to think about issues rather than sympathize with the characters or lose themselves in a story. His political ideas often got him into trouble. In this picture, Brecht is questioned before the House Un-American Activities Committee.

Americans who spend thousands of hours each year being drawn into television shows and yet seldom stop to critically think about what they are watching.

Brecht eliminated the vicarious experience of theatre by using various staging techniques. Sometimes he would have the actors step out of character and address the audience directly, or he might expose the theatrical lights and remove the curtains to remind the audience they are in a theatre. In this way, Brecht argued, the audience would never lose sight of the fact that the stage was a stage, and the actors were not real people, only actors. Alienated from the play, the audience would then be motivated to intelligently and objectively reflect on the moral issues of the story rather than being lulled into the theatrical illusion that puts the audience into a non-thinking, trance-like state where they accept what they are told without serious contemplation.

A few of Brecht's better-known plays are *The Threepenny Opera* (1928), *Galileo* (1945), *The Good Person of Setzuan* (1947), and *The Caucasian Chalk Circle* (1948). Perhaps his most famous is *Mother Courage and Her Children* (1941), set during the Thirty Years' War (1618–1648), a series of religious and political wars between the Protestants and Catholics that eventually involved most of Europe. The action of the play is epic: Mother Courage travels with her canteen wagon through Sweden, Poland, and Germany, profiting from the war by selling goods to the soldiers. *Mother Courage* makes a powerful statement about capitalism and war. Brecht's themes were often anti-capitalist, expressing the views that capitalism makes people work against one another and that it encourages selfishness and greed as well as injustice. During World War II, Brecht found sanctuary in Hollywood, where he wrote anti-Nazi films. However, he was later called before the House Un-American Activities Committee and forced to leave the country because of his Marxist ideas. He died in East Germany. (See the Spotlight "McCarthyism, Lillian Hellman, and the Theatre.")

The Threepenny Opera, one of Bertolt Brecht's best-known plays, incorporates many elements that foster the alienation effect. Political slogans are projected onto the back wall of the set, characters sometimes deliver their lines with their backs to the audience, and songs serve to keep the audience from getting too attached to the characters. This recent production staged by the University of Cincinnati College Conservatory of Music further enhances audience alienation by placing larger-than-life images of Brecht around the stage and prominently featuring signs that indicate settings, characters, and even the name of the play. Directed by Worth Gardner. Scenic design by Richard Finkelstein.

Richard Finkelstein Photography

SPOTLIGHT ON McCarthyism, Lillian Hellman, and the Theatre

The history of the United States is filled with attempts to censor plays for their content. After World War II, the United States endured one of its worst periods of censorship. McCarthyism, named for Joseph R. McCarthy, a Republican senator from Wisconsin, had actually begun in 1938 with a House committee's investigations of suspected "subversives" in Franklin Roosevelt's administration. After World War II ended, the Cold War began, and the House Un-American Activities Committee (HUAC) stepped up its work. In 1947 it gained notoriety by investigating alleged communist influence in Hollywood. The Hollywood Ten, a group of producers, directors, and screenwriters who refused to testify about their friends' political beliefs, were found guilty of contempt of Congress and sentenced to prison. The studios blacklisted, or refused to hire, anyone said to have an affiliation with or compassion for socialism or communism. In 1950 McCarthy formed a Senate subcommittee to conduct his own investigations of other sectors of U.S. society. Conformity was coerced and political messages were restricted through intimidation. In 1954, when McCarthy claimed without any solid evidence that the U.S. Army was riddled with communists, the Senate voted to censure him. However, the effects of McCarthyism and blacklisting lasted. For years plays and films in the United States had to champion capitalism and Christian ethics to be produced; meanwhile, in the Soviet Union, plays had to be in the style of social realism.

One of America's best-known playwrights in the middle of the twentieth century was Lillian Hellman (1905–1984). She is perhaps most famous for *The Children's Hour* (1934), a play about a spoiled, disturbed girl who ruins the lives of two female teachers by spreading rumors of an intimate relationship between them. On the play's opening night, there had been threats of injunctions and police actions to stop the production because it dared to suggest lesbianism. Before the Hays Office, the censor for Hollywood's studios, would let the script be used for a movie, they ordered it changed. The result was *These Three* (1936), a bowdlerized version of the play that had no hint of lesbianism. In the play, a young doctor loves one of the women, but the other woman loves her too. In the screen version, both women love the doctor. By 1961, a film version with Audrey Hepburn and Shirley MacLaine would be brave enough to vaguely allude to the central dramatic question, but it was still a pale imitation of Hellman's script.

When the play was re-staged in 1952, Hellman was called before HUAC. Her longtime companion, novelist Dashiell Hammett, had already been sent to prison for not cooperating with the committee. Hellman was willing to answer questions about herself but refused to answer any questions about her friends and acquaintances. She told the committee, "To hurt innocent people whom I knew many years ago in order to save myself is, to me, inhuman and indecent and dishonorable. I cannot and will not cut my conscience to fit this year's fashions." Hellman was blacklisted by the studios but not held in contempt of Congress.

While these witch hunts were silencing many voices in the United States, a few wrote plays that attacked the censorship and intimidation. Arthur Miller's *The Crucible* (1953), which was about the Salem witch trials, was a thinly veiled allegory, and *Inherit the Wind* (1955) by Jerome Lawrence and Robert E. Lee defended freedom of thought in its portrayal of the Scopes trial about teaching evolution in the schools.

In this original production of Lillian Hellman's *The Children's Hour*, student Mary Tilford is questioned about her allegation that two of her teachers are lovers. Because of its subject matter, *The Children's Hour* was banned initially in Boston, Chicago, and London. Even the Pulitzer Prize selection committee refused to attend the play. This 1934 production featured (l to r) Robert Keith as Dr. Cardin, Anne Revere as teacher Martha Dobie, Florence McGee as Mary, Katherine Emery as teacher Karen Wright, and Katherine Emmett as Mary's aunt. Directed by Herman Shumlin, Maxine Elliott's Theatre, New York.

Postwar Theatre in the United States

At the end of each world war, the United States, although paranoid about communism and suffering from the deaths of tens of thousands of its sons and daughters, seemed filled with optimism. Unlike most European plays, most American plays were still realistic. However, mixing various isms in one play soon became popular. For example, Arthur Miller's (1915–2005) *Death of a Salesman* (1949) mixes realism and expressionism. Most of this play—about the attempts of Willy Loman, an unsuccessful traveling salesman, to achieve the American dream—is in a realistic style and covers the last 24 hours of Willy's life as he attempts to pay his debts and decides to kill himself in order to leave his family a life insurance settlement. The expressionistic parts of the play are sequences from Willy's point of view; these express his rosy visions of the past, including the great hope that he has for his two sons. The realistic sections of the play show Willy's blind desire to attain the elusive, perhaps nonexistent, American dream, whereas the expressionistic moments illustrate Willy's limited view of what life should be.

Another form of realism is found in the works of Tennessee Williams (1911–1983), known for *The Glass Menagerie* (1945) and many other plays. This play tells the story of Tom; his disabled sister, Laura; and their controlling mother, Amanda, who tries to make a match between Laura and a gentleman caller. The style of *The Glass Menagerie* has been called **poetic realism** because the realism of the play is expressed through lyrical language.

Yet plenty of traditional realistic plays in post–World War II America also attacked the system and attempted to put real life on stage. Because realistic plays usually convey a social message, many activist writers used this style during the civil rights movement. One of the most famous plays of this period was Lorraine Hansberry's (1930–1965) *A Raisin in the Sun* (1959), a living-room drama about three generations of an African American family who struggle against economic, social, and political prejudices as well as self-doubt. Set in a small apartment in Chicago's South Side, the play tells the story of Walter Lee, a chauffeur, who dreams of a better life. He wants to use the life insurance money his family received after his father's death to open his own business, a liquor store. But his mother rejects his dream and wants to spend the money on his sister's aspiration of attending medical school and her own desire to move the family to a better neighborhood. Mama Younger even puts down a deposit on a new house in what happens to be an all-white neighborhood. When a con artist steals the majority of the life-insurance money, Walter Lee falls into despair. Then a representative of the all-white neighborhood tries to take advantage of the situation by offering to buy back their new house. Walter is ready to sell, but then he regains his integrity and decides that the family will take the house after all.

A Raisin in the Sun was based on Hansberry's own experiences. In 1938, when she was eight years old, her father bought a house in a white neighborhood. A few weeks later they were attacked by an angry white mob. A brick was thrown through Hansberry's bedroom window, narrowly missing her. Forced to leave the neighborhood, her father took his fight all the way to the Illinois Supreme Court where, in 1959, he won. That same year *A Raisin in the Sun* was produced and Lorraine Hansberry became the first black woman playwright to be produced on Broadway. It would go on to run for more than 500 performances.

Gordon Parks/Time Life Pictures/Getty Images

After a disappointing audience response during the Broadway preview of *A Raisin in the Sun*, Lorraine Hansberry thought the play would fail. However, at the premiere, the audience and the critics responded enthusiastically, and *A Raisin in the Sun* has become a pioneering example of African American theatre. Wanting to avoid stereotyped characters that audiences would dismiss, Hansberry created complex characters who struggled with a painfully realistic situation. Like the naturalist plays of the early twentieth century, *Raisin* was a glimpse of life that most Broadway patrons had not seen before. This original production featured Sidney Poitier (center) and Ruby Dee as Walter Lee and Ruth Younger. Directed by Lloyd Richards, Ethel Barrymore Theatre, New York, 1959.

Off Broadway, and Off-Off Broadway

The 1960s was a time of great social turmoil all over the world. During the 1950s, the United States had seen the Korean War, McCarthyism, the threat of mass annihilation with the Cold War, and the beginning of the civil rights movement. The new decade brought political assassinations, urban riots, the Vietnam War, peace protests, and the women's liberation movement—filling the streets with marches, demonstrations, and civil disobedience.

Starting in the late 1950s, small theatres had begun to spring up in several Manhattan neighborhoods to put on plays about the issues of the day. These theatres became collectively known as **Off Broadway**. Although the term was not coined until the 1950s, the movement had begun 50 years earlier as the **little theatre movement**, which staged inexpensive, noncommercial productions of artistically significant plays in small, out-of-the-way theatres. From the mid-1950s through the mid-1960s, there was a proliferation of little theatres in Manhattan, including Circle in the Square, The Phoenix Theatre, The Jewish Repertory, Circle Rep, The Manhattan Theatre Club, and The Negro Ensemble. Off-Broadway theatres produced new versions of commercial plays that had failed, neglected plays, plays of social protest, and experimental works. By 1959, there were 74 Off-Broadway productions, more than were playing on Broadway.

During the next 20 years, these small theatres introduced many playwrights who are well known today, including Edward Albee, Britain's Caryl Churchill, John Guare, Sam Shepard, Megan Terry, Jean-Claude van Itallie, and Lanford Wilson, as well as the actors Jason Robards, Colleen Dewhurst, Al Pacino, and Dustin Hoffman.

By the late 1960s, Off Broadway was becoming a victim of its own success, as actors, designers, and technical unions were demanding better working conditions and higher pay. Soon, production costs grew and therefore plays had to become more commercial and less experimental in order to attract a larger audience. The result was a new wave of even smaller, less expensive, alternative, experimental theatres: the **Off-Off-Broadway** movement. These tiny theatres—fewer than a hundred seats—flourished in lofts, basements, coffeehouses, storefronts, cafes, and in any found space that could be adapted for use as a theatre. At Off-Off-Broadway theatres, diverse and often formerly taboo topics such as homosexuality could be frankly discussed, and political plays that denounced the Vietnam War were the norm. At the Off-Off-Broadway theatre Caffe Cino, actors had an eight-by-eight-foot stage and had to pass a hat to cover expenses. At the Café La Mama, which opened in 1961, young, talented playwrights like Sam Shepard and Lanford Wilson were given a chance to break into the business.

Experimental theatre groups tested not only the premises of society but also of theatre. They questioned the idea that theatre had to take place in a theatre, with the audience sitting on one side and actors performing on the other. A few theatre companies even eliminated the need for a theatre by staging **happenings**, or unstructured theatrical events, on street corners, at bus stops, in lobbies, and virtually anywhere else people gathered. Some experimental theatre groups tried to bring ritual back into the theatre; others mixed movies and theatre into multimedia performances. In 1961 the **Bread and Puppet Theatre** began to use both giant puppets and actors to enact parables denouncing the Vietnam War and materialism. Many of these companies were inspired by the writings of Brecht, Beckett, Artaud, and the Polish Laboratory Theatre headed by Jerzy Grotowski (1933–1999). The Polish Laboratory was famous for taking theatre back to its basics. It limited the technical side of the theatre and promoted the actor audience relationship. Grotowski also changed the traditional seating arrangement and instead integrated the audience into the action of the play. For example, in *Kordian* (1962), a play that takes place in a mental institution, the audience sits on the stage with the actor-patients.

One of the most famous of these experimental theatres is **The Living Theatre**, which was founded in 1946 by Julian Beck (1925–1985) and Judith Malina (1926–2015). The Living Theatre has dedicated itself to contemporary social issues and highly political, aesthetically radical plays. In their heyday in the 1960s and 1970s, they staged works like *The Brig* (1963), which dramatized daily life in a Marine Corps prison, and *Paradise Now* (1968), in which actors asked the audience to join them in a protest calling for a social revolution or were asked to tear off their clothes and were led, naked, into the streets for an impromptu embrace with audience members. Julian Beck said, "We insisted on experimentation that was an image for a changing society. If one can experiment in theatre, one can experiment in life." Members of The Living Theatre spent a lot of time in jail for their nonviolent protests against the Vietnam War.

The experimental theatre movement spread across the United States, as hole-in-the-wall theatres tested new ground. In Chicago, the Off-Loop theatre movement mirrored the Off-Off-Broadway movement by staging experimental plays in theatres outside the downtown area (the Loop). In California, the San Francisco Mime Troupe promoted civil rights and women's rights, and El Teatro Campesino staged plays on the backs of flatbed trucks beside the picket lines of striking Chicano and Filipino migrant workers. Meanwhile, in New York City, the National Black Theatre incorporated both realistic acting and African ritual into plays like *Slave Ship* (1970), and Joseph Papp's Public Theater gave birth to the offbeat musical *Hair* (1967), the story of hippies fighting the draft during the Vietnam War.

Contemporary Theatre: It's Alive!

The five categories of theatre discussed in Chapter 1 are with us today: commercial, historical, political, experimental, and cultural. Commercial theatre— what we call "show business"— still dominates, as it always has, but the number of theatres that produce it has shrunk. Today, Broadway is dominated by small-cast comedies, blockbuster musicals, and—some feel— a lack of innovation. Theatre critics say that Broadway has turned into nothing more than one big theme park where only safe, profitable plays or Disney-imitation musicals can be staged. The major problem is cost. As with Hollywood movies, if a lot of money is at stake, producers are reluctant to take chances. Even Off-Broadway theatre, which was once the source of new ideas, has been forced to play it safe because of prohibitive costs. In spite of the problems, the commercial theatre continues to attract millions of people each year. Like most Hollywood blockbusters, the commercial theatre attracts an audience because it presents safe themes and reaffirms mainstream values.

Regional theatre is a strong force in the contemporary theatre world. A regional theatre is a permanent, professional theatre located outside of New York City. The regional theatre movement started in 1947, when Margo Jones

Photo Archives/University of Wyoming

The little theatre movement led to the opening of thousands of smaller noncommercial theatres located all over the country. These theatres are sometimes called "black boxes" because their walls are frequently painted black, and "99-seaters" because they often have fewer than 100 seats in order to comply with Equity rules. Here William L. Sircin III and Lindsay Neinast play a scene from the comedy *Seagulls in a Cherry Tree* in a black box theatre.

When we talk about the future of the American theatre, we have to talk about the future of our economic structure. There is none supporting the theatre. And that is becoming an increasing concern. Not only is it exorbitant to produce in New York, it's exorbitant everywhere. And the funding is tied up with the attitude of government officials, who can do a kind of benign censorship. So I think the whole economic infrastructure is at risk.

Paula Vogel, Playwright

founded the first fully professional, nonprofit, resident theatre in Dallas. A short time later, the Arena Stage was founded in Washington, D.C., and the Alley Theatre in Houston. A host of other regional professional theatres followed: the Guthrie Theatre in Minneapolis (1963), the Actors Theatre of Louisville (1964), the Mark Taper Forum in Los Angeles (1967), and many others. These theatres now do what Broadway did 50 years ago. By staging new plays alongside commercial hits and historical plays, they appeal to the intellectual audiences that Hollywood seldom serves. Playwright John Guare says, "Broadway is the place where tourists come. When I was a kid at Yale Drama School back in the 60s, you dreamed about having a play on Broadway. I don't think anybody dreams that today. You dream of having a play at the Seattle Rep, or Louisville, or the Goodman, or Trinity Rep. That's where the theatre is, and that's healthy."

Thanks in part to regional theatres, historical theatre is alive and well. Productions of dramas by such playwrights as Ibsen, Shaw, Goethe, Aeschylus, Sophocles, and Euripides still dot the landscape. In 2003, Aristophanes' 2,400-year-old comedy *Lysistrata* (see Chapter 13) was simultaneously produced in 59 countries as a protest against the war in Iraq. In any given week, more than 200 professional productions of Shakespeare's plays are taking place in theatres across the United States—and hundreds more in high school, community, and college theatres. College and regional theatres are the main source of historical theatre because they feel it is part of their mission to educate the public, as well as their actors, about the various styles and ideas in theatre over the centuries.

Experimental theatre is also flourishing, because playwrights, directors, designers, and actors always want to test their premises and reinvent their art. One new type of experimental theatre is **performance art**, a term used to describe performances that mix theatre, visual arts, music, dance, gesture, and rituals. Performance artists often use multimedia effects, sounds, and lighting effects to make a point and allow the audience to understand its deeper implications. They often reject the traditional elements of drama: plot, dialogue, characters, and setting. They are not interested in telling a story but in conveying a state of being. Like Dada and Theatre of Cruelty performers of the past,

Performance artists seek to challenge audiences, often by breaking social rules in order to force the observers to think about current issues. Instead of a traditional theatre or performance space, performance artists are interested in public arenas, such as galleries, parks, garages—or a Russian Orthodox Church. Pictured here are members of Pussy Riot, a Russian punk rock protest group, staging an unauthorized performance critical of the government and state sponsored religion, in Moscow's Cathedral of Christ the Savior.

ITAR-TASS Photo Agency/Alamy Stock Photo

performance artists seek to challenge the audience. They often break social rules in order to force the observers to think about current issues. Instead of a traditional theatre or performance space, performance artists are interested in public arenas, such as galleries, parks, garages—anywhere that fits their needs. (For information on the cultural diversity of performance art, see Chapter 3.)

Theatre in the Digital Age

In a world dominated by digital media, theatre may seem outdated to some. Today you buy your tickets online, computers control the special effects during the performance, and audiences tweet their reviews after the curtain. When it comes right down to it, the core elements of theatre are old-fashioned. There have been a few theatre companies that have tried to incorporate cutting-edge technology directly into their productions, but most theatres cannot afford such add-ons. And they are "add-ons"—theatre may be old-fashioned, but that's because its core element is human beings. Theatre does not need computers, or holographic imaging, or hoverboards to be relevant, the same as a book is not made more relevant because it is delivered to you on a screen. But a book does need a reader to be relevant, and the theatre needs an audience. And there's the rub. Will modern audiences (sated on a diet of Smartphones, Twitter, Tumbler, Snapchat, Vine, and whatever new forms of social media that are invented in the next ten minutes) find theatre relevant? Can audience members who cannot forgo texting or messaging for five minutes commit to and appreciate the two hours' traffic of the stage?

In addition, study after study finds that theatre audiences are getting older. For example, Broadway theatres reported that 18 – to 34-year-olds make up less than 25 percent of their audience. The average age of a person who attends a Broadway musical is 43, while the average age of a person who attends a Broadway play is 53. In order to attract younger audiences many theatres offer massive discounts for students. In addition they have raised the age limit on what they consider a "student" from under 21 to 25 and in some cases they even offer student discounts for audience members as old as 35.

The recent economic crisis has also hit the theatre hard. Declining attendance and the loss of government and patron support have forced many theatres to trim their budgets to the bone. In addition, corporate sponsors have reduced their support of the arts and at times demanded creative control in exchange for their backing. For example, the Trinity Repertory Company in Providence, Rhode Island, got in trouble with a production of *Nickel and Dimed*, a play based on social critic Barbara Ehrenreich's book about what it's like to be a minimum-wage worker in this country. Oskar Eustis, artistic director of the company, reported that the major corporate supporters called, "suggesting that we were doing something counterproductive to our own interests by producing this play. Now, none of those corporate supporters took their money back, but those phone calls made us sweat." In the future will the theatre have to conform to the will of corporations to pay its bills?

The current financial straits of the theatre have forced many artistic directors to put entertainment and big box office above social, educational, or intellectual agendas. Crowd-pleasing mindless musicals like *Always Patsy Cline* and farcical comedies like *Greater Tuna* dominate our theatrical landscape, leaving little room for classics by Ibsen, Shakespeare, and

When corporations partner with local theatres, they often want the theatre's productions to reflect their corporate values. Such was not the case with Joan Holden's *Nickel and Dimed*, a play about Americans who work full-time for poverty-level wages. The story follows the undercover research of social critic Barbara Ehrenreich, who worked minimum-wage jobs in three states to see whether she could make ends meet. This 2003 production at the Guthrie Theater in Minneapolis marks the first time the play was staged in one of the cities where Ehrenreich did her research. So that Minneapolis's working poor could attend the play, the Guthrie made tickets available for $2. Featuring Robynn Rodriguez as Ehrenreich, this production was directed by Bill Rauch.

Michal Daniel

Times Square is the heart of the Broadway Theatre Scene. Hundreds of thousands see plays and musicals there every year, producing nearly a billion dollars in revenue. Some critics question if Broadway is the future of the American Theatre, claiming that it has become little more than a tourist attraction.

William Missouri Downs

> As the economy worsens, fewer and fewer risks are taken. Some subjects are out of bounds altogether, including strong critiques of capitalism or American foreign policy, in others words, anything that might cause individual donors to stop donating.
>
> **Karen Mapede,** Playwright and director

Williams, or modern playwrights like Suzan-Lori Parks, Neil LaBute, David Mamet, Paula Vogel, or Yasmina Reza—playwrights who make you think. Leaving these great voices out of theatre could be catastrophic for it limits out ability to think. Playwright Donald Margulies points out, "Our government, our society, has created a generation of people who simply don't think in abstraction . . . I think that one needs to put on one's thinking cap when going to the theater . . . I think that we have fostered a mentality that somehow is ill-equipped to handle abstract thought."

For the last hundred years, theatre has struggled to find its voice in a world dominated by film and then television. Now it must struggle against social media and the ever-changing landscape of interconnected technology. What will it have to struggle against tomorrow? Virtual reality machines? Many have predicted the theatre's demise. But it has one saving grace, one bit of uniqueness, and that is: the theatre is *live*. It does not separate you from the actors through technology or time. It doesn't isolate you from life. Theatre is about here and now, face-to-face contact and that is something no technology has ever improved upon.

Ironically we close this chapter with a quote from a movie, number 16 on the American Film Institute's list of 100 best American Films. The classic Bette Davis drama *All About Eve* (1950) tells the story of an aging stage actress:

> Want to know what the Theater is? A flea circus. Also opera. Also rodeos, carnivals, ballets, Indian tribal dances, Punch and Judy, a one-man band - all Theater. Wherever there's magic and make-believe and an audience - there's Theater. Donald Duck, Ibsen, and The Lone Ranger, Sarah Bernhardt, Poodles Hanneford, Lunt and Fontanne, Betty Grable, Rex and Wild, and Eleanora Duse. You don't understand them all, you don't like them all, why should you? The Theater's for everybody—you included, but not exclusively—so don't approve or disapprove. It may not be your Theater, but it's Theater of somebody, somewhere.

Curtain Call

Of the five common categories of theatre mentioned in Chapter 1 (commercial, historical, political, experimental, and cultural) the one type of theatre that will most likely survive is commercial, because it reduces art to a leisurely activity, requires little intellectual effort, and is not a threat to governments, the corporate class, or the power elite. We live in an age when the freedom of the NEA to award funds on artistic merit—regardless of the artist's political point of view—has been compromised. Ours is a time wherein theatre companies often consider ticket sales before an artist's unique vision, and where some of the best playwrights, actors, and directors have been lured away from the poverty of the stage to the big bucks of Hollywood.

Artistic expression flourishes when it answers primarily to the uncompromised voice of the artist, when honest expression and expert craftsmanship are valued more highly than commercial concerns, and when it is encouraged to grow by a society that funds, attends, and embraces the many diverse voices of the people.

SUMMARY

MindTap

Test your knowledge with online printable flashcards and online quizzing.

Twentieth-century inventions such as the camera and electric lights changed the centuries-old art of theatre forever. There was a call for sets to be more "genuine," acting to be more "honest," and dialogue to sound like everyday speech. This trend led to realism and naturalism, styles that were also influenced by the ideas of the modern thinkers Charles Darwin, Sigmund Freud, and Karl Marx. Plays began to feature true-to-life, well-motivated characters and themes that examined problems of society. In an attempt to be more real, realistic plays used box sets that allowed audiences to feel as if they were spying on the action of the play. For some, realism wasn't real enough, so they developed naturalism.

In the early part of the twentieth century, the film industry began to take its toll on the theatre. Thousands of theatres were closed or converted into movie theatres. Movies could produce realism and naturalism better than the theatre, so theatre artists decided to "re-theatricalize" the theatre. Their efforts led to many avant-garde "isms." Symbolism was an attempt to show inner truth through symbolic acts and images. Expressionism attempted to show life from the point of view of a particular character. Dadaists attempted to mirror the madness of the world, and surrealists attempted to reveal the higher reality of the unconscious mind. Absurdism was a result of the atrocities of the world wars, World War II in particular, and especially in Europe. There are three broad categories of absurdism: fatalist, existentialist, and hilarious absurdism. Fatalists show people trapped in an irrational universe where even basic communication is impossible. The existentialists believe that God is dead and that we must now do everything for ourselves. The hilarious absurdist playwrights highlight the insanity of life in a comic way.

The plays of epic theatre have a grand scope: a large cast, a long period of time, and a wide range of sometimes unrelated incidents. One of its greatest proponents is Bertolt Brecht, who also advocated an "alienation effect" so that the audience would always be aware they are watching a play and must confront political, social, or economic injustices.

In the United States after World War II, mixing various isms in one play became popular. Some plays were part realism and part expressionism, whereas others told realistic stories with lyrical language. The social unrest of the 1960s led to the Off-Broadway and Off-Off-Broadway movements in which less-commercial, more-experimental plays tested the boundaries of theatre. Today, regional theatres are growing in number and importance, as they are often more willing than big Broadway houses to stage new and experimental plays.

THEATRE

MODERN THEATRE

THEATRICAL EVENTS AND PLAYS		HISTORICAL / CULTURAL EVENTS
• Gas lighting first used in theatres (1816)	**1810**	• Stethoscope invented (1819)
• First black theatre company in the United States (1821) • Henrik Ibsen (1828–1906) • Minstrel shows debut in the United States (1828)	**1820**	• Mexico, including the provinces of California and Texas, declares independence from Spain (1821) • Symphony No. 9 (Ninth Symphony), Ludwig von Beethoven (1824)
• *Faust*, part two, Johann Wolfgang von Goethe (1832) • First box set (1832)	**1830**	
• Astor Place riot (1849) • August Strindberg (1849–1912)	**1840**	• Photography invented (ca. 1840) • *The Communist Manifesto*, Karl Marx (1848) • California Gold Rush (1849)
• Advent of Realism (ca. 1850) • George Bernard Shaw (1856–1950)	**1850**	• *On the Origin of Species*, Charles Darwin (1859)
• Anton Chekhov (1860–1904) • *The Black Crook*, Charles M. Barras (1866)	**1860**	• Abraham Lincoln assassinated at Ford's Theatre (1865)

THEATRICAL EVENTS AND PLAYS

HISTORICAL / CULTURAL EVENTS

1870

- Duke of Saxe-Meiningen's theatre tours (1874–1890)
- *A Doll's House*, Henrik Ibsen (1879)
- *The Pirates of Penzance*, Gilbert and Sullivan (1879)

- Telephone invented (1876)
- Thomas Edison invents light bulb (1879)

1880

- Electricity first used in a theatre (1885)
- Eugene O'Neill (1888–1953)

- Coca-Cola invented (1882)

1890

- Vaudeville dominates U.S. musical entertainment (ca. 1880–1920)
- *The Importance of Being Earnest*, Oscar Wilde (1895)
- *A Trip to Coontown*, Bob Cole and Billy Johnson (1898)
- The Moscow Art Theatre opens (1898)
- Bertolt Brecht (1898–1956)

- First moving pictures (ca. 1890)
- First skyscraper (1891)
- Ellis Island begins accepting immigrants to the United States (1892)
- First professional football game (1895)

1900

- Expressionism thrives (ca. 1900–1920)
- *The Cherry Orchard*, Anton Chekhov (1904)
- Lillian Hellman (1905–1984)
- Samuel Beckett (1906–1989)

- Ragtime is popular (1900–1918)
- *Interpretation of Dreams*, Sigmund Freud (1900)
- Wright brothers' first flight (1903)
- Albert Einstein formulates special theory of relativity (1905)
- Earthquake and fire destroy much of San Francisco (1906)

1910

- First Western-style theatre opens in Japan (1911)
- Tennessee Williams (1911–1983)
- Women allowed on stage in China (1911)
- Actors' Equity founded (1912)
- *Pygmalion*, George Bernard Shaw (1912)
- Arthur Miller (1915–2005)

- The *Titanic* sinks (1912)
- World War I (1914–1918)

1920

- *The Hairy Ape*, Eugene O'Neill (1922)
- Moscow Art Theatre troupe tours the United States (1923–1924)
- *Show Boat*, Hammerstein and Kern (1927)
- Edward Albee (b. 1928)
- *Threepenny Opera*, Bertolt Brecht (1928)

- First scheduled radio broadcast (1920)
- U.S. women gain right to vote (1920)
- *The Jazz Singer*, first talking movie (1927)
- Charles Lindbergh makes solo flight across Atlantic (1927)
- Stock market crashes, sparking Great Depression (1929)

THEATRICAL EVENTS AND PLAYS

HISTORICAL / CULTURAL EVENTS

1930

- Lorraine Hansberry (1930–1965)
- Harold Pinter (b. 1930)
- Augusto Boal (b. 1931)
- Jerzy Grotowski (1933–1999)
- Wole Soyinka (b. 1934)
- Caryl Churchill (b. 1938)

- Orson Welles's radio broadcast *The War of the Worlds* causes mass panic (1938)
- World War II (1939–1945)

1940

- Jean-Paul Sartre's *No Exit* first performed (1944)
- Tennessee Williams' *The Glass Menagerie* opens on Broadway (1944)

- World War Two Ends (1945)
- The Soviet Union begins its Blockade of Berlin (1948)

1950

- Arthur Miller's witch trial play *The Crucible* opens on Broadway (1954)
- *The Sound of Music* opens on Broadway (1959)

- The Korean War Begins (1950)
- Julius and Ethel Rosenberg Executed (1953)
- Joseph McCarthy begins Senate hearings into alleged Communist influence in the United States Army (1954)

1960

- *Fiddler on the Roof*, Jerry Bock, Sheldon Harnick, and Joseph Stein (1964)
- Suzan-Lori Parks (b. 1964)
- El Teatro Campesino (The Farmworkers Theatre) founded (1965)
- Off-Off-Broadway theatre begins (ca. 1966)
- *Dance of the Forest*, Wole Soyinka (1966)
- *Hair*, Gerome Ragni, James Rado, and Galt MacDermot (1968)

- Berlin Wall constructed (1960)
- First Beatles record released (1962)
- Martin Luther King's "I have a dream" speech at the Lincoln Memorial (1963)
- Tonkin Gulf Resolution begins major U.S. involvement in Vietnam War (1964)
- China begins Cultural Revolution (1966)
- Woodstock Art and Music Festival in upstate New York (1969)

1970

- *Jesus Christ Superstar*, Tim Rice and Andrew Lloyd Webber (1971)
- *A Chorus Line*, Marvin Hamlisch and Edward Kleban (1975)
- *Zoot Suit*, Luis Valdez (1978)
- *Buried Child*, Sam Shepard (1979)

- Richard Nixon resigns to avoid impeachment for role in Watergate scandal (1974)
- First albums by Blondie and the Ramones bring punk rock to U.S. mainstream (1976)

1980

- *Cats*, Andrew Lloyd Webber (1982)
- *'night Mother*, Marsha Norman (1983)
- *Glengarry Glen Ross*, David Mamet (1984)
- *You Have Come Back*, Fatima Gallaire-Bourega (1986)
- *Fences*, August Wilson (1987)
- *M. Butterfly*, David Henry Hwang (1988)

- Mount St. Helens erupts in Washington State (1980)
- Former Hollywood actor Ronald Reagan elected U.S. President (1980)
- Macintosh debuts Apple personal computer (1984)
- Berlin Wall is destroyed (1989)
- *The Simpsons* debuts (1989)

1990

- *Angels in America*, Tony Kushner (1993)
- *Rent*, Jonathan Larson (1996)
- *The Vagina Monologues*, Eve Ensler (1996)
- *The Blue Room*, David Hare (1998)

- World Wide Web introduced (1993)
- *Pulp Fiction*, Quentin Tarantino (1994)

THEATRICAL EVENTS AND PLAYS

2000

- *Topdog/Underdog*, Suzan-Lori Parks (2001)
- *Hairspray*, Mark O'Donnell, Thomas Meehan, Marc Shaiman, and Scott Wittman (2002)
- *Anna in the Tropics*, Nila Cruz (2003)
- *Caroline, or Change*, Tony Kushner and Jeanine Tesori (2004)
- *Spamalot*, Eric Idle and John Du Prez (2005)
- Harold Pinter wins Nobel Prize in Literature (2005)

HISTORICAL / CULTURAL EVENTS

- September 11 attacks on New York City and Washington, DC (2001)
- Iraq War begins (2003)
- Final movie in *Matrix* trilogy (2003)
- Final episode of *Friends* draws about 52 million viewers in North America (2004)
- *Cat on a Hot Tin Roof* is produced on Broadway with an all-black cast (2008)
- *Rent*, final performance (September 7, 2008)
- Digital TV takes over (2009)
- *Spiderman: Turn Off the Dark* opens after 180 preview performances (2011)

KEY TERMS

Absurdism *377*

Alienation effect *381*

Avant-garde *374*

Box set *366*

Bread and Puppet Theatre *386*

Dadaism *377*

Epic theatre *381*

Existentialism *379*

Expressionism *374*

Fourth wall *366*

Happenings *386*

Kafkaesque *379*

Little theatre movement *385*

The Living Theatre *386*

Naturalism *372*

Off Broadway *385*

Off-Off-Broadway *386*

Performance art *388*

Poetic realism *384*

Problem play *366*

Realism *364*

Regional theatre *387*

Surrealism *377*

Symbolism *374*

Theatre of Cruelty *377*

GLOSSARY

A

absurdism An avant-garde "ism" that was the result of the two world wars. It has three types: fatalist, existentialist, and hilarious.

action The characters' deeds, their responses to circumstances, which in turn affect the course of the story.

Actors' Equity Association The union that represents stage actors; often shortened to "Actors' Equity" or "Equity." See also *Equity waiver*.

aesthetic distance The audience's awareness that art and reality are not the same. Closely tied to *willing suspension of disbelief*.

aesthetics The branch of philosophy that deals with the nature and expression of beauty.

Alexandrine Verse A common style of French tragic playwrights that had twelve syllables to a line. An actor would raise his voice for the first six syllables and lower it for the last six; each line was then followed by a slight pause.

alienation effect The result of techniques to keep the audience aware that what they are witnessing is only a play; used by Bertolt Brecht. Alienation techniques include having the actors address the audience out of character, exposing the lights, removing the proscenium arch and curtains, and having the actors perform on bare platforms or simple sets that are sometimes punctuated with political slogans.

allegory A dramatic device by which an actor represents or symbolizes an idea or a moral principle; common in medieval morality plays.

American Federation of Television and Radio Artists (AFTRA) The trade union, affiliated with the AFL-CIO, that represents talk-show hosts as well as announcers, singers, disc jockeys, newscasters, sportscasters, and even stuntpeople.

anagnorisis (an-ag-NOR-i-sis) Element of a Greek tragedy; the tragic hero's self-examination leading to realization of true identity; follows *peripeteia* (radical reversal of fortune).

antagonist (an-TA-guh-nist) The character who stands in the way of the protagonist's goals. See *protagonist*.

apron See *lip*.

arena theatre A type of theatre with the stage in the center, like an island, surrounded on all sides by audience; also called theatre-in-the-round.

Aristotelian Scholasticism (air-is-teh-TEEL-yen skeh-LAS-teh-sizm) A synthesis of Aristotle's philosophy and the dogma of the Roman Catholic Church that was widely taught in universities during the Middle Ages.

Arlecchino (Harlequin) (ar-leh-KEE-no; HAR-leh-kwen) A figure in commedia dell'arte; the crafty servant of Pantalone. His costume is covered with multicolored lozenges that represent the patches he used to repair his threadbare clothing. See also *commedia dell'arte* and *Pantalone*.

artistic director The person in charge of the overall creative vision or goal of the ensemble; often chooses which plays to produce, who will direct, and who will design; is also an ambassador to the community, a fundraiser, and the theatre's chief promoter.

Artists of Dionysus The first actors' union; formed by traveling companies of actors who traveled around the Mediterranean during the Hellenistic period.

assistant director A person who helps stage scenes and manage the production crew.

assistant stage manager A person who helps the stage manager run the show during performances and assists the director with the rehearsal process.

autos sacramentales (OW-toes sah-krah-mehn-TAH-lays) Religious dramas in Spain during the Middle Ages and Renaissance.

avant-garde (ah-vahnt-GARD) Any work of art that is experimental, innovative, or unconventional.

B

back story Dialogue about what happened to the characters before the play began and what happens between the scenes and offstage; also called *exposition*.

ballad A love song.

ballad opera Comic opera that mixed popular songs of the day with spoken dialogue; brought from England to the colonies during the colonial period.

basic elements of design Line, dimension, balance, movement, harmony, color, and texture.

beat A section of dialogue about a particular subject or idea; the smallest structural element of a script.

BFA (Bachelor of Fine Arts) An undergraduate degree awarded by many American universities for completing coursework in theatre, fine art, music, or dance.

black box theatre A small theatre that generally holds fewer than a hundred people and has moveable seats so that audience groupings can be changed for every production.

blackface Black makeup used by white performers playing African American roles, as in minstrel shows.

Blackfriars A famous indoor theatre that catered to wealthy clientele in late sixteenth-century London. James Burbage, who built the theatre in 1576, skirted London's anti-theatre laws by locating the theatre in the old Dominican friary called Blackfriars, which was legally church-owned land, not part of the city.

blocking The movement of the actors on stage during a production; the technique the director uses to achieve focus and "picturization."

blocking rehearsals A series of rehearsals in which the director and actors work out the *blocking*, or the movement of the actors on stage during the play.

book For a musical, the spoken lines of dialogue and the plot; written by the *librettist*. Compare *lyrics* and *music*.

book musical A musical with a particularly well-developed story and characters, such as *Fiddler on the Roof*.

book writer The person who creates the story, characters, and dialogue for a musical.

bourgeois (boorzh-WAH) **theatre** Commercial theatre productions that, like big-budget Hollywood films, pursue maximum profits by reaffirming the audience's values.

bowdlerize (bohd-luh-RISE) To edit out any vulgar, obscene, or otherwise possibly objectionable material before publication. The origin of the word is Thomas and Harriet Bowdler's prudishly sanitized edition of Shakespeare's plays for Victorian-era family consumption.

box office Ticket office of a theatre; named for the entry room in Elizabethan theatres where theatregoers dropped payment into a box.

box set Commonly used in realistic plays, a true-to-life interior containing a room or rooms with the fourth wall removed so that the audience feels they are looking in on the characters' private lives.

boy companies Professional theatre companies of boys who competed with adult acting troupes in Elizabethan London.

bread and circus A phrase of Roman origin which means to provide the people with plenty of food and distraction so that they will not rise up and overthrow those in power.

Bread and Puppet Theatre An experimental theatre troupe begun in 1961 that uses giant puppets as well as actors in political parables.

Bunraku (bun-RAH-koo) Japanese puppet theatre with large wooden puppets with many movable parts, onstage puppeteers dressed in black, and a narrator who chants the script.

burlesque (bur-LESK) A form of musical entertainment that features bawdy songs, dancing women, and sometimes striptease. Begun in the 1840s as a parody of opera and the upper class.

 C

call The time the actors arrive at the theatre.

callback list During auditions, a list directors keep of actors they want to call back for subsequent auditions as they narrow the field of candidates.

casting against type Casting an actor who is very different from, or even the opposite of, the type of person who would be expected to play the part.

casting director A person who specializes in finding the right actors for parts; especially common in Hollywood.

casting to type Casting an actor who physically matches the role or who has a deep understanding of the character's emotions and motivations.

catharsis An intense, twofold feeling of pity and fear that is the goal of Greek tragedy.

cattle call An audition to which anyone may come and be given a minute or so to perform for the director; also known as an "open call."

censorship The altering, restricting, or suppressing of information, images, or words circulated within a society.

character flaw An inner flaw that hampers a character's good judgment and leads the character to make unfortunate choices; sometimes called *fatal flaw* or *tragic flaw*.

character makeup Makeup that completely transforms the way actors look, such as shadows, wrinkles, and gray hair to turn a young actor into an elderly character; compare to *straight makeup*.

choregos (KOR-eh-gos) A wealthy citizen who financed productions performed at City Dionysia in ancient Greece. The choregos paid for special effects, costumes, and salaries.

choreographer The person who creates the dance numbers for a play or musical, or who teaches the dance numbers to the actors.

chorus In ancient Greek plays, an all-male group of singers and dancers who commented on and participated in the action.

climax The point of the greatest dramatic tension in the play; the moment the antagonist is defeated.

closed-shop union A union to which all employees *must* belong and which the employer formally recognizes as their sole collective bargaining agent; also called a "union shop." Compare *open-shop union*.

cold reading Audition in which actors read from a script without any preparation.

color-blind casting Casting actors without regard for their race or ethnic background.

comedy number A song in a musical that provides comic relief.

comedy of manners A form of Restoration comedy that features wit and wordplay and often includes themes of sexual gratification, bedroom escapades, and humankind's primitive nature when it comes to sex. See also *Restoration*.

comic opera A style of opera, including operetta, that developed out of *intermezzi*, or comic interludes performed during the intermissions of operas. Popularized by the work of Gilbert and Sullivan.

commedia dell'arte (kuh-MAY-dee-uh del-AHR-tay) Originating in sixteenth-century Italy, traveling acting companies that presented broad, improvisational comedy and were popular throughout Europe between 1550 and 1750.

commercial theatre The type of theatre that, like the majority of Hollywood screen entertainments, has entertainment and profitability as its reason for existence.

complications Story points in a play that make the protagonist's journey more difficult.

composer For a musical, the person who writes the music.

computer aided design (CAD) Programs used by set designers to create blueprints of set designs.

concept meeting An artistic gathering to interpret the playwright's script; the director and designers brainstorm, research, and experiment with different set, costume, and light possibilities.

concept production A production of a play dominated by the director's artistic vision, or concept.

conflict The key to the movement of a story; the element that qualifies a theatrical work as a "play."

convergent thinking Thinking that is measured by IQ and involves well-defined rational problems that have only one correct answer.

copyright A legal guarantee granted by the government to authors, composers, choreographers, inventors, publishers, and corporations that allows them to control and profit from their creative work and intellectual property.

corporate funding Money contributed to the arts, including the theatre, from companies of all sizes. Compare *government funding* and *patrons*.

corrales (koh-RAHL-layz) Crude platform stages built in courtyards of inns in Spain for performances of *autos sacramentales* and other plays.

costume renderings Drawings that indicate how a costume is shaped, where seams and folds are, how the costume flows, and what fabrics are to be used.

costume shop The sewing machines, fabric-cutting tables, fitting rooms, and laundry facilities needed to create and maintain the costumes for a theatrical production.

creative director A director who adds concepts, designs, or interpretations to a playwright's words.

creativity A moment of insight when something new is invented or something that already exists is transformed.

cross-cultural theatre Theatre that joins contrasting ideas—whether staging techniques or myths and rituals—from diverse cultures into a single work in order to find parallels between cultures and promote cultural pluralism.

cross-gender casting Intentionally casting men to play women's roles and women to play men's roles.

cultural theatre The type of theatre that is designed to support the heritage, customs, and point of view of a particular people, religion, class, country, or community.

culture The values, standards, and patterns of behavior of a particular group of people expressed in customs, language, rituals, history, religion, social and political institutions, and art and entertainment.

curtain Usually the start of a show, but can also be the end of a show or an act, signaled by the raising or lowering of the curtain.

curtain speech A brief speech given to the audience by the Artistic Director or a member of the theatre company before a play begins. During this speech, they often tell the audience about upcoming plays and ask for donations.

cyclorama (often shortened to "cyc" [SYK]) A large, stretched curtain suspended from a U-shaped pipe to make a background that can completely enclose the stage setting. Lights are often projected on the cyc to indicate a location or a mood.

D

Dadaism (DAH-dah-izm) A movement that was ignited by the atrocities of World War I and gained fame through staged performances designed to demonstrate the meaninglessness of life.

dance musical A musical that features the work of a director-choreographer such as Tommy Tune, Michael Bennett, or Bob Fosse.

dark moment The end of the middle section of a formula play, when the protagonist fails (for internal or external reasons), the quest collapses, and the goal seems unattainable.

dark night The one night of the week when a play is not performed and the theatre is closed; typically Monday night.

declamatory acting A style of acting popular from the Renaissance through the early twentieth century that features grand gestures and an exaggerated elocutionary style. The actors deliver their lines directly to the audience in a rhetorical manner typified by order, harmony, and decorum.

denouement (DAY-noo-MAH) The outcome of a play, a short final scene that allows the audience to appreciate that the protagonist, because of the preceding events, has learned some great or humble lesson.

deus ex machina (DAY-us eks MAH-kee-nah) Latin for "god from a machine"; an improbable plot twist, such as a god flying onto the stage via a special-effects crane (a *mechane*), that solves all the problems in the play.

deuteragonist (doo-ter-AG-oh-nist) In ancient Greek plays, the second actor. Compare *protagonist* and *tritagonist*.

dialogue The spoken text of the play; the words the characters say.

didaskalos (dih-DAH-sko-los) In ancient Greece, a playwright who staged the plays he wrote, instructing the performers and advising the designers and technicians.

dimmer A computerized light board.

Dionysus (dye-oh-NYE-sus) The ancient Greek god of wine and fertility; Dionysus was worshipped through theatre performances and sacrifices.

director The person who turns a printed script into a stage production, coordinating the work of theatre artists, technicians, and other personnel.

director's note A note in a program in which the director conveys to the audience his or her artistic or personal thoughts about a play.

disturbance An inciting incident that upsets the balance and starts the action of a play by creating an opportunity for conflict between protagonists and antagonists.

dithyramb (DIH-thih-RAM) A hymn sung at the altar of Dionysus, the ancient Greek god of wine and fertility; it was accompanied by dancing and perhaps improvisations by a chorus of as many as 50 men.

divergent thinking Thinking that involves fluency and the ability to generate a multitude of ideas from numerous perspectives.

domestic tragedy A type of play characterized by stories about common people, rather than ones of noble birth, who feel grand emotions and suffer devastating consequences.

downstage The area of the stage closest to the audience.

drama A form of theatre that tells a story about people, their actions, and the conflicts that result.

dramatic criticism A discriminating, often scholarly interpretation and analysis of a play, an artist's body of work, or a type or period of theatre.

Dramatists Guild of America (DGA) The playwrights' union in the United States; an open-shop union.

dramaturg (DRAH-mah-TURG) A literary advisor and expert in theatre history who helps directors, designers, and actors better understand the specifics and sensibilities of a play and who can also help playwrights find their voice (sometimes spelled *dramaturge*).

draper A person who, after studying the costume designer's drawings and renderings, cuts fabric into patterns that realize the design.

dresser A person just offstage who helps actors make quick costume changes.

dress parade A tryout of the completed costumes by the actors for the costume designer and director so that necessary changes can be made before opening night.

dress rehearsals The final rehearsals, when costumes and makeup are added, before the play opens.

E

ekkyklema (EH-kik-leh-muh) In ancient Greek theatres, a platform that could be rolled out from the skene to reveal a tableau.

elevations The views of a set design from front and back.

emotional memory An acting technique pioneered by Konstantin Stanislavsky in which the actor recalls the visual and auditory images, or physical circumstances, of a real-life (or imagined) event in order to relive the emotions accompanying it. Also called sense memory or affective memory.

empathy The ability to understand and identify with another's situation to the extent of experiencing that person's emotions.

enlightenment The protagonist's realization of how to defeat the antagonist; often related to the theme of the play.

Enlightenment A period in Europe (ca. 1650–1800) that glorified the human power to reason and analyze; a time of great philosophical, scientific, technological, political, and religious revolutions.

ensemble The crews of technicians, the assistants, and the artists including actors, directors, speech coaches, playwrights, and designers who use a wide variety of art forms including painting, drawing, writing, and acting as well as set, lighting, and costume design to create a theatre production.

epic theatre Features plays that have a grand scope, large casts, and cover a long period and a wide range of sometimes unrelated incidents. An innovation by Bertolt Brecht.

episode One scene in an ancient Greek play; alternates with *stasimons*.

Equity waiver An exception to Actors' Equity Association wage standards that allows members to work for free in small productions. See *Actors' Equity Association*.

ethnocentrism The practice of using one's own culture as the standard for judging other cultures.

event An unusual incident, a special occasion, or a crisis at the beginning of a play that draws the audience's interest.

Everyman The most famous morality play (ca. 1495); contains many allegorical characters encountered by Everyman as he seeks a companion for his reckoning before God.

existentialism A post-World War II philosophy that sees humans as being alone in the universe, without God, so they are entirely responsible for their destinies.

exodos (EKS-oh-dos) In ancient Greek theatre, the summation by the chorus on the theme and wisdom of the play.

experimental play A play that pushes the limits of theatre by eliminating the distance between actor and audience, trying out new staging techniques, or even questioning the nature of theatre.

exposition Dialogue about what happened to the characters before the play began and what happens between the scenes and offstage; also called *back story*.

expressionism A style that shows the audience the action of the play through the mind of one character. Instead of seeing photographic reality, the audience sees the character's own emotions and point of view.

F

fatal flaw See *character flaw; hamartia.*

Festival of Corpus Christi In 1264, the first occasion for which the medieval Church allowed a dramatic festival; the Thursday following Trinity Sunday.

fight director A specialist who choreographs stage combat from fistfights to swordplay.

final dress rehearsal The last rehearsal before an audience is invited. See *dress rehearsals.*

flats Originally, the wood-and-muslin units that made up three walls of a room on stage; now, plain wall units as well as doors, windows, and fireplaces.

floor plan The blueprint of a set design that shows the view from above.

fly system The elaborate network of pulleys, riggings, and counterweights that allows scenic pieces to be "flown" up and out of the audience's sight in a traditional proscenium arch theatre.

focus The actor, action, or spot on the stage to which the director draws the audience's attention. See also *sharing focus, stealing focus, triangulation,* and *upstaging.*

found, or **created, space** Spaces where theatre can be performed, such as parks, churches, town squares, basements, warehouses, gymnasiums, jails, subway stations, and street corners.

fourth wall An imaginary wall separating the actors from the audience; an innovation of Realism in the theatre in the mid-1800s.

french scene A structural element of a play that begins with any entrance or exit and continues until the next entrance or exit.

G

gels Sheets of colored plastic attached to the front of lighting instruments.

gender-neutral casting Casting without regard for the character's gender.

general working rehearsals Rehearsals during which the director and actors work on individual scenes and concentrate on understanding the characters' motivation, emotions, and personality.

genre (ZHAHN-ruh) A category of artistic works that share a particular form, style, or subject matter.

ghost light A single bare light bulb mounted on a portable pole left to burn all night in the middle of the stage as a safety precaution.

given circumstances Character-analysis approach that begins with examining characters' life circumstances: their situations, problems, and the limits life has placed on them. Can include general background such as upbringing, religion, and social standing, as well as

what happened to the character the moment before entering the scene.

gobos (GOH-bohz) Metal cutouts placed on the front of lighting instruments to project patterns (such as sunlight coming through the leaves of a tree) on the stage.

government funding The money spent each year on the arts by federal, state, and local governments. Compare *corporate funding* and *patrons.*

greenroom A small room for actors waiting for their cues, located just off the stage and out of the audience's earshot.

groundlings Audience members who stood on the main floor (and therefore paid the least for their tickets) in an Elizabethan theatre.

group dynamics The functioning of people when they come together into groups.

H

hamartia (heh-mar-TEE-eh) In ancient Greek tragedies, a personal weakness (also called a *tragic flaw* or *fatal flaw*) that leads to a tragic hero's downfall. A common hamartia is *hubris.*

hand props Any objects actors handle while on stage, such as pens, fans, cigars, money, and umbrellas.

happenings Unstructured theatrical events on street corners, at bus stops, in lobbies, and virtually anywhere else people gather.

Harlem Renaissance An African American literary, artistic, and musical movement during the 1920s and 1930s centered in the Harlem neighborhood in New York City.

Hellenistic period The two centuries when classical Greek culture spread around the Mediterranean Sea, including Egypt and the Middle East; dates approximately from the death of Alexander the Great in 323 BCE until the Roman conquest of Greece in 146 BCE. The word *Hellenistic* is derived from the Greek word meaning "to imitate the Greeks."

historical theatre Dramas that use the styles, themes, and staging of plays of a particular historical period.

house A theatre's seating area.

house manager In charge of all the ushers; deals with any seating problems and makes sure the audience finds their seats and that the play begins on time.

hubris (HYOO-bruhs) In classical Greek drama, a tragic hero's overbearing pride or arrogance. A type of *hamartia.*

humanists In fifteenth-century Italy, university students who rejected the traditional curriculum of theology in favor of the subjects studied in classical Greece, specifically rhetoric, literary criticism, grammar, history, poetry, painting, architecture, music, classical literature, and theatre.

I

Innamorata (ee-NAHM-oh-rah-teh) A stock character in commedia dell'arte; leading lady who is in love with Innamorato. See also *commedia dell'arte*.

Innamorato (ee-NAHM-oh-rah-toh) A stock character in commedia dell'arte; leading man who is in love with Innamorata. See also *commedia dell'arte*.

inner conflict Some sort of unfinished business that is so compelling that it handicaps the character until it is confronted.

interlude Secular play performed between other forms of entertainment at court in the late Middle Ages.

International Phonetic Alphabet (IPA) A system for transcribing the sounds of speech that is independent of any particular language but applicable to all languages.

interpretive director A director whose goal is to translate a script from page to stage as faithfully as possible.

J

jukebox musical A musical that features a particular band's song.

K

Kabuki (kuh-BOO-kee) A popular, robust, and spectacular version of the Japanese Noh theatre. The name comes from the characters for "song" (*ka*), "dance" (*bu*), and "skill" (*ki*). See also *Noh*.

Kafkaesque Marked by surreal distortion and senseless danger; a term that comes from the way that Czech writer Franz Kafka (1883–1924) depicted the world.

Kathakali (kahth-uh-KAH-lee) "Story play"; a form of Indian folk drama begun in the second century CE and based on the Hindu epic poems *Ramayana* and *Mahabharata*.

Ki In Kabuki theatre, wooden clappers whose beats accompany a *mie* pose at a particularly intense or profound moment.

L

La Ruffiana (lah ROO-fee-ah-neh) A stock character of commedia dell'arte; a gossipy old woman who meddles in the affairs of the lovers, Innamorata and Innamorato. See also *commedia dell'arte*.

League of Resident Theatres (LORT) An association of professional theatres that work together to promote the general welfare of the major regional theatres around the United States. Members of LORT also negotiate collective bargaining agreements with actors, directors, choreographers, and designers.

legs The curtains at the sides of a stage in a proscenium arch theatre.

Library of Alexandria One of the first universities; its holdings included original manuscripts by Aeschylus, Euripides, and Sophocles. Located in Alexandria, Egypt, a city founded by Alexander the Great.

librettist For a musical, the person who writes the *book*, or the spoken lines of dialogue and plot.

Licensing Act of 1737 An English law that gave the Lord Chamberlain the authority to censor plays. The term "legitimate theatre" comes from the time of the Licensing Act.

lighting plot A detailed drawing that shows the location of each lighting instrument on the hanging grid, where its light will be focused, its type, wattage and the circuitry needed, and its color.

limelight In the mid-1800s, a gas-powered spotlight in which a jet of oxygen and hydrogen was ignited with small bits of lime. Now, the word means "the center of attention."

lip Also called an *apron*, the area of a proscenium arch stage that extends into the audience's side of the picture frame.

literary arts Arts created with written language.

literary manager The liaison between playwrights, agents, and the theatre who reads and evaluates new scripts. Also, this person often writes grant applications to help support new play development and stage readings of new plays.

little theatre movement Inexpensive, noncommercial, artistically significant plays in small, out-of-the-way theatres. In the United States, flourished from the mid-1950s through the mid-1960s.

The Living Theatre A famous twentieth-century experimental theatre using aesthetically radical techniques to shake up audiences about social and political issues; founded in 1946 by Julian Beck (1925–1985) and Judith Malina (b. 1926).

lyricist For a musical, the person who writes the lyrics.

lyrics For a musical, the sung words; the writer is called a lyricist. See also *book* and *music*.

M

magic *if* A technique pioneered by Konstantin Stanislavsky for developing empathy with a character. It involves searching for the answers to the question "What would I do *if* I were this character in these circumstances?" The magic *if* allows actors to find similarities between themselves and a character and to explore the intimate emotions and thoughts that result.

major dramatic question (MDQ) The hook (or question) that keeps an audience curious or in suspense for the duration of the play; an element in the beginning of a formula play that results from the *disturbance* and the *point of attack*.

mansions Different settings ("houses") inside a church where the congregation gathered to watch the priest stage biblical playlets.

masque Originating in the early 1500s, a form of entertainment for monarchs and their invited audiences; characterized by grand dances, extravagant costumes with masks, lavish spectacle, poetry, and florid speeches all hung on a thin story line praising the monarch and demonstrating the need for loyalty.

mechane (MEH-kuh-nee) In ancient Greek theatres, a crane that could fly actors in over the skene to land gently in the orchestra or hover overhead.

medium The method, substance, and technique used to create a work of art.

melodrama Most popular in the late nineteenth century, a type of play that usually features working-class heroes who set out on a great adventure; story lines that praise marriage, God, and country; and florid background music. The word is a blend of "melody" and "drama."

method acting Also known as "the method," this system of realistic acting was distilled by followers of Konstantin Stanislavsky and has been taught primarily since the 1930s in America. See *Stanislavsky system.*

MFA (Master of Fine Arts) A graduate degree awarded by many American universities for completing advanced coursework in theatre, fine art, music or dance.

mie pose In Kabuki theatre, a sudden, striking pose (with eyes crossed, chin sharply turned, and the big toe pointed toward the sky) at a particularly intense or profound moment; accompanied by several beats of wooden clappers, the *Ki.*

minstrel show Stage entertainment consisting of songs, dances, and comic scenes performed by white actors in blackface makeup; originated in the nineteenth century.

miracle plays Plays in the Middle Ages in Europe that recounted stories about the lives, suffering, and miracles of particular saints.

mission statement A theatre's purpose and key objectives, which can include quality, diversity, and accessibility, as well as the type of theatre to be produced.

morality plays Allegorical plays in the late Middle Ages in Europe that taught moral lessons about how to conduct one's life.

Moscow Art Theatre A theatre company founded in the late nineteenth century by a group of Russian producers, actors, directors, and dramatists. Made famous by the plays of Anton Chekhov and the acting techniques of Konstantin Stanislavsky.

motivated light Stage lighting that comes from an identifiable source, such as a candle, a lamp, or the sun.

motivation The conscious or subconscious reason a character takes a particular action.

movement coach A specialist who instructs actors in various styles of movement.

multiculturalism The attempt to achieve a pluralistic society by overcoming all forms of discrimination, including racism, sexism, and homophobia.

music In a musical script, the orchestrated melodies, which are written by the *composer.* See also *book* and *lyrics.*

musical A type of theatre that features song and dance interspersed with spoken text. The genre includes not only modern musicals with popular songs and impressive spectacle (e.g., *Miss Saigon, Phantom of the Opera*) but also the masques, operas, burlesques, minstrel shows, variety shows, and music hall reviews of earlier periods. Compare *straight plays.*

musical comedy A type of musical characterized by a lighthearted, fast-moving comic story, whose dialogue is interspersed with popular music.

musical director A specialist who works with the musicians and teaches the actors the songs for a musical.

mystery cycle A group of plays about biblical stories performed outdoors by guilds during the Middle Ages in Europe.

mystery plays Liturgical plays performed outdoors by workers' guilds during the Middle Ages; *mystery* derives from *mesterie,* the Anglo-French word for "occupation."

N

National Endowment for the Arts (NEA) The federal agency that disburses tax dollars as grants to fund cultural programs.

naturalism "Sordid realism"; a style of theatrical design and acting whose goal is to imitate real life, including its seamy side. Also called "slice of life" theatre.

Natyasastra An encyclopedia of classical Indian dramatic theory and practice, written ca. 200 BCE–200 CE. Teaches actors dancing and stage gestures; also covers costume design, plot construction, music, and poetry.

New Comedy Greek comic plays with safe themes and mundane subject matter produced after Athens lost the Peloponnesian War to Sparta.

Noh (NOH) A form of traditional Japanese drama combining poetry, acting, singing, and dancing that was developed during the 1300s. Compare *Kabuki.*

nonmotivated light Stage lighting that reinforces the mood of a scene but doesn't necessarily come from an identifiable or onstage source.

O

off-book rehearsal The rehearsal when the actors must have their lines memorized because they no longer have the script ("book") with them on stage.

Off Broadway Originally, small experimental theatres that sprang up in the late 1950s outside Times Square to put on plays about current issues. They typically have much smaller houses than Broadway theatres.

Off Off Broadway Small, nontraditional, noncommercial theatres located in storefronts, coffeehouses, churches, and other public spaces in the New York City area.

Old Comedy Greek comic plays that directly or indirectly lampooned society and politics; they were filled with sight gags and obscene humor.

onnagata (oh-nah-GAH-tah) Men who play female roles in Kabuki theatre. See also *Kabuki*.

open-shop union A union in which membership is optional, such as the Dramatists Guild of America; compare *closed-shop union*.

opera A type of drama introduced at the end of the sixteenth century that is entirely sung.

operatic musical A musical that is mostly singing, with less spoken dialogue and usually a darker, more dramatic tone than an operetta has. Examples are *Les Misérables* and *Evita*.

operetta Like an opera, a drama set to music, but with a frivolous, comic theme, some spoken dialogue, a melodramatic story, and usually a little dancing. Also called "light opera." Popularized by Gilbert and Sullivan.

orchestra The circular playing area in ancient Greek theatres; derives from the Greek word for "dancing place." See also *skene* and *theatron*.

overture At the beginning of a musical; a medley of the songs played by the orchestra as a preview.

P

pageant wagon Wagon decorated with a set and used as a traveling stage for performances of mystery and miracle plays during the Middle Ages.

painted-face roles In the Peking opera, supernatural beings, warriors, bandits, and other stock characters whose makeup used elaborate geometrical designs and colors that symbolized character traits: red for loyalty, blue for vigor and courage, yellow for intelligence, black for honesty, and brown for stubbornness.

Pantalone (pahn-teh-LOW-nee) A stock character of commedia dell'arte; a stingy, retired Venetian merchant who often makes a fool of himself by courting young women. See also *commedia dell'arte*.

paper the house To give away free tickets to the families and friends of cast members in order to make it appear as though the play is popular.

parenthetical A short description such as (*loving*), (*angry*), or (*terrified*) to help the actor or the reader interpret a particular line of dialogue.

parodos The entrance of the chorus into the playing area in ancient Greek theatre.

parody The exaggerated imitations that are done for comic effect or political criticism.

patrons Individual contributors to the arts. Compare *corporate funding* and *government funding*.

Peking opera A synthesis of music, dance, acting, and acrobatics first performed in the 1700s in China by strolling players in markets, temples, courtyards, and the streets. Known in China as the "opera of the capital," or *ching-hsi*, it was founded by Qing dynasty Emperor Ch'ien-lung (1736–1795).

Peloponnesian War War between the city-states of Athens and Sparta and their allies (431–404 BCE). Athens's defeat by Sparta brought about the end of Athenian democracy and classic Greek theatre.

performance art An art form from the mid-twentieth century in which one or more performers use some combination of visual arts (including video), theatre, dance, music, and poetry, often to dramatize political ideas. The purpose is less to tell a story than to convey a state of being.

performance report Detailed notes to the actors and crew informing them of any problems that occurred and what needs to be fixed before the next performance.

performing arts Arts, such as theatre, music, opera, and dance, whose medium is an act performed by a person.

periakto (pehr-ee-AK-toh) In ancient Greek plays, a pivoting device used to quickly change all the paintings on the skene.

peripeteia (pehr-uh-puh-TEE-uh) In ancient Greek tragedies, a radical reversal of fortune experienced by the hero. See also *hamartia* and *anagnorisis*.

perspective scenery A technique of set design and scene painting that gives the illusion of depth; it gave birth to the proscenium arch theatre.

pictorial arts Arts, such as drawing and painting, created by applying line and color to two-dimensional surfaces.

picturization Composing pictures with the actors to reinforce an idea in the story; a technique used by directors.

playwright's note A note in a program in which the playwright conveys to the audience his or her artistic or personal thoughts about writing the play.

plot The causal and logical structure that connects events in a play.

plot-structure The playwright's selection of events to create a logical sequence and as a result to distill meaning from the chaos of life.

poetic realism A style of realism that is expressed through lyrical language.'

Poetics Written by Aristotle (384–322 BCE), the first known treatise on how to construct a dramatic story.

point of attack The point in the beginning of a formula plot where the protagonist must make a major decision that will result in conflict.

political theatre Theatre in which playwrights, directors, and actors express their personal opinions about current issues.

precolonial African theatre Indigenous African theatre that grew out of ritual and predates contact with Europeans. A combination of ritual, ceremony, and drama, it incorporates acting, music, storytelling, poetry, and dance; the costumed actors often wear masks. Audience participation is common.

presentational theatre Type of theatre that makes no attempt to offer a realistic illusion on stage. The actors openly acknowledge the audience, often playing to them and sometimes even inviting members to participate.

preview performance Performance of a play open to the public before the official opening night (and before the critics see it).

problem play A play that expresses a social problem so that it can be remedied.

producer or producing director In the United States, the person or institution responsible for the business aspects of a production. Producers can be individuals who finance the production with their own money or who control investors' money, or they can be institutions—universities, churches, community organizations, or theatre companies—that control the business side of the production.

production concept The thematic idea, symbol, or allegory that conveys the tone, mood, and theme of a play (e.g., a post-nuclear *Hamlet*).

production meeting One of a series of meetings between a director and designers to discuss how to realize the production concept as well as the play's philosophy, interpretation, theme, physical demands, history, and style.

profile An actor's position at a right angle to the audience; halfway between open and closed.

prologue In ancient Greek theatre, a short introductory speech or scene.

prompt book A copy of the play on which the production's sound and light cues, blocking notes, and other information needed for rehearsal and performance are recorded.

prop check The prop master ensures props are placed where they need to be and that they are in working order.

prop master A person who finds and buys props for productions, or designs and builds them; also in charge of *rehearsal props*.

props Short for *properties*; includes *set props* such as sofas and beds and *hand props*, or small objects actors handle on stage such pens, guns, cigars, money, umbrellas, and eyeglasses.

prop table A backstage table with each prop laid out and clearly labeled; where actors must place their props before leaving the area.

proscenium arch A formal arch that separates the audience from the actors, or a theatre with such an arch. Also called "picture frame" theatre.

protagonist (pro-TAG-uh-nist) In an ancient Greek play, the main actor. Now, the central character who pushes forward the action of a play. See also *antagonist, deuteragonist, tritagonist*.

public domain The legal realm of intellectual property that is not protected by a copyright or patent and belongs to the community at large.

publicity department People who promote a theatre and its upcoming productions.

Puritans A strict religious group in Elizabethan England who hated the theatre and lobbied to shut it down.

R

realism A style of theatre that attempts to seem like life, with authentic-looking sets, "honest" acting, and dialogue that sounds like everyday speech. See also *poetic realism, selective realism, simplified* (or *suggested*) *realism*.

realism The cultural movement behind theatrical realism began around 1850 and popularized the idea that plays could be a force for social and political change.

regional theatre Permanent, professional theatres located outside New York City.

rehearsal costume A temporary costume used during rehearsal so that the actors get a feel for the actual costume before it is ready.

rehearsal prop A temporary prop used during rehearsal to represent the real property that the actors will not be able to use until a few days before the play opens.

rehearsal report The stage manager's written report for the entire ensemble on how rehearsal went and about any concerns or ideas that affect the set, lights, props, or costume.

Renaissance Period in European history (ca. 1350–1650) when the wisdom of ancient Greek and Roman scholars was rediscovered and the dogma of the Church was challenged; characterized by a flowering of the arts and literature and the beginning of modern science. *Renaissance* comes from the Latin for "born again."

repertory A group of plays performed by a theatre company during the course of a season.

representational theatre A style of theatre in which the actors attempt to create the illusion of reality and go about their business as if there were no audience present.

reprise In a musical, the repetition of a song, sometimes with new lyrics, in a later scene. The new meaning or subtext makes a dramatic point.

Restoration Period of English history that began in 1660 with the reestablishment of the monarchy. It was characterized by scientific discovery, new philosophical concepts, improved economic conditions and a return of the theatre.

reviews Published or broadcast opinions of critics about whether a particular play is worth seeing. Compare to *dramatic criticism*.

revue A program of satirical sketches, singing, and dancing about a particular theme; also called a "musical review." Compare to *variety show*.

rigger A person who mounts and operates curtains, sets, and anything else that must move via the fly system above the stage; also called "flyman."

rising action The increasing power, drama, and seriousness of each subsequent conflict, crisis, and complication in a play.

ritual theatre The middle stage of theatre's evolution from rituals; the theatrical techniques of song, dance, and characterization were used, but the performances' purpose was that of rituals.

road house A theatre that has no resident company of actors of its own, but instead accepts productions from touring theatre companies.

rock musical A musical that uses rock and roll music, psychedelic rock, or contemporary pop and rock.

Roman mimes Troupes of actors in ancient Rome, whose shows were one of the most popular forms of entertainment. They were filled with jugglers, acrobats, and comic skits that include vulgar language, buffoonery, and nudity.

Romantics Enlightenment-era poets, novelists, and playwrights who questioned the Scientific Revolution's obsession with logic; they felt that science was not adequate to describe the full range of human experience, and stressed instinct, intuition, and feeling in their writings.

royalty payment Payment to playwrights or their estates in exchange for staging a copyrighted play.

running crew Everyone who helps out backstage during a play.

run-through A rehearsal to go through an act or the entire play from beginning to end with as few interruptions as possible.

S

Sanskrit drama One of the earliest forms of theatre in India, performed in Sanskrit by professional touring companies on special occasions in temples, palaces, or temporary theatres.

satyr play (SAY-tur) In ancient Greece, a comic-relief play performed between tragic plays at the City Dionysia. Often *burlesque*, these plays parodied the myths, gods, and heroes in the tragedies. Named for the half-beast, half-human creatures said to be companions of the god Dionysus.

Scapino (ska-PEE-noh) A stock character of commedia dell'arte; a servant who is smarter than his master; usually played by an acrobat. See also *commedia dell'arte*.

Screen Actors Guild (SAG) The union that represents film and television actors.'

scrim A curtain of open-mesh gauze that can be opaque or translucent depending on whether the light comes from in front or behind it.

The Second Shepherd's Play A comic play (ca. 1375) about what the three shepherds were doing just before the angel arrived to announce the birth of Jesus and they decided to go to Bethlehem bearing gifts (Luke 2:8–18).

selective realism A design style that mixes authentic-looking elements with stylized ones.

sentimental comedy A type of comedy that features middle-class characters finding happiness and true love.

set decoration A prop that is part of the set and is not touched by actors.

set designer The person who interprets a playwright's and director's words into visual imagery for a production; usually has a strong background in interior design, architecture, and art history, as well as theatrical conventions of various periods.

set prop Any prop that sits on the set, such as sofas, chairs, and beds. Compare *hand prop*.

shadow theatre A form of theatre created by lighting two-dimensional figures and casting their shadows on a screen. Probably originated in China around 100 BCE and later became popular in Islamic lands, where people were prohibited from playing characters.

sharing focus A position for two or more actors, each with a shoulder thrown back so that the audience can see them equally. See also *focus*.

showstopper In a musical, a big production number which receives so much applause that it stops the show.

sight lines Audience members' view of areas of the stage.

simplified, or **suggested, realism** A design style that suggests rather than exactly duplicates the look of a period.

skene (SKEEN) In ancient Greek theatre, the building behind the orchestra; it housed dressing rooms and storage spaces, and its façade was used as a backdrop for productions. See also *orchestra* and *theatron*.

sound board operator A person who runs the sound board during various sound cues throughout a production; also ensures that all the speakers, mixer, amplifiers, backstage monitor, and intercom are working prior to curtain.

sound designer A person who synthesizes and records the sounds for a production and designs systems to amplify an actor or singer's voice; has a detailed knowledge of acoustics, electronics, digital music editing programs, audio mixing boards and signal-processing equipment, microphones, effects processors, and amplifiers; and sometimes writes and plays transition music or underscore scenes with mood music.

souvenir program Programs sold at large professional performances that have more pictures and information about the production and cast than the basic program.

spatial arts Arts, such as sculpture and architecture, that are created by manipulating material in space.

special rehearsal A rehearsal for a special element, such as fight scenes, musical numbers, dance numbers, or dialects.

stage area One of the nine sections of the stage labeled according to the actors' point of view, such as downstage right, center stage, or upstage left.

stage directions Notes that indicate the physical movements of the characters.

stage door The back door that actors use to enter and leave the theatre.

stagehand A person who helps shift scenery and generally sets up the play for the next scene.

stage manager The most important assistant to a director; the person who is responsible for running the show during the performance and helping the director during auditions and the rehearsal process by taking notes, recording blocking, and scheduling rehearsals.

standing ovation When the audience stands to applaud a play—this is reserved for only the most extraordinary performances.

Stanislavsky system An individualized, psychological approach to acting pioneered by Konstantin Stanislavsky; also known as *method acting*.

stasimon In ancient Greek plays, a choral interlude between episodes.

stealing focus Taking focus out of turn; also known as *upstaging*. Compare *sharing focus*. See also *focus*.

stereotypes Generalized assumptions about people who are not like us.

stitcher The person who sews fabric patterns together creating the full costumes, and also builds or finds the *rehearsal costumes*.

straight makeup Makeup that does not change actors' looks but makes their faces look more three-dimensional and therefore more visible to the audience; compare to *character makeup*.

straight play In contrast to a *musical*, the category of plays without music.

Sturm und Drang (SHTURM oond DRAHNG; "storm and stress") The Romantic movement in Germany. Sturm und Drang plays exalted nature, emotions, and individualism; Johann Wolfgang von Goethe was the greatest Sturm und Drang playwright. See also *Romantics*.

subject What a work of art is about, what it reflects, and what it attempts to comprehend.

substitution Replacing a character's emotions with unrelated personal emotions; a technique used when the actor has not had the experience or emotional reaction of the character.

subtext The hidden meaning behind a line of dialogue; the real reason a character chooses to speak.

superobjective The driving force that governs a character's actions throughout the play.

surrealism A genre of theatre that emphasizes the subconscious realities of the character, usually through design, and often includes random sets with dreamlike qualities.

symbolism A design style or theatre genre in which a certain piece of scenery, a costume, or light represent the essence of the entire environment.

T

table work The first step in the rehearsal process; the actors read through the play while seated around a table. Afterward, the director and actors discuss the characters, motivations, and meaning, and the designers may present their ideas to the cast.

talent Natural ability; it is innate but also can be developed.

talk-back A post-performance discussion where the audience gets a chance to meet and perhaps ask questions of the director, actors, and sometimes the playwright.

teaser The curtain that frames the top of the stage. Compare *legs*.

technical approach Acting from the outside in, concentrating on physical details. Compare to *method acting*.

technical director The person who coordinates, schedules, and engineers all the technical elements of a production.

technique Proven procedure by which a complex task can be accomplished, such as raising a child, fixing a heart valve, auditing books, or acting in a play.

tech rehearsals Rehearsals that include the lights, sound, costumes, more complex props, and final set pieces.

theatre A performing art that is always changing and whose every performance is unique.

Theatre of Cruelty Originated by Antonin Artaud, stylized, ritualized performances intended to attack spectators' sensibilities and purge them of destructive tendencies.

Theatre of Dionysus The largest ancient Greek theatre, located in Athens; it could seat as many as 17,000 people.

theatre of identity Plays by and about a particular culture or ethnic group.

theatre of protest Plays that criticize the policies of the dominant culture and demand justice.

theatre of the people A type of theatre that provides a forum for everyday people to express themselves.

theatron (THAY-uh-tron) From the Greek term for "seeing place," the seating area in ancient Greek theatres. Compare *orchestra* and *skene*.

theme A play's central idea; a statement about life or a moral.

Thespis The first known Western actor. Created theatre by stepping from a dithyramb chorus in ancient Greece to play an individual role. In 534 BCE, wrote and acted in a play that won the City Dionysia. Source of the word "thespian," or a person who has studied the craft of acting.

three unities Rules for writing a play requiring (1) the action to take place within a 24-hour period, (2) settings that can all be reached within 24 hours, and (3) no commingling of comedy and tragedy. These rules for unity of time, place, and action were a misinterpretation of Aristotle's writings by Renaissance scholars.

thrust stage A theatre with a lip that protrudes so far into the house that the audience must sit on one of the three sides of the stage.

total theatre A form of postcolonial theatre in Africa that mixed traditional African ritual theatre and Western-style drama; appeared during the 1960s after African nations won their independence from European rule.

tragic flaw An unchangeable trait in a character that brings about his own ruin (e.g., Oedipus's arrogance in ignoring the oracle). Also known as *character flaw* and *fatal flaw*. See also *hamartia*.

tragic hero In ancient Greek tragedies, an extraordinary but empathetic person of noble birth or a person who has risen to prominence and makes a choice (due to bad judgment or to a character flaw) that leads to trouble, but who ultimately takes responsibility for the choice.

triangulation A technique for drawing focus when three actors or groups of actors are on stage; the person or group at the upstage or downstage apex of the triangle takes the focus. See also *focus*.

tritagonist (try-TAG-uh-nist) In ancient Greek plays, the third actor. Compare *protagonist* and *deuteragonist*.

trope A chanted or sung phrase incorporated into the Mass as an embellishment or commentary on a religious lesson.

U

University Wits In Elizabethan England, one of the groups of student actors writing and performing plays in the style of the ancient Greeks and Romans; included Thomas Kyd (1558–1594) and Christopher Marlowe (1564–1593).

upstage The area of the stage farthest from the audience.

upstaging Taking focus out of turn; also known as *stealing focus*.

V

values The principles, standards, and qualities considered worthwhile or desirable within a given society.

variety show A program of unrelated singing, dancing, and comedy numbers. Compare to *revue*.

vaudeville (VAHD-vill) A popular form of stage entertainment from the 1880s to the 1930s, descended from *burlesque*. Programs included slapstick comedy routines, song-and-dance numbers, magic acts, juggling, and acrobatic performances.

verbal scene painting A technique used by English and Spanish playwrights to set the mood or place of a scene. Because the words paint pictures, the audience "dresses" the stage in their imagination.

vocal coach A specialist who helps actors with speech clarity, volume, accent reduction or acquisition, and preservation of their voices for the long run of a show.

vomitories (often shortened to "voms") Tunnels, like those in sports stadiums, that run into and under the tiers of audience seats to allow actors quick access to the stage.

W

well-made play A sarcastic label for a formula play whose ending is happy and whose loose ends are neatly tied up; typified by the nineteenth-century melodramas of Eugene Scribe.

Western drama Drama that grew out of the theatre of Thespis in ancient Greece around 500 BCE. It passed from the Athenians to the Romans to the medieval Europeans and then to North America.

Will Call A booth or stand where audience members pick up the tickets they previously ordered by telephone or over the Internet.

willing suspension of disbelief The audience's acceptance of the quasi-reality of a work of art that enables the playwright, director, and actors to communicate perceptions about reality; the term was coined by English poet Samuel Taylor Coleridge. Closely tied to *aesthetic distance*.

wings Areas out of the audience's sight from which actors make their entrances and in which sets are stored.

writers for hire Writers, such as screen and television writers, who sell their words to production companies rather than retaining a copyright to them.

Writers Guild of America (WGA) The closed-shop union that represents screen and television writers.

Y

Yiddish Broadway The Jewish theatre district on Second Avenue in New York City in the late nineteenth and early twentieth century.

INDEX

M